SIXTH EDITION

Early Childhood Education Today

GEORGE S. MORRISON

Florida International University

MERRIL
an imprint of PRENTICE HALL
Upper Saddle River, New Jersey   Columbus, Ohio

Library of Congress Cataloging-in-Publication Data
Morrison, George S.
    Early childhood education today / George S.
Morrison.—6th ed.
      p.   cm.
    Includes bibliographical references and index.
    ISBN 0-02-384151-6
    1. Early childhood education—United
States.   I. Title.
LB1139.2.M67   1995
372'.21—dc20   94-8332
                          CIP

Cover art/photo: © Myrleen Ferguson Cate, Photo
   Network
Editor: Ann Castel Davis
Developmental Editor: Erin Haggerty
Production Editor: Linda Hillis Bayma
Photo Editor: Anne Vega
Text Designer: Thomas Mack
Cover Designer: Thomas Mack
Production Buyer: Patricia A. Tonneman
Electronic Text Management: Marilyn Wilson
   Phelps, Matthew Williams, Jane Lopez,
   Karen L. Bretz
Illustrations: Jane Lopez

This book was set in Korrina BT by Prentice Hall
and was printed and bound by R.R. Donnelley &
Sons Company. The cover was printed by Phoenix
Color Corp.

© 1995 by Prentice-Hall, Inc.
A Simon & Schuster Company
Upper Saddle River, New Jersey 07458

Earlier editions © 1991 by Macmillan Publishing
Company and © 1988, 1984, 1980, and 1976 by
Merrill Publishing Company.

Photo credits: AP Wide World Photos, p. 32; The
Bettman Archive, p. 52; Andy Brunk/Prentice Hall
and Merrill, pp. 210, 290; Ben Chandler/Prentice
Hall and Merrill, p. 65; Children's Hospital, Columbus, Ohio, p. 616; Scott Cunningham/Cunning-
ham/Feinknopf/Prentice Hall and Merrill, pp. 97,
213, 231, 380, 383, 403, 431, 437, 466, 481, 510,
518; Diane Elmer, p. 76; Rohn Engh/Sunrise Trinity
Photos, p. 26; Kevin Fitzsimmons/Prentice Hall and
Merrill, p. 617; Girl Scouts of America, p. 408;
Courtesy of IBM, p. 572; Korver/Thorpe Ltd., p. 66;
Lloyd Lemmerman/Prentice Hall and Merrill, pp.
474, 475, 493; George Morrison, pp. 181, 191,
579, 581; Courtesy of NationsBank, p. 173; Barbara Schwartz/Prentice Hall and Merrill, pp. 133,
214, 246, 308, 395, 400, 473, 596, 599, 629;
Michael Siluk, p. 263; Ann Vega/Prentice Hall and
Merrill, pp. 2, 10, 12, 39, 44, 55, 60, 68, 70, 71,
73, 75, 81, 90, 92, 94, 100, 106, 120, 130, 140,
154, 161, 208, 218, 227, 253, 258, 262, 265, 277,
286, 291, 326, 327, 331, 342, 344, 359, 363, 371,
373, 394, 446, 477, 498, 508, 523, 524, 534, 538,
545, 568, 606; Tom Watson/Prentice Hall and Merrill, pp. 418, 423, 430, 529, 591; Todd Yarrington,
p. 564; Todd Yarrington/Prentice Hall and Merrill,
pp. 7, 123, 270, 299, 302, 554, 604; Allen Zak, p.
159.

Printed in the United States of America

10 9 8 7 6 5 4 3 2

ISBN: 0-02-384151-6

Prentice-Hall International (UK) Limited, London
Prentice-Hall of Australia Pty. Limited, Sydney
Prentice-Hall of Canada, Inc., Toronto
Prentice-Hall Hispanoamericana, S. A., Mexico
Prentice-Hall of India Private Limited, New Delhi
Prentice-Hall of Japan, Inc., Tokyo
Simon & Schuster Asia Pte. Ltd., Singapore
Editora Prentice-Hall do Brasil, Ltda., Rio de
   Janeiro

This book is affectionately dedicated to Betty Jane

Preface

The world of early childhood is constantly changing, and the changes ahead promise to be rewarding and challenging. We professionals must be prepared to assist young children and their families in making the transition into the twenty-first century. The transition from one millennium to another in a few years will provide many opportunities and rewards. I believe this sixth edition of *Early Childhood Education Today* will help prepare professionals to rightfully, knowledgeably, confidently, and appropriately assume their roles of educating children, parents, and families for productive living.

GOALS AND COVERAGE

Early Childhood Education Today offers a thorough introduction to the field of early childhood education. It provides an up-to-date, cutting-edge, comprehensive overview of programs and practices, historic foundations, and the latest ideas and practices in the field. The content enables professionals at all levels to learn new knowledge and information, analyze issues, and apply practical, developmentally appropriate ideas and suggestions. Implications for practice abound throughout the text.

CONTEMPORARY THEMES

Essential contemporary themes and their implications for professional practice are included in the sixth edition of *Early Childhood Education Today*. These themes include multiculturalism and multiculturally appropriate practice; technology and its application to early childhood programs; equity and diversity issues, including gender and socioeconomic background; developmentally appropriate practice, curriculum, and assessment; the changing field of early childhood education; and the changing role of the early childhood professional.

NEW TO THE SIXTH EDITION

Users of the fifth edition will find major changes in the sixth edition. One chapter has been deleted, and two new chapters have been added. The sixth edition of *Early Childhood Education Today* is extensively revised to reflect changes in society and the field of early childhood education. Some of the book's key changes are these:

- A new chapter, "Multiculturalism: Education for Living in a Diverse Society," encourages professionals to consider how society is changing and how they can provide for the needs of all children according to their race and culture, gender, socioeconomic status, and family background through culturally sensitive practice, programming, and settings.

- A new chapter, "Technology and Early Childhood Education: Education for the Twenty-first Century," challenges professionals to promote technological literacy for themselves, children, and families. Society is becoming more technological, and professionals must keep up with the benefits and opportunities of technology.

- A new insert titled "A Look Inside," describes nine outstanding programs. These profiles, which are illustrated with color photographs, provide a visually appealing format to the sixth edition. They also reinforce the significant role business and industry play in early education and address the themes of multiculturalism, technology, and quality programming.

- Important vignettes, program descriptions, and personal philosophies by noted early childhood authorities (including Sue Bredekamp of the National Association for the Education of Young Children; James Comer of the Yale Child Development Center; Ellen Galinsky of the Families and Work Institute; and Sarah Greene, executive director of Head Start) provide a rich background of experiences and insight for professionals at all levels of their development.

- Every chapter has been thoroughly revised, new vignettes added, and the latest in theory, programming, and practice incorporated. Professionals at all levels can stay up-to-date with the sixth edition of *Early Childhood Education Today*.

Like all previous editions, this sixth edition was written with a deep sense of pride for all who teach, care for, and parent young children. I heartily agree with Froebel, Montessori, and Dewey that the care and education of young children is a redemptive calling. This vision of teaching is supported in chapter 16 by the vignettes submitted by the 1993 Teachers of the Year.

ACKNOWLEDGMENTS

In the course of my teaching, service, and consulting, I meet and talk with many professionals who are deeply committed to doing their best for young children and their families. I am always touched, heartened, and encouraged by the openness, honesty, and unselfish sharing of ideas that characterize these professional col-leagues. I take this opportunity to thank them publicly for helping me and all who reviewed the sixth edition of *Early Childhood Education Today*. Those who shared their time, talents, and ideas are Michelle R. Adkins, NationsBank Corporation, Charlotte, North Carolina; Tonia Alameda, Fienberg/Fisher Elementary School, Miami Beach, Florida; Kay Albrecht, director, HeartsHome Early Learning Center, Houston, Texas; Susie Armstrong, Montessori School at Greenwood Plaza, Engle-wood, Colorado; Margaret Baily, Audubon Head Start, Owensboro, Kentucky; Norma Beiler, Dade County Head Start, Miami, Florida; Barbara Bittner, Alexander D. Henderson University School, Florida Atlantic University, Boca Raton, Florida; Beverly Boals, professor, early childhood education, Arkansas State University; Lau-rie Brackett, The Stride Rite Corporation, Cambridge, Massachusetts; Patricia J. Callahan, Brigance Inventories and Screens, North Billerica, Massachusetts; Bernadette Caruso, University of Delaware; Nira Changwatchai, The Open Door, Austin, Texas; Ivonne Hatfield Clay, Longfellow School, Kansas City, Missouri; James Comer, Yale Child Study Center, New Haven, Connecticut; Shawn Cooper, Pacific Gas and Electric, San Francisco, California; Mary Ann Coulson, chair, Federation of FDCA, Education Project, Redwood City, California; Roger Croteau, Children's Home Society, Miami, Florida; Diane Cutshall, Indian Meadows Elementary, Fort Wayne, Indiana; Maria de la Torre, teacher, Charles R. Hadley Elementary School, Miami, Florida; Kathie Dobberteen, principal, Glen Murdock Elementary School, Bonita, California; Sarah A. Du Bosq, teacher, South Pointe Elementary School, Miami Beach, Florida; Fred Estrada, VISTA Magazine, Coral Gables, Florida; Betsy Evans, The Giving Tree School, Gill, Massachusetts; John Farie, director of human development, Metro-Dade County, Miami, Florida; Linda Harvey Filomeno, William D'Abate Elementary, Providence, Rhode Island; Karen Fleck, Head Start Transition Project, San Jose, California; Madeline Fried, The Thurgood Marshall Child Develop-ment Center, Herndon, Virginia; Cindy Gajdos, nursery teacher, Texas Woman's Uni-versity; Ellen Galinsky, Families and Work Institute, New York, New York; Lela Gan-dini, liaison to the United States for the Department of Early Education, Reggio Emilia; Violet Geib, first grade teacher, Stiegel Elementary School, Manheim, Penn-sylvania; Gail Gonzalez, health care director, San Jose, California; Janet Gonzalez-Mena, Napa Valley College, Suison, California; Sarah M. Greene, National Head Start Association, Alexandria, Virginia; Sara P. Grillo, Charles R. Hadley Elementary School, Miami, Florida; Cynthia Haralson, teacher, Miami, Florida; Chris Holicek, kindergarten teacher, Burleigh Elementary School, Brookfield, Wisconsin; Kathleen Holz, City and Country School, New York, New York; Kari Hull, Lemon Avenue Ele-mentary School, LaMesa, California; Cami Jones, director, Texas Education Agency, Austin, Texas; Ed Labinowicz, professor, Gresham, Oregon; Antonia Lopez, The Foundation Center for Phenomenological Research, Sacramento, California; Bar-bara Lord, teacher, Lexington Park Elementary School, Lexington Park, Maryland; Miriam Mades, kindergarten teacher, South Pointe Elementary School, Miami Beach, Florida; Dodie Magill, kindergarten teacher, Pelham Road Elementary School, Greenville, South Carolina; Beverly McGhee, headmistress, Alexander Montessori School, Miami, Florida; Shawn Michaud, The Open Door Infant Center,

Austin, Texas; Lynn Michelotti, teacher, Todd Hall School, Lincolnwood, Illinois; Richard A. Morris, Fel Pro Corporation, Skokie, Illinois; Lesley M. Morrow, professor, Rutgers University; Julie Morse, teacher, Lemon Avenue Elementary, La Mesa, California; Roger Myers, director, The Twenty-First Century School Program, Independence, Missouri; Judith A. Orion, consultant, The Montessori Institute, Denver, Colorado; Michele O'Shannessy, primary teacher, HeartsHome Early Learning Center, Houston, Texas; Carrie Peery, Hamilton Academic Achievement Academy, San Diego, California; Barry Pehrsson, chief executive officer, Southwinds, Inc., Middletown, New York; Maxine Roberts, professor of education, Pittsburgh, Pennsylvania; Gary Robertson, American Guidance Service, Circle Pines, Minnesota; Nancy B. Royal, kindergarten teacher, Elm Street Elementary, Newman, Georgia; Elizabeth Sears, The Open Door Preschool, Austin, Texas; Daniel D. Shade, director, Technology in Early Childhood Habitats, Department of Individual and Family Studies, University of Delaware; Margery Sher, The Thurgood Marshall Child Development Center, Herndon, Virginia; Linda Sholar, kindergarten teacher, Sangre Ridge Elementary School, Stillwater, Oklahoma; Peggy Sparks, Jostens Learning, San Diego, California; S. W. Stile, New Mexico State University; Bonnie Storm, U.S. Army Community and Family Support Center, Alexandria, Virginia; William Tamlyn, The St. Paul Companies, Inc., St. Paul, Minnesota; Michele Taylor, CDR, Lightfoot, Virginia; Kathryn Thomas, Educational Alternatives Inc., Bloomington, Minnesota; Mildred Vance, professor of education, Arkansas State University; Judith Vandergrift, Morrison Institute for Public Policy, Tempe, Arizona; David P. Weikart, High/Scope Educational Research Foundation, Ypsilanti, Michigan; Denise West, Public Health and Nutrition Program Director, Dade County Department of Public Health, Miami, Florida; Mary Ann Wilson, Sullivan County Community College, Loch Sheldrake, New York; M. Shirley Wormsbecker, program manager, Alberta Children's Hospital, Calgary, Alberta, Canada; and Marlene Zepeda, California State University, Los Angeles.

In addition, Millie Riley, Theresa Furye, and Sue Bredekamp, National Association for the Education of Young Children, and Carol Brunson Phillips, Council for Early Childhood Professional Recognition, have been very supportive of my requests for information and help and have been very generous in giving me permission to reprint from NAEYC publications.

I would also like to thank the reviewers of the previous five editions as well as the following people who offered helpful comments on this edition: Jerold Bauch, Vanderbilt University; Karen Colleran, Pierce College; Georgiana Cornelius, New Mexico State University; Anne Federlein, University of Northern Iowa; Florence Leonard, Towsend State University; Sima Lesser, Miami-Dade Community College; Mary Link, Miami University; Patricia Lowry, Jacksonville State University; Jacqueline Paulson, The College of Staten Island/CUNY; Judith Reitsch, Eastern Washington University; Kevin Swick, University of South Carolina; and C. Stephen White, University of Georgia.

My editors at Merrill are the greatest I have ever had the pleasure of working with. The efforts of Linda Bayma, Erin Haggerty, and freelance copy editor Laura Larson have been most appreciated. Their professional manner and expertise have contributed greatly toward making this text one of exceptional quality.

Contents

2

The Past: Prologue to the Present 53

3

Montessori Education:
Continuing Renaissance 91

4

Piaget: Constructivism
in Action 121

5

Child Care: Meeting the Needs of Children, Parents, and Families

**COLOR INSERT
A Look Inside . . .
Nine Model Programs**

Following page 206

6

Infants and Toddlers:
Development, Care,
and Education   209

Contents

9

The Primary Years: The Process of Schooling   343

10

The Federal Government, Children, and Families: Buiding for the Future   381

11

Teaching Children with Special Needs: Developing Awareness   419

12

Guiding Children: Developing Prosocial Behavior   467

13

Parent, Family, and Community Involvement: Keys to Successful Programs   499

14

Multiculturalism: Education
for Living in a Diverse Society   535

15

Technology and Early Childhood: Education for the Twenty-First Century 569

16

Early Childhood Professional Development: Becoming a Professional 605

APPENDICES

A

1

Current Issues
Early Childhood Today

After you read and study this chapter, you will be able to:

- ☐ Identify contemporary influences that create interest in early childhood education
- ☐ Confidently use terminology of the early childhood profession
- ☐ Identify and describe types of early childhood education programs
- ☐ Recognize the importance of the ecology of early childhood education
- ☐ Consider the influence corporations and other agencies have on early childhood programs
- ☐ Understand the need for public policy and how public policy is developed
- ☐ Examine adults' views of children and explain the implications these views have for rearing and educating children
- ☐ Examine social, political, economic, and educational issues that influence child rearing, teaching, and developing policy
- ☐ Review the procedures for observing children and plan to use observation as an early childhood professional

POPULARITY OF EARLY CHILDHOOD EDUCATION

In 1965, with the beginning of Head Start (see chap. 10), early childhood education entered its modern period. Over the past three decades, the field of early childhood education has been enormously popular, and interest in the field is at an all-time high. For all early childhood professionals, the years that close the twentieth century promise to be exciting and challenging. As one millennium ends and another begins, early childhood education continues to be in the spotlight. The issues and opportunities of the next quarter century will be an exciting and challenging time for all who work with young children and their families.

Today, the public at large is very enthusiastic regarding the importance of the early years in learning and later development. Given this attitude, early childhood education's popularity and interest in the early years will likely continue unabated.

Problems of child abuse, the numbers of children who live in poverty, infant mortality, and society's inability to meet the needs of all children are perennial sources of controversy and concern, to which early childhood professionals continue to seek solutions. The emergence of new ideas and issues relating to the education and care of young children and the quest to provide educationally and developmentally appropriate programs keep the field in a state of disequilibrium. Early childhood professionals are constantly challenged to determine what is best for young children and their families.

PUBLIC INTEREST IN EARLY CHILDHOOD

Daily newspapers provide ample evidence of the nation's interest in young children. These are a few newspaper headlines that called attention to young children, their parents, families, and agencies that serve them:

"Program for 'Welfare Dads' Aims to Get Them Working to Support Their Children" (*Christian Science Monitor*, April 24, 1993)

"Computers in Education, Technology Boosts Science and Math Creativity, Enlivens Reading Lessons" (*Chicago Tribune*, April 25, 1993)

"Day-Care Providers Say Parents' Priorities Askew: Cost—Not Quality—Comes First When Picking Service" (*Washington Post*, May 17, 1993)

"Kindergarten Quandary" (*Washington Post*, May 13, 1993)

"Pursuing Hope in the Trenches at Head Start" (*New York Times*, May 9, 1993)

"Business Urges Improvement in Child Care" (*Wall Street Journal*, March 19, 1993)

"Fortune 500 Group Finds Acute Lack of Child Care" (*Washington Post*, March 19, 1993)

Mass media magazines such as *Working Mother*, which includes child-rearing information, and *Parenting* help quench the insatiable desire of parents and the public for information about child care and rearing. Many agencies such as hospitals and health clinics also provide parent-oriented publications.

PARENTS AND EARLY CHILDHOOD

More parents have more disposable income and are willing to spend it on enriching their and their children's lives. Parents enroll themselves and their infants and toddlers in self-improvement programs promoted as physically and cognitively stimulating. Courses designed for expectant parents, new parents, and grandparents are now a standard part of the curriculum of many community colleges and schools. During one semester at a local community college, parents could select from these courses: Parent/Infant Enrichment, Play Activities with the Preschool Child, Discipline Strategies That Work, Movement and Play Activities, Creative Learning—Storytelling/Drama, Toilet Learning, Choosing a Preschool for Your Child, Building Your Child's Self-Esteem, and Developmental Screening for Infants. Many of the courses required registration of both parents and their young children!

Stimulation/enrichment programs help popularize the importance of the very early years. Infant-parent stimulation programs catch the fancy of young parents, who want "the best" for their children. They are willing to spend time, effort, and money to see that they get it, which in turn allows early childhood professionals to address the importance of the early years. It also creates a climate of acceptance for very early education and an arena in which early childhood professionals are heard. Infant stimulation programs stimulate more than infants.

Parent groups discuss how to help children get along with others, how to reduce stress in children's lives, the loss of childhood, how to nurture in the nineties, ways to accommodate diverse lifestyles, how to extend more rights to children, and how to parent in an electronic era in which children seemingly see all and know all.

FAMILIES AND EARLY CHILDHOOD

How to best meet children's needs and how to best meet these needs in culturally appropriate ways are always primary goals of early childhood education. Early childhood professionals agree that a good way to meet the needs of children is through their families, whatever that family unit may be (see Figure 1–1). Providing for children's needs through and within the *family system* makes sense for a number of reasons. First, it is the family system that has the primary responsibility for meeting many children's needs. So, helping parents and other family members meet their children's needs in appropriate ways means that everyone stands to benefit. Helping people in a family unit—mother, father, grandparents, and others—be better parents helps them and their children.

Second, for children to be helped effectively, family problems and issues often must be addressed first. For example, helping parents gain access to adequate, affordable health care means that the whole family, including children, will be more healthy.

FIGURE 1–1   Two Models Illustrating a New Paradigm for Providing Early Childhood Services

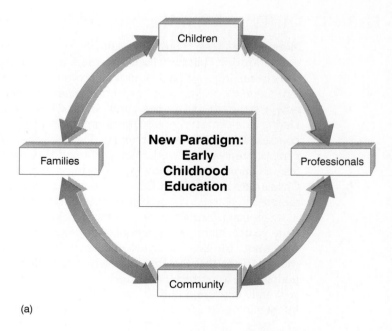

(a)

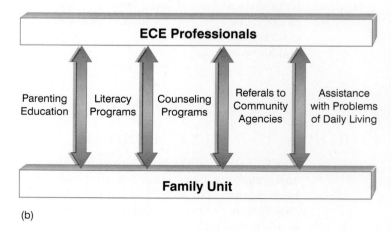

(b)

Third, early childhood professionals can do many things concurrently with children and their families that will benefit both at the same time. Literacy is a good example. Early childhood professionals are taking a family approach to helping children, their parents, and other family members learn how to read, write, speak, and listen. Teaching parents to read helps them understand the importance of supporting and promoting their children in the learning and teaching process.

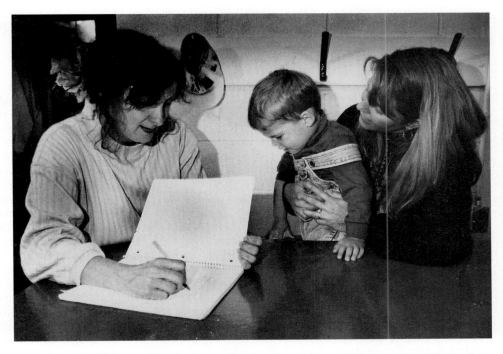

Children's development begins in the family system. The family system, with the help and support of early childhood programs, provides for children's basic needs. It makes sense for early childhood professionals to work with and through the family system in the delivery of their services.

Fourth, addressing the needs of children and their families as a whole, known as a *holistic* approach to education and the delivery of services, enables early childhood professionals and others to address a range of social concerns at the same time. Literacy, health education and care, abuse prevention, AIDS education, and parenting programs are some examples of the family-centered approach to assisting and developing children and their families. This approach will be expanded and refined by professionals throughout the coming years.

CHANGING FAMILIES

A major reason for new approaches to providing services to children and families is that families have changed and will continue to do so. Families are changing in the following ways:

1. *Structure.*   Families include many kinds of arrangements other than what is called the nuclear family. The definition of what a family is varies as society changes. Some of these changes result in

Program in Practice

NEW BEGINNINGS

New Beginnings is a collaborative effort involving San Diego, San Diego County, San Diego City Schools, the San Diego Housing Commission, and the San Diego Community College District. These five public agencies, along with the University of California–San Diego and the Children's Hospital and Health Center, are engaged in a long-term effort of institutional change as well as providing school-linked direct services to children and families.

The New Beginnings concept of inter-agency collaboration began in 1988 in a series of conversations among executives from the major public agencies serving children and families in San Diego County. The executives agreed that children and families in poverty in their communities had urgent needs and that their agencies provided services to many of the same children and families. They were concerned that none of the agencies were able to focus effectively on

preventing negative outcomes for children. From these initial conversations grew a commitment to refocus and restructure public services so that they would be more effective and accessible to families.

A feasibility study conducted in 1990 focused on the needs of families and children at Hamilton Elementary School, which serves nearly 1,300 children in grades K through 5 in a densely populated, ethnically diverse, low-income neighborhood of East San Diego. One aspect of the feasibility study placed a social worker from the Department of Social Services on the school site to work with families and children. Other components included interviews with families in their homes, meetings with families at the school, focus groups with line workers in each of the agencies, and a data match of clients served by multiple agencies. The information gathered was used to develop findings, conclusions, and a plan for implementation. A major conclusion of the

Contributed by Carrie Peery, principal, Hamilton Academic Achievement Academy—the site of New Beginnings, Integrated Services for Children and Families, San Diego, California.

- single-parent families, headed by mothers and fathers; and
- extended families, which include grandparents, uncles, aunts, and other relatives or individuals not related by kinship.

2. *Roles.*   As families change, so do the roles that parents and other family members perform. For example:

   - More parents work and have less time for their children and family affairs.
   - Working parents must combine many roles that go with being parents and employees. The many hats that parents wear increase as families change.

3. *Responsibilities.*   Responsibilities of families also are changing. As families change, many parents are not able to provide or cannot afford to pay for adequate and necessary care for their children. Other parents find that buffering

study was that most of the constraints limiting integrated services are issues of policy or practice, not insurmountable legal obstacles.

New Beginnings is not a project or program to be taken as a package and implemented. Rather, it is a set of basic principles:

■ Services and activities for families need to be focused on prevention.

■ Services need to be for families as a whole, not fragmented by the presenting "problem" or a single "client."

■ Services need to be responsive to the needs of families, not the convenience of agencies and their staff.

■ Agencies need to reallocate and realign resources that already exist before looking for infusions of new money.

■ Implementation of the collaborative process and the basic principles needs to be adapted to the needs of each community.

The first application of these concepts is at a demonstration site located on the campus of Hamilton Academic Achievement Academy. This is a multiservice center designed to provide accessible, nonfragmented access to families in the school's attendance area. Services provided at the center, opened in September 1991, include information and referral, parenting and adult education classes, workshops, counseling, case management, family advocacy, and service planning. The center also provides basic health care, including immunizations, Child Health and Disability Prevention (CHDP) exams, and minor treatment, as well as mental health services for children. The staff at the center includes a coordinator, an administrative assistant, a secretary/receptionist, and three full-time and three part-time family service advocates. Coming from existing partner agencies to work in new roles, staff members form an interdisciplinary service team to help meet the many needs of families and children. Other members of the extended team remain in their home agencies but provide services specifically targeted to families in the Hamilton attendance area.

their children from social ills such as drugs, violence, and delinquency is more than they can handle. Also, some parents are consumed by problems of their own so they have little time or attention for their children.

As families continue to change, early childhood professionals must continue to develop creative ways to meet the needs of children.

POLITICS AND EARLY CHILDHOOD EDUCATION

Whatever else can be said about education, one point holds true: education is political. Politicians and politics exert a powerful influence in determining what gets taught, how it is taught, to whom it is taught, and by whom it is taught. Early child-

Families are changing and will continue to change as society changes. Early childhood professionals must be willing and able to work with all kinds of families in the education of young children. What are the implications of changing family patterns that early childhood professionals need to remember as they work with families and children?

hood education is no exception. An important political and educational event occurred in 1989 when President George Bush and all governors of the fifty states met at the University of Virginia to set national education goals. A result of this meeting was the release in April 1991 of *America 2000: An Education Strategy.* The six goals of America 2000 are as follows:

1. All children in the United States will start school ready to learn.
2. The high school graduation rate will increase to at least 90 percent.
3. U.S. students will leave grades 4, 8, and 12 having demonstrated competency in challenging subject matter including English, mathematics, science, history, and geography; and every school in the country will ensure that all students learn to use their minds well, so they may be prepared for responsible citizenship, further learning, and productive employment in our modern economy.
4. U.S. students will be first in the world in science and mathematics achievement.
5. Every adult in the United States will be literate and will possess the knowledge and skills necessary to compete in a global economy and exercise the rights and responsibilities of citizenship.
6. Every U.S. school will be free of drugs and violence and will offer a disciplined environment conductive to learning.

In 1993, under Secretary of Education Richard Riley, the six national education goals became a formal national policy through Goals 2000: Educate America Act. The act also added competencies in arts and foreign languages as core subjects.

These goals have generated a great deal of debate, particularly concerning what they mean and how best to achieve them. Goals 1, 2, 5, and 6 have had and will continue to have particular implications for early childhood education. Goal 1 obviously impacts on children's readiness for school. Goal 2 is pertinent because the early childhood years are seen as the place to prevent school dropout. Many public school programs for three- and four-year-old children are funded with the specific purpose of beginning efforts to keep children in school at a later age. Goal 5 has encouraged many *intergenerational literacy and family literacy programs* in which children, their parents, and other family members are taught to read. Goal 6 supports the drug prevention programs implemented in early childhood programs, again on the premise that early prevention is much more effective than later treatment.

Readiness

Goal 1, known as "the readiness goal," has generated particular interest in early childhood education among politicians and early childhood professionals in determining precisely what readiness means. This examination has resulted in a reconceptualization of readiness.

Previously, readiness was generally viewed as the process of children getting ready for school. In this sense, readiness has been viewed in relation to school and the ability to read and write. This conception of readiness has traditionally placed the responsibility for "getting ready" on the child. It also implies that if a child is not ready, as judged by a test or some other criteria, then the child should not enter kindergarten or first grade or some other program. This practice often leads to children being kept out of school for a year while they get ready or being failed or held back in kindergarten or preschool.

The early childhood profession would like to get away from the use of the term *readiness*. Instead, they would like to couch their discussions and direct their actions around the ideas of "children's learning and development." The National Education Goals Panel, the group charged with assessing the nation's progress toward achieving the education goals by the year 2000, has identified five "critical dimensions" that they see as constituting children's early learning and development.

- *Physical well-being and motor development.*   Health and physical growth, ranging from being rested, fed properly, immunized, and healthy to being able to run, jump, use crayons, and work puzzles

- *Social and emotional development.*   The sense of personal well-being that allows a child to participate fully and constructively in classroom activities

- *Approaches toward learning.*   The curiosity, creativity, motivation, independence, cooperativeness, interest, and persistence that enable children from all cultures to maximize their learning

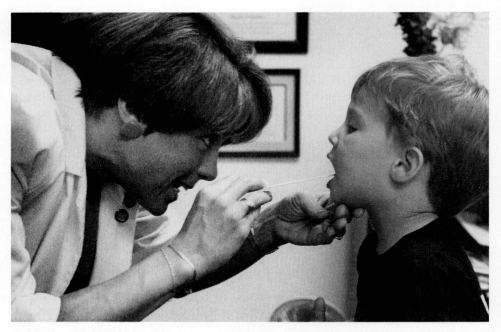

Readiness is now viewed as promoting children's learning and development in all areas. Readiness includes health and physical growth, such as being well rested, fed, and properly immunized. The United Nations estimates that worldwide, more than 8 million children a year die from five major diseases—pneumonia, diarrhea, measles, tetanus, and whooping cough.

- *Language usage.*   The talking, listening, scribbling, and composing that enable children to communicate effectively and express thoughts, feelings, and experiences

- *Cognition and general knowledge.*   Familiarity with basic information—including patterns and relationships and cause and effect—needed to solve problems in everyday life

The National Goals Panel will use these five areas to develop an Early Childhood Assessment System for assessing a sample representative of children during the kindergarten year.

NATIONAL READY TO LEARN COUNCIL

The National Ready to Learn Council, a nongovernmental consortium of thirty influential groups, is seeking bipartisan support for improving the well-being of preschool children. The council is cochaired by Ernest L. Boyer, president of the Carnegie Foundation for the Advancement of Teaching, and C. Everett Koop, former surgeon general. Participants include the Children's Defense Fund, Council of Chief State School Officers, Ecumenical Child Care Network, National Alliance of Business, American Academy of Pediatrics, American Association of Retired Persons, National Association for the Education of Young Children, and National Governor's Association.

The Ready to Learn Council's member groups plan to exchange information, encourage state and local programs that help children, monitor progress toward the goal of having children enter school ready to learn, and highlight successful preschool programs nationwide.

STATE INVOLVEMENT IN EARLY CHILDHOOD PROGRAMS

All the states are taking a lead in developing programs for young children, stimulated by several factors. One is the continuing federal reallocation of funds for early childhood and other human services programs. As federal dollars shift to other programs, states are responding by initiating programs of their own, funded from many sources—from lottery monies to taxes on commodities such as cigarettes.

Second, instead of giving monies directly to specific programs, federal dollars are consolidated into what are known as block grants—sums of money given to states to provide services according to broad general guidelines. In essence, the states, not the federal government, control how the money is spent and the nature of the programs funded. As federal support for early education is used to fund specific programs such as Head Start, the states will finance replacement, alternative, and substitute programs. This involvement will grow and strengthen as the states make greater commitments to child care and early education programs, especially for children from low-income families. For example, the majority of states have appropriated monies for prekindergarten programs to serve at-risk four-year-old children. This trend will accelerate. With direct funding comes control. When agencies contribute funding for programs, they also help determine the direction the programs will take, the policies that govern them, and which children and families they will serve.

CORPORATE INVOLVEMENT IN EARLY CHILDHOOD PROGRAMS

Many corporations are finding that early childhood education is a good investment, for a number of reasons. One is that corporations are increasingly dissatisfied with the products of the nation's schools. They have to spend millions of dollars teaching their employees such basic skills as reading and writing. Corporate executives think it makes more sense to invest in literacy in the early years than in the later years. In this sense, corporations see their investments in children and families as *social investments;* that is, investing in children and families is a good investment that pays dividends to all. This social investment approach to early childhood and other programs is also based in part on economics. A dollar invested in quality child care, drug prevention programs, literacy programs, and health programs (e.g., immunizations) will save money later through drug-free, literate, and healthy adults. In fact, a formula that corporate executives and politicians often use is that $1 invested in the early childhood years saves $7 in the adolescent and adult years.

Over the past decade, the following are some ways corporations have changed their patterns of involvement in early childhood programs:[1]

- They are developing programs that benefit the *communities* in which they operate as well as their own employees.

- They are leveraging their resources by teaming up on projects with local businesses and public agencies.

- They are extending their efforts to new groups, such as school-age and mildly ill children.

- They are helping bridge the gap between what good care costs and what parents can afford.

Consequently, companies such as American Telephone and Telegraph and Johnson and Johnson are spending considerable amounts of money on early childhood programs. The Stride Rite Corporation in particular has a reputation as a leader in providing programs for children and families. Stride Rite was the first company to provide on-site child care for its employees (see the Historical Time Line in chap. 2) and the first to offer intergenerational care for children and the elderly in the same facility. A description of this program appears in the color insert following page 206.

Increasingly, the private and governmental sectors are asking businesses to help them assist underserved populations. For example, the federal government is seeking business' aid in paying for a new pregnancy handbook designed to help reduce the infant mortality rate. The eighty-two-page *Health Diary* provides information on prenatal care and health care for children during the first two years of life. The publication, which costs $4.25, is also seen as a means of empowering parents and actively involving them in their health and that of their children. Federal officials will use the money from businesses to distribute free copies of the *Health Diary* in fifteen cities participating in Healthy Start, a federal program started in 1991 to improve prenatal care.

In short, early childhood education and young children have captured the attention of the nation. They compete with budget deficits, nuclear arms treaties, and summit meetings for media attention. Young children are prime-time subjects. Consequently, early childhood professionals must learn more about how to care for, educate, and rear children so they can advise parents, legislators, and those who formulate public policy when they look to them for guidance in determining what is best for the country's children.

THE RETURN OF CHILD-CENTERED EDUCATION

The field of early childhood has always been to a greater or lesser degree child centered, and today it is decidedly more so. This rediscovery and reemphasis on child-centered education is occurring for a number of reasons. First, society in general is much more interested in the whole child and efforts to address all of the needs that children have, not just their academic needs. As a result, there is much more concern for encouraging children to be healthy and lead healthy lifestyles. Consequently, interest in children's immunizations and seeing that all children are fully immunized by age two has received a lot of attention. Programs to help children be free of drugs are common in early childhood and primary programs. Concern for the welfare of children in all areas of their growth and development is evident.

TERMINOLOGY OF EARLY CHILDHOOD EDUCATION

Knowing the terminology is a necessity when discussing early childhood education. As an early childhood professional, you will want to have a command of the terminology used by the National Association for the Education of Young Children (NAEYC) and early childhood professionals (see Figure 1–2).

The term *professional* is used throughout this book to refer to all who work with, care for, and teach children between birth and age eight. This designation is used for several reasons. First, it avoids the obvious confusion between the use of such terms as *caregiver* and *teacher*. It is no longer easy or desirable to distinguish between someone who promotes care for and someone who teaches children. For example, the caregiving and educating roles are now blended so that a person who cares for infants is instructing them as well. However, in the preschool, kindergarten, and primary years, the term *teacher* is still and will continue to be used to designate professionals who *teach* children. Second, the early childhood profession is trying to upgrade the image and role of all those who work with young children. Referring to everyone as professionals helps achieve this goal.

Throughout this text, *early childhood* refers to the child from birth to age eight, which is a standard and accepted definition used by the NAEYC.[2] (At the same time, professionals recognize that prenatal development is also important.) The term frequently refers to children who have not yet reached school age, and the public often uses it to refer to children in any type of preschool.

Early childhood programs provide "services for children from birth through age eight in part-day and full-day group programs in centers, homes, and institutions; kindergartens and primary schools; and recreational programs."[3]

Early childhood education consists of the services provided in early childhood settings. It is common for professionals of young children to use the terms *early childhood* and *early childhood education* synonymously.

Other terms frequently used when discussing the education of young children are *nursery school* and *preschool*. *Nursery school* is a program for the education of two-, three-, and four-year-old children. Many nursery schools are half-day programs, usually designed for children of mothers who do not work outside the home, although many children who have two working parents do attend. The purpose of the nursery school is to provide for active learning in a play setting. In some instances the kindergarten curriculum has been pushed down into the nursery school. As a result, a child-centered program in an informal play setting that characterizes a good nursery school has been replaced by a formal teacher-centered set-

FIGURE 1–2   Types of Early Childhood Programs

Program	Purpose	Age
Early childhood program	Multipurpose	Birth to grade 3
Child care	Play/socialization; baby-sitting; physical care; provides parents opportunities to work; cognitive development; full-quality care	Birth to 6 years
High school child care programs	Provide child care for children of high school students, especially unwed parents; serve as an incentive for student/parents to finish high school and as a training program in child care and parenting skills	6 weeks to 5 years
Drop-off child care centers	Provide care for short periods of time while parents shop, exercise, or have appointments	Infancy through the primary grades
After-school care	Provides care for children after school hours	Children of school age; generally K to 6
Family day care	Provides care for a group of children in a home setting; generally custodial in nature	Variable
Employer child care	Different settings for meeting child care	Variable; usually as early as 6 weeks to the beginning of school
Corporate child care	Same as employer child care	Same as employer child care
Proprietary care	Provides care and/or education to children; designed to make a profit	6 weeks to entrance into first grade
Nursery school (public or private)	Play/socialization; cognitive development	2 to 4 years
Preschool (public or private)	Play/socialization; cognitive development	2½ to 5 years
Parent cooperative preschool	Play/socialization; preparation for kindergarten and first grade; baby-sitting; cognitive development	2 to 5 years
Baby-sitting cooperatives (co-op)	Provide parents with reliable baby-sitting; parents sit for others' children in return for reciprocal services	All ages
Prekindergarten	Play/socialization; cognitive development; preparation for kindergarten	3½ to 5 years
Junior kindergarten	Prekindergarten program	Primarily 4-year-olds
Senior kindergarten	Basically the same as regular kindergarten	Same as kindergarten

FIGURE 1–2 *Continued*

Program	Purpose	Age
Kindergarten	Preparation for first grade; developmentally appropriate activities for 4½- to 6-year-olds; increasingly viewed as the grade before first grade and as a regular part of the public school program	4 to 6 years
Pre-first grade	Preparation for first grade; often for students who "failed" or did not do well in kindergarten	5 to 6 years
Interim first grade	Provides children with an additional year of kindergarten and readiness activities prior to and as preparation for first grade	5 to 6 years
Transitional or transition classes	Classes specifically designed to provide for children of the same developmental age	Variable
Developmental kindergarten	Same as regular kindergarten; often enrolls children who have completed one or more years in an early childhood special education program	5 to 6 years
Transitional kindergarten	Extended learning of kindergarten preparation for first grade	Variable
Preprimary	Preparation for first grade	5 to 6 years
Primary	Teaches skills associated with grades 1, 2, and 3	6 to 8 years
Toy lending libraries	Provide parents and children with games, toys, and other materials that can be used for learning purposes; housed in libraries, vans, or early childhood centers	Birth through primary years
Lekotek	Resource center for families who have children with special needs; sometimes referred to as a *toy* or *play library* (*lekotek* is a Scandinavian word that means play library)	Birth through primary years
Infant stimulation programs (also called parent/infant stimulation and mommy and me programs)	Programs for enhancing sensory and cognitive development of infants and young toddlers through exercise and play; activities include general sensory stimulation for children and educational information and advice for parents	3 months to 2 years
Multiage grades or groups	Groups or classes of children of various ages; generally spanning 2 to 3 years per group	Variable
Dual-age classroom	An organizational plan in which children from two grade levels are grouped together; another term for multiage grouping and for maintaining reasonable student-teacher ratios	Variable

FIGURE 1–2 *Continued*

Program	Purpose	Age
Learning families	Another name for multiage grouping. However, the emphasis is on practices that create a family atmosphere and encourage living and learning as a family. The term was commonly used in open education programs. Its revival signifies the reemergence of progressive and child-centered approaches.	Variable
Junior first grade	Preparation for first grade	5 to 6 years
Split class	Teaches basic academic and social skills of grades involved	Variable, but usually primary
Head Start	Play/socialization; academic learning; comprehensive social and health services; prepares children for kindergarten and first grade	2 to 6 years
Follow Through	Extended Head Start services to grades 1, 2, and 3	6 to 8 years
Private schools	Provide care and/or education	Usually preschool through high school
Department of Children, Youth, and Families	A multipurpose agency of many state and county governments; usually provides such services as administration of state and federal monies, child care licensing, and protective services	All
Health and Human Services	Same as Dept. of Children, Youth, and Families	All
Health and Social Services	Same as Dept. of Children, Youth, and Families	All
Home Start	Provides Head Start service in the home setting	Birth to 6 or 7 years
Laboratory school	Provides demonstration programs for preservice teachers; conducts research	Variable; birth through senior high
Child and Family Resource Program	Delivers Head Start services to families	Birth to 8 years
Montessori school (preschool and grade school)	Provides programs that use the philosophy, procedures, and materials developed by Maria Montessori (see chapter 3)	1 to 8 years
Open education	Child-centered learning in an environment characterized by freedom and learning through activities based on children's interests	2 to 8 years
British primary school	Implements the practices and procedures of open education	2 to 8 years
Magnet school	Specializes in subjects and curriculum designed to attract students; usually has a theme (e.g., performing arts); designed to give parents choices and to integrate schools	5 to 18 years

ting. *Preschool* generally means any educational program for children prior to their entrance into kindergarten.

Preschool programs for three- and four-year-old children are rapidly becoming a part of the public school system, particularly those designed to serve low-income children and their families. For example, the Dade County, Florida, public schools operate 143 preschool programs for three- and four-year-old children.

When a public school or other agency operates one program for five-year-olds and another for four-year-olds, the term *kindergarten* is applied to the former and *nursery school* or *preschool* to the latter. Public school kindergarten is now almost universal for five-year-old children (see chap. 8), so it can no longer be thought of as "preschool." Kindergarten is now part of the elementary grades K through 6, and the designation is almost universally used.

The term *prekindergarten* is growing in use and refers to programs for four-year-olds attending a program prior to kindergarten. Another term, *transitional kindergarten*, designates a program for children who are not ready for kindergarten and who can benefit from another year of the program. The term *transitional* also refers to grade school programs that provide additional opportunities for children to master skills associated with a particular grade. Transitional programs do not usually appear beyond the second and third grades.

Junior first grade or *pre–first grade* are transitional programs between kindergarten and first grade designed to help five-year-olds get ready to enter first grade. Not all children are equally "ready" to benefit from typical first grade because of the wide range of mental ages and experiential backgrounds, and children frequently benefit from such special programs. However, the goal of many early childhood professionals is to have all children learning at levels appropriate for them.

Preprimary refers to programs for children prior to their entering first grade; *primary* means first, second, and third grades. In some school districts primary grade children are taught in classes that include two grade levels. In these *split* or *nongraded classes*, first and second graders and second and third graders are taught in a single class. Split classes are seldom composed of upper-elementary children. Reasons for split classes are increasing or decreasing school enrollments, influences of child-centered practices, and teacher contracts that limit class size.

A *parent cooperative* preschool is a school formed and controlled by parents for their children. Programs of this type are generally operated democratically, with the parents hiring the staff. Often, some of the parents are hired to direct or staff the program. Being part of a cooperative means parents have some responsibility for assisting in the program.

The term *child care* encompasses many programs and services for preschool children. *Day care* is a term used for child care, but most people engaged in the care of young children recognize this as outmoded. *Child care* is more accurate and descriptive because it focuses on children themselves. The primary purpose of child care programs is to care for young children who are not in school and school-age children before and after school hours. Child care programs may have a total quality orientation or an educational orientation, and some may offer primarily baby-sitting or custodial care. Many programs have a sliding-fee schedule based on parents' ability to pay. Quality child care programs are increasingly characterized by their comprehensive services that address children's total needs—physical, social, emotional, creative, and intellectual. Today, parents, the public, and the profession understand that *child care* means providing physical care *and* educational programs for the whole child.

A large number of *family day care* programs provide child care services in the homes of the caregivers. This alternative to center-based programs usually accommodates a maximum of four or five children in a *family day care home. Home care* programs were formerly custodial in nature, but there is a growing trend for caregivers to provide a full range of services in their homes.

Church-related or *church-sponsored* preschool and elementary programs are quite common and becoming more popular. These programs usually have a cognitive, basic skills emphasis within a context of religious doctrine and discipline. The reason for the popularity of these church-sponsored programs, which often charge tuition, is their emphasis on the basic skills and no-nonsense approach to learning and teaching.

Head Start is a federally sponsored program for children from low-income families. Established by the Economic Opportunity Act in 1964, Head Start is intended to help children and their families overcome the effects of poverty. *Follow Through* extends Head Start programs to children in grades 1 through 3 and works with school personnel rather than apart from the schools.

Public and private agencies, including colleges, universities, hospitals, and corporations, operate many kinds of *demonstration programs*. Many colleges and universities with schools of education have a *laboratory school* used primarily for research in teaching methods, demonstration of exemplary programs and activities, and teacher training. Many of these schools also develop materials and programs for children with physical and learning disabilities.

As the name implies, a *toy library* makes toys and other learning materials available to children, parents, child care providers, and teachers. Toy libraries may be housed in libraries, shopping malls, churches, preschools, and mobile vans. Many toy libraries are supported by user fees and parent and community volunteers.

Names for Children

Professionals in early childhood education use certain labels to refer to children of different ages, as outlined in Figure 1–3. Just as professionals use certain terms to refer to children, so too are there labels for the various adults who work with young children, as shown in Figure 1–4.

ISSUES WITH NAMES AND CERTIFICATION

A growing issue in early childhood education is what to call professionals who work with young children and what certification they should have. As early childhood programs become more closely tied with the public schools and profit-oriented private sectors, certification is becoming more of an issue. Certification is an issue for two

FIGURE 1–3   Labels for Children

Name	Description	Age
Baby	Generic term referring to a child from birth through the first 2 years of life	Birth to 2 years
Neonate	Child during the first month of life, from Latin words *neo* (new) and *natus* (born); usually used by nurses, pediatric specialists, and people working in the area of child development	Birth to 1 month
Infants	Children from birth to the beginning of independent walking (about 12 months of age)	Birth to 1 year
Toddlers	Children from the beginning of independent walking to about age 3; the term *toddler* is derived from the lunging, tottering, precarious balanced movement of children as they learn to walk.	13 months to 3 years
Preschoolers	Children between toddler age and age of entrance into kindergarten or first grade; because kindergarten is becoming more widespread, it is customary to refer to 4-year-olds as preschoolers.	3 to 5 years
Child/children	Generic term for individuals from birth through the elementary grades	Birth to 8 years
The very young	Used to identify and specify children from birth through preschool	Birth to 5 years

reasons. The first relates to *what* certification a person who works with young children should have. Public school teachers generally must have a four-year degree and state certification in early childhood education. Some have certification to teach grades K through 3, others to teach pre-K, meaning three- and four-year-old children. Some states have certification for teachers who want to work with infants and toddlers. However, some think that a four-year degree and state certification is not necessary for persons who want to teach and care for children from birth to age four. There is a decided movement toward having the child development associate (CDA) credential be the certification of choice for teachers of children from birth to four years, with four-year-degree people with certification acting as supervisors, mentors, and programs directors. The CDA competency goals and functional areas are found in Appendix A.

Economics is one of the primary factors fueling the certification issue. As public schools in particular establish programs for children at earlier and earlier ages, the cost of providing four-year certified teachers becomes increasingly expensive. Many school districts want to save money by hiring teachers with less than four-year

FIGURE 1–4   Labels for Adults Who Work with Young Children

Title	Description
Early childhood professional	This is the preferred title for anyone who works with young children in any capacity. This designation reflects the growing belief of the early childhood profession that people who work with children at any level are professionals and as such are worthy of the respect, remuneration, and responsibilities that go with being a professional.
Early childhood educator	Works with young children and has committed to self-development by participating in specialized training and programs to extend professional knowledge and competence
Early childhood teacher	Responsible for planning and conducting a developmentally and educationally appropriate program for a group or classroom of children; supervises an assistant teacher or aide; usually has a bachelor's degree in early childhood, elementary education, or child development
Early childhood assistant teacher	Assists the teacher in conducting a developmentally and educationally appropriate program for a group or classroom; frequently acts as a coteacher but may lack education or training to be classified as a teacher (many people who have teacher qualifications serve as an assistant teacher because they enjoy the program or because the position of teacher is not available); usually has a high school diploma or associate degree and is involved in professional development
Early childhood associate teacher	Plans and implements activities with children; has an associate degree and/or the CDA credential; may also be responsible for care and education of a group of children
Aide	Assists the teacher and teacher assistant when requested; usually considered an entry-level position
Director	Develops and implements a center or school program; supervises all staff; may teach a group of children
Home visitor	Conducts a home-based child development/education program; works with children, families, and staff members
Child development associate	Has completed a CDA assessment and received the CDA credential[*]
Caregiver	Provides care, education, and protection for the very young in or outside the home; includes parents, relatives, child care workers, and early childhood teachers
Parent	Provides the child with basic care, direction, support, protection, and guidance
Volunteer	Contributes time, services, and talents to support staff. Usually are parents, retired persons, grandparents, and university/college/high school students

[*]CDA National Credentialing Program, *Child Development Associate Assessment System and Competency Standards* (Washington, D.C.: CDA National Credentialing Program, 1985), p. 551.

degrees and state certification to teach infants, toddlers, and preschoolers. This trend will likely continue, with professional organizations such as the NAEYC collaborating with other professional organizations and state and local education agencies to develop certification guidelines for teachers of infants, toddlers, and preschoolers.

As far as names for professionals are concerned, the professional designation *teacher* will likely be used to designate all those whose primary responsibility is to teach children of all ages. Thus, there will be infant teacher/educator, toddler teacher/educator as well as preschool teacher, kindergarten teacher, and so forth. However, the term *early childhood professional* is used more often to designate anyone working with young children up to age eight. (See also chap. 16.)

THE ECOLOGY OF EARLY CHILDHOOD

Ecology is the study of how people interact with their environments and the consequences (good and bad) of these interactions. Interest is growing in how children interact with their environments—family, home, child care center, and school—and the effect of these interactions on children.

Early childhood ecological considerations apply at three levels. The first level is an examination of the environments and how they are structured and arranged to promote children's maximum growth. For example, early childhood professionals are more aware than ever of the role the child care environment has in influencing health, safety, and physical and intellectual development. Sensitive professionals seek ways to structure environments so they are less stressful, more healthful, less dangerous, and more accommodating to children's developmental needs.

At the second level, early childhood professionals focus on how environments interact with each other. Professionals are part of children's environments, and how they interact with parents, who are also part of children's environments, affects children. For example, the extent to which a child's home and family does or does not support her literacy development greatly influences how well she learns to speak, write, and read. An unfavorable ecological setting, one without printed materials—books, magazines, and newspapers—and in which language is not encouraged, greatly influences a child's literacy development. Early childhood professionals demonstrate their attunement to the importance of interactions between educational settings and homes when they initiate programs of parent involvement and family support.

Political and social environments represent a third, more abstract level of interaction. For example, in Florida, kindergarten is compulsory for all children five years of age as of September 1. What effects does such political policy have on young children? Some people worry that children who are five by September 1 are "too old" when they enter kindergarten. Others are concerned about the cost and trauma parents undergo to find quality child care because their children were born a month or a day too late. Others see an advantage to the September 1 age limit in that children are older when they come to school and therefore are more "ready" to learn.

Ecological considerations interest early childhood and child development researchers in another way. They want to know how children's natural environments—their homes, families, child care centers, peer groups, and communities—

influence their behavior. Say, for example, that a researcher is interested in knowing more about the factors that affect young children's toy selection. She designs a laboratory experiment, gathers data, and arrives at certain conclusions. But these conclusions may not be equally valid for explaining how young children choose toys in their homes. This is one reason there is so much interest in ecological settings by those who are searching for answers to why children behave as they do. The point is that members of the early childhood profession, parents, social workers, legislators, and others are beginning to care about such ecological relationships, which will undoubtedly play an even more important role in early childhood as the years go by.

PUBLIC POLICY AND EARLY CHILDHOOD EDUCATION

Public policies in the field of early childhood education are policies that affect and influence the lives of children, parents, and families. They are implemented through official statements, pronouncements, and legislation. Many child care programs and most public schools, for example, have policies that require full immunization against childhood diseases before entering the program. As you might suspect, several public policies determine what ages children can enter school, how child care programs should operate, and how to provide appropriate care and education for children with special needs. Throughout this text, you will find many instances in which public policy outlines specific kinds of programs for children and families and the circumstances and funding under which they are delivered.

As early childhood professionals become increasingly involved in advocacy activities, they and their professional organizations issue position statements designed to influence public policy prior to its enactment and implementation. Child advocacy agencies draft position papers on topics ranging from developmentally appropriate practices for young children to the pros and cons of developing public school programs for four-year-olds. The NAEYC, for example, is a strong advocate for developmentally appropriate practices in early childhood programs. Agencies such as the Children's Defense Fund influence national and state legislation for programs to help children and families. (In chap. 16, you will learn more about your professional roles and responsibilities in advocating for public policy that supports children and their families.)

At no time in U.S. history has there been so much interest and involvement on the part of professionals in the development of public policy. This political reality is beneficial to all—children, parents, families, and early childhood professionals—for it helps assure that children's families' best interests will be considered when decisions are made that affect them.

ENDANGERED CHILDHOOD

Concern is growing that childhood as we knew or remember it is disappearing. Children are often viewed as pseudo-adults; they even dress like adults, in designer clothes, and expensive athletic shoes. Some believe that childhood is not only endangered but already gone. Others add that children are hurried and forced to grow up too fast too soon. In addition, childhood and children are endangered in another way. The circumstances in and under which parents must rear their children have worsened over the past decade. Growing numbers of families lack the necessary resources to raise their children well. Figure 1–5 identifies eight indicators of children's well-being that are used to measure how well the nation's children are doing. In all areas, children have lost ground.

Improving the conditions that affect and influence these indicators is a major challenge facing early childhood professionals and all child- and family-serving organizations. The nature and extent of what is required to help children and families underscore the necessity for collaboration among and between early childhood professionals and community agencies.

VIEWS OF CHILDREN: INFLUENCES ON EARLY CHILDHOOD

Views of children determine how people teach and rear them. As you read about the different views of children, try to clarify and change, when appropriate, what you believe. Also, identify social, environmental, and political factors that tend to support each particular view. Sometimes, of course, views overlap, so it is possible to synthesize ideas from several perspectives into a particular personal view.

FIGURE 1–5   National Indicators of Child Well-Being

Indicators	From	To	Difference
Percentage of low-birth-weight babies	1985 (6.7)	1990 (7.0)	+0.3
Infant mortality rate (per 1,000 live births)	1985 (10.6)	1990 (9.2)	−1.4
Death rate, ages 1–14 (per 100,000 children)	1985 (33.8)	1990 (30.5)	−3.3
Teen violent death rate, ages 15 to 19 (per 100,000 teens)	1985 (62.8)	1990 (70.9)	+8.1
Percentage of all births that are to single teens	1985 (7.5)	1990 (8.7)	+1.2
Percentage graduating high school	1985 (71.6)	1990 (68.7)	−2.9
Percentage of children in poverty	1985 (20.5)	1987–91 (19.8)	−0.7
Percentage of children in single-parent families	1985–87 (22.7)	1988–92 (24.7)	+2.0

Sources: Center for the Study of Social Policy and the Annie E. Casie Foundation.

A major problem facing every-one is the growing number of children who live in or who are affected by poverty. As report-ed in the 1993 Kids Count Data Book, *"The highest child poverty rates persist in the South. More than one third of the children in Louisiana and Mississippi are poor." Helping children and their families requires more than education: it also requires assistance with employment, housing and social services.*

Miniature Adults

What early childhood professionals and parents identify as childhood has not always been considered a distinct period of life. During medieval times, the notion of child-hood did not exist; little distinction was made between children and adults. The con-cept of children as miniature adults was logical for the time and conditions of medieval Europe. Economic conditions did not allow for a long childhood depen-dency. The only characteristics that separated children from adults were size and age. Children were expected to act as adults in every way, and they did so.

In many respects the twentieth century is no different, because children are still viewed and treated as adults. In many third world countries of Latin America, Africa, and Asia, children are, of necessity, expected to be economically productive. They are members of the adult working world at age four, five, or six. The United Nations Educational, Scientific and Cultural Organization (UNESCO) estimates that 100 mil-lion children around the world work and live in city streets. In many countries chil-dren are involved in war as active participants and casualties. Almost daily, newspa-pers show these children dead or wounded and waiting for help.

In the United States, where child labor laws protect children from the world of adult work and exploitation, some people advocate allowing children to enter the workplace at earlier ages and for lower wages. In some rural settings, young children still have economic value. Approximately one million migrant children pick crops and help their parents earn a livelihood (see chap. 10). At the other end of the spectrum, child actors and models engage in highly profitable and what some call glamorous careers.

Encouraging children to act like adults and hurrying them toward adulthood causes conflicts between capabilities and expectations, particularly when early childhood professionals demand adultlike behavior from children and set unrealistic expectations. Problems associated with learning, behavior, and social skills can occur when children are constantly presented with tasks and activities that are developmentally inappropriate for them.

The Competent Child

The 1960s ushered in a renewal of interest in very young children and how they learn. Many research studies (see chap. 2) have focused on the importance of the early years and challenged professionals and parents to reconsider the role early learning plays in lifelong learning. As a result of this renewed interest in the early years, parents placed great *intellectual* importance on early learning. This change in parental attitudes toward early learning resulted in what David Elkind calls the "concept of the competent infant." He believes the image of the competent infant is promoted and reinforced by such social conditions as divorce, increasing numbers of single parents, and two-career families. According to Elkind, "The concept of the competent infant is clearly more in keeping with these contemporary family styles." As Elkind explains,

> A competent infant can cope with the separation from parents at an early age. He or she is able to adjust with minimal difficulty to babysitters, day care centers, full-day nursery schools and so on. If some parents feel residual pangs of guilt about leaving their young offspring in out-of-home care, they can place their youngster in a high-pressure academic program. If the child were not in such a program, the parents tell themselves, he or she would fall behind peers and would not be able to compete academically when it is time to enter kindergarten. From this perspective, high pressure academic programs are for the young child's "own good."[4]

Many parents embrace the concept of the competent infant as compatible with what they want to achieve in their own lives. An upwardly mobile, career-oriented parent wants a child who can achieve at an early age. Parents want to begin early to assure success and advancement for their competent children. Susan Littwin sums up this attitude toward child rearing:

> What the child care experts did do, at least indirectly, was create the idea of the professional parent. With all the advice available on television talk shows and in magazines and paperback books, raising children could no longer be something that you did by tradition or whim or common sense. There was a right way and a wrong way to put a child to bed, to leave him with a baby-sitter, to get him started at school, to have a friend over. Being a parent was a career; the harder you worked the more you gained.[5]

The view of the competent child is alive and well in the United States. Indeed, some parents believe that their children possess the competence and resiliency to deal with the problems associated with growing up as well as divorce, poverty, and lack of health care.

The Child as Sinful

Based primarily on the religious belief in original sin, the view of the child as sinful was widely accepted in the fourteenth through eighteenth centuries, particularly in colonial North America during the Puritan era of the sixteenth and seventeenth centuries. Misbehavior was a sign of this inherent sin. Making children behave and using corporal punishment whenever necessary were emphasized. Misbehavior was taken as proof of the devil's influence, and beating the devil out of the child was an acceptable solution.

This view of inherent sinfulness persists, manifested in the belief that children need to be controlled through rigid supervision and insistence on unquestioning obedience to and respect for adults. Educational institutions are perceived as places in which children can be taught "right" behavior. The number of private and parochial or religious schools that emphasize respect, obedience, and correct behavior is growing because of parents' hopes of rearing children who are less susceptible to the temptations of crime, drugs, and declining moral values. Also, the Christian Right preaches a biblical approach to child rearing, encouraging parents to raise their children to obey them. Disobedience is viewed as sinful, and obedience is promoted, in part, through strict discipline.

Blank Tablets

The English philosopher John Locke (1632–1704) believed that children were born into the world as *tabula rasa*, or blank tablets. After extensive observations, Locke concluded, "There is not the least appearance of any settled ideas at all in them; especially of ideas answering the terms which make up those universal propositions that are esteemed innate principles."[6] Locke believed that children's experiences, through sensory impressions, determined what they learned and consequently what they became. The blank tablet view presupposes no innate genetic code or inborn traits; that is, children are born with no predisposition toward any behavior except what is characteristic of human beings. The sum of what a child becomes depends on the nature and quality of experience; in other words, environment is the primary determinant of what a person becomes.

The blank tablet view has several implications for teaching and child rearing. If children are seen as empty vessels to be filled, the teacher's job is to fill them—to present knowledge without regard to needs, interests, or readiness for learning. What is important is that children learn what is taught. Children become what adults make of them.

This view of children de-emphasizes individual differences and assumes that as children are exposed to the same environmental influences, they will tend to behave and even think the same. This concept is the basis for many educational beliefs and practices in socialist countries. Children begin schooling early, often at six weeks of age, and are taught a standard curriculum that promotes a common political consciousness. They are expected to behave in ways that are consistent with and appropriate to how a citizen of the state should behave.

Growing Plants

A perennially popular view of children envisages them as growing plants with the educator or parent acting as gardener. Classrooms and homes are greenhouses in which children grow and mature in harmony with their natural growth patterns. A consequence of growth and maturing is that children *unfold,* much as a flower blooms under the proper conditions. In other words, what children are to become results from natural growth and a nurturing environment. Two key ingredients of this natural growth and unfolding are *play* and *readiness.* The content and process of learning are included in play, and materials and activities are designed to promote play.

Children become ready for learning through motivation and play. This concept prompts teaching subjects or skills when children reach the point at which they can benefit from appropriate instruction. Lack of readiness to learn indicates that the child has not sufficiently matured; the natural process of unfolding has not occurred.

Belief in the concept of unfolding is evident in certain social and educational policies, such as proposals to raise the age requirements for entry into kindergartens and first grade so that children have more time to mature and get ready for school. Many people also believe each child's maturation occurs in accordance with an innate timetable, that there is a "best time" for learning specific tasks. They feel it is important to allow time for children's inner tendencies to develop and that teachers and parents should not "force" learning. This maturation process is as important, if not more so, than children's experiences. Many contemporary programs operate on the unfolding concept, whether or not it is explicitly stated.

Evidence for the widespread view of children as growing plants is poignantly illustrated by one father's reflections on the results and implications of his son's kindergarten screening test. This father was struck by the fact that his son had performed adequately, but not perfectly, and wondered what relevance the kindergarten screening test actually had to his son's future school performance.

> We then went upstairs to water some late seedlings that go into our garden for fall. Radicchio . . . broccoli, lettuce and cauliflower. Noah ran his finger over the sprouts and giggled. They tickled. There they were, uncounted dozens of sprouts, all green, all about the same height.
>
> And it came to me.
>
> As I nurture and fertilize and pull the weeds that will want to clog this boy's growing-up years, he, too, will come to fruition. I'll have some control over that—some, not total, I realize. He may turn out to be the finest of the group, the biggest broccoli, the finest head of radicchio. He may command respect, praise and a high price in the marketplace of life.[7]

Property

The view that children are property has persisted throughout history. Its foundation is that children are the property of their parents or institutions. This view is justified in part by the idea that, as creators of children, parents have a right to them and their labors. Children are, in a real sense, the property of their parents. Parents have broad authority and jurisdiction over their children. Interestingly, few laws interfere with the right of parents to control their children's lives, although this situation is changing somewhat as children are given more rights and the rights they have are protected.

Laws (although difficult to enforce) protect children from physical and emotional abuse. Where there are compulsory attendance laws, parents must send their children to school. Generally, however, parents have a free hand in dealing with their children. Legislatures and courts are reluctant to interfere in what is considered a sacrosanct parent-child relationship. Parents are generally free to exercise full authority over their children. Within certain broad limits, most parents feel their children are theirs to do with as they please. Parents who embrace this view see themselves as decision makers for their children and may place their own best interests above those of their children.

Investments in the Future

Closely associated with the notion of children as property is the view that children represent future wealth or potential for parents and a nation. Since medieval times, people have viewed child rearing as an investment in the future. Many parents assume (not always consciously) that, when they are no longer able to work or must retire, their children will provide for them. Consequently, having children becomes a means to an end. Seeing that children are clothed and fed assures their future economic contribution to their parents.

This view of children as investments, particularly in their parents' future, is being dramatically played out in contemporary society. More middle-age adults are becoming parents to their aging and ill parents. This group, known as the "sandwich generation," is taking care of both their grandchildren, as a result of divorce, death, abandonment, and other circumstances, *and* their elderly parents. Many of these middle-age parents who thought they were investing in their future through their children may not have any investment at all.

Over the last several decades, several social policies in the United States have been based partly on the view that children are future investments for society in general. Many programs are built on the underlying assumption that preventing problems in childhood leads to more productive adulthood. An extension of this attitude is that preventing a problem is less expensive than curing one. Some local educational programs thus emphasize identifying the problems of children and their families early, in order to take preventive rather than remedial action. As professionals, we also know that besides being more expensive, remediation is not as effective as prevention.

Particularly during the 1960s, many federal programs were based on the idea of conserving one of the country's greatest resources—its children. Head Start, Follow Through, and child welfare programs are products of this view, which has resulted in a "human capital" or "investment" rationale for child care and other services.

The public believes a primary goal of education is to develop children who will be productive and help protect the nation against foreign competition. Therefore, the early education of young children in "good" programs is seen as one way to strengthen the United States economically. Thus, the country's best defense against outside economic forces is a well-educated, economically productive population. From this perspective, then, investing in children is seen as an investment in the country. Also, the view that children are our greatest wealth implies that we cannot and should not waste this potential.

Some believe, however, that this perspective of children as an investment in the future fails to consider children's intrinsic human worth. Trying to make a nation stronger through its children tends to emphasize national priorities over individuals. Also, solving a nation's "problems" is not and should not be viewed primarily as a "children's" problem.

CHILDREN AS PERSONS WITH RIGHTS

A contemporary legal and humanistic view recognizes children as individuals with rights of their own. While children are often still treated as economic commodities and individuals who need protection, their rights are beginning to be defined, promoted, and defended. Since children are not organized into political groups, others must act as their advocates. Courts and social service agencies are becoming particular defenders.

In 1989, the United Nations (UN) Convention on the Rights of the Child was adopted by 159 member states of the UN General Assembly. The convention, in reality a human treaty, went into effect on September 2, 1990, after ratification by more than twenty nations. It has the status of a legally binding treaty for all nations who sign it.

The convention contains fifty-four articles, and the highlights are printed in Appendix B. The articles convey a very strong view of the child as a family member and individual. You will note that the convention combines political, civil, economic, and cultural rights. In this sense, the convention acknowledges that health and economic well-being are also essential to political freedoms and rights. In addition, by extending rights to individual children, the convention challenges the view of children as property.

The National Education Association (NEA), the nation's largest teachers' professional organization, adopted the following *Bill of Rights for Children* as presented to the NEA Representative Assembly on July 4, 1991:

> We, the People of the United States, in order to achieve a more perfect society, fulfill our moral obligations, further our founding ideals and preserve the continued blessings of liberty, do hereby proclaim this Bill of Rights for Children.

I.   No child in a land of abundance shall be wanting for plentiful and nutritional food.

II. A society as advanced in medical knowledge and abilities as ours shall not deny medical attention to any child in need.

III. Whereas security is an essential requirement for a child's healthy development, the basic security of a place to live shall be guaranteed to every child.

IV. To ensure the potential of the individual and nation, every child at school shall have the right to a quality education.

V.   The government, whose primary role is to protect and defend at all levels, shall assure that children are safeguarded from abuse, violence, and discrimination.

Although children of the world and nation are gaining more rights, societal attitudes toward children's rights are often still ambivalent. Some children's rights supporters believe children need advocates to act on their behalf. They maintain children are politically disenfranchised, economically disadvantaged, the personal property of their parents, vulnerable to abuse and exploitation because of their lack of experience, and have passive legal status. On the other hand, many people, including some parents, feel they should be allowed to raise their children as they think best, free of interference from children's rights advocates.

Rights are being extended to children in ways that would not have been thought possible ten years ago. Particularly in the area of fetal rights, parents are encountering conflicts between their rights and the lives of their unborn children. Many states require places that sell liquor to post a sign that says, "Warning: Drinking alcoholic beverages during pregnancy can cause birth defects." Major controversies are arising between the right of the unborn and the rights of pregnant women. Questions

Today, children and youth are granted more rights than ever before. Kimberly Mays won the right to decide whom she would live with, her natural parents or her adoptive father. What rights do children have today that they didn't have a decade ago? Do you agree with the trend toward granting children more rights?

such as "What rights of the pregnant woman supersede those of her unborn child?" and "Does the government or other agency have the right to intervene in a woman's life on behalf of her unborn child?" are not easy to answer. Controversy continues between those groups that advocate for the rights of the unborn fetus and groups that advocate for a mother's rights, including privacy, emotional and physical integrity, and self-determination. Questions as to whose rights take precedence—the fetus's or the mother's—are becoming increasingly polarized.

The debate regarding children's rights will continue as the rights of children become further defined and clarified through the judicial system. The rights of all children will be examined, and more special interest groups will join the trend to gain even more rights for children.

Children as Potential Persons

Another view of children, the child as a potential person, is closely associated with the future investment view. This perspective became popular about 1950 and is still so today. It considers the child to be a "person" in his or her own right, allowing for the basis of advocacy and supporting children's rights and for laws and programs designed to provide the child with self-determination. Children are thus given more rights to make decisions for and on behalf of themselves.

A landmark example of children's right of self-determination is the case of twelve-year-old Gregory Kingsley. In 1992, he took legal action on his own behalf to break his ties to his mother, which enabled him to be adopted by his foster parents. According to many child advocates, the most significant thing about Gregory's case, for Gregory and other children, is that the judge in the case allowed the boy to sue on his own behalf. As a result, a child had a standing before the law to initiate a case that affected him. This, of course, sets a precedent for other children as well.

A review of the ways we view children leads to some intriguing questions. In this generation, are parents and professionals as child centered as they should be? Are early childhood professionals interested in helping children receive the best so they can realize their best? What we know we should do and what we do are often two different things. Public and social policies often supersede our interest in children. Wars, national defense, and economics sometimes take precedence over questions of what is best for children.

CONTEMPORARY SOCIAL ISSUES AFFECTING EARLY CHILDHOOD EDUCATION

Women's Movement

The women's movement has had a tremendous and long-lasting influence on young children and early childhood education. A major reason for the interest in infants and infant care is that women want quality out-of-home care for their infants. True equality for women depends partly on relieving them of the constant care of children. As women have more choices about how best to conduct their lives and the lives of their children, there is increased demand for more and better comprehensive child care. The women's movement has helped enlighten parents regarding their rights as parents, including helping them learn how to advocate on behalf of themselves and their children for better health services, child care, programs for earlier education and parenting, and family-friendly work environments.

Working Parents

More and more families find that both parents must work to make ends meet. Almost 60 percent of mothers with children under six are currently employed, which creates a greater need for early childhood programs (see Figure 1–6). This demand brings a beneficial recognition to early childhood programs and encourages early childhood professionals to meet parents' needs. Unfortunately, the urgent need for child care has encouraged some ill-prepared people who do not necessarily have children's or parents' best interests in mind to establish programs. Demand is high enough that good programs have not yet had a chance to drive inferior programs from the child care marketplace.

FIGURE 1–6   Increase in Percentage of Mothers in the Labor Force

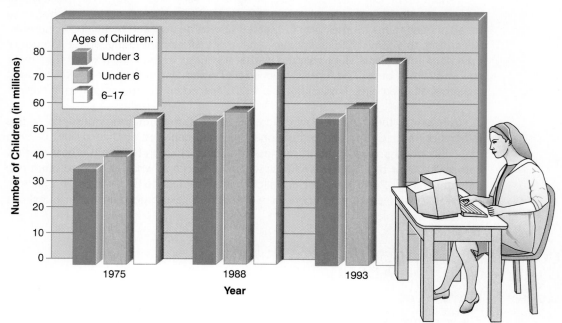

Source: National Commission on Children, *Beyond Rhetoric: A New American Agenda for Children and Families*.

For their part, some parents are not able or willing to evaluate programs and select the best ones for their children, which also encourages poor-quality programs to stay in operation.

Rising Incomes

Ironically, while the need for two incomes generates interest in early childhood, rising incomes are also a factor. Many parents with middle-level incomes are willing to invest money in early education for their children. They look for nursery schools and preschool programs they feel will give their children a good start in life. Montessori schools and franchised operations have benefited in the process. In the last several years, the Montessori system especially has experienced a tremendous boom, in the number of both individuals seeking Montessori teacher training and preschool enrollments (see chap. 3). Some parents of three- and four-year-olds spend almost as much in tuition to send their children to good preschools as parents of eighteen-year-olds do to send their children to state-supported universities.

Single Parents

The number of one-parent families is increasing while the number of two-parent households is declining, as shown in Figure 1–7. In 1990, almost 25 percent of U.S. children were in families headed by a single parent. People become single parents for a number of reasons. Half of all marriages end in divorce. Some people choose single parenthood, and some, such as many teenagers, become parents by default. In addition, liberalized adoption procedures, artificial insemination, surrogate childbearing, and general public support for single parents make this lifestyle an attractive option for some people. The reality is that more women are having babies without marrying (see Figure 1–8).

Awareness of the growing number of single-parent families is not enough; we must also understand that within the population as a whole, certain cultural groups are disproportionately represented in single-parent families. Figure 1–9 shows the rapid rise in the number of children in families headed either by the mother or the father by race.

These increases are attributable to a number of factors. For instance, pregnancy rates are higher among lower socioeconomic groups. Also, teenage pregnancy rates in poor white, Hispanic, and African-American populations are sometimes higher because of lower education, economics, and fewer opportunities. A complex interplay among other personal issues, such as family, religious, and cultural views, also factors into the prevalence of teen pregnancy.

No matter how people become single parents, the extent of single parenthood has tremendous implications for early childhood professionals. In response to growing single parenthood, early childhood programs are developing curricula to help children and their parents deal with the stress of family breakups. Professionals are called on to help children adjust to the guilt they often feel about the family breakup

FIGURE 1–7 Living Arrangements of Children

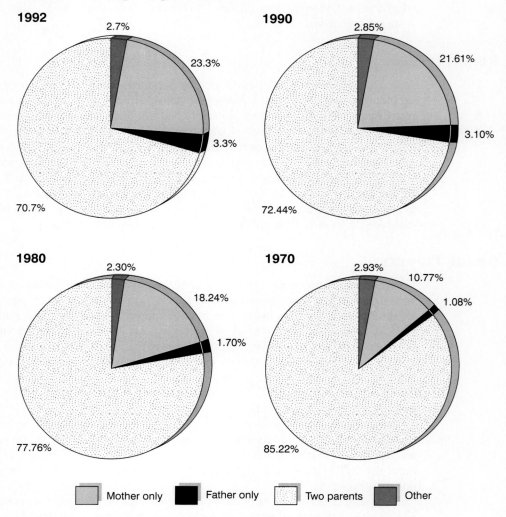

1992
2.7%
23.3%
3.3%
70.7%

1990
2.85%
21.61%
3.10%
72.44%

1980
2.30%
18.24%
1.70%
77.76%

1970
2.93%
10.77%
1.08%
85.22%

Mother only   Father only   Two parents   Other

Source: U.S. Department of Commerce, Bureau of the Census.

and their changed family pattern and lifestyle. In addition to needing assistance with child care, single parents frequently seek help in child rearing, especially in regard to discipline. Early childhood professionals are often asked to conduct seminars to help parents gain these skills.

A decade ago, early professionals were not as concerned about how to assist and support unwed parents and children from single-parent families, but today they recognize that these parents want and need their help. How well early professionals meet the needs of single parents can make a difference in how successful single parents are in their new roles.

FIGURE 1–9   Percentage of Never-Married Women Age Eighteen to Forty-Four Who Have Children

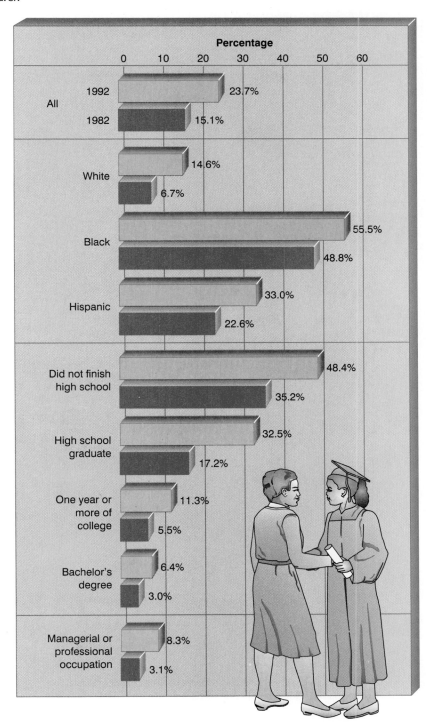

Source: *Education Week,* August 4, 1993, p. 22. Used by permission.

FIGURE 1–9   Children in Single-Parent Families by Race

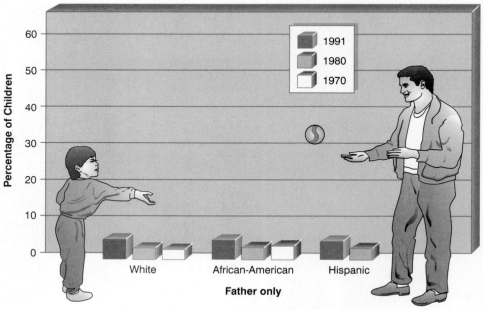

Note: 1970 data on Hispanic single-parent families are not available.
Source: U.S. Department of Commerce, Bureau of the Census.

Teenage parenting is on the increase. The 1993 Kids Count Data Book reports that in 1990, 360,645 babies were born to single women under 20, representing almost 9 percent of all births. One implication of teenage parenting is that mothers are less likely to complete their education. What impact does this have on children? What can early childhood professionals do to support teenage parents as their children's first teachers?

Fathers

A continuing change in early childhood today is that fathers have rediscovered the joys of parenting and working with young children. Men are playing an active role in providing basic care, love, and nurturance to their children. The definition of fatherhood has changed; a father is no longer stereotypically unemotional, detached from everyday responsibilities of child care, authoritarian, and a disciplinarian. Fathers no longer isolate themselves from child rearing only because they are male. Men are more concerned about their role of fatherhood and their participation in family events before, during, and after the birth of their children. Fathers want to be involved in the whole process of child rearing. Because so many men feel unprepared for fatherhood, agencies such as hospitals and community colleges are providing courses and seminars to introduce fathers to the joys, rewards, and responsibilities of fathering.

Fathers no longer quietly acquiesce to giving up custody of their children in a divorce. Men are becoming single parents through adoption and surrogate childbearing. Figure 1–7 indicates the percentage of single families headed by fathers. Fathers' rights groups have tremendous implications for the family court system and traditional interpretations of family law. Fathers are also receiving some of the employment benefits that have traditionally gone only to women. Paternity leaves, flexible work schedules, and sick leave for family illness are just a few examples of how fathering has come to the workplace.

Teenage Parents: Children Having Children

Teenage pregnancies continue to be a problem. Each year one out of ten, or 1.1 million, teenagers become pregnant. The following facts about teenage pregnancy dramatically demonstrate its extent and effects:[8]

- In 1991, for women aged fifteen through nineteen, there were 62.1 births per 1,000, up from 59.9 in 1990. (Note that this is the *birth rate,* not the *pregnancy rate.* Many states do not report the number of teenagers who have had abortions, so there is really no way of determining the pregnancy rate for the nation as a whole.)
- For states that do report pregnancy rates, Georgia had the highest, with 110.6 per 1,000 teenage women.
- Mississippi has the highest birth rate for teenagers, with 81 births per 1,000.

Concerned legislators, public policy developers, and national leaders view teenage pregnancy as symptomatic of what is wrong with society in general. They worry about the demand for public health and welfare services, envision a drain on taxpayer dollars, and decry the loss of future potential because of school dropouts. From an early childhood point of view, teenage pregnancies create greater demand for infant and toddler child care and programs to help teenagers learn how to parent. The staff of an early childhood program must often provide nurturance for both children and parents, because the parents themselves may not be emotionally mature. Emotional maturity is necessary for parents to engage in a giving relationship with children. When teenage parents lack parenting characteristics of any kind, early childhood professionals must help them develop them.

The Federal Role in Social Service and Education Programs

Beginning about 1980, the federal government began cutting many program budgets, and private agencies and state governments had to take over support of some programs. Other programs had to close, so that some families and children had to cope with reduced services or no services at all. Federal monies had a stimulating effect on early childhood programs in the 1960s and 1970s, but cuts during the 1980s had a dampening effect. Federal support for early childhood and related programs will likely continue to be scarce, with the exception of Head Start. Increased support from private agencies, contributions, and volunteerism constitute legitimate alternatives to federal funds.

Critics of the declining federal presence in early childhood programs maintain that the results are harmful for women, children, and families. They specifically cite increases in the number of women and children living in poverty and a higher infant mortality rate. Figure 1–10 illustrates the extent of family poverty, particularly that experienced in single-female-headed families.

FIGURE 1–10   Families with Children Living in Poverty

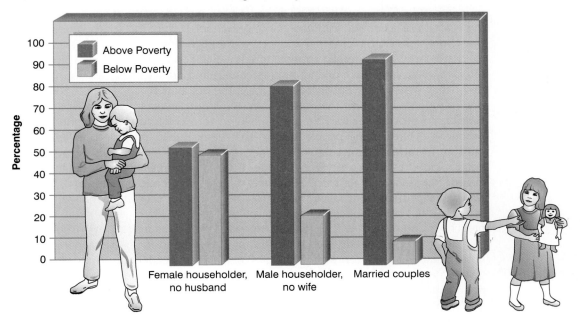

Source: U.S. Department of Commerce, Bureau of the Census.

Advocacy

Reduced funding for early childhood programs requires early childhood profession-als to be strong advocates on behalf of children and their families. Early profession-als should be in the vanguard of efforts to influence public policy and develop public awareness about providing for children in the early years. Programs that commit to and depend on federal monies must recognize their vulnerability to shifts in political attitude and swings, both up and down, in federal support. Agencies that provide money can also take it away. Strong advocacy is part of the solution to this dilemma.

THE PUBLIC SCHOOLS AND EARLY EDUCATION

Traditionally, the majority of preschool programs were operated by private agencies or agencies supported wholly or in part by federal funds to help the poor, unem-ployed, working parents, and disadvantaged children. But times have changed. All parents exert great pressure on public school officials and state legislatures to spon-sor and fund additional preschool and early childhood programs. The public schools of many states provide some degree of funding for programs for three- and four-year-olds. Consequently, public school programs for these children are a growing reality. For example, the Dade County School District in Florida operates 103 preschool classrooms for three- and four-year-old children.

Parents lobby for public support of early childhood education for a number of reasons. First, because working parents cannot find quality child care for their children, they believe the public schools hold the solution to child care needs. Second, the persistent belief that children are a nation's greatest wealth makes it seem sensible to provide services to young children to avoid future school and learning problems. Third, many people believe that early public schooling, especially for children from low-income families, is necessary if the United States is to promote equal opportunity for all. They argue that low-income children begin school already far behind their more fortunate middle-class counterparts, and the best way to keep them from falling hopelessly behind is for them to begin school earlier. Fourth, some parents cannot afford quality child care. They believe preschools, furnished at the public's expense, are a reasonable, cost-efficient way to meet child care needs. A fifth reason for the demand for public school involvement relates to the "competent child." Parents want academic programs for their children at an earlier age and look, naturally, to the public schools to provide programs that will help their children succeed in life. Sixth, today's parents are the best educated in U.S. history. These well-educated parents are causing a boom in preschool programs that emphasize earlier and more comprehensive education for young children.

The alignment of the public schools with early childhood programs is becoming increasingly popular. Many public schools have already moved into the area of child care and preschool programs for three- and four-year-old children. There are several arguments in favor of such an alignment. First, some professionals think it is not wise to train nonteachers for preschool positions when trained professionals are available. Second, some professionals think it makes sense to put the responsibility for educating and caring for the nation's children under the sponsorship of one agency—the public schools. For their part, public school teachers and the unions that represent them are anxious to bring early childhood programs within the structure of the public school system.

There is by no means consensus that universal public schooling or even anything approaching it for very young children should be available. Critics of the effort to place preschool programs in the public schools give three reasons against such a policy. First, they cite the failure of public education to do a good job of teaching young children for whom they currently provide programs. They ask, "How can public schools handle an expanded role if they have not done a good job with what they are already supposed to do?" Second, some critics say that public school teachers are not trained in the specific skills needed in Head Start, child care, and other preschool programs. A third, more convincing argument relates to money: the cost of having the public schools assume the responsibility of preschool programs would probably cost over several billion dollars, which taxpayers are unlikely to be willing to pay.

Nonetheless, it seems inevitable that the growing presence of the public schools in and on early childhood education will continue to expand. Given the fact that so many public schools offer programs for threes and fours, can programs for infants and toddlers be far behind? Probably not.

PARADIGM SHIFTS IN EARLY CHILDHOOD EDUCATION

From all of what we have discussed in this chapter, it is apparent that the field of early childhood education is in constant flux. It can truly be said about early childhood education that change, often dramatic change, is predictable. The changes in early childhood education that occurred within the past decade have resulted in some identifiable *paradigm shifts*. A paradigm is a model for how things occur or happen. The following are some of the critically important paradigm shifts occurring in early childhood education today, discussed earlier:

- *Family-centered programs.*   Early childhood professionals are now working with families within the family system in order to provide the most meaningful education and services to children and their families.

- *Two-generation programs.*   It is common now for early childhood professionals to work with children and families across generations. Early childhood professionals are helping children and their parents, and in many cases grandparents, develop literacy skills. Consequently, three-generational programs are becoming more commonplace.

- *Collaborative efforts with other agencies.*   More and more early childhood professionals are working cooperatively and collaboratively with professionals from other agencies to combine resources and to work in an integrative manner.

- *An ecological/holistic approach.*   Early childhood professionals now realize that they have to deliver a wide range of services to children and their families in family and community settings. Early childhood professionals also recognize now more than ever they have to provide for children's physical, social, and emotional needs as well as their cognitive needs.

- *Child-centered programs.*   Increasingly, what early childhood professionals do in their programs focuses on the needs of children and their families rather than their own needs or those of their agencies. In addition, child-centered programs emphasize that children and their active involvement in learning is the preferred method of education and the process by which children learn best. Consequently, an emphasis is on involving children in their own learning, which enables them to develop their knowledge and intelligence. Today, the teaching/learning process centers on having children involved as active participants in their own learning and cognitive development as opposed to passive recipients of knowledge through teacher-directed learning, worksheets, and the like. Active learning is in; passivity is out.

Two- and three-generation programs are now a regular part of many early childhood programs. Why are they so necessary? How have professionals' roles changed as a result?

Evidence for the rebirth of child-centered approaches to early childhood education is also seen in such pedagogical practices as cooperative learning (see chap. 9), having children make choices about what they will learn and how, and the use of activities and strategies to promote children's thinking. Other child-centered approaches very much in evidence are programs designed to promote children's self-esteem; multiage grouping; having professionals stay with or teach the same group of children for more than one year; transition programs that help children move easily from program to program, grade to grade, and agency to agency; and concern for children's health, safety, and nutrition.

OBSERVING CHILDREN'S BEHAVIOR

Today, professionals are stressing observation as a means of collecting information about children and families. *Observation* is the systematic examination, noting, or conscious attention to a child, setting, program, or situation for the purpose of gathering information on which to base a judgment, make a recommendation, or develop a plan or strategy. It is an intentional activity for the purpose of influencing behavior or programs.

Professionals recognize that children are more than what is measured by a particular test. Utilizing more "authentic" means for assessing children, professionals realize that observation is one of the most authentic means of learning about children and what they know and are able to do, especially when it occurs in *naturalistic settings* such as classrooms, child care centers, playgrounds, and homes. Observation also enables professionals to gather information about children that they might not be able to gather in other ways.

Sometimes, when professionals and parents look at children, they do not really see what they are doing or understand why they are engaged in a particular behavior or activity. Children's behaviors provide insight into them, but because professionals do not observe in any systematic way, the significance and importance goes undetected. This is why it is important for early childhood professionals to understand the importance of and how to use observation to gather data about young children.

When used for data collection and informational purposes, observation is entirely different from the casual and unsystematic "looking" we use in daily interactions with children. For example, a professional may notice that there is a new child from Vietnam in the center attended by Hispanic and Anglo children. Through systematic observation she will be able to determine the attitudes of children to children of other races and then plan accordingly for appropriate multicultural activities and experiences.

Advantages of Observation

There are a number of advantages to gathering data through observation:

- Observation provides for *intentional* and *systematic* collecting of data.
- Observation enables the observer to gather data that cannot be gleaned by conducting paper-and-pencil tests or questioning a young child. If we want to study the reactions of four-year-old preschoolers to a new room arrangement, for example, observation will probably provide us with more valid data than other methods. Observation enables professionals to gain information directly that could otherwise be gathered only indirectly. You can learn a lot about children's peer interactions through observation.
- Observation effectively assesses children's abilities, that is, what they are able to do, and determines areas in which they need additional support and help.
- Observation can be used to develop a source of data that can be used to assess children's performance over time. Daily, weekly, and monthly observations of children's behaviors and activities provide such a database and form a framework for evaluation of each child's achievement and development.
- Observation helps professionals gather information for use in reporting to and conferencing with parents (see chap. 13). Increasingly, reports to parents about children involve professionals' observations and children's work samples.

Steps in Observing

A credible and professional job of observing requires several steps.

Step 1: Planning the Observation

This step includes developing and stating your goals for observation. These goals state *why* you want to observe and help direct your efforts to *what* you will observe. Stating goals provides direction for your observation and helps focus your attention on the observational process. A goal for observing might be "To determine the effectiveness of activities used to mainstream children with disabilities into the day care program" (see chap. 11). Another goal might be "To determine what modifications will be necessary in the classroom setting to facilitate the mainstreaming of children with disabilities."

Step 2: Conducting the Observation

In conducting your observation, it is important to be objective, specific, and as thorough as possible. For example, during your objective observation, you may write, "Dana states that she is going to color a picture for her daddy. There is not enough room for Dana's wheelchair to fit between the art table and the easel so she can have access to the art shelf. She had to ask someone to get the crayons for her."

Step 3: Interpretation

All observations can and should result in some kind of interpretation. Interpretation serves several important functions. First, it puts our observations into perspective, that is, in relation to what we know. Second, it helps us make sense of what we have observed. Third, it has the potential to make us grow. For example, interpreting the lack of access of the child with a disability to crayons raises the legitimate question "Should Dana have access to all parts of the learning environment that other children have access to?" To answer this question, you will probably need to extend your knowledge of laws and practices relating to children with disabilities in regular classrooms. Fourth, interpretation is the foundation for implementing results of observation. Without interpretation of some kind, it would be difficult to do much about what you observed. You may interpret your observations this way: "The fact that a wheelchair-bound child cannot reach an integral part of the classroom without assistance indicates that the room arrangement must be modified."

Step 4: Implementation

The implementation phase means that you will do something with the results or "findings" of your observation. Of course, how you use your observational results will depend largely on why you observed in the first place. Most often, observation is done for a specific reason. In our case, you could implement the findings several ways. You could write up your results in the form of a paper in which you recommend activities and classroom settings appropriate for children with disabilities such as Dana. Or, you could meet with Dana's teacher and share your observational results. Perhaps Dana's teacher will seek your further assistance and cooperation in making her classroom more accessible for children with disabilities. The observational guide shown in Figure 1–11 will help you with observations you may want to conduct as you read this text.

This information will help you think more about observing children and the important role it can have in directing and promoting their development. Throughout this book, we will have more to say about observation and the particular role it plays in the education of infants, toddlers, preschoolers, and primary grade children.

FIGURE 1–11   Observational Guide

Observer's name: _____

Children observed (e.g., Cindy H., Silvia L.): _____

Children's ages (e.g., 4–5 or kindergarten): _____

Observation setting: _____

Date and time of observation: _____

Observation goal—Purpose of observation: _____

Objective observation:

1.

2.

3.

4.

Interpretations:

Implementation recommendations:

READINGS FOR FURTHER ENRICHMENT

Bozett, Frederick W., and Shirley M. H. Hanson, eds. *Fatherhood and Families in Cultural Context* (New York: Springer, 1991)

Provides the research to explain the cultural impacts on fatherhood today. Each chapter explains a different phase of fatherhood. Some topics are social change, components of culture and fatherhood, effects of social class on fatherhood, religious impact on fathers, and future cultural changes.

Brooks, Andrée Aelion. *Children of Fast-Track Parents: Raising Self-Sufficient and Confident Children in an Achievement-Oriented World* (New York: Viking, 1989)

Brooks identifies a new American childhood, populated by baby-boom parents whose drive for success and accomplishment has created a generation of angry, distressed children. The author provides specific suggestions to counteract the effects of the resulting alienation.

Cleverley, Joan, and D. C. Phillips. *Visions of Childhood: Influential Models from Locke to Spock*, rev. ed. (New York: Teachers College Press, 1986)

Updated focus on major ideas and theories of child rearing and educational practices. Examines major contributions of Freud, Piaget, Dewey, and many others; provides a solid foundation of the philosophy and fundamentals of early childhood education.

Galinsky, Ellen, and Judy David. *The Preschool Years: Family Strategies That Work from Experts and Parents* (New York: Time Books, 1988)

A contemporary view of parenting that recommends strategies for balancing commitments of parents to child rearing, home, and careers. Includes information on child and parent development, models for problem solving, and insights into conflicts between parents and preschoolers.

Lerner, Jacqueline, and Nancy Galambos. *Employed Mothers and Their Children* (New York: Garland, 1991)

Discusses several ways to balance work and family. Chapters range from "Infant Day Care: Concerns, Controversies, Choices" to "Children in Self-Care: Figures, Facts, and Fiction."

Schorr, Lisbeth B., and Daniel Schorr. *Within Our Reach: Breaking the Cycle of Disadvantage* (New York: Doubleday, 1988)

A valuable book that has created a great deal of interest in what works and does not work in national efforts to break cycles of poverty and dependency. Suggests many progressive solutions to social and educational problems in the 1990s.

Spodek, Bernard, and Olivia N. Saracho. *Issues in Early Childhood Curriculum* (New York: Teachers College Press, 1991)

The second yearbook in early childhood education, this volume presents a timely and thought-provoking look at some of the critical issues in early childhood education today, such as multiculturalism, technology, family systems, and developmentally appropriate practices that are influencing curriculum developers for young children.

ACTIVITIES FOR FURTHER ENRICHMENT

1. Review early childhood literature and daily newspapers to identify statements of public policy and issues relating to public policy. What are the issues involved in each? In what ways do you agree or disagree with these policies?

2. Interview parents and determine how their current family is similar to and different from their family when they were children. Which family pattern do they prefer? Why?

3. Interview parents who have children under age eight to determine how they view their children: miniature adults, the competent child, the child as sinful, blank tablets, growing plants, property, or investments in the future. How do they think their view(s) influences their child-rearing patterns?

4. Contact agencies that provide services to single parents, teenage parents, and families in need. How do these programs influence early childhood education programs in your local community?

5. Interview single parents and determine what effects and influences single parenting has on children. In what ways is single parenting stressful to parents and children? How can early childhood programs support and help single parents?

6. Observe parent-child relationships in public settings such as supermarkets, laundries, and restaurants. What do these relationships tell you about parent-child interactions and how parents rear their children? What implications do these relationships have for how children are taught in school?

7. Recall your own childhood. Do you think your parents pushed you through childhood too quickly, or did you have a relaxed, unhurried childhood?

8. The emphasis on early education has prompted some critics and experts to charge that parents and early childhood professionals are making children grow up too soon, too fast. Interview parents and preschool teachers to determine their views on this topic. Do you agree or disagree with the data you gathered?

9. Find out what problems early childhood professionals in local preschools and child care centers face as a result of divorce, abuse, and other types of stress in children's lives. How do they help with these problems?

10. Find out what types of preschool programs are available in your community. Who may attend them? How are they financed? What percentage of the children who attend have mothers working outside the home?

11. Over a period of several weeks or a month, collect articles from newspapers and magazines relating to infants, toddlers, and preschoolers. Then categorize these articles by topics (e.g., child abuse). What topics were given the most coverage? Why? What are the emerging topics or trends in early education, according to newspaper and magazine coverage? Do you agree with everything you read? Can you find instances in which information or advice may be inaccurate, inappropriate, or contradictory?

12. Visit attorneys, legal aid societies, juvenile courts, and other agencies. List the legal rights children already have. Do you think children have some rights they should not have? Which ones? Why?

13. List factors that support the argument that childhood is disappearing or has disappeared. Then make a list to support the opposite viewpoint—that childhood is not disappearing.

14. Visit corporations and businesses in your area, and determine what they are doing to support education and family programs.

15. List at least five social, political, and economic conditions of modern society, and explain how these conditions influence how people view, treat, and care for the very young.

16. List at least five significant contributions you believe good early childhood education programs can make in the lives of young children.

NOTES

1. Diane Harris, "Big Business Takes on Child Care," *Working Woman,* June 1993, p. 51.

2. National Academy of Early Childhood Programs, *Accreditation Criteria and Procedures* (Washington, D.C.: National Association for the Education of Young Children, 1984), p. x.

3. National Association for the Education of Young Children, *Early Childhood Teacher Education Guidelines* (Washington, D.C.: Author, 1982), p. xii.

4. David Elkind, "Formal Education and Early Education: An Essential Difference," *Phi Delta Kappan* 67 (1986), p. 634.

5. Susan Littwin, *The Postponed Generation: Why America's Grown-Up Kids Are Growing Up Later* (New York: Morrow, 1986), p. 21.

6. John Locke, *An Essay Concerning Human Understanding* (New York: Dover Publications, 1959), pp. 92–93.

7. Paul Wilkes, "The First Test of Childhood," *Newsweek* 114 (1989), p. 8.

8. "Teen Pregnancy Rates Increase for Fifth Year," *Miami Herald,* October 3, 1993.

2

The Past
Prologue to the Present

After you have read and studied this chapter, you will be able to:

- [ ] Identify why it is important to know the ideas and theories of great educators
- [ ] Analyze and develop a basic understanding of the beliefs of Luther, Comenius, Locke, Rousseau, Pestalozzi, Owen, Froebel, Montessori, Dewey, Piaget, Vygotsky, and Gardner
- [ ] Understand how the beliefs and ideas of great educators have influenced and continue to influence early childhood programs
- [ ] Identify basic concepts that are essential to high-quality early childhood programs and education
- [ ] Develop an appreciation for the professional accomplishments and contributions of great educators to the field of early childhood education
- [ ] Develop knowledge of and respect for events that have significantly influenced the field of early childhood education
- [ ] Understand how people, agencies, and legislation influence early childhood education

IMPORTANCE OF THE PAST

There are at least five reasons to know about the ideas and theories of great educators who have influenced the field of early childhood education. First, by reading of the hopes, ideas, and accomplishments of people our profession judges famous, we realize that today's ideas are not necessarily new. Old ideas and theories have a way of being reborn. Good ideas and practices persist over time and tend to be recycled through educational thought and practices in ten- to twenty-year periods. For example, many practices popular in the 1970s, such as family grouping, child-centered education, and active learning, are now popular again as the twenty-first century approaches.

Old ideas and practices seldom get recycled exactly in their previous form. The recycling of former ideas and practices results in changes and modifications necessary for contemporary society and situations. Knowing about these former ideas and practices helps us recognize them when they do come around again. Most important, knowing about former practices enables you to be an active participant in the recycling process of applying good practices of previous years to contemporary practice. We can more fully appreciate the recycling of thought and practices in early education if we have an understanding of the root of our profession.

Second, many ideas of famous educators are still dreams, despite the advances we attribute to modern education. In this regard, we are the inheritors of a long line of thinkers as far back as Socrates and Plato. We should acknowledge this inheritance and use it as a base to build meaningful teaching careers and lives for children and their families. We have an obligation to continue to build the dream.

Third, ideas expressed by the early educators help us better understand how to implement current teaching strategies whatever they may be. For instance, Rousseau, Froebel, and Montessori all believed children should be taught with dignity and respect. This attitude toward children is essential to an understanding of good educational practice and often makes the difference between good and bad teaching.

Fourth, theories about how young children grow, develop, and learn decisively shape educational and child-rearing practices. Some parents and teachers may not realize, however, what assumptions form the foundations of their daily practices. Studying and examining beliefs of the great educators helps parents and early childhood educators clarify what they do and gives them insight into their actions. In this sense, knowing about theories liberates the uninformed from ignorance and empowers professionals and parents. As a consequence, they are able to implement developmentally appropriate practices with confidence.

Fifth, exploring, analyzing, and discovering the roots of early childhood education helps *inspire* professionals. Recurring rediscovery forces people to examine current practices against what others have advocated. Examining sources of beliefs helps clarify modern practice, and reading and studying others' ideas make us rethink our own beliefs and positions. In this regard, the history of the great educators and their beliefs can keep us current. When we pause long enough to listen to what they have to say, we frequently find a new insight or idea that motivates us to continue our quest to be the best we can be.

HISTORIC INFLUENCES
Martin Luther

While the primary impact of the Protestant Reformation was religious, other far-reaching effects were secular. Two of these were *universal education* and *literacy*, both topics very much in the forefront of educational practice today.

In Europe, the sixteenth century was a time of great social, religious, and economic upheaval, partly because of the Renaissance and partly because of the Reformation. Great emphasis was placed on formal schooling to teach children how to read, the impetus for which is generally attributed to Martin Luther (1483–1546) and the Reformation he spurred.

The question of what to teach is an issue in any educational endeavor. Does society create schools and then decide what to teach, or do the needs of society determine what schools it will establish to meet desired goals? This is a question early childhood professionals wrestle with today. In the case of European education of that time, Luther emphasized the necessity of establishing schools to teach children to read. Simply stated, Luther replaced the authority of the hierarchy of the Catholic Church with the authority of the Bible. Believing that each individual was free to work out his own salvation through the Scriptures meant that people had to learn to read the Bible in their native tongue.

The great educators believed that parents are their children's primary teachers. Teaching parents to read is as important as teaching children to read. When parents are literate, there is an intergenerational basis for literacy.

This concept marked the real beginning of teaching and learning in people's native language, the *vernacular*, as opposed to Latin, the official language of the Catholic Church. Before the Reformation, only the wealthy or those preparing for a religious vocation learned to read or write Latin. Luther translated the Bible into German, making it available to the people in their own language. In this way, the Protestant Reformation encouraged and supported popular universal education.

Luther believed the family was the most important institution in the education of children. To this end, he encouraged parents to provide religious instruction and vocational education in the home. Throughout his life Luther remained a champion of education. He wrote letters and treatises and preached sermons on the subject. His best-known letter on education is the *Letter to the Mayors and Aldermen of All the Cities of Germany in Behalf of Christian Schools*, written in 1524. In this letter, Luther argues for public support of education:

> Therefore it will be the duty of the mayors and council to exercise the greatest care over the young. For since the happiness, honor, and life of the city are committed to their hands, they would be held recreant before God and the world, if they did not, day and night, with all their power, seek its welfare and improvement. Now the welfare of a city does not consist alone in great treasures, firm walls, beautiful houses, and munitions of war; indeed, where all these are found, and reckless fools come into power, the city sustains the greatest injury. But the highest welfare, safety, and power of a city consists in able, learned, wise, upright, cultivated citizens, who can secure, preserve, and utilize every treasure and advantage.[1]

Out of the Reformation came other religious denominations, all interested in preserving the faith and keeping their followers within the fold of their church. Most of the major denominations such as Calvinism and Lutheranism established their own schools to provide literacy and knowledge about the faith. Education and schooling were considered not only socializing forces but also means of religious and moral instruction. Many religious groups have always had rather extensive school programs, for this is one way to help assure that children born into the faith will continue in the faith. Religious schools are a means of defending and perpetuating the faith as well as a place in which converts can learn about and become strong in the faith.

Today, many churches and synagogues operate early childhood programs. A growing number of parents want an early childhood program that supports their values, beliefs, and culture. They look for and find such programs operated by religious organizations. Furthermore, religious preschools tend to provide programs that emphasize cognitive and social learning through play. Parents see such programs as a satisfactory alternative to what they consider to be the pushing and hurrying of some academically based preschool programs.

John Amos Comenius

John Amos Comenius (1592–1670) was born in Moravia, a former province of the Czech Republic, and became a Moravian minister. He spent his life serving as a bishop, teaching school, and writing textbooks. Of his many writings, those that have received the most attention are *The Great Didactic* and the *Orbis Pictus (The World in Pictures)*, considered the first picture book for children.

Just as Luther's religious beliefs formed the basis for his educational ideas, so too with Comenius. In fact, throughout this discussion of the influence of great men and women on educational thought and practice, you will see a parallel interest in religion and education. It has always been obvious to religious followers that what they believe gives shape, form, and substance to what they teach, and, to a large degree, what is taught determines the extent to which religious beliefs are maintained and extended.

Comenius believed that humans are born in the image of God. Therefore, each individual has an obligation and duty to be educated to the fullest extent of one's abilities so as to fulfill this godlike image. Since so much depends on education, then, as far as Comenius was concerned, it should begin in the early years.

> It is the nature of everything that comes into being, that while tender it is easily bent and formed, but that, when it has grown hard, it is not easy to alter. Wax, when soft, can be easily fashioned and shaped; when hard it cracks readily. A young plant can be planted, transplanted, pruned, and bent this way or that. When it has become a tree these processes are impossible.[2]

Comenius was an advocate of universal education beginning at an early age and continuing through adulthood. Because Comenius believed that people are essentially good, he felt education should be a positive learning experience that includes freedom, joy, and pleasure. This view contrasts sharply to the concept of education as discipline, consisting partly of a rigid, authoritarian atmosphere designed to control children's natural inclination to do bad things. Today, in modern terms, the argument is whether children learn better in an authoritarian setting characterized by traditional classrooms or in a child-centered setting that encourages autonomy and self-regulation.

Comenius also believed that education should follow the order of nature. Following this natural order implies a timetable for growth and learning, and early childhood professionals must observe this pattern to avoid forcing learning before children are ready. This belief is reflected in Montessori's concept of sensitive periods, Piaget's stages of development, and the developmentally appropriate practices of today. Comenius also thought that learning is best achieved when the senses are involved and that sensory education forms the basis for all learning:

> Those things, therefore, that are placed before the intelligence of the young, must be real things and not the shadows of things. I repeat, they must be *things*; and by the term I mean determinate, real, and useful things that can make an impression on the senses and on the imagination. But they can only make this impression when brought sufficiently near.
>
> From this a golden rule for teachers may be derived. Everything should, as far as is possible, be placed before the senses. Everything visible should be brought before the organs of sight, everything audible before that of hearing. Odors should be placed before the sense of smell, and things that are testable and tangible before the sense of taste

and of touch respectively. If an object can make an impression on several senses at once, it should be brought into contact with several.[3]

We see an extension and refinement of Comenius's principle in the works of Montessori and Piaget and contemporary programs that stress manipulation of concrete objects, the project approach, and active learning.

Comenius gave some good advice when he said that the golden rule of teaching should be to place everything before the senses. Because of his belief in sensory education, Comenius thought children should not be taught the names of objects apart from the objects themselves or pictures of the objects. *Orbis Pictus* helped children learn the names of things and concepts, as they appeared during Comenius's time, through pictures and words. Comenius's emphasis on the concrete and sensory is a pedagogical principle early childhood professionals still try to grasp fully and implement. Many contemporary programs stress sensory learning, and several early childhood materials promote learning through the senses.

A broad view of Comenius's total concept of education is evident by examining some of his principles of teaching:

Following in the footsteps of nature we find that the process of education will be easy

i.   If it begins early, before the mind is corrupted.

ii.   If the mind be duly prepared to receive it.

iii.   If it proceeds from the general to the particular.

iv.   And from what is easy to what is more difficult.

v.   If the pupil be not overburdened by too many subjects.

vi.   And if progress be slow in every case.

vii.   If the intellect be forced to nothing to which its natural bent does not incline it, in accordance with its age and with the right method.

viii. If everything be taught through the medium of the senses.

ix.   And if the use of everything taught be continually kept in view.

x.   If everything be taught according to one and the same method.

These, I say, are the principles to be adopted if education is to be easy and pleasant.[4]

A noticeable trend in education today is to make learning, as Comenius suggested, simpler and more pleasant. Comenius's two most significant contributions to today's education are books with illustrations and the emphasis on sensory training found in many early childhood programs. We take the former for granted and naturally assume that the latter is a necessary basis for learning.

John Locke

As mentioned in chapter 1, John Locke (1632–1704) popularized the *blank tablet* view of children. This and other of his beliefs influence modern early childhood education and practice. Indeed, the extent of Locke's influence is probably unappreciated by many who daily implement practices based on his theories. More precisely,

Locke developed the theory of and laid the foundation for *environmentalism*—the belief that it is the environment, not innate characteristics, that determine what children will become.

Locke, born in Somerset, England, was a physician, philosopher, and social scientist. His ideas about education were first applied when his cousin and her husband asked him for child-rearing advice. His letters to them were published in 1693 as *Some Thoughts Concerning Education.* Many of his philosophical ideas that directly relate to education are also found in *An Essay Concerning Human Understanding.* Locke's assumption of human learning and nature was that there are no innate ideas. This belief gave rise to his theory of the mind as a blank tablet or "white paper." As Locke explains:

> Let us suppose the mind to be, as we say, white paper void of all characters, without ideas. How comes it to be furnished? Whence comes it by that vast store which the busy and boundless fancy of man has painted on it with an almost endless variety? Whence has it all the materials of reason and knowledge? To this I answer, in one word, from *experience*; in that all our knowledge is founded, and from that it ultimately derives itself.[5]

For Locke, then, environment forms the mind. The implications of this belief are clearly reflected in modern educational practice. The notion of the primacy of environmental influences is particularly evident in programs that encourage and promote early education as a means of overcoming or compensating for a poor or disadvantaged environment. Based partly on the idea that all children are born with the same general capacity for mental development and learning, these programs also assume that differences in learning, achievement, and behavior are attributable to environmental factors such as home and family conditions, socioeconomic context, early education, and experiences. Programs of early schooling, especially the current move for public schooling for three- and four-year-olds, work on the premise that disadvantaged children fail to have the experiences of their more advantaged counterparts. In fact, it is not uncommon to provide public funding for early schooling for those who are considered disadvantaged and to design such programs especially for them.

Because Locke believed that experiences determine the nature of the individual, sensory training became a prominent feature in the application of his theory to education. He and others who followed him believed that the best way to make children receptive to experiences was to train their senses. In this regard, Locke exerted considerable influence on others, particularly Maria Montessori, who developed her system of early education based on sensory training.

Jean-Jacques Rousseau

Jean-Jacques Rousseau (1712–1778) was born in Geneva, Switzerland, but spent most of his life in France. He is best remembered by educators for his book *Émile*, in which he raises a hypothetical child from birth to adolescence. Rousseau's theories were radical for his time. The opening lines of *Émile* set the tone not only for

Rousseau's educational views but many of his political ideas as well: "God makes all things good; man meddles with them and they become evil."[6]

Rousseau advocated a return to nature and an approach to educating children called *naturalism*. To Rousseau, naturalism meant abandoning society's artificiality and pretentiousness. A naturalistic education permits growth without undue interference or restrictions. Indeed, Rousseau wanted Émile to admire and emulate Daniel Defoe's Robinson Crusoe as an example of a resourceful person living close to and in harmony with nature. Rousseau would probably argue against such modern practices as dress codes, compulsory attendance, minimum basic skills, frequent and standardized testing, and ability grouping, because they are "unnatural."

There is some tendency in American education to emphasize naturalism by replacing practices such as regimentation, compulsory assignments, and school-imposed regulations with less structured processes. Indeed, contemporary practices stress naturalism in this approach regardless of whether or not practitioners are always aware of it. For example, family grouping seeks to create a more natural familylike atmosphere in schools and classrooms, literacy programs emphasize literature from the natural environment (e.g., using menus to show children how reading is important in their everyday lives), and conflict resolution programs teach children how to get along with others.

According to Rousseau, natural education promotes and encourages qualities such as happiness, spontaneity, and the inquisitiveness associated with childhood. In his method, parents and teachers allow children to develop according to their natural abilities, do not interfere with development by forcing education, and tend not to overprotect them from the corrupting influences of society. Rousseau felt that Émile's education occurred through three sources: nature, people, and things. As Rousseau elaborates:

Rousseau maintained that parents and the environment are important and powerful influences on the development of children. What are some ways they shape the course of development?

All that we lack at birth and need when grown up is given us by education. This education comes to us from nature, from men, or from things. The internal development of our faculties and organs is the education of nature. . . . It is not enough merely to keep children alive. They should learn to bear the blows of fortune; to meet either wealth or poverty, to live if need be in the frosts of Iceland or on the sweltering rock of Malta.[7]

Rousseau believed, however, that although parents and others have control over education that comes from social and sensory experiences, they have no control over natural growth. In essence, this is the idea of *unfolding,* in which the nature of children—what they are to be—unfolds as a result of maturation according to their innate timetables. We should observe the child's growth and provide experiences at appropriate times. Some educators interpret this as a *laissez-faire* or "let alone" approach to parenting and education.

Educational historians point to Rousseau as dividing the historic and modern periods of education. Rousseau established a way of thinking about the young child that is reflected in innovators of educational practice such as Pestalozzi and Froebel. His concept of natural unfolding echoes Comenius and appears in current programs that stress promoting children's readiness as a factor in learning. Piaget's developmental stages also reinforce Rousseau's thinking about the importance of natural development. Educational practices that provide an environment in which children can become autonomous and self-regulating have a basis in his philosophy. The common element in all the approaches that advocate educating in a free, natural environment is the view of children as essentially good and capable of great achievement. It is the responsibility of early childhood professionals and parents to apply appropriate educational strategies at the right time, enabling all children to reach their full potential.

Perhaps the most famous contemporary example of the laissez-faire approach to child rearing and education is found in A. S. Neill's book *Summerhill,* which was also the name of his famous school. Neill presents a strong case for freedom and self-regulation. He and his wife wanted "to make the school fit the child—instead of making the child fit the school." Therefore:

We set out to make a school in which we should allow children freedom to be themselves. In order to do this, we had to renounce all discipline, all direction, all suggestion, all moral training, all religious instruction. We have been called brave, but it did not require courage. All it required was what we had—a complete belief in the child as good, not an evil, being. For almost forty years, this belief in the goodness of the child has never wavered; it rather has become a final faith.[8]

Johann Heinrich Pestalozzi

Johann Heinrich Pestalozzi (1746–1827) was born in Zürich, Switzerland. He was greatly influenced by Rousseau and his *Émile.* In fact, Pestalozzi was so impressed by Rousseau's back-to-nature concepts that he purchased a farm he hoped would become a center for new and experimental methods in agriculture. While engaged in farming, Pestalozzi became more and more interested in education and, in 1774, started a school at his farm called Neuhof. There Pestalozzi developed his ideas of the integration of home life, vocational education, and education for reading and writing. Because the cost of trying his ideas was much greater than the tuition he was able to collect, this educational enterprise went bankrupt.

Pestalozzi spent the next twenty years writing about his educational ideas and practices. From such writings as *Leonard and Gertrude*, which was read as a romantic novel rather than for its educational ideas, Pestalozzi became well known as a writer and educator. He spent his later years developing and perfecting his ideas at various schools throughout Europe.

Rousseau's influence is most apparent in Pestalozzi's belief that education should follow the child's nature. His dedication to this concept is demonstrated by his rearing his only son, Jean-Jacques, using *Émile* as a guide. His methods were based on harmonizing nature and educational practices:

> And what is this method? It is a method which simply follows the path of Nature, or, in other words, which leads the child slowly, and by his own efforts, from sense-impressions to abstract ideas. Another advantage of this method is that it does not unduly exalt the master, inasmuch as he never appears as a superior being, but, like kindly Nature, lives and works with the children, his equals, seeming rather to learn with them than to teach them with authority.[9]

Unfortunately, Pestalozzi did not have much success rearing his son according to Rousseau's tenets, as evidenced by Jean-Jacques's inability to read and write by age twelve. This may be due to either his physical condition (he was thought to be epileptic) or Pestalozzi's inability to translate Rousseau's abstract ideas into practice. Pestalozzi was able, however, to refine his own pedagogical ideas as a result of the process.

Probably the most important lesson from Pestalozzi's experience is that in the process of education, early childhood professionals cannot rely solely on children's own initiative and expect them to learn all they need to know. Although some children do teach themselves to read, parents and others have created the climate and conditions for that beginning reading process. To expect that children will be or can be responsible for learning basic skills and appropriate social behaviors by themselves is simply asking too much.

Pestalozzi believed all education is based on sensory impressions and that through the proper sensory experiences, children can achieve their natural potential. This belief led to "object lessons." As the name implies, Pestalozzi thought the best way to learn many concepts was through manipulatives, such as counting, measuring, feeling, and touching. Pestalozzi believed the best teachers were those who taught children, not subjects. He also believed in multiage grouping. Pestalozzi anticipated by about 175 years the many family-centered programs of today that help parents teach their young children in the home. He believed mothers could best teach their children and wrote two books, *How Gertrude Teaches Her Children* and *Book for Mothers*, detailing procedures for how to do this. He felt that "the time is drawing near when methods of teaching will be so simplified that each mother will be able not only to teach her children without help, but continue her own education at the same time."[10]

Robert Owen

As is often the case, people who affect the course of educational thought and practice are visionaries in political and social affairs as well. Robert Owen (1771–1858) is no exception. Owen's influences on education resulted from his entrepreneurial activities associated with New Lanark, Scotland, a model mill town he managed. Owen was an *environmentalist*; that is, he believed that the environment in which children are reared is the main contributing factor to beliefs, behavior, and achievement. Consequently, he maintained that society and persons acting in the best interests of society can shape children's individual characters. Owen and other *Utopians* like him believed that by controlling the circumstances and consequent outcomes of child rearing, it was possible to build a new and perhaps more perfect society. Such a deterministic view of child rearing and education pushes free will to the background and makes environmental conditions the predominate force in directing and determining human behavior. This is how Owen explained it:

> Any character, from the best to the worst, from the most ignorant to the most enlightened may be given to any community, even to the world at large, by the application of proper means; which means are to a great extent at the command and under the control of those who have influence in the affairs of men.[11]

Owen believed that good traits were instilled at an early age and that children's behavior was influenced primarily by the environment. Thus, in Owen, we see influences of both Locke's theory of blank tablet and Rousseau's theory of innate goodness.

To implement his beliefs, Owen opened an infant school in 1816 at New Lanark, designed to provide care for about a hundred children age eighteen months to ten years while their parents worked in his cotton mills. This led to the opening of the first infant school in London in 1818.[12] Part of Owen's motivation for opening the infant schools was to get the children away from their uneducated parents. Indeed, to provide education for his workers and transform them into "rational beings," Owen opened a night school for them.

While we tend to think that early education for children from low-income families began with Head Start in 1965, Owen's infant school came over a hundred years before! Owen also had Utopian ideas regarding communal living and practice. In 1824, he purchased the village of New Harmony, Indiana, for a grand experiment in communal living. Part of the community included a center for a hundred infants. The New Harmony experiment failed, but Owen's legacy lived on in the infant schools of England. These eventually developed into kindergartens, influenced by European educators.

Several things about Owen's efforts and accomplishments are noteworthy. First, his infant school preceded Froebel's kindergarten by about a quarter of a century. Second, Owen's ideas and practices influenced educators as to the importance of early education and the relationship between education and societal improvements, which is an idea much in vogue in current educational practice. In addition, early childhood professionals and other professionals today, not unlike Owen's time, seek through education to reform society and provide a better world for all humankind.

Friedrich Wilhelm Froebel

Friedrich Wilhelm Froebel (1782–1852), born in Germany, devoted his life to developing a system for the education of young children. While his contemporary, Pestalozzi, with whom he studied and worked, advocated a system for teaching, Froebel developed a curriculum and methodology for educating young children. In the process, Froebel earned the distinction as the "father of the kindergarten." As a result of his close relationship with Pestalozzi and of reading the works of Rousseau, Froebel decided to open a school and put his ideas into practice.

Like some great people, Froebel was not eminently successful in his personal or professional lives. Some reasons for a lack of recognition during his lifetime were his inability to find educators who were interested in his ideas and his many personal problems. In his early years, Froebel was supported both financially and emotionally by his brother's widow, who as a result of this support had expectations of marriage. When this union did not materialize, Froebel's relatives mounted an attack on him and his ideas. This animosity lasted throughout his life and prevented, in several instances, the adoption of his ideas by others. It was only at the end of his life that he and his methods received the recognition they so richly deserved.

Froebel's primary contributions to educational thought and practice are in the areas of learning, curriculum, methodology, and teacher training. His concept of children and how they learn is based, in part, on the idea of unfolding, held by Comenius and Pestalozzi before him. The educator's role, whether parent or teacher, is to observe this natural unfolding and provide activities that will enable children to learn what they are ready to learn when they are ready to learn. The teacher's role is to help children develop their inherent qualities for learning. In this sense, the teacher is a designer of experiences and activities. This notion of teacher as facilitator was reinforced later by both Montessori and Piaget, both undoubtedly influenced by Froebel, who believed:

> Therefore, education in instruction and training, originally and in its first principles, should necessarily be *passive*, following (only guarding and protecting), *not prescriptive, categorical, interfering.*
>
> Indeed, in its very essence, education should have these characteristics; for the undisturbed operation of the Divine Unity is necessarily good—cannot be otherwise than good. This necessity implies that the young human being—as it were, still in process of creation—would seek, although still unconsciously, as a product of nature, yet decidedly and surely, that which is in itself best; and, moreover, in a form wholly adapted to his condition, as well as to his disposition, his powers, and means. [13]

Consistent with his idea of unfolding, comparable to the process of a flower blooming from a bud, Froebel compared the child to a seed that is planted, germinates, brings forth a new shoot, and grows from a young, tender plant to a mature fruit-producing one. He likened the role of educator to that of gardener. In his kindergarten, or "garden of children," he envisioned children being educated in close harmony with their own nature and the nature of the universe. Children unfold their uniqueness in play, and it is in the area of unfolding and learning through play that Froebel makes one of his greatest contributions to the early childhood curriculum.

> Play is the purest, most spiritual activity of man at this stage, and, at the same time, typical of human life as a whole—of the inner hidden natural life in man and all things. It gives, therefore, joy, freedom, contentment, inner and outer rest, peace with the world. It holds the sources of all that is good. A child that plays thoroughly, with self-active determination, persevering until physical fatigue forbids, will surely be a thorough, determined man, capable of self-sacrifice for the promotion of the welfare of himself and others. Is not the most beautiful expression of child-life at this time a playing child?—a child wholly absorbed in his play?—a child that has fallen asleep while so absorbed?
>
> As already indicated, play at this time is not trivial, it is highly serious and of deep significance. Cultivate and foster it, O mother; protect and guard it, O father! To the calm, keen vision of one who truly knows human nature, the spontaneous play of the child discloses the future inner life of the man.
>
> The plays of childhood are the germinal leaves of all later life; for the whole man is developed and shown in these, in his tenderest dispositions, in his innermost tendencies. [14]

Froebel knew from experience, however, that unstructured play represented a potential danger and that it was quite likely, as Pestalozzi learned with his son Jean

Froebel compared children to seeds and likened parents and professionals to gardeners. As discussed in chapter 1, the view of children as growing plants and their development, similar to the unfolding of a blooming flower, has been and is a prevalent and influential belief in how children grow and develop.

Jacques, that a child left to his own devices may not learn much. Without guidance and direction and a prepared environment in which to learn, there was a real possibility that little or the wrong kind of learning would occur.

According to Froebel, the teacher is responsible for guidance and direction so children can become creative, contributing members of society. To achieve this end, Froebel developed a systematic, planned curriculum for the education of young children. The basis for his curriculum were "gifts," "occupations," songs he composed, and educational games. Gifts were objects for children to handle and use in accordance with teachers' instructions, so they could learn shape, size, color, and concepts involved in counting, measuring, contrasting, and comparison. The first gift was a set of six balls of yarn, each a different color, with six lengths of yarn the same colors as the balls. Part of the purpose of this gift was to teach color recognition.

Froebel felt that the ball (meaning a spherical object) played an important role in education; consequently, he placed a great deal of emphasis on its use. He also believed the ball was a perfect symbol for humankind's unity with the divine, a concept he felt was important but is difficult for us to understand. Froebel said of the ball:

> Even the word *ball*, in our significant language, is full of expression and meaning, pointing out that the ball is, as it were, an image of the all; but the ball itself has such an extraordinary charm, such a constant attraction for early childhood, as well as for later youth, that it is beyond comparison the first as well as the most important plaything of childhood especially.[15]

The second gift was a cube, a cylinder, and a sphere. Directions for the use of the second gift give insight into Froebel's educational methods and philosophy.

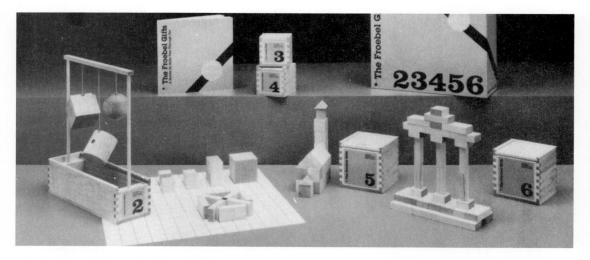

These modern reproductions of some of Froebel's "gifts" attest to the renewed interest in Froebelian ideas and materials. They also reinforce the importance of concrete, manipulative materials in learning and in emphasizing the role of active learning.

The importance of the consideration of the presence and absence of an object and its utilization for play, and in playing with the child, has been already noticed (with the ball . . .). With this we will now add a continuation to the play; for repeating the same experience in different ways with the same object serves to develop as well as to strengthen the child. Hence the mother hides the cube in her hand while she sings to her child:

I see now the hand alone.
Where, oh, where can cube be gone?

The mother thus leads the gaze and attention of the child to her hand, which he will therefore watch intently; the gaze, and even the little hand of the child, will make an effort to find the cube. As if yielding to this effort, the concealing hand opens, and the mother says or sings to the child:

Aha! aha!
My hand has hid the cube with care,
While you looked for it everywhere.
See, it is here!
Look at it, dear.

By this play the child is not only again made to notice that the cube fills space, but his attention is also called to the precise form of the cube; and he will look at it sharply, unconsciously comparing it with the hand, to which his eyes were first attracted. But the form of the cube appears to him, up to this point, as too large a whole, and composed of too many kinds of parts; the child's view of it must therefore be clarified by single perceptions.

Therefore the mother or nurse clasps the cube again in her hand, but so that one surface is still perceptible, singing to the child:

Only one side here you see
Where can now the others be?[16]

Occupations were materials designed for developing various skills, primarily psychomotor, through activities such as sewing with a sewing board, drawing pictures by following the dots, modeling with clay, cutting, stringing beads, weaving, drawing, pasting, and folding paper. Many of the games or plays Froebel developed were based on his gifts.

Froebel is called the "father of the kindergarten" because he devoted his life to developing both a program for the young child and a system of training for kindergarten teachers. Many of the concepts and activities of the gifts and occupations are similar to activities that many kindergarten and other early childhood programs provide.

Froebel's recognition of the importance of learning through play is reinforced by contemporary early childhood professionals who plan and structure their programs around play activities. Other features of Froebel's kindergarten that remain are the play circle, where children sit in a circle for learning, and singing songs to reinforce concepts taught with "gifts" and "occupations." Froebel was the first educator to develop a planned, systematic program for educating young children and the first to encourage young, unmarried women to become teachers. This break with tradition caused Froebel no small amount of criticism and was one reason his methods encountered opposition.

All the great educators believed play is the basis for learning and incorporated play into their curriculum. When planning programs and activities, early childhood professionals should provide many opportunities for children to participate in play. What would you say to parents who asked you about the importance of play in their child's growth and development?

Common Beliefs

All the educators discussed so far had certain basic premises in common. First, they believed strongly in the important role of the family in educating children and laying the foundation for all future learning. Second, they believed in the importance of educating children early in life. Consequently, they advocated schooling either in the home or in a school setting. Third, they felt parents needed training and help to be good parents and their children's first teachers. They recognized that for education to begin early in life, it was imperative that parents have materials and training to do a good job (as we will discuss in chap. 13). Educators and politicians are rediscovering how important parents are in the educational process. Parent involvement is being encouraged in public schools and other agencies, and we are learning what great educators knew all along: that parents are their children's first, and perhaps best, teachers.

MODERN INFLUENCES

Maria Montessori

Maria Montessori (1870–1952) was born in Italy and devoted her life to developing a system for educating young children. Her system has influenced virtually all subsequent early childhood programs. A precocious young woman who thought of undertaking either mathematics or engineering as a career, she instead chose medicine. Despite the obstacles to entering a field traditionally closed to women, she became the first woman in Italy to earn a medical degree. Following this achievement, she was appointed assistant instructor in the psychiatric clinic of the University of Rome. At that time, it was customary not to distinguish between the mentally retarded children and the insane, and her work brought her into contact with the mentally retarded children who had been committed to insane asylums. Although Montessori's first intention was to study children's diseases, she soon became interested in educational solutions for problems such as deafness, paralysis, and idiocy.

At that time she said, "I differed from my colleagues in that I instinctively felt that mental deficiency was more of an educational than medical problem."[17] Montessori became interested in the work of Edouard Seguin, a pioneer in the development of an educational system for mentally defective children, and of Jean Itard, who developed an educational system for deaf mutes. Montessori credits Itard and Seguin with inspiring her to continue her studies with mentally retarded children. Of her initial efforts at educating children, she said:

> I succeeded in teaching a number of the idiots from the asylums both to read and to write so well that I was able to present them at a public school for an examination together with normal children. And they passed the examination successfully.[18]

This was a remarkable achievement, which aroused interest in both Montessori and in her methods. Montessori, however, was already considering something else:

> While everyone else was admiring the progress made by my defective charges, I was trying to discover the reasons which could have reduced the healthy, happy pupils of the ordinary schools to such a low state that in the intelligence test they were on the level with my own unfortunate pupils.[19]

While continuing to study and prepare herself for the task of educating children, Montessori came upon the opportunity to perfect her methods and implement them with normal school-age children quite by chance. In 1906 she was invited by the director general of the Roman Association for Good Building to organize schools for young children of families who occupied the tenement houses constructed by the association. In the first school, named the *Casa dei Bambini*, or Children's House, she tested her ideas and gained insights into children and teaching that led to the perfection of her system.

Montessori was profoundly religious, and a religious undertone is reflected throughout her work. She often quoted from the Bible to support her points. For example, at the dedication ceremonies of the first Children's House, she read from Isaiah 60:1–5 and ended by saying, "Perhaps, this Children's House can become a new Jerusalem, which, if it is spread out among the abandoned people of the world, can bring a new light to education."[20] Her religious dedication to the fundamental sacredness and uniqueness of every child and subsequent grounding of educational processes in a religious conviction undoubtedly account for some of her remarkable achievements as a person and educator. Thus, her system functions well for those who are willing to dedicate themselves to teaching as if it were a religious vocation.

Montessori's philosophical and pedagogical ideas are evident in many early childhood programs. As much as any other single individual, Montessori influenced the nature and direction of American preschool education. One of her concepts, daily living skills, is incorporated into almost every early childhood program.

John Dewey

John Dewey (1859–1952) represents a truly American influence on U.S. education. Through his positions as professor of philosophy at the University of Chicago and Columbia University, his extensive writing, and the educational practices of his many followers, Dewey did more to alter and redirect the course of education in the United States than any other person.

Dewey's theory of schooling, usually called *progressivism*, emphasizes children and their interests rather than subject matter. From this child-centered emphasis comes the terms *child-centered curriculum* and *child-centered schools*. The progressive education philosophy also maintains that schools should be concerned with preparing children for the realities of today rather than some vague future time. As expressed by Dewey in *My Pedagogical Creed*, "education, therefore, is a process of living and not a preparation for future living."[21] Thus, out of daily life should come the activities in which children learn about life and the skills necessary for living.

What is included in Dewey's concept of children's interests? "Not some one thing," he explained; "it is a name for the fact that a course of action, an occupation, or pursuit absorbs the powers of an individual in a thorough-going way."[22] In a classroom based on Dewey's ideas, children are involved with physical activities, utilization of things, intellectual pursuits, and social interaction. Physical activities include running, jumping, and active involvement with materials. In this phase the child begins the process of education and develops other interest areas that form the basis for doing and learning. The growing child learns to use tools and materials to construct things. Dewey felt that an ideal expression for this interest was daily living activities or occupations such as cooking and carpentry.

To promote an interest in the intellectual—solving problems, discovering new things, and figuring out how things work—children are given opportunities for inquiry and discovery. Dewey also believed that *social interest,* referring to interactions with people, was encouraged in a democratically run classroom.

While Dewey believed the curriculum should be built on the interests of children, he also felt it was the teacher's responsibility to plan for and capitalize on opportunities to integrate or weave traditional subject matter through and around the fabric of these interests. Dewey describes a school based on his ideas:

> All of the schools . . . as compared with traditional schools . . . [exhibit] a common emphasis upon respect for individuality and for increased freedom; a common disposition to build upon the nature and experience of the boys and girls that come to them, instead of imposing from without external subject-matter standards. They all display a certain atmosphere of informality, because experience has proved that formalization is hostile to genuine mental activity and to sincere emotional expression and growth. Emphasis upon activity as distinct from passivity is one of the common factors.[23]

Teachers who integrate subjects, use thematic units, and encourage problem-solving activities and critical thinking are philosophically indebted to Dewey.

There has been a great deal of misinterpretation and criticism of the progressive movement and Dewey's ideas, especially by those who favor a traditional approach that emphasizes the basic subjects and skills. Actually, Dewey was not opposed to teaching basic skills or topics. He did believe, however, that traditional educational

John Dewey believed that working on projects promoted active learning and helped children learn many academic and social skills such as cooperation, consideration for others, and learning how to work in a group. Today, active learning, cooperative learning, and projects are very much a part of early childhood programs.

strategies *imposed* knowledge on children, whereas their interests should be a springboard for involvement with skills and subject matter.

> The accumulation and acquisition of information for purposes of reproduction in recitation and examination is made too much of. "Knowledge," in the sense of information, means the working capital, the indispensable resources of further inquiry; of finding out, or learning, more things. Frequently it is treated as an end itself, and then the goal becomes to heap it up and display it when called for. This static, cold-storage ideal of knowledge is inimical to educative development. It not only lets occasions for thinking go unused, but it swamps thinking. No one could construct a house on ground cluttered with miscellaneous junk. Pupils who have stored their "minds" with all kinds of material which they have never put to intellectual uses are sure to be hampered when they try to think. They have no practice in selecting what is appropriate, and no criterion to go by; everything is on the same dead static level.[24]

Dewey not only influenced educational thought and practice in the United States but also exerted a strong influence on the educational thought and practice of other countries who embrace his concept of incorporating work and education. We find the idea of "socially useful education" particularly evident in contemporary China, Russia, and other socialist countries.

Jean Piaget

Jean Piaget (1896–1980) was born in Switzerland. He was a precocious child who published his first article at the age of ten. He received his baccalaureate degree from college at eighteen and earned his doctorate three years later. His training in biology was influential in the development of his ideas about knowledge, and it forms the primary basis for his theory of intellectual development.

Piaget studied in Paris, where he worked with Theodore Simon at the Alfred Binet laboratory, standardizing tests of reasoning for use with children. (Binet and Simon developed a scale for measuring intelligence.) This experience provided the foundation for Piaget's clinical method of interviewing, used in studying children's intellectual development. As Piaget recalls, "Thus I engaged my subjects in conversations patterned after psychiatric questioning, with the aim of discovering something about the reasoning process underlying their right, but especially their wrong, answers."[25] The emphasis on this method helps explain why some developers of a Piaget-based early childhood curriculum encourage the teacher's use of questioning procedures to promote thinking.

Following his work with children in Paris, which established the direction of his life work, Piaget became associated with the Institute J. J. Rousseau in Geneva and began studying intellectual development. Piaget's own three children played a major role in his studies, since many of his consequent insights about children's intellectual development are based on his observations and work with them. Using his own children in his studies caused some to criticize his findings. His theory, however, is based on not only his research but also literally hundreds of other studies involving thousands of children. Based on his research, Piaget came to these conclusions about early childhood education:

- Children play an active role in their own cognitive development.
- Mental and physical activity are important for children's cognitive development.
- Experiences constitute the raw materials children use to develop mental structures.
- Children develop cognitively through interaction with and adaptation to the environment.
- Development is a continuous process.
- Development results from maturation and the *transactions* or interactions between children and the physical and social environments.

Piaget also popularized the age/stage approach to cognitive development and influenced others to apply the theory to other processes such as moral, language, and social development. He encouraged and inspired many psychologists and educators to develop educational curricula and programs utilizing his ideas and promoted interest in the study of young children's cognitive development that has in turn contributed to the interest in infant development and education.

Piaget believed children develop their intelligence through active *learning. This is the theory of* constructivism. *Early childhood professionals promote active learning by providing opportunities for children to be actively involved with concrete activities that promote questioning and thinking. We can hear this child asking himself, "Where does this piece fit?"*

Lev Vygotsky

Lev Vygotsky (1896–1934), a contemporary of Piaget, increasingly inspires the practices of early childhood professionals. Vygotsky was born in Russia, the second of eight children. An intellectually precocious child, he graduated from Moscow University, where he studied law. Like so many great people, what he studied at the university was not what determined his life work, but it laid the foundation. Vygotsky suffered from tuberculosis and died at thirty-seven.

Although his career was short-lived, Vygotsky was a prolific writer and wrote widely in many areas, including linguistics and his theory of psychology and development. Vygotsky's theory of development is particularly useful in describing children's mental, language, and social development. His theory also has many implications for how children's play promotes language and social development.

Vygotsky believed that children's mental, language, and social development is supported and enhanced by others through social interaction. This view is opposite from the Piagetian perspective in which children are much more solitary developers of their own intelligence and language. For Vygotsky, development is supported by social interaction, and "learning awakens a variety of developmental processes that are able to operate only when the child is interacting with people in his environment and in collaboration with his peers. Once these processes are internalized, they become part of the child's independent developmental achievement."[26] Further, Vygotsky believed that beginning at birth, children seek out adults for social interaction, and development occurs through these interactions.

For early childhood professionals, one of Vygotsky's most important concepts is the "zone of proximal development." Vygotsky defined this zone as

> that area of development into which a child can be led in the course of interaction with a more competent partner, either adult or peer. . . . [It] is not some clear-cut space that exists independently of the process of joint activity itself. Rather, it is the difference between what the child can accomplish independently and what he or she can achieve in conjunction with another, more competent person. The zone is thus *created* in the course of social interaction.[27]

From Vygotsky's point of view:

> Learning is not development; however, properly organized learning results in mental development and sets in motion a variety of developmental processes that would be impossible apart from learning. Thus, learning is a necessary part and universal aspect of the process of developing culturally organized, specifically human, psychological functions.[28]

For Vygotsky, learning is directly related to the course of child development.

Intersubjectivity is a second Vygotsky concept. Intersubjectivity is based on the idea that "individuals come to a task, problem, or conversation with their own subjective ways of making sense of it. If they then discuss their differing viewpoints, shared understanding may be attained. . . . In other words, in the course of communication participants may arrive at some mutually agreed-upon, or intersubjective,

Vygotsky emphasized the importance of collaboration in learning and social development. Collaboration of children with other children and adults enables them to use skills learned in the collaboration even when the competent person is not present.

understanding."[29] Communication or dialogue between teacher and child literally becomes a means for helping children "scaffold," that is, develop new concepts and think their way to higher-level concepts.

This intersubjectivity is similar to Piaget's theory that disequilibrium sets the stage for assimilation and accommodation, and, consequently, new schemes develop. Furthermore, Vygotsky believed that as a result of teacher-child collaboration, the child uses concepts learned in the collaborative process to solve problems when the teacher is not present. As Vygotsky said, the child

> continues to act in collaboration even though the teacher is not standing near him. . . .
> This help—this aspect of collaboration—is invisibly present. It is continued in what looks
> from the outside like the child's independent solution of the problem.[30]

According to Vygotsky, social interactions and collaboration are essential ingredients in the processes of learning and development.

Many current practices such as cooperative learning, joint problem solving, coaching, collaboration, mentoring, and other forms of assisted learning are consistent with Vygotsky's theory of development.

Howard Gardner

Born in Scranton, Pennsylvania, Howard Gardner (1943–) graduated from Harvard University with his bachelor's and Ph.D. degrees. He is a professor of education and adjunct professor of psychology at Harvard University, adjunct professor of neurology at the Boston University School of Medicine, and codirector of Harvard Project

Zero. Gardner directs research on such themes as children's appreciation of figurative language, children's drawings, early symbolization, the mastery of notations in middle childhood, children's play and narrative abilities, the development of musical competence, and children's facility with media and technology, including television and computers.

Gardner personifies how the past, present, and future are integrated with each other. As a contemporary theorist, he is changing our ideas about children's intellectual development and how to promote their cognitive development. Gardner challenges early childhood professionals—indeed, all professionals—with his *theory of multiple intelligences.*

According to Piaget, mature biological thinking, or intelligence, consists of mainly logical/mathematical activities, such as classification, seriation, numeration, time, and spatial relations. This view of intelligence as a single set of mental skills, measurable by an intelligence test, is the way intelligence is generally conceived by educators and the public. Gardner, on the other hand, maintains:

> a human intellectual competence must entail a set of skills of problem solving—enabling the individual to *resolve genuine problems or difficulties* that he or she encounters and, when appropriate, to create an effective product—and must also entail the potential for *finding or creating problems* thereby laying the groundwork for the acquisition of new knowledge.[31]

Based on this view of intelligence, Gardner identifies seven intelligences: linguistic, musical, logical-mathematical, spatial, bodily-kinesthetic, interpersonal, and

According to Gardner's theory of multiple intelligences, children demonstrate intelligence across a range of seven intelligences, including musical intelligence as shown here. Why is Gardner's theory so popular? How would you apply his theory in early childhood programs?

intrapersonal. This view of intelligence as seven components has and will undoubtedly continue to influence educational thought and practice. (See chap. 9 for an expanded discussion of the seven intelligences.)

FROM LUTHER TO VYGOTSKY: BASIC CONCEPTS ESSENTIAL TO GOOD EDUCATIONAL PRACTICES

As They Relate to Children

- Everyone needs to learn how to read and write.
- Children learn best when they use all their senses.
- All children are capable of being educated.
- All children should be educated to the fullest extent of their abilities.
- Education should begin early in life.
- Children should not be forced to learn but should be appropriately taught what they are ready to learn and should be prepared for the next stage of learning.
- Learning activities should be interesting and meaningful.
- Social interactions with teachers and peers are a necessary part of development.

As They Relate to Teachers

- Teachers must show love and respect for all children.
- Teachers should be dedicated to the teaching profession.
- Good teaching is based on a theory, a philosophy, goals, and objectives.
- Children's learning is enhanced through the use of concrete materials.
- Teaching should move from the concrete to the abstract.
- Observation is a key means for determining children's needs.
- Teaching should be a planned, systematic process.
- Teaching should be child centered rather than adult or subject centered.
- Teaching should be based on children's interests.
- Teachers should collaborate with children as a means of promoting development.

As They Relate to Parents

- The family is an important institution in children's education and development.
- Parents are their children's primary educators.
- Parents must guide and direct young children's learning.
- Parents should be involved in any educational program designed for their children.
- Everyone should have knowledge of and training for child rearing.

THE RECENT PAST

To fully understand the current basis for the public's interest in early childhood education and young children, we need to look back almost half a century to three significant events: (1) the general acceptance of claims that the public schools were not successfully teaching reading and related skills; (2) the boycott of city buses by blacks in Montgomery, Alabama, on December 1, 1955; and (3) the launching of *Sputnik* by the Soviet Union on October 4, 1957.

These events changed early childhood education in two important ways. First, in and of themselves, they influenced specific policies, programs, and legislation affecting young children and their families. Second, they affected people's attitudes toward and ways of thinking about what is best for young children.

How the United States educates its children and how well the schools fulfill their appointed tasks are always topics of national discussion and debate. Hardly a day passes that the schools are not criticized in some way. Schooling and public criticism go hand in hand. During the 1950s, a host of articles and books detailed "why children cannot read," followed in 1955 by the publication of Rudolf Flesch's *Why Johnny Can't Read*. Flesch criticized the schools for the way reading was taught. Critics and parents began to question the methodology and results of the teaching of reading and other basic skills. Parents demanded schools and programs that would teach these skills. Many parents felt that traditional play-oriented preschools and public school programs that emphasized socialization were not preparing their children for attending college or earning a living. Programs that stressed cognitive learning became popular with parents who wanted to give their children both an early start and a good foundation in learning.

Flesch's criticism of reading methods laid the groundwork for introducing the phonetic approach to reading, a system based on having children learn that letters represent sounds. As children learn such skills as initial consonant sounds, blends, digraphs (a pair of letters representing a specific speech sound), silent consonants, and medial and final consonants, they can "sound out" the majority of words they encounter. This phonetic method, championed by Jeanne Chall, replaced the "look-say" or "whole-word" method popular at the time. As you might expect, given the inevitable swing of the education pendulum, the phonetic approach is currently encountering criticism and challenges in the name of whole language and emerging literacy (see chaps. 7 and 8).

The Montgomery bus boycott set in motion a series of court cases and demonstrations for civil rights and human dignity. The fight for civil liberties spread quickly to the school arena. As a result, the rights of children and parents to public education were clarified and extended. Many of the new federal and state regulations and laws that affect children with disabilities, the disadvantaged, and abused children are essentially civil rights legislation rather than purely educational legislation.

Included in this legislation, and undoubtedly the two most important for early childhood, are Public Law 94-142, the *Education for All Handicapped Children Act*, and Public Law 99-457, the *Education of the Handicapped Act Amendments*, both of which extend rights to educational and social services to special needs children

and their parents and families. Both laws, with their tremendous educational implications, also broaden and extend civil rights. Consequently, children have been
granted rights to a free, appropriate, individualized education, as well as humane
treatment.

Spurred by the Soviet Union's launching of *Sputnik* in 1957, the U.S. government in 1958 passed the National Defense Education Act to meet national needs,
particularly in the sciences. What made it possible for the Soviets to launch *Sputnik?* Examination of the Soviet educational system led to the conclusion that it provided educational opportunities at an earlier age than did the U.S. public schools.
Some educators began to wonder if we too should not teach children at a younger
age; as a result, there was a surge of interest in early education.

Research

At the same time that Soviet space achievements brought a reappraisal of our educational system, research studies were also influencing our ideas about how children
learn, how to teach them, and what they should learn. These studies led to a major
shift in basic educational premises concerning what children can achieve. Research
by B. S. Bloom and J. M. Hunt enabled early childhood professionals to arrive at
these conclusions:

1. The period of most rapid intellectual growth occurs before age eight. The extent
   to which children will become intelligent, based on those things by which we
   measure intelligence and school achievement, is determined long before many
   children enter school. The notion of promoting cognitive development implies
   that children benefit from home environments that are conducive to learning
   and early schoollike experiences, especially for children from environments that
   place children at risk for developing their full potential.

2. It is increasingly evident that children are not born with fixed intelligences. This
   outdated concept fails to do justice to people's tremendous capacity for learning
   and change. In addition, evidence supports developmental intelligence. The
   extent to which individual intelligence develops depends on many variables, such
   as experiences, child-rearing practices, economic factors, nutrition, and the quality of prenatal and postnatal environments. Inherited genetic characteristics set a
   broad framework within which intelligence will develop. Heredity sets the limits,
   while environment determines the extent to which the limits are achieved.

3. Children reared in homes that are not intellectually stimulating may also lag
   intellectually behind their counterparts reared in more advantaged environments. Implications concerning the home environment are obvious. Experience
   shows that children who lack an environment that promotes learning opportunities may be at risk throughout life. On the other hand, homes that offer intellectual stimulation tend to produce children who do well in school.

How should early childhood professionals respond to research that indicates the
family has an extremely powerful influence on children's achievement? As with so

many things in life, the middle ground is often the best position. We cannot ignore or minimize the influence of the family. Schools and society should do everything possible to involve parents in schooling and help do the best job of nurturing, rearing, and educating. On the other hand, schools and early childhood professionals must be willing to respond creatively and with a broad range of services to all children without blaming anyone or any institution. The responses of all to family conditions and their effects on the child are critical in determining how well schools fulfill the functions of education and socialization.

Poverty

During the 1960s, the United States rediscovered the poor and recognized that not everyone enjoyed affluence. In 1964, Congress enacted the Economic Opportunity Act (EOA). The EOA was designed to wage a war on poverty on several fronts. Head Start, created by the EOA, attempted to break intergenerational cycles of poverty by providing education and social opportunities for preschool children of families living in poverty (see chap. 10).

Head Start played as big a role, if not the biggest, as any other single force in interesting the nation in educating young children. Although programs for children had been sponsored by the federal government during the Great Depression and World War II, these were primarily designed to free mothers for jobs in defense plants. Head Start marked the first time that children and their families were the intended beneficiaries of the services.

The Open Education Movement

We can trace the foundations of open education to Pestalozzi, Froebel, Montessori, and Dewey, although they did not use the same terminology. Montessori might be called the first modern open educator, because she allowed children to enjoy freedom within a prepared environment. She also encouraged individualized instruction, and most important, insisted on respect for children.

Interest in open education in the United States began in the 1960s when many educators and critics called attention to the ways schools were stifling student initiative, freedom, and self-direction. Schools were compared to prisons; critics described students sitting apathetically in straight rows, passively listening to robot-like teachers, with little or no real learning taking place. In short, classrooms and learning were assumed to be devoid of enthusiasm, joy, and self-direction. Educators and schools were challenged to involve students in learning and abolish policies and procedures that were detrimental to students' physical and mental health. In essence, schools were challenged to become happy places of learning.

Concurrently, school reformers in the United States discovered the British Primary School, a comprehensive education program characterized by respect for children, responsiveness to children's needs, and learning through interests.

Open education is an attempt to restructure preschool and primary classrooms into settings that support individuality, promote independence, encourage freedom, and demonstrate respect for children. In this context, open education is a logical extension of many of the ideas of Montessori, Dewey, and Piaget. It encourages children to become involved in their own learning, and teachers allow children to make choices about how and what they learn. Teachers can conduct an open program regardless of the physical, social, or financial setting of the school or community.

Open education is an environment in which children are free from authoritarian adults and arbitrary rules. Contrary to popular misconception, children are not free to do everything they choose. Within broad guidelines, however (ideally established by teachers, students, and administrators), children are free to move about the room, carry on conversations, and engage in learning activities based on their interests.

Open education is child-centered learning. Adults do not do all the talking, decision making, organizing, and planning when it is children who need to develop these skills. Open education seeks to return the emphasis to the child, where it rightfully belongs.

Just as Montessori conceptualized a new role for teachers, so does open education encourage redefinition of the role. Teachers who believe that open education is possible have surmounted the first obstacle—many teachers are afraid to try it. Open education teachers respect students and believe children are capable of assuming responsibility for their own learning. Teachers consider themselves primarily teachers of children, not of subject matter, and feel confident with all students in all subject areas. They are keen observers, for many of the decisions regarding instruction and activities depend on thorough knowledge of what the children have accomplished. Adjectives that describe open teachers' role include *learner, guide, facilitator, catalyst,* and *director*.

Many of the ideas of progressive education and open education which have their foundations in Dewey's ideas are back. These include such practices as child-centered learning, integration of subjects into themes and activities, and as we see here, cooperative learning in which children help each other and learn from each other.

The Death and Rebirth of Open Education

During the 1980s, the pendulum of change swung toward a "back to basics," sub-ject-centered, teacher-centered, highly organized system of education and away from a child-centered, activity-centered program characterized by freedom and open education. The pendulum has now swung back toward concepts embodied in open education, although we now apply other names such as *active learning* to convey practices similar to these embodied in open education. The open education concept was always most popular and successful with early childhood professionals, perhaps because of a combination of young children's natural ability to work well in an open setting and the fact that preschool teachers are generally comfortable in an informal classroom atmosphere.

Open education is full of excitement and challenge. The opportunities for an individualized, self-paced program, operated within a context of freedom, choice, active learning, respect for children, and relevance, appeal to the early childhood profession.

A familiar maxim in the worlds of fashion, design, and education says, "If it's good, it will be back in ten or fifteen years." Open education and its accompanying practices have been reborn. The following signs of new life have arisen:

- Developmentally appropriate curricula and practices designed to meet chil-dren's developmental needs (see chap. 6)
- Whole language, emergent literacy, and other practices designed to integrate processes of reading, writing, and speaking (see chaps. 8 and 9)
- Renewed interest in child-centered versus teacher- and subject-centered teach-ing and learning
- Multiage and family grouping. Interestingly, many early educators have always attempted to make their programs resemble a family. This same tendency is evident today in classrooms in which children are grouped as "families," con-sisting of different ages, responsibilities are shared, and children arrive at deci-sions after discussion among "family" members. Grouping children into families provides not only structure but an identity and security in which to learn.
- Programs that involve children in active learning and choices (see, e.g., the High/Scope curriculum, chap. 4; South Pointe Elementary School, chap. 9)
- The project approach
- Cooperative learning (see chap. 8)
- Family-centered programs. The emphasis on parent involvement underscores the historic importance of the family as a context in which to conduct education.

RECURRING THEMES

Certain processes are common to good teaching regardless of time or place. Respecting children, attending to individual differences, and getting children inter-ested and involved in their learning are the framework of quality educational programs. Reading about and examining the experiences of great educators help keep this vision before us.

All great educators have believed in the basic goodness of children, that is, that children by nature tend to behave in socially acceptable ways. They believed it was the role of the teacher to provide the environment for this goodness to manifest itself. Young children learn to behave in certain ways according to how they are treated, the role models they have to emulate, and the environments in which they have to grow. Children do not emerge from the womb with a propensity toward badness but tend to grow and behave as they are treated and taught.

A central point that Luther, Comenius, Pestalozzi, Froebel, Montessori, and Dewey sought to make about our work as educators, no matter in what context—parent or early childhood professional—is that we must do it well and act as though we really care about those for whom we have been called to serve.

TIME LINE: THE HISTORY OF EARLY CHILDHOOD EDUCATION

The following material summarizes key events cumulatively affecting early childhood education as we know it today.

1524   Martin Luther argued for public support of education for all children in his *Letter to the Mayors and Aldermen of All the Cities of Germany in Behalf of Christian Schools.*

1628   John Amos Comenius's *The Great Didactic* proclaimed the value of education for all children according to the laws of nature.

1762   Jean-Jacques Rousseau wrote *Émile*, explaining that education should take into account the child's natural growth and interests.

1780   Robert Raikes initiated the Sunday School movement in England to teach Bible study and religion to children.

1801   Johann Pestalozzi wrote *How Gertrude Teaches Her Children*, emphasizing home education and learning by discovery.

1816   Robert Owen set up a nursery school in Great Britain at the New Lanark Cotton Mills, believing that early education could counteract bad influences of the home.

1817   Thomas Gallaudet founded the first residential school for the deaf in Hartford, Connecticut.

1824   The American Sunday School Union was started with the purpose of initiating Sunday schools around the United States.

1836   William McGuffey began publishing the *Eclectic Reader* for elementary school children; his writing had a strong impact on moral and literary attitudes in the nineteenth century.

1837   Friedrich Froebel, known as the "father of the kindergarten," established the first kindergarten in Blankenburgh, Germany.

1837   Horace Mann began his job as secretary of the Massachusetts State Board of Education; he is often called the "father of the common schools" because of the role he played in helping set up the elementary school system in the United States.

1837   Edouard Seguin, influenced by Jean Itard, started the first school for the feeble-minded in France.

1856   Mrs. Carl Schurz established the first kindergarten in the United States in Watertown, Wisconsin; the school was founded for children of German immigrants, and the program was conducted in German.

1860   Elizabeth Peabody opened a private kindergarten in Boston, Massachusetts, for English-speaking children.

1869   The first special education class for the deaf was founded in Boston.

1871   The first public kindergarten in North America was started in Ontario, Canada.

1873   Susan Blow opened the first public school kindergarten in the United States in St. Louis, Missouri, as a cooperative effort with William Harris, superintendent of schools.

1876   A model kindergarten was shown at the Philadelphia Centennial Exposition.

1880   First teacher-training program for teachers of kindergarten began in Oshkosh Normal School, Philadelphia.

1884   The American Association of Elementary, Kindergarten, and Nursery School Educators was founded to serve in a consulting capacity for other educators.

1892   The International Kindergarten Union (IKU) was founded.

1896   John Dewey started the Laboratory School at the University of Chicago, basing his program on child-centered learning with an emphasis on life experiences.

1905   Sigmund Freud wrote *Three Essays of the Theory of Sexuality*, emphasizing the value of a healthy emotional environment during childhood.

1907   Maria Montessori started her first preschool in Rome called Children's House; her now-famous teaching method was based on the theory that children learn best by themselves in a properly prepared environment.

1909   The first White House Conference on Children was convened by Theodore Roosevelt.

1911   Arnold Gesell, well known for his research on the importance of the preschool years, began child development study at Yale University.

1911   Margaret and Rachel McMillan founded an open-air nursery school in Great Britain, in which the class met outdoors and emphasis was on healthy living.

1912   Arnold and Beatrice Gesell wrote *The Normal Child and Primary Education*.

1915   Eva McLin started the first U.S. Montessori nursery school in New York City.

1915   The Child Education Foundation of New York City founded a nursery school using Montessori's principles.

1918   The first public nursery schools were started in Great Britain.

1919   Harriet Johnson started the Nursery School of the Bureau of Educational Experiments, later to become the Bank Street College of Education.

1921   Patty Smith Hill started a progressive, laboratory nursery school at Columbia Teachers College.

1921   A. S. Neill founded Summerhill, an experimental school based on the ideas of Rousseau and Dewey.

1922   With Edna Noble White as its first director, the Merrill-Palmer Institute Nursery School opened in Detroit, with the purpose of preparing women in proper child care; at this time, the Institute was known as the Merrill-Palmer School of Motherhood and Home Training.

1922   Abigail Eliot, influenced by the open-air school in Great Britain and basing her program on personal hygiene and proper behavior, started the Ruggles Street Nursery School in Boston.

1924   *Childhood Education*, the first professional journal in early childhood education, was published by the IKU.

1926   The National Committee on Nursery Schools was initiated by Patty Smith Hill at Columbia Teachers College; now called the National Association for the Education of Young Children, it provides guidance and consultant services for educators.

1926   The National Association of Nursery Education (NANE) was founded.

1930   The IKU changed its name to the Association for Childhood Education.

1933   The Work Projects Administration (WPA) provided money to start nursery schools so that unemployed teachers would have jobs.

1935   First toy lending library, Toy Loan, was founded in Los Angeles.

1940   The Lanham Act provided funds for child care during World War II, mainly for day care centers for children whose mothers worked in the war effort.

1943   Kaiser Child Care Centers opened in Portland, Oregon, to provide twenty-four-hour child care for children of mothers working in war-related industries.

1944   The journal *Young Children* was first published by the NANE.

1946   Dr. Benjamin Spock wrote the *Common Sense Book of Baby and Child Care*.

1950   Erik Erikson published his writings on the "eight ages or stages" of personality growth and development and identified "tasks" for each stage of development; the information, known as "Personality in the Making," formed the basis for the

1950   White House Conference on Children and Youth.

1952   Jean Piaget's *The Origins of Intelligence in Children* was published in English translation.

1955   Rudolf Flesch's *Why Johnny Can't Read* criticized the schools for their methodology in teaching reading and other basic skills.

1957   The Soviet Union launched *Sputnik,* sparking renewed interest in other educational systems and marking the beginning of the "rediscovery" of early childhood education.

1958   The National Defense Education Act was passed to provide federal funds for improving education in the sciences, mathematics, and foreign languages.

1960   Katharine Whiteside Taylor founded the American Council of Parent Cooperatives for those interested in exchanging ideas in preschool education; it later became the Parent Cooperative Preschools International.

1960   The Day Care and Child Development Council of America was formed to publicize the need for quality services for children.

1964   At its Miami Beach conference, the NANE became the National Association for the Education of Young Children (NAEYC).

1964   The Economic Opportunity Act of 1964 was passed as the beginning of the war on poverty and was the foundation for Head Start.

1965   The Elementary and Secondary Education Act was passed to provide federal money for programs for educationally deprived children.

1965   The Head Start Program began with federal money allocated for preschool education; the early programs were known as child development centers.

1966	The Bureau of Education for the Handicapped was established.	1980	The first American lekotek (toy-lending library) opened its doors in Evanston, Illinois.
1967	The Follow Through Program was initiated to extend the Head Start Program into the primary grades.	1980	The White House Conference on Families was held.
1968	B. F. Skinner wrote *The Technology of Teaching*, which outlines a programmed approach to learning.	1981	The Head Start Act of 1981 (Omnibus Budget Reconciliation Act of 1981, Public Law 97-35) was passed to extend Head Start and provide for effective delivery of comprehensive services to economically disadvantaged children and their families.
1968	The federal government established the Handicapped Children's Early Education Program to fund model preschool programs for children with disabilities.	1981	The Education Consolidation and Improvement Act (ECIA) was passed, consolidating many federal support programs for education.
1970	The White House Conference on Children and Youth was held.		
1971	The Stride Rite Corporation in Boston was the first to start a corporate-supported child care program.	1981	Secretary of Education Terrell Bell announced the establishment of the National Commission on Excellence in Education.
1972	The National Home Start Program began for the purpose of involving parents in their children's education.	1982	The Mississippi legislature established mandatory statewide public kindergartens.
1975	Public Law 94-142, the Education for All Handicapped Children Act, was passed mandating a free and appropriate education for all children with disabilities and extending many rights to parents of such children.	1983	An Arkansas commission chaired by Hillary Clinton calls for mandatory kindergarten and lower pupil-teacher ratios in the early grades.
1979	The International Year of the Child was sponsored by the United Nations and designated by Executive Order.	1984	The High/Scope Educational Foundation released a study that it said docu-

READINGS FOR FURTHER ENRICHMENT

Dewey, John. *Experience and Education* (New York: Collier Books, 1938)

Dewey's comparison of traditional and progressive education.

Dropkin, Ruth, and Arthur Tobier, eds. *Roots of Open Education in America: Reminiscences and Reflections* (New York: City College Workshop Center for Open Education, 1976)

Papers that grew out of a 1975 conference at Lillian Weber's Center trace roots of open education back to the Mohawk nation. Settlement houses, one-room schoolhouses, Dewey, and progressivism are cited for their significant or in some cases overrated contributions.

Hymes, J. L., Jr. *Twenty Years in Review: A Look at 1971–1990* (Washington, D.C.: National Association for the Education of Young Children, 1991)

A treasure trove of detail about recent history in early childhood education. Each chapter contains a year's history of the past two decades.

Korn, Claire V. *Alternative American Schools: Ideals in Action* (Albany: State University of New York Press, 1991)

mented the value of high-quality preschool programs for poor children. This study will be cited repeatedly in coming years by those favoring expansion of Head Start and other early-years programs.

1985   Head Start celebrated its twentieth anniversary with a Joint Resolution of the Senate and House "reaffirming congressional support."

1986   The U.S. secretary of education proclaimed this the Year of the Elementary School, saying, "Let's do all we can this year to remind this nation that the time our children spend in elementary school is crucial to everything they will do for the rest of their lives."

1986   Public Law 99-457 (the Education of the Handicapped Act Amendments) established a national policy on early intervention that recognizes its benefits, provides assistance to states to build systems of service delivery, and recognizes the unique role of families in the development of their children with disabilities.

1987   Congress created the National Commission to Prevent Infant Mortality.

1988   Vermont announced plans to assess student performance on the basis of work portfolios as well as test scores.

1989   The United Nations Convention on the Rights of the Child was adopted by the UN General Assembly.

1990   The United Nations Convention on the Rights of the Child went into effect following its signing by twenty nations.

1990   Head Start celebrated its twenty-fifth anniversary.

1991   Education Alternatives, Inc., a for-profit firm, opened South Pointe Elementary School in Miami, Florida, the first public school in the nation to be run by a private company.

1991   The Carnegie Foundation issued "Ready to Learn," a plan to ensure children's readiness for school.

1994   The United Nations declared 1994 the Year of the Indigenous Child.

Examines alternative schools in the United States. Korn points out that perhaps the future of education depends on traveling off the beaten educational track. She looks at alternative schools that employ the philosophies of the great educators.

Montore, Will S. *Comenius and the Beginnings of Educational Reform* (New York: Arno, 1971)

The author traces the reform movement in education before and up to Comenius, who was responsible for the movement's most significant contributions. He also talks about the life of John Amos Comenius and his educational writings.

Winsor, Charlotte, ed. *Experimental Schools Revisited* (New York: Agathon, 1973)

Series of bulletins published by Bureau of Educational Experiments, a group of professionals dedicated to cooperative study of children, from 1917 to 1924. The book documents roots of modern education and relates the first serious attempts to provide educational programs for toddlers and experiences based on children's maturational levels. Chapters dealing with "Play School" and "Playthings" demonstrate philosophical and methodological bases for learning through play.

ACTIVITIES FOR FURTHER ENRICHMENT

1. Compare classrooms you attended as a child to early education classrooms you are now visiting. What are the major similarities and differences? How do you explain the differences?

2. Do you think most teachers are aware of the historic influences on their teaching? Why is it important for teachers to be aware of these influences?

3. Many teachers of young children are more Froebelian in their approach to teaching than they realize. Can you find evidence to support this statement?

4. Some critics of education feel that schools have assumed (or have been given) too much responsibility for teaching too many things. Do you think certain subjects or services could be taught or provided through another institution or agency? If so, which ones? Why?

5. Reflect on your experiences in elementary school. What experiences were most meaningful? Why? What teachers do you remember best? Why?

6. Interview the parents of children who attend a parochial school. Find out why they send their children to these schools. Do you agree or disagree with their reasons?

7. Reexamine Comenius's ten basic principles of teaching. Are they applicable today? Which do you agree with most and least?

8. Is it really necessary for children to learn through their senses? Why?

9. To what extent do religious beliefs determine educational practice? Give specific examples from your own experiences and observations to support your answer.

10. Why does society in general and education in particular not always follow the best educational practices advocated by many great educators?

11. Have you observed instances in which children were left to their own whims in a laissez-faire school environment? What were the results, and why did they occur?

12. Besides the recurring themes of the great educators presented in this chapter, are there others you would list? Tell why you selected other themes.

13. List people, agencies, and legislation that are influencing early childhood education. Give specific examples. Do you think the influences will be long-lasting or short-lived?

14. What evidence can you find that Piaget has influenced early childhood programs?

15. List ways you have been or are being influenced by ideas and theories of the people and events discussed in this chapter. Do schools make a difference?

NOTES

1. From F. V. N. Painter, *Luther on Education,* © 1928 by Concordia Publishing House, pp. 180–181. Used by permission.

2. John Amos Comenius, *The Great Didactic of John Amos Comenius,* trans. and ed. M. W. Keatings, 1986, 1910 (New York: Russell & Russell, 1967, p. 58.

3. Ibid., pp. 184–185.

4. Ibid., p. 127.

5. John Locke, *An Essay Concerning Human Understanding,* ed. Peter H. Nidditch (Oxford: Oxford University Press, 1975), p. 104.

6. Jean-Jacques Rousseau, *Émile; Or, Education,* trans. Barbara Foxley, Everyman's Library Edition (New York: Dutton, 1933), p. 5.

7. Jean-Jacques Rousseau, *Émile,* trans. and ed. William Boyd (New York: Teachers College Press, by arrangement with Heinemann, London, 1962), pp. 11–15.

8. Alexander S. Neill, *Summerhill* (New York: Hart, 1960), p. 4.

9. Roger DeGuimps, *Pestalozzi: His Life and Work* (New York: Appleton, 1890), p. 205.

10. Ibid., p. 1691.

11. S. Bamford, *Passages in the Life of a Radical* (London: London Simpkin Marshall, 1844).

12. *The New Encyclopaedia Britannica in Thirty Volumes,* 15th ed. (Chicago: University of Chicago, 1978), vol. 14, p. 990.

13. Friedrich Froebel, *The Education of Man* (Clifton, NJ: Kelley, 1974), pp. 7–8.

14. Friedrich Froebel, *The Education of Man,* trans. M. W. Hailman (New York: Appleton, 1887), p. 55.

15. Friedrich Froebel, *Pedagogics of the Kindergarten,* trans. Josephine Jarvis (New York: Appleton, 1902), p. 32.

16. Ibid., pp. 83–84.

17. Maria Montessori, *The Discovery of the Child,* trans. M. J. Costelloe (Notre Dame, IN: Fides, 1967), p. 22.

18. Maria Montessori, *The Montessori Method,* trans. Anne E. George (Cambridge, MA: Bentley, 1967), p. 38.

19. Montessori, *The Discovery of the Child,* p. 28.

20. Ibid., p. 37.

21. Reginald D. Archambault, ed., *John Dewey on Education—Selected Writings* (New York: Random House, 1964), p. 430.

22. Henry Suzzallo, ed., *John Dewey's Interest and Effort in Education* (Boston: Houghton Mifflin, 1913), p. 65.

23. Archambault, *John Dewey on Education,* pp. 170–171.

24. From John Dewey, *Democracy and Education.* Copyright 1916 by Macmillan Company; copyright renewed 1944 by John Dewey. Reprinted with permission of Macmillan Publishing Co.

25. Edwin G. Boring et al., eds., *A History of Psychology in Autobiography,* vol. IV (Worcester, MA: Clark University Press, 1952; New York: Russell & Russell, 1968), p. 244.

26. L. S. Vygotsky, *Mind in Society* (Cambridge, MA: Harvard University Press, 1978), p. 90.

27. Jonathan R. H. Tudge, "Processes and Consequences of Peer Collaboration: A Vygotskian Analysis," *Child Development* 63 (1992), p. 1365.

28. Ibid.

29. Vygotsky, *Mind in Society,* p. 90.

30. Tudge, "Processes and Consequences," p. 1365.

31. L. S. Vygotsky, *The Collected Works of L. S. Vygotsky.* Vol. I. Problems of General Psychology (New York: Plenum, 1987), p. 216.

32. Howard Gardner, *Frames of Mind* (New York: Basic Books, 1983), pp. 60–61.

3

Montessori Education
Continuing Renaissance

After you have read and studied this chapter, you will be able to:

- ☐ Comprehend events in Maria Montessori's career that influenced her educational methods
- ☐ Compare and contrast the Montessori philosophy with those of other early childhood education programs
- ☐ Identify the main philosophical and pedagogical principles of the Montessori program
- ☐ Analyze, understand, and critique the basic characteristics of a good Montessori program
- ☐ Describe features of the prepared environment that are unique to the Montessori method
- ☐ Classify materials used in a Montessori program and understand their purpose
- ☐ Evaluate and explain reasons for the popularity of Montessori programs today
- ☐ Describe the essential roles of teachers and children in Montessori programs
- ☐ Explain how the Montessori system can be adapted to a regular classroom setting

Montessori education is extremely popular. Many parents and professionals consider it to be an ideal program that encourages independence and responsibility in child-centered settings. What are the appeals that Montessori has for the public?

If we were to single out one person to credit with a revival of early childhood education, it would be Maria Montessori. The Montessori method helped create and renew interest in early childhood education beginning about 1965. When parents and professionals were searching for exemplary early childhood programs, Montessori is one of the models they turned to.

What is so attractive and mesmerizing about the Montessori system? It is intriguing for a number of reasons. First, Montessori education has always been identified as a quality program for young children. Second, parents who observe a *good* Montessori program like what they see: orderliness, independent children, self-directed learning, a calm environment, and *children* at the center of the learning process. Third, Montessori's philosophy is based on the premise that education begins at birth, and the idea of early learning has been and remains popular with parents. Fourth, public schools include Montessori in their magnet programs, giving parents choices in the kind of program their children will have at a particular school. It is also used as a means of desegregation.

Over the past decade the implementation of Montessori education has increased tremendously in public school early childhood programs. Montessori would probably smilingly approve of the contemporary use of her method once again to help change the nature and character of early childhood education.

PRINCIPLES OF THE MONTESSORI METHOD

The following principles are a synthesis of Montessori ideas and practices. They fairly and accurately represent how Montessori educators implement the Montessori method in many kinds of programs across the United States.

Respect for the Child

Respect for the child is the cornerstone on which all other Montessori principles rest. Montessori said:

> As a rule, however, we do not respect children. We try to force them to follow us without regard to their special needs. We are overbearing with them, and above all, rude; and then we expect them to be submissive and well-behaved, knowing all the time how strong is their instinct of imitation and how touching their faith in and admiration of us. They will imitate us in any case. Let us treat them, therefore, with all the kindness which we would wish to help to develop in them. And by kindness is not meant caresses. Should we not call anyone who embraced us at the first time of meeting rude, vulgar and ill-bred? Kindness consists in interpreting the wishes of others, in conforming one's self to them, and sacrificing, if need be, one's own desire.[1]

Because each child is unique, education should be individualized for each child:

> The educator must be as one inspired by a deep *worship of life*, and must, through this reverence, respect, while he observes with human interest, the *development* of the child life. Now, child life is not an abstraction; *it is the life of individual children*. There exists only one real biological manifestation: the *living individual*; and toward single individuals, one by one observed, education must direct itself.[2]

Children are not miniature adults and should not be treated as such. Montessori was firm in her belief that a child's life must be recognized as separate and distinct from that of the adult. She attributed most of the responsibility for restricting the education of young children to adults who impose their ideas and dreams on children, failing to distinguish between children's lives and their own.

> In their dealings with children adults do not become egotistic but egocentric. They look upon everything pertaining to a child's soul from their own point of view and, consequently, their misapprehensions are constantly on the increase. Because of this egocentric view, adults look upon the child as *something empty* that is to be filled through their own efforts, as *something inert* and helpless for which they must do everything, as *something lacking an inner guide* and in constant need of direction. In conclusion we may say that the adult looks upon himself as the child's creator and judges the child's actions as good or bad from the viewpoint of his own relations to the child. The adult makes himself the touch stone of what is good and evil in the child. He is infallible, the model upon which the child must be molded. Any deviation on the child's part from adult ways is regarded as an evil which the adult hastens to correct.
>
> An adult who acts in this way, even though he may be convinced that he is filled with zeal, love, and a spirit of sacrifice on behalf of his child, unconsciously suppresses the development of the *child's own personality*.[3]

Respect for children is a cornerstone of the Montessori method. Indeed, it should be a guiding principle for all who work with young children. What are some ways adults show disrespect for children? What are some ways professionals can show respect for children as they engage them in meaningful learning activities?

Educators and parents show respect for children in many ways. Helping children do things and learn for themselves, for example, encourages and promotes independence. At the same time, it also demonstrates a basic respect for their needs as individuals to be independent and self-regulating. When children have choices, they are able to develop the skills and abilities necessary for effective learning, autonomy, and positive self-esteem. These practices are so much more respectful of children than always doing for them or insisting that they do things as adults want them to. (The theme of respect for children resurfaces in our discussion of guiding behavior in chap. 12.)

The Absorbent Mind

Montessori believed that children are not educated by others. Rather, one must educate oneself: "It may be said that we acquire knowledge by using our minds; but the child absorbs knowledge directly into his psychic life. Simply by continuing to live, the child learns to speak his native tongue."[4] This is the concept of the absorbent mind.

There are unconscious and conscious stages in the development of the absorbent mind. From birth to three years, the *unconscious absorbent mind* develops the senses used for seeing, hearing, tasting, smelling, and touching. The child literally absorbs everything.

From three to six years, the *conscious absorbent mind* selects sensory impressions from the environment and further develops the senses. In this phase children are selective in that they refine what they know. For example, children in the unconscious stage merely see and absorb an array of colors without distinguishing among them; however, from three on, they develop the ability to distinguish, match, and grade colors. Montessori challenged the teacher to think through the concept of the absorbent mind:

> How does a child, starting with nothing, orient himself in this complicated world? How does he come to distinguish things, by what marvelous means does he come to learn a language in all its minute details without a teacher but merely by living simply, joyfully, and without fatigue, whereas an adult is in constant need of assistance to orient himself in a new environment to learn a new language, which he finds tedious and which he will never master with the same perfection with which a child acquires his own mother tongue?[5]

Montessori wanted us to understand that children cannot help but learn. Simply by living, children learn from their environment. Jerome Bruner expresses this idea when he says that "learning is involuntary." Children learn because they are thinking beings. What they learn depends greatly on the people in their environment, what those people say and do, and how they react. In addition, available experiences and materials also help determine the type and quality of learning—and thus the individual.

Early childhood professionals in their work with young children are reemphasizing the ideas that children are born into the world learning and with constant readiness and ability to learn. We will discuss these concepts further in chapter 6.

Sensitive Periods

Montessori believed there are sensitive periods when children are more susceptible to certain behaviors and could learn specific skills more easily:

> A sensitive period refers to a special sensibility which a creature acquires in its infantile state, while it is still in a process of evolution. It is a transient disposition and limited to the acquisition of a particular trait. Once this trait or characteristic has been acquired, the special sensibility disappears. . . .
>
> A child learns to adjust himself and make acquisitions in his sensitive periods. These are like a beam that lights interiorly or a battery that furnishes energy. It is this sensibility which enables a child to come in contact with the external world in a particularly intense manner. At such a time everything is easy; all is life and enthusiasm. Every effort marks an increase in power. Only when the goal has been obtained does fatigue and the weight of indifference come on.
>
> When one of these psychic passions is exhausted, another area is enkindled. Childhood thus passes from conquest to conquest in a constant rhythm that constitutes its joy and happiness.[6]

The secret of using sensitive periods in teaching is to recognize them when they occur. While all children experience the same sensitive periods (e.g., a sensitive period for writing), the time at which the periods occur is different for each child.

Therefore, it becomes the role of the directress (as Montessori teachers are often called) or the parent to detect these times of sensitivity for learning and provide the setting for optimum fulfillment. Observation thus becomes crucial for teachers and parents. Indeed, many educators believe that observation of children's achievement and behavior is more accurate than the use of tests (see chap. 1).

The sensitive period for many learnings occurs early in life, during the time of rapid physical language and cognitive growth. Experiences necessary for optimum development must be provided at this time. Through observation and practice, for example, Montessori was convinced the sensitive period for development of language was a year or two earlier than originally thought.

Once the sensibility for learning a particular skill occurs, it does not arise again with the same intensity. For example, children will never learn languages as well as when the special sensitivity for language learning occurs. Montessori said, "The child grows up speaking his parent's tongue, yet to grownups the learning of a language is a very great intellectual achievement."[7]

Teachers must do three things: recognize that there are sensitive periods, learn to detect them, and capitalize on them by providing the optimum learning setting to foster their development. Much of what early childhood professionals mean by *readiness* is contained in Montessori's concept of sensitive periods.

The Prepared Environment

Montessori believed children learn best in a prepared environment, which can be any setting—classroom, a room at home, nursery, or playground. The purpose of the prepared environment is to make children independent of adults. It is a place in which children can *do things for themselves*. The ideal classrooms Montessori described are really what educators advocate when they talk about child-centered education and active learning. In many respects, Montessori was the precursor of many practices in use today.

Following their introduction to the prepared environment, children can come and go according to their desires and needs, deciding for themselves which materials to work with. Montessori removed the typical school desks from the classroom and replaced them with tables and chairs at which children could work individually or in small groups. In a modern Montessori classroom, much of a child's work is done on the floor. Montessori saw no reason for a teacher's desk, since the teacher should be involved with the children where they are doing their work. She also introduced child-sized furniture, lowered chalkboards, and outside areas in which children could, at will, take part in gardening and other outdoor activities.

Her concept of a classroom was a place in which children could do things for themselves, play with material placed there for specific purposes, and *educate themselves*. She developed a classroom free of many of the inhibiting elements in some of today's classrooms. Freedom is essential characteristic of the prepared environment. Since children are free, within the environment, to explore materials of their own choosing, they absorb what they find there.

A Montessori environment is characterized by orderliness, with a place for everything and everything in its place. The low shelving gives children ready access and encourages use of the materials. Why is it important to have an organized environment?

Many adults fear children will automatically abuse freedom or not know how to act in an environment in which they are responsible for governing their own actions. When a Montessori teacher anticipates inappropriate behavior, she quickly diverts the child to other materials or activities. Although the Montessori teacher believes in freedom for children and children's ability to exercise that freedom, children are not free to make unlimited choices. For example, children must know how to use materials correctly before they are free to choose materials. Students are free to pick within the framework of choices provided by the teacher. Choice, however, is also a product of discipline and self-control that children learn in the prepared environment.

Self- or Autoeducation

Montessori referred to *autoeducation* as the concept that children are capable of educating themselves:

> The commonest prejudice in ordinary education is that everything can be accomplished by talking (by appealing, that is, to the child's ear), or by holding one's self up as a model to be imitated (a kind of appeal to the eye), while the truth is that the personality can only develop by making use of its own powers.[8]

Children who are actively involved in a prepared environment and exercising freedom of choice literally educate themselves. The role freedom plays in self-education is crucial:

> And this freedom is not only an external sign of liberty, but a means of education. If by an awkward movement a child upsets a chair, which falls noisily to the floor, he will have an evident proof of his own incapacity; the same movement had it taken place amidst stationary benches would have passed unnoticed by him. Thus the child has some means by which he can correct himself, and having done so will have before him the actual proof of the power he has gained: the little tables and chairs remain firm and silent each in its own place. It is plainly seen that the *child has learned* to command his movements.[9]

Our universal perception of the teaching learning act is that the teachers teach and children learn, a view that overlooks everyone learns a great deal through one's own efforts. Through the principle of autoeducation, Montessori focuses our attention on this human capability. The art of teaching includes preparing the environment so that children, by participating in it, educate themselves. Think of the things you learned by yourself and the conditions and circumstances under which you learned them. Your reflections will remind you of the self-satisfaction that accompanies self-learning and the power it has to generate further involvement.

Obviously, it is sometimes quicker, more efficient, and more economical to be told or shown what to do and how to do it. Teachers and parents need to understand, however, that autoeducation should have a more dominant role in education than we have been willing to give it. In this sense, education should become more child centered and less teacher centered.

THE ROLE OF THE TEACHER

The Montessori teacher should demonstrate certain behaviors in order to implement the principles of this child-centered approach. The teacher's roles include these:

1. *Making children the center of learning.*   As Montessori said, "The teacher's task is not to talk, but to prepare and arrange a series of motives for cultural activity in a special environment made for the child."[10]

2. *Encouraging children to learn* through the freedom provided for them in the prepared environment.

3. *Observing children* in order to prepare the best possible environment, recognizing sensitive periods, and diverting inappropriate behavior to meaningful tasks.

Montessori believed, "It is necessary for the teacher to *guide* the child without letting him feel her presence too much, so that she may be always ready to supply the desired help, but may never be the obstacle between the child and his experience."[11]

A MONTESSORI TEACHER

In August 1980, I happened upon Montessori quite by accident. A friend suggested I volunteer in the classroom she was working in, to fill some of my summer afternoons. I did this, and now fourteen years later I find myself writing this personal story.

When I first started, I knew next to nothing about Montessori and her methods but was immediately intrigued with what I saw in the classroom. My expectations were of chaos; what I found was harmony. The children were busy, focused, and happy. My curiosity had been aroused. After two years assisting full-time in the classroom, I still was not satisfied with what I knew about Montessori. So I made the decision to pursue the formal training to become certified.

One of the prevailing attitudes throughout the training was that Maria Montessori discovered, through observation, that children learn by doing. I have found the same to be true of myself. After all my formal classroom training had been completed, educational materials had been read, I went into the classroom knowing I had many of the answers, but I found I did not even know the questions. With all the knowledge I had gained, experience would prove to be the answer to the equation.

In a Montessori classroom, one of the primary responsibilities of the teacher is to become a catalyst between the materials and the child. This is achieved by giving lessons either individually or in a small group. But the lessons I provide are equal to the ones given to me by the children. For example, a coworker and I were struggling to get a printer hooked up to a new computer. As we did this, Travis, a four-year-old, walked up, looked at the back of the machine, and said, "Miss Susie, you need a different interface cable." My coworker and I looked at him then looked at one another in disbelief. After further investigation we found he was right.

Through this experience I learned not to take the children for granted. Oftentimes they are much more aware than they are given credit for, simply because of their young age.

Another lesson was given to my staff and me, in flexibility, on last year's kindergarten camping trip. We started out on our annual two-day overnight trip to the mountains with food for a small army, chaperons galore, and nothing but fun on our agenda. Shortly after we arrived at our destination we found Mother Nature's agenda to be contrary to ours. As the thunderheads moved in, we knew we had to move out. Breaking the news to the children had to be done with care because they had been looking forward to the trip for some time. To raise their dampened spirits, we changed the name of the outing to the "kindergarten overnight pajama party at school." To most of the children, sleeping at the school was rather amusing. To cap off the event, when we awoke the next morning, we found three of the children covered with chicken pox.

As I am sure you have noticed, the episodes mentioned here have a humorous side. The ability to laugh at disasters in the classroom and at oneself is an important tool to possess. In addition to a sense of humor, one needs to have certain personality characteristics. These include patience, understanding, enthusiasm, and dedication. In my opinion, one needs to possess all of these qualities to be successful in a career in early childhood education.

The unconditional love the children offer and the joy I receive in watching them grow have no equal. Becoming a Montessori teacher for me has proven to be not only a career choice but also a life choice. It has been a very eye-opening, rewarding, and fulfilling experience. While another career may have been more financially profitable, another career could never have given me the daily satisfaction I have received—satisfaction that money cannot buy.

Contributed by Susie Armstrong, three- to six-year-old primary class, Montessori at Greenwood Plaza, Englewood, Colorado.

THE MONTESSORI METHOD IN PRACTICE

In a prepared environment, certain materials and activities provide for three basic areas of child involvement: *practical life* or motor education, *sensory materials* for training the senses, and *academic materials* for teaching writing, reading, and mathematics. All these activities are taught according to a prescribed procedure.

Practical Life

The prepared environment emphasizes basic, everyday motor activities, such as walking from place to place in an orderly manner, carrying objects such as trays and chairs, greeting a visitor, learning self-care skills, and other practical activities. For example, the "dressing frames" are designed to perfect the motor skills involved in buttoning, zipping, lacing, buckling, and tying. The philosophy for activities such as these is to make children independent of the adult and develop concentration. Water activities play a large role in Montessori methods, and children are taught to scrub, wash, and pour as a means of developing coordination. Practical life exercises also include polishing mirrors, shoes, and plant leaves; sweeping the floor; dusting furniture; and peeling vegetables.

Montessorians believe that as children become absorbed in an activity, they gradually lengthen their span of concentration; as they follow a regular sequence of actions, they learn to pay attention to details. Montessori practitioners believe that without concentration and involvement through the senses, little learning takes

Practical life activities help children learn about and practice everyday activities such as folding napkins, polishing, cleaning vegetables, and washing dishes. Children enjoy doing practical life activities. Why do you think they do?

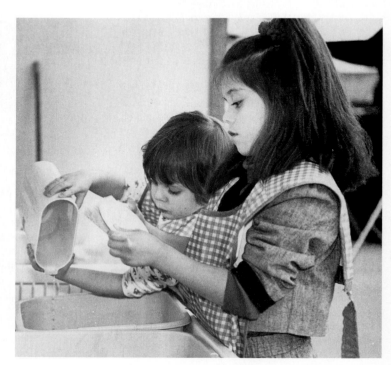

place. Although most people assume that we learn practical life activities inciden-
tally, a Montessori teacher shows children how to do these activities through precisely detailed instructions. Verbal instructions are minimal; the emphasis in the
instructional process is on *showing how*—modeling and practice.

Montessori believed children's involvement and concentration in motor activities
lengthens their attention span. In a Montessori classroom, it is not uncommon to
see a child of four or five polish his shoes or scrub a table for twenty minutes at a
time! The child finds the activity intrinsically rewarding and pleasurable.

Practical life activities are taught through four different types of exercises. *Care
of the person* involves activities such as using the dressing frames, polishing shoes,
and washing hands. *Care of the environment* includes dusting, polishing a table,
and raking leaves. *Social relations* include lessons in grace and courtesy. The fourth
type of exercise involves *analysis and control of movement* and includes locomotor
activities such as walking and balancing. Figures 3–1, 3–2, and 3–3 are directions
for some of the practical life activities in a Montessori classroom. Notice the procedures and the exactness of presentation.

Sensory Materials

These are some materials found in a typical Montessori classroom (the learning purpose appears in parentheses):

- *Pink tower* (visual discrimination of dimension)—ten wood cubes of the same
  shape and texture, all pink, the largest of which is ten centimeters cubed. Each
  succeeding block is one centimeter smaller. Children build a tower beginning
  with the largest block.

- *Brown stairs* (visual discrimination of width and height)—ten blocks of wood, all
  brown, differing in height and width. Children arrange the blocks next to each
  other from thickest to thinnest so the blocks resemble a staircase.

- *Red rods* (visual discrimination of length)—ten rod-shaped pieces of wood, all
  red, of identical size but differing in lengths from ten centimeters to one meter.
  The child arranges the rods next to each other from largest to smallest.

- *Cylinder blocks* (visual discrimination of size)—four individual wood blocks that
  have holes of various sizes; one block deals with height, one with diameter, and
  two with the relationship of both variables. Children remove the cylinders in random order, then match each cylinder to the correct hole.

- *Smelling jars* (olfactory discrimination)—two identical sets of white, opaque
  glass jars with removable tops through which the child cannot see but through
  which odors can pass. The teacher places various substances, such as herbs, in
  the jars, and the child matches the jars according to the smell of the substance
  in the jars.

- *Baric tablets* (discrimination of weight)—sets of rectangular pieces of wood that
  vary according to weight. There are three sets, light, medium, and heavy, which
  children match according to the weight of the tablets.

FIGURE 3–1   Pouring

Materials: Tray, rice, two small pitchers (one empty, the other containing rice)

Presentation: The child must be shown how to lift the empty pitcher with the left hand and with the right, raise the pitcher containing rice slightly higher. Grasping the handle, lifting, and tilting are practiced. The spout of the full pitcher must be moved to about the center of the empty pitcher before the pouring begins. Set down both pitchers; then change the full one to the right side, to repeat the exercise.

   When rice is spilled, the child will set the pitchers down, beside the top of the tray, and pick the grains up, one at a time, with thumb and forefinger.

Purpose: Control of movement.

Point of Interest: Watching the rice.

Control of Error: Hearing the rice drop on the tray.

Age: 2¹/₂ years.

Exercise: A container with a smaller diameter, requiring better control of movement. Control the amount of rice for the smaller container.

Note: Set up a similar exercise, using colored popcorn instead of rice.

Rice or Popcorn

- *Color tablets* (discrimination of color and education of the chromatic sense)—two identical sets of small, rectangular pieces of wood used for matching color or shading.
- *Sound boxes* (auditory discrimination)—two identical sets of cylinders filled with various materials, such as salt and rice. Children match the cylinders according to the sound the materials make.

FIGURE 3–2 Plant Shining

Materials: Apron, green-leafed plant, sheet of white freezer paper, basket with small sponge, caster, bottle of plant polish, orange stick, cotton ball.

Presentation:
1. Lay out all the material in order of use from left to right.
2. Bring a plant to the table and place it on the paper.
3. Dampen the sponge at the sink and gently wipe off the top side of the leaf with forward strokes. Hold the leaf on the underside with the other hand. Stroke several leaves to remove the dust.
4. Pour small amount of polish into caster.
5. Wrap a small portion of the cotton ball on the orange stick.
6. Dip the stick in the polish and again stroke gently on the leaf in the manner described above.

Clean up:
1. Remove cotton from the stick and put it in the wastebasket.
2. Take the caster to the sink and wash and dry it.
3. Wash the sponge and bring it back to the table.
4. Place the material back in the basket.
5. Replace the plant on the shelf.
6. Fold the paper. Discard only if necessary.
7. Return basket and paper to the shelf.

Purpose: Coordination of movement; care of plants.

Point of Interest: Seeing the leaves get shiny.

Control of Error: Dull leaves and polish on white paper.

Age: 3 years and up.

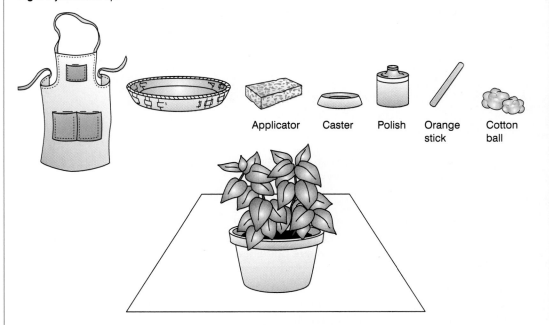

Applicator   Caster   Polish   Orange stick   Cotton ball

FIGURE 3–3   Dusting

Materials: Basket with a duster, soft brush, and feather duster; table to be dusted

Presentation:
Look for dust, with the eyes at the level of the surface of the table. Start with one half of the table, the one immediately in front of you.
Wipe the surface first, as most of the dust will be lying on the top and will give the greatest result.
Always dust away from the body, starting at one end working progressively to the other end, using circular movements.
After the top dust the sides, after the sides dust the legs. Don't forget the corners, the insides of the legs, and underneath the tabletop. The brush is to be used for the corners.
Shake the duster over the wastebasket or outdoors.

Purpose: Coordination of movements, care of the environment, indirect preparation for writing

Point of Interest: The dust to be found in the duster; shaking the dust off the cloth

Control of Error: Any spot of dust left behind

Age: $2\frac{1}{2}$ to $4\frac{1}{2}$ years.

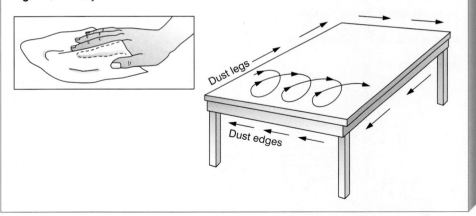

Source: *A Montessori Teacher's Manual* by Elizabeth and Charles Caspari and Friends. © E. G. Caspari, 1974. All rights reserved. Used by permission.

- *Tonal bells* (sound and pitch)—two sets of eight bells, alike in shape and size but different in color; one set is white, the other brown. The child matches the bells according to the tone they make.
- *Cloth swatches* (sense of touch)—two identical swatches of cloth. Children identify them according to touch, first without a blindfold but later using a blindfold.

- *Temperature jugs or thermic bottles* (thermic sense and ability to distinguish between temperatures)—small metal jugs filled with water of varying temperatures. Children match jugs of the same temperature.

Materials for training and developing the senses have these characteristics:

- *Control of error.*   Materials are designed so that children can see if they make a mistake; for example, if a child does not build the blocks of the pink tower in their proper order, she does not achieve a tower effect.
- *Isolation of a single quality.*   Materials are designed so that other variables are held constant except for the isolated quality or qualities. Therefore, all blocks of the pink tower are pink because size, not color, is the isolated quality.
- *Active involvement.*   Materials encourage active involvement rather than the more passive process of looking.
- *Attractiveness.*   Materials are attractive, with colors and proportions that appeal to children.

Basic Purposes of Sensory Materials

One purpose of Montessori sensory materials is to train children's senses to focus on some obvious, particular quality; for example, with the red rods, the quality is length; with pink tower cubes, size; and with bells, musical pitch. Montessori felt it is necessary to help children discriminate among the many stimuli they receive. Accordingly, the sensory materials help make children more aware of the capacity of their bodies to receive, interpret, and make use of stimuli. In this sense, the Montessori sensory materials are labeled *didactic*, designed to instruct.

Second, Montessori thought that perception and the ability to observe details were crucial to reading. The sensory materials help sharpen children's powers of observation and visual discrimination as readiness for learning to read.

A third purpose of the sensory materials is to increase children's ability to think, a process that depends on the ability to distinguish, classify, and organize. Children constantly face decisions about sensory materials: which block comes next, which color matches the other, which shape goes where. These are not decisions the teacher makes, nor are they decisions children arrive at by guessing; rather, they are decisions made by the intellectual process of observation and selection based on knowledge gathered through the senses.

Finally, all the sensory activities are not ends in themselves. Their purpose is to prepare children for the occurrence of the sensitive periods for writing and reading. In this sense, all activities are preliminary steps in the writing-reading process.

Academic Materials for Writing, Reading, and Mathematics

The third area of Montessori materials is academic; specifically, items for writing, reading, and mathematics. Exercises are presented in a sequence that encourages writing before reading. Reading is therefore an outgrowth of writing. Both processes, however, are introduced so gradually that children are never aware they are learning to write and read until one day they realize they are writing and reading. Describing

Sensory training plays a major role in the Montessori method. What knowledge, skills, and concepts is this child learning through her involvement with these materials?

this phenomenon, Montessori said that children "burst spontaneously" into writing and reading. Montessori anticipated contemporary practices such as the whole language approach in integrating writing and reading and in maintaining that through writing children learn to read.

Montessori believed many children were ready for writing at four years of age. Consequently, a child who enters a Montessori system at age three has done most of the sensory exercises by the time he is four. It is not uncommon to see four- and five-year-olds in a Montessori classroom writing and reading. Following are examples of Montessori materials that lay the foundation for and promote writing and reading:

- *Ten geometric forms and colored pencils.*   These introduce children to the coordination necessary for writing. After selecting a geometric inset, children trace it on paper and fill in the outline with a colored pencil of their choosing.

- *Sandpaper letters.*   Each letter of the alphabet is outlined in sandpaper on a card, with vowels in blue and consonants in red. Children see the shape, feel the shape, and hear the sound of the letter, which the teacher repeats when introducing it.

- *Movable alphabet, with individual letters.*   Children learn to put together familiar words.

- *Command cards.*   These are a set of red cards with a single action word printed on each card. Children read the word on the card and do what the word tells them to do (e.g., *run, jump*).

Examples of materials for mathematics are the following items:

- *Number rods*—a set of red and blue rods varying in length from ten centimeters to one meter, representing the quantities one through ten. With the help of the teacher, children are introduced to counting.
- *Sandpaper numerals*—each number from one to nine in sandpaper on a card. Children see, touch, and hear the numbers. They eventually match number rods and sandpaper numerals. Children also have the opportunity to discover mathematical facts through the use of these numerals.
- *Golden beads*—a concrete material for the decimal system. The single bead represents one unit. A bar made up of ten units in a row represents a ten; ten of the ten bars form a square representing one hundred; and ten hundred squares form the cube representing one thousand.

Additional Features

Other features of the Montessori system are *mixed-age grouping* and *self-pacing*. A Montessori classroom always contains children of different ages, usually from two-and-a-half to six years. This strategy is becoming more popular in many classrooms and has long been popular in the British Infant Schools. Advantages of mixed-age groups are that children learn from one another and help each other, a wide range of materials is available for all children, and older children become role models and collaborators for younger children. Contemporary instructional practices of student mentoring and cooperative learning all have their roots in and are supported by multiage grouping.

In a Montessori classroom, children are free to learn at their own rate and level of achievement. They determine which activities to participate in and work at their own pace. However, children are not allowed to dally at a task. Through observation, the teacher determines when children have perfected one exercise and are ready to move to a higher level or different exercise. If a child does not perform an activity correctly, the teacher gives him or her additional help and instruction.

Figure 3–4 outlines the basic characteristics of a good Montessori program that you can use as a guideline when you observe Montessori classrooms. Perhaps you can add other criteria you think make a good early childhood program. You will be able to understand further what Montessori education is all about when you read "A Day in a Children's House," which follows. Keep in mind that although details of educational programs vary from center to center, the basic constructs of a good Montessori program should be present.

INFANT MONTESSORI

Montessori for children under three is growing ever more popular, as illustrated by the rapidly expanding Montessori infant programs. The description of the Nido (Nest) on pages F and G in the color insert provides an example of what is included in the Montessori infant program.

FIGURE 3–4 Basic Characteristics of a Montessori Program for Three- to Six-Year-Old Children

Growth in the Child	Program Organization	Adult Aspects
Toward independence and problem solving	Ungraded three year age span: 2.6 to 6 years.	Certified Montessori teachers at the 3-6 year level
Toward the enjoyment of learning	Parental commitment to a three year cycle of attendance	Continuing professional development
Toward the development of order, concentration, and coordination	Five day week with a minimum daily three hour session	Observational skills to match students' developmental needs with activities
Toward skills in oral communication	Personal and group instruction	Strategies to facilitate the unique and total growth of each individual
Toward respect for oneself, other people, and the planet	Child: adult ratio of 15:1	Leadership skills to foster a nurturing environment supportive of learning
Toward responsible group membership	Observational records of the child	A partnership developed with parents
	Regularly scheduled parent conferences	Supervision and education of auxiliary classroom personnel
	Public observation policy	

Learning Environment	Program Emphasis	Administrative Support
Diverse set of Montessori materials, activities and experiences	To encourage intrinsic motivation, spontaneous activity, and self–education	Organized as a legally and fiscally responsible entity
Schedule that allows large blocks of uninterrupted learning time	To provide sensory education for intellectual development	Non-discriminatory admissions policy
Classroom atmosphere that encourages social interaction	To encourage competencies through repetitive concrete experiences	Written educational policies and procedures
Space for personal, small group, and whole class learning activities	To encourage cooperative learning through peer teaching and social interaction	Adherence to state laws and health requirements
Lightweight, proportionate, movable child-sized furnishing	To provide learning opportunities through physical activity and outdoor work	Current school affiliation with AMS and other professional groups.
Identifiable ground rules	To provide learning activities for creative expression	
Aesthetically pleasing environment		
Outdoor space to accommodate rigorous physical activity		

Source: American Montessori Society, *Basic Characteristics of a Montessori Program for Children Ages 3 to 6 Years,* pamphlet (New York: Author, 1991). Copyright April 1991. Used by permission.

Program in Practice

A DAY IN A CHILDREN'S HOUSE

Billy Smith arrives at the Alexander Montessori School at 8:30 A.M. He is left off at the entrance to the school by his mother, who is on her way to work as a secretary at the headquarters of a national airline.

Billy is greeted by one of the classroom aides as he gets out of the car. He has gained a great deal of independence in his year and a half at the school and goes into his classroom by himself. If a child is new to the school, he is escorted to his classroom, or children's house, by an aide until he is able to go by himself. Billy, who is four years old, has a brother and a sister. He will attend the school until he is six, when he will enter first grade in a Montessori elementary or a local public school.

Billy is greeted by his teacher, Frances Collins, as he enters the classroom. "Good morning, Billy. How are you this morning?" Mrs. Collins greets Billy while shaking his hand. She engages him in a brief conversation about his baby sister.

The previous day, Billy checked out, by himself, a book from the children's house library. This morning, Billy goes to the library card file and finds the card to the book he checked out. He places the card in the book and returns the book to the library. Billy does all the checking out and in of books, including writing his own name, without help. The key to this independence is the arrangement of the library. Mrs. Collins has the library, book cards, and the check-out and check-in systems arranged so the children can do all these things themselves.

In Mrs. Collins's class of thirty-three children, ages range from two and a half to five and a half years. Mrs. Collins has two aides to help her.

Since Billy is the first child to arrive in the children's house this morning, he takes the chairs down from all the tables. He also puts down pieces of carpeting (approximately two by three feet) on the floor for each child and places a name card for each child on each piece of carpet. When the children come into the class, they will find their name card, pick it up, and place it on a pile. This is one way Mrs. Collins takes roll and, at the same time, helps the children learn their printed names.

Next, Billy goes to the language area, takes a set of geometric insets to a table (writing is always done on a table), and uses the frame and insets to make a geometric design, of his choice, on a sheet of paper. When his design is finished, he fills in the design with straight lines using colored pencils. Billy uses an ink stamp to stamp lines on the back of his paper, writes his name on the paper, and files his paper in his own file. The materials in his file will be made into a booklet that will be sent home at the end of the week.

Billy is in the sensitive stage for writing, which means his motor skills make him capable of writing on paper, and he is always eager to write. Billy goes to the other side of the language corner to the movable alphabet cabinet and takes a set of word pictures to the carpet. Using the movable alphabet, he constructs a sentence using the picture card and movable alphabet letters. Billy's sentence is "The king is fat." After he has constructed his sentence, Billy takes paper and pencil and goes to a table where he writes this sentence. After he finishes writing, he puts the paper in his file.

At about 10:15 A.M., Billy takes a break for juice. The snack in the Montessori house is on an "as needed" basis, and Billy helps himself,

This account of a day in a children's house is based on the program and activities of the Alexander Montessori School in Miami, Florida. There are nine directresses at the Alexander School, all of whom are AMS certified.

pouring his own drink. Sometimes he and one of his friends take their break together. No attempt is made to force children to take a break or take it all at once or in groups.

After his snack, Billy goes to the practical life area and polishes a table. This activity takes about fifteen minutes. Billy gets all the materials needed for the activity, completes the task, and puts things away by himself. Through exercises of practical life, Billy develops good work habits and extends his span of concentration. Polishing the table involves him in a gross-motor activity that has to be performed in a certain way—setting up the material in a specific sequence (from left to right) and then polishing the table. When he has finished polishing, it is Billy's responsibil-

ity to replace the materials and return everything to the shelf.

After polishing the table, Billy goes to the math center. Here he and another student set up the addition strip board and see how many ways they can make "nine." This activity usually takes about ten minutes. After he finishes in the math area, Billy goes to a directed lesson shared by Mrs. Collins and a group of six children. Each child is given a reading booklet (published by a major publishing company), and they discuss the pictures. The children who can, read the story while those who cannot follow along. Emphasis in this activity is on listening, sequencing, and comprehension. This activity usually lasts from ten to fifteen minutes.

FIGURE A

Two Metal Insets. In the example shown on the left, the child chose the shapes and colors, stimulating the child's visual motor development; in the example shown on the right, the child wrote a message, illustrating spontaneous, inventive writing.

From 11:00 to about 11:20, the children go outside, where they engage in free play for about ten minutes, then have a directed movement lesson consisting of jumping rope, throwing, or catching. In addition to free or directed play, this outdoor time may be used for nature walks and other kinds of field experiences.

When Billy comes in from outdoor play, he joins the other children in a circle activity with Mrs. Collins to learn songs and sing songs previously learned. The songs are usually based on a monthly theme selected by Mrs. Collins. In addition to a song, the children will also do finger plays, recite poems, and use rhythm band instruments. In the circle time (the children sit on a circle or ellipse marked on the floor), Billy holds the flag while

FIGURE B

A Writing Sample by Montessori Student Alba Gosalbez

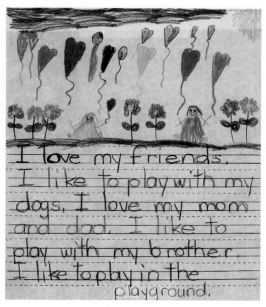

the children say the Pledge of Allegiance, another child leads the group in song about good health habits, and each child is given an opportunity to share an experience that is important to him. Billy tells about his cousin visiting him over the weekend. The circle time also provides an opportunity to talk about matters of interest to the whole group. Children are free to join the circle time as they wish. The teacher respects children's personal independence and concentration on the task they are working on, so no one need stop what they are doing just to join the circle time. Because the circle time activities are so interesting, however, children generally want to join. The circle time provides an opportunity to all the children, who have been working at their own pace all morning, to come together.

When circle time is over, usually after about twenty minutes, the children eat their lunch. They wash their hands, get paper place mats, place them on a table, and set their lunch pails on them. At Billy's children's house, all the children bring their own lunch. Sometimes a child or several children who did not go outside during the recess time will set the tables.

Billy is responsible for helping clean up the table where he eats. In a children's house, children do everything they might normally do in their own homes: cleaning up, setting the table, getting a snack. After lunch, children can take part in games and songs. This activity is directed by the teacher. Lunchtime usually lasts about an hour. During lunchtime, the children are also free to visit with each other and use materials of their choice.

After lunch, Billy checks his folder to see whether there is any unfinished work. If there is, he finishes it. If there is no work to be finished, the teacher suggests several things for him to do. On this particular day, Billy chooses to work with the geometry cabinet. This activity involves matching a set of cards to their corresponding geometric shapes. This matching activity takes Billy about twenty minutes. After he puts his materials away, Billy chooses easel painting. Again, Billy is responsible for putting on his own apron, getting the paper, putting it on the easel, and painting his own picture. This activity also encourages creativity.

In Billy's children's house, there is no special time for rest. Children rest when they feel a need for it. Even with the two-and-a-half-year-olds, there is no attempt to force a nap time or rest period. The two-and-a-half- and three-year-old children go home for the day at noon, so there are only four- and five-year-olds in the school during the afternoon. Billy and his classmates, as a general rule, do not rest.

When his art activity is finished, Billy's teacher offers him a new lesson with the hundred board. Billy is invited to a table, and the teacher brings the materials to the table. Part of Billy's task is to pay attention to the directed lesson so he will know how to do the lesson independently. When the teacher feels he is ready, Billy can begin to participate, and he gradually takes over the activity. This does not mean that Billy has entirely absorbed the lesson. If his teacher thinks it is necessary, she will give him another, or a more directed, lesson. This directed activity usually lasts about half an hour.

The last activity of the day is a birthday party for one of the classmates. The day ends at 3:00 P.M. Mrs. Collins says good-bye to Billy and tells him she is looking forward to seeing him tomorrow. Billy goes to the area where the children are picked up by their parents or other caregivers. Billy is picked up by a caregiver.

There is really no such thing as a "typical" day in a children's house. On any particular day, children may work only in the areas of math and practical life. Also, if children are undecided about what to do at any time, they will check their work folders to get ideas about what to do or to see what needs to be finished. They will also confer with the teacher to get direction.

How Billy's Teacher Keeps Her Records

Each child has a work folder with his or her name on it. Inside are four sheets listing the lessons from each of the four areas or avenues (practical life, sensorial, math, and language) of the Montessori system. Mrs. Collins marks each lesson with a yellow marker when she presents it to the child. When the child has mastered the lesson, she marks it in red, which indicates that the child is ready to go to another lesson.

All written work, such as words, sentences, numbers, geometric shapes, and tracing, is kept in children's work folders. When a child has completed five papers of each activity, Mrs. Collins makes it into a booklet to take home. Reports to parents are made in both conferences and writing. The Montessori program is explained to the parents before their children are enrolled. Periodic parent programs are also conducted to keep the parents informed and involved.

CRITICISMS OF THE MONTESSORI METHOD

The Montessori system is not without critics. One criticism deals with the didactic nature of the materials and the program. Some say the system teaches a narrow spectrum of activities in which concepts are learned in a prescribed manner, following prescribed methods, using a prescribed set of material. Montessori believed children learned best from the materials when they were shown how to use them, which seems to make sense, rather than just allowed to mess around with them. In many Montessori programs but by no means all, children are encouraged to use and experiment with the materials in creative ways after they have mastered them. One Montessori teacher related that she has seen children use the pink tower blocks in over a hundred ways!

Critics also claim the Montessori classroom does not provide for socialization. They cite the lack of group play, games, and other activities normally present in traditional kindergarten programs. This criticism, of course, is no truer for a Montessori setting than for any other classroom. No method or teacher can stop social interactions unless the teacher is determined to do so or the children are afraid of her. Many Montessori activities promote and offer opportunities for sharing tasks, cooperation, collaboration, and helping. Also, outdoor time and lunchtime (when children eat in pairs, threes, or small groups) afford ample opportunity for social interaction.

A related criticism is that children do not have opportunities to participate in dramatic make-believe and pretend play. Montessori believed that "play is the child's work." As such, children's play sets the stage for later roles and functions necessary for successful adult living. Thus, according to Montessori, fantasy play had little value. This is one Montessori area professionals have to examine in terms of what we know about children and learning *today*.

The charge is frequently heard that Montessori schools represent an elitist or middle-class system. This claim likely stems from the fact that many Montessori schools were at one time operated by individuals for profit with high tuition. In most towns and cities, the Montessori program is now widely used in many Head Start, day care, and public school programs.

One reason some parents and teachers feel the Montessori program is rigid is that its ideas and methodologies are so detailed. Another reason is that they have nothing to compare this system to other than the free-play programs they are more accustomed to. When parents and teachers compare the Montessori system, which organizes the environment and learning experiences in a specific, purposeful way, to a free-play setting, they tend to view the Montessori setting as rigid. Parents and teachers need to focus instead on the results of the system.

SELECTING A MONTESSORI SCHOOL

Parents frequently ask early childhood professionals advice about placing their children in a Montessori program. Unfortunately, there is no guarantee that a Montessori program is of the kind and quality advocated by Maria Montessori. Selecting a Montessori preschool is like making other consumer choices; the customer must beware of being cheated. No truth-in-advertising law requires operators of a Montessori school to operate a quality program. Because the name has such appeal to parents, some schools call themselves Montessori without either the trained staff or facilities to justify their claim.

Not only do some schools misrepresent themselves, but some teachers do so as well. There is no requirement that a teacher must have Montessori training of any particular duration or by any prescribed course of instruction. The American Montessori Society (AMS) approves training programs that meet its standards for teacher training, and the Association Montessori Internationale (AMI) approves teacher training programs that meet the standards of the international organization.

Early childhood professionals can advise parents to consider these points when selecting a Montessori program:

- Is the school affiliated with a recognized Montessori association (AMS or AMI)?
- Is the teacher a certified Montessori teacher or trained in the Montessori method?
- Are practices of the Montessori method part of the program?
- Contact parents of former students to determine their satisfaction with the program; ask them, "Would you again send your child to this school? How is your child doing in first grade? How was the Montessori program beneficial to your child?"
- Compare tuition rates of the Montessori school to other schools. Is any difference in tuition worth it?
- Why do you want your child to attend a Montessori school? Is it social status? Prestige? Do you feel your child will achieve more by attending a Montessori school? Visit other preschool programs to determine whether a Montessori program is best for your child.
- Interview the director and staff to learn about the program's philosophy, curriculum, rules and regulations, and how the program differs from others that are not Montessori.
- Following enrollment, pay attention to children's progress through visits, written reports, and conferences to be sure they are learning what will be needed for an easy transition to the next grade, program, or school.

MONTESSORI AND THE PUBLIC SCHOOLS

Over the past decade, Montessori programs have been implemented in public school programs, especially preschool programs and kindergartens. The first implementation of the Montessori program in the public schools occurred in Cincinnati, Ohio, in 1975. Now more than two thousand public school classrooms offer Montessori Programs.[12]

A number of reasons account for the public school popularity of Montessori. First, Montessori is used to *restructure* contemporary education. Montessori is one of many programs of early childhood education that the public schools have used to *restructure* or fundamentally change the way they educate children. This restructuring of the schools is closely associated with the retraining of teachers. Restructuring provides opportunities for retraining. So, a second reason for the growth of popularity of public school Montessori is that it is used as a means for retraining teachers. A successful Montessori program depends on well-trained teachers. Thus, by implementing a Montessori program, this provides the opportunity to train teachers in "new" and "alternative" approaches to educating young children.

Third, public school Montessori programs are often used as *magnet* schools, schools designed to give parents a choice of kinds of educational programs to send their children. While the basic purpose of magnet schools is to integrate schools racially, at the same time they give parents choice about what kind of program to give their children. Magnet schools as a means of integration have enabled professionals to use federal dollars that otherwise would not be available to them. Without a doubt the availability of federal dollars has been a major factor for public school implementation of the Montessori program. If Montessori is implemented *to the level it should be,* the cost can be $20,000 a classroom.

Fourth, inclusion of Montessori in the public schools is a way of giving parents choices in the kind of program their children will have at a particular school. This providing for parental choice is often tied to the magnet school approach and integration. Nonetheless, it does provide opportunities for parents about where their children will attend school and the curriculum that they will study.

Fifth, over the past decade parents who have had positive experiences with Montessori programs for their children have been strong advocates for the expansion of Montessori to public schools. This advocacy by parents has played a major role in both the popularity of Montessori and its growth.

Sixth, since Montessori developed her program for children with disabilities, some public schools see the Montessori method as an ideal way to meet the learning needs of today's children with disabilities.

The application of Montessori to the public school settings is so popular that these professionals have their own publication, the *Public School Montessorian* (published by Jola Publications, Box 8354, Minneapolis, MN 55408).

BILINGUAL MONTESSORI PRESCHOOL

A unique integration of native language instruction, preschool education, and the Montessori method is taking place in more than twenty child development centers throughout California. The centers, administered by the Foundation Center for Phenomenological Research in Sacramento, serve nearly 1,900 Spanish-speaking children six weeks to six years of age.

The Foundation Center provides a supportive learning environment for children through the Montessori method, home (i.e., native) language instruction, and multicultural environment. The staff relies exclusively on the child's primary language for instruction, interacting with the children only in Spanish throughout the day. Some children may respond occasionally in English, but staff members always use Spanish when communicating with the children.

"If you respect a child's home language, the transition to the second language will happen miraculously," comments Antonia López, director of education and staff development for the Foundation Center. "A lot of people think that if a child learns to speak English sooner, they'll be better off. But they don't realize what you're doing is separating the child from its parents."

All staff are recruited from the community the centers serve. After working as teaching assistants, they begin the process of being certified as Montessori teachers.

OFTEN ASKED QUESTIONS ABOUT MONTESSORI

Does attending a Montessori program stifle a child's creativity?

People who ask this question for some reason think the prepared environment and didactic materials somehow keep or prohibit children from becoming or being creative. A Montessori program, *in and of itself,* does not inhibit children's creative impulses or activities. How parents and teachers encourage, support, and promote children's behaviors determines how "creative" they are. Oddly, this "creativity" question is seldom asked about other programs.

After attending a Montessori program, do children have trouble adjusting to a regular program?

Embedded in this question is the belief that children who engage in active, independent learning inherent in a Montessori program will have trouble adjusting to a more "rigid" public school program. Fortunately, as we have described above, increasing numbers of public schools are implementing the Montessori system. In addition, transition programs—programs designed to help children make smooth adjustments from one school program to another—are growing in popularity and use (see chaps. 7, 8, and 10). Most Montessori programs have such programs of transition for children and their families.

How long should a child attend a Montessori program?

I was recently asked this question by a university student whose sister has her child in a Montessori program. The sister's worry is based on her fears that her daughter will have problems adapting to a public school setting.

Public school administrators and teachers are responding to parents' demands for Montessori programs for preschool through grade 6. Growing numbers of parents want the benefits of Montessori for the children throughout the elementary grades. So, some parents address the adapting question by advocating for elementary Montessori programs.

THOROUGHLY MODERN MONTESSORI

One of the many things that strikes a first-time observer to a Montessori classroom is how modern Montessori is both in terms of ideas and practice. Let us examine some features of Montessori that illustrate how modern it is.

1. *Integrated curriculum.*   Montessori provides an integrated curriculum in which children are actively involved in manipulating concrete materials across the curriculum—writing, reading, science, math, geography, and the arts. The Montessori curriculum is integrated in other ways, across ages and developmental levels. Montessori materials are age appropriate for a wide age range of children.

2. *Active learning.* In Montessori classrooms, children are actively involved in their own learning, as the vignette about Billy indicates. Manipulative materials provide for active and concrete learning.

3. *Individualized instruction.* Curriculum and activities should be individualized for children. Montessori does this through individualizing learning for *all* children. Individualization occurs though children's interactions with the materials as they proceed at their own rates of mastery.

4. *Independence.* The Montessori environment emphasizes respect for children and promotes success, both of which encourage children to be independent. Indeed, independence has always been a hallmark of Montessori.

5. *Appropriate assessment.* Observation is the primary means of assessing children's progress, achievement, and behavior in a Montessori classroom. Well-trained Montessori teachers are skilled observers of children and adept at translating their observation into appropriate ways for guiding, directing, facilitating, and channeling children's active learning.

6. *Developmentally appropriate practice.* From the preceding illustrations, it is apparent that the concepts and process of developmentally appropriate curriculum and practice are inherent in the Montessori method. What is specified in developmentally appropriate practice (see chaps. 6–9) is included in Montessori practice. Indeed, it may well be that some of the most developmentally appropriate practices are conducted by Montessori practitioners. Furthermore, I suspect that quality Montessori practitioners understand, as Maria Montessori did, that children are much more capable than what some early childhood practitioners think they are capable of.

SOME FURTHER THOUGHTS

In many respects, Maria Montessori was a person for all generations, and her method is proving to be a program for all generations. Montessori contributed greatly to early childhood programs and practices. Through her method she will continue to do so. Many of her practices—such as preparing the environment, providing child-size furniture, promoting active learning and independence, and using multiage grouping—have been incorporated into many early childhood classrooms. As a result, it is easy to take her contributions, like Froebel's, for granted. We do many things in a Montessorian way without thinking too much about it.

As we have noted, today Montessori education is enjoying another rebirth, especially in the public schools' embracing of its method. What is important is that early childhood professionals adopt the best of Montessori for children of the twenty-first century. As with any practice, professionals must adopt approaches to fit the children they are teaching while remaining true to what is best in that approach. Respect for children is never out of date and should be accorded to all children regardless of culture, gender, or socioeconomic background.

We have the tremendous benefit of hindsight when it comes to evaluating and analyzing educational thought and practice. In this process we need to consider what was appropriate then and determine what is appropriate today based on what we know now. When appropriate, early childhood professionals need to make reasoned and appropriate changes in educational practice. This is what growing the profession is all about.

More information about Montessori programs and training can be obtained by writing to the following organizations:

- The American Montessori Society, 150 Fifth Avenue, #203, New York, New York 10011; (212) 924-3209

- Association Montessori International. This is the oldest international Montessori organization, founded by Maria Montessori in 1929. Address inquiries to AMI/USA, 170 W. Scholfield Road, Rochester, New York 14617; (716) 544-6709

- North American Montessori Teachers' Association (NAMTA), 11424 Bellflower Rd. NE, Cleveland, Ohio 44106; (216) 421-1905

READINGS FOR FURTHER ENRICHMENT

Albanseia, Franco. *Montessori Classroom Management* (New York: Crown, 1990)

Provides insight on how to set up and manage a Montessori classroom. An asset for teachers who are hesitant about teaching in a Montessori setting but understand how a Montessori class can make a world of difference.

Gordon, Cam. *Together with Montessori* (Minneapolis: Jola, 1993)

A practical guide to help teachers, administrators, and parents work cooperatively together in developing quality Montessori programs.

Hainstock, Elizabeth G. *The Essential Montessori* (New York: New American Library, 1986)

Outlines the positive attributes found in Montessori schools. Examines the philosophy behind the program and concepts.

Kahn, David, ed. *Implementing Montessori Education in the Public Sector* (N.p.: 1990) (ERIC Document Reproduction Service Number ED 327 286)

Given the tremendous explosion of Montessori programs in the pubic schools, this is a good book to read. Discusses the use of the Montessori as a means of national public school reform. Provides information about equipment and curriculum as well as a discussion of language arts, bilingual education, and mixed age groups given the current trends in these areas.

Kramer, Rita. *Maria Montessori* (New York: Putnam's, 1976)

Well-researched and documented biography.

Montessori, Maria. *Spontaneous Activity in Education* (New York: Schocken Books, 1965)

Continuation of ideas and methodologies begun in *The Montessori Method*. Deals with concepts of attention, intelligence, imagination, and moral development and discusses provisions for them in a Montessori setting.

Montessori, Mario M., Jr., and Paula Polk Lillard, ed. *Education for Human Development: Understanding Montessori* (New York: Schocken Books, 1976)

Written by the grandson of Maria Montessori, essays in this book provide fresh insight into many Montessorian concepts. Addresses some traditional criticisms of the Montessori method and gives a modern approach to the Montessori system. Should be read after one has a knowledge of Montessori and her ideas.

Orem, R. C., and Marjorie Coburn. *Montessori Prescription for Children with Learning Disabilities* (New York: Putnam's, 1978)

> Applies and adapts Montessori methods to the needs of the child with learning disabilities. There is a lot of interest in applying Montessori to programs for children with disabilities, so this book is timely despite its date.

ACTIVITIES FOR FURTHER ENRICHMENT

1. Write three or four paragraphs describing how you think Montessori has influenced early childhood educational practice.

2. Compare Montessori materials to those in other kindergartens and preschool programs. Is it possible for teachers to make Montessori materials? What advantages or disadvantages would there be in making and using these materials?

3. What features of the Montessori program do you like best? Why? What features do you like least? Why? What features are best for children?

4. After visiting a Montessori classroom and talking with teachers, evaluate the criticisms of the system mentioned in the chapter. Are the criticisms valid? Are there any you would add? Why? In addition, make a list of the aspects of the Montessori classroom you liked and disliked and explain why.

5. A mother of a four-year-old asks your advice about sending her child to a Montessori school. What is your response?

6. Write to the AMS, AMI, and NAMTA for information about becoming a certified Montessori teacher. Compare the requirements for becoming a certified Montessori teacher with your university training. What are the similarities and differences?

7. Although there is a tremendous rise in the implementation of the Montessori in the public schools, some educators think that this boom is not entirely good for both the Montessori system and the public schools. What do you think some of their concerns are?

8. Interview public and private school teachers about their understanding of the Montessori program. Do they have a good understanding of the program? What are the most critical areas of understanding or misunderstanding? Do you think *all* early childhood professionals should have knowledge of the Montessori program? Why?

9. Interview a Montessori school director to learn how to go about opening a Montessori school. Determine what basic materials are needed and their cost, then tell how a particular community would determine how one would "market" the program.

10. Multiage grouping is one of the aspects of the Montessori program that appeal to many early childhood professionals. Make a list of the advantages and disadvantages of multiage grouping. What conclusions based on your list can you draw?

NOTES

1. Maria Montessori, *Dr. Montessori's Own Handbook* (New York: Schocken Books, 1965), p. 133.

2. Maria Montessori, *The Montessori Method,* trans. Anne E. George (Cambridge, MA: Bentley, 1967), p. 104.

3. Maria Montessori, *The Secret of Childhood,* trans. M. J. Costello (Notre Dame, IN: Fides, 1966), p. 20.

4. Maria Montessori, *The Absorbent Mind,* trans. Claude A. Claremont (New York: Holt, Rinehart & Winston, 1967), p. 25.

5. Montessori, *The Secret of Childhood,* p. 48.

6. Ibid., pp. 46, 49.

7. Montessori, *The Absorbent Mind,* p. 6.

8. Ibid., p. 254.

9. Ibid., p. 84.

10. Ibid., p. 8.

11. Montessori, *Dr. Montessori's Own Handbook,* p. 131.

12. Interview August 16, 1993, with Denny Shapiro, editor of *The Public School Montessorian.*

4

Piaget
Constructivism in Action

After you have read and studied this chapter, you will be able to:

☐ Critically examine and develop an understanding of Piaget's theory of intellectual development

☐ Identify the cognitive processes Piaget considered integral parts of intellectual development

☐ Summarize and interpret Piaget's stages of intellectual development

☐ Explain the characteristics of children's thinking at each stage of intellectual development

☐ Use the terminology necessary to understand Piaget's theory.

☐ Analyze Piaget's stages of intellectual development in their relationship to children's development of knowledge

☐ Identify the major features and common concepts of educational curricula based on Piaget's theory

☐ Explain the role of autonomy in children's learning

☐ Discuss and evaluate issues and controversies associated with Piaget's theory

The Swiss epistemologist (one who studies how knowledge is acquired) Jean Piaget developed the *cognitive theory* approach to learning (see chap. 2). Piaget was interested in how humans learn and develop intellectually, beginning at birth and continuing across the life span. He devoted his life to conducting experiments, observing children (including his own), and writing about his theory. Piaget has enriched our knowledge about children's thinking, and his influence on early childhood education continues to be significant.

Piaget's theory of intelligence is basically a logicomathematical theory; that is, intelligence is perceived as consisting primarily of logical and mathematical abilities. Compare this to Howard Gardner's theory of multiple intelligences presented in chapter 2.

Generally, the term *intelligence* suggests intelligence quotient or IQ—that which is measured on an intelligence test. This is not what Piaget meant by intelligence; rather, intelligence is the cognitive, or mental, process by which children acquire knowledge; hence, *intelligence* is "to know." It is synonymous with *thinking* in that it involves the use of mental operations developed as a result of acting mentally and physically in and on the environment. Basic to Piaget's cognitive theory is the active involvement of children through direct experiences with the physical world. A second point is that intelligence develops over time, and a third premise is that children are *intrinsically* motivated to develop intelligence.

Piaget conceives of intelligence as having a biological basis; that is, all organisms, including humans, adapt to their environments. You are probably familiar with the process of physical adaptation, in which an individual, stimulated by environmental factors, reacts and adjusts to that environment; this adjustment results in physical changes. Piaget applies the concept of adaptation to the mental level and uses it to help explain how intellectual development evolves through stages of thinking. Humans mentally adapt to environmental experiences as a result of encounters with people, places, and things; the result is cognitive development.

Constructivism and Intellectual Development

Piaget's theory is a *constructivist* view of development. Children literally construct their knowledge of the world and their level of cognitive functioning. "The more advanced forms of cognition are constructed anew by each individual through a process of 'self-directed' or 'self-regulated' activity."[1] The constructivist process

> is defined in terms of the individual's organizing, structuring and restructuring of experience—an ongoing lifelong process—in accordance with existing schemes of thought. In turn, these very schemes become modified and enriched in the course of interaction with the physical and social world.[2]

Children continuously organize, structure, and restructure experiences in relation to existing schemes of thought. Experiences provide a basis for constructing schemes.

In explaining the role of constructivism, Constance Kamii, a leading Piaget scholar, states, "Constructivism refers to the fact that knowledge is built by an active child from the inside rather than being transmitted from the outside through the senses."[3]

Play with materials and caring for animals provides children opportunities to be physically and mentally involved. Piaget believed such involvement is necessary for mental development in the early years.

Active Learning

Active learning is an inherent part of constructivism, as both a concept and process. As a concept, active learning means that children develop—construct—knowledge through active physical and mental activity. As a process, active learning means that children are actively involved with a variety of manipulative materials in problem-setting and problem-solving activities. The NAEYC and the majority of early childhood professionals support active learning as the preferred practice in early childhood programs.

INTELLECTUAL DEVELOPMENT AND ADAPTATION

According to Piaget, the adaptive process at the intellectual level operates much the same as at the physical level. The newborn's intelligence is expressed through reflexive motor actions such as sucking, grasping, head turning, and swallowing. Through the process of adaptation to the environment via these reflexive actions, the young child's intelligence has its origin and is developed.

Adaptation is for Piaget the essence of intellectual functioning, just as it is the essence of biological functioning. It is one of the two basic tendencies inherent in all species; the other is organization, the ability to integrate both physical and psychological structures into coherent systems. Adaptation takes place through organization; the organism discriminates among the myriad stimuli and sensations by which it is bombarded and organizes them into some kind of structure.[4]

Through this interaction with the environment that results in adaptation, children organize sensations and experiences. The resulting organization and processes of interaction are called *intelligence*. Obviously, therefore, the quality of the environment and the nature of children's experiences play a major role in the development of intelligence. For example, the child with various and differing objects available to grasp and suck, and many opportunities for this behavior, will develop differentiated sucking organizations (and therefore an intelligence) quite different from that of the child who has nothing to suck but a pacifier.

The Process of Adaptation

Piaget believed the adaptive process is composed of two interrelated processes, assimilation and accommodation. On the intellectual level, *assimilation* is the taking in of sensory data through experiences and impressions and incorporating them into knowledge of people and objects already created as a result of these experiences.

> Every experience we have, whether as infant, child, or adult, is taken into the mind and made to fit into the experiences which already exist there. The new experience will need to be changed in some degree in order for it to fit in. Some experiences cannot be taken in because they do not fit. These are rejected. Thus the intellect assimilates new experiences into itself by transforming them to fit the structure which has been built up. This process of acting on the environment in order to build up a model of it in the mind, Piaget calls assimilation.[5]

Accommodation is the process by which individuals change their way of thinking, behaving, and believing to come into accord with reality. For example, a child who is familiar with cats because she has several at home may, upon seeing a dog for the first time, call it a cat. She has assimilated dog into her organization of cat. However, she must change (accommodate) her model of what constitutes "catness" to exclude dogs. She does this by starting to construct or build a scheme for dog and thus what "dogness" represents.

> Now with each new experience, the structures which have already been built up will need to modify themselves to accept that new experience, for, as each new experience is fitted in to the old, the structures will be slightly changed. This process by which the intellect continually adjusts its model of the world to fit in each new acquisition, Piaget calls accommodation.[6]

The twin processes of assimilation and accommodation, viewed as an integrated, functioning whole, constitute *adaptation*.

Equilibrium is another process in Piaget's theory of intelligence. *Equilibrium* is a balance between assimilation and accommodation. Individuals cannot assimilate new data without to some degree changing their way of thinking or acting to fit those new data. People who always assimilate without much evidence of having

FIGURE 4–1   The Adaptation Process

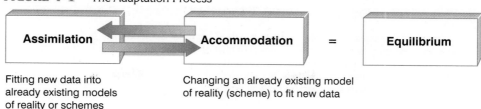

Fitting new data into
already existing models
of reality or schemes

Changing an already existing model
of reality (scheme) to fit new data

changed are characterized as "flying in the face of reality." Yet, individuals cannot always accommodate old ideas to all the information they receive. If this were the case, no beliefs would ever be maintained. A balance is needed between the two. Diagrammed, the process would look something like that in Figure 4–1.

Upon receiving new sensory and experiential data, children assimilate or fit these data into their already existing knowledge (scheme) of reality and the world. If the new data can be immediately assimilated, then equilibrium occurs. If unable to assimilate the data, children try to accommodate and change their way of thinking, acting, and perceiving to account for the new data and restore equilibrium to the intellectual system. It may well be that a child can neither assimilate nor accommodate the new data; if so, he or she rejects the data entirely. Figures 4–2 and 4–3 and accompanying text illustrate the construction of a new concept.

Instances of rejection are common if what children are trying to assimilate and accommodate is radically different from their past data and experiences. This partially accounts for Piaget's insistence that new experiences must have some connection or relationship to previous experiences. Present school experiences should build on previous life and school experiences.

More important, early childhood professionals must try to assess children's cognitive structures and determine the suitability of learning activities in promoting cognitive growth. Before giving children activities in classification, for example, the teacher must determine at what level the children are functioning in relation to classification structures. It is also imperative that the teacher does not have children do tasks for which they lack the cognitive structure. Undoubtedly, some of the reasons for school failure can be attributed to teachers who insist that children engage in tasks for which they have no experiential background and consequently lack the necessary cognitive structure. For example, a child must "know" what a circle is before being able to "find something shaped like a circle in the room." Likewise, a child should not be asked to separate red beads from blue and yellow beads if unable to discriminate yet among colors.

Schemes

Piaget used the term *scheme* to refer to units of knowledge children develop through the adaptation process. (In reality, children develop many schemes.) Newborns have only reflexive actions. By using reflexive actions such as sucking and grasping, children begin to build their concept and understanding of the world. When a child uses primarily reflexive actions to develop intellectually, he or she is in what Piaget calls the *sensorimotor stage*, which begins at birth and usually ends

FIGURE 4–2   A Child's Construction of a New Concept

Consider three-year-old Betty, who meets cats in her neighborhood daily. From her observations, she is able to organize a mental category or concept built on cats' similarities, despite their differences. She can recall the category for use when needed. Organizing her observations in this way gives her an effective means of handling new observations. We can infer this from Betty's observed behavior.

One day she notices a squirrel for the first time . . .

Having focused on the squirrel's similarities with cats only, she mentally placed this new information from the environment into her category for cats. However, curiosity aroused, she approaches the squirrel and it runs off.

Later in the day, she is surprised to see a squirrel standing on its hind legs. After a momentary puzzlement her expression changes as she calls after the squirrel.

Source: *The Piaget Primer: Thinking, Learning, Teaching* by Ed Labinowitz, Reading, MA: Addison-Wesley, 1980, p. 29. ©
1980 by Addison-Wesley Publishing Co., Inc. Used by permission.

FIGURE 4–3   A Child's Construction of a New Concept (cont.)

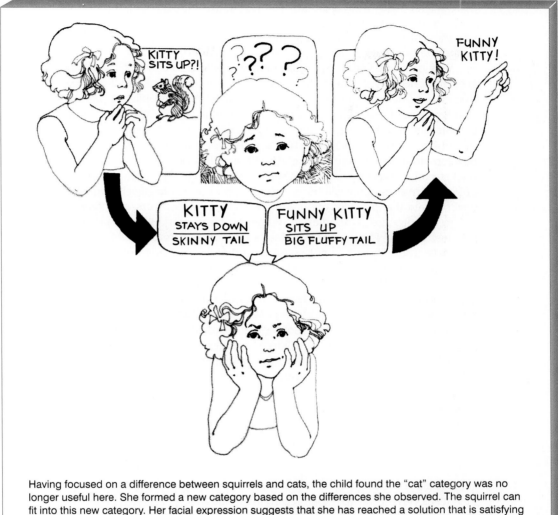

Having focused on a difference between squirrels and cats, the child found the "cat" category was no longer useful here. She formed a new category based on the differences she observed. The squirrel can fit into this new category. Her facial expression suggests that she has reached a solution that is satisfying to her mental framework and is compatible with her experience.

On another occasion, when she used the "funny kitty" label in her mother's presence, she was given the correct label. The name "squirrel" fitted into her framework.

Source: *The Piaget Primer: Thinking, Learning, Teaching* by Ed Labinowitz, Reading, MA: Addison-Wesley, 1980, p. 30. © 1980 by Addison-Wesley Publishing Co., Inc. Used by permission.

between eighteen months and two years. Reflexive actions help children construct a mental scheme of what is suckable and what is not (what can fit into the mouth and what cannot) and what sensations (warm and cold) occur by sucking. Children also use the grasping reflex in much the same way to build schemes of what can and cannot be grasped.

Why do some children develop or create different schemes? This depends on the environment in which the child is reared and the quality of the child's experiences in that environment. To a great extent, the environment establishes parameters for the development of intelligence. A child who is confined to a crib with no objects to suck or grasp is at a disadvantage in building mental structures through sensorimotor responses. Another child who has a variety of materials has more opportunity to develop alternative schemes. A child with a variety of materials and a caring adult to help stimulate sensory responses will do even better. By the same token, as children grow and mature, they will have greater opportunities to develop intellectually in an environment that provides for interaction with people, objects, and things.

In this process of adaptation, Piaget ascribed primary importance to the child's physical activity. Physical activity leads to mental stimulus, which in turn leads to mental activity. Thus, it is not possible to draw a clear line between physical activity and mental activity in infancy and early childhood. Settings should provide for active learning by enabling children to explore and interact with people and objects. Early childhood professionals' understanding of this key concept helps explain their arranging infant and toddler settings so children can be active. It also helps explain the growth of programs that encourage and provide active learning for all children.

Everyone recognizes that children should play, but we have not always recognized the importance of play as the context in which children construct mental schemes to form a basis for all other schemes. Play, to Piaget, is a powerful process in intellectual development. Parents seem to sense this intuitively in wanting their children to play, particularly with other children. Many early childhood professionals have an understanding of the importance of play and include play in their curricula.

Maturation and Intellectual Development

Piaget believed maturation, children's development over time, also influences intellectual development. Factors that in turn influence maturation are (1) genetic characteristics of the child, (2) the child's unique characteristics as a human being, and (3) environmental factors such as nutrition. Maturation in part helps explain why children's thinking is not the same as the thinking of adults and why we should not expect children to think as adult do. A child who has adults to interact with, as through conversation that solicits and promotes the child's involvement, has the opportunity to develop schemes that differ from those of the child who lacks this involvement.

Social Transmission and Intellectual Development

Piaget felt social transmission is important because some information and modes of behavior are best transmitted to children by people rather than by other methods, such as reading. (When discussing environmental influences, I include people;

Piaget considers them a separate factor.) Examples of social transmission include behavior appropriate to certain situations, such as not running in front of cars, and many curriculum skills involving the three Rs. From the cognitive development viewpoint, however, there is a difference between being told what something is ("This block is large") and understanding what "large" means as a result of playing and experimenting with blocks of different sizes. Telling a child that something is large involves no thinking processes on the child's part; to develop thinking processes teachers must provide the child with many experiences to perform operations—for example, stacking, sorting, seriating, experimenting, and building with blocks.

Stages of Intellectual Development

Figure 4–4 summarizes Piaget's developmental stages and provides examples of stage-related characteristics. Piaget contended that developmental stages are the same for all children, including the atypical child, and that all children progress through each stage in the same order. The ages are only approximate and should not be considered fixed. The sequence of growth through the developmental stages does not vary; the ages at which progression occurs do vary.

Sensorimotor Stage

During the period from birth to about two years, children use senses and motor reflexes to build knowledge of the world. They use their eyes to see, their mouths to suck, and their hands to grasp. Through these innate sensory and reflexive actions, they continue to develop an increasingly complex, unique, and individualized hierarchy of schemes. What children are to become physically and intellectually is related

FIGURE 4–4   Piaget's Stages of Cognitive Development

Stage	Characteristic
Sensorimotor (Birth to18 months/ 2 years)	Uses sensorimotor system of sucking, grasping, and gross-body activities to build schemes; begins to develop object permanency
Preoperational (2 to 7 Years)	Dependent on concrete representations; uses the world of here and now as frame of reference; enjoys accelerated language development; internalizes events; is egocentric in thought and action; thinks everything has a reason or purpose; is perceptually bound; makes judgments primarily on basis of how things look
Concrete operations (7 to 12 years)	Is capable of reversal of thought process; able to conserve; still is dependent on how things look for decision making; becomes less egocentric; structures time and space; understands number; begins to think logically
Formal operations (12 to 15 years)	Is capable of dealing with verbal and hypothetical problems; can reason scientifically and logically; no longer is bound to the concrete; can think with symbols

Piaget's theory has many implications for how professionals interact with children and design learning experiences for them. Among the implications are that children think differently at different stages of cognitive development and that their thinking is not like adult thinking and should not be compared to it.

to these sensorimotor functions and interactions. Furth says, "An organism exists only insofar as it functions."[7] This important concept stresses the necessity of an enriched environment for children.

The sensorimotor period has these major characteristics:

- Dependency on and use of innate reflexive actions
- Initial development of object permanency (the idea that objects can exist without being seen)
- Egocentricity, whereby children see themselves as the center of the world and believe events are caused by them
- Dependence on concrete representations (things) rather than symbols (words, pictures) for information
- By the end of the second year, children rely less on sensorimotor reflexive actions and begin to use symbols for things that are not present. (We will discuss intellectual development in infants, toddlers, preschoolers, and primary grade children in more detail in later chapters.)

Preoperational Stage

The preoperational stage begins at age two and ends at approximately seven years. Preoperational children are different from sensorimotor children in these ways:

- Language development begins to accelerate rapidly.
- There is less dependence on sensorimotor action.
- There is an increased ability to internalize events and think by utilizing representational symbols such as words in place of things.

Preoperational children continue to share common characteristics such as egocentricity with sensorimotor children. At the preoperational level, egocentricity is characterized by being perceptually bound. This is making judgments, expressing ideas, and basing perceptions mainly on an interpretation of how things are physically perceived by the senses. How things look to preoperational children is in turn the foundation for several other stage-related characteristics. First, children faced with an object that has multiple characteristics, such as a long, round, yellow pencil, will "see" whichever of those qualities first catches their eye. Preoperational children's knowledge is based only on what they are able to see, simply because they do not yet have operational intelligence or the ability to think using mental images.

Second, absence of operations makes it impossible to *conserve,* or determine that the quantity of an object does not change simply because some transformation occurs in its physical appearance. For example, show preoperational children two identical rows of checkers (see Figure 4–5). Ask whether there are the same number of checkers in each row. The children should answer affirmatively. Next, space out the checkers in each row, and ask whether the two rows still have the same number of checkers. They may insist that there are more checkers in one row "because it's longer." These children base their judgment on what they can see, namely the spatial extension of one row beyond the other row. This is also an example of *reversibil-*

FIGURE 4–5   Conservation of Number—A Lasting Equivalence

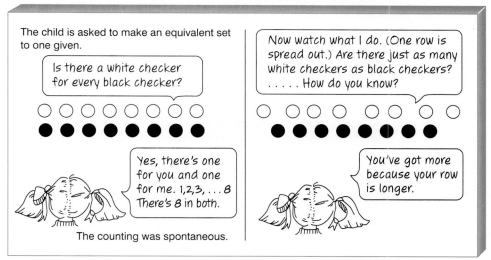

Source: *The Piaget Primer: Thinking, Learning, Teaching* by Ed Labinowitz, Reading, MA: Addison-Wesley, 1980, p. 101. © 1980 by Addison-Wesley Publishing Co., Inc. Used by permission.

ity; in this case, the children are not capable of reversing thought or action, which would require mentally putting the row back to its original length.

Preoperational children act as though everything has a reason or purpose; that is, they believe every act of their parents and teacher or every event in nature happens for a specific purpose. This accounts for children's constant and recurring questions about why things happen, how things work, and the corresponding exasperation of adults in trying to answer these questions.

Preoperational children also believe everyone thinks as they think and therefore act as they act for the same reasons. Because preoperational children are egocentric, they cannot put themselves in another's place. To ask for sympathy or empathy with others is asking them to perform an operation beyond their developmental level.

Preoperational children's language illustrates their egocentrism. For example, in explaining to you about a dog that ran away, a child might say something like this: "And we couldn't find him . . . and my dad he looked . . . and we were glad." In this case, because of egocentrism, the child assumes you have the same point of view and know the whole story. The details are missing for you, not for the child. Young children's egocentrism also helps explain why they tend to talk at each other rather than with each other. This dialogue between two children playing at a day care center reveals egocentrism:

Jessica: My mommy's going to take me shopping.

Mandy: I'm going to dress this doll.

Jessica: If I'm good I'm going to get an ice cream cone too.

Mandy: I'm going to put this dress on her.

The point is that egocentrism is a fact of cognitive development in the early childhood years. Our inability always to see clearly someone else's point of view is evidence that egocentrism in one form or another is part of the cognitive process across the life span.

Concrete Operations Stage

Piaget defined *operation* as follows:

> First of all, an operation is an action that can be internalized; that is, it can be carried out in thought as well as executed materially. Second, it is a reversible action; that is, it can take place in one direction or in the opposite direction.[8]

Unlike preoperational children, whose thought goes in only one direction (using the body and sensory organs to act on materials), children in the concrete stage begin to use mental images and symbols during the thinking process and can reverse operations. Although children are very much dependent on the perceptual level of how things look to them, development of mental processes can be encouraged and facilitated during this stage through the use of concrete or real objects as opposed to hypothetical situations or places.

Keep in mind, however, that telling is not teaching. Professionals should structure learning settings so children have experiences at their level with real objects,

Classroom activities such as classifying, seriating, and ordering help children develop an understanding of how things are related. Piaget believed that these activities as well as those involving numeration and time and spatial relationships contributed to children's intellectual development.

things, and people. Teachers often provide activities that are too easy rather than activities that are too difficult; for example, instead of just giving the children a basket of small plastic colored beads to play with, ask them to sort the beads into a red group, a blue group, a yellow group, and a green group.

A characteristic of concrete operational children is the beginning of the ability to conserve. Unlike preoperational children, who think that because the physical appearance of an object changes it therefore follows that its quality or quantity changes, concrete operational children begin to develop the ability to understand that change involving physical appearances does not necessarily change quality or quantity (see Figures 4–6 and 4–7).

Children also begin to reverse thought processes, by going back over and "undoing" a mental action they have just accomplished. At the physical level, this relates to conservation. Other mental operations children are capable of during this stage are these:

- One-to-one correspondence
- Classification of objects, events, and time according to certain characteristics
- Classification involving multiple properties of objects (see Figure 4–7)
- Class inclusion operations
- Complementary classes

PICK OUT THE TWO CLAY BALLS THAT HAVE THE SAME AMOUNT OF CLAY. 	NOW WATCH WHAT I DO. I'M GOING TO MAKE THIS ONE INTO A SAUSAGE. 	DO YOU STILL HAVE THE SAME AMOUNT OF CLAY, <u>OR</u>, DO YOU HAVE MORE IN ONE OF THE PIECES? 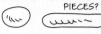	WHAT MAKES YOU THINK SO? 
Equivalence Established	One Object Transformed	Child Judges Conservation	Child Justifies Response

Preoperational (2–7)

> THE SAUSAGE IS MORE. IT'S LONGER.

Preoperational children are strongly influenced by appearances. When two dimensions are altered at the same time the preoperational child will center his attention on only one dimension and ignore the other. Most children younger than 7–8 years experience *centration* as they are unable to mentally hold two dimensions at the same time. They may have already constructed rules such as "longer is more" and "skinnier is less" but are unable to coordinate the rules.

When questioned, the children may agree that it's still the same clay. This knowledge of the *identity* of the clay is not enough to overcome the perceptual pull of the dominant dimension.

Children of this age tend to focus on the end result rather than on the act of transformation that neither adds nor subtracts any clay. Their responses reflect an *irreversibility* of such transformations to return to the original state. The children are unable to take a mental round trip back to the original shape of the clay.

Concrete Operational (7–11)

> YOU MADE IT LONGER, BUT IT'S SKINNIER. IT'S STILL THE SAME AMOUNT.

> IT'S THE SAME CLAY. YOU DIDN'T ADD ANY OR TAKE ANY AWAY.

> IF YOU ROLLED IT BACK IT WOULD BE JUST AS BIG.

Seven to eight-year olds

Each child here justifies his conservation response with at least one of three logical arguments, as above. Children seldom offer more than two logical arguments in their justification. Children in the concrete operational stage have the following logical capacities:

Compensation: To mentally hold two dimensions at the same time (decenter) in order to see that one compensates for the other.

Identity: To incorporate identity in their justification. Identity now implies conservation.

Reversibility: To mentally reverse a physical action to return the object to its original state.

These related and reversible mental actions that operate in the presence of physical objects are called *concrete operations*.

Understanding of the conservation concept applied to most other properties requires more time and experience to develop.

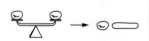

Does the clay ball weigh the same as the sausage, or does one weigh more?

Conservation of Weight (10 Years)

Will the water levels still be the same or will one be higher when the sausage is put in?

Conservation of Displacement Volume (11 Years)

Source: *The Piaget Primer: Thinking, Learning, Teaching* by Ed Labinowitz, Reading, MA: Addison-Wesley, 1980, p. 73. © 1980 by Addison-Wesley Publishing Co., Inc. Used by permission.

FIGURE 4–7   Classification

Preoperational Stage (2–7)

Classification is the act of grouping objects according to their similarities. It is an activity in which young children naturally get involved.

"Put things together that are alike and go together."

Rather than arrange objects according to some chosen property, young children (four years) will arrange them according to the requirements of a picture.

Graphic representation

Children make piles of objects that look alike in one way.

Resemblance sorting

When two colors are present the child's grouping shows a lack of consistency. The child begins by grouping according to shape but soon loses track and allows color to become the basis for grouping.

Concrete Operational Stage (7–11)

Seven- to eight-year-old children can place objects in two overlapping classes and justify their choice.

Seven- to eight-year-old children can respond to the *class inclusion* tasks in the presence of objects, e.g., green + yellow chips.

Eight- to nine-year-old children demonstrate a refinement in approaching classification. When presented with groups of flowers they are able to respond correctly to the following questions:

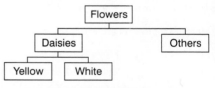

(invisible relationship of groups)

"Which will make a bigger bunch, all the daisies or all the yellow daisies? . . . all of the flowers or all the daisies?"

"If you picked all the flowers in the garden would you have any daisies left?"

"Can you put a daisy in the box marked flowers without changing the label?"

"If you take all the daisies out of the box would you have any flowers left?"

Source: *The Piaget Primer: Thinking, Learning, Teaching* by Ed Labinowitz, Reading, MA: Addison-Wesley, 1980, p. 74. © 1980 by Addison-Wesley Publishing Co., Inc. Used by permission.

During the concrete operations stage, children are less egocentric. They learn that other people have thoughts and feelings that differ from their own. One of the more meaningful methods of helping children develop beyond this innate egocentrism is through interaction with other individuals, especially peers. The teacher's role is not to "teach" children to share or tell them when to apologize for something they have done. It is through involvement with others, interacting and talking about social encounters, that children gradually become less egocentric.

This stage does not represent a period into which children suddenly emerge, after having been preoperational. The process of development is a gradual, continual process occurring over a period of time and resulting from maturation and experiences. No simple sets of exercises will cause children to move up the developmental ladder. Experiences with people and objects result in activities that lead to conceptual understanding.

Formal Operations Stage

The next stage of development, the second part of operational intelligence, is called *formal operations*. It begins at about eleven years of age and extends to about fifteen years. During this period, children become capable of dealing with increasingly complex verbal and hypothetical problems and are less dependent on concrete objects to solve problems. Children become free of the world of "things" as far as mental functioning is concerned. Thinking ranges over a wide time span that includes past, present, and future. Children in this stage develop the ability to reason scientifically and logically, and they can think with all the processes and power of adults. How one thinks is thus pretty well established by the age of fifteen, although adolescents do not stop developing new schemes through assimilation and accommodation.

PROGRAMS BASED ON PIAGET

The High/Scope Educational Approach

The High/Scope Educational Research Foundation is a nonprofit organization that sponsors and supports the High/Scope Educational Approach. The program is based on Piaget's intellectual development theory and

> is an innovative, open-framework educational program that seeks to provide broad, realistic educational experiences for children. The curriculum is geared to the child's current stage of development to promote the spontaneous and constructive processes of learning and to broaden the child's emerging intellectual and social skills.[9]

Since part of the Piagetian theory of intellectual development maintains that children must be actively involved in their own learning through experiences and encounters with people and things, the High/Scope Educational Approach promotes children's active involvement in their own learning. The program identifies these three fundamental principles:

- Active participation of children in choosing, organizing, and evaluating learning activities, which are undertaken with careful teacher observation and guidance in a learning environment replete with a rich variety of materials located in various classroom learning centers

- Regular daily planning by the teaching staff in accord with a developmentally based curriculum model and careful child observations

- Developmentally sequenced goals and materials for children based on the High/Scope Key Experiences[10]

Objectives

The High/Scope program strives to

> develop in children a broad range of skills, including the problem solving, interpersonal, and communication skills that are essential for successful living in a rapidly changing society. The curriculum encourages student initiative by providing children with materials, equipment, and time to pursue activities they choose. At the same time, it provides teachers with a framework for guiding children's independent activities toward sequenced learning goals.
>
> The teacher plays a key role in instructional activities by selecting appropriate, developmentally sequenced material and by encouraging children to adopt an active problem-solving approach to learning. . . . This teacher-student interaction—teachers helping students achieve developmentally sequenced learning goals while also encouraging them to set many of their own goals—uniquely distinguishes the High/Scope Curriculum from direct-instruction and child-centered curricula.[11]

The High/Scope approach influences the arrangement of the classroom, the manner in which teachers interact with children, and the methods employed to assess children. The High/Scope curriculum can be defined by looking at the five interrelated components shown in Figure 4–8. Active learning forms the hub of the "wheel of learning" and is supported by the key elements of the curriculum.

The Five Elements of the High/Scope Approach

Active Learning.   At the center of the High/Scope curriculum is the idea that children are the mainspring of their own learning. The teacher supports children's active learning by stocking the classroom with a variety of materials, making plans and reviewing activities with children, interacting with and carefully observing individual children, and leading small- and whole-group activities that provide active learning activities.

Classroom Arrangement.   The High/Scope classroom arrangement invites children to engage in personal, meaningful, educational experiences. In addition, the classroom contains five or more interest areas that encourage choice. Figure 4–9 shows a room arrangement for kindergarten.

The plan-do-review process, detailed later, is the child-initiated experience that implements the High/Scope Educational Approach. The organization of materials and equipment in the classroom supports the plan-do-review process in that children know where to find materials and what materials can be used, which encourages development of self-direction and independence. Small-group tables are used for seating, independent work space, center time activities, and teacher-directed instruction. Flexibility and versatility contribute to the learning function. The floor plan in Figure 4–9 shows how room arrangement can support and implement the program's philosophy, goals, and objectives and how a center approach (books, blocks, computers, dramatic play, art, construction) provides space for large-group activities and meetings, small-group activities, and individual work. In a classroom in

FIGURE 4–8   High/Scope Curriculum Wheel

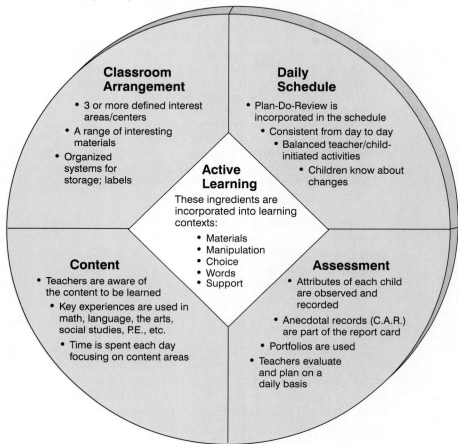

Classroom Arrangement
- 3 or more defined interest areas/centers
- A range of interesting materials
- Organized systems for storage; labels

Daily Schedule
- Plan-Do-Review is incorporated in the schedule
- Consistent from day to day
- Balanced teacher/child-initiated activities
- Children know about changes

Active Learning
These ingredients are incorporated into learning contexts:
- Materials
- Manipulation
- Choice
- Words
- Support

Content
- Teachers are aware of the content to be learned
- Key experiences are used in math, language, the arts, social studies, P.E., etc.
- Time is spent each day focusing on content areas

Assessment
- Attributes of each child are observed and recorded
- Anecdotal records (C.A.R.) are part of the report card
- Portfolios are used
- Teachers evaluate and plan on a daily basis

Source: Used with the permission of David P. Weikart, president, High/Scope Educational Research Foundation, 600 N. River St., Ypsilanti, Michigan 48198-2898.

which space is a problem, the teacher must work at making one area serve many different purposes.

The teacher selects the centers and activities to use in the classroom based on several considerations:

- Interests of the children (e.g., kindergarten children are interested in blocks, housekeeping, and art)
- Opportunities for facilitating active involvement in seriation, number, time relations, classification, spatial relations, and language development
- Opportunities for reinforcing needed skills and concepts and functional use of those skills and concepts

FIGURE 4–9 A High/Scope Kindergarten Classroom Arrangement

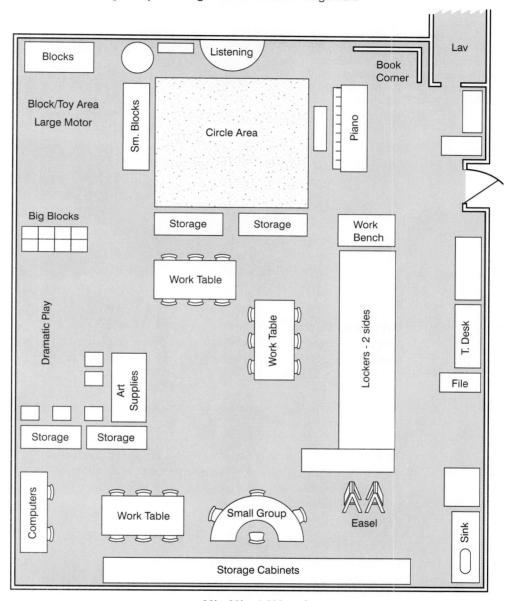

36′ × 30′ = 1,080 sq. ft.

Source: Used with the permission of David Weikart, president, High/Scope Educational Research Foundation, 600 N. River St., Ypsilanti, Michigan, 48198-2898.

Observation serves as a basis for assessing children's abilities and achievements. It also provides a basis for planning and for assuring that past learning is matched to present learning. What specific information can professionals gather through observation? (See chap. 1.)

Daily Schedule.   The schedule considers developmental levels of children, incorporates a sixty-to seventy-minute plan-do-review process, provides for content areas, is as consistent throughout the day as possible, and contains a minimum number of transitions.

Content.   The High/Scope key experiences are lists of observable learning behaviors (see later discussion).

Assessment.   Teachers keep notes about significant behaviors, changes, statements, and things that help them better understand a child's way of thinking and learning. Teachers use two mechanisms to help them collect data, the key experience note form and the portfolio.

The Professional's Role

The adult's role in the High/Scope curriculum encompasses behaviors in three broad areas. Adults must (1) know from where children are starting; (2) provide an environment in which children can become self-initiating decision makers and problem solvers; and (3) guide children. These aspects of the teacher's role are supported by cooperation with adults similarly concerned with children's education. Working in these three areas enables the teacher to come to know each child well. It is important that teachers know at what developmental level each child is functioning. Children benefit most from experiences that match their developmental capacities.

By knowing the developmental stages, the teacher can involve children in appropriate activities. For example, if a child is at the preoperational level, the teacher might use a classification activity involving how objects are similar and different, whereas if the child were at the concrete operational level, a classification activity involving sorting objects into increasingly higher orders of classes would be more appropriate. The teacher can thus provide an individualized program for each child. These are ways to identify a child's developmental level:

1. Observe what children are doing, things they make, and pictures they draw.
2. Question children about their work, actions, and activities.
3. Simulate an activity designed to reveal how the child acts, works, behaves, and interacts.

The teacher must also continually encourage and support children's interests and involvement in activities, which occurs within an organized environment and a consistent routine. The teacher must involve children in planning for their own learning. Teachers plan from *key experiences* through which children's emerging abilities may be broadened and strengthened. Children generate many of these experiences on their own; others require adult guidance. Many key experiences arise naturally throughout the daily routine. Key experiences are not limited to specific objects or places; they are natural extensions of children's projects and interests. Figure 4–10 lists some key experiences that support learning in the areas of speaking and listening, writing and reading.

A team-teaching concept provides children and adults with greater support, involvement, ideas, attention, help, and expertise. Just as children plan and work, so does the teaching team plan daily for the classroom. The recommended adult-child ratio is one to ten, so a High/Scope classroom of thirty children would have three adults—perhaps one teacher, one paid aide, and a volunteer, or one teacher, one assistant teacher, and one aide.

In the High/Scope approach, the learning process is based on matching children's developing levels of intellectual ability to learning tasks and activities. No effort is made to push children, speed up the learning process, teach for achievement of a developmental level, or teach facts as a substitute for thinking. The children's emerging abilities are "broadened and strengthened" rather than "taught" in the conventional sense.

To match learning tasks with developmental levels, children are involved in activities according to their interests, in a framework based partly on ideas from open education (see chap. 2). Open education need not occur in an open space but can take place in a self-contained classroom. In the open framework, children are involved in decision making, self-direction, and problem solving.

FIGURE 4–10   Key Experiences in Language and Literacy for a High/Scope K–3 Curriculum

Speaking and Listening
Speaking their own language or dialect

Asking and answering questions

Stating facts and observations in their own words

Using language to solve problems

Participating in singing, storytelling, poetic and dramatic activities

Recalling thoughts and observations in a purposeful context

Acquiring, strengthening, and extending speaking and listening skills
Discussing to clarify observations or to better follow directions
Discussing to expand speaking and listening vocabulary
Discussing to strengthen critical thinking and problem-solving abilities

Writing
Observing the connections between spoken and written language

Writing in unconventional forms
Scribbles
Drawings
Letters—random or patterned, possibly including elements of names copied from the environment
Invented spelling of initial sounds and intermediate sounds

Writing in conventional forms

Expressing thoughts in writing

Sharing writing in purposeful context

Using writing equipment (e.g., computers, typewriters)

Writing in specific content areas

Plan-Do-Review Process

The basic instructional/learning model of the High/Scope approach is the *plan-do-review model*. Children plan their activity, work at it, and represent the activity in some way, as they review or recall how they carried out their plan. Figure 4–11 shows sample schedules for children in a variety of programs using the High/Scope approach.

Plan.   Children plan for the work they will do. For example, a child may plan to plant a cutting that has been rooted, his or her interest aroused by a science unit on plants. Other related activities are available in the science center. During the planning process, children are asked to think about, communicate verbally or in pictures, and/or write about these items:

FIGURE 4–10 *Continued*

Acquiring, strengthening, and extending writing skills
  Letter formation
  Sentence and paragraph formation
  Capitalization, punctuation, and grammatical usage
  Editing and proofreading for mechanics, content, and style
Expanding the forms of composition
  Expressive mode
  Transactional mode—expository, argumentative, descriptive
  Poetic mode—narrative poetry
Publishing selected compositions

Reading
Experiencing varied genres of children's literature

Reading own compositions

Reading and listening to others read in a purposeful context

Using audio and/or video recordings in reading experiences

Acquiring, strengthening, and extending specific reading skills
  Auditory discrimination
  Letter recognition
  Decoding—phonetic analysis (letter/sound associations, factors affecting sounds, syllabication), structural analysis (forms, prefixes, suffixes)
  Vocabulary development
Expanding comprehension and fluency skills
  Activating prior knowledge
  Determining purpose, considering context, making predictions
  Developing strategies for interpreting narrative and expository text
  Reading varied genres of children's literature

- The area where one will implement the plan
- The kind and amount of materials one will need
- The sequence one will follow in completing the plan
- How long it will take to complete the plan and the problems one might encounter

The planning format of the plan-do-review process progresses through several stages as children develop their ability to communicate. During the plan part of the activity, children engage in *representing,* expressing how they want to engage in an activity. The youngest children simply tell the group where they plan to go and what they plan to do. As the children begin to learn letter formation and sounds, they are encouraged to use a combination of invented spelling and drawings to put their plans on paper. They may use words found in the classroom (labels) or look for

FIGURE 4–11 Sample Schedules under the High/Scope Approach

Preschool Program, Half Day

8:30	Greeting/circle time
8:45	Planning time
9:00	Work time
9:45	Clean-up time
10:00	Recall time
10:10	Snack time
10:30	Small-group time
10:50	Circle time
11:00	Outside time

Head Start Program, Half Day

8:30	Greeting/circle time
8:45	Breakfast, toothbrushing
9:15	Planning time
9:30	Work time
10:15	Clean-up time
10:30	Recall time
10:45	Snack time
11:00	Small-group time/circle time
11:20	Outside time
11:45	Lunchtime

Day Care Center, Full Day

7:30	Free choice/breakfast
8:00	Outside time
8:45	Bathroom
9:00	Circle/planning time
9:15	Work time
10:15	Clean-up time
10:30	Recall/snack time
11:00	Small-group time
11:30	Outside/lunch preparation
12:00	Lunch
12:30	Circle time
1:00	Nap time
2:00	Planning time
2:15	Work time
3:15	Clean-up time
3:30	Recall time
3:45	Outside time
4:30	Departure time

Source: Warren Buckleitner, "A Trainer's Perspective: Six Steps to High/Scope Curriculum Implementation," *High/Scope Resource* 8(3), Fall 1989, pp. 4–9. Published by the High/Scope Educational Research Foundation, 600 N. River St., Ypsilanti, Michigan 48198-2898. Used by permission.

words in their individual dictionaries. As writing and spelling skills emerge, the children become more independent plan writers.

Do. Children then carry out the activity in the classroom's learning centers, in this case by planting the cutting, labeling it, and beginning a journal to record the plant's growth. They may also represent their activities or products. In the case of the plant, the child writes and tells about the activity of planting the cutting and beginning the journal. The teacher tries to move the child through a hierarchy of thinking levels during the representation: taking photographs, making tape recordings; building a model with paper, clay, sticks, or spaghetti and telling about it; drawing a picture, cartoon sequence, puzzle, or painting; writing stories, books, songs, puppet shows, plays, and journals; and making graphs with real objects, pictures, or symbols. Language is incorporated into all these activities; for example, children are asked to label parts and tell about what they are doing (Figure 4–12).

Review. Children then participate in an evaluation or review of their activities. The review process involves having children mentally review and recall what they did based on their original plans. This review can take the form of telling, describing,

FIGURE 4–12   Representation

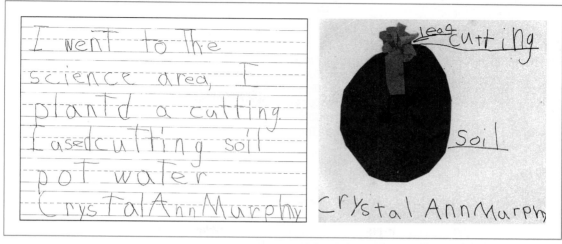

demonstrating (role playing), drawing, building, journal writing, and so forth. In small or large groups, they describe the attributes and details of their products and relate what they have done and how they have done it. The teacher also encourages children in evaluating the activity, asking whether there were any problems to solve, what steps were followed during work time, and what follow-up, if any, is planned. Children also have many opportunities to ask questions about other children's projects, so that the children as well as the teacher engage other children in the review process.

Implementing the plan-do-review model in the classroom depends on

- the teacher's understanding of the High/Scope approach and the plan-do-review process,
- the teacher's knowledge and understanding of child development and intellectual development,
- the teacher's knowledge of subject areas,
- materials available,
- how the teacher views children, and
- the teacher's personal philosophy of education.

Common Themes of Piaget-Based Curricula

Four recurring themes appear in curricula based on Piaget's ideas. One is that children's thinking is substantially different from that of adults, and adults must not try to impose their way of thinking on children. Adults should provide a setting in which children can think their own ideas and construct their own model of the world. Appropriate teacher behaviors include tolerance, support, acceptance of wrong answers, and encouragement to make hypotheses.

Program in Practice

HIGH/SCOPE IN ACTION

According to the *High/Scope Assessment Participant Guide* (Ypsilanti, MI: High/Scope Educational Research Foundation, 1994), "The High/Scope educational approach for three- to five-year-olds is a developmental model based on the principle of active learning. The following beliefs underlie this approach:

■ Children construct knowledge through their active involvement with people, materials, events, and ideas, a process that is intrinsically motivated.

■ While children develop capacities in a predictable sequence, adult support contributes to children's intellectual, social, emotional, and physical development.

■ Consistent adult support and respect for children's choices, thoughts, and actions strengthen the child's self-respect, feelings of responsibility, self-control, and knowledge.

■ Careful observation of children's interests and intentions is a necessary step in understanding their level of development and planning and carrying out appropriate interactions with children" (p. 2).

Full-Day Preschool Program (approximate times)

8:30	Greeting Circle
9:00	Small-Group Time
9:20	Planning
9:30	Work Time
10:40	Cleanup
10:50	Recall
11:00	Snack
11:15	Outside
11:45	Departures/Lunch
12:30	Rest Time
1:15	Planning
1:25	Work Time
2:35	Cleanup
2:45	Recall
2:55	Snack
3:05	Circle
3:25	Outside/Departures

The High/Scope daily routine and the teacher's role support these principles throughout the child's day. Beginning with Greeting Circle and through all the time period, there is a balance of child- and adult-initiated activity. At Greeting Circle, children gather as the teacher begins an animal finger play well-known by the children, who join in immediately. Then the teacher suggests that they make a circus of animals and their movements. Two children do not want to be animals, and the teacher asks whether they would be the "audience." They get chairs and prepare to watch. Children suggest elephants, bears, and alligators, and they all move to music in a parade of animals for the audience. The teachers says, if they like, they can choose an animal to be as they move to Small Group. At Small Group they make "inventions" of their choice with the recyclable materials Jacob has brought and the pine cones they had collected the previous day.

Including children in the decisions about activities and materials used in their day is an important way of supporting their intrinsic motivation. Research indicates that five factors are essential to learning: enjoyment, interest, control, probability of success, and

Contributed by Betsy Evans, The Giving Tree School, Gill, Massachusetts.

feelings of competence. During Greeting Circle and Small Group, the children have been actively involved in choices of activities and materials, and at Small Group they have each used the materials in their own way. As they play, they notice and describe their actions and observe how others do things similarly and differently.

As Small Group activities are completed, Planning begins. The teacher asks the younger children to get something they will use and the older ones to draw or copy the symbols or letters from an area in which they will play. Charlie, age three, gets a small hollow block and brings it back. "I'm going to make a train. That's all," he says. Aja, age four, brings a dress and a roll of tape. "I'm going to the playhouse to be the mommy, and then I'm going to the Art Area to make something with tape," she explains. Five-year-old Ashley shows the teacher her drawn plan of the Tub Table and the scoops she will use with the rice.

During Work Time, the teachers participate in children's play, riding on Charlie's train, showing Tasha how to make a *3* and a *5* for train "tickets," joining two children playing a board game, and listening to Aja as she explains how she made a doll bed out of tape and a box. One teacher helps Nicholas and Charlie negotiate a conflict over a block, encouraging them by listening and questioning until they agree on a solution. The teachers also write five to six anecdotes throughout the morning as they observe significant play episodes. They then move through the room, reminding children that in a few minutes the cleanup bell will ring. Ashley has suggested that for cleanup they make two trains, moving around the room to music and pausing when the music stops to clean up an area. The children really enjoy this activity, and Cleanup happens quickly.

At Recall, the teacher brings a hoola hoop, and the children each hold on, turning the hoop as they sing a short song. When the song ends, the child by the colored tape recalls. Charlie tells about the train they made out of blocks. Nicholas describes the special "speed sticks." Aja shows her doll bed, and Tasha describes her "tickets." After Snack, the children get their coats on and discuss what they will do outside. "Let's collect more pine cones. We can use them for food for the baby alligators"; "Let's go on the swings. I just learned how to pump"; "Let's see if we can find more bugs hiding under the rocks. They go there for winter." The teacher responds, "I'd like to help you look for bugs."

Children who are actively involved in solving problems with materials and each other participate in many of the ten High/Scope "Key Experiences" during their play: Social Relation and Initiative, Language, Creative Representation, Music, Movement, Classification, Seriation, Number, Space, and Time. These Key Experiences are important guides for understanding development, planning activities, and describing the thinking and actions involved in children's play.

The High/Scope approach to learning supports developmentally appropriate, active-learning activity for each child, as it encourages decision making, creative expression, problem solving, and other emerging abilities.

HISTORY OF HIGH/SCOPE

The High/Scope curriculum was initiated with the establishment of the High/Scope Perry Preschool Project in 1962. I was struck by the significant school failure rates of black youth from the south side and white youth along the central Michigan Avenue corridor in Ypsilanti. Both these areas were marked by poor housing, welfare families, and general unemployment. Something had to be done.

As school psychologist and director of special services for the Ypsilanti public schools, I had the responsibility of providing programs to such youth. When these young people were referred to me, it was for academic or behavior problems. The referring teacher often believed, naively, that if a psychologist would only test the child, the youngster would improve. However, as school psychologist, I became very disillusioned with my craft when I found I provided little real help and could predict IQ scores for youth from either of these two areas simply by knowing their addresses.

The late 1950s and early 1960s were a simpler time. There was a heady sense of potential for change represented by the energies in the early civil rights movement. With the naive enthusiasm of the young professional, I presented a challenging program of academic change to the principals of the elementary and junior high schools at a regular administrators' meeting. Backed by several reform-minded principals, I tried to see whether the schools could change their teaching strategies to meet the need of children from poor families. The meeting was a disaster. Some of the principals actually left the room during the presentation because, I now realize, the change necessary to reverse these failures was more than the system could tolerate.

In this atmosphere, the High/Scope Perry Preschool Project was initiated to prepare chil-dren before they entered school. There was no commitment at the start of the project to the power of early childhood education or to the later rhetoric of "critical periods" that ushered in Head Start. It was simply mechanically convenient to work with children before the schools had authority.

Fortunately, three years before the project began, in the fall of 1959, Michigan passed legislation permitting state funds to be used for children under age five if a special need was certified by a school psychologist. With that small window, the High/Scope Perry Project was designed and funded.

Initially, the service was not a research project. It was set up to draw children from the two areas of poverty within Ypsilanti and to provide services to them before school. Upon bringing in a group of outside experts from local universities, we were informed, fairly assertively, that our program would probably cause three- and four-year-olds harm. Thus, the strategy was shifted from delivering a program of general service to creating a controlled research project. It was the fidelity to good research procedures that was essential to the project's long-term service to the nation. Had we operated just as a service project, our preschool program would be no different than others and our data would never be useful to policymakers. However, set up as a study with a random sample assignment of children to preschool service or no service, the research backbone of the study was established.

Our first application for outside funds was rejected. Small school districts do not do research. The project was simplified from one serving both white and black youth to one serving only youngsters from the black section who seemed most in need. We resubmitted our proposal, and the project was funded.

The development of the High/Scope preschool curriculum began immediately in the

Contributed by David P. Weikart, president, High/Scope Educational Research Foundation, 600 N. River St., Ypsilanti, Michigan 48198-2898.

fall of 1962. After visiting both middle- and lower-class nursery schools, we were not impressed with the general curriculum philosophy of the day. A manners-and-morals approach to early education, with a commitment to the maturation theory "play is children's work," without carefully considered support from teachers would not work.

While the first year did not fully reflect the pattern the curriculum was to become, the approach we adapted was one of careful teacher planning from a developmental perspective. We encouraged close teacher support of the child's individual interests and efforts. Our small-group time had more planned teacher activities than we now recommend, but the significant characteristics of the High/Scope curriculum, such as children's control of their own activities, were evident. Probably, the essential nature of the High/Scope approach was not fully realized by us as program developers until we ran the research experiment investigating the impact of three different curriculum styles. In the 1967 film *This Is the Way We Go to School,* which contrasts three different curriculum styles, one can see the central elements of the High/Scope approach firmly in place from those early days.

Essential Contributions of the High/Scope Approach

The High/Scope methodology has made several contributions to the field, but some stand out as unique and central to our work. First, the emphasis on the plan-do-review or the intention-action-reflection cycle is of special importance. This process structures the teacher-child relationship. It opens the door by permitting the child free choice while at the same time giving the teacher a strong support role. The cycle is also important because it encourages a number of other curriculum procedures. For example, High/Scope classrooms typically label all

objects in their room as to their location. Since children make their own plans, they then have access to materials on their own and not through a teacher intermediary. Labeling also permits children to put everything away with general teacher support.

The cycle also gives the teacher a role of supporting and extending children's activities. This role means that the teacher uses a questioning style that supports children's thinking, such as, "How do you get all those calves in such a small space?"; "I wonder why the light is on now"; "Can you tell me how you made this?" This questioning approach gives the child a strong incentive to use language in conversation with the teacher and peers.

A second important aspect of the High/Scope curriculum is that it is an approach to education and not a specific curriculum. Thus, it is a method that helps organize the day, frames teacher-child relationships and interaction, encourages use of child development principles both in planning support for children and observing them, and permits a strong connection between the program at the school and the parents' work with their children at home. As such, the actual practice in any given classroom is developed by the teacher for his or her own students. Thus, while the content of what children experience varies widely from classroom to classroom, the approach remains constant.

Development of the observation assessment procedures, the High/Scope Child Observation Record (COR), is a third contribution. Rather than a screening checklist, a standard paper-and-pencil test, or a work record approach, this system records the best performance by the child as observed by the teacher. It is completely scorable and not subject to the same kinds of judgment problems that, say, the "portfolio" or "work record" style of assessment is subject to.

What Is the Future of High/Scope?

The High/Scope curriculum methodology is used widely in the United States as a major school reform effort. But rather than focusing on the structure and administration of schools, it centers on the interaction between adults and children in carefully designed settings. Presently, approximately fifteen hundred endorsed High/Scope trainers are working throughout the United States and in twelve foreign countries. At a minimum, these trainers serve about twenty-five thousand teacher-aide classroom units enrolling about three hundred thousand children.

An international registry of these participants certifies programs with the best High/Scope practice in the field. Over the long run, this registry of professionals working with the High/Scope approach will become an independent governing body to manage the curriculum and assure its quality. Institutes are being developed in fifteen countries at this time.

Second, children must be actively involved in learning. A child who is a passive recipient of information does not have the proper opportunity to develop intelligence to its fullest.

A third theme is that learning should involve concrete objects and experiences with many children and adults, particularly at the sensorimotor and preoperational stages. Children are too often asked to deal with abstractions such as words and numbers when they have no idea what these symbols represent.

Finally, the fourth common theme of Piagetian programs pertains to the quality and relatedness of experiences. What a child is like at a particular stage is largely a function of past experiences. Good experiences lead to intellectual development. Our job as teachers and parents is to maximize the quality of experiences. In addition, children's comprehension of an event depends greatly on the proximity of the event to the concepts involved. If children have nothing to associate an experience to, it is meaningless. Assimilation and accommodation cannot function unless experiences closely parallel each other.

ISSUES

A number of issues are associated with a comprehensive understanding of Piaget's theory. First, some difficulties associated with Piaget and his theory of intelligence arise from the complexity of his writings, which can be difficult to read and interpret. As a result, it takes a great deal of time, effort, and energy to determine their implications for education. One is never sure of interpreting Piaget correctly, so individuals must be willing to change their interpretations and constantly strive to improve the understanding and conceptualization of his theory.

In addition, some people think that Piaget's theory of intellectual development is an educational theory, and some educators confuse Piagetian experiments with a

Piagetian curriculum. Well-meaning teachers often believe that by having students replicate Piagetian experiments, they are "teaching Piaget." The experiments do have merit as a diagnostic process for determining how children think; the results, however, should be used to develop meaningful experiences. As Duckworth points out, "Piaget has no answer to the questions of *what* it is children ought to learn. But once, as educators, we have some sense of what we would like children to learn, then I think that Piaget has a great deal to say about *how* we can go about doing that."[12]

A third issue relates to early childhood curricula that call themselves Piaget based. Educators run the risk of blindly accepting and adopting such programs without thorough knowledge and understanding of Piaget's theory. To accept a curriculum without understanding its inherent concepts can be as ineffectual as applying a curriculum that has no theory as its foundations. The issue here is the same as that regarding Montessori programs; simply naming a program after Piaget does not guarantee it is based on his theory.

Finally, some people would like to teach more at an earlier age, in the hope of "speeding up" development. Piaget called this "the American issue." Piaget's stages are not designed to challenge teachers or students and should not be viewed as something to master as quickly as possible. Programs that seek to implement a Piaget-based curriculum should provide classroom environments rich in materials and opportunities for children to participate actively in learning. Teachers who understand Piaget and who are willing to support and stimulate children in their efforts to construct their own knowledge are essential to any quality early childhood program. Piaget's theory has much to offer parents and teachers who believe that children can and are the major players in the process of cognitive development.

PIAGET RECONSIDERED

Like all things designed to advance our knowledge and understanding of children, theories must stand the tests of time, criticism, and review. Theories are subject to the scrutiny, testing, and evaluation of professionals. This is the way theories are accepted, rejected, modified, and refined. Researchers have conducted thousands of studies to test the validity of Piaget's ideas. This constant review has prompted professionals to rethink some of their practices and applications.

First, Piaget seems to have underestimated the ages at which children can perform certain mental operations. For example, children in the preoperational stage can perform operations assigned to the concrete operations stage. This observation does not invalidate Piaget's work. Rather, it means that professionals must readjust their thinking and practices based on new discoveries about his ideas.

Second, Piaget's emphasis on a logicomathematical view of intelligence tends to deemphasize other views of intelligence. For many years, Piaget's theory was literally the preeminent theory of intelligence and the one practitioners discussed and sought to translate into educational practice. Professionals now have broadened their vision and have turned their attention to other views of intelligence; for example, in chapter 2 we discuss the currently popular views of Lev Vygotsky and Howard Gardner.

Third, Piaget's theory emphasizes the role of the *individual* child in the development of intelligence. The child literally creates his or her own intelligence. This solitary approach to cognitive development tends to downplay the role of social interactions and the contributions of others to this process. Many professionals who believe there is a social interaction basis for the development of intelligence are rediscovering Vygotsky's theory.

While Piaget's theory is constantly reviewed and refined, and although other theories of intelligence are in the cognitive development spotlight, Piaget's contributions will continue to influence early childhood programs and professionals for decades to come. We have much more to learn from Piaget.

READINGS FOR FURTHER ENRICHMENT

Case, Robbie. *The Mind's Staircase: Exploring the Conceptual Underpinnings of Children's Thought and Knowledge* (Hillsdale, NJ: Erlbaum, 1992)

Gives general and specific views of the mind, its structure, and development. Highlighted is the Piagetian approach to the issue of cognitive generality and specificity and advantages and limitations of the new Piagetian position.

Dodd, A. W. *A Parent's Guide to Innovative Education: Working with Teachers, Schools, and Your Children for Real Learning* (Chicago: Nobel, 1992)

Discusses innovative teaching practices, some of which are based on Piaget's theory of intellectual development, and explains benefits of such approaches to real learning.

Hohmann, Mary, Bernard Banet, and David P. Weikart. *Young Children in Action: A Manual for Preschool Educators* (Ypsilanti, MI: High/Scope Press, 1979)

In spite of the date, this is still *the* High/Scope book. An excellent guide to understanding and implementing the High/Scope approach, it remains the book professionals use.

Hohmann, M., and D. P. Weikart. *Developing Young Children* (Ypsilanti, MI: High/Scope Press, 1994)

A comprehensive guide to and explanation of the High/Scope approach. Provides a special focus on the adult's role in supporting young children's learning. Includes chapters on social development, music, and movement.

Kamii, Constance. *Number in Preschool and Kindergarten* (Washington, D.C.: National Association for the Education of Young Children, 1982)

Excellent, easy-to-read discussion of applying Piaget's theory to teaching numbers by one of the leading Piagetian interpreters. Contains many practical ideas and activities for teaching numerical thinking. The appendix "Autonomy as the Aim of Education: Implications of Piaget's Theory" should be read by every teacher and parent.

Kamii, Constance, and Georgia DeClark. *Young Children Reinvent Arithmetic* (New York: Teachers College Press, 1985)

A must for those who are serious about Piaget's theory and about young children, this book translates Piaget's theory into a program of games and activities.

ACTIVITIES FOR FURTHER ENRICHMENT

1. Observe three children at the ages of six months, two years, and four years. Note in each child's activities what you consider typical behavior for that age. Can you find examples of behavior that correspond to one of Piaget's stages?

2. Observe a child between birth and eighteen months. Can you cite any concrete evidence, such as specific actions or incidents, to sup-

port the view that the child is developing schemes of the world through sensorimotor actions?

3. In this chapter you are provided with a floor plan for a High/Scope classroom. Design your own floor plan, and provide a rationale for why you designed the plan as you did. Tell how and why it differs from the floor plan in the chapter.

4. The High/Scope approach is very popular in early childhood programs. What accounts for this popularity? Would you implement this curriculum in your program? Why?

5. Interview a trainer for the High/Scope approach, and identify the key issues in training professionals in the philosophy and methods of this program.

6. Compare Piaget's theory to another theory, such as Montessori's. How are they similar and different?

7. Plan a kindergarten lesson incorporating the plan-do-review process and the key experiences. Write about the benefits for children of the plan-do-review process.

8. List five concepts or ideas about Piaget's theory that you consider most significant for how to teach and rear young children. Explain how learning about Piaget's beliefs and methods influences your philosophy of teaching.

9. Visit an early childhood classroom, and find examples of egocentrism and conservation. Also, identify any other characteristics of children's thinking as described by Piaget.

10. If an early childhood professional said he did not think it was important to know about Piaget's theory, how would you respond?

NOTES

1. Deanna Kuhn, "The Role of Self-Directed Activity in Cognitive Development," in *New Directions in Piagetian Theory and Practice,* ed. Irving E. Sigel, David M. Brodzinsky, and Roberta M. Golinkoff (Hillsdale, NJ: Erlbaum, 1981), p. 353.

2. David M. Brodzinsky, Irving E. Sigel, and Roberta M. Golinkoff, "New Directions in Piagetian Theory and Research: An Integrative Perspective," in *New Directions in Piagetian Theory and Practice,* ed. Irving E. Sigel, David M. Brodzinsky, and Roberta M. Golinkoff (Hillsdale, NJ: Erlbaum, 1981), p. 5.

3. Constance Kamii, "Application of Piaget's Theory to Education: The Preoperational Level," in *New Directions in Piagetian Theory and Practice,* ed. Irving E. Sigel, David M. Brodzinsky, and Roberta M. Golinkoff (Hillsdale, NJ: Erlbaum, 1981), p. 234.

4. Mary Ann Spencer Pulaski, *Understanding Piaget* (New York: Harper & Row, 1980), p. 9.

5. P. G. Richmond, *An Introduction to Piaget* (New York: Basic Books, 1970), p. 68.

6. Ibid.

7. Hans G. Furth, *Piaget for Teachers* (Englewood Cliffs, NJ: Prentice-Hall, 1970), p. 15.

8. Jean Piaget, *Genetic Epistemology,* trans. Eleanor Duckworth (New York: Columbia University Press, 1970), p. 21.

9. High/Scope Education Research Foundation, *The High/Scope® K–3 Curriculum: An Introduction* (Ypsilanti, MI: Author, 1989), p. 1.

10. Ibid.

11. Ibid., p. 3.

12. Eleanor Duckworth, "Learning Symposium: A Commentary," in *New Directions in Piagetian Theory and Practice,* ed. Irving E. Sigel, David M. Brodzinsky, and Roberta M. Golinkoff (Hillsdale, NJ: Erlbaum, 1981), p. 363.

5

Child Care
Meeting the Needs of Children, Parents, and Families

After you have read and studied this chapter, you will be able to:

☐ Appraise families' needs for child care services

☐ Use and apply terminology and definitions associated with child care

☐ Evaluate and critique the purposes of child care programs

☐ Assess the economic issues of child care and determine how they influence the delivery of quality child care

☐ Develop an understanding of quality child care and how quality programs operate

☐ Evaluate the nature and types of child care services and programs

☐ Identify and understand the sources of child care funding

☐ Compare and evaluate the effectiveness of child care programs in meeting the needs of children, parents, and families

☐ Review proprietary child care and the reasons for its growth

☐ Assess the importance of child development associate training for early childhood professionals and programs

☐ Evaluate issues associated with the care of the nation's children

☐ Verify future trends in child care services and needs

☐ Analyze the findings of research studies regarding the effects and influences of child care

At the end of chapter 4, we discussed issues relating to Piagetian-based programs. We said that *any* program that desires to provide for children's developmental needs must offer an environment rich in human and learning resources and conducive to children's active learning and involvement. These factors and others apply to child care programs as well and are illustrated in the description of the Thurgood Marshall Child Development Center on pages D and E of the color insert. That program description also serves as a good introduction to our discussion of child care.

POPULARITY OF CHILD CARE

The need for child care is high and will continue to grow, owing to maternal employment, dual-career families, changing family patterns, and changes in child care practices by U.S. families. Over 58 percent (almost 60) of mothers with children under six are employed in the work force.

The need for affordable child care is further influenced by the fact that 55 percent of female-headed families live below the poverty level (see Figure 5–1). The number of single mothers living in poverty, 2.3 million, is better understood when compared to the 375,000 single fathers living in poverty. Single-parent mothers in poverty represent 53 percent of their group, whereas single-parent fathers in poverty represent 24 percent of their group.

Also, there is an increasing need for child care for infants. Although about 54 percent of mothers with children under three years of age are in the work force, infant care is not readily available; when it is available, it is expensive.

While more programs are available for three-, four-, and five-year-olds, many operate on a part-time basis. Most parents do not work part-time. Therefore, unavailability of full-time child care necessitates alternate care arrangements in the course of a day. This situation is inconvenient, expensive, and disruptive to children's needs for continuity.

Changing family patterns also create a need for child care (see chap. 1). Both men and women are deciding to become parents—natural or adoptive—without marrying. According to the Census Bureau, in 1992, nearly one in four—24 percent—of all single women had given birth. This increase contrasts sharply with a 15 percent (one in seven) birth rate by single women in 1982. Interestingly, the sharpest increase in single parenthood is among affluent and well-educated women. For

FIGURE 5–1   Single Mothers with Children Under Six Living in Poverty*

Age of Mother	One Child (%)	Two or More Children (%)	Total (%)
16 to 24 years	294 (76.0)	246 (90.1)	551 (70.3)
25 to 34 years	205 (44.5)	507 (80.7)	720 (59.4)
16 years and older	602 (53.2)	916 (80.1)	1609 (53.1)

*Numbers in thousands.
Source: *Poverty in the United States: 1992,* Current Population Reports, Series P-60, No. 185, Table 13, p. 79.

FIGURE 5–2   Percentage of Never-Married Mothers Ages 15–44

Race	1982	1992
Black	48.8	55.5
White	6.7	14.6
Hispanic	22.6	33.0

Source: Jason DeParle, "Census Reports a Sharp Increase Among Never-Married Mothers," *New York Times*, July 14, 1993, pp. 1 and A9.

example, the percentage of unmarried women with one or more years of college who gave birth rose from 5.5 percent in 1982 to 11.3 percent in 1993 (refer to Figure 1–8). Figure 5–2 shows the increase in never-married mothers in a ten-year period for three major ethnic groups.

The implications of these social conditions are obvious: children need care by people other than their parents, frequently in places other than their homes. As more women enter the labor force and as the demand for child care increases, the challenge is clear. Early childhood professionals must advocate for and participate in the development of quality, licensed child care programs.

THE TERMINOLOGY OF CHILD CARE

Child care terminology can be confusing, especially for persons not involved in the field. Sometimes the term *child care* is used interchangeably with other terminology such as *family day care, baby-sitting,* and *early childhood education*. The term *child care* is preferable to *day care,* because children are the central focus of any program provided for them.

The currently accepted concept of child care is that it is a *comprehensive* service to children and families and *supplements* the care children receive from their families. Care is *supplemental* in that parents delegate responsibility to caregivers for providing care and appropriate experiences in their absence that supplements the care children receive at home. Care is *comprehensive* in that, although it includes custodial care such as supervision, food, shelter, and other physical necessities, it goes beyond these to include activities that encourage and facilitate learning and are responsive to children's health, social, and psychological needs. A comprehensive view of child care considers the child to be a whole person; therefore, the major purpose of child care is to facilitate optimum development. Figure 5–3 shows the various kinds of child care programs with important and interesting information about them, especially as it relates to staff turnover, wages, and hourly fees.

TYPES OF CHILD CARE PROGRAMS

Child care is offered in many places, by many types of persons and agencies who provide a wide variety of care and services. A program may operate twenty-four hours a day, with the center or home open to admit children at any hour. There are also

FIGURE 5-3 Profiles of Early Education and Care Settings, 1990

	Head Start	Nonprofit Centers				For-Profit Centers		Regulated Home-Based Programs
		Public Schools	Religious-Sponsored	Other Sponsor	Independent	Chain	Independent	
Average Total Enrollment	50	58	73	58	63	91	67	6
Average Percentage of Children Enrolled Who Are Age 3 to 5	99%	83%	74%	74%	69%	48%	59%	39%
Average Percentage of Children Enrolled Who Are Members of Minority Groups	57%	48%	22%	45%	27%	21%	21%	19%
Average Percentage of Children Enrolled Who Are From Families Receiving Public Assistance	68%	n.a.	5%	30%	10%	6%	8%	5%
Average Percentage of Teachers Who Have a College Degree	45%	88%	50%	52%	49%	31%	35%	11%
Average Hourly Wage of Teachers	$9.67	$14.40	$8.10	$8.46	$7.40	$5.43	$6.30	$4.04
Average Annual Teacher Turnover Rate	20%	14%	23%	25%	25%	39%	27%	n.a.
Average Child-Staff Ratio in Groups in Which the Youngest Child is Age 3	8.4	7.4	8.7	8.8	8.4	11.0	9.0	6.4
Percentage of Programs that Provide:								
Physical examinations	71%	31%	44%	16%	7%	4%	2%	n.a.
Cognitive testing	97%	77%	36%	51%	36%	31%	29%	n.a.
Percentage of Programs that Charge Parental Fees	3%[a]	39%	99%	91%	98%	100%	99%	99%
Average Hourly Fee Charged by Programs that Charge Fees	—[b]	$1.19[b]	$1.65	$1.39	$1.73	$1.47	$1.53	$1.64
Sample Size	231	255	240	131	402	94	459	583

Source: Profile of Child Care Settings Study (Princeton, NJ: Mathematica Policy Research, Inc., 1990).

Note: n.a. means not available

[a]A few Head Start programs reported caring for and charging fees for school-age children.

[b]Small sample size.

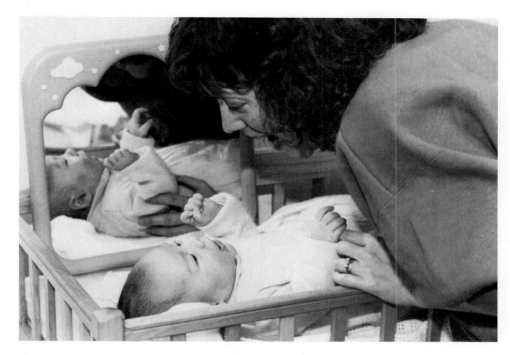

Growing numbers of parents in the work force have created demand for quality infant care, which includes nurturing professionals and an enriched evironment. There is increasing evidence that poor quality programs that do not provide adequately for infants' social, cognitive, and language needs fail to help them achieve their full potential. Professionals are concerned that we as a nation may be placing generations of children at risk. What are your thoughts?

whole-day programs that usually operate on a 6:30 A.M.–6:00 P.M. schedule to accommodate working parents. Half-day programs, such as those operated in many Head Start centers, usually run from 8:30 or 9:00 A.M. to 1:00 or 2:00 P.M., although more Head Start programs are becoming full-day programs. Parents who work usually supplement half-day programs with other forms of child care or a baby-sitter.

Full-Service Child and Family Programs

While child care programs have traditionally focused on children's needs, the trend is toward providing a wide range of services to children and their families. *Family-centered* programs go beyond providing child care. They help parents cope with daily living problems (e.g., help parents find adequate housing), enhance their parenting skills (e.g., provide parenting classes), and otherwise assist parents (e.g., connect parents with health services). In this regard, child and family programs are linking up with other agencies, such as health clinics, so that they can meet children's, parents', and families' needs.

FIGURE 5–4 Who's Caring for the Nation's Children Under Five?

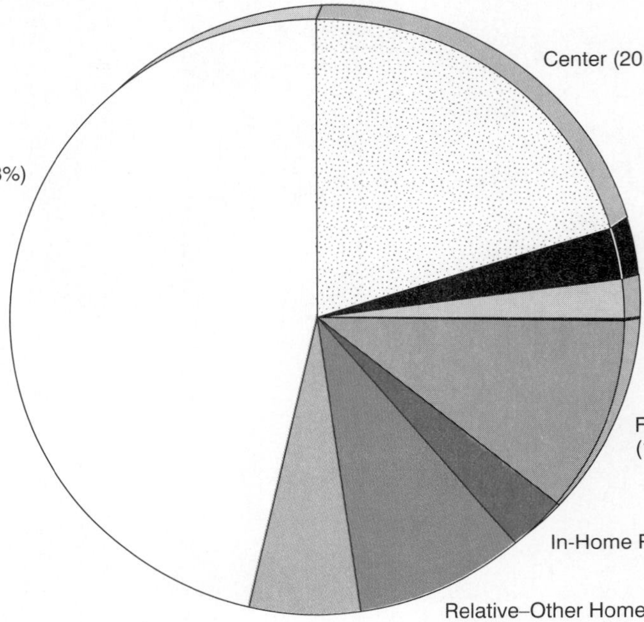

- Parent (46.3%)
- Center (20.5%)
- Other (2.8%)
- Lesson (2%)
- Self-Care (0.1%)
- Family Dare Care (10.7%)
- In-Home Provider (3%)
- Relative–Other Home (8.7%)
- Relative–Child's Home (5.9%)

Source: Compiled with data from S. L. Hofferth, A. Brayfield, S. Deich, and P. Holcomb, *National Child Care Survey 1990* (Washington, D.C.: Urban Institute Press, 1991).

Child Care by Family and Relatives

Child care arranged within nuclear and extended families or with friends is the most used child care arrangement (see Figure 5–4). Parents handle these arrangements in various ways. Some mothers and fathers work different shifts, so one parent cares for the children while the spouse is at work. These families do not need out-of-home care. In some cases, children are cared for by grandparents, aunts, uncles, or other relatives. These arrangements satisfy parents' needs to have their children cared for by people with similar lifestyles and values. Such care may be less costly, and compensation may be made in ways other than direct monetary payments. For example, one couple converted part of their house into an efficiency apartment where an elderly aunt lives rent-free in return for caring for the couple's two-year-old child. These types of arrangements allow children to remain in familiar environments with people they know. Child care by family members provides children with continuity and a sense of safety and security.

The number of children who are cared for through informal arrangements exceeds the number enrolled in centers or family care, primarily for two reasons. First, there is a lack of available quality child care programs. Second, many parents prefer to take care of their own children. When people search for child care, they often turn, out of necessity, to people who are available and willing to take care of children. These two criteria, however, are not the best or only ones people who provide child care or baby-sitting services should meet. There is a tremendous difference between placing a child in a high-quality, comprehensive program and placing him or her with an individual who provides primarily custodial care.

Family Day Care

When child care is provided in a child's own family or familylike setting, it is known as *family day care*. In this arrangement an individual caregiver provides care and education for a small group of children in her or his home. Eleven percent of the children under five in child care are cared for in family day care. Family day care generally involves three types of settings: homes that are unlicensed and unregulated by a state or local agency, homes that are licensed by regulatory agencies, and homes that are licensed and associated with an administrative agency.

Many parents leave their children at homes that are unregulated and unlicensed, and the kind of care a child receives depends on the skill, background, and training of the person who offers it. Some family day care providers are motivated to

As families change, grandparents are becoming parents again. For early childhood professionals, what are the implications of grandparents as primary caregivers of a growing number of children?

meet state or local standards for child care so they can be licensed. Family day care providers may also be associated with a child care agency. They meet state and agency standards for care and, in return, receive assistance, training, and referrals of parents who need child care. The agency usually subsidizes the cost of the children's care when the parents are eligible for subsidies.

Definitions of Family Day Care

Definitions of family day care vary from state to state. California defines family day care as "[r]egularly provided care, protection and supervision of children, in the caregiver's own home, for periods of less than twenty-four hours per day while the parents or guardians are away."[1] In Pennsylvania, a family day care home is defined as "[a] home other than the child's own home operated for profit or not for profit, in which child day care is provided at any one time to four, five, or six children, unrelated to the operator."[2]

After you have read the vignette of Patrick at family day care, it will be obvious that *good family day care is much more than baby-sitting.* In the past there was a tendency to equate family care with custodial care. Care providers today, however, are becoming more diligent about interacting with and stimulating the children they care for. The quantity and quality of specific services provided in family homes varies from home to home and from agency to agency. However, caregivers (almost 50 percent) spend a substantial amount of their time in direct interaction with children. Undoubtedly, one reason parents prefer family child care is that it offers the opportunity for a family atmosphere, especially for younger children.

Intergenerational Child Care

Intergenerational child care programs take two forms. One kind integrates children and the elderly into an early childhood and adult care facility. The elderly derive pleasure and feelings of competence from helping care for and interact with children, and young children receive attention and love from older caregivers. In today's mobile society, families often live long distances from each other, and children may be isolated from the care that grandparents can offer. Intergenerational programs blend the best of both worlds: children and the elderly receive care and attention in a nurturing environment.

For example, the Stride Rite Intergenerational Day Care Center, located in Cambridge, Massachusetts, enables children and elders to come together for activities including reading, baking, and painting. The Intergenerational Center is the daytime home (7:30 A.M. to 5:30 P.M.) for elders over the age of sixty and children aged fifteen months to six years. This program is discussed on pages B and C of the color insert.

A second type of intergenerational child care utilizes older adults, often retirees, as employees and volunteers to help care for children. Older citizens are valued as untapped resources of skills and knowledge who have much to offer children and programs.

Center Child Care

Care of children in center settings, also called *center child care* or *group child care*, is conducted in specially designed and constructed centers, churches, YMCAs and YWCAs, and other such settings. Again, states have definitions for what constitutes a center-based program. The definition for group or center care in Florida is

> [to] serve groups of six (6) or more children. It utilizes subgrouping on the basis of age and special need but provides opportunity for experience and learning that accompanies a mixing of ages. Group day care centers may enroll children under two years of age *only* if special provisions are made for the needs of the infants to be consistently met by one person, rather than a series of people; and which permits the infant to develop a strong, warm relationship with one mother figure. This relationship should approximate the mothering the infant would receive in a family day care home.[3]

In Texas, on the other hand, "[a] day care center is a child care facility that provides care less than twenty-four hours a day for more than twelve children under age fourteen."[4]

Many center programs are comprehensive, providing a full range of services. Some are baby-sitting programs, while some offer less than good custodial care. The quality of day care services among settings depends on those who provide the services, which makes conclusively defining child care difficult. Variations from state to state also make it hard to do anything but generalize.

FEDERALLY SUPPORTED CHILD CARE

Social Services Block Grant

Child care centers often receive federal funds because they serve low-income families who are eligible for cash assistance under Title IV A of the Social Security Act, or they are eligible for social services under the Social Services Block Grant (formerly Title XX).

Congress authorized Title XX in 1974 as a block grant to fund and administer what had been separate adult and child welfare programs. It was revised in 1980 and renamed Social Services Block Grant. Its level of funding has changed very little since its inception, and there are no requirements for state match. Some states require a local match from their subdistricts. The Child Care and Development Block Grant of 1990 passed Congress after several attempts to produce a day care bill that would recognize the need for child care apart from other social services.

States use Social Services Block Grant funding to cover its highest priorities apart from Title IV A. They include children

- who are at risk for neglect and abuse;
- who have special needs (disabilities); or
- whose parents are working with incomes just above AFDC, including farm worker families. The level depends on the amount of money available in each state.

Program in Practice

PATRICK'S DAY AT FAMILY DAY CARE

I enjoy being a child care provider because I realize I can enhance a good family situation but cannot replace it. I am open from 7:00 A.M. to 5:00 P.M. If these hours are not convenient for a family, other child care homes in my city have more flexible hours. I encourage parents to interview with as many care providers as possible before they make a decision about a particular home.

The Day

7:45 A.M. Patrick is four and a half years old and has been coming to my family day care home since he was ten weeks old. He is dropped off by his dad. Melanie, three and a half years; Bret, two and a half years; and Marina, four months, have already arrived. Marina has been fed and is napping. Bret and Melanie are playing with puzzles or stringing beads at the kitchen table. Patrick's dad sits down for about five minutes, chats a moment with Patrick and me, gives Patrick a kiss, and says good-bye. (I do not like sneak-out good-byes; these can lead to distrust.) Patrick joins the activities at the table and after fifteen to twenty minutes goes to the blocks, as he loves to build. Tyler, twenty-three months, arrives and is fussy. He has been out ill for several days and is having a rough time getting into the swing of things. I recommend that Tyler's dad make his good-bye quick and firm to end the turmoil Tyler is working himself into. Tyler gets a hug and love from Dad and me, and he tells me he would like to take a little rest. Five minutes later he wants to get up and play with his friends.

8:40–9:00 A.M. The children have breakfast. Patrick and Melanie help set the table,

and everyone, even Tyler, helps clean up their own places after eating. Patrick leads everyone to the bathroom for wash-up time.

9:10 A.M. The children all help pick up toys, so we can get ready for music time. There is approximately twenty to thirty minutes of dancing, shaking, stomping, singing, and music making. I encourage the children to express their creativity, and each child gets a chance also to perform individually. Melanie and Patrick love to use the wooden microphones and sing solo or duet. Tyler wants to copy everything anyone else does.

9:40 A.M. We have circle time, when everyone reviews the calendar, weather, shapes, and colors. Patrick reminds us he wants to do the alphabet mystery draw, where each child reaches into a bag and draws out a letter of the alphabet. One of the children draws a letter, and everyone tries to name it, even Tyler. Everyone helps him guess! Patrick loves this game and excels.

We then do fingerpaints, poster paints, felt pens, crayons, and chalking. Paper cutting and pasting is a constant favorite. Patrick will stick to a project until completed and then will "teach" a younger child how to complete his work. He is very kind and sincere in his efforts, and Bret appreciates the thoughtfulness. Tyler has to be included in all activities, or he will fuss until he is. His efforts are sincere, and he is very proud of himself. So are we all.

10:30 A.M. We go outdoors, play in the yard, go for a hike, or ride bikes around the block. The yard is large and fenced, and the children utilize all the territory. One area has

Contributed by Mary Ann Coulson, past president, California Federation of Family Day Care Associations, Inc., and chair of the Federation of FDCA Education Project.

climbing apparatuses, another has kitchen equipment, and another has a playhouse. An easel occupies a creative area. Patrick loves to paint as well as dig and plant. Of course, digging is the best part, according to Melanie. All the children come in rough-and-tumble clothes so I do not spend a lot of time worrying about staying clean.

12:00 Noon   Lunch. Once again Patrick leads the way to wash-up and helps supervise the younger ones. Melanie, Bret, and Patrick set the table, and lunch is served. Everyone cleans their place. Even Tyler carries his plate and cup to the sink.

12:15 P.M.   Baby Ben, six months old, arrives and joins the lunch crowd.

12:45 P.M.   Wash-up and nap time. Everyone appreciates this quiet time of day. The children's day has started early at home and has been busy in our home. They sleep in separate beds but are two or three to a room. Patrick and Melanie may wake up early, go potty, and back to bed. Sometimes they whisper back and forth until it is time to wake up. "Shush, here comes Mary Ann," says Patrick.

3:00 P.M.   Diapers, potty, wash-up, and baby bottles for the two infants and snack time for the older children. We read stories 'til my voice cracks, and then we go outside

again. Baby, toddler, and preschooler—all together we swing, crawl, run, jump, hop, learn simple games, do finger plays, explore the garden, work, and play. We check the progress of our butterfly cocoons and what flowers are blooming.

4:00 P.M.   Patrick's mom arrives, we visit for five to ten minutes, and they leave. The rest of the children play outdoors, or we come back inside and read. The remainder of the time is spent in free play; by 5:00 everyone is gone. The last few minutes are spent in picking up and cleaning up.

Concluding Remarks

Over the course of a year we visit museums, aquariums, zoos, parks, take train rides, and learn to cooperate with and respect each other. I try to keep my group small and stable, raising over 50 percent of the children to kindergarten age. Some leave the area or want extended hours, so I can no longer meet their needs. Once they go to school they are welcome to come visit, but I think at that point they need a different caregiver. It is terrific to see the development and personal growth of a six-week-old infant as he or she matures to happy, competent living. What a wonderful process life is. This is a very satisfying and rewarding way to make a living.

Program in Practice

A DAY IN THE LIFE OF AN INFANT AT THE OPEN DOOR INFANT CENTER IN AUSTIN, TEXAS

Center Schedule for Children and Staff

Center open: 7:30–5:30, Monday–Friday

Teachers and Hours

Shawn: 7:15–1:15   Marie: 7:45–12:45

Rong: 9:00–12:00   Beckie: 11:30–5:30

Teresa: 12:30–6:00   Tanya: 1:00–5:30

Infants and Ages in Months

Cason, 9   Alex, 8

Jando, 6   Colleen, 7

Piper, 7   Alyson, 4

Jared, 2 (twin)   Justin, 2 (twin)

Emily, 3

A Typical Day

The center is dark and quiet when I arrive at 7:15 A.M. I have fifteen minutes to prepare the room. I turn on lights, unlock doors, then begin to ready the infant room. We need hot water in the "coffee maker" to heat bottles, wet paper towels for diapering, a trash bag in the can, a blanket on the floor for the babies, and a variety of toys—noisemakers, soft squeeze toys, cause-and-effect boxes, balls, and some paper towel rolls. Toys hang from the bottom of the cribs, because the babies crawl around underneath them; the mirror is at baby height; the swings, high chairs, and rocking chairs are clean and ready to go. The daily record sheet is ready for the parents to begin and the teachers to complete. I put a tape of cheerful morning music on the tape player, and the door opens as the first family arrives.

It is 7:30 A.M. Cason and his dad come in, with Emily and her mom close behind. Both infants are put on the blanket with toys while the parents put away diapers, bottles, food, and daily supplies. I listen as they tell about the previous night, the sleeping schedule, and morning routine. My coteacher arrives along with three more babies and their parents. Two children have not had their bottles yet, so Marie begins to prepare them. I check diapers, then sit on the floor and visit. Both babies who need bottles are older than six months, so they can sit in infant seats and hold their own bottles. Alex is beginning to make fussy sounds, so I check the chart. He has had no cereal, so I mix it and feed him in the high chair. Colleen arrives and needs a snack. I turn the two babies in high chairs to face each other, with a window at their sides. They babble and watch each other. When I open the window, the breeze blows in and they smile.

Marie has four babies on the floor when our two-month-old twins arrive. We sit them in infant swings so they will not get crawled over while we put away all their belongings. Alyson and Emily are showing sleepy signs, so I put Emily in her crib and Alyson in the swinging bassinet. I wind the bassinet and pat Emily to sleep. Marie begins cereal for Jando, who has just arrived. Our aide, Rong Fong, arrives, and we are all glad to see her. Piper, the ninth and last infant of the day, arrives as well. It is 9:00. We prepare the rest of the needed bottles and breakfast. One teacher is at the high chairs, one is on the floor, and one is giving an infant a bottle.

Contributed by Shawn Michaud, site director, the Open Door Infant Center, Austin, Texas.

At about 10:00, some babies are ready for a morning nap. We know by individual signals—whining, putting her head on the floor, pulling an ear, rubbing eyes, or crying—all signals we have come to recognize. We put four sleeping babies in their cribs and, one at a time, jiggle or pat them to sleep. One baby is swinging, and each of us has one baby now to rock, sing, and tickle. It is a quiet time, 10:30. As the older babies begin to awaken, around 11:15 to 11:30, the younger infants seem ready to rest. When babies awaken in their cribs, we get them up, kiss, cuddle, and change diapers. I wind up some music toys on the floor. The tired, tiny infants begin to cry, unable to fall asleep. I pull the cribs close and pat one baby while jiggling the other's crib. They drop off in about four minutes.

Now comes an active time. One afternoon staff member, Beckie, arrives, and we roll the ball, pull the "see and say" sounds, play patty-cake, and do some infant massage. We prepare lunches for those who will need them soon and change diapers. Alex and Cason get lunch in the high chairs; Colleen and Jando take bottles in the infant seats. I give a bottle to Alyson. The twins and Emily are still asleep. Piper is chewing a teething toy. We anticipate Emily's waking soon and call her mom to plan for her lunchtime breast feeding. She will come at 12:30 unless we call to say Emily needs her sooner. Warm water will be given if she needs it to help her wait. Teresa, another afternoon staff member, arrives; Rong Fong has left; and Marie is about to leave. We exchange anecdotes and information about the morning. Our times are staggered so the change for the babies can be gradual.

The noon hour tends to be somewhat loud with greetings and activity. Jared begins to cry; he is not hungry, sleepy, or wet; from his clenched fists and drawn-up knees, it seems like gas. I pat him and carry him on my shoulder. He does not improve. We call his mom and get permission to give him Mylicon. He burps soon and settles down comfortably. Emily's mom has come in to breast-feed during the busy time; mother and baby spend their time in the rocking chair.

Lunches get finished, and Alex and Cason go outside with Beckie. They play in the infant area and swing in the infant swing. Inside, Teresa blows bubbles and holds the stick in front of the fan. The room fills with bubbles, and the babies' eyes follow the bubbles everywhere. Afternoon juice and formula bottles are prepared. Alex and Cason return from outside hot and tired. They both accept juice in cups in the high chairs. Several babies show sleepy signs and go down for afternoon naps. Beckie takes time to do Jando's "exercises" recommended by his therapist. Teresa dances to Chuck Berry with Alyson. One baby claps hands. Emily rolls over for the first time, and we all laugh and clap. A prospective family comes to visit. Alex cries and needs to sit on a lap while they are in the room. Cason needs afternoon medicine. He then falls asleep while having his bottle in Tanya's arms. Jared wakes up and lies on the floor over a rolled blanket. He is beginning to hold up his head. Justin lies on his back and watches the musical mobile. Alyson is in the infant seat with the rainbow bars over her. She bats at Mickey Mouse. As parents arrive, they read the babies' charts and pick up bottles while we help get the baby ready. We tell parents of a happy incident during the day and kiss the baby good-bye. Beckie helps the twins' parents carry them to the car with all their belongings.

When only two babies remain, Teresa begins to wash the toys with soap and water, then sprays them with a solution of water and bleach. The swings, chairs, and large toys are sprayed, and the sink is wiped down. When the last baby has gone, the windows are locked, the blinds pulled down, hot water emptied, diapers restocked, table washed, lights turned out—and the room is dark and quiet once more.

States use Child Care and Development Block Grant funds to provide services to those children related to Title IV A. They include children of parents who are

- employed and receiving partial AFDC,
- in training and receiving AFDC, or
- employed and on AFDC in the past year.

CHILD CARE COMPONENT OF THE CHILD AND ADULT CARE FOOD PROGRAM

A second source of federal support comes through the U.S. Department of Agriculture (USDA) Food and Nutrition Service, Child Nutrition Division, Child Care Component (CCC). Through this program, the USDA works through state agencies that administer the program. Nutritional support is provided in two ways: commodities and money.

For example, the USDA will provide commodities such as cheese, dry milk, and peanut butter to child care centers and family day care homes to support their nutritional programs. In lieu of commodities, programs can choose to receive cash equal to 14 cents per child for each lunch or supper served, in addition to the regular reimbursement (this cash-in-lieu-of-commodities rate is adjusted annually based on the cost of living). Children twelve years of age and younger are eligible for participation. In addition, children with disabilities, regardless of age as long as they are in a center in which the majority of children enrolled are eighteen years or younger, and migrant children up to age fifteen are also eligible. In fiscal 1993, the USDA provided $1.3 billion of support through CCC.[5]

WOMEN, INFANTS, AND CHILDREN (WIC)

A third source of federal support, also through the USDA, funds the Special Supplemental Food Program for Women, Infants, and Children (WIC). The WIC program, funded in each of the fifty states, provides basic nutritious foods to low- and moderate-income women and children. These foods are rich in protein, iron, calcium, and vitamins A and C, key nutrients often lacking in the diets of the WIC population. Participants also receive nutrition education and counseling as well as breast-feeding promotion and support.

WIC is available to women who are pregnant, breast-feeding, and postpartum (the period of time after childbirth); infants (birth to one year); and children from age one up to their fifth birthday. Postpartum women who are breast-feeding are eligible for up to twelve months, and non-breast-feeding women are eligible for up to six months.

To participate in WIC, these groups must meet the following criteria:

1. *Income guidelines.*   The income criteria varies from state to state. In Florida, for example, the criteria is an income of 185% of poverty (U.S. Poverty Income Guidelines are listed in chap. 10). For example, for a nonfarm family of three, the poverty level is $11,890. Multiplying $11,890 by 185 percent totals $21,996.50, the income below which a nonfarm family of three is eligible for WIC food supplements. States must use an income eligibility between 100 percent to 185 percent of poverty.

2. *Medical or nutritional risk.*   Such risks include a pregnant woman who is not gaining enough weight, a child who is anemic, and an infant who needs a special formula.

Women and children who meet the criteria are eligible for supplemental foods— milk, eggs, dried beans or peanut butter, iron-fortified cereal, cheese, vitamin C–rich juices, and iron-fortified infant formula and infant cereal. In addition, women who are totally breast-feeding also receive tuna fish and fresh carrots.

The method of payment varies from state to state. Florida recipients receive a check or voucher for the specific food items. In fiscal 1994, the USDA contributed $3.2 billion to the WIC program.

CHILD CARE TAX CREDITS

A fourth federal source of support is the child care tax credits for individuals and corporations. The federal tax code provides employers with certain "tax breaks" or benefits for providing child care services to their employees.

Since 1975, parents have been able to itemize the cost of child care as a credit against their federal income taxes under the Federal Child and Dependent Care Credit. Currently, the amount that can be deducted is based on a sliding scale. From $0 to $10,000 of annual adjusted taxable income, 30 percent of the cost of child care can be deducted. As adjusted income increases by $2,000, the percentage that can be deducted decreases by 1 percent until it reaches 20 percent. For example, for $11,000 of adjusted income, 29 percent of the cost of child care can be deducted; for $12,000 adjusted income, 28 percent, and so forth. The maximum amount of the cost of child care a family can use toward determining their credit is $2,400 for one child and $4,800 for two children.

For example, Valerie and Jack Lewis have three children. Last year they spent $5,200 on child care. Their combined adjusted income is $46,000. Their credit against their income taxes for child care is $960 ($4,800 multiplied by 20 percent). Even though Jack and Valerie paid $5,200 for child care, the maximum amount they could use was the $4,800 allowed by law. Likewise, they could only deduct 20 percent of the cost of child care, because each $2,000 of their income over $10,000 reduced the 30 percent rate by 1 percent. Figure 5–5 helps explain the deduction calculations.

Although the Federal Child and Dependent Care Credit is available to parents, only 31 percent of families with an employed mother use it. Interestingly, families with income above the poverty level are more likely to use the credit than families living in poverty.[6]

WHO SUPPORTS CHILD CARE?

The most common sources for funding and support for child care are

- parents, who pay all or part of the cost;
- state programs, especially Health and Human Services;
- federal agencies (Administration for Children, Youth, and Families; Social Security Administration; Child Care Food Program of the USDA);
- private and charitable foundations (United Way, Easter Seal Society);
- organizations (YMCA, YWCA, YMHA), and religious groups that provide care to members and the public, usually at reduced rates;
- employers; and
- parent cooperatives.

FIGURE 5–5   Federal Child Care Credit Calculation

Gross Adjusted Income	Percentage of the Cost of Child Care to Be Deducted	Cost of Child Care, 2 or More Children
$0–10,000	30	$1,440
$10,001–12,000	29	$1,392
$12,001–14,000	28	$1,344
$14,001–16,000	27	$1,296
$16,001–18,000	26	$1,248
$18,001–20,000	25	$1,200
$20,001–22,000	24	$1,152
$22,001–24,000	23	$1,104
$24,001–26,000	22	$1,056
$26,001–28,000	21	$1,008
$28,000+	20	$ 960

After food, housing, and taxes, child care is the fourth largest budget item for a working family. Many families spend at least 10 percent of their income on child care, and the average single mother may spend up to one-fourth of her income (see Figure 5–6). Families with employed mothers spend over $21 billion a year on child care services. The average weekly expenditure for child care by employed mothers with preschool children is $63.[7] However, only 40 percent of the families requiring child care paid someone to do it. This is consistent with the data in Figure 5–4.

Employer-Sponsored Child Care Programs

Today, almost everyone is expected to work, including women with young children. But many of society's institutions were designed during an era of male breadwinners and female homemakers. What is needed are child care programs and workplace policies that ensure that women can participate fully in their jobs and careers and can have the time and resources to invest in their children.

New responses to child care arise as more and more parents enter the work force. The most rapidly growing segment of the work force, in fact, is married women with children under one year old. To meet the needs of working parents, employers are increasingly called upon to provide affordable, accessible, quality child care. Corporate-supported child care is one of the fastest-growing employee benefits, as identified by the U.S. Chamber of Commerce.

FIGURE 5–6   Child Care Costs

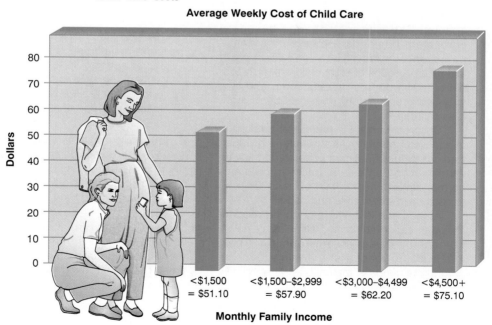

Average Weekly Cost of Child Care

Monthly Family Income:
- <$1,500 = $51.10
- <$1,500–$2,999 = $57.90
- <$3,000–$4,499 = $62.20
- <$4,500+ = $75.10

Source: U.S. Census Bureau.

Program in Practice

NATIONSBANK CHILD CARE CENTER

NationsBank, the South's largest banking company, has earned national recognition as a leader in developing progressive and flexible programs for working parents. The results of an employee survey in the mid-1980s revealed child care to be the number one need. The company responded with an expanding and evolving array of work-family programs. The NationsBank Child Care Center in Charlotte, North Carolina, is a model representing an added dimension in the company's efforts to aid employees.

The center is designed with its primary users in mind: children. Natural lighting and play space are given priority. Each classroom opens directly to one of six outdoor playgrounds. Large, interior central foyers turn into recreational areas on foul-weather days.

The capacity for full-year care is 160 children. Forty spaces (25 percent) are reserved for children of eligible tenants of the Nations-Bank Corporate Center. Also, there are thirty Back-Up Care spaces and ten Get Well Care spaces. Capacity may change based on enrollment demands. However, the anticipated enrollment structure is forty-eight infants (six groups of eight children), forty toddlers (four groups of ten children), and seventy-two preschoolers (four groups of eighteen children).

Children enrolled in the center participate in a developmentally appropriate, individualized curriculum. Teachers understand the variety of learning styles and paces in children's normal development. Their job is to respond to each child's own style and pace.

At the heart is a warm, nurturing relationship with caring adults in a stimulating, developmentally designed environment. Thus, much of the teachers' planning revolves around the needs of the children—individually

and as a group. Each day there is both indoor and outdoor activity, small-group and independent projects, and active and quiet play.

The program begins with an understanding that children are active learners and that there is no clear separation between learning and caring, play and work. The NationsBank Child Care Center is committed to promoting all aspects of development, including these:

- *Motor development*—using large muscles for skills such as throwing and running as well as small muscles for activities such as stacking and writing

- *Perceptual development*—for example, learning to look deliberately, thinking about what one sees, and distinguishing parts of a whole scene

- *Social/emotional development*—how to be a constructive member of a group as well as an individual; recognizing and understanding feelings, how to act on or cope with them; allowing each child to develop his or her unique, individual talents; developing a foundation that promotes success in school, including problem-solving skills, a high self-esteem, and a love of learning; providing an environment that is free of racial and gender bias or stereotypes

- *Language development*—using words to express and understand needs, feelings, and ideas; reading and prereading skills; and appreciation for books and other written language

The center's yard, enclosed by a brick and wrought iron fence, has playground equipment for children to enjoy during recreation time. The ample exterior play space allows

Providing for children in developmentally appropriate ways is a major goal of NationsBank Child Care Center. Professionals respond to children's interests and learning styles in warm, nurturing ways. Corporations across the country are including child care in the benefits provided employees and their families and are leading the way in designing environments and programs that are child centered and family focused.

children to crawl, run, jump, skip, and enjoy outdoor activities on sunny days. Each of the six play areas serve as the "backyard" for children at their daytime home away from home.

Get Well Care

A program for children who are mildly ill is included among the services of the Full-Year Care. Parents receive detailed guide-lines for Get Well Care upon enrollment. However, the following description may also be helpful.

When children in Full-Year Care are under the weather and not up to the demands of their regular activity, but well enough to leave home, care can be provided in Get Well Care. This is a separate area, staffed by a full-time registered nurse.

Parent Involvement

NationsBank is committed to promoting active parent participation in the center. Parents are encouraged to visit the center and are welcome at any time. Extensive communication with parents about their child, their child's room, and the center is an important part of the program.

In addition to many written and verbal means of communication with parents, the parent representative system (parent reps) is a formal way parents can give feedback and input. Each month volunteer parent reps call other parents to learn how things are going and obtain ideas, questions, or suggestions about the center. Parent reps meet monthly to discuss these comments; these meetings are open to parents.

Administration

Resources for Child Care Management (RCCM) manages and supervises Nations-Bank Child Care Center. RCCM's unique approach to the management of workplace child care centers assures NationsBank will have a strong influence on the program and policy at its center. This partnership is based on a mutual commitment to well-accepted standards of high-quality care.

During the last decade, employer-sponsored child care has become one of the more talked-about and most frequently implemented child care programs. Although not new (the Stride Rite Corporation started the first on-site corporate child care program in Boston in 1971), there is a surge in these services. The number of employer-sponsored child care programs has grown from 110 in 1972 to over 4,500 in 1993, partly because of the increase of mothers in the work force but also because of the realization that child care is good business. Yet, despite its numerous advantages, child care remains the least frequently offered employee benefit. Only an estimated 4,500 of the 44,000 employers with a hundred or more workers currently offer any type of child care support to their employees.

Employers can provide child care services in a number of ways:

- *Resource and referral services.*   Corporations supply several services in this area, such as information and counseling for parents on selecting quality care and referrals to local child care providers. These services can be offered in-house (i.e., on site) or through a community or national resource and referral agency.

- *On-site or near-site child care centers for their employees' children.*   The corporation supplies space, equipment, and child care workers. Some corporations contract with an outside agency to provide child care service. Some corporations also maintain a list of family day care homes and contract with the day care provider for spaces in the home. They may also assist in equipping the providers' homes for child care services.

- *Direct aid.*   Some companies provide a flat subsidy—a specific amount to their employees to help cover the cost of child care. For example, NationsBank, the largest bank in the South, pays its associates with limited incomes up to $35 per week to pay for child care.

- *Voucher system.*   Corporations give employees vouchers with which to purchase services at child care centers.

- *Vendor system.*   Corporations purchase slots at child care centers and make them available to employees either free or at reduced rates.

- *Consortium.*   Two or more corporations share the cost of an on-site or near-site child care.

- *Contributions to a child care center where many of the corporation's employees place their children.*   The subsidy results in reduced rates for employees and/or priority on a center waiting list.

- *Parent-family leave.*   A corporation provides a paid or subsidized leave of absence for the parent in lieu of specific child care services.

If they do not extend direct child care benefits, employers can make child care arrangements easier for their employees in other ways. They can offer a flexible work schedule, so parents may not need child care or as much of it. Other possibilities are maternity leave extensions, paternity leaves, and use of sick leave to include absence from work for a sick child.

Payroll Deductions for Child Care

Federal tax law allows employee payroll deductions for a flexible spending account for child care. The employee reimbursement system works as either a salary reduction plan or as a direct employee benefit. As a benefit, the employee sets aside a certain amount of salary to be paid directly by the employer to the child care provider. More common are employee salary reductions that allow child care payments to be made from pretax earnings, often at a considerable discount for most employees. The type of child care the employee can use is not limited. This plan provides a significant benefit to workers in higher tax brackets. Under such plans, present tax law requires that employees forfeit any of the amount specifically set aside that they do not spend on child care by the end of the calendar year. Employees pay no federal or social security taxes on money they spend for child care. The current maximum salary reduction allowed for child care is $5,000 a year.

Advantages of Employer-Sponsored Child Care

Many advantages accrue to corporations that sponsor or support child care. The presence of a corporate child care program can be an excellent recruiting device; hospitals, in particular, find child care services an added incentive in recruiting personnel.

Other claims for corporate-sponsored child care are that it promotes employee morale and reduces absenteeism. A possible side benefit is that the corporation

THE FAMILY-FRIENDLY WORKSITE

Increasing numbers of employers are providing employees a wide range of benefits relating to their children and families. FEL-PRO Incorporated, an industrial and automotive gaskets manufacturer in Skokie, Illinois, provides many benefits to its employees, including the following:

- State-licensed, on-site child care for up to forty-five children. Parents pay $85 per month, and the company pays the $120 balance.

- Child development seminars on a variety of issues to help parents better deal with raising a family

- Summer camp for six- to fifteen-year-olds at the company's 220-acre ranch

- Subsidized tutoring programs for children with learning difficulties

- $1,000 treasury bonds for the parents of new babies and $5,000 toward legal expense for parents who adopt a child

- Up to five days per year of company-subsidized emergency home care of sick children and other dependents

- Up to $3,000 per year for undergraduate studies and up to $6,500 for graduate studies for employees; $3,300 for four years for their dependents to attend an accredited college or university; and financial counseling for students and parents

- Up to ten weeks of half- to fully paid maternity leave, plus up to two months unpaid family care leave

- Flexible start times for some office departments

may be eligible for a variety of tax benefits through business expenses, charitable gifts, and depreciation. Knowing they need not worry about child care may motivate employees to stay with a company. In fact, corporate child care can be viewed as a family support system, which tends to encourage positive feelings toward the company and perhaps offset negative feelings about other factors such as pay and working conditions. Employees may also be more inclined to work different shifts when child care is available.

Similarly, there are advantages to employees. Parents can be more relaxed and confident about their children's care. Many parents can visit their children during breaks or even eat lunch with them. Being near their children is particularly advantageous for nursing mothers. Also, if a child becomes ill, the employee is immediately available. When parents have long commuting distances, parents and children get to spend more time together.

Financial benefits of employer child care include the possibility of deducting the cost of child care from an employee's salary, which represents a forced means of budgeting; employers can usually provide high-quality care at reasonable cost; and when child care is provided as part of an employee's work benefits package, the cost is not taxable.

What's New in Corporate Involvement?

Corporations now recognize more and more that they have both a social responsibility and a responsibility to their future work forces to be involved in child care and early childhood programs. Some of the ways corporations are becoming more involved are described here:

- They are more proactive in outreach efforts to involve the community in their child care programs, in two ways. First, they are inviting the community to reserve slots for children in their child care programs. Second, corporations are providing monies to child care programs in the community to train personnel and upgrade their services.

- Corporations are collaborating with other agencies to address issues of supply, demand, and quality. For example, the DuPont Company, through its Flying Colors Program, encourages and supports child care programs to become NAEYC accredited. To date, seventy-five programs have been accredited through DuPont's Flying Colors Program.

- Corporations are looking at child care programs in industrialized countries, to determine what unique and beneficial features they can apply to their child care programs in the United States. As companies examine how other countries excel in world economic markets, it is only natural that they should also look at how those nations care for and educate their future work force.

- Corporations are interested in investing in quality. They want quality programs for their employee's children and families. Corporations also want to promote quality child care in communities, particularly communities in which they have plants and offices.

- Corporations are becoming more involved in programs for older children. They are investing in before- and after-school care programs, summer camps, and institutes, especially those that focus on math, science, and technology.

- Corporations believe that they are laying the groundwork for the future work force. More and more, corporate executives discuss the need to invest in the quality of the future work force by investing in children today. In this sense, corporations are becoming more oriented not only to their future needs but to the needs of society as well.

The descriptions of the Children's Center at the St. Paul and the Pacific Gas and Electric Company Children's Center on pages A and N and O of the color insert illustrate how business and industry are fast becoming leaders in setting the standards for child care programming. These straightforward and extensive involvements of companies in providing child care and family-related services are a primary example of the restructuring occurring in the nation's business sector and how these changes in turn change the child care landscape. As you read and study these descriptions, think about how these programs and others like them across the country are changing how businesses take care of employees' children. Also, develop a list of such changes and predict how you think business-supported and -sponsored child care will change over the next decade.

Proprietary Child Care

Some child care centers are run by corporations, businesses, and individual proprietors for the purpose of making a profit. Some for-profit centers provide custodial services and preschool and elementary programs as well. Many of these programs emphasize their educational component and appeal to middle-class families who are willing to pay for the promised services. About 35 percent of all child care centers in the United States are operated for profit, and the number is likely to grow. Child care is a big service industry, with more and more entrepreneurs realizing that there is money to be made in caring for the nation's children. Figure 5–7 shows the agencies that operate child care programs.

Foster Child Care

Almost every state uses foster child care. Children are placed in foster care because their parents cannot or will not take care of them, or because they have been abused or abandoned. As many as 429,000 children live in foster care homes or foster group homes.[8] Many children in foster care facilities have some disability that makes them less attractive to some for adoption.

A growing phenomenon in the United States is the number of *hand-me-down children*; many parents find they cannot afford to raise their children or can no

FIGURE 5–7   Center Care by Auspices

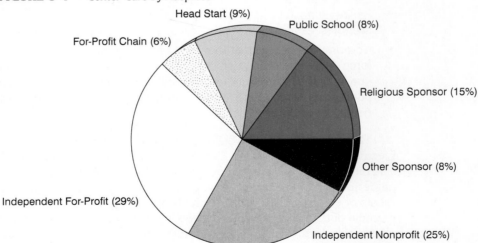

Source: Ellen Eliason Kisker, Sandra L. Hofferth, Deborah A. Phillips, and Elizabeth Farquhar, *A Profile of Child Care Settings: Early Education and Care in 1990,* vol. I (Princeton, NJ: Mathematica Policy Research, 1991), p. 36.

longer discipline them effectively, so they simply turn them over to the courts, which in turn place them in foster care.

Baby-Sitters

Children are their parents' most valuable assets, so parents should not seek the lowest common denominator either in quality or pay when deciding about the kind of person to whom they will entrust their children. These are important qualities early childhood professionals can encourage parents to look for in anyone who acts as a baby-sitter:

- *The necessary age and maturity to provide basic care for children.*   While no particular chronological age makes a person qualified to give basic care, a certain degree of maturity is necessary.
- *Education in providing child care.*   Training might come through a course offered by a school or service organization or through caring for younger brothers and sisters. In any case, a sitter should know how to diaper, feed, and interact with children.
- *Basic training in first aid and emergency procedures*
- *Trustworthiness*
- *Child-rearing values that agree with those of the parents.*   Parents must tell baby-sitters how they want certain situations handled and how they want their children disciplined.
- *Neatness, good grooming, and acceptable verbal skills*
- *Good recommendations and references from others who know and/or have used the sitter*

Drop-In or Casual Child Care

Many parents with part-time jobs or flexible schedules need a place to leave their children. Some child care services meet such needs in the form of storefront child care centers, child care services in shopping centers, and parents who do occasional baby-sitting in their homes. These services are convenient, but they do have some drawbacks. First, the quality of care may be low simply because the children are transient, and it is difficult to build continuity into a program whose population base is unstable. A second disadvantage is that sporadic contact with strangers can be stressful to a child.

CHILD CARE FOR CHILDREN WITH MEDICAL NEEDS

One of the trends associated with child care is that it is becoming more specialized. Consequently, more and more programs are providing care for children with medical needs.

Ill Child Care

For most parents, balancing the demands of a job and the obligations of parent-hood is manageable as long as children are healthy. But, when children get sick, parents must find someone who will take care of them or stay home. The National Child Care Survey 1990 data reveal that 35 percent of mothers employed outside the home reported that in the month previous to the survey their child was sick on a day they were supposed to work. Fifty-one percent of these women missed an aver-age of 2.2 days of work per month because of their sick child.

Fortunately, working parents increasingly have flexible employee benefits that enable them to stay home with sick children, but many do not. Also, when children are only mildly ill or do not have a contagious illness, parents feel there should be other options to losing a day's work. Child care providers have begun to respond to parents' needs. Some centers provide care for sick children as part of their program, and other providers are opening centers exclusively for the care of ill children.

These are some of the ways to manage care of an ill child:

- *In the home.*   Child care aide goes into homes to care for ill children.
- *Hospital based.*   Some hospitals have programs for providing for sick children.
- *Center based.*   Ill child care is part of a center's program of services, usually in a separate room.
- *A separate facility specifically designed, built, and staffed to provide child care on an as-needed basis for sick children.*
- *Family care.*   Ill children are provided for in a family day care home.

Staff training for those who provide care for ill children is also a critical concern. Some factors in training include these:

- What caregivers and parents can expect in behaviors and symptoms of typical childhood illnesses
- How to care for ill children according to different kinds of illnesses
- How to respond to the needs of ill children
- When to exclude the child from ill child care
- Curriculum—how to provide learning opportunities for ill children within the lim-its of their illness
- Administering first aid and CPR
- Infection control

The National Association of Sick Child Day Care (NASCDC) has the following recommendations for programs that offer sick child care:

- They should be medically safe and sound.
- A health professional who is well versed in ambulatory pediatric care and famil-iar with the child care field should be represented in the operation of the service.

A fast-growing and greatly needed area of child care is for services for mildly ill and, in some cases, chronically ill children. Many child care programs recognize that when children are sick, parents often face a crisis in their jobs and careers. These concerns cannot be casually dismissed by saying that parents should stay home with their ill children.

- Children should have many opportunities to be involved in play and school-related activities. Children's development does not end just because they are ill.
- Programs should screen children prior to admittance for diseases that are too contagious or serious.
- When medically fragile and technologically dependent children are admitted to the rest program, a professional nurse should be on site.
- Parents should visit a program and evaluate it prior to using its services. Some things to look for:

    Is the facility clean, and does the staff disinfect furniture, materials, and equipment?

Program in Practice

RAINBOW RETREAT: "R AND R" FOR ILL CHILDREN

Rainbow Retreat in Pasadena, California, is one of only a few programs that provide care, at three sites, for mildly ill children. Before using its services, parents preregister their children while they are well. Rainbow Retreat provides care for children between the ages of two months and twelve years. After they have registered, parents call the center when they need care for their ill children. One of the staff members goes over a checklist to determine whether the child can be admitted directly from the home to the center or whether he or she must first see a physician. When parents bring their children in, a staff member does a health assessment regarding the nature of the illness and confirms whether they can attend. Care at Rainbow Retreat costs $5 an hour, with a four-hour minimum stay. Some employers pay for this.

Rainbow Retreat will not admit children with measles, mumps, or chicken pox; otherwise, children with almost any other illness are admitted as long as the child's physician feels he or she can be in the program. Rainbow Retreat will accept children with fevers, ear infections, vomiting, diarrhea, or colds; it will also accept an asthmatic child who has seen a doctor and whose asthma is under control; postsurgical children who have had,

for example, an appendectomy or tonsillectomy; and children in casts who have sprains or fractures.

Although children can stay at Rainbow Retreat for as long as they need ill care, the average stay is two days. Some children stay only one day. Rainbow Retreat can care for ten children at one time; the daily average is six children. During their stay, children are involved in developmentally appropriate activities that take into consideration their illness and physical condition. At the end of each day, parents receive a report that includes temperature, diet, output, activity participation, and recommendation for future care.

National Pediatric Support Services is the parent organization of Rainbow Retreat as well as a number of regular child care centers. Rainbow Retreat shares a site with each of the child care centers. In addition to a registered nurse, the staff includes a licensed practical nurse and a teaching assistant. The staff takes special precautions to assure that furniture, equipment, and materials are disinfected daily to control infections, yet at the same time they allow children freedom to use the center. As a further precaution to limit the spread of germs, no one wears shoes into Rainbow Retreat.

Does the staff meet the needs of children quickly, pleasantly, and respectfully?

Are licenses, staff qualifications, menus, and daily schedules clearly posted?

Does each child have a written record of his or her medical and educational progress while in the program?

According to Gail D. Gonzalez, past president of NASCDC, "Every program, despite its design, should have a yearly evaluation to assure that there are appropriate procedures in place to prevent contamination and infections. In any quality sick day care program, children are happy, parents are trustful of the care, and health professionals are comfortable with the services."[9]

DAY CARE FOR CHILDREN WITH AIDS

What do you do for child care if you and/or your child has AIDS? One solution is to send your child to a child care center designed especially for children with AIDS. Although children with AIDS are covered under the provisions of the Americans with Disabilities Act (see chap. 11), some child care centers take children with AIDS and others will not. Both these situations pose a problem if a parent with AIDS must work, is sick, or needs to go to the doctor. (See the Program in Practice feature on page 184.)

BEFORE- AND AFTER-SCHOOL CARE

In many respects, public schools are logical places for before-and after-school care. They have the administrative organization, facilities, and staff to provide such care. Many taxpayers and professionals have always believed that schools should not sit empty in the afternoons, evenings, holidays, and summers. So, using the resources already in place for child care seems to make good sense. This is why in many communities public schools are helping meet the need for after-school child care.

The Dade County, Florida, public schools provide after-school care for 17,000 students in 189 elementary schools. The school district operates eighty-seven after-school centers with its own personnel, fifty-eight are operated by the YMCA, twenty-one by the YWCA, and twenty-three by the Family Christian Association of America. The district also operates seventy-nine before-school care sites at seventy-nine centers; twenty-seven are operated by the YMCA, two by the YWCA, and fifty are school based.

Special-needs students are mainstreamed at eighty-three schools with over 700 students in after-school care. Parents pay from $15 to $25 per week depending on the per-child cost at the individual school. Because the programs are school based and managed, the costs of services vary depending on the nature and cost of each program. Services begin at dismissal and end at 6:00 P.M. The curriculum of the child care programs includes Boy and Girl Scouts, 4-H, fun activities based on skills and concepts measured by state assessment tests for grades 3 and 5, drama, and ballet.

In other localities, after-school care may be no more than baby-sitting, with large groups of children supervised by a few adults. The cost of after-school care may be more than parents can afford. Also, when the program follows the school calendar, parents are left to find other care when school is not in session.

According to the *National Study of Before and After School Programs*,[10] about 1.7 million children in kindergarten through grade 8 are enrolled in 49,500 programs. The three most common sponsors of before- and after-school child care are the public schools, for-profit corporations, and nonprofit organizations. Nationally, as with the Dade County program described earlier, most care is provided after school. The study states that the ability of agencies to serve more poor families and to enhance the developmental nature of the programs is hampered by a reliance on paid tuition, a lack of access to "child friendly" space, high staff turnover, and inadequate programming for children beyond third grade.

Program in Practice

CARING FOR CHILDREN WITH AIDS

A unique program for some families is a child care center for children who have AIDS or whose parents have AIDS. One such center is operated by Children's Home Society of Florida, Southeastern Division, in Miami, Florida. After New York, Florida has the highest number of children with AIDS. The day care center enrolls ten children between the ages of eighteen months and five years. Eight are HIV positive or have AIDS; two are HIV negative.

Roger Croteau, a registered nurse, established the center with the help of a state grant because parents who have AIDS or whose children have AIDS have few options regarding child care. As Roger says, "Although times are changing and people are more understanding about AIDS, the fact remains that especially in children, AIDS carries a stigma."

When three-year-old Christopher entered the program, he had a mother and father. However, he lived with his mother and grandmother. His mother was having kidney failure as a result of AIDS and had trouble taking care of him, so his grandmother helped. His father was working twelve hours days and lived alone in their apartment.

Christopher is HIV infected and has AIDS. When he entered the day care program, he did not exhibit any signs of infection and took AZT (an antiviral drug) four times a day. Socially, Christopher was introverted and shy and would cling to his parents. His grandmother was also working full-time, and his

mother could not spend much time with him because of her condition. The need for child care was obvious.

The day care program is a social and academic development program modeled after Head Start. The day care contracts with a local health agency for special services such as speech and hearing therapy and developmental assessment. Field trips are conducted once a week. Roger believes getting children out into the community is a good way to provide for their needs. As he says, "It is important for the children go on field trips once a week to provide the emotional, physical, and social stimulation that a lot of the families can't provide for their children due to the family conditions and parents' failing health."

In addition to Roger, the program is staffed by a certified teacher and teacher aide. This provides a five-to-one child-staff ratio.

Christopher has blossomed as a result of being in the program. He gets along well with other children and adults, is very talkative, and is no longer as shy as he used to be. Christopher is a very bright child and cognitively is developmentally above average.

Six months after enrolling in the day care program, Christopher's mother died. Prior to her death, she was as involved in Christopher's day care as much as her illness would allow her. She volunteered in the classroom and attended parent meetings. She was a strong advocate for the children. She

LATCHKEY CHILDREN

Every day, many children stay home by themselves until it is time to go to school or their parents return from work. Children who care for themselves before and/or after school are referred to as *latchkey* or *self-care children*. While there are risks associated with young children providing themselves self-care, one reality of contemporary

attended a conference of the Association for the Care of Children's Health in Washington, D.C., and took part in a parent networking weekend. At such conferences, parents learn about similar programs and are encouraged to return to their hometown and build a support network and advocate for chronically ill children.

Christopher's father is involved in his care and is supportive of his attendance at the child care center. He may be HIV positive but refuses to be tested.

A number of things make this child care program unique:

- ■ It provides a nondiscriminatory environment for children with AIDS. Although child care programs cannot legally discriminate, some nonetheless do. The staff acknowledges from the beginning the HIV status of the children. They are willing to administer AZT to the children, with parental consent.

- ■ The staff makes a point of academically stimulating the children to try to maintain their developmental levels. They feel this is important because the children may be absent because of their illness.

- ■ The staff meets once a month with a special immunology team from a local hospital to discuss families' and children's health statuses and medical treatments.

- ■ A monthly parent meeting is parent driven; that is, the agenda is family focused,

and parents set the topics of discussion, such as emphasizing infection control and disease reduction. For example, they discuss the do's and don'ts of home hygiene, such as the need for cleanliness and the types and uses of solutions that kill HIV. They address the dangers of exposure to childhood diseases such as chicken pox. Children with AIDS are much more vulnerable to the side effects of childhood diseases. Therefore, they require additional medication to help them battle effects of the diseases. They also talk about topics that other parents might not consider important, such as not allowing their children to play in sandboxes which are bacteria breeding grounds.

- ■ The staff helps parents learn the necessity of providing a balanced nutritional program that is appropriate for their children's HIV symptoms.

A primary goal of the program is to mainstream the children into Head Start, early intervention programs, and other pre-K programs. Roger and the staff work for *full inclusion* of the children in regular programs. Roger believes there is currently a need for child care for children with AIDS, but the long-term goal is to not have such programs. "Kids need to be with kids and have as normal a childhood as possible," he explains.

life is that thousands do, as many as 2.1 million children between the ages of 5 and 13. Some states have laws against leaving children under a certain age (usually 12) alone without supervision. Many parents may not be aware of these laws or may feel they really have no choice. In fact, for some parents, self-care for their children is a positive choice. The following example illustrates that some children are successful in the process of self-care.

Eight-year-old Myra Martinez, an only child, takes the school bus home each day from school. With the house-key hung around her neck, she lets herself in and cares for herself from 3:30 until 6:30 P.M., when her parents arrive home.

Myra follows a routine she and her parents have worked out for her well-being and safety. When she gets home, Myra immediately "beeps" her mother at work. This way, her mother knows Myra is home and returns her call. Myra stays in the house, does not answer the door for strangers, and does not have friends over while her parents are not home. In addition, Myra and her parents have rehearsed what to do in an emergency. Myra is very happy and self-confident about taking care of herself. As she says, "I feel very independent, and I like being able to take care of myself."

Early childhood professionals are in unique positions to advise and work with parents about the self-care of their children. Some guidelines to share with parents are as follows:

- Do not expect children to assume more responsibilities than they are capable of. Some children are more responsible than others. Parents and professionals can help children assume responsibilities by helping them learn to do things for themselves.
- Establish rules that children must follow when they are caring for themselves. Some rules to consider:

  Do not leave the house.

  No other children or adults are allowed to visit.

  Decide who is in charge when more than one child is involved.

  Decide whether the child is *not* to answer the door for anybody *or* whether the child may answer the door for relatives and previously approved adults such as the next-door neighbor.

- Set up emergency procedures.

  Post a list of all emergency numbers: police, fire, 911.

  Instruct children about what to do in an emergency.

- Show children how to do certain things *or* tell them they cannot do certain things. If children can fix a snack, what kind? Can they use the stove? Microwave? Some parents have children do chores such as washing clothes. Other parents view this time as a good time for children to do their homework.
- When possible, have children call a parent when they get home from school. Parents, friends and relatives can periodically check on their children.

MILITARY CHILD CARE

The Army, Navy, Air Force, Marine Corps, and Coast Guard operate Child Development Programs at over seven hundred locations throughout the world and within the United States. The armed services are the largest providers of employer child care services. The programs offer care of all kinds—hourly, part-day, full-day, before and after school, evening and weekend—to children of military families and other Department of Defense personnel. Furthermore, the armed services operate center programs ranging in size from 29 to 450 children. Infant care accounts for 40 percent of all child care services provided by the armed services. These programs help family members meet their military responsibilities secure in the knowledge that their children are receiving quality care.

Military child care programs are funded through Defense Department appropriations, parents fees, and funds from local programs. Department of Defense funds usually cover the costs of facilities, utilities, supplies, and equipment; parent fees cover the cost of staff salaries.

The armed forces provides great career opportunities for early childhood professionals. It offers one of the best job opportunities in the world; in fact, the military offers many job opportunities *around* the world. A so-called horizontal employment pathway is the opportunity to be a teacher in a center or a home child care provider. A vertical pathway is entering as a teacher, moving up to an assistant center director, then a center director, and so forth (see Figure 5–8).

The military also offers a full range of professional training that enables personnel to assume a wide range of jobs; in other words, the military grows its own professionals. The needs of military child care are just too vast for the military to rely on other agencies (i.e., community colleges, colleges, universities). Consequently, the military trains its personnel and promotes from within.

NANNIES

Nannies were in great demand as child care providers during the 1980s. The demand for nannies has somewhat abated partly because of the cost of hiring a nanny and partly because parents are rethinking their and their children's lifestyles. More parents are committed to doing with less rather than more, as was typical of the 1980s. Still, some upwardly mobile parents who can afford to do so are hiring nannies (or *mannies*, as males are called). Although an *au pair*, the traditional mother's helper (often from Europe) has always been part of the child care scene, nannies are more highly skilled. A nanny is usually trained in child development, infant care, nutrition, grooming, manners, and family management.

Nannies' living arrangements, compensation, and duties vary greatly from family to family. Some live and work in the home twenty-four hours a day, while others work an eight- to ten-hour day and have their own homes. Some nannies have responsibility for child care only; others also assume household responsibilities, including meal preparation; others include teaching their charges as part of their responsibilities. In addition to a salary, some nannies receive paid vacations, medical benefits, and use of a car. Besides providing quality child care, a nanny is a constant presence in a child's life. A trained nanny is a valuable addition to the family and provides more than just child care.

FIGURE 5–8   Army Child Development Services

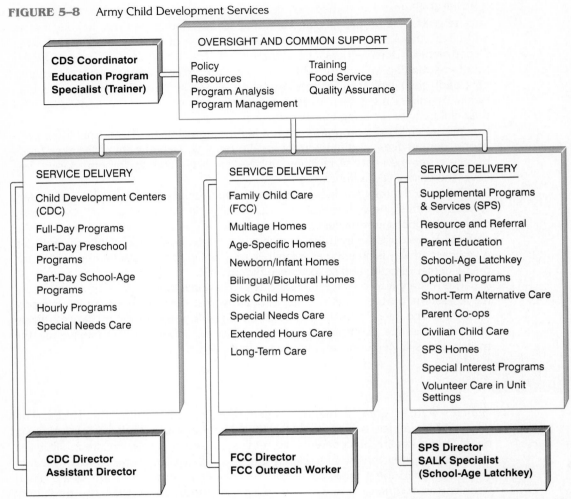

OVERSIGHT AND COMMON SUPPORT

Policy	Training
Resources	Food Service
Program Analysis	Quality Assurance
Program Management	

CDS Coordinator

Education Program Specialist (Trainer)

SERVICE DELIVERY

Child Development Centers (CDC)

Full-Day Programs

Part-Day Preschool Programs

Part-Day School-Age Programs

Hourly Programs

Special Needs Care

CDC Director
Assistant Director

SERVICE DELIVERY

Family Child Care (FCC)

Multiage Homes

Age-Specific Homes

Newborn/Infant Homes

Bilingual/Bicultural Homes

Sick Child Homes

Special Needs Care

Extended Hours Care

Long-Term Care

FCC Director
FCC Outreach Worker

SERVICE DELIVERY

Supplemental Programs & Services (SPS)

Resource and Referral

Parent Education

School-Age Latchkey

Optional Programs

Short-Term Alternative Care

Parent Co-ops

Civilian Child Care

SPS Homes

Special Interest Programs

Volunteer Care in Unit Settings

SPS Director
SALK Specialist
(School-Age Latchkey)

Source: U.S. Army Community and Family Support Center, 2461 Eisenhower Ave., Alexandria, Virginia 22331. Used by permission.

TRAINING AND CERTIFICATION FOR EARLY CHILDHOOD PERSONNEL

A major challenge facing all areas of the early childhood profession is the training and certification of those who care for and teach young children. Training and certification requirements vary from state to state, but more states are tightening standards for child care, preschool, kindergarten, and primary personnel. Many states have mandatory training requirements that an individual must fulfill before being certified as a child care worker. The curriculum of these training programs frequently specifies mandatory inclusion of topics. For example, in Florida, all child care personnel must complete the Department of Health and Rehabilitation Services' twenty-hour child care training course. The course is composed of four modules:

1.   State and local rules and regulations governing child care
2.   Health, safety, and nutrition
3.   Identifying and reporting child abuse and neglect
4.   Child growth and development

In addition, all child care personnel must complete an annual eight-hour in-service training program.

Certificate Programs

Many high schools and vocational education programs conduct training leading to an entry-level certificate. This training certifies people to act as child care aides.

Associate Degree Programs

Many community colleges provide training in early childhood education that qualifies recipients to be child care aides, primary child care providers, and assistant teachers.

Baccalaureate Programs

Four-year colleges provide programs that result in early childhood teacher certification. The ages and grades to which the certification applies vary from state to state. Some states have separate certification for prekindergarten programs and nursery schools; in other states, these certifications are "add-ons" to elementary (K–6, 1–6, 1–4) certification.

Master's Degree Programs

Depending on the state, individuals may gain initial early childhood certification at the master's level. Many colleges and universities offer master's level programs for people who want to qualify as program directors or assistant directors or who may want to pursue a career in teaching.

The CDA National Credentialing Program

At the national level, the Child Development Associate (CDA) National Credentialing Program offers early childhood professionals the opportunity to develop and demonstrate competencies for meeting the needs of young children. A CDA is "able to meet the specific needs of children and who, with parents and other adults, works to nurture children's physical, social, emotional, and intellectual growth in a child development framework."[11]

The CDA program, begun in 1971, is a major national effort to evaluate and improve the skills of caregivers in center-based preschool settings, center-based infant/toddler settings, family day care homes, home visitor settings, and bilingual settings—programs that have specific goals for bilingual development children. The CDA National Credentialing Program is operated by the Council for Early Childhood Professional Recognition. The council has two options for obtaining the CDA credential. One option, the CDA Professional Preparation Program–P3, allows candidates to work in postsecondary institutions as part of the credentialing process. The second option is the direct assessment method, which is designed for candidates who have child care work experience in combination with some early childhood education training.

A candidate for the CDA credential in any setting must first meet these eligibility requirements:

- Be eighteen years old or older
- Hold a high school diploma or equivalent

To obtain the CDA national credential, candidates under the direct assessment option must meet these additional eligibility requirements:

- 480 hours of experience working with children within the past five years
- 120 hours of formal child care education and training within the past five years

The candidate must then feel competent in the six CDA competency areas (see Appendix A).

The CDA Professional Preparation Program

To obtain credentialing by means of this option, the candidate must meet the two general eligibility requirements and must also identify an advisor to work with during the year of study, which is made up of three phases.

The first phase of this model is the fieldwork phase. It involves study of the Council Model Curriculum, "Essentials for Child Development Associates Working with Young Children." This curriculum includes the six competency areas listed in Appendix A. The second phase is the course work, in which the candidate participates in seminars offered in community colleges and other postsecondary educational institutions. These seminars are designed to supplement the curriculum and are administered by a seminar instructor. The third and last phase is the final evaluation, which takes place in the candidate's work setting or field placement.

The results of all three phases of the Professional Preparation Program are sent to the council office for review and determination of whether the candidate has successfully completed all aspects of the CDA Professional Preparation Program. To date, more than fifty thousand persons have been awarded the CDA credential.

Additional information about the CDA can be obtained from the Council for Early Childhood Professional Recognition, 1341 G Street, NW, Suite 400, Washington, D.C. 20005-3105. The toll-free number is 1-800-424-4310; the fax number is (202) 265-9161.

Bryan Keith Davis was awarded the milestone 50,000th credential in 1993. One of the few males to be awarded the CDA credential, Brian says, "The most exciting part about being a caregiver is when a child learns something for the first time. Knowing I've made a difference in their lives is rewarding."

WHAT CONSTITUTES QUALITY CHILD CARE?

It is easy to say that parents should seek out and insist on quality child care. For their part, many parents do try to find what they believe is quality child care for their children.

How Parents Define Quality

When parents select child care they view the following as important factors:[12]

1.	Quality	37%
2.	Care by relatives	30%
3.	Convenient location	10%
4.	Reasonable cost	9%
5.	Other	14%

When parents say they want quality, what do they mean? Parents report that the most important aspects of quality for them are

- child-related characteristics, including child-staff ratios, group size, and age ranges;
- provider-related characteristics, including a warm and loving teaching/parenting style, reliability, training, and credentials;
- program-related characteristics, including preparation for school, cognitive and social development, religious instruction, and instruction in own culture; and
- facility-related characteristics, including toys, equipment, homelike setting, and health and safety issues.[13]

We know from our previous discussions that there is more to quality than these elements. So, while professionals applaud and support parents' quest for quality, much still needs to be done to educate parents and the public about the full dimensions of child care.

The following guidelines can assist early childhood professionals as they educate parents to a deeper understanding of the dimensions of quality care.

Developmental Needs

Good child care provides for children's needs and interests at each developmental stage. For example, infants need good physical care as well as continual love and affection and sensory stimulation. Toddlers need safe surroundings and opportunities to explore. They need caregivers who support and encourage active involvement.

Appropriate and Safe Environment

At all age levels, a safe and pleasant physical setting is important. Such an area should include a safe neighborhood free from traffic and environmental hazards; a fenced play area with well-maintained equipment; child-sized equipment and facilities (toilets, sinks); and areas for displaying the children's work, such as finger painting and clay models. The environment should also be attractive and cheerful. The rooms, home, or center should be clean, well lit, well ventilated, and bright.

Caregiver-Child Ratio

The ratio of adults to children should be sufficient to give children the individual care and attention they need. The NAEYC guidelines for child care ratio of caregivers are 1:3 or 1:4 for infants; 1:3 or 1:4 for toddlers; and 1:8 to 1:10 for preschoolers, depending on group size.

Research supports the belief that when children are cared for in programs that follow these guidelines for group size, they receive better care. In a study by Howes, Phillips, and Whitebook on the effects of adult-child ratios on quality they found:

> When five or more children were cared for by one adult in infant classrooms and nine children in toddler and preschool classrooms, at least 50 percent of the children were in classrooms rated as inadequate in caregiving. When five or more children were cared for by one adult in infant groups, eight or more children in toddler groups and preschool groups, at least 50 percent of the children were in classrooms rated as inadequate in activities. Children in infant classrooms with 1:3 or less ratios, toddler classrooms with 1:4 or less ratios, and preschool classrooms with 1:9 or less were more likely than children in classrooms with worse (higher) ratios to experience both caregiving and activities rated as good or very good.[14]

Policy recommendations and state laws governing child-adult ratios in child care programs are frequently at odds with each other. The ratios vary greatly from state to state and are often higher than child care professionals prefer. The recommendations of NAEYC regarding staff-child ratios are shown in Figure 5–9.

Figure 5–10 shows current child-staff ratios by age and program auspices and compares these ratios to NAEYC's recommendations.

Developmentally Appropriate Program

The program should have a written, developmentally based curriculum for meeting children's needs. The curriculum should specify activities for children of all ages that caregivers can use to stimulate infants, provide for the growing independence of toddlers, and address the readiness and literacy skills of four- and five-year-olds. The program should go beyond good physical care to include good social, emotional, and cognitive care as well. It should include a balance of activities, with time for playing indoors and outdoors and for learning skills and concepts.

Family Involvement

Parents and other family members should learn about the child care setting and their children's growth and development. Parents need encouragement to make the child care services part of their lives, so they are not detached from the center, its staff, or what happens to their children.

FIGURE 5–9   Staff-Child Ratios and Group Size

Age of Children*				Group Size						
	6	8	10	12	14	16	18	20	22	24
Infants (birth to 12 months)	1.3	1.4								
Toddlers (12 to 24 months)	1.3	1.4	1.5	1.4						
2-year-olds (24 to 36 months.)		1.4	1.5	1.6†						
2- and 3-year-olds			1.5	1.6	1.7†					
3-year-olds						1.7	1.8	1.9	1.10†		
4-year-olds							1.8	1.9	1.10†		
5-year-olds							1.8	1.9	1.10†		
6- to 8-year-olds (school age)							1.8	1.9	1.10	1.11	1.12

Source: *Accreditation Criteria and Procedures of the National Academy of Early Childhood Programs* (Washington, D.C.: National Association for the Education of Young Children, 1984), p. 24.

*Multiage grouping is both permissible and desirable. When no infants are included, the staff-child ratio and group size requirements shall be based on the age of the majority of the children in the group. When infants are included, ratios and group size for infants must be maintained.

†Smaller group sizes and lower staff-child ratios are optimal. Larger group sizes and higher staff-child ratios are acceptable only in cases where staff are highly qualified.

FIGURE 5–10   Average Group Size and Number of Children per Staff Member in Centers by Age of Child and Auspices

	Group Size	Children per Staff Member
By Age of Child*		
Under 1 year only	7 (6–8)	4.0 (3–4)
1-year-olds only	10 (6–12)	6.2 (3–5)
2-year-olds only	12 (8–12)	7.3 (4–6)
3- to 5-year-olds	17 (14–20)	9.9 (7–10)
By Auspices†		
Nonprofit		
Head Start	19	8.4
Public school	16	7.4
Religious sponsor	16	8.7
Other sponsor	20	8.8
Independent	16	8.4
For-profit		
Chain	18	11.0
Independent	15	9.0
All Centers	**16**	**8.8**

Source: Barbara Willer, "An Overview of the Demand and Supply of Child Care in 1992," *Young Children* (January 1992), p. 21. Copyright © 1992 by the National Association for the Education of Young Children. Reprinted by permission.
*NAEYC recommendations in parentheses.
†Groups of 3-year-olds only.

Staff Training and Development

Whether in a family or center setting, child care providers should be involved in an ongoing program of training and development. The CDA program is a good way for staff members to become competent and maintain the necessary skills. Program administrators should have a background and training in child development and early childhood education. A director of a child care program or agency should have a bachelor's degree in early childhood education, certification, or, at least, special college work in this area. Knowledge of child growth and development is essential for caregivers. Films, books, training in clinical settings, and experiences with children help professionals know about development. Professionals need to be developmentally and child oriented rather than self- or center oriented.

Knowledge of Children

Child care providers, especially those of infants, should be sensitive to the adjustments children make when they come into a child care setting. The environment and the people are new to them. A baby who has been the only child at home and cared for only by the mother or father has a lot to adapt to in a center setting, where there are more infants and more caregivers. Many center infant programs make sure that one care provider takes care of the same infants, to give them the security that comes from familiarity. Likewise, new caregivers must also adjust when they come into the home or center, since every child has a unique personality, preferences, and ways of responding to the world.

Quality and Professionalization Organizations

Many professional organizations are involved in determining criteria for quality programs. The Southern Early Childhood Association (SECA) issued a position statement listing the following fundamental needs that must be met in child care:

- The child needs to feel that the situation is a safe and comfortable place for him to be.
- The child needs to learn to feel good about himself.
- A child needs to be fully employed in activities that are meaningful to him—that support him in his full-time quest to learn.
- A child needs to develop ability to live comfortably with other children and adults.
- A child needs to have his physical development supported and be helped to learn health, nutritional, and safety practices.
- The child in care needs to feel that there is consistency in his life and a shared concern for him among the important people in his life—his parents and his caregivers. [15]

Program Accreditation

In any discussion of quality, the question invariably arises, "Who determines quality?" Fortunately, the NAEYC has addressed the issue of a standard in its Center Accreditation Project (CAP). The CAP is a national, voluntary accreditation process for child care centers, preschools, and programs that provide before- and after-school care for school-age children. Accreditation is administered through NAEYC's National Academy of Early Childhood Programs. The NAEYC cites these benefits of accreditation:

- Accredited programs are recognized as quality programs.
- Parents will seek out accredited programs.
- The staff learns through the accrediting process.

The criteria addressed in the accreditation project are interactions among staff and children, curriculum, staff and parent interactions, administration, staff qualifications and development, staffing patterns, physical environment, health and safety, nutrition and food service, and program evaluation. [16]

ADVOCACY AND QUALITY CHILD CARE: CHILD CARE AWARE

Child Care Aware is a large national public awareness effort to help parents select quality child care. It is sponsored by the Dayton Hudson Foundation, Mervyn's, and Target Stores in cooperation with the National Association of Child Care Resource and Referral

Program in Practice

ACCREDITING A PROGRAM

The Decision

The idea of getting our two centers, Open Door Preschools, accredited by NAEYC was exciting for all of us. Accreditation requires higher standards than licensing. The accreditation process would provide a good way to evaluate and improve our centers' programs. We had always felt that we were providing excellent care for our children; accreditation would confirm this belief. This would also be an excellent opportunity for the staff, parents, and teachers to work together toward a major goal. The decision to apply for accreditation was made, and as educational director of Open Door, I would oversee the accreditation process.

Preparation

Following the NAEYC guidelines, we examined and evaluated our programs in various areas, such as goals and philosophy, long-range written curriculum plan, interaction among staff and children, staff-parent communication, policies, staff-training plans, and so on. After a comprehensive evaluation of all these aspects, we identified their strengths and weaknesses. Also, through weekly staff meetings, we came up with a set of plans to accomplish our goal.

We looked for areas in which to strengthen our programs, including health and safety, environment, and nutrition. We also added several pieces of playground equipment and rearranged the classroom environment. To better prepare our teachers, we invited special speakers to meet with the staff and had our staff attend conferences and workshops. Among the topics were providing appropriate activities for the children, interacting with the children, handling inappropriate behavior, and promoting communication among parents and staff.

Also, at this time we had the staff evaluate the program and themselves, and I conducted classroom observations of the teachers, followed by evaluations and discussions of their performance. Parents as well as teachers of both centers answered questionnaires. We had some difficulty getting questionnaires back from parents and realized that we should have communicated better with the parents. We would have received better response if we had gone over items in the questionnaires with the parents and made them aware of the whole process. Also, we should have taken more time at each step in the process to make sure that teachers were prepared for self-evaluation, the staff questionnaires, and classroom observation.

Contributed by Dr. Nira Changwatchai, site director, The Open Door (South Location), Austin, Texas.

Agencies (NACCRRA), Child Care Action Campaign (CCAC), NAEYC, and the National Association for Family Day Care (NAFDC). In addition to the goal of helping parents recognize quality child care, the initiative also is noteworthy for the partnership between national child care organizations and philanthropic organizations.

LOCATING CHILD CARE

The majority of parents (66 percent) find child care for their children through friends, neighbors, and relatives. Parents obviously feel more comfortable using this informal system, probably believing they can trust these people's judgments.

Occasionally, during this self-study, the professionals became worried about being observed (after we submitted the materials to NAEYC, validators would come to observe the professionals and centers). After all, what would we do if something went wrong or if somebody were sick? In this case, at the end of the day, validators would talk with the director and staff to clear up these points. I also worried about the paperwork that needed to be compiled and organized. However, we overcame these worries and were ready to move on with all the support from our board of directors and parents.

After the improvements were made and the documents prepared, I mailed all the documentation—which included the Program Description and Center Profile, summary sheets of classroom observation, staff questionnaires, and parent questionnaires—to NAEYC.

Validator Visiting Day

About a month later, the validators arrived. Everyone was excited and nervous at the same time. Even though the validators were very friendly, we each felt as if we were once again student teachers. The difference was that this time we had volunteered to partici-

pate. However, things went smoothly. Everyone tried to be calm and act as we normally would. As the days went by, we began to relax. It was not as hard as we had anticipated.

Success

After the visits, we had to wait for the results. The validators were here only to confirm our evaluation of our center; the actual decision would be made by a commission. Finally, in June we were informed that both centers, Open Door North and Open Door South, had received accreditation. We were two of the first five centers in Austin to be accredited.

It was certainly worthwhile to go through the process, although everyone had to work hard. We were proud to be recognized as having high-quality programs by the early childhood profession, and we were proud to provide quality care and education for children. After accreditation, centers must report any changes or improvements to NAEYC annually until it is time to reaccredit again in three years. Having learned a lot our first time around, we had our third center accredited one year after it opened. From now on, accreditation should not be as hard.

Thirteen percent of parents locate their child care through newspaper advertisement and bulletin boards; 9 percent use a resource and referral system.[17] The use of child care information and referral systems is increasing. These referral systems, usually computer based and operated by municipal governments, universities, corporations, and nonprofit agencies, help parents gain access to information about competent, convenient, and affordable care. Information supplied to parents includes names, addresses, and phone numbers of providers and basic information about the services, such as hours of operation, ages of children cared for, and activities provided.

CHILD CARE ISSUES

As in any profession, child care is not without controversies. The following sections explore some of the issues that confront society as a whole, child care professionals, and the profession.

Who Does Child Care Serve?

Children

One issue concerns whether child care should benefit parents or children. There is a tendency to interpret child care as a service primarily for parents, which critics feel has caused the quality of child care programs to suffer. The needs of children should not be secondary to those of parents. A primary concern for all caregivers should be quality care for children.

Families

Child care is increasingly seen as a comprehensive service for *families*. This means that child care programs are not only providing services for children. They consider the entire family—children, parents, and extended relatives—as the recipients of their services. This expansion of services is in keeping with the trend by early childhood professionals to pay greater attention to *ecology*—the environment in which children are reared and the influences these environments have on children. These environments include family, home life and settings, siblings, community agencies, and so forth. All these influence children's growth and development. It makes sense to consider *family systems* when providing services to and for children.

Which Children

Ultimately, a system of child care must be available to all parents and their children. Until this is possible, the nation needs priorities. Should child care be aimed at low-income parents who need to work or engage in work training programs? Or should priority be given to abused and neglected children? Questions such as these are not easy to answer given the limited resources the United States allocates to quality child care.

Interactions Among the Home, the Workplace, and Child Care

Child care professionals are increasingly aware that the family and workplace environments are critical to the final outcome of children's well-being. Accordingly, professionals are seeking ways to help parents in their demanding, stressful roles as modern parents and employees. These interactions take many forms, as we have discussed in this chapter, but the link between the home and the child care program must be strengthened as a means of providing both quality family life situations and quality child care. More and more, early childhood professionals recognize that child care is a family support system and not a substitute for the home and family. The parenting and developmental information child care programs provide and the skills they help parents develop are as important as the quality of their care.

Likewise, what happens in the workplace and the benefits parents have or do not have affects their performance as both employees and parents. A corporation that has a program of benefits that helps support families (e.g., leave for caring for sick children, flexible work schedules) has more productive workers as it simultaneously contributes to an enhanced quality of life for its parent/employees.

State and National Licensing Standards

Some early childhood advocates maintain that one way, perhaps the only way, to increase the quality of child care is to have a system of national standards that all child care programs would have to meet. These standards would relate particularly to child-staff ratios, group size, and staff training. Advocates of such standards believe they would bring a badly needed uniformity to child care regulations. The closest that the United States comes to having a system of national standards is through programs that are federally funded and supported, such as Head Start.

As you might expect, not everyone agrees that a system of national standards is necessary or desirable. Some bemoan the federal control that standards would bring. Others think that child care is and should be a state- and locally regulated function. What will likely happen is that as more federal support is given to child care, attempts will be made to provide federal regulations as well.

The Effects of Child Care on Children

Quite often in discussions about and conceptualization of child care, we have a homogenized view of what it is and what it should be; that is, we think one universal kind of quality child care exists that is good for all children. And, in a sense, this is exactly true; the profession can and does maintain, for example, that low caregiver-child ratios and small group size indicate quality child care. But is the same kind of child care necessarily good for all children? As we become more knowledgeable about the effects of child care on children in general, we must pay more attention to its influence on different children. Caregivers must continue to think about how to tailor different kinds of child care services based on children's individual differences, cultures, and family situations. (Chap. 14 discusses in detail how to provide culturally sensitive care for infant and toddlers.) This is precisely the kind of response professionals are taking in relation to children with special needs.

We must also recognize that to a large extent, how parents view child care is a product of their culture, upbringing, and education. Some parents see child care as a service they should use only for the least amount of time, while others may consider child care a major contributor to their children's rearing and are perfectly willing to have their children in a program most of the day.

The particular effects of child care on children is a much debated topic. In an effort to address conflicting research results and the profession's response to research studies, the National Center for Clinical Infant Programs (NCCIP), the National Academy of Science, and the Institute of Medicine issued this statement about child care:

> When parents have choices about the selection and utilization of supplementary care for their infants and toddlers and have access to stable child care arrangements featuring skilled, sensitive and motivated care givers, there is every reason to believe that both children and families can thrive. Such choices do not exist for many families in America today, and inadequate care poses risks to the current well-being and future development of infants, toddlers and their families.[18]

This policy statement makes it clear that the nation, states, and individual programs must work toward developing an agenda for ways to provide all the nation's children with stable child care arrangements and skilled, sensitive, and motivated child care workers.

Recent research reveals that child care may have significant educational benefits for children. Some evidence indicates that toddlers have a remarkable ability to learn new skills from each other. Also, the abilities one toddler learns can quickly spread to others. In other words, infants and toddlers can learn and remember what they see other children do. Furthermore, what they learn in the play or child care group is retained outside the group setting.[19] This kind of research illustrates the increasing numbers of studies that attest to the positive benefits for children in quality preschool and child care programs.

Improving the Quality of Child Care

One obvious way to improve the quality of child care programs and personnel is through more stringent facility licensing and training requirements. Also, parents can and should be educated to the need for quality child care. Parents often help perpetuate poor child care by accepting whatever kind of care they can find. If they are properly educated and involved in programs, they can help make child care better for everyone.

Quality Child Care for All

Although we talk a great deal about quality child care and identify the criteria that constitute quality, the fact remains that quality child care is not widely available to the majority of families. One challenge is determining how to provide quality programs that will enhance and promote families' optimum development. Not only does the quality of child care differ from program to program, it also varies from one state to another, as we see in the variations in mandated adult-child ratios and the training guidelines required as a condition for employment.

Furthermore, when families and children at risk receive poor-quality child care, this places children in double jeopardy. While all children must have quality care, those who are at risk will benefit the most from quality care because it helps moderate the effects of risk factors. However, as we previously stated in this chapter, children from middle-class families are the most likely to receive poor-quality care. A constant challenge to all involved in the education and development of young children must be to upgrade all child care programs.

In addition, the comprehensive nature of good child care programs must be extended. Many still believe that if a program provides germfree custodial care, it is a good one. Unfortunately, however, some of these programs have sterile philosophies and activities as well.

Who Should Pay for Child Care?

The federal government's support for child care services has been shrinking over the past decade, although Head Start receives enhanced funding (see chap. 10). This means that the three other available sources for child care support—state agencies, private agencies, and consumers—will, of necessity, have to increase their support.

As fewer and fewer federal dollars become available, more parents will be called on to help pay the real cost of their children's care. Yet the fact remains that most parents who have to work probably cannot and will not be able to afford the cost of quality child care programs. Efforts to have child care subsidized by employers, foundations, and charitable groups will have to increase.

How Much Should Child Care Cost?

Traditionally, child care has been a low-cost and low-paying operation. Many programs emphasize keeping costs low so that working and low-income parents will not be overburdened; this results in a very low pay scale for child care workers. Thus, as the cost of child care is kept low, the true cost is subsidized by low-paid workers. Yet, if child care costs rise to provide workers with fairer wages, many families who can hardly afford what they now pay would be priced out of the services. Also, as more public schools offer programs for four-year-olds, many child care workers with degrees will be attracted to these programs by the higher salaries. This shift could tend to lower the quality of child care programs and further decrease salaries.

Two noteworthy efforts are currently under way to help address issues associated with the cost of child care and low child care worker wages.

Worthy Wages Coalition

The Worthy Wage Coalition is an association of organizations whose primary focus is specifically to address issues of inadequate compensation in child care. Inadequate compensation for child care workers, which includes salaries and benefits, cannot be considered in isolation of other factors. These include quality for children and affordability for families. The Worthy Wage Coalition is coordinated by the Child Care Employees Project, a national organization dedicated to improving child care wages, working conditions, and access to training. Its address and phone number are 6536 Telegraph Avenue, Suit A-201, Oakland, California 94609; (510) 653-9889.

Full Cost of Quality

The Full Cost of Quality program is an initiative of NAEYC. It is designed to highlight public awareness regarding what constitutes quality in early childhood services and the cost of fully meeting professional recommendations regarding high quality.

Parents need to know and understand that quality child care costs money. In addition, when parents understand what constitutes quality, they are more likely to seek it out and demand it. All early childhood professional have an obligation to promote and provide high-quality programs, help parents understand the importance and cost of quality, and advocate to the public regarding quality child care. For more information about the Full Cost of Quality program, contact the Public Affairs Division of the National Association for the Education of Young Children, 1509 16th St., NW, Washington, D.C. 20036; (800) 424-2460.

Agreement Between Parents and Care Providers

As we noted at the beginning of this chapter, increasing numbers of parents turn over their children to outside child care providers. Many parents entrust their children to people they know very little about. They may be reliable and trustworthy, or they may not. Parents are now better informed as to what constitutes quality child care. Although they are becoming more selective, they still leave their children with people who are relative strangers. It is therefore extremely important for quality child care providers to work closely with parents from the time of their initial contact, usually at registration. Professionals must demonstrate to parents their competence in areas such as child development, nutrition, and planning and implementing developmentally appropriate curricula. They must also assure parents that they will maintain daily communication about the child's progress. Additionally, parents and professionals must agree on discipline and guidance procedures, and professionals and social service agencies need to guide parents as to what constitutes good child rearing and appropriate discipline practices.

FUTURE TRENDS IN CHILD CARE

What does the future hold for child care? Listed here are some continuing trends:

- The number of women who enter the work force, full- or part-time, will increase. In particular, women with children under three will represent the fastest-growing group of parents seeking child care. For many working parents, staying home with their children is not an option or desire.

- The number of employer-sponsored or -assisted child care programs will grow because of employees' demands for child care and the obvious advantages to employers. The greater the benefits to the employer, the more likely they will increase their involvement in child care.

- Public schools will participate to an even greater extent in providing child care, especially before- and after-school care. Also, preschool programs for three- and four-year-olds are a rapidly growing part of public schools programs. In reality, these programs ease parents' needs for child care. Within the next decade, programs for infants and toddlers may become part of the regular services of some public schools.

- The federal government's role in child care will become less significant, and the influence of individual states will increase. The federal government will not make comprehensive services available to all children because the expense of a national child care program would necessitate reordering federal budget priorities. The trend in federal support to social service programs is to return monies to the states in the form of block grants, which allows states greater freedom and autonomy in determining how funds are spent. The block grant procedure also reduces direct federal control of state and local programs.

- Policymakers and early childhood professionals will seek to expand alternatives to traditional child care as we know it. More emphasis will be placed on alternatives to child care such as parenting leaves from work for child care, flexible work schedules, and work-at-home options.

- More child care will be tied to parent employment training. That is, child care will be used as one means of helping parents get employment by providing care for their children while they undergo employment training.

- The distinction between child care and preschool will further disappear until the two concepts are a unified whole. We already see evidence of this in many early childhood programs, and in many respects, Head Start is leading the way in this unified approach to early childhood education. Also, the public school entry into the child care arena, on an ever-accelerating scale, helps erode the boundaries between child care and preschool programs.

- Probably one of the most significant changes in child care already under way is that child care will be more family centered and more dedicated to helping parents achieve their goals. As child care strives to involve families, it will also be more collaborative with other programs and agencies that can assist in family-centered programs. Both of these new directions will have many implications for new professional roles.

Child care represents, in many respects, the new frontier in early childhood education. Many more families need full-service, comprehensive programs. More opportunities for enhanced collaboration and greater linkages are apparent with each passing year. What is necessary is for early childhood professionals to continue to professionalize the field and make child care the program that can and is willing to provide for families' and children's needs.

READINGS FOR FURTHER ENRICHMENT

American Academy of Pediatrics. *Child Care: What's Best for Your Family* (Elk Grove Village, IL: American Academy of Pediatrics, 1992)

Guidelines for selecting quality child care based on twenty-one questions about "What parents should ask about. . . ." Ideal resource to distribute at parent meetings and seminars. One free copy of this booklet can be obtained by sending a self-addressed, stamped envelope to American Academy of Pediatrics, Department C, Child Care Brochure. P.O. Box 927, Elk Grove Village, IL 60009-0927.

Beardsley, Lyda. *Good Day/Bad Day: The Child's Experience of Child Care* (New York: Teachers College Press, 1990)

A typical day is described in both good and mediocre child care centers, which gives insight into what happens to children in different kinds of settings, especially for those who have not spent much time in such places.

Blum, Lauri. *Free Money for Day Care* (New York: Simon & Schuster, 1992)

Provides information on funding assistance available, in all fifty states and for parents of all income levels, to aid parents in meeting the necessary costs of day care. Gives names of corporations that fund day care.

Clarke-Stewart, Alison. *Daycare*, rev. ed. (Cambridge, MA: Harvard University Press, 1993)

Discusses day care, as an issue of concern to parents, with an attempt to educate all Americans about the importance of quality day care. Describes the history, problems, needs, and effects of child care on children.

Flating, Sonja. *Child Care: A Parent's Guide* (New York: Facts on File, 1991)

Systematic handbook of advice on how to find the best child care. Guides the reader through each step of the decision-making process, beginning with a self-test and concluding with an action plan for implementing the child care

choice and the impact of that choice on the family. Includes discussions of the types of care presently available.

Gillis, Margaret McCusker, Anne M. Kealey, Margaret M. Sawyer, and Michele Dempsey-Dubrow. *Little People: Big Business, A Guide to Successful In-Home Day Care* (Whitehall, VA: Betterway, 1991)

A complete guide to setting up a day care business. Provides advice about equipment needed, licensing, record keeping, contracts and agreements as well as how to establish and maintain professional standards and quality care. Suggests a year's curriculum.

Gonzalez-Mena, J. *Tips and Tidbits: A Book for Family Day Care Providers* (Washington, D.C.: National Association for the Education of Young Children, 1991)

Provides practical information and advice designed to help family day care providers solve problems they confront in daily work with children.

Klein, Abbie Gordon. *The Debate over Child Care 1969–1990* (Albany: State University of New York Press, 1992)

New and interesting perspective on problems facing child care in the United States. Identifies social factors and ideologies that have prevented a unified social policy for child care services. In particular, analyzes the advantages and disadvantages of five different sponsors of child care: public schools, the church, private enterprise, nonprofit organizations, and corporations.

Kontos, S. *Family Day Care: Out of the Shadows and into the Limelight* (Washington, D.C.: National Association for the Education of Young Children, 1992)

A thorough, readable examination of research on family day care. Responds to questions such as, Who are the nation's family day care providers? What services do they provide to what families and children?

Lusk, Diane, and Bruce McPherson. *Making Day Care Work for You and Your Child* (New York: Morrow, 1992)

Deals with how to live with day care. The most frustrating problems experienced by parents, children, and teachers in an early childhood program are pinpointed, using real-life examples, and multiple solutions are offered.

Seligson, Michelle, and Michael Allenson. *School-Age Child Care: An Action Manual for the 90s and Beyond*, 2d ed. (Westport, CT: Greenwood, 1993)

Explores the challenges that child care providers will encounter as the twenty-first century approaches. This action manual guides readers through the processes of designing, implementing, and managing programs for children ages five to twelve.

U.S. Department of Labor. *Employers and Child Care: Benefitting Work and Family* (Washington, D.C.: Author, 1991)

Child care is a critical labor force issue, and this book was designed for employers and employees who are concerned with developing programs and policies to assist in quality, cost-effective child care programs.

Zigler, Edward F., and Mary E. Lang. *Child Care Choices* (New York: Free Press, 1991)

Helps answer many perplexing questions about child care and early childhood education in the United States—for example, what are the special needs of infants, toddlers, and preschoolers in various settings? Reviews different approaches to child care that have been attempted in the United States. Offers a comprehensive strategy for enabling parents to choose from among a wide variety of child care options.

ACTIVITIES FOR FURTHER ENRICHMENT

1. Survey parents in your area to determine what services they desire from a child care program. Are most of the parents' child care needs being met? How is what they want in a child care program similar to and different from standards for quality child care?

2. Visit child care center programs for infants and toddlers. What makes each program unique? Which program would you feel most comfortable working in? Why? Which program would you feel most comfortable enrolling your infant or toddler in? Why?

3. Determine the legal requirements for establishing center and home child care programs in your state, city, or locality. What kind of funding is available? What are the similarities and differences of establishing home and center programs? What is your opinion of the guidelines?

4. Invite people from child care programs, welfare departments, and social service agencies to speak to your class about child care. Find out who may attend child care programs. Also, determine what qualifications and training are necessary to become a child care employee.

5. After visiting various child care programs, including center and home programs, discuss similarities and differences. Which of the programs provides the best services? What changes or special provisions need to be made to improve the success of these kinds of programs?

6. Gather information on franchised early childhood programs. What are the similarities and differences? In your opinion, what factors are necessary for the success of these kinds of programs?

7. Review the yellow pages of the your telephone directory for child care programs. Call several for information about their programs. What conclusions can you draw from your calls?

8. Develop a checklist to show parents what to look for in a quality child care program.

9. Visit an employer-sponsored child care program, and describe it to your classmates. List the pros and cons for parents and for employers of employer-sponsored child care.

10. Survey parents to determine the strengths and weaknesses of the child care programs they use.

11. Conduct a survey to learn the cost of child care services in your area. Arrange your data in a table. What conclusions can you draw?

12. Tell why or why not you would leave your six-week-old infant in center child care, and list the pros and cons for such care. Share this information with your classmates.

13. Compare and contrast the child care systems of other countries presented in this chapter with child care in the United States. Could we improve the U.S. system using the ideas of other countries? What determines the type of child care a particular nation provides?

14. Is the CDA credential recognized in your state? If yes, find out how many centers are participating in the CDA program.

NOTES

1. State of California Health and Welfare Agency, *Family Day Care Homes for Children* (July 1992), Division 12, Chapter 3 (Sacramento: Department of Social Services, 1992), p. 1.

2. *Pennsylvania Family Day Care Regulations* (1992), p. 3290-8.

3. *Minimum Standards for Child Care Services* (Miami: State of Florida, Department of Health and Rehabilitative Services, 1986), p. 4.

4. John H. Winters, *Minimum Standards for Day Care Centers* (Austin: Texas Department of Human Services, May 1985), p. 2.

5. Program fact sheet, Child Nutrition Division of the Food and Nutrition Service, U.S. Department of Agriculture.

6. Sandra L. Hofferth, April Brayfield, Sharon Deich, and Pamela Holcomb, National Child Care Survey 1990 (Washington, D.C.: Urban Institute Press, 1991), p. 199.

7. Ibid., p. 198.

8. Children's Defense Fund, State of America's Children (Washington, D.C.: Author, 1992), p. 63.

9. Interview with Gail D. Gonzalez, October 1993.

10. U.S. Department of Education, Office of Policy and Planning.

11. Carol Brunson Phillips, *Field Advisor's Guide for the CDA Professional Preparation Program* (Washington, D.C.: Council for Early Childhood Professional Recognition, 1991), p. 2.

12. Hofferth et al., *National Child Care Survey 1990*, p. 215.

13. Ibid.

14. Carrollee Howes, Deborah Phillips, and Marcy Whitebook, "Thresholds of Quality: Implications for the Social Development of Children in Center-Based Child Care," *Child Development* 63 (1992), p. 454. Used by permission.

15. Southern Association on Children under Six, *Position Statement on Quality Child Care* (pamphlet).

16. National Association for the Education of Young Children, *Accreditation by the National Academy of Early Childhood Programs* (Washington, D.C.: Author, 1991), p. 2.

17. Hofferth et al., *National Child Care Survey 1990*, p. 213.

18. National Center for Clinical Infant Programs, *Infants, Families, and Child Care: Toward a Research Agenda* (Washington, D.C.: Author, 1988), p. 6.

19. Daniel Goleman, "Baby Sees, Baby Does, and Classmates Follow," *New York Times*, July 21, 1993, p. B7.

THE CHILDREN'S CENTER AT THE ST. PAUL

The St. Paul Companies, a worldwide insurance organization based in downtown St. Paul, Minnesota, operates a new $1.6 million on-site child care center for its employees. Called The Children's Center at The St. Paul, the facility is part of the company's new $70 million addition to its headquarters complex.

Already a leader in family-oriented benefits design, The St. Paul's employees research on child care showed that headquarters employees have some thousand children age ten and younger; of that group, 75 percent said they depend on child care services from someone other than spouses or partners. The center can accommodate 118 children in its eight classrooms: 24 infants (the largest infant program in

the state), 30 toddlers, and 64 preschoolers. The 12,500-square-foot facility allows for 55 square feet of classroom space per child. This is 20 square feet more than that required by state codes.

In the infant rooms, antimicrobial carpet with extra padding creates a comfortable and bacteria-free crawl area. Additional sound-proofing also has been installed in the infant sleeping rooms. The toddler and preschool rooms feature eating areas, with meals served family-style, play areas, and bathroom facilities. All water temperatures are preset for the children's safety.

The center features both indoor and outdoor play areas. The "large-muscle" playroom, at the west end of the facility, is primarily for use during inclement weather. It has portable basketball hoops, slides, crawl blocks, and an indoor tricycle path. The 15,000-square-foot outdoor play area is made up of a garden area and two playgrounds with equipment sized to fit specific ages. Each playground features child-safe equipment and a two-inch rubber safety surface to cushion falls and reduce the risk of injuries.

Contributed by Diane Cushman, health and family program specialist, The St. Paul Companies, St. Paul, Minnesota; photos © 1991 Mike Haber-mann.

A

S tride Rite's intergenerational day care center is the first center in American business to pair the care of children and the elderly.

On a Tuesday morning at the Stride Rite Corporation's headquarters in Cambridge, Massachusetts, an unusual scene is unfolding. Two elderly women, Eva DaRosa and Margaret Donovan, are ferrying preschoolers, two at a time, from their classroom to the lunchroom where the staff is working with the children and elders to make a handprint mural. Everyone is enjoying the project, but the real fun of the day has turned out to be the ride in Margaret's wheelchair. Each pair of children takes turns riding in her lap and pushing the chair with Eva's help. One child gets to ride on the way out, the other on the way back to their classroom. The women are enjoying the event almost as much, and after a dozen runs have dubbed themselves the pony express.

The center's design allows a traffic pattern that encourages the informal interaction between children and elders while also providing privacy for each group. It is divided into two separate wings that are connected through a large central area. The children's wing has four classrooms for different age groups; the elders' wing has three rooms designed for a variety of quiet and noisy activities. The central or middle core houses administrative offices, a kitchen and dining facility, and a resource center that includes conference rooms and a library. Among the special features of the facility are wide doorways to accommodate wheelchairs, and floor surfaces that make mobility easier for frail elders. An outdoor space was built to accommodate and stimulate both groups of clients.

B

The Stride Rite program meets the physical, social, and intellectual needs of each group through a carefully planned and supervised curriculum that fosters regular daily contact between the elders and children. Intergenerational curricula include (for children and elders separately and together) reading and writing stories, table games, celebrating holidays and birthdays, cooking and eating, arts and crafts, and taking field trips.

The intergenerational aspects are proving to be a great success for both children and elders.

"The relationship between the children and the elders has really exceeded our expectations," says Karen Leibold, director, Work and Family Programs. "We thought we'd need to bring them together slowly, with a lot of staff direction and with specific projects to do. What we've found is that they're like magnets with each other. They just come together. They enjoy each other's company. Sometimes it can be for five minutes at the end of the day, when they meet in the entryway. Sometimes it's waving across the lunchroom at each other. Sometimes it can be an extended period of time, reading books together, or cooking, or making things with blocks or Play-Doh."

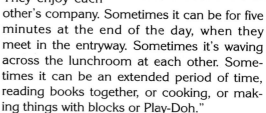

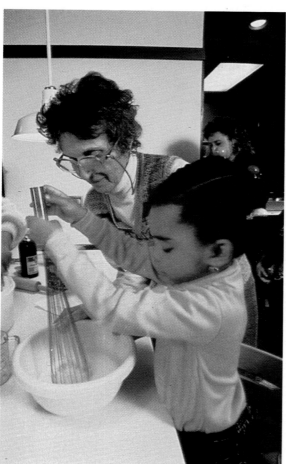

The intergenerational day care program is an outstanding example of how the needs of employees, employers, children, and elders can be met through collaborative planning.

Contributed by Stride Rite Corporation, Cambridge, Massachusetts; photos by Rick Friedman.

The Thurgood Marshall Child Development Center is sponsored by the United States Supreme Court, the Administrative Office of the U.S. Courts, the Federal Judicial Center, the Judicial Panel on Multidistrict Litigation, and the U.S. Sentencing Commission. The Thurgood Marshall Child Development Center is built around a philosophy of caring, flexibility, and choice for children. The dynamic Marshall environment satisfies the young child's sense of wonder, sociability, and eagerness to explore. A bowl of water and a sponge, for instance, offers a chance for a child and teacher to talk, laugh, and explore together.

Marshall teachers are talented, highly trained, and academically credentialed. They nurture and

facilitate integrated learning continuously, making sure to follow a child's own rhythms. Teachers understand that children are learning all the time through active and purposeful involvement with people, materials, and ideas.

An atmosphere of ongoing learning energizes and vitalizes the center, characterized by play-oriented, child-initiated curriculum. Moms and dads visit for story time or lunch. Children, staff, and parents take walks in the neighborhood and trips to museums and monuments.

Staff enjoys playing with the children on the carpet and feeding them while seated comfortably on the sofa or rocking chairs. Infants are on totally individual schedules as requested by their parents. Plenty of stimulating toys are available

D

for the babies and their caregivers to enjoy. The staff understands the importance of talking and singing to the babies throughout the day.

There is a great respect for toddlers and two-year-olds. Each new step is applauded and cheered. The children are marching (or rather toddling!) toward more independence each day and need to have many choices of activities throughout the day. Toys and equipment such as soft building blocks are selected to help toddlers develop gross- and fine-motor skills.

The preschoolers' area provides preschoolers opportunities to explore and choose activities as they see fit. Art, music, gross- and fine-motor activities, dramatic play, blocks, science, and books are some of the interesting centers around the room. The staff plans activities for the groups as well as for individual children in order to foster their development in all areas. The Marshall Center is a busy, happy place where children are respected and loved.

Contributed by Madeline Fried and Margery Sher, Fried & Sher, Inc., Herndon, Virginia; photos by Fried & Sher, Inc.

E

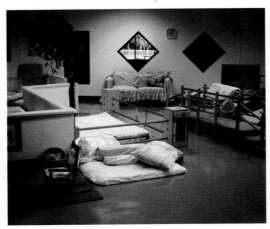

A Nido consists of nine babies from two months to twelve to fourteen months (when the child is walking well). With three adults, a three-to-one child-caregiver ratio is maintained at all times. The Montessori Nido environment is divided into four main areas. The first area, the **movement area**, is equipped with a thin covered mattress with kiosks and bars the babies use for pulling up; other mattresses may be available around the room depending on the space. The movement area usually includes a stair as well.

The **sleeping area**, the second area of the Nido environment, is an isolated area with individual futons (the tiniest babies' futons are enclosed in a Plexiglas "crib" that sits on the floor). This area provides a quiet place for the babies to sleep whenever they need to, but it also has easy access to the rest of the environment so that when a baby awakens, he or she can crawl or walk to the adults. The children are free to go onto their futons when they are sleepy and come off when they awake.

The third area, the **eating area**, is equipped with low, heavy "weaning" tables and chairs instead of high chairs. The children are capable of getting into and out of the chairs with ease. The adults sit on low stools facing the children when feeding them. This area is not carpeted; the children are encouraged to feed themselves as soon as possible but are never left to eat alone as eating is a "social occasion." An area is provided for nursing moms to come and nurse their babies, and several adult areas are available for giving bottles to those babies who take them.

The last area, the **physical care area** (changing, bathing), is beside a water source. Elsewhere in the room there is a rocking chair for comforting babies. Most of the room is tiled—not carpeted—except for the sleeping area. This allows the babies to move around more easily and

makes cleaning and sterilizing the floor possible. A low stool is used to accommodate children learning to change their own panties. Panties are used instead of diapers so that babies can move more easily and become more aware of their bodily functions. This environment has no walkers, swings, playpens, cribs, high chairs—none of the devices sold to "aid" a baby's movement. Babies are placed on the floor and move everywhere.

There is no program, so to speak, in the Nido. The children spend their time as they would at 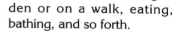 home: sleeping, being awake and interacting with adults and other children, using the materials provided for their development, moving about the environment, going outside—either in the garden or on a walk, eating, bathing, and so forth.

Contributed by Judith Orion, director, A. M. I. Assistance to Infancy Training, Denver, Colorado; photos provided by The Montessori Institute, Denver, Colorado.

Reggio Emilia is a city in northern Italy. The excellent educational program the city offers its children, based on providing an educational environment that encourages learning, is known as the Reggio Emilia approach. Reggio Emilia sponsors infant programs for children three months to three years and programs for children three to six years.

Each of the Reggio schools can accommodate seventy-five children, with each group or class consisting of about twenty-five children with two coteachers. Children of single parents and children with disabilities have priority in admission. The other children are admitted according to a scale of needs. Parents pay on a sliding scale based on income.

The Reggio Emilia approach is unique in that the children are encouraged to learn by investigating and exploring topics that interest them. Learning is a social and cultural process that does not occur in isolation from other children, adults, and the environment. The Reggio school environment is designed to accommodate the child's developmental culture and provide a wide range of stimulating media and materials for children to express their learning, such as words, sounds and music, movement, drawing, painting, sculpting and modeling clay or wire, making collages, using puppets and disguises, photography, and more.

Reggio children typically explore topics by way of group projects. This approach fosters a sense of community, respect for diversity, and a collaborative approach to problem solving—both important aspects of learning. Two coteachers are present during the project to guide the children and widen the range of learning. This is the way Carlina Rinaldi, *pedagogista* (consultant, resource person), describes a project:

> A project, which we view as sort of an adventure and research, can start through a suggestion from an adult, a child's idea, or from an event such as a snowfall or something else unexpected. But every project is based on the attention of the educators to what the children say and do as well

H

as what they do not say and do. The adults must allow enough time for the thinking and actions of children to develop.*

The children pictured here are working on a special "Shadows" project. The exploration of shadows has great attraction for children and many implications for learning with pleasure. Children discuss their ideas about shadows and formulate hypotheses about shadows' origin and destiny. Exploration of shadows in the schools for Reggio Emilia continues to be a favorite theme for children and teachers. In this specific episode, after exploring shadows outside (at different times of day) and inside (with artificial

light and flashlights), the teacher extends the interest of a child who has represented a little girl with full skirt by posing a question-problem to her.

*Carlina Rinaldi, "The Emergent Curriculum and Social Constructivism," in Carolyn Edwards, Lella Gandini, and George Forman, eds., *The Hundred Languages of Children* (Norwood, NJ: Ablex, 1993), p. 108.

Contributed by Lella Gandini, Northhampton, Massachusetts. Photos from the city of Reggio Emilia, teachers, and children of the preprimary schools Diana and Gulliver, Tutto ha un'ombra meno le formiche *(Everything but the ant has a shadow) (City of Reggio Emilia, Italy: Department of Education Via Guido da Castello, 1990), p. 12; photos provided by Lella Gandini.*

TEACHING AND LEARNING WITH COMPUTERS: ONE SCHOOL'S SUCCESSFUL EXPERIENCE

The Alexander D. Henderson University School, a K–8 public school in Boca Raton, Florida, is the perfect example of the successful incorporation of computers to foster learning. Learning at this school is accomplished through a series of related computer activities that involve all the child's senses. The program is called "Teaching and Learning with Computers," or TLC, and is a complete instructional model. At Henderson, students first encounter computers in kindergarten.

In Elaine Lewis's kindergarten class, students work with the literacy program *Writing to Read 2000*, which includes using books and audio tapes. They also spend time in a "Make Words" center that contains tactile letters of plastic and felt or stencils for creating letters and words.

The program at this stage is a useful diagnostic tool. Lewis says she often observes children as they work at the various centers to see eye-hand coordination, audio discrimination, and if they are following directions.

In the first grade and higher, the TLC program expands to include science and mathematics programs as well. The incorporation of computers in these grades is more comprehensive.

Suzanne Sturrock, one of Henderson's first grade teachers, says her children are in learning centers all day. In the morning, she talks to the whole class for about thirty minutes to preview the day's lessons and to review what they did the day before. Then the students form small groups and begin moving through the room's five centers. At the end of the rotation, everyone gathers to talk about what they have

done. At this point Sturrock evaluates the effectiveness of the tasks and assigns enrichment or review tasks for students as needed.

Additionally, Sturrock likes the integrated nature of the program, which addresses social, educational, and technological learning skills simultaneously. "It seems to meet the needs of all children by using a variety of activities. I can remediate slower learners and provide enrichment for gifted ones," she says.

As the children progress through each grade, the program grows and changes with them to suit their needs. The technology component in the program provides an element of recency other educational materials cannot maintain.

Contributed by Barbara Bittner, director, Alexander D. Henderson University School, Boca Raton, Florida; photos supplied by International Business Machines Corporation.

K

VISTAKIDS COMPUTER LITERACY PROGRAM

Hispanics consider education one of the keys to the future. Unfortunately, report after report reveals the high school dropout rate and underachievement of Hispanic children. One solution to these problems is the VistaKids program. It is designed to boost the reading, writing, and math skills of low-income Hispanic children and improve their sense of competence and self-esteem through the use of computers.

Another issue facing Hispanic children is technological literacy. Research shows that Hispanic children are less likely to have access to computers than their non-Hispanic counterparts. Thus technological literacy is another goal of VistaKids.

VistaKids is a project sponsored by VISTA Magazine in collaboration with SER-Jobs for Progress, a nonprofit educational and employment training organization serving Hispanics.

The VistaKids program is located at Shenandoah Elementary School in Miami, Florida, an intercity school with an enrollment of 1,295 students in grades 1–5. (The pre-K and kindergarten children are in a satellite facility at a nearby middle school.) The school serves many recently arrived families from Cuba, Nicaragua, Guatemala, and El Salvador. When the children enter school, they speak little if any English. Most are eligible for free breakfast and lunch programs.

The VistaKids program is an after-school program that begins at 2:00 P.M. and runs until 5 P.M. The children in the 2 P.M.–3 P.M. class ride the buses home. The children in the 3 P.M.–5 P.M. classes

are in the after-school child care program. The program also operates on Saturday from 10 A.M. to 12 P.M., and the parents are actively involved in bringing their children, learning to assist in the program, and learning the value their English fluency plays in their children's lives. Parents also realize the importance of learning English and supporting their children's English use in out-of-home settings.

Enrollment in VistaKids is open to all children. However, space and the number of computers are limited, so only sixty children are enrolled at one time. Approximately 240 children are served throughout the school year. Enrollment is based on children's English for Speakers of Other Languages (ESOL) level. All children in VistaKids are at the lowest ESOL

L

level, which means they do not know enough English to get by.

Becky Bolivar, director of the program, and eight aides work with the children after school and on Saturdays. As Becky explains, "To promote comprehension and to help the children to become English-proficient as soon as possible, we avoid translating into Spanish, and the VistaKids program is entirely in English."

Teresa Estrada, a VISTA director and the driving force behind the program explains: "When underprivileged immigrant children start the early grades with practically no knowledge of English because in most cases they do not even hear English at home, unless they get some specialized attention at school, they are likely to fall well behind their learning

potential. If the trend continues beyond third grade, it becomes in many cases a hopeless situation, and by the time they enter high school, they are at-risk students very likely to drop out. The objective of our program is to make sure that all kids enrolled in the program enter third grade at a level of learning at least equal to that of their more affluent Anglo counterparts." And Teresa continues: "The results so far have been outstanding and even beyond our expectations. The minds of those recently arrived children are like sponges, and it is incredible how much and how fast they learn under the proper learning environment. We are very encouraged and feel confident that VistaKids is a program that is making a difference."

Children such as Licet Ramirez, Carlos Ortiz, Jeanette Martinez, and Katrine Arauz are enthusiastic about the program, too. As Carlos says, "I want to come all the time." Katrine has bigger plans: "I want my parents to get me a computer so I can work at home!"

Principal Maria Llerena wishes there were more space and more computers and says, "When our young students join the VistaKids program, they begin to see school as a positive place to be, and they soon realize that learning can be fun."

Used with permission of VISTA Magazine, 999 Ponce de Leon Blvd., Coral Gables, Florida; photos by Michael Upright.

M

The Pacific Gas and Electric Company (PG&E) Children's Center is the first major corporate child care center to locate in downtown San Francisco. For PG&E, opening the Children's Center brings a new advantage to its downtown location, offering a way for employees to balance the demands for work and family.

The 9,000-square-foot Children's Center on the mezzanine floor of the headquarter building can accommodate up to sixty-six infants, toddlers, and preschoolers. The center's central location allows parents to leave their children in the morning, visit them at lunch or during breaks, and pick them up at the end of the day.

Inside the center, designers created an environment for learning, safety, and comfort. Classrooms and alcoves provide quiet space for reading, storytelling, or napping, while lofts and platforms offer ample practice for climbing and exploring—all in view of the center's professional caregivers.

Meeting individual needs is evident in the center's approach to physical activity. Opportunities for movement are a daily part of the indoor and outdoor environment.

The center upholds the premise that children learn by doing. Throughout the day, children have opportunities to participate in hands-on learning activities. Whether they are measuring sand, pouring water, or rattling instruments, children can feel, manipulate, and experiment with objects in an atmosphere of discovery. The center also places a high value on the learning acquired through play. Development of language, problem-solving skills, cooperation with others, as well as introductions to such cognitive concepts as mathematics are all important outcomes of children's play.

Infants enjoy a homelike environment with soft lighting, colorful spaces, and comfortable furnishings. Activities such as feeding, holding, talking, and playing seek to meet individual needs and schedules.

N

Toddlers enjoy their own component of the curriculum, in which they have a primary caregiver who supports their growing independence while emphasizing eating, toileting, language, and movement. As toddlers become more independent, they are able to play and interact with others in a challenging and fun setting.

The final component of the center's curriculum concentrates on preschoolers. The preschool program promotes the development of creativity and self-esteem through play activities in science, art, music, reading, drama, cooking, and blocks. Such activities build emotional and social skills while enhancing learning and achievement.

Contributed by Pacific Gas and Electric Company, San Francisco, California.

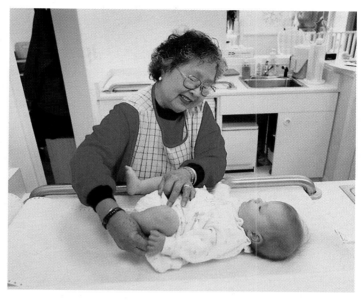

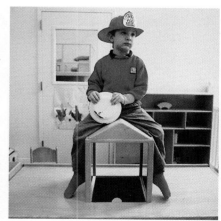

A *tesseract®* (in case you were wondering!) is a wrinkle in time. It is an imaginary corridor for traveling through space introduced in Madeline L'Engle's book *A Wrinkle in Time* (New York: Dell, 1962). The Tesseract® Way as a belief and educational system defines South Pointe Elementary School's approach to learning.* This philosophy places the child as the major focus and active participant within daily school activity.

South Pointe maintains a ratio of two teachers (one teacher and one associate teacher) for each group of thirty students. A Personal Education Plan™ is developed for each child. Within this

plan students and teachers work together to create and evaluate curriculum and learning. Teachers use learner outcomes to help students plan what they will learn, how they will learn it, and evaluate their own learning.

The math program is a great example of the Tesseract® Way in practice. At South Pointe math concepts are taught using manipulatives to small groups of children. In math class, children plan with their teacher what practice they will do each day and then they work independently at their own level and pace. Teachers model appropriate behaviors, observe, listen, respond, and guide children as they learn.

Parents are also actively involved. Four parent-teacher conferences are held per year. A unique feature is that the first conference is held before the school year begins, which allows parents to tell the school about their child.

At South Pointe everyone—parents, teachers, and students—works together to set new learning goals and find exciting, interesting ways to reach these goals!

*On September 3, 1991, South Pointe Elementary School in Miami, Florida, became the first public school in the nation operated by Education Alternatives, Inc., a for profit firm. Tesseract® is a registered trademark and Personal Education Plan™ is a trademark of Education Alternatives, Inc.

Photos by Michael Upright.

P

Infants and Toddlers
Development, Care, and Education

After you have read and studied this chapter, you will be able to:

- ☐ Identify reasons the number of programs for infants and toddlers has increased
- ☐ Comprehend infant and toddler development in the physical, motor, psychosocial, cognitive, and language areas
- ☐ Explain Piaget's cognitive theory as it relates to infants and toddlers
- ☐ Compare theories about the process of language development and acquisition
- ☐ Explain Erikson's theory of psychosocial development in the infant and toddler years
- ☐ Distinguish the developmental differences between infants and toddlers and the need to provide developmentally appropriate programs for each
- ☐ Analyze and understand the features that contribute to quality infant and toddler programs
- ☐ Identify what constitutes developmentally appropriate curricula for infants and toddlers
- ☐ Articulate and analyze issues involved in quality care and education for infants and toddlers

Interest in infants and toddlers is at an all-time high and will continue during the next decade. The growing demand for infant and toddler care and education stems primarily from the large number of women entering the labor force, the high divorce rate, and the economic need for both parents to work. It is also fueled by parents who want their children to have an "early start" and get off on the "right foot" so they can have an even better life than their parents. The acceptance of early care and education is also attributable to a changing view of the very young and the discovery that infants are remarkably competent individuals. Parents and early childhood professionals have combined forces to give infants and toddlers quality care and education without harmfully and needlessly pushing and hurrying them. This collaborative effort will continue.

PHYSICAL DEVELOPMENT

The infant and toddler years between birth and age three are full of many developmental milestones and social events. Infancy, life's first year, includes many firsts: the first breath, the first smile, first thoughts, first words, and first steps. Many significant developments also occur during toddlerhood, the period between one and three years; two are unassisted walking and rapid language development. Language and mobility are the cornerstones of autonomy that enable toddlers to become independent. These unique developmental events are significant for children as well as those who care for and teach them. How early childhood professionals and par-

Quality programs provide materials and activities for a wide range of infants' and toddlers' abilities. Good programs do not limit their activities and materials to the "average" infant or toddler but provide for each child's individual temperament, learning style, likes, dislikes, and developmental ability.

FIGURE 6–1   Height and Weight of Infants and Toddlers

Age	Males		Females	
	Height (inches)	**Weight (pounds)**	**Height (inches)**	**Weight (pounds)**
Birth	19.9	7.2	19.6	7.1
3 months	24.1	13.2	23.4	11.9
6 months	26.7	17.3	25.9	15.9
9 months	28.5	20.2	27.7	18.9
1 year	30.0	22.4	29.3	21.0
1½ years	32.4	25.3	31.9	23.9
2 years	34.5	27.8	34.1	26.2
2½ years	36.3	30.1	35.9	28.5
3 years	38.0	32.4	37.6	30.7

Source: Based on data in P. V. V. Hamill et al., "Physical Growth: National Center for Health Statistics Percentiles," *American Journal of Clinical Nutrition* 32 (1979), pp. 607–629.

ents respond to infants' firsts and toddlers' quest for autonomy helps determine how children grow and master the life events that await them.

To fully grasp their roles as educators and nurturers, early childhood professionals need to understand major events and processes of normal growth and development. To begin, we must recognize that infants and toddlers are not the miniature adults many baby product advertisements picture them to be. Children need many years to develop fully and become independent. This period of dependency and professionals' responses to it are critical for the developing child. Professionals must constantly keep in mind that "normal" growth and development are based on averages, and the "average" is the middle ground of development. (Figure 6–1 gives average heights and weights for infants and toddlers.) To assess children's progress, or lack of it, professionals must know the milestones of different stages of development. At the same time, to assess what is "normal" for each child, they must consider the whole child. They must look at cultural and family background, including nutritional and health history, to determine what is normal for that child. Professionals must also keep in mind that when children are provided with good nutrition, health care, and a warm, loving emotional environment, development tends toward what is "normal" for each child.

MOTOR DEVELOPMENT

Motor development is an important part of infant and toddler development because, as we have discussed in chapter 4, it contributes to intellectual and skill development. Human motor development is governed by certain basic principles:

FIGURE 6–2   Infant and Toddler Motor Milestones

Behavior	Age of Accomplishment for 90% of Infants/Toddlers
Chin up momentarily	3 weeks
Arms and legs move equally	7 weeks
Smiles responsively	2 months
Sits with support	4 months
Reaches for objects	5 months
Smiles spontaneously	5 months
Rolls over	5 months
Crawls	7 months
Creeps	10 months
Pulls self to stand	11 months
Walks holding onto furniture	13 months

Source: William K. Frankenburg, William Sciarillo, and David Burgess, "The Newly Abbreviated and Revised Denver Developmental Screening Test," *Journal of Pediatrics* 99 (Dec. 1981), pp. 996. Used by permission.

- Motor development is sequential (see Figure 6–2).
- Maturation of the motor system proceeds from gross (large) to fine behaviors. When learning to reach, for example, an infant sweeps toward an object with the whole arm; as a result of development and experiences, gross reaching gives way to specific reaching and grasping.
- Motor development is from *cephalo* to *caudal*—from head to foot (tail). This process is known as *cephalocaudal* development. The head is the most developed part of the body at birth; infants hold their heads erect before they sit, and sitting precedes walking.
- Motor development proceeds from the *proximal* (midline or central part of the body) to the *distal* (extremities), known as *proximodistal* development. Infants are able to control their arm movements before they can control finger movements.

Toilet Training

Toilet training (or *toilet learning* as it is sometimes called) is a milestone of the toddler period. This process often causes a great deal of anxiety for parents, professionals, and toddlers. American parents want to accomplish toilet training as quickly and efficiently as possible, but frustrations arise when they start too early and expect too much of children. Toilet training is largely a matter of physical readiness, and most child-rearing experts recommend waiting until children are two years old before beginning. Although some parents claim that their children are trained as early as one year, it is probably the parent rather than the child who is trained.

Toilet training is the process of helping children gain control over elimination. It is often not the quick and easy process parents and some caregivers hope for, because so many factors are involved—among them, the child's emotional and physical readiness and the parent's willingness to make it a cooperative effort. And, as this picture illustrates, learning to flush is also part of the process!

The principle of toilet training is that parents and professionals are helping children develop control over an involuntary response. When an infant's bladder and bowel are full, the urethral and sphincter muscles open. The goal of toilet training is to teach the child to control this involuntary reflex and use the toilet when appropriate. Training involves timing, patience, modeling, preparing the environment, establishing a routine, and developing a partnership between the child and parents/professionals. Another necessary partnership is between parents and professionals who are assisting in toilet training, especially when parents do not know what to do, are hesitant about approaching toilet training, or want to start the training too soon.

INTELLECTUAL DEVELOPMENT

As we learned in chapter 4, the first schemes are sensorimotor. According to Piaget, infants do not have "thoughts of the mind." Rather, they come to know their world by actively acting on it through their senses and motor action. According to Piaget, infants *construct* (as opposed to absorb) schemes using sensorimotor reflexive actions.

Infants begin life with only reflexive motor actions that are used to satisfy biological needs. In response to specific environmental conditions, the reflexive actions are modified through accommodation and adaptation to the environment. Patterns of adaptive behavior are used to initiate more activity, which leads to more adaptive behavior, which in turn yields more schemes. Consider sucking, for example, an innate sensorimotor scheme. The child turns the head to the source of nourishment, closing the lips around the nipple, sucking, and swallowing. As a result of experiences and maturation, this basic sensorimotor scheme is adapted or changed to include anticipatory sucking movements and nonnutritive sucking such as sucking a pacifier or blanket.

New schemes are constructed or created through the processes of assimilation and accommodation. Piaget believed children are active *constructors* of intelligence through assimilation (taking in new experiences) and accommodation (changing existing schemes to fit new information), which results in *equilibrium*.

Stages of Cognitive Development

Sensorimotor Intelligence

Sensorimotor intellectual development consists of six stages, shown in Figure 6–3.

Stage I: Birth to One Month.   During this stage, infants suck and grasp everything. They are literally ruled by reflexive actions. Reflexive responses to objects are undifferentiated, and infants respond the same way to everything. Sensorimotor

Professionals in quality programs plan developmentally appropriate activities for all children that are based on their interests and encourage active involvement. Helping children do things for themselves supports that independence. Toddlers need support in doing things for themselves. How can professionals help children become independent?

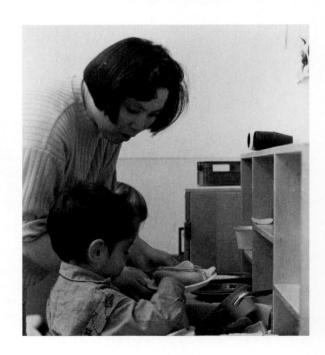

FIGURE 6–3 Stages of Sensorimotor Intellectual Development

Stage	Age	Behavior
I: Reflexive action	Birth to 1 month	Reflexive actions of sucking, grasping, crying, rooting, swallowing
		Through experiences, reflexes become more efficient (e.g., amount of sucking required for nourishment)
		Little or no tolerance for frustration or delayed gratification
II: Primary circular reactions	1 to 4 months	Acquired adaptations form
		Reflexive actions gradually replaced by voluntary actions
		Circular reactions result in modification of existing schemes
III: Secondary circular reactions	4 to 8 months	Increased responses to people and objects
		Able to initiate activities
		Beginning of object permanency
IV: Coordination of secondary schemes	8 to 12 months	Increased deliberation and purposefulness in responding to people and objects
		First clear signs of developing intelligence
		Continuing development of object permanency
		Actively searches for hidden objects
		Comprehends meanings of simple words
V: Experimentation (tertiary circular reactions)	12 to 18 months	Active experimentation begins through trial and error
		Spends much time "experimenting" with objects to see what happens; insatiable curiosity
		Differentiates self from objects
		Realization that "out of sight" is not "out of reach" or "out of existence"
		Beginning of understanding of space, time, and causality
VI: Representational intelligence (intention of means)	18 to 24 months	Development of cause-effect relationships
		Representational intelligence begins; can mentally represent objects
		Engages in symbolic imitative behavior
		Beginning of sense of time
		Egocentric in thought and behavior

schemes help infants learn new ways of interacting with the world, and the new ways of interacting promote cognitive development.

Grasping is one infant sensorimotor scheme. At birth, the grasping reflex consists of closing the fingers around an object placed in the hand. Through experiences and maturation, this basic reflexive grasping action becomes coordinated with looking, opening the hand, retracting the fingers, and grasping. In this sense, the scheme develops from a pure, reflexive action to an intentional grasping action. As an infant matures, in response to experiences, the grasping scheme is combined with a delightful activity of grasping and releasing things.

Stage II: One to Four Months.   The milestone of this stage is the modification of the reflexive actions of Stage I. Sensorimotor behaviors not previously present in the infant begin to appear: habitual thumb sucking (which indicates hand-mouth coordination), tracking moving objects with the eyes, and moving the head toward sounds (which indicates the beginning of the recognition of causality). Infants start to direct their own behavior rather than being totally dependent on reflexive actions. The first steps of intellectual development have begun.

Primary circular reactions begin during Stage II. A circular response occurs when an infant's actions cause a reaction in the infant or another person that prompts the infant to try to repeat the original action. The circular reaction is similar to a stimulus-response, cause-and-effect relationship.

Stage III: Four to Eight Months.   Piaget called this stage that of "making interesting things last." Infants manipulate objects, demonstrating coordination between vision and tactile senses. They also reproduce events with the purpose of sustaining and repeating acts. The intellectual milestone of this stage is the beginning of *object permanence*. When infants in Stages I and II cannot see an object, it does not exist for them—a case of "out of sight, out of mind." During the later part of Stage III, however, there is a growing awareness that when things are out of sight, they do not cease to exist.

Secondary circular reactions begin during this stage. This process is characterized by an infant's repeating an action with the purpose of getting the same response from an object or person; for example, an infant will repeatedly shake a rattle to repeat the sound. Repetitiveness is a characteristic of all circular reactions. "Secondary" here means that the reaction is elicited from a source other than the infant. The infant interacts with people and objects to make interesting sights, sounds, and events last. Given an object, the infant will use all available schemes, such as mouthing, hitting, and banging; if one of these schemes produces an interesting result, the infant continues to use the scheme to elicit the same response. Imitation becomes increasingly intentional as a means of prolonging an interest.

Stage IV: Eight to Twelve Months.   During this stage, the infant uses means to attain ends. Infants move objects out of the way (means) to get another object (end). They begin to search for hidden objects, although not always in the places they were hidden, indicating a growing understanding of object permanence.

Stage V: Twelve to Eighteen Months.   This stage, the climax of the sensorimotor period, marks the beginning of truly intelligent behavior. Stage V is the stage of experimentation. Toddlers experiment with objects to solve problems, and their experimentation is characteristic of intelligence that involves *tertiary circular reactions*, in which they repeat actions and modify behaviors over and over to see what will happen. This repetition helps develop an understanding of cause-and-effect relationships and leads to the discovery of new relationships through exploration and experimentation.

Physically, Stage V is also the beginning of the toddler stage, with the commencement of walking. Toddlers' physical mobility, combined with their growing ability and desire to experiment with objects, makes for fascinating and often frustrating child rearing. They are avid explorers, determined to touch, taste, and feel all they can. Although the term *terrible two's* was once used to describe this stage, professionals now recognize that there is nothing terrible about toddlers exploring their environment to develop their intelligence. Novelty is interesting for its own sake, and toddlers experiment in many different ways with a given object. They use any available item—a wood hammer, a block, a rhythm band instrument—to pound the pegs in a pound-a-peg toy, for instance.

Stage VI: Eighteen Months to Two Years.   This is the stage of transition from sensorimotor to symbolic thought. Stage VI is the stage of symbolic representation. *Representation* occurs when toddlers can visualize events internally and maintain mental images of objects not present. Representational thought enables toddlers to solve problems in a sensorimotor way through experimentation and trial and error and predict cause-and-effect relationships more accurately. Toddlers also develop the ability to remember, which allows them to try out actions they see others do. During this stage, toddlers can "think" using mental images and memories, which enables them to engage in pretend activities. Toddlers' representational thought does not necessarily match the real world and its representations, which accounts for a toddler's ability to have other objects stand for almost anything: a wooden block is a car; a rag doll is a baby. This type of play is also known as *symbolic play* and becomes more elaborate and complex in the preoperational period.

We need to keep in mind several important concepts of infant and toddler development:

1. The chronological ages associated with Piaget's stages of cognitive development are approximate. In fact, as we discussed in chapter 4, children can do things earlier than the ages assigned by Piaget. Professionals should not be preoccupied with children's ages but should focus on cognitive behavior, which gives a clearer understanding of a child's level of development. This is the true meaning of developmentally appropriate caregiving.

2. Infants and toddlers do not "think" as adults do; they come to know their world by acting on it and need many opportunities for *active* involvement.

Through experimentation and by talking with children, Piaget documented that they construct their own intelligence. It is important for professionals to provide young children opportunities and materials to actively explore and "experiment" within a safe, supportive environment.

3. Infants and toddlers are actively involved in *constructing* their own intelligence. Children's activity with people and objects stimulates them cognitively and leads to the development of mental schemes.

4. Parents and professionals need to provide *environments* and *opportunities* for infants and toddlers to participate in active involvement. These are two important conditions for intellectual development. Reflexive actions form the basis for assimilation and accommodation, which enable the development of cognitive structures. Professionals must ensure that infants and toddlers have experiences that will help assure success in the task of intellectual construction.

5. At birth, infants do not know that there are objects in the world and, in this sense, have no knowledge of the external world. They do not and cannot differentiate between who they are and the external world. For all practical purposes, the infant is the world. All external objects are acted on through sucking, grasping, and looking. This acting on the world enables infants to construct schemes of the world.

6. The concept of causality, or cause and effect, does not exist at birth. Infants' and toddlers' concepts of causality begin to evolve only through acting on the environment.

7. As infants and toddlers move from one stage of intellectual development to another, the previous stage is not replaced by the new; rather, later stages evolve from earlier ones. Schemes developed in Stage I are incorporated into and improved on by the schemes constructed in Stage II, and so forth.

LANGUAGE DEVELOPMENT

Language development begins at birth. Indeed, some argue it begins before birth. The first cry, the first coo, the first "da-da" and "ma-ma," the first word are auditory proof that children are participating in the process of language development. Language helps define us as human. Language acquisition represents one of humans' most remarkable intellectual accomplishments. How does the infant go from the first cry to the first word a year later? How does the toddler develop from saying one word to over fifty words a year later? While everyone agrees children learn language, not everyone agrees how children learn language. How does language development begin? What forces and processes prompt children to participate in one of the uniquely human endeavors? Let us examine some of the explanations.

Language Acquisition

Heredity plays a role in language development in a number of ways. First, humans have the respiratory and laryngeal systems that make rapid and efficient vocal communication possible. Second, the human brain makes language possible. The left hemisphere is the center for speech and phonetic analysis and the brain's main language center. But the left hemisphere does not have the exclusive responsibility for the language process. The right hemisphere plays a role in our understanding of speech intonations, which enables us to distinguish between declarative, imperative, and interrogative sentences. Without a brain that allows us to process, language as we know it would be impossible. Third, heredity plays a role in language development in that some theorists believe that humans are innately endowed with the *ability* to produce language.

Noam Chomsky is one proponent of the theory that humans are born with the ability to acquire language. He hypothesizes that all children possess a structure or mechanism called a language acquisition device (LAD) that permits them to acquire language. The young child's LAD uses all the language sounds heard to process many grammatical sentences, even sentences never heard before. The child hears a particular language and processes it to form grammatical rules.

Eric Lenneberg has studied innate language acquisition in considerable detail in many different kinds of children, including the deaf. According to Lenneberg:

All the evidence suggests that the capacities for speech production and related aspects of language acquisition develop according to built-in biological schedules. They appear when the time is ripe and not until then, when a state of what I have called "resonance" exists. The child somehow becomes "excited," in phase with the environment, so that the sounds he hears and has been hearing all along suddenly acquire a peculiar prominence. The change is like the establishment of new sensitivities. He becomes aware in a new way, selecting certain parts of the total auditory input for attention, ignoring others.[1]

The fact that children generate sentences they have never heard before is often cited as proof of innate ability. What would language be if we were only capable of reproducing the sentences and words we heard? The ability of children in all cultures and social settings to acquire language at a relatively immature age tends to support the thesis that language acquisition and use is more than a product of imitation or direct instruction. Indeed, children learn language without formal instruction.

The idea of a sensitive period of language development makes a great deal of sense and had a particular fascination for Montessori, who believed there were two sensitive periods for language development. This first sensitive period begins at birth and lasts until about three years. During this time, children unconsciously absorb language from the environment. The second period begins at three years and lasts until about eight years. During this time, children are active participants in their language development and learn how to use their power of communication. Milestones of language development for infants and toddlers are shown in Figure 6–4.

Environmental Factors

Theories about a biological basis of language should not be interpreted to mean that children are born with the particular language they will speak. While the ability to acquire language has a biological basis, the content of the language—vocabulary—is acquired from the environment, which includes other people as models for language. Therefore, development depends on talk between children and adults, and between children and children. Optimal language development ultimately depends on interactions with the best possible language models. The biological process of language acquisition may be the same for all children, but the content of their language will differ according to environmental factors. A child left to his or her own devices will not learn the language as well as the child reared in a linguistically rich environment.

For example, imagine the case of Genie, a modern-day "wild child." During her early days, Genie had minimal human contact, and her father and brother barked at her like dogs instead of using human language. She did not have an opportunity to learn language until she was thirteen-and-a-half years old, and even after prolonged treatment and care, Genie remained basically language deficient and conversationally incompetent.[2]

Behaviorism

One popular view of language development is that language is acquired through associations resulting from stimulus-response learning. Thus, learning theorists see language acquisition as a product of parents' and the environment's rewarding chil-

FIGURE 6–4   Language Development in Infants and Toddlers

Months of Age	Language
Birth	Crying
1½	Social smile
3	Cooing (long pure vowel sound)
5	"Ah-goo" (the transition between cooing and early babbling)
5	Razzing (child places tongue between lips and produces a "raspberry")
6½	Babbling (repetition of consonant sounds)
8	"Dada/Mama" (inappropriate)
10	"Dada/Mama" (appropriate)
11	One word
12	Two words
14	Three words
15	Four–six words
15	Immature jargoning (sounds like gibberish; does not include any true word)
18	Seven–twenty words
18	Mature jargoning
21	Two-word combinations
24	Fifty words
24	Two-word sentences
24	Pronouns (*I, me, you*; used inappropriately)

Source: A. J. Capute and P. J. Accardo, "Linguistic and Auditory Milestones during the First Two Years of Life," *Clinical Pediatrics* 17(11) (Nov. 1978), p. 848. Used by permission.

dren's language efforts. Parents, for example, reward children for their first sounds by talking to them and making sounds in response to the children's sounds. First words are reinforced in the same way, with parents (and others) constantly praising and encouraging. Modeling and imitation also play important roles in this view of language acquisition. Children imitate the sounds, words, sentences, and grammar they hear modeled by other children and adults. The child's parents reinforce or reward the child when the sounds made are a part of the language and do not reinforce sound patterns not in the language; in this way, the child learns the language of the parents.

The question of innate language acquisition versus language acquisition based on environmental factors is similar to the controversy of nature versus nurture in intellectual development. One cannot reject one viewpoint at the expense of the other. We must consider language acquisition as the product of both innate processes and environmental factors.

Early Childhood Professionals and Language Learning

People who care for children and are around them in the early stages of language learning greatly influence how and what they learn. Children's language experiences can make the difference in their school success. Many children enter a preschool or child care setting without much experience in talking and listening to other children or adults in different social settings.

Parents and professionals should focus on the content of language: learning names for things, how to speak in full sentences, and how to use and understand language. Many of these language activities relate directly to success in preschool, kindergarten, and first grade. These guidelines are useful in promoting children's language development:

- Treat children as partners in the communication process. Many infant behaviors, such as smiling, cooing, and vocalizing, serve to initiate conversation, and professionals can be responsive to these through conversation.

- Conversations are the building blocks of language development. Attentive and caring adults are infants' and toddlers' best stimulators of cognitive and language development.

- Talk to infants in a soothing, pleasant voice, with frequent eye contact, even though they do not "talk" to you. Most mothers and professionals talk to their young children differently from the way they talk to adults. They adapt their speech so they can communicate in a distinctive way called *motherese*. Mothers' language interactions with their toddlers are much the same as with infants. When conversing with toddlers who are just learning language, it is a good idea to simplify verbalization—not by using "baby talk," such as "di-di" for diaper or "ba-ba" for bottle, but rather by speaking in an easily understandable way. For example, instead of saying, "We are going to take a walk around the block so you must put your coat on," you would instead say, "Let's get coats on."

- Use children's names when interacting with them, to personalize the conversation and build self-identity.

- Use a variety of means to stimulate and promote language development, including reading stories, singing songs, listening to records, and giving children many opportunities to interact with other adults and children who have conversations with them.

- Encourage children to converse and share information with other children and adults.

- Help children learn to converse in various settings by taking them to different places so they can use their language with a variety of people. This approach also gives children ideas and events for using language.

- Have children use language in different ways. Children need to know how to use language to ask questions, explain feelings and emotions, tell what they have done, and describe things.

- Give children experiences in the language of directions and commands. Many children fail in school settings not because they do not know language but because they have little or no experience in how language is used for giving and following directions. It is also important for children to understand that language can be used as a means to an end—a way of attaining a desired goal.

- Converse with children about what they are doing and how they are doing it. Children learn language through feedback—asking and answering questions and commenting about activities—which shows children that professionals are paying attention to them and what they are doing.
- Talk to children in the full range of adult language, including past and future tenses.

PSYCHOSOCIAL DEVELOPMENT

Erik H. Erikson (1902–1994) is noted for his *psychosocial theory* of development. According to Erikson, children's personalities grow and develop in response to social institutions such as families, schools, child care centers, and early childhood programs. Of course, adults are principal components of these environments and therefore play a powerful role in helping or hindering children in their personality development.

Stages of Psychosocial Development

Erikson's theory has eight stages, which he also classifies as *ego qualities*. These qualities emerge across the human life span. Erikson maintains psychosocial development results from the interaction between maturational processes such as biological needs and the social forces encountered in everyday living. Socialization provides the context for conflict and crisis resolution during the eight developmental stages. Four of these stages apply to children from birth to age eight (see Figure 6–5).

Stage I: Basic Trust versus Mistrust (Birth to About Eighteen Months)

During this stage, children learn to trust or mistrust their environments and professionals. Trust develops when children's needs are met consistently, predictably, and lovingly.

Stage II: Autonomy versus Shame and Doubt (Eighteen Months to About Three Years)

This is the stage of independence, when children want to do things for themselves. Lack of opportunities to become autonomous and independent and professional overprotection result in self-doubt and poor achievement. As a result, instead of feeling good about their accomplishments, children come to feel ashamed of their abilities.

Stage III: Initiative versus Guilt (Three Years to About Five Years)

During the preschool years children need opportunities to respond with initiative to activities and tasks, which gives them a sense of purposefulness and accomplishment. Erikson believes children can feel guilty when they are discouraged or prohibited from initiating activities and are overly restricted in attempts to do things on their own.

FIGURE 6–5 Erikson's Stages of Psychosocial Development in Early Childhood

Stage	Approximate Ages	Characteristics	Role of Early Childhood Educators	Outcome for Child
Basic trust vs. mistrust	Birth to 18 months or 2 years	Infants learn either to trust or mistrust that others will care for their basic needs, including nourishment, sucking, warmth, cleanliness, and physical contact.	Meet children's needs with consistency and continuity	Views the world as safe and dependable
Autonomy vs. shame	18 months to 3 years	Toddlers learn to be self-sufficient or to doubt their abilities in activities such as toileting, feeding, walking, and talking.	Encourage children to do what they are capable of doing; avoid shaming for any behavior	Learns independence and competence
Initiative vs. guilt	3 to 5 years (to beginning of school)	Children are learning and want to undertake many adultlike activities, sometimes overstepping the limits set by parents and thus feeling guilty.	Encourage children to engage in many activities; provide environment in which children can explore; promote language development	Able to undertake a task, be active and involved
Industry vs. inferiority	Elementary	Children actively and busily learn to be competent and productive or feel inferior and unable to do things well.	Help children win recognition by producing things; recognition results from achievement and success	Feelings of self-worth and industry

Stage IV: Industry versus Inferiority (The Elementary School Years)

In this period, children display an industrious attitude and want to be productive. They want to build things, discover, manipulate objects, and find out how things work. Productivity is important during this stage. They also want recognition for their productivity, and adult response to children's efforts and accomplishments helps develop a positive self-concept. Feelings of inferiority result when children are criticized, belittled, or have few opportunities for productivity.

Basic Human Needs

Abraham Maslow (1890–1970) identified a basic hierarchy of human needs (see Figure 6–6): (1) life essentials, (2) safety and security, (3) belongingness and love, (4) achievement and prestige, (5) aesthetic needs, and (6) self-actualization. All professionals must endeavor to provide the conditions, environments, and opportunities for children at all ages to have these basic needs met. A comprehensive discussion of these needs and examples of how to provide for them, especially as a means of guiding children's behavior, is found in chapter 12.

In chapter 3, we discussed in detail the Montessori approach to educating young children and emphasized the use of Montessori educational materials. The description of the Montessori Nido on pages F and G of the color insert illustrates the great respect Montessorians have for children and their development. Montessori believed children begin their mental development at birth and must receive active care to children in the first years of life. Pay particular attention to the Nido as a prepared environment and the "knowledgeable care" provided.

Characteristics of Professionals

Regardless of who provides care for infants and toddlers, professionals should have certain qualities to provide for children's *total* needs on all levels: physical, cognitive, language, social, and emotional. These traits include love of children, caring about children, warmth, kindness, patience, good physical and mental health, compassion, courtesy, dedication, empathy, enthusiasm, honesty, and intelligence. Some may think infants and toddlers are not capable of learning much in the early years, so it does not make much difference if caregivers do much with them. Infants and toddlers *are* very capable persons, and it does matter who takes care of and educates them. Alice Honig believes that *nurturing* is a necessary quality for all professionals: "The high-quality infant professional is a special kind of nurturing person, with keen observation skills. Flexible, creative, comforting—she or he has a calm style that radiates secure commitment to an infant's well-being."[3]

Quality professionals really *know* the children they care for. This knowledge, combined with knowledge of child growth and development, enables them to provide care that is appropriate for *each* child. They also *care* about the children. They accept and respect all children and their cultural and socioeconomic backgrounds. Furthermore, quality professionals *care about themselves*. This self-caring appears

FIGURE 6–6   Hierarchy of Needs

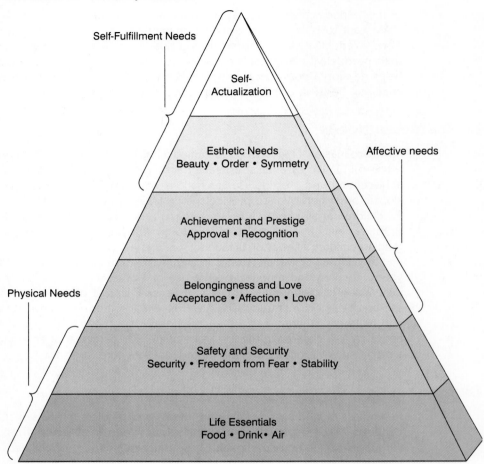

Source: MASLOW'S HIERARCHY OF NEEDS DATA from MOTIVATION AND PERSONALITY, 3RD ED. by ABRAHAM H. MASLOW. Revised by Robert Frager, James Fadiman, Cynthia McReynolds, and Ruth Cox. Copyright 1954, (c) 1987 by Harper & Row, Publishers, Inc. Copyright (c) 1970 by Abraham H. Maslow. Reprinted by permission of HarperCollins Publishers, Inc.

in their commitment to the child care profession and includes learning and developing the skills necessary to be a good care provider. It is further evidenced through good grooming, neatness, and cleanliness.

PROGRAMS FOR INFANTS AND TODDLERS

Infants and toddlers are cared for and educated in many kinds of programs and ways. These include child care centers (some of which specialize in infant care), family day care homes, baby-sitting cooperatives, mothers' day-out programs, and the child's own home under a caregiver's supervision. Regardless of the type of program, a good-quality one has these basic features:

- *Quality professionals.*   It is impossible to have a quality program without a quality staff. Those who are responsible for administering and conducting programs for the very young should make every effort to hire a staff with the characteristics that contribute to high quality. Patient, warm adults who understand how infants and toddlers grow and develop are probably the most important factor in a developmentally appropriate early childhood program.

- *Acceptable staff-child ratios.*   The NAEYC guidelines (presented in chap. 5) suggest ratios every program should strive to achieve. Program directors often say they comply with state guidelines for staff-child ratios and therefore provide a quality program. State regulations for staff-child ratios may, however, be too high to enable professionals to do their best.

- *Responsive environment.*   An environment is responsive when it is sensitive to the unique needs of *all* children and not merely satisfied to meet the needs of the "average" child.

Routines such as sleeping, feeding, diapering, and comforting are an important and necessary part of any child care program and become the context in which a curriculum is developed. Caregivers and parents must keep each other informed about a child's behavior and any deviations in routines. Transitions such as this one, when parents give their children over to the caregiver, provide one opportunity to share information.

Program in Practice

A DAY AT HeartsHome EARLY LEARNING CENTER

Walking into my classroom at 8:30 A.M., I greet Melinda, the coteacher who opens our classroom and two of the children in my primary teaching group that have already arrived. Christina, ten months old, greets me with a big smile. While babbling incessantly about how her morning with Melinda has gone so far, she cautiously toddles over to me and gives me a hug. Christopher, eight months old, says "hello" with a big smile that lights up his entire cereal-covered face! As I put my things away, Melinda tells me how the children are and what they might be needing as I take over their care for the rest of the day. Ashby, eight months old, comes in with her father around 8:45 A.M. He checks her in on the Heart-to-Home Exchange (a daily pattern sheet), writing the time they arrived, how long she slept the night before, when she awoke, whether she has had breakfast, how her behavior is, and any extra information he would like me to know. He writes me a note that Ashby's mother will be in around 3:00 P.M. to take her to her well-baby checkup.

As the day unfolds, I record daily events, diaper changes, what each child eats and drinks, and what activities they did. These pattern sheets are kept on clipboards in each child's cubbie, which makes recording information and checking them to see what a child might need handy. Ashby joins Christina and Christopher on the floor in a carpeted area to play with the toys, rattles, and manipulatives located on a nearby shelf, look at toys hanging from a toy suspension bar, or pull up on a play gym. Adam, twelve months old, comes in soon after his mother and his older sister, a preschooler who also attends HeartsHome. My whole group of four is at school, and we settle in for another day.

Throughout the day I have certain goals based on observation and a developmental assessment instrument that helps me chart where each child is developmentally in the domains of development. The goals guide my curriculum planning—which includes preparing the environment, planning to stimulate emerging skills with specific activities, and planning time for exploring and manipulating objects around the indoor and outdoor environment.

Another important role that I have is to maintain strong communication with the parents. When parents first enroll their children, there is a period of gradual enrollment. It usually lasts from a week to ten days. During this period, the parent and the child visit the school together to help the parent, teacher, *and* the child get to know one another and become comfortable with each other. I conducted an intake interview recently with Ashby's parents that allowed them to tell me everything there is to know about her, from what she does and does not eat (she is just starting vegetables and is trying one at a time), to the way she likes to be held (she likes to drink her bottle and cuddle close), to how she likes to be put to sleep (patted down in her bed with a blanket in her hand).

In addition to the intake interview and the Heart-to-Home Exchange, I hold quarterly conferences to discuss children's developmental progress. The parents of my children also meet with me, the director, and other parents quarterly to discuss their baby's growth and development, what comes next, and any other issues of concern to parents. Monthly newsletters from teachers to parents complete the written communication cycle, while a Parent Advisory Board meets regularly with

Contributed by Michele O'Shannessy, a primary teacher at HeartsHome Early Learning Center, Houston, Texas.

the director to make sure the input is considered. All of these help maintain strong communication and satisfaction among the teachers, parents and school.

As the day progresses, I follow the lesson plans for the week, performing routine care as needed and remembering to make routines a part of the stimulation experience. Developmentally appropriate lesson plans allow children to demonstrate skills in the areas of social-emotional, cognitive, language, gross motor, and fine motor. By developing lesson plans that encourage a wide range of activities, children become more involved in activities and maintain interest in what is going on in the classroom. Today, I have planned two activities: imitating sounds such as "Dada" and "Mama" to encourage language development and body painting. When I body-paint, I take the infants' clothes off except their diapers and put them on a piece of large white paper with nontoxic, washable paint on it. They love to crawl on the paint, eat it, and literally paint their diapers. I let them do this until they want to go to another activity or want me to hold them. Then it is time to get cleaned up. These activities are done throughout the day as time allows—I did the painting activity with Ashby and Adam while Christina was taking a nap and Christopher was bouncing the bouncer, giving me time to enjoy the messy activity with Ashby and Adam and to clean it up before Christina woke up or Christopher got tired of the bouncer. Christina and Christopher got a chance to do the painting activity while Ashby and Adam had their naps.

To make my day go smoother, each child sets her or his own pace during the day. For example, Christopher usually goes down for a nap around 9:00 or 9:30 every morning while Ashby will go down around 11:00. By taking advantage of their different schedules, I am able to spend quality time with each child during the day. By spending time with each child I learn more about them and pick up on cues that tell me what each baby might need. This really helps out when I have more than one or two children who need something at the same time. Individual scheduling means that rarely do all four children need something at the same time.

A developmental challenge has arisen in my classroom. Christina is going through separation anxiety. She shows a strong attachment toward her parents and me. When she successfully completes this stage, she will be ready to move on to relationships with other children and people. But right now only I will do! This stage has required me to accommodate Christina as I go about the day. For example, she likes to be held more than usual now and prefers that I spend most of my time with her. When I am helping or holding another child, she usually protests. When she does, I narrate to her what I am doing while assuring her that I will give her my attention as quickly as I can. If I cannot respond at once, I try redirecting her attention toward activities that she enjoys until I can tend to her needs or narrating to her that I will help her out as soon as I finish with another child. I am also holding her as often as I can when I am free to do so. These efforts are gradually paying off as she increases her independent behavior.

Another important part of the day is preparing to leave for lunch. Before leaving, Stacie, a familiar assistant teacher, and I exchange information about what each baby might need while I am at lunch—diaper change, bottle or lunch, nap, or to play. Making sure each child is happy and busy, I tell them where I am going and say good-bye. The end of all days goes much the same way except I make sure that I have written experience notes about the day on all the Exchanges about what the children have done during the day.

The most beneficial part of working at HeartsHome is being able to develop an intimate relationship with my group of children through *primary teaching*. I will stay with the same children until they are three. We will change classrooms, but that is all. Staying with the same children is very rewarding—I get to see them grow and learn. And, I get to know the parents so well that we share a special, relaxed relationship. Finally, primary teaching makes my job much easier because I get to know and understand my children better each day. I go home tired—it is really very hard work to take care of four infants, but I feel satisfied that my group and I shared a special day.

APPROPRIATE CURRICULUM AND ACTIVITIES

Developmentally Appropriate Infant and Toddler Programs

Many issues we have discussed in earlier chapters, particularly chapter 5, relate to the area of infant and toddler education. First is the issue of developmental appropriateness. All early childhood professionals who provide care for infants and toddlers—indeed, for all children—must understand and recognize this important concept, which provides the solid foundation for any program. The NAEYC defines *developmentally appropriate* as having two dimensions:

- *Age appropriateness.*   Human development research indicates that there are universal, predictable sequences of growth and change during the first nine years of life. These predictable changes occur in all domains of development—physical, emotional, social, and cognitive. . . .
- *Individual appropriateness.*   Each child is unique, with an individual pattern of growth as well as individual personality, learning style, and family background.[4]

In addition, the NAEYC has developed "Guidelines for Developmentally Appropriate Practice" to help staff plan for activities. These are among the suggestions:

- A developmentally appropriate curriculum provides for all areas of children's development—physical, emotional, social, and cognitive—through an integrated approach.
- Curriculum planning is based on professionals' observations and recordings of each child's special interests and developmental progress.
- Curriculum planning emphasizes an interactive process.
- Learning activities and materials should be concrete and real.

- Programs should provide for a wider range of developmental interests and abilities than the chronological age range of the group would suggest.
- Professionals should offer a variety of activities and materials and increase the difficulty, complexity, and challenge of an activity as children develop understanding and skills.
- Adults should provide opportunities for children to choose from among a variety of activities, materials, and equipment and time to explore through active involvement.
- Multicultural and nonsexist experiences, materials, and equipment should be provided for children of all ages.
- Adults should arrange a balance of rest and active movement for children throughout the program day.
- Outdoor experiences should be provided.[5]

Early childhood professionals must also understand the importance of providing programs for infants and toddlers that are uniquely different from programs for older children. This is what the NAEYC has to say about the necessity for unique programming for infants and toddlers:

Developmentally appropriate programs for children from birth to age 3 are distinctly different from all other types of programs—they are not a scaled-down version of a good program for preschool children. These program differences are determined by the unique characteristics and needs of children during the first 3 years:

- Changes take place far more rapidly in infancy than during any other period in life.

Professionals must learn about the cultural and family background of parents and children as a means of truly providing multi-culturally sensitive care and for authentically meeting the needs of children and families. What kind of family background information should professionals gather?

- During infancy, as at every other age, all areas of development—cognitive, social, emotional, and physical—are intertwined.
- Infants are totally dependent on adults to meet their needs.
- Very young children are especially vulnerable to adversity because they are less able to cope actively with discomfort and stress.

Infants and toddlers learn through their own experience, trial and error, repetition, imitation, and identification. Adults guide and encourage this learning by ensuring that the environment is safe and emotionally supportive. An appropriate program for children younger than three invites play, active exploration, and movement. It provides a broad array of stimulating experiences within a reliable framework of routines and protection from excessive stress. Relationships with people are emphasized as an essential contribution to the quality of children's experiences.[6]

Based on these dimensions, professionals must provide different programs of activities for infants and toddlers. To do so, early childhood professionals must get parents and other professionals to recognize that infants, as a group, are different from toddlers and need programs, curricula, and facilities specifically designed for them. Based on this recognition, it is then necessary to design and implement developmentally appropriate curricula. The early childhood profession is leading the way in raising consciousness about the need to match what professionals do with children to children's development as individuals. There is a long way to go in this regard, but part of the resolution will come with ongoing training of professionals in child development and curriculum planning.

Finally, we will want to match professionals to children of different ages. Not everyone is emotionally or professionally suited to provide care for infants and toddlers. Both groups need adults who can respond to their particular needs and developmental characteristics. Infants need especially nurturing professionals; toddlers, on the other hand, need adults who can tolerate and allow for their emerging autonomy and independence.

Curricula for Infants and Toddlers

Curriculum for infants and toddlers consists of all the activities and experiences they are involved in while under the direction of professionals. Consequently, professionals plan for *all* activities and involvements: feeding, washing, diapering/toileting, playing, learning and stimulating interactions, outings, involvements with others, and conversations. Professionals must plan the curriculum so it is developmentally appropriate. In addition to the ideas that professionals can ascertain from the NAEYC guidelines for a developmentally appropriate curriculum, these concepts may also be included:

- Self-help skills
- Ability to separate from parents
- Problem solving

- Autonomy and independence
- Assistance in meeting the developmental milestones associated with physical, cognitive, language, personality, and social development

Providing Multicultural Environments and Activities for Infants and Toddlers

As noted previously, the NAEYC endorses multicultural experiences, materials, and equipment as an integral part of developmentally appropriate practices. The NAEYC validates multicultural education in this way:

Providing a wide variety of multicultural, nonstereotyping materials and activities helps ensure the individual appropriateness of the curriculum and also

1. enhances each child's self-concept and esteem,
2. supports the integrity of the child's family,
3. enhances the child's learning processes in both the home and the early childhood program by strengthening ties,
4. extends experiences of children and their families to include knowledge of the ways of others, especially those who share the community, and
5. enriches the lives of all participants with respectful acceptance and appreciation of differences and similarities among them.

Multicultural experiences should not be limited to a celebration of holidays and should include foods, music, families, shelter, and other aspects common to all cultures.[7]

Early childhood professionals in all programs must endeavor to make their programs as multicultural and nonsexist as possible. The following ideas of Kimberlee Whaley and Elizabeth Blue Swadener will help you achieve this goal:

Translating these theories and ideas into practice can be difficult at best. When you work in a program with a number of infants or toddlers it becomes very easy to get caught up in routine "custodial" duties and to forget you are dealing with unique individuals. The following suggestions will help bring multicultural education into the infant/toddler classroom:

- Create classrooms that are less conforming and more individualized. Is it really necessary for all toddlers to sit during "circle," or could there be a quiet option for those who would prefer it? Make an effort to recognize the special qualities of each child.
- Learn the background and culture of each family. The importance of continuity between center and home can't be overemphasized.
- Build self-esteem by allowing the child to feel competent. Encourage independence and allow the child to do things for him/herself. Plan this into the day—it takes twice as long but it's worth the effort.
- Encourage creativity. Allow children to do their own work regardless of how you think it looks. Allow them to be pleased and satisfied with their own work. Encourage creative and unique responses to question.

- Portray both genders in nurturing roles. Let toddlers visit and help with infants on a regular basis.
- Avoid gender-stereotyped toys, puppets, puzzles and books.
- Use different types of music in programs. Classical, country and popular music is often important in homes. Use music from other countries as well. Tapes of the parents singing or reading can also be effective.
- Talk about feelings often. Give labels to emotions. Research indicates that acquiring labels for emotions appears to be important for children to identify their own experiences as well as develop empathy for others.
- Be aware that toddlers from families whose first language is not English may be learning two languages simultaneously. Allow children to become competent in their first language. Expose them to English, but don't push. For example, write their names in both languages and ask parents to provide translations of frequently used phrases.
- Put up pictures of different experiences, ethnic groups and customs in the infant/toddler area. Show different ways of meeting the same needs.
- Encourage positive attention seeking behavior in both genders. Give boys the words to get their needs for nurturance met.
- Be sure your materials represent many cultures and lifestyles. Dolls, books, puppets, music and dramatic play materials are just some of the things that can be easily adapted.[8]

CHILDPROOFING HOMES AND CENTERS

As infants become more mobile and as toddlers start their constant exploration, safety becomes a major concern. Professionals can advise parents about childproofing the home. In addition, professionals must childproof centers and other settings.

Home
- Remove throw rugs so toddlers do not trip.
- Put breakable objects out of toddlers' reach.
- Cover electrical wall outlets with special covers.
- Remove electrical cords.
- Install gates in hallways and stairs (make sure gates are federally approved so the toddlers cannot get their heads stuck and strangle).
- Take knobs off stoves.
- Purchase medicines and cleaners with childproof caps.
- Store all medicines and cleaning agents out of reach; move all toxic chemicals from low cabinets to high ones (even things like mouthwash should be put in a safe place).
- Place safety locks on bathroom doors that can be opened from the outside.
- Cushion sharp corners of tables and counters with foam rubber and tape or cotton balls.

- If older children in the home use toys with small parts, beads, and so forth, have them use these when the toddler is not present or in an area where the toddler cannot get them.
- When cooking, turn all pot handles to the back of the stove.
- Avoid using cleaning fluids while children are present (because of toxic fumes).
- Place guards over hot water faucets in bathrooms so toddlers cannot turn them on.
- Keep wastebaskets on tops of desks.
- Keep doors to the washer and dryer closed at all times.
- Keep all plastic bags, including garbage bags, stored in a safe place.
- Shorten cords on draperies; if there are loops on cords, cut them.
- Immediately wipe up any spilled liquid from the floor.

Center
- Cover toddler area floors with carpeting or mats.
- Make sure storage shelves are anchored well and will not tip over; store things so children cannot pull heavy objects off shelves onto themselves.
- Use only safe equipment and materials, nothing that has sharp edges or is broken.
- Store all medicines in locked cabinets.
- Cushion sharp corners with foam rubber and tape.
- Keep doors closed or install gates.
- Fence all play areas.

HEALTH ISSUES IN EARLY CHILDHOOD PROGRAMS

The spread of diseases in early childhood programs is a serious concern to all who care for young children (see Figure 6–7). Part of the responsibility of all caregivers is to provide healthy care for all children. One of the most effective ways to control the spread of disease in early childhood programs and promote the healthy care of young children is by washing hands. These are generally accepted procedures for hand washing:

1. Turn on the faucet. In some programs, faucets have control levers that can be turned on and shut off with the elbows. This is the preferable method since it eliminates the spread of germs and fecal matter by the hands.
2. Wet hands, wrists, and forearms.
3. Apply liquid soap. Liquid soap is preferred because cake soap can transmit germs and fecal matter.

(Text continues on p. 240.)

Program in Practice

DESCRIPTION OF A TODDLER PROGRAM

Toddlers Are Unique

Toddlers are broadly defined as young children who have achieved the walking stage to the age of approximately thirty-six months. They are unique because they are always in transition, exploring the environment, testing new developmental skills, and achieving new growth patterns. More specifically, toddlers

- want control of themselves and their body (developing autonomy: e.g., want to feed and dress themselves; become toilet trained);
- are developing social skills but still in the solitary or parallel stage of play;
- begin to play pretend games;
- listen to simple stories;
- want to participate in real-life tasks (washing dishes, cooking, other household chores);
- benefit from close contact with others;
- want to make their own decisions and choices (e.g., about what to wear, eat, play);
- become increasingly curious about surroundings and set off on their own to explore;
- say two or more words together and use gestures and words to make their wants known;
- begin to understand and use abstract words such as *up, down, now,* and *later;*
- can identify body parts;
- develop better motor skills (e.g., can walk up and down stairs, run with good coordination, jump, hop on one foot);
- respond to verbal requests;
- imitate actions;
- are aware of their own clothing and toys;
- are affectionate (e.g., return a kiss or hug);
- express fear of strangers;
- show trust and love;
- express preferences strongly;
- develop a sense of humor; and
- become easily frustrated.

Exciting new motor skills and changing problem-solving abilities are noticeable each day. Individuality is strong, so programs must be individualized and personalized. To effectively plan a developmental program for toddlers, one must understand this unique transitory phase of development.

Unique Developmental Qualities

- *Toddlers are mobile*—walk, run, dart, and disappear; climb stairs and crawl around furniture; pull and push items; jump; begin to ride a tricycle.
- *Toddlers are explorers*—open and close doors, jars, boxes; crawl into shelves, under furniture; investigate trash baskets, toy chests, and supply shelves; can find almost any object.
- *Toddlers' appetites decline*—growth rate slows down drastically as body has less demand for food; do not need or want large amounts of food; small servings of nutritious food are necessary; teething begins at about seven or eight months of age, by eighteen months they have twelve teeth, and by age three they have a full set of twenty.
- *Toddlers are not toilet trained*—certain levels of neurological and motor develop-

Contributed by Beverly M. Boals and Mildred B. Vance of Arkansas State University.

ment have not been reached, so frequent accidents will occur; do not have control of the sphincter muscles of bladder and bowel and, therefore, are not consistent in toileting habits; are able to achieve bowel control before bladder control; girls are typically ready earlier, at about two and a half years, than boys, who are not ready until three years.

■ *Toddlers' cognitive development expands rapidly*—able to see relationship of objects; make comparisons; able to draw, use pegs, build with blocks, look at books; able to imitate others, engage in pretend play.

■ *Toddlers achieve milestones in language acquisition*—use productive speech and receptive speech; use telegraphic speech with only two- or three-word sentences; language comprehension is more advanced than language production; language becomes fundamental to social activities; love stories, books, records, television, singing, and word games like "Patty-Cake"; ask lots of questions.

■ *Toddlers have unique social and emotional behaviors*—attachment behaviors have been developed; exhibit stranger and separation anxiety; respond to distress of others; enjoy other children's company; respond with smiles and laughter; vocalize with others; develop prosocial behavior.

A Toddler Program

A program designed for toddlers will consist of a number of interactive components focused on the physical, mental, social, and emotional care and needs of the child. These components include the

■ caregiver,

■ environment,

■ curriculum, and

■ parents.

Characteristics of an Effective Caregiver   Caregivers, to meet toddlers' needs effectively, should understand the true nature of the toddler. They should be

■ child centered—attentive and loving to toddlers, willing to meet toddlers' needs before own;

■ self-confident—relaxed and anxiety free, skilled in physical and emotional care;

■ flexible—able to rearrange schedule and activities to meet individual needs;

■ spontaneous and open—able to recognize developmental and growth stages and plan accordingly;

■ sensitive—understanding of cultural family differences and expectations, empathetic toward differences, purposeful in interaction with toddlers;

■ positive in life and career—positive in affective expressions and communication with toddlers and parents, void of evidence of anger or displeasure; and

■ appreciative of toddlers—able to express appropriate affection and show obvious pleasure in involvement with toddlers.

The Toddler Environment   The toddler program requires an environment designed especially for the small child. When planning each component in a toddler program, safety should be the primary consideration. A variety of indoor spaces are necessary: spaces to explore, rest, move, pretend, and eat.

Activity areas for individuals and small groups of two or three must be readily available and offer a view of an entire area. Indoor space should provide the equipment and materials needed to facilitate a developmentally appropriate curriculum. Outdoor spaces should also include a variety of areas:

- Grassy areas
- Areas for running
- Movable equipment for active play
- Play structures for gross-motor development
- Opportunities for climbing
- Shady areas for quiet time
- Spaces for wheel toys
- Areas for outdoor art
- Sand and water exploration
- Nature areas for plants and animals
- Observation areas for bird feeders and animal cages
- Spaces for outdoor story and snack

In planning and designing outdoor toddler areas, further consideration should be given to the following:

- Balance between activities and quiet activities—designated areas for certain activities: active—running, jumping, climbing, swinging; quiet—painting, resting, housekeeping
- Moveable, creative equipment—boxes, tires, tunnels (obstacle courses)
- Balance between shady and sunny areas
- Variety of textures: hard/cement; soft/garden and grass; grainy/sand; rough/bark; cool/water

- Covered area for wheel toys and rainy days
- Sitting space
- Different levels: hills or mounds, flat areas
- Designated areas for certain ages if outside at the same time

Suggested outdoor activities also include these:

- Cardboard boxes
- Dirt for digging
- Wagons
- Housekeeping props
- Fence painting
- Colored chalk on sidewalk
- Texture rubs
- Seeds, bulbs, flowers, vegetable gardens

The Toddler Curriculum   The developmentally appropriate curriculum for toddlers should fulfill the need to explore and know; therefore, inviting areas of exploration need to be established frequently. Play activities should be the core of the curriculum. A daily curriculum should include a theme and a variety of related play activities. A developmentally appropriate curriculum should offer the following:

- Freedom to explore and manipulate
- Opportunities to participate in activities utilizing many senses
- Opportunities to develop physically—space to move about and to increase gross-motor development
- Large blocks
- Sand play/water play

- Cardboard boxes for pushing and pulling and/or similar commercial toys such as wagons, grocery carts
- Wheel toys, large wooden trucks, airplanes, cars
- Objects to climb on, over, and under
- Dolls, carriages, strollers
- Nesting toys, puzzles, manipulative games
- Plastic bowls, lids
- Graduated sizes of paper towel tubes
- Music—chimes, music boxes, records, tapes
- Books
- Nondictated art
- Dramatic play/housekeeping/pretend play
- Manipulatives
- Nature experiences
- Language experiences
- Cooking and mixing experiences

Daily Program Sequence   All daily schedules will need to be modified to meet the special needs of the children enrolled and the time spent at the facility. Programs should be designed to enhance specific cultural and ethnic backgrounds.

8:30–9:30   Greet children; help children with wraps and belongings; help children say good-bye to parents (attachments are very strong). Involve children in a play area as quickly as possible. Play music to set the mood for the day. Encourage toddlers to bring and keep something of their own to help them feel at home. Have an assistant stationed in a book area to invite children to listen to or to do finger plays or rhyme games.

Have toys placed at designated areas; provide opportunities for pretend play. Children need time to settle into activities; they do not like to be rushed. Have snacks available during this period of time for those who did not eat breakfast or need nourishment. Bite-size pieces of fruit, oranges, cereal, buttered toast cut into small strips, small pieces of cheese, tuna, chicken, or crackers make nourishing snacks.

9:30–9:45   Story time. Toddlers love actual stories about familiar events such as *Taking a Bath, Pat the Bunny,* or *Goodnight Moon.* Stories should be short, told to an individual or small group, and toddlers should feel free to come and go at will.

9:45–10:00   Toileting. Even though toddlers will need to go to the bathroom throughout the day, frequent reminders are a must at this stage. Helping with potty training is a part of the program. Children learn by observing and being reminded.

10:00–10:25   Outdoor play time or walking tours.

10:25–11:25   Selected play areas—table activities, books, small muscle activities. When toddlers play together, adults need to provide duplicate toys and materials, large-piece puzzles, peg boards, art activities, cars, trucks, easel painting, block building, dramatic play.

11:25   Cleanup, toileting—getting ready for lunch. Staff members need to be friendly helpers.

11:30–12:00   Quiet activity prior to lunch. Lunch with quiet music and family-style meals. The meal should have a variety of colors, textures, and temperatures and a balance of strongly flavored, bland, and mild foods. Children can be helpers with assigned tasks—setting table, cleanup, etc. Lunch is an opportunity to introduce new and different foods one at a time and develop social skills in a relaxed atmosphere.

12:00–1:30/1:45   Nap time—individual cots or beds (some children are fearful of falling off cots). Place chair backs draped with blankets, quilts, or pieces of fabric between cots to provide privacy. Rocking chairs should be available for adults to use if needed. Nap time (as all other activities throughout the day) should be nonthreatening. Each child should have his or her own cot covers, wash cloths, towels, and clothing. Sheets from beds or cots need to be placed in a hamper for laundering. All items should be washed with nonallergic detergent. Liquid soap with a spoonful of bleach should be used for cleaning surfaces. Each state has minimum licensing requirements that should be followed.

1:30–1:45/2:00   Getting up from nap—check to see whether pants and/or diapers need to be changed. Wash hands and face, give toddler time to adjust.

2:00–2:30   Arrange a small snack of finger foods and juice for children to select from in self-service. Allow play activities to continue during this time, but encourage each child to participate in snack.

2:30–3:00   Selected play activities–music, movement, stories, toys, stuffed animals, real objects, animals, or plants can be used for conversation and interaction.

3:00–3:45   Outdoor time with planned curricular activities such as art, easel painting on paper clipped to a fence, pretend props such as cardboard boxes used as a train and cars. Toddlers approach the world without preconceived ideas about how things should work—an approach that often leaves them in precarious and dangerous positions.

3:45–5:00   Indoor small-group/individual curricular experiences, such as art, stories, or tape recordings of books.

5:00–6:00   Departure—do not rush children; give them time to become reacquainted with parents or other person who is responsible for picking up child. Talk with child about favorite activities. Assure child that you will be present the next day.

4. Scrub hands, wrists, and forearms, making sure that enough pressure is applied to produce friction.
5. Rinse hands, wrists, and forearms.
6. Dry hands, wrists, and forearms completely with a disposable paper towel.
7. Use a disposable paper towel to turn off the faucet.

The spread of germs can also be greatly reduced through the use of sanitary diapering techniques. Diapering is another prime vehicle for germ transmission. It is imperative that sanitary procedures be followed while diapering children. The NAEYC's guidelines for sanitary diaper changing are as follows:

1. Place paper or other disposable cover on diapering surface.
2. Pick up the child. If the diaper is soiled, hold the child away from you.

Communicating with Parents

Caregivers need to give vital information to parents, from "not feeling well," to minor accidents, to a special accomplishment or achievement throughout the day. Written information may be provided describing curricular activities, visitors in the classroom, special events, and suggestions for parents. Mail boxes for parents, an exchange counter, and forms for parents to convey needed information to staff are useful. Educational programs designed to enhance parenting and communication skills are recommended. Educational programs can also facilitate management of family and community resources and can give parents and families additional strategies for coping and providing enriching home and family lives.

Summary

A toddler program consists of the interactive components of

- a quality caregiver,
- appropriate indoor and outdoor environments,
- a developmentally appropriate curriculum, and
- active parents.

All programs must have a safe and healthy environment and caregivers who are knowledgeable about the developmental stages of this age group. Materials and equipment should be available to create a daily environment. Opportunities should abound for language, cognitive, creative, physical, and social development. Toddlers establish reciprocal behaviors with nurturing adults both in and out of the home. A commitment to quality programming by parents and program caregivers and administrators will provide the best opportunity for joint happiness and toddlers' maximum growth and development.

3. Lay the child on the diapering surface. *Never leave the child unattended.* If you use them, put on disposable gloves now.

4. Remove soiled diaper and clothes. Fold disposable diapers inward and reseal with their tapes.

5. Put disposable diapers in a lined, covered step can. Put cloth diapers in a plastic bag securely tied, then put into a larger, labeled, plastic bag to go home. Do not put diapers in toilet. Bulky stool may be emptied into toilet.

6. Put soiled clothes in doubled, labeled plastic bags to be taken home.

7. Clean the child's bottom with a moist disposable wipe. Wipe front to back using towelette only once. Repeat with fresh wipes if necessary. Pay particular attention to skin folds. Pat dry with paper towel. Do not use any kind of powder, as inhaling it can be dangerous. Use a skin care product only on a parent's request.

FIGURE 6–7   Spread of Contamination in Child Care Centers

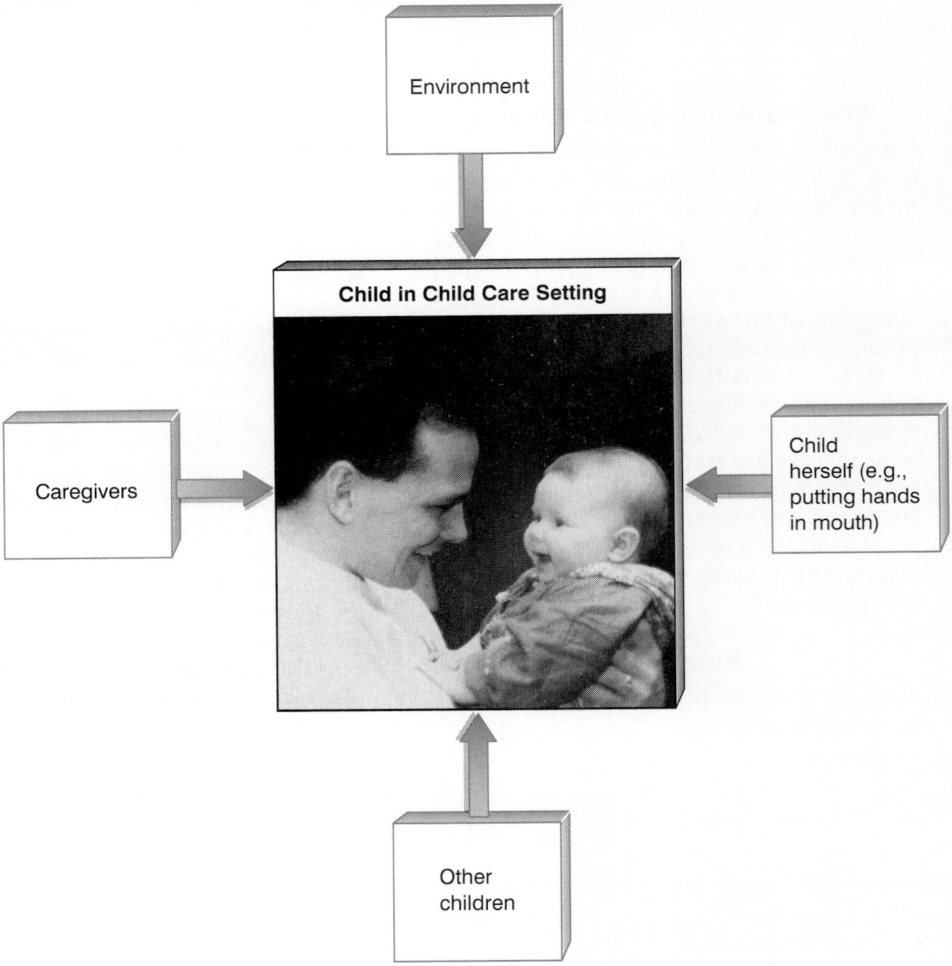

8. Dispose of the towelette or paper towel in a lined, covered step can. *If you used disposable gloves, discard them now.*

9. Wipe your hands with a disposable wipe. *Dispose it* in the lined, covered step can.

10. Diaper or dress the child. Now you can hold her or him close to you.

11. Wash the child's hands. Assist the child back to the group.

12. Remove disposable covering from the diapering surface.

13. Wash and rinse the area with water (use soap if necessary), and sanitize it with bleach solution (quarter cup bleach to one gallon water) made fresh daily.

14. Wash your own hands thoroughly.

It is important for early childhood professionals to protect themselves and the children from AIDS. Here are some basic guidelines:

- Staff and children should wash their hands before eating
- Staff and children should wash their hands before and after using the toilet
- Staff should wash their hands before and after changing a diaper
- Staff should wash their hands before and after treating a cut or wound
- Staff should wear gloves if there is contact with blood or blood-containing body fluids or tissue discharge[9]

It sounds trite, but health in child care and preschool programs truly begins with the people who conduct the programs. Hand-washing policies, diapering procedures, and AIDS precautions, however well stated and intended, will do little good if they are not followed. It is important, therefore, for caregivers and teachers to do all that they can to protect and promote the health of children.

Infants and toddlers are interesting and remarkably competent individuals, as we have discussed throughout this chapter. The developmental and educational milestones of these years are foundational for all that follow throughout life. All professionals must use their knowledge, understanding, energy, and talents to assure that the foundation is the best it can be.

READINGS FOR FURTHER ENRICHMENT

Balter, Lawrence, and Anita Shreve. *Dr. Balter's Child Sense: Understanding and Handling the Common Problems of Infancy and Early Childhood* (New York: Poseidon, 1987)

Covering the period from birth to age five, this book provides many answers for parents and professionals of young children. Includes responses to problems of the young infant up to concerns of the preschool child, such as another baby, divorce, and other family considerations.

Biber, Barbara. *Early Education and Psychological Development* (New Haven, CT: Yale University Press, 1987)

Biber, a leading proponent of the developmental-interaction approach to early childhood education, advocates a whole-child approach that encourages children to exercise control over their learning, with professionals as guides for interactions between students and staff. Valuable insight into the development of the child-centered approach at Bank Street College.

Greenman, Jim. *Caring Spaces, Learning Places* (Redmond, WA: Exchange, 1988)

This book discusses important aspects of indoor and outdoor environments for infants and young children. It covers safety, age appropriateness, aesthetics, planning and design, comfort, different surfaces, remodeling, storage, ideas for setting up a classroom, and the impact of the environment on children and staff.

Hass, Carolyn Buhai. *Look at Me: Activities for Babies and Toddlers* (Chicago: Chicago Review Press, 1987)

Easy-to-use activities: Toys to Make, Learning Games, Indoor/Outdoor Fun, Books and Reading, Positive Self-Image, Imaginative Play, Arts and Crafts, Easy and Nutritious Recipes, and others.

Maxim, George. *The Sourcebook: Activities for Infants and Young Children,* Second Edition (New York: Merrill/Macmillan, 1990)

Activities to encourage infants and young children in physical, emotional, motor, and creative development; guidelines for evaluations.

McLane, Joan, and Gillian McNamee. *Early Literacy* (Cambridge, MA: Harvard University Press, 1990)

An excellent source for expanding the readers understanding of language development. Authors answer questions such as, What is literacy? When does literacy begin? What are some bridges to literacy?

Morrison, George S. *The Education and Development of Infants, Toddlers, and Preschoolers* (Glenview, IL: Scott, Foresman, 1988)

Developmental theory and practical applications professionals need to provide developmentally appropriate curriculum; includes charts and vignettes. One reviewer said it qualifies as both a textbook and a good read for parents.

Stewart, Bernice, and Julie S. Vargas. *Teaching Behavior to Infants and Toddlers* (Springfield, IL: Charles C Thomas, 1990)

Describes positive methods for teaching appropriate behaviors to infants and toddlers.

ACTIVITIES FOR FURTHER ENRICHMENT

1. Visit at least two programs that provide care for infants and toddlers. Observe the curriculum to determine whether it is developmentally appropriate. What suggestions would you make for improving the curriculum? Explain what you liked most and least about the program.

2. Develop five activities professionals do to promote children's basic trust needs.

3. You have been asked to speak to a group of parents about what they can do to promote their children's language development in the first two years of life. Outline your presentation, and list five specific suggestions you will make to the parents.

4. Observe children between the ages of birth and eighteen months. Identify the six stages

of sensorimotor intelligence by describing the behaviors you observed. Cite specific examples of secondary and tertiary reactions. For each of the six stages, list two activities that would be cognitively appropriate.

5. In addition to the qualities cited in this chapter, list and explain five other qualities you think are important for professionals of infants and toddlers.

6. Why is motor development important in the early years? What are five things early childhood educators can include in their programs to promote motor development?

7. Most of Sylvia's friends and family members criticized her for sending her three-week-old baby, Katrina, to a child care center. Sylvia honestly weighed the pros and cons of this decision and believes this was the best one for her and her child. List the positive and negative factors involved in putting a three-week-old infant in a child care center program. Does the law in your state specify how old a child has to be before enrolled in a child care center? If so, what is this age and what other standards must be followed when providing care for infants?

8. Identify customs that are passed down to infants and toddlers as a result of the family's cultural background. How do these customs affect young children's behavior?

9. Visit centers that care for young children of different cultures. List the differences you find. What areas are most similar?

10. Interview parents of young infants from different cultures. What are their five top expectations for their babies? How are expectations different and alike?

11. Interview professionals who work in family day care homes and others who work in child care centers. How does the care for infants and toddlers differ in the two settings? In which kind of program would you prefer to be a professional? Why?

12. Develop a set of activities for mothers and their infants to use at home. Try these activities out with parents and infants, and tell what went well and what you would change.

13. Every morning, Maria, the professional of an infant group, reads a story to the children.

But one day, a new parent went storming to see the program director. The parent claimed that Maria's very heavy Spanish accent would negatively affect his son's language development. Do you think the parent was right or wrong? Why? What would you do if you were the program director?

14. Interview mothers about their concerns in leaving their infants in the care of others. Identify the concerns of fathers in relation to the same situation. Do parents' concerns differ according to the age or sex of their children?

15. Identify at least ten games or activities that are beneficial to the developing infant and the growing toddler. Describe the benefits of each of the games or activities you list.

NOTES

1. Eric H. Lenneberg, "The Biological Foundations of Language," in Mark Lester, *Readings in Applied Transformational Grammar* (New York: Holt, Rinehart & Winston, 1970), p. 8.

2. Susan Curtiss, *Genie: A Psycholinguistic Study of a Modern-Day "Wild Child"* (New York: Academic Press, 1977).

3. Alice C. Honig, "High Quality Infant/Toddler Care," *Young Children* 4 (Nov. 1985), p. 40.

4. Sue Bredekamp, ed., *Developmentally Appropriate Practice in Early Childhood Programs Serving Children from Birth through Age 8,* expanded ed. (Washington, D.C., National Association for the Education of Young Children, 1987), pp. 7–8. © 1987 by the National Association for the Education of Young Children. Reprinted by permission.

5. National Association for the Education of Young Children, "Position Statement on Developmentally Appropriate Practice in Early Childhood Programs Serving Children from Birth through Age 8," *Young Children* 41(1) (Sept. 1986), pp. 4–29.

6. National Association for the Education of Young Children, *Developmentally Appropriate Practice in Early Childhood Programs Serving Infants* (Washington, D.C.: Author, 1989), no. 547.

7. Bredekamp, *Developmentally Appropriate Practice,* p. 2.

8. Kimberlee Whaley and Elizabeth Blue Swadener, "Multicultural Education in Infant and Toddler Settings," *Childhood Education* 66(4) (1990), pp. 239–240. Reprinted by permission of K. Whaley and E. B. Swadener and the Association for Childhood Education International, 11501 Georgia Ave., Suite 315, Wheaton, Maryland. Copyright © by the Association.

9. National Academy of Early Childhood Programs, "Preventing HIV/AIDS Transmittal," *Newsletter of the National Academy of Early Childhood Programs,* 66(2), p. 5.

7

The Preschool Years
Foundations for Learning and Living

After you have read and studied this chapter, you will be able to:

☐ Describe and explain preschoolers' basic growth and development

☐ Relate the history of preschool and nursery education from the McMillan sisters to the present

☐ Discuss various definitions and purposes of play in preschool programs

☐ Explain the various ways play promotes children's learning

☐ Identify reasons for the current interest in preschool programs

☐ Summarize reasons for developing preschool programs for young children

☐ Advise others regarding goals and objectives for preschools

☐ Appraise and critique preschool curricula and schedules

☐ Analyze issues concerning preschool programs

This chapter is about the preschool years, when children are between the ages of three and five. While the term *preschool years* has been traditionally used to describe the period before children enter school, this designation is rapidly becoming obsolete. Today, it is common for many children to be in a school of some kind beginning as early as age two and three. And child care beginning at six weeks is becoming de rigueur for children of working parents. Additionally, many states such as Texas, Florida, California, New York, and North Carolina have public preschool programs for four-year-olds; the term *preschool* hardly applies to threes and fours anymore.

Many parents view the preschool years as the time children "get ready" to enter kindergarten or first grade, the beginning of what they consider "formal" schooling. Early childhood professionals view the events of the preschool years as the cornerstone of later learning. Some parents, however, still think of this period as a time when children should be unburdened by learning and allowed to play and enjoy life, perhaps, as some feel, for the last unstructured time. For many, though, the preschool years are the beginning of a period of at least fourteen years during which their lives will be dramatically influenced by teachers and schooling.

For our purposes, *preschools* are programs for two- to five-year-old children, before kindergarten. In this chapter we will also discuss *nursery schools*, programs for three- and four-year-olds.

Early childhood professionals generally distinguish between preschool and child care. Applying the term *preschool* to a program usually means it has an educational purpose and a curriculum designed to involve children primarily in learning activities. Parents usually enroll their children in preschools because they believe in early learning and want their children to learn. Child care, on the other hand, is primarily intended to provide care for children so parents can work. The purposes of child care and preschool are not mutually exclusive, however, and the better programs of either emphasize both quality care and learning. Some preschools have broadened their programs to include child care components. The preschool program may be conducted in the morning, with a child care program in the afternoon; the preschool may have before- and after-school child care programs; or child care and preschool programs may be conducted in the same building but separately.

HISTORY OF PRESCHOOL EDUCATION

The history of preschool education is really the history of nursery school education, which cannot be separated from the history of kindergarten education. The origin of nursery schools as it affects the United States was in Great Britain. In 1914, Margaret and Rachel McMillan started an open-air nursery with an emphasis on health care and healthy living, without ignoring cognitive stimulation. They also began a program of visiting homes to work with mothers. Their work led to the passage, in 1918, of the Fisher Act, which provided national support for nursery education and led to the establishment of the first public nursery schools in Great Britain.

In 1914, Caroline Pratt opened the Play School (now the City & Country School) in New York City. One of the nation's first truly progressive schools, it was patterned on the philosophy of John Dewey and designed to take advantage of what Pratt called children's "natural and inevitable" desire to learn.

Patty Smith Hill was a champion of the nursery school movement in the United States and started a progressive laboratory school at Columbia Teachers College in New York in 1921. Abigail Eliot, another nursery school pioneer, studied in Great Britain for six months with the McMillan sisters, then started the Ruggles Street Nursery School in Boston in 1922. Meanwhile, also in 1922, the Merrill-Palmer Institute Nursery School opened in Detroit, under the direction of Edna White. The Institute and White were responsible for training many nursery school teachers.

A temporary impetus to nursery education occurred in 1933, when the federal Works Progress Administration provided funds to hire unemployed teachers in nursery school programs. In 1940, the Lanham Act provided money for child care for mothers employed in defense-related industries. One of the best examples of these programs were the Kaiser Child Service Centers built by Edgar Kaiser to provide child care for children of workers in the Kaiser shipyards. Each center was designed to provide care for about a thousand children between the ages of eighteen months and six years. Open 364 days a year, 24 hours a day, these centers were staffed by people with degrees in child development. This support ended with the war in 1945.

From the 1940s to the present, preschools have been mainly private, sponsored by parent cooperatives, churches, and other agencies. Federal involvement in preschool education has been through Head Start and support for child care programs directed at low-income families and children. Interest and enrollment in preschools for all children, however, has increased over the past decade.

THE GROWING POPULARITY OF PRESCHOOLS

The acceleration of preschool programs began with Head Start in 1965. This trend continues to grow, with greater numbers of four-year-olds entering preschools, many operated by public schools (see Figure 7–1). In addition, the ages at which children enter preschool is decreasing; that is, children are entering preschool at a younger age.

Reasons for the rapid increase in and demand for preschool programs for three- and four-year-old children are best understood within the context of societal changes over the last two decades and contemporary societal problems and concerns. Keep in mind that social events and issues determine the nature and kinds of current educational programs and those we can expect to see in the next decade. Whenever we ask "why" about a particular educational program, we can always find the answer in societal needs and political concerns, because society traditionally and legitimately looks to educational institutions to help it address its short- and long-term goals. In fact, it is fair to say that education is one of the principal facilitators of society. With these concepts in mind, we can identify the following reasons to explain the current popularity of preschool programs, particularly public preschool programs for three- and four-year-olds:

• Changing family patterns, especially single-parent families

Program in Practice

THE CITY & COUNTRY SCHOOL TODAY

The City & Country School, founded by Caroline Pratt in 1914, is an example of a progressive school that continues to educate children using the curriculum structure that was set forth nearly eighty years ago: "giving children experiences and materials that will fit their stage of development and have inherent in them unlimited opportunities for learning." Pratt, a teacher, sought to provide a school environment that suited the way children learn best—by doing.

The younger groups (ages two through seven) use basic, open-ended materials to reconstruct what they are learning about the world and organize their information and thinking in meaningful ways. Materials such as blocks, clay, water, paint, and wood are chosen because of their simplicity, flexibility, and the challenging possibilities that they offer. The blocks, developed by Pratt, are the mainspring of the curriculum today as they were in the early days of the school. It is City & Country School's belief that an early childhood curriculum based on open-ended mate-

rials fosters independence, motivation, and interest, all essential components of learning.

The Lower School curriculum provides a firm foundation for the more formal academic skills that children must master in later years. The Jobs Program was developed to play the central role in groups aged eight through thirteen. Each group has a specific job to perform related to the school's functioning as an integrated community. These jobs provide a natural impetus for perfecting skills in reading, writing, spelling, and mathematics and a relevant framework for the exploration of social studies and the arts.

Beyond their work with blocks and jobs, children at City & Country are given opportunities to experience art, music, dramatics, science, computer, and woodworking, often integrated with their classroom work.

Located in the Greenwich Village district of New York City on 13th Street, the school currently has an enrollment of 195 students between the ages of two and thirteen. It continues to exemplify child-centered education.

Contributed by Kathleen Holz, principal of the City & Country School.

- Changing economic patterns, with more women in the work force
- Changing attitudes toward work and careers. The shift away from homemaking as a career to outside employment and careers causes the early childhood profession to provide more programs and services, including programs for threes and fours.
- The view by parents, public policy planners, and researchers that intervention programs (to deal with such problems as substance abuse) work best in the early years. Research verifies the positive short- and long-term benefits of quality preschool programs to children and society.
- Growing concern on the part of corporations and businesses as to the quality of the contemporary and future work force. They see early education as one way of developing a literate work force.
- Advocacy for publicly supported and financed preschools as a means of preventing the exclusion of poor children and their families from the early education movement.

FIGURE 7–1   Preschool Enrollment

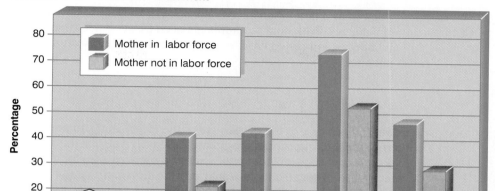

Source: U.S Bureau of the Census, "School Enrollment—Social and Economic Characteristics of Students," *Current Population Reports,* Series P-20 (April 1990).

- The increasingly popular notion that three- and four-year-old children are ready, willing, and able to learn.

    Paradigm shifts in preschool programs over the past twenty years, and particularly in the past decade, have resulted in a number of significant changes in programs and purposes. Previously, the predominate purposes of preschools were to help children become socialized—to enhance their social-emotional development and get children ready for school. There is a decided move away from using socialization as the sole justification for preschooling, and, as we have seen, the definition of readiness and ways to promote it are changing also. Preschools are now promoted as ways to accomplish the following things:

- *Support and develop children's innate capacity for learning.*   Thus the responsibility for "getting ready for school" is shifted from being primarily a child's and parent's responsibility to a cooperative venture between child/family/home and school.

- *Provide a centralized agency (i.e., the school) and a support system (i.e., school personnel) to deliver services at an early age to children and their families.*

- *Deliver a full range of health, social, economic, and literacy services to families.*   Thus, *family welfare* is also seen as a justification for operating preschools.

- *Solve or find solutions for pressing social problems.*   The early years are viewed as a time when interventions are most likely to have long-term positive influences. Preschool programs are seen as ways of lowering the number of dropouts, improving children's health, and reducing substance abuse and delinquency.

SCHOOLS FOR THE TWENTY-FIRST CENTURY

Edward Zigler, one of the developers of the Head Start program, proposes an alternative model for preschool programs. Called *Schools for the Twenty-First Century,* Zigler's model suggests that public schools serve as sites for a comprehensive child care system. These schools would provide developmental child care for children ages three to five, half-day care for kindergarten children, before and after school care, and child care during vacations. (In chap. 8 we discuss the trend toward full-day kindergartens.) Public school personnel would also provide parent education and training for family day care providers. A description of the Twenty-First Century School in Independence, Missouri, appears in chapter 9.

WHO IS PRESCHOOL FOR?

Whenever we discuss educational programs of any kind, the question sooner or later arises regarding who should attend the programs. Preschool programs are no different. A quick and easy answer is that all three- and four-year-old children should attend schools; given unlimited resources, this is the appropriate solution. In fact, the national trend is toward universal public education for three- and four-year-olds; however, we will probably not see this trend become a reality before the first decade of the twenty-first century. So for now, the children who attend public preschools are generally those who are members of a particular risk group—that is, children of low-income parents, children of teenage parents, and children with special needs. At the other end of the economic spectrum, parents who *can* afford to send their children to private preschools do so, especially to academically oriented preschools. Such parents will continue to seek out and pay for the best for their children.

PURPOSES OF PRESCHOOLS

Another dimension to the discussion of public preschools always involves that of aims and purposes. It is easy to say that the preschool should stress teaching the basic skills: reading, writing, and arithmetic and getting children ready for kindergarten. However, given the needs of today's children and the fact that more are becoming at risk all the time, a purely academic curriculum hardly meets their needs. For many children, an academically oriented program with ample opportunities for social interactions meets their needs and those of their parents. A more appropriate response for at-risk children seems to be a program that combines education with a broad range of social services. In fact, a trend in preschool and early childhood programming is to focus on the social services approach as a way to meet all needs of the child and family (see chap. 9). Head Start is considered a model for providing comprehensive services (see chap. 10).

WHO SHOULD PROVIDE PRESCHOOL SERVICES?

Many agencies provide services for preschool children, including child care programs, Head Start, cooperative preschools, and others (see chap. 1). There is a growing consensus, however, that the public schools should provide programs and services for three- and four-year-olds. This preference is based on several factors. First, public schools and the infrastructure (teachers, cafeteria workers, custodians, and administration) are already in place; it makes sense, therefore, for them to open their facilities to this younger population. Second, as long as parents pay taxes to support the public schools, they often conclude that these schools should provide services for their children rather than their paying other programs to do so. Third, the public schools are viewed as institutions that can offer all children equal access to educational and other services. If the public schools enroll three- and four-year-old children, other programs that traditionally offer programs to this age group will turn their attention to serving the needs of children from birth to age two.

Society and parents are demanding more quality preschool programs because they view the preschool years as a valuable time for learning. Preschool children need opportunities to use open-ended materials in order to organize their information and develop thinking. How do activities such as this one promote these processes?

WHO IS THE PRESCHOOLER?

Today's preschoolers are not like the children of previous decades. Many have already attended one, two, or three years of child care or nursery school. They have watched hundreds of hours of television. Many have experienced the trauma of family divorces, and many have experienced the psychological effects of abuse. Both collectively and individually, the experiential backgrounds of preschoolers are quite different from those of previous generations. But it is precisely this background of experiences, its impact and implications, that early childhood professionals must understand to meet preschoolers' needs effectively.

Physical and Motor Development

An understanding of preschoolers' physical and motor development enables you to acknowledge why active learning is so important. To begin with, a noticeable difference between preschoolers and their infant and toddler counterparts is that preschoolers have lost most of their baby fat and taken on a leaner, lankier look. This "slimming down" and increasing motor coordination enables the preschooler to participate with more confidence in the locomotor activities so vitally necessary during this stage of growth and development. Both girls and boys continue to grow several inches per year throughout the preschool years (see Figure 7–2).

Preschool children are in an age of rapid motor skill development. They are learning to use and test their bodies. It is a time for learning what they can do and how they can do it as individuals. *Locomotion* plays a large role in motor and skill development and includes activities of moving the body through space—walking, running, hopping, jumping, rolling, dancing, climbing, and leaping. Children use these activities to investigate and explore the relationships between themselves, space, and objects in space.

Preschoolers demonstrate the principles of cephalocaudal and proximodistal development mentioned in chapter 6. The cephalocaudal development enables the preschooler to participate in many physical activities; likewise, the concentration of motor development in the small muscles of the arms and hands lets them participate in fine-motor activities such as drawing, coloring, painting, cutting, and past-

FIGURE 7–2   Height and Weight of Preschoolers

| Age | Males | | Females | |
	Weight (pounds)	Height (inches)	Weight (pounds)	Height (inches)
3 years	32.4	38.0	30.7	37.6
4 years	36.8	40.5	35.2	40.0
5 years	41.2	43.3	38.9	42.7

Source: Adapted from P. V. V. Hamill et al., "Physical Growth: National Center for Health Statistics Percentiles," *American Journal of Clinical Nutrition* 32 (1979), pp. 607–629.

ing. Consequently, preschoolers need programs that provide action and play, supported by proper nutrition and healthy habits of plentiful rest and good hygiene.

Good educational practices also dictate that preschool programs deemphasize activities that require preschoolers to wait or sit for extended periods of time. Although learning self-control is part of preschoolers' socialization process, developmentally appropriate practices call for activity. It is also important to incorporate health education into programs for three-, four-, and five-year-olds. Children should participate in activities that promote good hygiene and nutrition. Preschool and elementary curricula should incorporate lifelong goals and objectives for healthy living. The goal is to promote, encourage, and develop good habits early in life rather than to have children grow up using bad habits.

Cognitive Development

Preschoolers are in the preoperational stage of intelligence. As we saw in chapter 4, these are characteristics of the preoperational stage: (1) children grow in their ability to use symbols, including language; (2) children are not capable of operational thinking (an *operation* is a reversible mental action), which explains why Piaget named this stage preoperational; (3) children center on one thought or idea, often to the exclusion of other thoughts; (4) children are unable to conserve; and (5) children are egocentric.

Characteristics during the preoperational stage have particular implications for early childhood professionals. Because preschool children are egocentric, they believe everyone sees what they see and think as they think. This egocentrism influences how preschoolers respond to things and interact with others. Piaget believed the underlying reason for many of preoperational children's "errors" of reasoning stem from their inability to see other viewpoints. This egocentrism is not selfishness but rather a lack of awareness. Early childhood educators recognize that many children are able to engage in cognitive activities earlier than Piaget thought and that many do not demonstrate a characteristic at the age or to the degree Piaget maintained.

Language Development

The preschool years are a period of rapid language growth and development. Vocabulary increases, and as children continue to master syntax and grammar, sentence length increases. The first words infants or toddlers use are *holophrases*, one word that conveys the meaning of a sentence. For example, a child may say "milk" to express "I'd like some more milk, please."

At one year, infants know two or more words; by the age of two, about 275. During the second year of life, toddlers' language proficiency increases to include *telegraphic speech*—two- or three-word utterances acting as a sentence. "Amy go," for example, can mean that Amy wants her mother to take her for a walk in the stroller. During the third year, children add helping verbs and negatives to their vocabulary, for example, "I don't want milk." Sentences also become longer and more complex. During the fourth and fifth years, children use noun or subject clauses, conjunctions, and prepositions to complete their sentences.

During the preschool years, children's language development is diverse, comprehensive, and it constitutes a truly impressive range of learning. An even more impressive feature of language acquisition during the preschool years is that children learn intuitively, without a great deal of instruction, the rules of language that apply to words and phrases they use.

PRESCHOOL PLAY

What Is Play?

There are many definitions of play and ideas about why children play. Children's play results in learning. Therefore, *play is the process through which children learn*. In this sense, play is a tool for learning.

The notion that children learn through play begins with Froebel, who built his system of schooling on the educative value of play. As discussed in chapter 2, Froebel believed that natural unfolding (development) occurs through play. Since his time, most early childhood programs have incorporated play into their curricula or have made play a major part of the day.

Montessori viewed children's active involvement with materials and the prepared environment as the primary means through which they absorbed knowledge and learn. John Dewey also advocated and supported active learning and believed that children learned through play activities that were based on their interests. Dewey thought too that children should have opportunities to engage in play that is associated with everyday activities (e.g., the house center, post office, grocery store, and doctor's office). He felt that play helps prepare children for adult occupations. This reasoning may explain why curriculum developers and teachers base many activities, such as a dress-up corner, around adult roles.

Piaget believed play promotes cognitive knowledge and was a means by which children construct knowledge of their world. He identified three kinds of knowledge: physical, logical-mathematical, and social. According to Piaget, through active involvement, children learn about things and the physical properties of objects; knowledge of the environment and their role(s) in it; and logical-mathematical knowledge—numeration, seriation, classification, time, space, and number. Regarding social knowledge, vocabulary, labels, and proper behavior, Piaget believed children learn this material from others.

Unlike Piaget, Vygotsky viewed the social interaction that occurs through play as essential to children's development. Through social interactions with others (see chap. 2), children learn language and social skills—cooperation and collaboration—that promote and enhance their cognitive development. Viewed from Vygotsky's perspective, adults' play with children is as important as children's play with their peers. Thus, play promotes cognitive development and provides for a way to develop social skills.

Play as a means of expending surplus energy has historically been a popular theory about why children play. This theory resembles the *cathartic theory*, which holds that children use play as a means of relieving frustrations and emotions. Play is certainly an excellent means of relieving stress, and early childhood professionals now recognize that play is one antidote for stressful situations and events.

Purposes of Play

Children learn through play, and play occupies a major part of most children's lives. Play activities are essential to their development, helping them

- learn concepts;
- develop social skills;
- develop physical skills;
- master life situations;
- practice language processes;
- develop literacy skills (see description later);
- enhance self-esteem; and
- prepare for adult life and roles (e.g., learn to become independent, how to think, make decisions, cooperate/collaborate with others).

Without the opportunity for play and an environment that supports it, a child's learning is limited. Early childhood programs that provide time for play increase and enhance the limits of children's learning.

Montessori thought of play as children's work and the home and preschool as "workplaces" where learning occurs through play. This linking of play and work is unfortunate in some respects because it attaches many of the negative connotations of adult work to children's play. However, the comparison does convey the total absorption, dedication, energy, and focus children demonstrate through their play activities. Children engage in play naturally and enjoy it; they do not select play activities because they intentionally set out to learn. For example, a child does not choose to put blocks in order from small to large because he wants to learn how to seriate, nor does he build an incline because he wants to learn the concept of "down" or the principles of gravity; however, the learning outcomes of his play are obvious. Children's play is full of opportunities for learning, but there is no guarantee that children will learn all they need to know when they need to know it through play. Providing opportunities for children to choose among well-planned, varied learning activities enhances the probability that they will learn through play.

Kinds of Play

Social Play

Most children's play occurs with or in the presence of other children. Social play occurs when children play with each other in groups. Mildred Parten developed the most comprehensive description and classification of children's play. Her terminology, developed in 1932, is still valid for today's children:

In solitary play, shown here, the child focuses on what she is doing. Onlooker play is merely observing the play of others. Children engaged in parallel play are doing what others are doing but are not really playing together. In associative play, there is some interaction.

Parten's Types of Social Play

- *Unoccupied play.* The child does not play with anything or anyone; the child merely stands or sits, without doing anything observable.

- *Solitary play.* Although involved in play, the child plays alone, seemingly unaware of other children.

- *Onlooker play.* The child watches and observes the play of other children; the center of interest is others' play.

- *Parallel play.* The child plays alone but in ways similar to and with toys or materials similar to those of other children.

- *Associative play.* Children interact with each other, perhaps by asking questions or sharing materials, but do not play together.

- *Cooperative play.* Children actively play together, often as a result of organization of the teacher (the least frequently witnessed play in preschools).[1]

Social play supports many important functions. First, it provides the means for children to interact with others and learn many social skills. Play provides a context in which children learn: how to compromise ("OK, I'll be the baby first and you can be the mommy"), gain impulse control ("I can't always do what I want when I want to do it"), learn to be flexible ("We'll do it your way first and then my way"), resolve conflicts, and continue the process of learning who they are. Children learn what skills they have, for example, skills relating to leadership. Second, social play provides a vehicle for practicing and developing literacy skills. Children have others with whom to practice language and learn from. Third, it helps children learn impulse control; they realize they cannot always do whatever they want. And fourth, in giving a child other children with whom to interact, social play negates isolation and helps children learn the social interactions so vital to successful living.

Cognitive Play

Froebel, Montessori, and Piaget recognized the cognitive value of play. Froebel through his gifts and occupations and Montessori through her sensory materials saw children's active participation with concrete materials as a direct link to knowledge and development. Piaget's theory influences contemporary thinking about the cognitive basis for play. From a Piagetian perspective, play is literally cognitive development (see chap. 4 and the High/Scope Curriculum).

Piaget and Stages of Play

Piaget describes four stages of play through which children progress as they develop, including functional play, symbolic play, playing games with rules, and constructive play.

Functional Play.   Functional play, the only play that occurs during the sensimotor period, is based on and occurs in response to muscular activities and the need to be active. Functional play is characterized by repetitions, manipulations, and self-imitation. Piaget described functional play (which he also called *practice play* and *exercise play*) this way: "The child sooner or later (often even during the learning period) grasps for the pleasure of grasping, swings [a suspended object] for the sake of swinging, etc. In a word, he repeats his behavior not in any further effort to learn or to investigate, but for the mere joy of mastering it and of showing off to himself his own power of subduing reality."[2]

Repetition of language is common at this level. Functional play allows children to practice and learn physical capabilities while exploring their immediate environments. Very young children are especially fond of repeating movements for the pleasure of it. They engage in sensory impressions for the joy of experiencing the functioning of their bodies.

Symbolic Play.   The second stage is symbolic play, which Piaget also referred to as the "let's pretend" stage of play. During this stage, children freely display their creative and physical abilities and social awareness in a number of ways. A child's pretending to be something else, such as an animal, is an example of symbolic play. Symbolic play also occurs when children pretend that one object is another—that a building block is a car, for example. Symbolic play may also entail pretending to be another person—a mommy, daddy, or caregiver. As toddlers and preschoolers grow older, their symbolic play becomes more elaborate and involved.

Playing Games with Rules.   The third stage of play, games with rules, begins around the ages of seven or eight. During this stage, children learn to play within rules and limits and adjust their behavior accordingly. During this stage, children can make and follow social agreements. Games with rules are very common in middle childhood and adulthood.

Constructive Play.   A fourth stage of play, constructive play, develops from symbolic play and represents children's adaptations to problems and their creative acts. Constructive play is characterized by children being involved in play activities in order to construct their knowledge of the world. They first manipulate play materials and then use these materials to create and build things (a sand castle, a block building, a grocery store) and experiment with the ways things go together.

Value of Play

Play serves an important process for promoting children's learning and development. Play enhances social interaction and the development of social skills—learning how to share, getting along with others, taking turns, and generally learning how to live in a community. Play promotes physical development and body coordination and develops and refines small- and large-motor skills. Play helps children discover their bodies: how they function and how they can be used in learning.

Lifetime attitudes toward play develop in early childhood. Children learn motor skills they will use as adults and discover that play can be restful, therapeutic, and satisfying. If children are taught that play is something one does only after all one's work is finished, or that it takes away from productive work, or is only for special occasions, children will have a negative attitude toward play, feel guilty about participating in it, and have a hard time integrating it into their adult lives.

Play assists in personality and emotional development because it enables children to try out different roles, release feelings, express themselves in a nonthreatening atmosphere, and consider the roles of others. Play enhances and promotes development in the cognitive, affective, and psychomotor areas. It helps children learn, acquire information, and construct their own intelligence. Through play, children develop schemes, find out how things work (and what will not work), and lay the foundation for cognitive growth. Because play activities are interesting, play becomes naturally, or intrinsically, rewarding, and children engage in it for its own value. Children's interest in their play also leads to a continually lengthened attention span.

Professionals' Roles in Promoting Play

Early childhood professionals are the key to whether meaningful play, and therefore learning, occurs in the preschool. What professionals do and the attitudes they have toward play determine the quality of the preschool environment and the events that occur there. Professionals have these responsibilities in a quality play curriculum:

• Planning to implement the curriculum through play and integrating specific learning activities with play to achieve specific learning outcomes. Play activities should match children's developmental needs and be free of sex and cultural stereotypes. Professionals have to be clear about curriculum concepts and ideas they want children to learn through play.

• Providing time for learning through play and including it in the schedule as a legitimate activity in its own right

- Creating environments and structuring time for learning through play, including indoor and outdoor areas that encourage play and support its role in learning
- Organizing the classroom or center environment so that cooperative learning is possible and active learning occurs
- Providing materials and equipment that are appropriate to the children's developmental level and support a nonsexist and multicultural curriculum
- Educating assistants and parents in how to promote learning through play
- Supervising play activities and participating in children's play. In these roles, professionals help, show, and model when appropriate and refrain from interfering when appropriate.
- Observing children's play. Teachers can learn how children play and the learning outcomes of play to use in planning classroom activities.
- Questioning children about their play, discussing what children did during play, and "debriefing" children about what they have learned through play

Informal or Free Play

Proponents of learning through spontaneous, informal play activities maintain that learning is best when it occurs in an environment that contains materials and people with whom children can interact. Learning materials may be grouped in centers with similar equipment: a kitchen center, a dress-up center, a block center, a music and art center, a water or sand area, and a free-play center, usually with items such as tricycles, wagons, and wooden slides for promoting large-muscle development.

The atmosphere of this kind of preschool setting tends to approximate a home setting, in which learning is informal, unstructured, and unpressured. Talk and interactions with adults are spontaneous. Play and learning episodes are generally determined by the interests of the children and, to some extent, professionals, based on what they think is best for children. The expected learning outcomes are socialization, emotional development, self-control, and acclimation to a school setting.

Three problems can result from a free-play format. One is that some professionals interpret it to mean that children are free to do whatever they wish with whatever materials they want to use. Second, aside from seeing that children have materials to play with, some professionals do not plan for special play materials, how children will interact with the materials, or what children are to learn while playing. Third, sometimes professionals do not hold children accountable for learnings from free play. They rarely question children about concepts or point out the nature of the learning. Such professionals are seldom part of the play process. They act as disinterested bystanders, with their primary goal being to see that children do not injure themselves while playing. In a quality program of free play both indoors and outside, professionals are active participants. Sometimes they observe, sometimes they play with the children, sometimes they help the children, but they never intrude or impose. Avoiding the possible pitfalls of the free-play format enables children to learn many things as they interact with interesting activities, materials, and people in their environment.

Preschool programs must provide children with the opportunity for play, the materials for play, and an environment that supports play. What are some important roles of early childhood professionals as they facilitate and guide children's play?

Dramatic (Pretend) Play

Dramatic play allows children to participate vicariously in a wide range of activities associated with family living, society, and their cultural heritage. Dramatic play is generally of two kinds: sociodramatic and fantasy. *Sociodramatic play* usually involves everyday realistic activities and events, whereas *fantasy play* typically involves fairy tale and superhero play. Dramatic play centers often include areas such as housekeeping, dress-up, occupations, dolls, school, and other situations that follow the children's interests. A skillful professional can think of many ways to expand their interest and then replace old centers with new ones. For example, after a visit to the police station, a housekeeping center might be replaced by an occupations center.

In the sociodramatic play area, children have an opportunity to express themselves, assume different roles, and interact with their peers. Sociodramatic play centers thus act as a nonsexist and multicultural arena in which all children are equal. Professionals can learn a great deal about children by watching and listening to their dramatic play. For example, one professional heard a child remark to the doll he was feeding that "you better eat all of this 'cause it's all we got in the house." As a result of further investigation, the professional linked the family with a social service agency that helped them obtain food and money.

Professionals must assume a proactive role in organizing and changing the dramatic play areas. They must set the stage for dramatic play and participate in play with the children. They must also encourage those who "hang back" and are reluctant to play and involve those who may not be particularly popular with the other children. Surprisingly, because of their background and environment, some children have to be taught how to play. In other words, as in all areas of early childhood education, professionals must deal with children's dramatic play in an individual and holistic way.

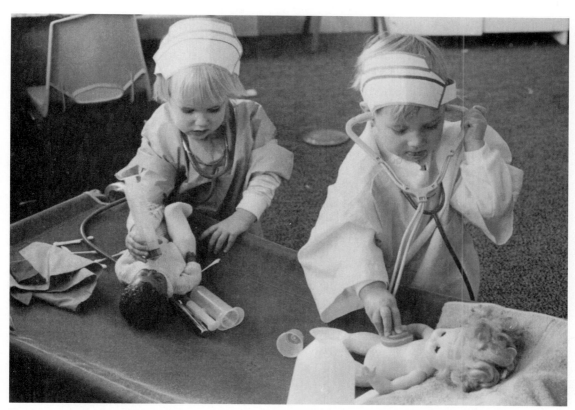

Dramatic play serves an important function of promoting children's understanding of concepts and processes. Here, play allows children to symbolically engage in health care procedures and helps alleviate their fears of doctors, nurses, and other medical practitioners as well as medical settings.

Outdoor Play

Children's play outside is just as important as that inside. However, outdoor play is often considered relatively unimportant and needed only as an opportunity for children to let off steam and get rid of excess energy. Children do need to relieve stress and tension through play, and outdoor activities provide this opportunity. Professionals should plan for what children will do and the equipment available. Outdoor play is not a chance for children to run wild.

Outdoor environments and activities promote large- and small-muscle development and body coordination as well as language development, social interaction, and creativity. Professionals should plan for a particular child or group of children to move through progressively higher skill levels of running, climbing, and throwing. The outdoor area is a learning environment, and as such, the playground should be designed according to learning objectives.

Many teachers also enjoy bringing the indoor learning environment "outdoors," using easels, play dough, or dramatic play props to further enhance learning opportunities. In addition, taking a group of children outdoors for story or music time, sitting in the shade of a tree, brings a fresh perspective to daily group activities.

Safety

Providing a safe and healthy environment is an important part of an early childhood professional's responsibilities and applies to the playground as well as to the inside facilities. Outdoor areas should be safe for children to play. Usually, states and cities have regulations requiring the playground to be fenced and have a source of drinking water, a minimum number of square feet of play area for each child, and equipment that is in good repair. As with indoor activities, provisions for outdoor play involve planning, supervising, and helping children be responsible for their behavior.

Rough-and-Tumble Play

All children, to a greater or lesser degree, engage in rough-and-tumble play. One theory of play says that children play because they are biologically programmed to do so; that is, it is part of children's—and adults'—genetic heritage to engage in play activities. Indeed, there is a parallel in children's rough-and-tumble play and behaviors in the animal kingdom, for example, run-and-chase activities and "pretend" fighting. Rough-and-tumble play activities enable children to learn about themselves (e.g., lead/follow, develop physical skills, experiment and practice roles physically and vicariously).

Issues Associated with Play

First is the issue of early childhood professionals' willingness, ability, and skill in explaining to parents in particular and the public in general the value of play and that children can and do learn through play. Early childhood professionals constantly must educate parents and the public about the function and value of play in preschool settings. When professionals do not do a good job of explaining, the value of play tends to lessen in the public's eye, which further encourages those who advocate a strictly academic approach to preschool programs.

Second, preschool professionals must plan for children's play to assure that they have time for play, the appropriate materials for play, and an appropriate environment that supports, promotes, and encourages developmentally appropriate play for all children. The unwillingness of some to do this or not do it well means that children will not gain the benefit from play that they need.

THE PRESCHOOL CURRICULUM

How do we determine an appropriate curriculum for three- and four-year-olds? Some say society determines the curriculum according to what it thinks children should learn and do. For example, Western society values academic skill related to reading, writing, and math as well as social skills and getting along with others.

Therefore, preschool activities that help children do these things should be included in the curriculum. Others say the curriculum should be based on what children will learn and do in kindergarten and first grade. This kind of preschool curriculum should, therefore, include many "readiness" activities. Still others say the individual child should determine the curriculum according to what each knows or does not know; thus, the starting place is the needs and interests of children.

Play as Curriculum

In the continuing debate about what the preschool curriculum should be, many people respond that play is the most appropriate curriculum. However, play is the *process* by which the curriculum is implemented. Although it is true that children learn *through* play, to say play is the curriculum begs the issue of what children are to learn.

What good preschool programs do—what any good educational program does—is to take each child at whatever point in development he or she is at and provide a set of appropriate experiences enabling that child to go as far as possible *without* pushing, hurrying, or overstressing. The essence of early education is a set of guided experiences, both cognitive and affective. Early childhood educators

Literacy development is one of the important goals of the preschool. Professionals can read to and involve children in print materials as a means of helping them develop literacy skills. Why does our society place such an important emphasis on literacy development?

should always start with children and base their curriculum on them. What we teach is and should be based on child development, the needs of children, and what they are like as individuals. If this is done, then the curriculum will be child centered and developmentally appropriate.

The vignette on pages 268–269 illustrates how literacy can be promoted through play.

PRESCHOOL GOALS

All programs should have goals to guide activities and on which to base teaching methodologies. Without goals, it is easy to end up teaching just about anything without knowing why. Goals of individual preschools vary, but all programs should have certain essential goals. Simply because programs have goals, however, does not necessarily mean their teaching methods support or achieve those goals. Many preschools suffer this weakness—there is a difference between what they say they do and what they actually do. Most good preschools, however, plan goals in these areas: social and interpersonal skills, self-help and intrapersonal skills, building self-esteem, academics, thinking skills, learning readiness, language, and nutrition.

Social and Interpersonal Goals

- Helping children learn how to get along with other children and adults and how to develop good relationships with teachers
- Helping children learn to help others and develop caring attitudes

Self-Help Skills and Intrapersonal Goals

- Modeling for children how to take care of their personal needs such as dressing (tying, buttoning, zipping) and knowing what clothes to wear
- Eating skills (using utensils, napkins, and a cup or glass; setting a table)
- Health skills (how to wash and bathe, how to brush teeth)
- Grooming skills (combing hair, cleaning nails)

Self-Esteem Goals

- Promoting self-help skills to help children develop good self-image and high self-esteem
- Helping children learn about themselves, their family, and their culture
- Developing a sense of self-worth by providing experiences for success and competence
- Teaching about body parts and their function

Academic Goals

- Teaching children to learn their names, addresses, and phone numbers
- Facilitating children's learning of colors, sizes, shapes, and positions such as under, over, and around

- Facilitating children's learning of numbers and prewriting skills, shape identification, letter recognition, sounds, and rhyming
- Providing for small-muscle development

Thinking Goals

- Providing environments and activities that enable children to develop the skills essential to constructing schemes in a Piagetian sense—classification, seriation, numeration, and knowledge of space and time concepts. These form the basis for logical-mathematical thinking.
- Giving children opportunities to respond to questions and situations that require them to synthesize, analyze, and evaluate

Learning Readiness Goals

- Facilitating readiness skills related to school success, such as following directions, learning to work alone, listening to the teacher, developing an attention span, learning to stay with a task until it is completed, staying in one's seat, and controlling impulses

Literacy Goals

- Providing opportunities for interaction with adults and peers as a means of developing oral language skills
- Helping children increase their vocabularies
- Helping children learn to converse with other children and adults
- Building proficiency in language
- Developing emergent literacy skills (prewriting and reading skills)

Nutrition Goals

- Providing experiences that enable children to learn the role of good nutritional practices and habits in their overall development
- Providing food preparation experiences
- Introducing children to new foods, a balanced menu, and essential nutrients

Developing Independence

Besides the goals of promoting the skill areas, but subsumed within them, are two other goals of the preschool experience: to foster independence and a positive attitude toward learning. In many respects, the major goal for all education from preschool to university is to help students become independent. In addition, they should develop an attitude of liking to learn and wanting to come to school. In a sense, the entire school program should help children do things for themselves, to become autonomous.

PROMOTING LITERACY IN PLAY

Early childhood educators have recognized the value of play for social, emotional, and physical development. The use of play to promote literacy development, however, is at an earlier stage. The prevalent concept of reading readiness as a set of abstract skills taught in a formal pencil-and-paper setting assigns no role to play, especially during free-choice cooperative play periods.

Recently, play has attracted greater importance as a medium for literacy development. It is recognized now that literacy develops in meaningful, functional social settings. Literacy development involves a child's active engagement in cooperation and collaboration with peers; it builds on what the child already knows with the support and guidance of others. Play provides this setting. During observations of children at play, one can note the functional uses of literacy that children incorporate into their play themes. When the environment is appropriately prepared with literacy materials in play areas, children have been observed to engage in attempted and conceptional reading and writing in collaboration with other youngsters. In similar settings lacking literacy materials, the same literacy activity did not occur.[3]

To demonstrate how play in the appropriate setting can nurture literacy development, I take you into a classroom in which the teacher has designed a veterinarian's office to go along with their animal theme, with a concentration on pets. The dramatic play area was designed with a waiting room; chairs; a table filled with magazines, books, and pamphlets about pet care; posters about pets; office hour notices; a "No Smoking" sign; and a sign advising visitors to "Check in with the nurse when arriving." On a nurse's desk were patient forms on clipboards, a telephone, an address and telephone book, appointment cards, and a calendar. The office contained patient folders, prescription pads, white coats, masks, gloves, a toy doctor's kit, and stuffed animals for patients.

Ms. Meyers, the teacher, guided students in using the various materials during free-play time in the veterinarian's office, for example, by reminding the children to read to pets in waiting areas or to fill out forms with information about a patient's condition, treatments, recommended prescriptions, and appointment times. In addition to giving directions, Ms. Meyers also modeled behaviors by participating in play with the children when the materials were first introduced. This setting provided a literacy-rich environment with books and writing materials; modeled reading and writing by teachers that children could observe and emulate; provided the opportunity

Contributed by Lesley Mandel Morrow, professor and chair, Department of Learning and Teaching, Rutgers University.

Unfortunately, some preschool programs and teachers foster an atmosphere of dependence, helplessness, and reliance on others by doing things for the children instead of helping children learn to do things for themselves. A good rule-of-thumb for all preschool professionals is to avoid doing anything for children that they can do or learn to do for themselves. We can encourage independence by having children take care of their own environment. Children should be responsible for dusting, cleaning, washing, wiping, polishing, emptying waste baskets, vacuuming, sweeping, and helping care for classroom pets. Whether programs promote dependence or independence can be ascertained by comparing them to the scale in Figure 7–3 (see p. 271).

to practice literacy in real-life situations that had meaning and function; and encouraged children socially to interact, collaborate, and perform reading and writing with peers.[4] The following anecdotes relate the type of behavior that was observed in the play area.

Jessica was waiting to see the doctor. She told her stuffed animal dog Sam not to worry, that the doctor would not hurt him. She asked Jenny, who was waiting with her stuffed animal cat Muffin, what the kitten's problem was. The girls agonized over the ailments of their pets. After a while they stopped talking, and Jessica picked up a book and pretended to read *Are You My Mother?* to her dog Sam. Jessica showed Sam the pictures as she read.

Preston examined Christopher's teddy bear and wrote a report in the patient's folder. He read his scribble writing out loud and said, "This teddy bear's blood pressure is twenty-nine points. He should take sixty-two pills an hour until he is better and keep warm and go to bed." At the same time he read, he showed Christopher what he had written so he would understand what to do.

When selecting settings to promote literacy in play, choose those that are familiar to children and relate to themes being studied. Some suggestions for literacy materials and settings to add to dramatic play areas include the following:

- A fast-food restaurant, ice cream store, or bakery suggests menus, order pads, a cash register, specials for the day, recipes, and lists of flavors or products.

- A newspaper office yields writing paper, telephones, directories, maps, typewriters, computers, and areas that focus on sports, travel, general news, and weather.

- A supermarket or local grocery store can include labeled shelves and sections, food containers, cash registers, telephones, shopping receipts, checkbooks, coupons, and promotional flyers.

- A post office to serve for mailing the children's letters would need paper, envelopes, address books, pens, pencils, stamps, cash registers, and mailboxes. A mail carrier hat and bag are important for children who deliver the mail by reading names and addresses.

- A gas station and car repair shop can be designed in the block area. Toy cars and trucks can be used for props. There can be receipts for sales, road maps for help with directions to different destinations, auto repair manuals for fixing cars and trucks, posters that advertise automobile equipment, and empty cans of different products found in stations.[5]

Texas Essential Elements for Preschool

The following are the Texas Essential Elements for Preschool in the areas of social/emotional and intellectual development. In order to identify this baseline information, the Texas Education Agency (TEA, the state Department of Education) reviewed literature, requested suggestions from teachers across the state, talked with curriculum experts, and held public hearings to determine what children should learn and be able to do.

Prekindergarten Education

Social/emotional development, prekindergarten, shall include the following essential elements:

Promoting good nutrition for children and their families is an important part of the preschool curriculum and helps establish lifelong attitudes toward healthy living. An emphasis on nutrition illustrates professionals' concern for the whole child.

I.   Emotional development (knowledge, understanding, and positive acceptance of self). The student shall be provided opportunities to:

   A.   recognize successes and feel pride in work

   B.   recognize and appreciate his or her uniqueness

   C.   persevere with most self-chosen tasks and

   D.   demonstrate emerging self-discipline and autonomous behaviors through decision making and self-selected activities

II. Social development (interactions with others). The student shall be provided opportunities to:

   A.   experience positive, supportive interactions with adults and peers

   B.   develop a sense of belonging to a group

   C.   engage in cooperative activities

   D.   learn how to make and maintain friendships and

   E.   show respect for individuals in the diverse school population

III. Social responsibilities (behaviors of a socially responsible person). The student shall be provided opportunities to:

   A.   observe and role play socially responsible behaviors in a variety of situations

   B.   learn school and classroom routines

   C.   develop an emerging awareness of the care of property and materials

   D.   develop an emerging awareness of environmental issues

FIGURE 7–3   Preschool Environment Rating Scale for Independence

Practices That Foster Dependence	Practices That Encourage Independence
Teachers put children's wraps on for them.	Teachers teach children how to put on their own wraps.
Adults set tables, put out napkins, pour drinks, etc.	Children set tables, put out napkins, pour their own drinks.
Adults serve children lunch, snacks.	Children serve themselves; preferably they eat family style.
Adults clean up after children.	Children clean up after themselves.
Adults feed children.	Children are taught how to feed themselves and other self-help skills.
Children have to ask adults for materials and equipment.	Children have reasonably free access to equipment and materials.
Adults pass out and collect materials.	Children are responsible for passing out, collecting, and organizing materials.
Adults clean up after children.	Children clean up after themselves and put away all materials.

E.   value and respect individual similarities and differences and

F.   value and respect similarities and differences in cultural identities and heritage including linguistic variations.

Intellectual development, prekindergarten, shall include the essential elements:

I.   Knowledge of communication. Receptive/expressive language integrated through meaningful listening/speaking and print-related experiences. [Note: The essential elements for primary language for bilingual education, prekindergarten, and English as a second language, prekindergarten, are described in chap. 14.] The student shall be provided opportunities to:

A.   focus attention on adult and peer speakers during individual and group interactions

B.   enjoy repetition, rhyme, and rhythm through poems, chants, and fingerplays individually or with a group

C.   enjoy daily listening and responding to stories and books

D.   follow simple oral directions

E.   recognize voice tone and nonverbal cues to aid in communication

F.   acquire vocabulary related to concepts in a meaningful context

G.   engage in conversation to achieve a variety of purposes including getting needs met, requesting, inquiring, sharing information, and playing

H.   select books for individual needs and interests

I.   associate print with spoken language

    J.   become familiar with personally meaningful environmental print

    K.   share ideas, feelings, and stories through activities such as dictating stories, conversation, dramatic play and

    L.   recognize that experiences can be written about

II.   Knowledge of integrated content. Integrated content acquired through processes of identifying, comparing and contrasting, classifying, sequencing and ordering, predicting cause/effect relationships, and exploring. The student shall be provided opportunities to:

    A.   identify:

        1.   match objects in one-to-one correspondence

        2.   become familiar with a variety of geometric shapes in the environment

        3.   use the senses to gain information about objects from the environment emphasizing color, texture, taste, odor, sound, size, shape, direction, motion, heat/cold, and sink/float

        4.   celebrate special events (e.g., birthdays, holidays) including those that are culturally related and

        5.   discuss ways people can help and learn from each other.

    B.   compare and contrast:

        1.   recognize that there are different types of families, homes, and communities and

        2.   compare similarities and differences of a variety of objects.

    C.   classify:

        1.   classify a variety of objects by function and

        2.   classify a variety of objects by a single attribute.

    D.   sequence and order:

        1.   repeat and create a simple pattern using concrete objects (e.g., beads, blocks) and

        2.   describe sequences in basic family and school routines.

    E.   predict cause/effect relationships:

        1.   observe changes in nature and daily events

        2.   draw conclusions and predict outcomes based on experience and

        3.   assist in setting class rules including rules of safety.

    F.   explore:

        1.   demonstrate creative thinking through fluency, flexibility, elaboration, creation of new ideas, spontaneity

        2.   construct structures using blocks and other manipulative materials of different sizes and shapes

        3.   construct basic concepts of weight, mass, and volume through water play, sand play, and cooking

        4.   explore positional relationships such as in, on, under and

        5.   interpret simple visuals (e.g., photographs, pictures).[6]

Developing the Whole Child

Preschool professionals have always been concerned with the development of the whole child. This concern requires providing activities and experiences that promote growth in the physical, emotional, social, and cognitive realms. These areas are not separate and mutually exclusive—they are interrelated. Good programs try to balance activities to address these areas.

The Daily Schedule

Although there are various ways to implement a preschool's goals, most preschools operate according to a play-oriented program that includes self-selection of activities and learning centers. A daily schedule in preschool programs is illustrated in the following sections.

Opening Activities

As children enter, the professional greets each individually. Daily personal greetings make the child feel important, build a positive attitude toward school, and provide an opportunity to practice language skills. They also give the professional a chance to check each child's health and emotional status. Children usually do not arrive all at one time, so the first arrivals need something to do while others are arriving. Free selection of activities or letting children self-select from a limited range of quiet activities, such as puzzles, pegboards, or markers to color with, are appropriate. Some professionals further organize this procedure by having children use an "assignment board" to help them make choices, limit the available choices, and practice concepts such as colors, shapes, and recognizing their names. Initially, the teacher may stand beside the board when children come and tell each child what the choices are. The teacher may hand children their name tags and put them on the board. Later, children can find their own tags and put them up. At the first of the school year, each child's name tag can include his or her picture (use an instant camera) or a symbol or shape the child has selected.

Group Meeting/Planning

After all the children arrive, they and the teacher plan together and talk about the day ahead. This is also the time for announcements, sharing, and group songs.

Learning Centers

After the group time, children are free to go to one of various learning centers, organized and designed to teach concepts. Figure 7–4 lists types of learning centers and the concepts each is intended to teach.

Bathroom/Hand Washing

Before any activity in which food is handled, prepared, or eaten, children should wash and dry their hands.

FIGURE 7–4   Learning Centers

Center	Concepts	Center	Concepts
Housekeeping	Classification	Woodworking	Following directions
	Language skills	(pinewood, cardboard,	Functions
	Sociodramatic play	Styrofoam)	Planning
	Functions		Whole/Part
	Processes		
Water/sand	Texture	Art	Color
	Volume		Size
	Quantity		Shape
	Measure		Texture
Blocks	Size		Design
	Shape		Relationships
	Length		
	Seriation	Science	Identification of odors
	Spatial relations		Functions
Books/language	Verbalization		Measure
	Listening		Volume
	Directions		Texture
	How to use books		Size
	Colors, size		Relationships
	Shapes		
Puzzles/perceptual development	Names	Manipulatives	Classification
	Size		Spatial relationships
	Shape		Shape
	Color		Color
	Whole/part		Size
	Figure/ground		Seriation
	Spatial relations		

Snacks

After center activities, a snack is usually served. It should be nutritionally sound and something the children can serve (and often prepare) themselves.

Outdoor Activity/Play/Walk

Ideally, outside play should be a time for learning new concepts and skills, not just a time to run around aimlessly. Children can practice climbing, jumping, swinging, throwing, and body control. Many walking trips and other events can be incorporated into outdoor play.

Bathroom/Toileting

Bathroom/toileting times offer opportunities to teach health, self-help, and intrapersonal skills. Children should also be allowed to use the bathroom whenever necessary.

Lunch

Lunch should be a relaxing time, and the meal should be served family style, with professionals and children eating together. Children should set their own tables and decorate them with placemats and flowers they can make in the art center or as a special project. Children should be involved in cleaning up after meals and snacks.

Relaxation

After lunch, children should have a chance to relax, perhaps to the accompaniment of stories, records, and music. This is an ideal time to teach children breathing exercises and relaxation techniques.

Nap Time

Children who want or need to should have a chance to rest or sleep. For those who do not need to or cannot sleep on a particular day, quiet activities should be available. Under no circumstances should children be forced to sleep or lie on a cot or blanket if they cannot sleep or have outgrown their need for an afternoon nap.

Bathroom/Toileting

See the previous comments.

Snack

See the previous comments.

Centers or Special Projects

Following nap time is a good time for center activities or special projects. (Special projects can also be conducted in the morning, and some may be more appropriate then, such as cooking something for snack or lunch.) Special projects might be cooking, holiday activities, collecting things, work projects, art activities, and field trips.

Group Time

The day can end with a group meeting to review the day's activities. This meeting develops listening and attention skills, promotes oral communication, stresses that learning is important, and helps children evaluate their performance and behavior.

This preschool schedule is for a whole-day program; many other program arrangements are possible. Some preschools operate half-day programs five days a week with only a morning session; others operate both a morning and afternoon session; others operate only two or three days a week. In still other programs, parents choose how many days they will send their children. Creativity and meeting parent needs seem to be hallmarks of preschool programs.

SELECTING A GOOD EARLY CHILDHOOD PROGRAM

Parents often wonder how to select a good early childhood program. Early childhood professionals can use these guidelines to help others arrive at an enlightened preschool decision:

- What are the physical accommodations like? Is the facility pleasant, light, clean, and airy? Is it a physical setting one would want to spend time in? If not, children will not want to, either. Are plenty of materials available for the children to use?

- Do the children seem happy and involved or passive? Is television used as a substitute for a good curriculum and quality professionals?

- What kinds of materials are available for play and learning?

- Is there a balance of activity and quiet play and of individual, small-group, and group activities? Child-directed and professional-directed activities? Indoor and outdoor play?

- Is the physical setting safe and healthy?

- Does the school have a written philosophy, objectives, and curriculum? Does the program philosophy agree with the parents' personal philosophy of how children should be reared and educated? Are the philosophy and goals age appropriate for the children being served?

- Does the staff have written plans? Is there a smooth flow of activities, or do children wait for long periods "getting ready" for another activity? Does the curriculum provide for skills in self-help; readiness for learning; and cognitive, language, physical, and social-emotional development? Lack of planning indicates lack of direction. Although a program whose staff does not plan is not necessarily a poor program, planning is one indicator of a good program.

- What is the adult-child ratio? How much time do teachers spend with children on a one-to-one or small-group basis? Do teachers take time to give children individual attention? Do children have an opportunity to be independent and do things for themselves?

- Are there opportunities for outdoor activities?

- What kind of education or training does the staff have? The staff should have training in the curriculum and teaching of young children. The director should have at least a bachelor's degree in childhood education or child development.

- Are staff personnel sensitive to the gender and cultural needs and backgrounds of children and families?

- Is the staff stable?

- How is lunchtime handled? Are children allowed to talk while eating? Do staff members eat with the children?

- Is the director well trained? Can she or he explain the program? Describing a typical day can be helpful. Is she or he actively involved in the program?

- How does the staff treat adults, including parents? Does the program address the needs of children's families?

- Is the program affordable? If a program is too expensive for the family budget, parents may be unhappy in the long run. Parents should inquire about scholarships, reduced fees, fees adjusted to income level, fees paid in monthly installments, and sibling discounts.

- Are parents of children enrolled in the program satisfied?

- Do the program's hours and services match parents' needs?

- How does the staff relate to children? Are the relationships loving and caring?

- How do staff members handle typical discipline problems, such as disputes between children? Are positive guidance techniques used? Are indirect guidance techniques used, for example, through room arrangement, scheduling, and appropriate activity planning? Is there a written discipline philosophy that agrees with the parents' philosophy?

- What are the provisions for emergency care and treatment? What procedures are there for taking care of ill children?

Quality Programs in Public Schools

Many child-serving and professional organizations recognize the need to develop guidelines for what their constituents believe makes quality and appropriate programming. The Southern Early Childhood Association, concerned about the effects of public preschools for four-year-olds, has issued a position statement on quality four-year-old programs in public schools, suggesting the following standards and procedures:

Happy and joyful involvement should be a major goal for all who are involved in preschool programs. When parents select early childhood programs for their children they should assure that joyful learning is promoted in the program. What can professionals do to assure that learning is joyful for children and their families?

- The administrator or building principal should have a minimum of nine semester hours of early education courses, with a focus on developmental characteristics of young children and appropriate programming.

- The teacher must hold a valid early childhood certificate; training must have included work with prekindergarten children; the training should meet the criteria of the NAEYC guidelines adopted as NCATE Standards for programs in four-year institutions.

- The child must be age four by the same date identifying eligibility for entrance in kindergarten.

- The adult-child ratio should be 1:7, not to exceed 1:10; enrollment that exceeds ten requires the assignment of an additional responsible adult with training in early childhood education/child development.

- The session for the child should not be less than one half-day.

- The daily schedule must be flexible, include a balance of free-choice and teacher-initiated large- and small-group activities, and reflect the developmental needs of the whole child.

- The early childhood curriculum must be designed specifically for four-year-olds and must be appropriate for their developmental level and interests.

- The learning environment must be arranged in interest centers that provide for individual and group learning experiences.

- Materials, equipment, and supplies appropriate for a developmental curriculum must be available in sufficient quantities.

- The classroom must be equipped with movable furniture of correct size, have a water supply available, and supply restroom facilities to accommodate four-year-old children.

- The outside play area must be accessible for flexible use; be properly equipped for climbing, riding, and enjoying gross-motor activities; and designed for the safety of the child including fencing.

- Minimum space requirements should be based on fifty square feet per child inside and one hundred square feet per child outside.

- The program must include a parent component: education, classroom visitation, and regular conferences to support the child's educational experience.

- A process must be established to provide communication among the early childhood programs in the school: four-year-olds, kindergarten, and primary grades.

- Appropriate developmental evaluation and observations must be conducted periodically to provide information for effective planning for meeting the individual needs of children.

Quality programs should *avoid* the following elements:

- The reassignment of upper elementary teachers who have no specialized training in early childhood education

- The elimination of play and the opportunity for child-selected activities

- The use of watered-down first grade curriculum that includes formal readiness activities, workbooks, and ditto sheets

- The placement of children in desks or rows of chairs that inhibit an active learning environment
- The accommodation of young children in facilities such as classroom, playground, cafeteria, and bathrooms that are designed for older children
- The use of standardized skill tests rather than observations and informal evaluations to assess the needs of the young child[7]

The National Association of Elementary School Principals states that quality early childhood programs do the following things:

- Develop a positive self-image
- Enhance social and emotional development
- Improve all communication skills
- Stimulate interest in the natural world
- Increase the child's capacity for self-discipline
- Advance the development of fundamental motor skills and abilities
- Identify special individual mental, social, emotional, or physical needs
- Further the development of respect for human dignity and for the rights of others
- Promote aesthetic appreciation and expression
- Encourage creativity
- Give and receive sincere affection[8]

EFFECTIVENESS OF PRESCHOOL PROGRAMS

The eternal question about early childhood programs is, Do they do any good? During the last several years, a number of longitudinal studies were designed to answer this question. The Perry Preschool Study came to this conclusion:

Results to age 19 indicate lasting beneficial effects of preschool education in improving cognitive performance during early childhood; in improving scholastic placement and achievement during the school years; in decreasing delinquency and crime, the use of welfare assistance, and the incidence of teenage pregnancy; and in increasing high school graduation rates and the frequency of enrollment in post-secondary programs and employment.[9]

From an analysis of seven exemplary preschool programs, Schweinhart and Weikart reached this conclusion:

The documented effects of early childhood education may be organized according to the major outcomes for participants at each period of their lives. These outcomes and the ages at which they occurred are: improved intellectual performance during early childhood; better scholastic placement and improved scholastic achievement during the elementary school years; and, during adolescence, a lower rate of delinquency and higher rates of both graduation from high school and employment at age 19. The best-documented preschool effect is an immediate improvement in intellectual performance as represented by intelligence test scores.[10]

ISSUES OF PRESCHOOL EDUCATION

Placement of Preschools in Public Schools

A major issue of preschool education is whether preschool programs should be operated by public schools. The fact remains, more and more four-year-olds are enrolled in preschool programs operated by the public schools. Some question whether public schools are the appropriate agencies to provide schooling for three- and four-year-olds. Many feel that public school professionals lack the training to meet the unique needs of this age group and that the public schools are motivated by a desire to gain control of this segment of education rather than to serve preschoolers' educational needs.

Developmentally Appropriate Curriculum

Many preschool programs are academic in nature; the curriculum consists of many activities, concepts, and skills traditionally associated with kindergarten and first grade. Critics of public school programs for three- and four-year-children think this kind of program puts too much pressure on them because they are not developmentally ready. A persistent and long-standing issue in early childhood education, "pushing" children usually revolves around overemphasis on learning basic skills and other skills associated with school success. The issue is complex. First, we need a precise understanding of what it means to push children. Some children are able to do more than others at earlier ages; some respond better to certain kinds of learning situations than others. Some parents and children are able to be involved in more activities than are others. So, we must always relate the topic of pushing to individual children and their family contexts. (Of course, when we feel parents may be pushing their child, we need to advise them of the potential harm they may be doing.)

Research is emerging about the effects of pushing young children. Researchers at Temple University, for example, found that children of mothers "who pushed them to attain academic success in preschool were less creative, had more anxiety about tests, and, by the end of kindergarten, had failed to maintain their internal academic advantage over their less-pressured peers."[11] Given this kind of data, both parents and early childhood educators must remember to provide opportunities for children to learn and develop at their own rates.

How to conduct a preschool program that is developmentally appropriate will likely remain an issue. Unfortunately, some preschool curricula are more suited to the kindergartner or first grader. Many programs operate under the false assumption that if it is good for kindergarten or first grade, the watered-down version is suitable for preschool. Professional and public organizations are calling public attention to the need to match the curriculum and activities of preschool programs to preschoolers' developmental levels, physically, cognitively, socially, and emotionally.

In response to the developmentally appropriate issue, many public schools and early childhood educators are calling for a restructuring of preschool early childhood programs that would result in an early childhood unit. Such a recommendation comes from *The Report of the NASBE Task Force on Early Childhood Education,* which states:

> We recommend that early childhood units be established in elementary schools, to provide a new pedagogy for working with children ages 4–8 and a focal point for enhanced services to preschool children and their parents.[12]

Certificate Training

Another issue is the problem of providing quality early childhood professionals. The growing number of preschools for three- and four-year-olds has created a need for more teachers and caregivers. Unfortunately, programs often hire unqualified personnel. In some cases this situation brings new revelations of child abuse in centers and makes more apparent an inadequacy in screening people who work with children. In our rush to provide programs, we must not cut corners or compromise standards. Professionals have moral, ethical, and legal obligations to protect children and provide them with teachers of the highest quality. Part of this issue involves teacher certification: people who work with or teach preschoolers should have specific training and/or certification for that age group. To allow someone with inappropriate education to teach preschoolers does an injustice to the concept of a developmentally appropriate curriculum.

Child-Centered Programs

Quality in preschool programs is an issue in another way, focusing on how to provide a balance between the best of those characteristics we define as quality: desirable teacher-child ratios, encouraging independence, and a learning environment that promotes child-centered learning while providing children with the skills necessary for future academic success. Some preschool proponents tend to focus almost exclusively on the basic skills of reading, writing, and arithmetic, with an accompanying tendency to minimize the importance of nurturing development in children's social and emotional areas. As early childhood professionals, we must strive to provide a balance between academics and all areas of development.

Should Three- and Four-Year-Olds Be in Public Preschools?

Despite the trend toward earlier schooling for three- and four-year-old children, some express the view that school can wait:

> Above all, the preschool years are a time for play. Let your child enjoy them. Parents today are being bombarded with advice and suggestions about ways in which, if they just do the right thing, they can make their children smarter and quicker and altogether more effective than they would have been without these special efforts.
> "Maybe I don't spend enough time with him," "Maybe I ought to do more about teaching him to read," "Maybe I'm losing time when I just let him grow up naturally," are doubts that worry many young parents today. Even if you don't read the books that tell you how to increase your child's intelligence or how to raise a brighter child, there is a feeling in the air that parents ought to be doing something special about their children's minds.

We assure you, no matter what you read or what anybody tells you, it is not necessary to push your preschooler.[13]

Who Are Preschools For?

The question to ask is, Should *all* three- and four-year-old children attend public preschools? As you might expect, there is more support for four-year-old attendance than for the three-year-old group. Some think that preschool programs should be for all children, not just for those who are at risk for school failure. However, not all agree. Others believe that attendance of all children is too costly. (Some school districts, such as Dade County, Florida, provide public preschools for threes and fours, but they charge parents tuition for their children's attendance.) Still others think that the inclusion of children with disabilities in public preschool programs places too many demands on other children and early childhood professionals. However, it is the children who are at risk for school failure and children with disabilities who are most likely to benefit from taxpayer support of public preschools.

THE FUTURE OF PRESCHOOL EDUCATION

The further spread of public preschools for three- and four-year-old children is inevitable. This growth, to the point where all children are included, will take decades but *will* happen. Most likely, the public schools will focus more on programs for four-year-old children and then, over time, include three-year-olds. A logical outgrowth of this long-term trend will be for the public schools to provide services for even younger children and their families. One thing is certain: preschool as it was known a decade ago is not the same today, and ten years from now, it will not be the same as it is today.

READINGS FOR FURTHER ENRICHMENT

Brickman, Nancy Altman. *Supporting Young Learners: Ideas for Preschool and Day Care Providers* (Ypsilanti, MI: High/Scope, 1991)

Includes ideas on planning by children and schedule planning by teachers, as well as strategies for active learning, home day care, playgrounds, and children's use of computers. An excellent source book with many ideas for first-year teachers as well as experienced teachers.

Jones, Elizabeth, and Gretchen Reynolds. *The Play's the Thing: Teachers' Roles in Children's Play* (New York: Teachers College Press, 1992)

Discusses the teacher's role in children's play: teachers as stage manager, mediator, player, scribe, assessor, and planner. Considers actual activities teachers can incorporate in the classroom that will not inhibit children's creative play.

Mitchell, Anne, Michelle Seligson, and Fern Marx. *Early Childhood Programs and the Public Schools: Between Promise and Practice* (Dover, MA: Auburn House, 1989)

A comprehensive look at all aspects of early childhood public school programs: history, results of state and district surveys, administration, financing, regulation, eligibility criteria, coordination of programs, staffing, types of programs, responsiveness to families, and a view toward the future. A good guide for anyone interested in early childhood programs.

Morrow, L. M. *Literacy Development in the Early Years: Helping Children Read and Write* (Boston: Allyn & Bacon, 1993)

An outstanding practical and informative book that provides the theory as well as the "how to" for promoting and helping children become literate.

Townsend-Butterworth, Diana. *Your Child's First School: A Handbook for Parents* (New York: Walker, 1992)

This excellent book provides much needed information to parents about the choices they have to make in selecting their child's first school. Some questions the book helps parents answer are, How do you decide whether your child is ready for school? How do you find a quality early childhood school? How can a parent be a partner in a child's education? How can a busy parent help a child get the most out of school?

Warner, Cynthia. *A Resource Guide to Public School Early Childhood Programs* (Alexandria, VA: Association for Supervision and Curriculum Development, 1988)

A guide to issues and concerns that surround the decisions administrators and teachers make regarding preschool programs.

ACTIVITIES FOR FURTHER ENRICHMENT

1. Visit preschool programs in your area. Determine their philosophies and find out what goes on in a typical day. Which would you send your children to? Why?

2. Observe children at play. Identify the types of social play listed in the chapter. Give descriptive examples of children's play for each stage.

3. Piaget believed that children construct schemes through play. Observe children's play, and give examples of schemes developed through play.

4. Identify the basic purposes of a preschool program. Ask your classmates to rank these in order. What conclusions can be drawn from their rankings?

5. Survey preschool parents to learn what they expect from a preschool program. How do parents' expectations compare to the goals of preschool programs you visited?

6. Tell how you would promote learning through a specific preschool activity. For example, what learning outcomes would you have for a sand/water area? What, specifically, would be your role in helping children learn?

7. Write a philosophy of a preschool program, and develop goals and objectives for it. Write a daily schedule that would support your goals.

8. Visit a preschool program, and request to see their program goals. How do they compare to those listed in this chapter? What would you change, add, or delete?

9. Read and review five articles that relate to today's trend in establishing quality preschool programs. What are the basic issues discussed? Do you agree with these issues?

10. Develop a file of activities you can use in a preschool program. Use the following headings to help organize your file:

      Activity name

      Objective

      Description

      Materials needed

      Is it easier to find materials for some areas than for others? Why?

11. How do parents and others "push" children? How can pushing harm children? Do you think some children need a push? What is the difference between constructive and destructive pushing?

NOTES

1. Mildred Parten, "Social Play among Preschool Children," *Journal of Abnormal and Social Psychology* 27 (1932), pp. 243–269.

2. Jean Piaget, *Play, Dreams and Imitations in Childhood* (London: Routledge & Kegan Paul, 1967), p. 162.

3. See L. M. Morrow, "The Impact of Classroom Environment Changes to Promote Literacy during Play," *Early Childhood Research Quarterly* 5, pp. 537–554.

4. See L. M. Morrow, *Literacy Development in the Early Years: Helping Children Read and Write,* 2d ed. (Boston: Allyn & Bacon, 1993).

5. For more information, see L. M. Morrow and M. Rand, "Promoting Literacy during Play and Designing Early Childhood Classroom Environments," *The Reading Teacher* 44 (1991), pp. 396–402.

6. Cami Jones, *TEA Update: New Directions in Early Childhood Education* (Austin, TX: TEA Division of Curriculum Development; Prekindergarten and Kindergarten Education, 1991), pp. 1–3. Used by permission.

7. *Position Statement on Quality Four-Year-Old Programs in Public Schools* (Little Rock, AR: Southern Association on Children under Six, 1991). Used by permission.

8. National Association of Elementary School Principals, *Early Childhood Education Standards for Quality Programs for Young Children and the Elementary School Principal* (Alexandria, VA: Author, 1990), p. 2. Reprinted with permission. Copyright 1990, National Association of Elementary School Principals. All rights reserved.

9. John R. Berrueta-Clement et al., *Changed Lives: The Effects of the Perry Preschool Program on Youths through Age 19* (Ypsilanti, MI: High/Scope Press, 1984), p. 1.

10. Lawrence J. Schweinhart and David P. Weikart, "Evidence That Good Early Childhood Programs Work," *Phi Delta Kappan* 66(8) (1985), p. 547.

11. Chris Raymond, "New Study Reveals Pitfalls in Pushing Children to Succeed Academically in Preschool Years," *Chronicle of Higher Education,* Nov. 1, 1989, p. A4.

12. National Association of State Boards of Education, *Right from the Start: The Report of the NASBE Task Force on Early Childhood Education* (Alexandria, VA: Author, 1988), p. vii.

13. Louis Bates Ames and Joan Ames Chase, *Don't Push Your Preschooler* (New York: Harper & Row, 1980), p. 2.

8

Kindergarten Education
Learning All You Need to Know

After you have read and studied this chapter, you will be able to:

☐ Explain the history of kindergarten programs from Froebel to the present

☐ Identify and critique goals and objectives for kindergarten programs

☐ Analyze the concepts of and issues surrounding readiness for learning

☐ Evaluate the benefits and disadvantages of different entrance ages for kindergarten

☐ Assess issues of full- and half-day kindergarten programs

☐ Explain the nature of developmentally appropriate and inappropriate kindergarten curricula

☐ Evaluate and critique kindergarten screening and assessment programs

☐ Analyze the nature and importance of transitions for kindergarten children

☐ Identify and evaluate issues confronting kindergarten education

☐ Develop and write a personal philosophy of kindergarten education

Perhaps the title of this chapter struck you as a little odd or puzzling. Read it again. I got the idea for the title from Robert Fulghum's best-selling book, *All I Really Needed to Know I Learned in Kindergarten*. Fulghum says these suggestions form the essentials of kindergarten education:

Share everything.

Play fair.

Don't hit people.

Put things back where you found them.

Clean up your own mess.

Don't take things that aren't yours.

Say you're sorry when you hurt somebody.[1]

It is doubtful anyone would argue with these kindergarten learning outcomes. But today, most people would expect *more* of kindergarten. Kindergarten is seen as an essential year, perhaps *the* essential year in the schooling experience. And, it is for this reason that expectations are high for children to learn the essentials and be successful.

THE HISTORY OF KINDERGARTEN EDUCATION

Froebel's educational concepts and kindergarten program were imported into the United States virtually intact by individuals who believed in his ideas and methods. Froebelian influence remained dominant for almost half a century, until John Dewey and his followers challenged it in the early 1900s. While Froebel's ideas seem perfectly acceptable today, they were not acceptable to those in the mid-eighteenth century who subscribed to the notion of early education. Especially innovative and hard to accept was that learning could be based on play and children's interests—in other words, child centered. Most European and American schools were subject oriented and emphasized teaching basic skills. In addition, Froebel was the first to advocate a communal education for young children *outside* the home. Until Froebel, young children were educated in the home, by their mothers. Although Froebel advocated this method too, his ideas for educating children as a group, in a special place outside the home, were revolutionary.

Credit for establishing the first kindergarten in the United States is accorded to Margarethe Schurz. After attending lectures on Froebelian principles in Germany, she returned to the United States and, in 1856, opened her kindergarten at Watertown, Wisconsin. Schurz's program was conducted in German, as were many of the new kindergarten programs of the time, since Froebel's ideas of education appealed especially to bilingual parents. Schurz also influenced Elizabeth Peabody, the sister-in-law of Horace Mann, when, at the home of a mutual friend, Schurz explained the Froebelian system. Peabody was not only fascinated but converted.

Peabody opened her kindergarten in Boston in 1860. She and her sister, Mary Mann, also published a book, *Kindergarten Guide*. Peabody almost immediately

"EVERYTHING I NEED TO KNOW" ACCORDING TO MRS. SHOLAR'S AFTERNOON KINDERGARTEN CHILDREN

- Use good manners.
- Help make our room clean and neat and safe.
- Be nice and share.
- Use centers right.

- Listen when someone else is talking.
- Take bathroom, water fountain, and library breaks during center or recess time.
- Use inside voices inside.
- Walk in the classroom.
- Keep your shoes on.
- Flush the toilet and wash your hands when you go to the bathroom.

Contributed by Linda Sholar, Sangre Ridge Elementary School, Stillwater, Oklahoma.

realized that she lacked grounding in the necessary theory to implement Froebel's ideas adequately. She visited kindergartens in Germany, then returned to the United States to popularize Froebel's methods. Peabody is generally credited as the main promoter of the kindergarten in the United States. An event that also helped advance the kindergarten movement was the appearance of appropriate materials. In 1860, Milton Bradley, the toy manufacturer, attended a lecture by Peabody, became a convert to the concept of kindergarten, and began to manufacture Froebel's gifts and occupations.

The first *public* kindergarten was founded in St. Louis, Missouri, in 1873 by Susan E. Blow, with the cooperation of the St. Louis superintendent of schools, William T. Harris. Elizabeth Peabody had corresponded for several years with Harris, and the combination of her prodding and Blow's enthusiasm and knowledge convinced Harris to open a public kindergarten on an experimental basis. Endorsement of the kindergarten program by a public school system did much to increase its popularity and spread the Froebelian influence within early childhood education. In addition, Harris, who later became the U.S. commissioner of education, encouraged support for Froebel's ideas and methods.

Training for kindergarten teachers has figured prominently in the development of higher education. The Chicago Kindergarten College was founded in 1886 to teach mothers and train kindergarten teachers. In 1930, the Chicago Kindergarten College became the National College of Education. In 1888, Lucy Wheelock opened a kindergarten training program in Boston. Known as the Wheelock School, it became Wheelock College in 1949.

The kindergarten movement in the United States was not without growing pains. Over a period of time, the kindergarten program, at first ahead of its time, became rigid and centered around methods and the teacher rather than the child.

In Chapter 2, we discussed Vygotsky's ideas regarding the role social interaction plays in cognitive development and learning. Froebel and other great educators have viewed working with and getting along with others as important parts of the kindergarten curriculum. What can professionals do to promote kindergartners' social interactions?

By the turn of the century, many kindergarten leaders thought kindergarten programs and training should be open to experimentation and innovation rather than rigidly follow Froebel's ideas. The chief defender of the Froebelian status quo was Susan Blow. In the more moderate camp was Patty Smith Hill, who thought that, while the kindergarten should remain faithful to Froebel's ideas, it should nevertheless be open to innovation. She believed that to survive, the kindergarten movement would have to move into the twentieth century and was able to convince many of her colleagues. More than anyone else, Blow is responsible for kindergarten as we know it today.

Hill's influence is evident in the format of many present-day preschools and kindergartens. Free, *creative* play, in which children can use materials as they wish, was Hill's idea and represented a sharp break with Froebelian philosophy. She also introduced large blocks and centers where children could engage in housekeeping, sand and water play, and other activities.

Many preschool activities have their basis in adult occupations. Froebel had children engage in building, carpentry, sewing, and sweeping; Montessori conceived many other real-life activities (see chap. 3). They chose these activities because many adult roles, such as building with blocks and carpentry, appeal to children; educators have also long believed that learning materials and activities could be used to introduce children to the world of work. For example, William Harris was interested in the kindergarten because he thought children could be better prepared for industrial society if they had some understanding of adult occupations.

Were Froebel alive today, he would probably not recognize the program he gave his life to developing. Many kindergarten programs are subject centered rather than child centered as Froebel envisioned them. Furthermore, he did not see his program as a "school" but a place where children could develop through play. Although kindergartens are evolving to meet the needs of society and families, we must not forget the philosophy and ideals on which the first kindergartens were based.

WHO IS KINDERGARTEN FOR?

Froebel's kindergarten was for children three to seven years of age; in the United States, kindergarten has been considered the year before children enter first grade. Since the age at which children enter first grade varies, the ages at which they enter kindergarten also differ. People tend to think that kindergarten is for five-year-old children rather than four-year-olds, and most professionals tend to support an older rather than a younger entrance age because they think older children are more "ready" for kindergarten and learn better. Whereas in the past children had to be five years of age prior to December 31 for kindergarten admission, today the trend is toward an older admission age. Many school districts require that children be five years old by September 1 of the school year.

The entrance age for kindergarten often creates controversy, usually because parents want an earlier entrance age and professionals want a later entrance age. Some states and districts make exceptions to age requirements by evaluating children for early admittance, which creates further controversy over what test to use and what score to use as a cutoff point. Decisions for early entrance are sometimes based on children's behaviors in a kindergarten setting. Children and their parents may attend a special kindergarten day during the summer or early fall, before the beginning of school, so professionals can judge children's readiness for school and learning.

There is wide public support for compulsory *and* tax-supported public kindergartens. A Gallup poll showed that 80 percent of the respondents favored "making kindergarten available for all those who wish it as part of the public school system,"

Today, kindergarten is a universal part of the schooling experience, enrolling children from all cultures and socioeconomic backgrounds. Kindergarten children are not all the same, and the kindergarten experience should not be the same for all children. How can professionals help assure that kindergarten programs meet the unique needs of children?

FIGURE 8–1   Kindergarten Enrollment

Source: *New York Times,* September 8, 1993, p. B8. Copyright © 1993 by the New York Times Company. Adapted by permission.

71 percent favored compulsory kindergarten attendance, and 70 percent think children should start school at ages four or five (29 percent favored age four and 41 percent favored age five).[2] In keeping with this national sentiment, most children attend kindergarten, though it is mandatory in only seven states (Arkansas, Delaware, Florida, South Carolina, South Dakota, Virginia, and Oregon) and the District of Columbia.

Kindergarten has rapidly become universal for the majority of the nation's five-year-olds. Today, kindergarten is either a whole- or half-day program and within the reach of most of the nation's children. As with four-year-olds, the number of five- and six-year-olds attending kindergarten has risen steadily (see Figure 8–1).

SCHOOL READINESS: WHO GETS READY FOR WHOM?

In discussions of preschool and kindergarten programs, school readiness is a major topic of debate. Raising entrance ages for admittance to kindergarten and first grade is based on the reasoning that many children are "not ready," and teachers therefore have difficulty teaching them. The early childhood profession is reexamining "readiness," its many interpretations, and the various ways the concept is applied to educational settings and children.

For most parents, readiness means the child's ability to participate and succeed in beginning schooling. From this perspective, readiness includes a child's ability, at a given time, to accomplish activities and engage in processes associated with schooling, whether nursery school, preschool, kindergarten, or first grade. Readiness does not exist in the abstract—it must relate to something. Readiness is measured against the process of formal public schooling. By the same token, a child's lack of readiness may be considered a deficit and detriment, because it indicates a lack of what is needed for success in kindergarten and first grade.

However, as we discussed in chapter 1, goal 1 of Goals 2000, the readiness goal, states, "Readiness for school: By the year 2000, all children in America will start school ready to learn." This goal has renewed debate and discussion about readiness. In focusing on Goal 1, we sometimes forget that there are three subgoals as well:

- All children who are disadvantaged or have disabilities will have access to high-quality and developmentally appropriate preschool programs that help prepare children for school.

- Every parent in the United States will be a child's first teacher and devote time each day helping his or her preschool child learn; parents will have access to the training and support they need.

- Children will receive the nutrition and health care needed to arrive at school with healthy minds and bodies, and the number of low-birth-weight babies will be significantly reduced through enhanced prenatal systems.

Most important, this discussion has changed our definition and attitude about readiness and what it means. Today, the term *readiness* is being replaced with the concept of *early development and learning*. Readiness is no longer seen as consisting of a predetermined set of capabilities that must be attained before entering kindergarten or first grade. Furthermore, responsibility for children's early learning and development is no longer placed solely on the child or parents but rather is seen as a shared responsibility among children, parents, families, early childhood professionals, and communities.

The National Association for the Education of Young Children (NAEYC) has adopted the following position statement on school readiness:

> The National Association for the Education of Young Children (NAEYC) believes that those who are committed to promoting universal school readiness must be committed to
>
> 1. addressing the inequities in early life experience so that all children have access to the opportunities which promote school success;
> 2. recognizing and supporting individual differences among children; and
> 3. establishing reasonable and appropriate expectations of children's capabilities upon school entry.[3]

Maturation and Readiness

Some early childhood professionals and many parents believe that time cures all things, including a lack of readiness. They think that as time passes, a child grows and develops physically and cognitively and, as a result, becomes ready to achieve. This belief is manifested in school admissions policies that advocate children's remaining out of school for a year if they are not ready for school as measured by a readiness test. Assuming that the passage of time will bring about readiness is similar to the concept of unfolding, popularized by Froebel. *Unfolding* implies that development is inevitable and certain and that what a child will be, his or her optimum degree of development, is determined by heredity and a biological clock. Froebel likened children to plants and parents and teachers to gardeners whose task is to nurture and care for children so they can mature according to their genetic inheritance and maturational timetable. The concept of unfolding continues to be a powerful force in early childhood education, although many challenge it as an inadequate, outmoded concept.

The modern popularizer of the concept of unfolding was Arnold Gesell (1880–1961), whose ideas and work continue at the Gesell Institute of Human Development in New Haven, Connecticut. Gesell made fashionable and acceptable the notion of inherent maturation that is *predictable, patterned,* and *orderly.*[4] He also created a number of tests to measure this development, from which he constructed a series of developmental or behavioral norms that specify in detail children's motor, adaptive, language, and personal-social behavior according to chronological age. Gesell also coined the concept of *developmental age* to distinguish children's developmental growth from chronological age; for example, a child who is five years old may have a developmental age of four because he demonstrates the behavioral characteristics of a four-year-old rather than a five-year-old. Gesell believed that parents make their greatest contribution to readiness by providing a climate in which children can grow without interference to their innate timetable and blueprint for development. The popularity of this *maturationist view* has led to a persistent sentiment that children are being hurried to grow up too soon. More critics of early education say that we should let children be children, allow them to enjoy the only childhood they will ever have, and not push them into learning.

Self-Education Through Play

In addition to time and maturation, self-education through play and appropriate activities also promotes readiness. The self-education viewpoint stresses the roles children play in their own learning. In most discussions of readiness, people talk as though children take no part in it, giving all the credit to maturation and heredity. All great educators, however, have stressed the role children play in their own development. Froebel talked about unfolding, Montessori advocated auto- or self-education, and Piaget stressed the active involvement of the child in the process of cognitive development. Time alone is not sufficient to account for or provide children with the skills they need for school success.

For Froebel, play was the energizer, the process that promotes unfolding. He developed his "gifts" and "occupations" to help teachers involve children in play. Montessori believed the prepared environment, with its wealth of sensory materials specifically designed to meet children's interests, is the principal means to help children educate themselves. For Piaget, the physically and mentally active child in an environment that provides for assimilation and accommodation develops the mental schemes necessary for productive learning.

Self-education is child centered, not subject or teacher centered. Children play the star roles in the drama of learning; teachers are the supporting cast. Child-centered readiness programs provide children with enriched environments of material and human resources in which they can play and enhance their own development while they construct the cognitive schemes essential for readiness and, ultimately, school success. Concerning self-education, Caroline Pratt said about her famous Play School, "The attempt in the play school has been to place children in an environment through which by experiment with that environment they may become self-educated."[5]

For some children, the home is such an environment; other children lack the enriched environment necessary to support self-education fully. Unfortunately, some five-year-olds are denied admission to kindergarten programs because they are not "ready" and spend another year in a sterile home or program environment that has failed to support the growth and development necessary to be ready for the schooling experience. For these reasons, we now have an expanded vision of what readiness is and what is necessary to achieve this union.

Quality Programs

Providing young children with *quality* preschool programs is one way to promote and assure that they will enter school ready to learn. As more and more kindergarten teachers see that children are not ready for basic skills curricula, agencies such as Head Start, child care centers, and public schools have implemented programs for three- and four-year-olds to provide the activities and experiences necessary for kindergarten success.

Readiness Skills

In all the rhetoric associated with readiness, readiness skills and behaviors are frequently overlooked. The areas of readiness skills and behaviors include language, independence, impulse control, interpersonal skills, experiential background, and physical and mental health.

Language

Language is the most important readiness skill. Children need language skills for success in school and life. Important language skills include *receptive language,* such as listening to the teacher and following directions; *expressive language,* demonstrated in the ability to talk fluently and articulately with teacher and peers, the ability to express oneself in the language of the school, and the ability to communicate needs and ideas; and *symbolic language,* knowing the names of people, places, and things, words for concepts, and adjectives and prepositions.

Independence

Independence means the ability to work alone on a task, take care of oneself, and initiate projects without always being told what to do. Independence also includes mastery of self-help skills, including but not limited to dressing skills, health skills (toileting, hand washing, using a handkerchief, and brushing teeth), and eating skills (using utensils and napkins, serving oneself, and cleaning up).

Impulse Control

Controlling impulses includes working cooperatively with others and not hitting others or interfering with their work, developing an attention span that permits involvement in learning activities for a reasonable length of time, being able to stay seated for a while. Children who are not able to control their impulses are frequently (and erroneously) labeled hyperactive or learning disabled.

Interpersonal Skills

Interpersonal skills are those of getting along and working with both peers and adults. Asked why they want their child to attend a preschool program, parents frequently respond, "To learn how to get along with others." Any child care or preschool program is an experience in group living, and children have the opportunity to interact with others so as to become successful in a group setting. Interpersonal skills include cooperating with others; learning and using basic manners; and most important, learning how to learn from and with others.

Experiential Background

Experiential background is important to readiness because experiences are the building blocks of knowledge, the raw materials of cognitive development. They provide the context for mental disequilibrium, which enables children to develop higher levels of thinking. Children must go places—the grocery store, library, zoo—and they must be involved in activities—creating things, painting, coloring, experimenting, and discovering. Children can build only on the background of information they bring to a new experience. If they have had limited experiences, they have little to work with and cannot develop well.

Physical and Mental Health

Children must have good nutritional and physical habits that will enable them to participate fully in and profit from any program. They must also have positive, nurturing environments and professionals to develop a self-image for achievement.

Dimensions of Readiness

Readiness has many dimensions that make it much more than a skill-focused process. *Readiness is a never-ending process.* It does not exist only in the preschool and kindergarten years, although we often think of it this way. We should not think of readiness as something children do or do not have but rather as a continuum throughout life—the next life event is always just ahead, and what experiences children are currently engaging in should prepare them for it.

All children are always ready for some kind of learning. Children always need experiences that will promote learning and get them ready for the next step in the process of schooling. As early childhood educators, we should constantly ask such questions as, What does the child know? What can I do to help the child move to the next level of understanding?

Schools and professionals should promote readiness for children, not the other way around. In this regard, schools should get ready for children and offer a curriculum and climate that allows for children's inevitable differences. Rather than subscribe only to notions of what learning is about, early childhood professionals should rededicate themselves to the ideal that schools are for children. Public schools that want children to be ready for predetermined programs have their priorities reversed. Schools should provide programs based on the needs of children and families, not on preconceived notions of what children ought to be able to do.

Children's readiness for learning should be viewed as a collaborative effort among children, the school, early childhood professionals, families, and the community. (In this regard the "community" can be defined as local, state, and national). No longer can we or should we place the primary responsibility for children's readiness solely on children themselves or on their families. We all, individually and collectively, are responsible for helping children gain all they can from the process of schooling while assuring that they can be all they are capable of becoming.

Readiness is individualized. Five- and six-year-old children exhibit a wide range of abilities. While we have said previously that all children are ready for particular learning experiences, not all children are ready for the same thing. It is not abnormal for some children to be behind in certain skills and behaviors and other children to be ahead. What is abnormal is to expect all children to be the same.

Readiness is a function of culture. Professionals have to be sensitive to the fact that different cultures have different values regarding the purpose of school, the process of schooling, children's roles in the schooling process, and what the family's and culture's role is in promoting readiness. Professionals must learn about other cultures, talk with parents, and try to find a match between the process and activities of schooling and families' cultures. (See chap. 7 for a discussion of culturally sensitive caregiving.)

Making Readiness a National Agenda

Ernest L. Boyer and the Carnegie Foundation for the Advancement of Teaching have set a national agenda for helping assure that all children will enter school ready to learn. They propose a seven-step agenda for achieving this goal.[6] The steps are listed here with some of the suggested subgoals:

Step 1:   *A Healthy Start.* Good health and good schooling are inextricably interlocked, and every child, to be ready to learn, must have a healthy birth and be well nourished and protected in the early years of life. As part of step 1, Boyer proposes a network of neighborhood-based Ready-to-Learn Clinics in every underserved community to assure basic health care for all mothers and preschool children.

Step 2:   *Empowered Parents.* The home is the first classroom. Parents are the most essential teachers; all children, as a readiness requirement, should live in a secure environment in which empowered parents encourage language development. Boyer recommends a new Ready-to-Learn Reading Series with recommended books for preschoolers, prepared under the leadership of the American Library Association.

Step 3:   *Quality Preschool.* Since many young children are cared for outside the home, high-quality preschool programs are required that not only provide good care but also address all dimensions of school readiness. Boyer suggests that every school district establish a preschool program as an optional service for all three- and four-year-olds not participating in Head Start.

Step 4:   *A Responsive Workplace.* If each child in the United States is to come to school ready to learn, we must have workplace policies that are family-friendly, ones that offer child care services and give parents time to be with their young children.

Step 5:   *Television as Teacher.* Next to parents, television is the child's most influential teacher. School readiness requires television programming that is both educational and enriching. In this area, Boyer proposes a Ready-to-Learn cable channel, working collaboratively with public television, to offer programming aimed exclusively at the educational needs and interests of preschool children.

Step 6:   *Neighborhoods for Learning.* Since all children need spaces and places for growth and exploration, safe and friendly neighborhoods are necessary. Efforts to achieve this goal would include a network of well-designed outdoor and indoor parks in every community to give preschoolers opportunities for exercise and exploration.

Step 7:   *Connections across the Generations.* Connections across the generations will give children a sense of security and continuity, which will contribute to their readiness in the fullest sense. Boyer envisions a "Grandteacher Program" in communities across the country in which older people participate as mentors in day care centers and preschools.

The readiness goal is a popular one with professionals and parents. Popularity is not enough, however. It will take the concerted efforts of all—professionals, parents, communities, state governments, the federal government, business, and citizens—to move from rhetoric to reality.

Children are born learning. Learning is not something children "get ready for," but is a continuous process. The support of children's learning in the home and kindergarten is everyone's responsibility—professionals, parents, families, schools, and communities. What can kindergarten professionals and community leaders do to help parents support their children's learning?

DEVELOPMENTAL KINDERGARTENS

The developmental kindergarten is a prekindergarten for developmentally or behaviorally delayed kindergarten children. It is seen as one means of helping at-risk children succeed in school. There is a specific procedure and rationale for placing children in such a program:

- Test kindergarten-eligible children prior to their entrance to kindergarten to determine which children are at risk (developmentally delayed).

- Give at-risk children an extra year to develop by placing them in a less cognitively oriented kindergarten classroom in which developmental needs can be addressed.

- Promote them to a regular kindergarten classroom the following year.

- As a result of having had an extra year to mature in the developmental kindergarten, a reduction in later school failure will be achieved.[7]

TRANSITION CLASSES

A *transition class* is designed to give children the time they need to achieve what is required for entry into another grade. Children are really getting two years to achieve what they normally would achieve in one. What is different about the transition class from a nongraded program is that the transition class consists of children of the same age, whereas the nongraded classroom has multiage children.

The concept and practice of transition classes implies and should involve linear progression. Children are placed in a transition class so that they can continue to progress at their own pace. The curriculum, materials, and teaching practices should be appropriate for each child's developmental age or level.

Proponents of transitional programs believe they offer the following advantages:

- Placement in a transition program promotes success, whereas retention is a regressive practice that promotes failure.
- The program provides for children's developmental abilities.
- Children are with other children of the same developmental age.
- The program provides children with an appropriate learning environment.
- The program puts children's needs ahead of the need to place a child in a particular grade.
- The program provides time for children to integrate learning. This extra time is often referred to as "the gift of time."

On the other hand, opponents of such programs make these points:

- Transition programs are another form of failure and are really retention in disguise.
- Transition programs are really another form of tracking in which the less ready children are removed from their more able peers.
- Transition programs can reinforce a basic skills orientation to kindergarten. Some school districts have eliminated or prohibit transitional programs.

WHAT SHOULD KINDERGARTEN BE LIKE?

When making decisions about what kindergarten should be like, we can apply the critical ideas and philosophies of the historic figures discussed in chapter 2 to contemporary practice. Consider Froebel, for example:

> The Kindergarten is an institution which treats the child according to its nature; compares it with a flower in a garden; recognizes its threefold relation to God, man and nature; supplies the means for the development of its faculties, for the training of the senses, and for the strengthening of its physical powers. It is the institution where a child plays with children.[8]

By comparing Froebel's vision of the kindergarten to today's kindergartens, we see that many of today's kindergartens are much different than what Froebel envisioned. This situation is entirely appropriate in many ways, for society is vastly different today than is was in Froebel's time. However, we still need to remember Froebel's and others' visions of what kindergartens can be like.

Program in Practice

AN ITALIAN TAKE ON EARLY CHILDHOOD EDUCATION

Reggio, Reggio, Reggio! The name at first sounds like some exotic vegetable propagated especially for the latest Italian cuisine. In fact, Reggio Emilia is a method for educating children, a quite good one that is very popular. Early childhood educators' fascination with and interest in Reggio Emilia exemplifies their interest in the educational practices of other countries and their willingness to apply the best of these practices to their own programs.

Some questions to keep in mind as you read pages H and I of the color insert are these: What makes Reggio so appealing to U.S. educators? What might be some barriers to implementing the Reggio method in early childhood programs?

DEVELOPMENTALLY APPROPRIATE PRACTICE

This book has emphasized that in all things professionals do for and with children, their efforts should be *developmentally appropriate*. Developmentally appropriate practice—that is, teaching and caring for young children—facilitates learning that is in accordance with their physical, cognitive, social, and linguistic development. In other words, professionals will help children learn and develop in ways that are compatible with their age and who they are as individuals (e.g., their background of experiences, culture).

Talking about developmentally appropriate practice is one thing; putting it into practice is another. Here are some of the implications of such practice for kindergarten programs (indeed, all programs involving young children):

- Learning must be meaningful to children and related to what they already know. Children find things meaningful when they are interesting to them and they can relate to them.

- Children do not learn in the same way or are interested in learning the same thing as everyone else all the time. Thus, teachers must individualize their curriculum as much as possible. Montessori understood this point (see chap. 3), and the High/Scope educational approach provides for it (see chap. 4).

- Learning should be physically and mentally *active;* that is, children should be actively involved in learning activities by building, making, experimenting, investigating, and working collaboratively with their peers.

- Children should be involved in *hands-on* activities with concrete objects and manipulatives. Emphasis is on real-life activities as opposed to workbook and worksheet activities.

Individualized learning activities focus on specific needs and abilities and allow teachers to continually assess children's achievement. Individualized attention also helps keep children at the center of the teaching/learning process and is an important part of developmentally appropriate practice.

Full- or Half-Day Kindergarten

Both half- and full-day kindergarten programs are available. A school district that operates a half-day program usually offers one session in the morning and one in the afternoon, so that one teacher can teach two classes. Although many kindergartens are half-day programs, there is not general agreement as to whether this system is best. Those who argue for the half-day session say that this is all the schooling the five-year-old child is ready to experience and that it provides an ideal transition to the all-day first grade. Those in favor of full-day sessions generally feel that not only is the child ready for and capable of a program of this length but also that such an approach allows for a more comprehensive program. Kindergartens are about evenly divided between whole- and half-day programs across the United States (thus, descriptions of both appear in this chapter).

Regardless, the trend is toward full-day kindergarten programs for all five-year-old children. However, essentially two factors stand in the way of a more rapid transition to full-day programs: tradition and money. Kindergartens are historically and traditionally half-day programs, although there is ample evidence of full-day programs for four- and five-year-old children. As time passes and society's needs begin to point to full-day programs to prepare children for living in an increasingly complex world, more kindergarten programs will become full-day.

(Text continues on p. 308.)

Program in Practice

DEVELOPMENTALLY APPROPRIATE PRACTICE: GENIUS OR JARGON?

The nation's largest professional organization of early childhood educators, the National Association for the Education of Young Children (NAEYC) published position statements on developmentally appropriate practice (DAP) in early childhood programs serving children from birth through age eight in 1987 (Bredekamp, 1987). Those documents, based on input from hundreds of early childhood professionals, have been the most widely disseminated of NAEYC's position statements with almost 400,000 copies distributed. The term *developmentally appropriate* has been used informally for decades by early childhood educators to describe high-quality early education experiences for young children or as the major criterion for qualifying an experience, such as "[fill in the blank] is fine as long as it's done in a developmentally appropriate way."

These documents were developed in a specific political and pedagogical context. In the mid-1980s, NAEYC members became alarmed over the nationwide trend toward pushed-down curriculum and emphasis on formal instruction in academics with increasingly younger children. Among the results of this trend was an alarming rise in the number of children struggling and failing in kindergarten and first grade and an overemphasis on passing a readiness test for entrance to kindergarten or promotion to first grade.

The documents were specifically designed to counter this trend by promulgating greater understanding of more appropriate expectations for young children and also by promoting an approach to education that is based on the likelihood that individual children will vary in their rate of development,

interests, learning styles, and many other dimensions. Therefore, DAP promotes a more child-centered approach supporting children's own construction of knowledge through active exploration of materials and interaction with other people (adults and children), and supporting children's ability to choose good learning experiences from a variety the teacher plans or the children initiate. Such an approach precludes a traditional educational model in which all the children are expected to do the same thing at the same time on the same day and to acquire the same quality of predetermined skills and knowledge within the same nine-month time frame or go back and try again.

In codifying the definition of developmentally appropriate, the NAEYC attempted to achieve several goals. First, the documents provide a general definition of the construct of "developmentally appropriate" as having two dimensions: age-appropriate and individually appropriate. Such a definition demands that programs be built on a framework of generalized knowledge about child development and learning, while also necessitating adaptation of specific program practices, environments, and experiences to individual and cultural differences among children and groups. In other words, developmentally appropriate programs cannot all look alike because all children are not alike. Everyone knows intuitively that no two children are exactly alike, yet this simple fact is so often overlooked in structuring educational experiences and institutions of groups of children. Somehow, because we have traditionally grouped children by chronological age and excluded those with disabilities, education systems have been based on

Contributed by Sue Bredekamp, director of professional development, National Association for the Education of Young Children.

the assumption that some norm could be predicted and programs could be geared toward that norm. Now that all programs are required by federal law not to discriminate against children with disabilities and all programs are serving increasingly diverse populations of children from different socioeconomic, cultural, and linguistic backgrounds, the tyranny of the "norm" must be overturned. Developmentally appropriate practices, although drawing on general information about child development and learning, are by definition practices that are adapted for individual and cultural differences.

A second goal was achieved with the publication of DAP: expansion of the definition with both positive and negative exemplars. The framers of the document believed that it was not sufficient to advise teachers on what to do to be developmentally appropriate; they felt that it was also necessary to state more specifically what not to do. This decision grew out of a history of stating standards or guiding principles in the positive only to discover in practice that misinterpretations were rampant. For instance, during an on-site visit for NAEYC's accreditation system during which the validator observed four-year-olds engaged in teacher-directed activity for one hour and questioned the lack of child choice, the director replied that there was a balance of

teacher-directed and child-initiated activity because the children were allowed to choose the poem that was read to them. Experiences such as this convinced us of a well-known aspect of conceptual development: humans develop concepts from exposure to both positive and negative exemplars. Therefore, with a little trepidation, we added examples of inappropriate practice contrasted with more positive descriptions of appropriate practice.

The format of opposing inappropriate and appropriate practices is one of the most frequently praised—and also one of the most commonly criticized—aspects of the document. The format contributes to some of the myths about developmentally appropriate practices that have surfaced over the years. Kostelnik (1992) presents some of the common misinterpretations of developmentally appropriate practice or myths: "There is one right way to implement a developmentally appropriate program. Developmentally appropriate programs can be defined according to dichotomous positions; one position is always right, the other always wrong."

Another concern about the format is that it conveys that practice is prescriptive rather than individualized and varying, which is not the document's intent. Another criticism is that the "language of imperative" limits academic freedom and reflective practice. Others report that the negative examples have been very effective mechanisms for bringing about change or causing teachers and administrators to reflect on their practices. In retrospect, despite the potential for misunderstanding the negative examples, the decision to include them was perhaps the greatest genius in the document; including examples of inappropriate practice ensured that the document would be somewhat controversial and even threatening, which in turn ensured that it would not easily disappear as one more bromidic discussion of nice things about children.

Including examples of inappropriate and appropriate practices was also a tremendous risk because it may have communicated to some untrained audiences that it is possible to identify a cookbook response for any situation; of course, it is not possible to dictate specific responses in advance for every situation. For example, in theory a group of early childhood professionals may agree that it is inappropriate to leave an infant to cry for a long period of time. But ask those same professionals to describe an appropriate response, and they would have a myriad of questions: How old is the infant? What is the context, home or center? What sort of a cry is it—hunger, pain, boredom? What is the family's preferred cultural style of comforting? The fact is that appropriate practice can only be described in terms of general principles (based on what we know about child development and learning); the specific behaviors of teachers and children will always vary depending on an enormous array of variables.

So we see that a concept like "developmentally appropriate practice" is deceptively simple and enormously complex. Implementing programs that strive to be developmentally appropriate demand educated professionals who continually reflect on their practice; study their children; and adapt their practices, environments, expectations, and responses to the needs and interests of the children. Without such professionals, DAP becomes just another example of educational jargon. The genius of developmentally appropriate practice lies not in the words on the page but in the teachers and children who create learning communities in which to live and learn together.

References

Bredekamp, S., ed. *Developmentally Appropriate Practice in Early Childhood Programs Serving Children from Birth through Age 8,* expanded edition (Washington, D.C.: National Association for the Education of Young Children, 1987).

Kostelnik, M. "Myths Associated with Developmentally Appropriate Program." *Young Children* 47(4), 17–23.

Program in Practice

THE FULL DAY KINDERGARTEN: "HOW DO YOU DO IT ALL?"

All the children are lined up outside the door bursting to come in—everyone is talking and in constant motion. They explode with enthusiasm as they enter, all chattering at once wanting to know what is for lunch. "I forgot my note for you", "Is today music?", "Here's money for the field trip." How, you ask, do you maintain order or even get the day started? Our class has structure within the room that was initiated by the students. We have read many books and had class discussions and then as a group we posted our Class Super Rules. During our busy day we may need to check our rules and make adjustments to our behavior. Cooperative classroom rules are posted on a large piece of chart paper for everyone to see.

The all-day kindergarten program is unique in that it is housed in a campus setting. Lincolnwood Schools have three buildings. The early primary building, Todd Hall, has grades pre-K to 2. Rutledge Hall has grades 3 to 5, and Lincoln Hall has sixth through eighth grades. This setting allows other grades to come in and volunteer time in the kindergarten rooms, such as eighth graders working with young five-year-olds or a fourth grade class interviewing kindergarten children and then writing a book for each child. The kindergarten classes are small— eighteen to twenty students—with a part-time aide. In a typical classroom, a third or fourth of the students speak a language other than English.

In order to maintain young children's enthusiasm, an integrated theme approach is being used. All areas of the curriculum are integrated, and each child is achieving at his or her own level of development. A spirit of cooperation and unity builds as each child is succeeding. When children are succeeding, their self-esteem is developing. Success builds on success.

A chant or a poem starts the day. The entire class meets together for whole-group activities. Other discussions include calendar patterning, weather graphing, and news of the day. Children are actively involved and share many of their ideas.

Shared reading or a time when a variety of literature and language experiences are introduced is natural extension. We have a strong literature-based reading program with a wide variety of authors, games, and multicultural books. During the morning the children are rested, ready, and eager for new experiences–capitalize on it! Depending on the theme or unit of study many different ideas may be presented, such as KWL (what do you *k*now? What do you *w*ant to know? What have you *l*earned?), webbing, language experience stories, and writing. One of the important things to model and share with children is the reading of good literature. The more sound effects and voice inflections the better it is. A book may be a springboard for many ideas and activities that are integrated into different areas or centers of interest in the room.

Children can bring in signs of spring from a nature walk around the school. They can observe seeds, plants, and cuttings in the science area with magnifying glasses; draw or write in science journals about their observations; make classroom spring murals; label items with invented spelling; review library books about spring that are displayed; or listen to tapes with books in a listening center. Items brought in from the nature walk can be sorted and labeled.

Contributed by Lynn Michelotti, Todd Hall School, Lincolnwood, Illinois.

We attempt to integrate and relate what we are doing in the classroom so it makes sense to children and is relevant. Children are actively engaged using all their senses and learn best when able to touch, smell, and feel real objects. As the children are involved in choosing their area of interest, I move around and talk with children one on one or in a small group or just watch and listen. This is the time I make notes about children. Some days the group may need more teacher assistance than others depending on the activities planned. This is when parent volunteers are a great help in the room. Other activities that children choose are the housekeeping area, block construction, learning games, puzzles, flannel board area, puppet dramatization, sand or water table, and computer center. The classroom is humming with activity as children move about and talk with their classmates.

The computer area has many varied and challenging levels of instruction. After the children are familiar with basic computer instruction, they are able to choose their disk and work on their level of competency. Center time varies depending on our daily activities.

Gym, music, and library are taught by other teachers in their rooms. Math activities are presented to the entire class or small groups. Specific activities using manipulatives are incorporated in the Math Their Way activities that are used in our school. These range from exploration, patterning, categorizing, numbers, graphing, estimating, and cooking. Parent volunteers help out in small-group activities. We use many hands-on manipulatives—unifix cubes, geo boards, and polydrons. Hands-on activities make learning relevant and meaningful.

Being an all-day kindergarten, lunch is a big part of the day for the children. All six kindergarten classes eat together and go outside for recess. When the children come inside, they usually need to rest. To make it a more enjoyable time they listen to classical music, look at books, and as the year progresses are read chapter books such as *Charlotte's Web* or *The Box Car Children.* Chapter books are a wonderful way to stretch children's imagination, remember events, and predict happenings.

Afternoons go by quickly. More in-depth activities can be continued from the morning or theme-related projects begun. This block of time allows children their special interests or choices. Journal writing using invented spelling is done. Experimentation is encouraged, as is asking peers for help. The classroom is noisy as children share their ideas with each other.

The afternoon allows an extended block of time to work with children on their portfolios. You can schedule time to sit and conference one on one with each child. What is important in this process is to let the children decide what they want to include in their portfolio. They learn to organize their material and reflect on what is included.

When closing the day, some children share an important project with their classmates. This may be from school or home. Children are encouraged to develop their questioning techniques. To bring closure to the day we read a story and talk about the events of the day.

A vital element in developing an outstanding kindergarten program is parent involvement. We have open houses to explain our program, and we encourage parents to volunteer in the classroom. Even many working parents find time to take a day off to accompany the class on a field trip or attend an event at school. Many programs and conferences are held at night to accommodate working parents. Another strong link with the parent is a weekly newsletter from me that provides information about activities and happenings in our room that week. At times the children can draw pictures and write with invented spelling to produce a class newspaper that can go home to parents.

How do you possibly do it all? It helps tremendously when administrators believe young children should be taught using developmentally appropriate techniques. From the principal to the superintendent, all support provides an atmosphere in which teachers can grow and develop to their fullest potential.

An all-day kindergarten can be exhausting but very rewarding. Eager minds, like sponges, absorb all you say and do. Children at this age are fun, honest, open, and always full of questions. I value and honor all children and their innate curiosity.

Money is the most important obstacle to the growth of full-day kindergarten programs. Without a doubt, it takes twice as many teachers to operate full-day programs as half-day programs. But as society continues to recognize the benefits of early education and as kindergartens and early childhood programs are seen as one means for solving societal problems, more funding will be forthcoming.

Computer literacy and involvement with technology should begin in the preschool and continue in the kindergarten. Children enjoy working with computers and through developmentally appropriate involvement they can develop thinking and social skills and learn much information that supports learning.

Program in Practice

KINDERGARTEN AT THE DAWN OF THE TWENTY-FIRST CENTURY

Burleigh Elementary School, a part of the Elmbrook School District, is located in Brookfield, a western suburb of Milwaukee, Wisconsin. It houses 920 kindergarten through sixth grade students, with five sections of kindergarten. The kindergarten children are taught by four teachers (three regular education teachers and one special education teacher) and three teaching assistants. All the early childhood students with special needs are also located at Burleigh. Students are mainstreamed as much as possible. In the morning, one of the kindergarten teachers team-teaches with an early childhood teacher in order to provide an integrated setting for regular and special needs children. Burleigh also is part of a program offering opportunities for city children to attend suburban schools. Presently African American and Mung students are in the kindergarten classes.

Each year the staff chooses an all-school theme such as oceans or space. The current theme is a multicultural one: Burleigh—A Great Mix for a Better World. Each grade level picked a subtopic to explore. The kindergarten and early childhood level chose the theme of family. We started by working on the concept of what is a family. Then we talked about Burleigh as our school family and how we can get along with our school friends. We then extended it to families around the world and how they are alike and different. Many multicultural books were shared with the children, and .the concept of family was emphasized in several activities. Children drew their houses and then dictated directions on how to get there from school. All the children's directions were compiled in a class booklet and placed in the classroom library. The children also got to write a family story on the classroom computer. They did all the typing themselves with guidance from the teacher.

Our kick-off activity was an all-school field trip to the Milwaukee Symphony's multicultural youth concert entitled Kaleidoscope. All classes at Burleigh have buddy classes who accompanied each other on the trip. During the unit we had many guest speakers and programs representing different cultures such as a Japanese tea party, a program on African music and instruments, and a Native American storyteller. We also had an artist in residence, who painted a large wall mural of Burleigh's students.

The unit culminated with an open house at night during which children could bring their families to share with them all our projects and activities. Folk dance groups from our own Burleigh families performed, and apple pie was served in the cafeteria.

The kindergarten year started out with all three kindergarten teachers using cooperative planning. All classes participate in a program called "Safety Town." This program had been previously offered by the Junior Women's League in the summer with a limited enrollment. Because the program was so beneficial, Burleigh's kindergarten staff decided to incorporate it as part of their kindergarten curriculum. The program covers daily lessons on such things as bus safety, pedestrian safety, fire safety, and saying no to strangers. Field trips to the city's police and fire stations are part of the program. Police officers and fire fighters also come to our classes to present lessons on safety.

Each day the children also get to practice

Contributed by Chris Holicek, kindergarten teacher, Burleigh Elementary School, Brookfield, Wisconsin.

being pedestrians and motorists. A city with streets and sidewalks was painted on the playground. Big-wheel trikes are used for the motorists. While half the children practice being pedestrians (walking on the sidewalks, stopping at corners and stop signs, and looking both ways), the other half ride on the trikes, also stopping at corners and stop signs. There is also a working traffic light so that children can practice stopping on red and starting on green. Parent volunteers and teachers work together to manage the "traffic." Safety town activities ended by inviting parents to come and see the children demonstrate their skills as good pedestrians and motorists.

In my afternoon kindergarten section, curriculum is presented in units of study based on themes. During a water cycle theme, for example, the process of scientific inquiry is developed. Children are young scientists who ask questions, experiment to find answers, and record their findings. Children work cooperatively in small groups, to make discoveries about absorption, how water changes form, sinking and floating, and evaporation. Sometimes I team with a first grade teacher in many activities. The whole unit is integrated also through language arts. Books and poems are read about rain and water. Art activities and daily projects are based on the books read that day. Big books on sinking and floating are read during the shared book time. Oral language is encouraged during small-group activities. Children utilize writing and drawing to record their discoveries each day. Science units are always presented in a "Hands-on discovery" approach. This active involvement is a natural motivator and helps children be enthusiastic about their learning.

Reading and writing activities occur daily. When children come into school at 12:40, they sit down and write in their jour-nals. This is free writing—children choose what and how they want to write. There are many stages of writing that children go through as emergent literacy learners including scribbling, copying environmental print, writing classmate's names, and using temporary spelling (writing down the sounds they know). All children are working at their own developmental level.

The room is immersed in print—alphabet letters, words based on the theme, children's names, schedules, and so forth, are displayed around the room. Children talk to each other a great deal during journal time and do a lot of sharing with each other. About 90 percent of composing in kindergarten is oral.

I individually assess each child at the beginning of the year on such things as letter and sound recognition, concepts of print and book handling, and attitudes about reading and writing. I use this information to guide children individually in their quest to make sense of written language. Assessment guides instruction, so I repeat these assessments throughout the year and modify my lessons in order to meet children's needs. During journal time I walk around the room observing children and jotting down notes.

When children are finished with their journal writing, they individually "read" it to me. This sharing of their work is actually a daily conference with me and gives me daily information I need to guide the children's growth.

As children finish journaling, they sit on the carpet for "noisy reading" time. It is called noisy reading time because children at this age usually retell stories, read aloud, or read with buddies. During this time, I engage in "kid watching" or observing the reading behaviors of the children. I may be looking to see whether a child can retell a story using pictures, is paying attention to the print, or has voice print match (can point to each word when reading). I use this information, again, to guide children individually in their reading development.

At 1:00 the children gather together as a group on the carpet. During the first part of this group time, children can share the journal writing with the whole class. I select four or five children based on their table arrangement. Each table gets to share weekly. This sharing is an important part of the writing process in kindergarten. Children feel good about themselves, and the other children learn different strategies to use in their own journals.

I use the next part of group time to introduce the concepts that the children will be learning that day. During this time, children also participate in calendar and math activities on counting. About 1:20 children are involved in a large-group shared book reading time when I read a big book to the children. Children usually join in on repetitive phrases.

Big books are read daily to children for the enjoyment of reading but also the shared book is the major instructional vehicle in which to teach strategies and skills. An example is a phonics skill—pointing out words that start with the same letter. Using letters and sounds to unlock words is an important cuing system in reading and is emphasized in the actual process of reading and not as an isolated activity. Visual clues and meaning clues are also taught during shared book time in order to present a balanced reading program.

Many activities can spin off from the shared book experience. Children can illustrate the story and take it home to read. They can act out the story with props and puppets. They can read the big book itself and copies of the same book in little book form available in baskets on the carpet. They might watercolor a scene from the book. The opportunities are endless.

Children do an art activity each day about 1:45 based on the big book read or on the theme we are studying. Creativity is encouraged. Projects are presented in an open-ended fashion so that individual differences can be taken into account. Art is a key component of my program. I believe art is a basic component of an early childhood program and that used effectively; it develops individuality, imagination, aesthetic appreciation, hand-eye coordination, and creativity; and provides children concrete ways to respond to their environment.

When children are done with their project, they then can choose discovery learning centers. Individual choice and learning time is highly valued. They usually have thirty minutes of free-choice time. The reading corner is set up with lots of books, big books, pillows, rocking chairs, and stuffed animal book characters to read to.

A writing center—a table with paper, pencils, crayons, markers, a stapler, and tape—is available during free-choice time. Children are free to write or make their own books.

Another center open to the children is a publishing center. I serve as the editor, discussing with the child what he or she wants to write about. Then the child comes up with the title and illustrates the cover. The child may dedicate the book to someone on the inside cover. The child dictates a sentence for each page and illustrates it. Children share their books with the class and their families. A note is placed in the back of the book that says, "Dear Family, How do you like my book? Please write some comments below. Please return my book tomorrow so that it can go in our library."

Other centers include blocks, housekeeping corner, painting, play dough or clay, dramatic play props (a castle when doing a unit on England), computer, hands-on math and science activities, and games. The housekeeping corner changes with the units of study—during a water unit it becomes a plumbing store, during a food unit it becomes a grocery store.

Graphing is incorporated in many units of study. For instance, children are asked to bring in a piece of fruit during a unit on healthy food in order to make a fruit salad. Before cutting up the fruit, the children graph it on a large vinyl floor graph by types and colors. As a group they count and compare which type has more or less.

Patterning, concept of number, estimation, sorting, and classifying are other math strands incorporated into daily or thematic activities. Math stations are also set up so that children get direct hands-on experiences with math manipulatives.

Children also have the opportunity once a week to go to art, music, physical education, and the media center classes taught by specialists in this area. As much as possible the classroom and specialist teachers try to coordinate activities based on the theme studied.

Our balanced reading program has two other exciting features. "Take home" books are available for students. Lots of books on the emergent level in reading are available in baskets. Children can choose to take home a book each night and read it to/with their family. A note accompanies the book in order that parents can communicate back to me on how their child did with that book. The take-home book program must be voluntary. If a child is not interested, forcing the issue could have negative results. Our goal is to have kids who love to read and want to read and who eventually become lifelong readers.

Texas Essential Elements for Kindergarten

The following are the Texas Essential Elements for Kindergarten in the areas of social-emotional development and intellectual development. (See chap. 7 for the Texas Essential Elements for Preschool.)

Social/emotional development, kindergarten, shall include the following essential elements:

I.   Emotional development (knowledge, understanding, and positive acceptance of self). The student shall be provided opportunities to:

A.   recognize successes and feel pride in work

B.   recognize and appreciate his or her uniqueness

C.   persevere with most self-chosen tasks

D.   demonstrate emerging self-discipline and autonomous behaviors through decision making and self-selected activities; and

E.   develop an emerging awareness of consequences of behavior.

II. Social development (interactions with others). The student shall be provided opportunities to:

    A.   experience positive, supportive interactions with adults and peers

    B.   develop a sense of belonging to a group

    C.   engage in cooperative activities

    D.   learn how to make and maintain friendships

    E.   show respect for individuals in the diverse school population

    F.   accept uniqueness of others; and

    G.   participate in leadership as well as follower roles.

III. Social responsibility (behaviors of a socially responsible person). The student shall be provided opportunities to:

    A.   observe and role play socially responsible behaviors in a variety of situations

    B.   develop an emerging awareness of the care of property and materials

    C.   develop an emerging awareness of environmental issues

    D.   value and respect individual similarities and differences; and

    E.   value and respect similarities and differences in cultural identities and heritage including linguistic variations.

Intellectual development, kindergarten, shall include the following essential elements:

I.   Knowledge of communication. Receptive/expressive language integrated through meaningful listening/speaking and print-related experiences. The essential elements for primary language for bilingual education, kindergarten, are described in subsection (e) of this section and the essential elements for English as a second language, kindergarten, are described in subsection (f) of this section. The student shall be provided opportunities to:

    A.   focus attention on adult and peer speakers during individual and group interactions

    B.   enjoy repetition, rhyme, and rhythm through poems, chants, and fingerplays individually or with a group

    C.   enjoy daily listening and responding to stories and books

    D.   follow simple oral directions

    E.   recognize voice tone and nonverbal cues to aid in communication

    F.   acquire vocabulary related to concepts in a meaningful context

    G.   engage in conversation to achieve a variety of purposes including getting needs met, requesting, inquiring, sharing information, and playing

    H.   select books for individual needs and interests

    I.   associate print with spoken language

    J.   become familiar with personally meaningful environmental print

    K.   make predictions of what will happen next in a story

    L.   share ideas, feelings, and stories through activities such as spontaneous drawing, conversation, dramatic play, and informal experimentation with letter-like forms or invented spellings; and

    M. recognize that experiences can be written about.

II.   Knowledge of integrated content. Integrated content acquired through processes of identifying, comparing and contrasting, classifying, sequencing and ordering, predicting cause/effect relationships, and exploring. The student shall be provided opportunities to:

A.   identify:

1.   match objects in one-to-one correspondence

2.   become familiar with a variety of geometric shapes in the environment

3.   use the senses to gain information about objects from the environment emphasizing color, texture, taste, odor, sound, size, shape, direction, motion, heat/cold, and sink/float

4.   celebrate special events (e.g., birthdays, holidays) including those that are culturally related

5.   identify ways people can help and learn from each other

6.   count objects orally through the highest number conceptualized

7.   recognize and describe changes in objects, organisms, and events

8.   recognize traffic and danger symbols critical to the safety of children; and

9.   identify how basic human needs (e.g., food, clothing, shelter) are met by different people.

B.   compare and contrast:

1.   recognize that there are different types of families, homes, and communities

2.   compare sets using concepts such as more than, as many as, and less than to solve relevant problems

3.   recognize part and whole relationships with manipulative materials; and

4.   compare two concrete objects as to length, height, capacity, and size.

C.   classify:

1.   form groups by sorting and matching objects using more than one attribute; and

2.   classify a variety of objects from the environment as being living or non-living.

D.   sequence and order:

1.   copy, extend, and record linear patterns made up of concrete objects (e.g., beads, blocks); and

2.   describe sequences in basic family and school routines.

E.   predict cause/effect relationships:

1.   observe changes in nature and daily events

2.   draw conclusions and predict outcomes based on experience; and

3.   assist in setting class rules including rules of safety.

F.   explore:

1.   demonstrate creative thinking through fluency, flexibility, elaboration, creation of new ideas, spontaneity

2.   construct structures using blocks and other manipulative materials of different sizes and shapes

3.   explore basic concepts of weight, mass, and volume through water play, sand play, and cooking

4.   explore positional relationships such as under, over, above, below, in front of, far away from, inside, outside, between

5.   interpret simple visuals (e.g., photographs, pictures, rebus charts); and

6.   use sensory information to explore and recognize attributes, patterns, and relationships using concrete objects.[9]

ASSESSMENT IN THE KINDERGARTEN

Because of federal mandates and state laws, school districts usually evaluate children in some way before or at the time of their entrance into school. Also, some type of screening occurs at the time of kindergarten entrance to evaluate learning readiness. Unfortunately, children are often classified on the basis of how well they perform on these screenings. When assessment is appropriate and the results are used to design developmentally appropriate instruction, it is valuable and worthwhile.

Assessment tests serve basically seven purposes:

1.   To identify what children know
2.   To identify special needs
3.   To assist in referral decisions
4.   To determine appropriate placement
5.   To help develop lesson plans and programs
6.   To identify behavioral and developmental levels as opposed to chronological level
7.   To inform parents about their children's developmental status

Screening Processes

Screening measures give school personnel a broad picture of what children know and are able to do, as well as their physical and emotional status. As gross indicators of children's abilities, screening procedures provide much useful information for decisions about placement for initial instruction, referral to other agencies, and what additional testing may be necessary to pinpoint a learning or health problem. Many school districts conduct a comprehensive screening program in the spring for children who will enter kindergarten in the fall. Screening can involve the following tasks:

•   Gathering parent information about health, learning patterns, learning achievements, personal habits, and special problems

•   Health screening, including a physical examination, health history, and a blood sample for analysis

- Vision, hearing, and speech screening
- Collecting and analyzing data from former programs and teachers, such as preschools and child care programs
- Administering a cognitive and/or behavioral screening instrument

Comprehensive screening programs are conducted in one day or over several days. Data for each child are usually evaluated by a team of professionals who make instructional placement recommendations and, when appropriate, advise additional testing and make referrals to other agencies for assistance.

Screening Instruments

Several screening instruments provide information for grouping and planning instructional strategies. Most can be administered by people who do not have specialized training in test administration. Parent volunteers often help administer screening instruments, many of which can be administered in about thirty minutes.

BRIGANCE® K and 1 Screen

The BRIGANCE® K and 1 Screen is an evaluation instrument for use in kindergarten and grade 1. The kindergarten pupil data sheet for the BRIGANCE® K and 1 screen shows the skills, behaviors, and concepts evaluated in the kindergarten portion of the screening instrument (see Figure 8–2). Samples of test items and directions for administration are shown in Figures 8–3 and 8–4.

DIAL-R

The DIAL-R (Developmental Indicators for the Assessment of Learning—Revised) is an instrument designed for screening large numbers of prekindergarten children. Requiring approximately twenty-five to thirty minutes to administer, it involves individual observation for motor skills, concepts, and language skills. The screening team consists of a coordinator, an operator for each of the skills areas screened, and aides or volunteers to register parents and children. The DIAL-R score sheet is shown in Figure 8–5.

Developmentally Appropriate Assessment

A great deal of controversy exists in the early childhood professions about appropriate and inappropriate uses of assessment. According to the NAEYC, developmentally appropriate assessment of young children should incorporate the following features:

(Text continues on p. 324.)

FIGURE 8–2 The Kindergarten Pupil Data Sheet for the BRIGANCE® K and 1 Screen

A. Student's Name   Colin Killoran

Parents/Guardian   Kristin and Edmund Killoran

Address   310 Locke Street

	Year	Month	Day
Date of Screening	91	6	15
Birth date	86	1	10
Age	5	5	5

School/Program   Vinal School

Teacher   Leslie Feingold

Assessor   Dennis Dowd

B. Basic Screening Assessments

			C. Scoring		
Page	Assessment Number	Skill (Circle the skill for each correct response and make notes as appropriate.)	Number of Correct Responses	Point Value	Student's Score
3	1A	**Personal Data Response:** Verbally gives: ①first name ② full name ③ age 4. address (street or mailing) 5. birth date (month and day)	3 x	2 points each	6/10
4 & 5	2A	**Color Recognition:** ① red ② blue ③ green ④ yellow ⑤ orange 6. purple ⑦ brown ⑧ black ⑨ pink 10. gray	8 x	1 point	8/10
6	3A	**Picture Vocabulary:** Recognizes and names pictures of: ① dog ② cat ③ key ④ girl ⑤ boy ⑥ airplane ⑦ apple ⑧ leaf 9. cup 10. car	8 x	1 point each	8/10
7	4A	**Visual Discrimination—Forms and Uppercase Letters:** Visually discriminates which one of four symbols is different: ①○○ ②③○ ④◇○ ⑤○○ ⑥○ 7. I ⑧ P 9. V 10. X	7 x	1 point each	7/10
8	5A	**Visual-Motor Skills:** Copies:① — ②○ ③+ ④□ 5. △	4 x	2 points ea.	8/10
9 & 10	6A	**Gross-Motor Skills:** ① Hops two hops on one foot. ② Hops two hops on the other foot ③ Stands on one foot momentarily. ④ Stands on the other foot momentarily. ⑤ Stands on one foot for five seconds. ⑥ Stands on the other foot for five seconds. ⑦ Walks forward heel-to-toe four steps. 8. Walks backward toe-to-heel four steps. ⑨ Stands on one foot momentarily with eyes closed. 10. Stands on the other foot momentarily with eyes closed.	8 x	1 pt. ea.	8/10
11	7A	**Rote Counting:** Counts by rote to: (Circle all letters prior to the first error.) ① ② ③ ④ ⑤ ⑥ 7 8 9 10	6 x	.5 point each	3/5
12	8A	**Identifies Body Parts:** Identifies by pointing to or touching: ① chin ② fingernails ③ heels ④ ankles ⑤ jaw ⑥ shoulders ⑦ elbows 8. hips ⑨ wrists 10. waist	8 x	.5 point each	4/5
13 & 14	9A	**Follows Verbal Directions:** Listens to, remembers, and follows: ① one-step direction 2. two-step direction	1 x	2.5 points each	2.5/5
15	10A	**Numeral Comprehension:** Matches quantity with numerals:② ① ④ ③ 5	4 x	2 points ea.	8/10
16	11A	**Prints Personal Data:** Prints first name Reversals: Yes No ✓	1 x	5 points	5/5
17	12A	**Syntax and Fluency:** ① Speech is understandable. ② Speaks in complete sentences.	2 x	5 points ea.	10/10
				Total Score:	77.5 /100

D. Observations:

1. Handedness: Right ✓ Left ___ Uncertain ___
2. Grasps pencil with: Fist ___ Fingers ✓
3. Hearing appeared to be normal: (See p. vii) Yes ___ No ✓ Uncertain ___
4. Vision appeared to be normal: (See p. vii) Yes ✓ No ___ Uncertain ___
5. Record other observations on another sheet.

E. Recommendations:

Place in: Preschool ___   Low Kindergarten ___   Average Kindergarten ✓   High Kindergarten ___

Other (Indicate) ___

Refer for: (Indicate if needed.)   Ask nurse to check hearing.

Source: From BRIGANCE® Diagnostic Inventory of Basic Skills, © 1976, 1977, Curriculum Associates, Inc. BRIGANCE® is a registered trademark of Curriculum Associates, Inc. Used by permission.

FIGURE 8-3 Sample BRIGANCE® Test Items

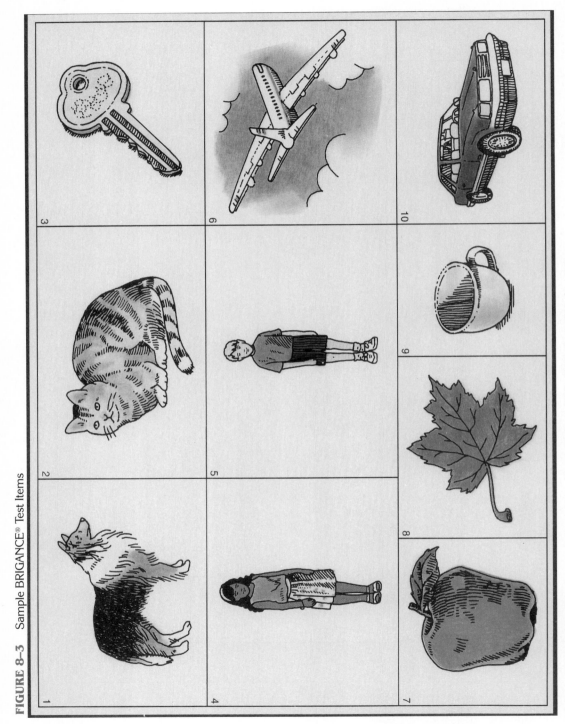

Source: From BRIGANCE® *Diagnostic Inventory of Basic Skills*, © 1976, 1977, Curriculum Associates, Inc. BRIGANCE® is a registered trademark of Curriculum Associates, Inc. Used by permission.

318

FIGURE 8–4 Directions for Administering the BRIGANCE® Picture Vocabulary Screening Instrument

Skill: Names pictures.

1. dog	2. cat	3. key
4. girl	5. boy	6. airplane
7. apple	8. leaf	9. cup	10. car

Data Sheet: Kindergarten.

Assessment Method: Individual oral response.

Material: S-6.

Discontinue: After two consecutive errors.

Time: Your discretion; however, five seconds per picture is recommended.

Accuracy: Give credit for each correct response.

Point Value: 1 point for each picture.

Notes:

1. **Possible Observations:** As the student names the pictures, you may wish to observe and make note of the following:

   a. *Articulation Problems:* Do the student's articulation skills appear typical for his or her age, or are there indications of articulation problems such as substituting, adding, or distorting sounds? (See "Articulation of Sounds" on pages S-45 and 45.)

   b. *Syntax and Fluency:* Is the student's speech understandable and are some of the responses in sentences? (See "Syntax and Fluency" on page 17.)

   c. *Focusing Difficulties:* Does the student appear to have difficulty focusing on one picture because he or she is distracted by the other pictures on the page? (See **Note 4.**)

   d. *Attention to Task:* Does the student consistently attend to your requests, or does he or she have difficulty attending for reasons such as a short attention span or distractions?

   e. *Interest Level:* Does the student appear to have an interest in looking at and talking about the pictures? Does the student want to talk about a particular picture? Does the student volunteer additional information about the picture?

   f. *Confidence Level:* Does the student appear relaxed, or is he or she anxious about responding?

   g. *Assurance of Response:* Does the student respond automatically or hesitantly?

Directions: This assessment is made by pointing to each picture on S-6 and asking the student to name it. Pause after each picture for the student's response. Give encouragement, if necessary.

Point to each picture, and

Ask: **What is this?** or **What do you call this?**

Request the picture names in the following order:

1. dog	2. cat	3. key
4. girl	5. boy	6. airplane
7. apple	8. leaf	9. cup	10. car

2. **Supplemental Assessments:** You may wish to use the pictures for an informal assessment of the student's comprehension and language development. This may be accomplished by asking questions such as the following:

   - Which two are pets?
   - Which two are people?
   - Which two grow on trees?
   - Which two can we ride in?
   - Which two have four legs?
   - Which two can talk?
   - Why do we have keys?
   - Airplanes? Cars? Cups?
   - Which ones do you have at home?

3. **Assessing the Student with Limited Speech or the Student Who Is Reluctant to Respond Orally:** The "Picture Vocabulary" assessment is made by asking the student to name each picture (*expressive skill*). If there is difficulty in getting the student to respond orally, you may wish to ask the student to point to each picture as you name it (*receptive skill*). You may wish to note the results of this assessment, but do *not* give credit.

4. **Screen If Necessary:** If it appears that the student is having difficulty focusing on one picture at a time because of the visual stimuli from the entire page, cover the other pictures with blank sheets of paper.

5. **Advanced Skills:** The "Responds to Picture" assessments on pages 40 and 41 assess more advanced skills. You may wish to use one of them to informally assess the skill level of the more capable student.

6. **Referencing:** The objects used in this assessment are common to the reading readiness materials of the programs listed in the *References* on page 68. Eight of the ten programs included all ten of the objects. The airplane was included in eight of the ten programs.

Source: From BRIGANCE® *Diagnostic Inventory of Basic Skills*, © 1976, 1977, Curriculum Associates, Inc. BRIGANCE® is a registered trademark of Curriculum Associates, Inc. Used by permission.

FIGURE 8–5 DIAL-R Score Sheet

AGS Edition

DIAL-R™

RECORD BOOKLET

Carol Mardell-Czudnowski
Dorothea S. Goldenberg

Developmental Indicators for the Assessment of Learning–Revised

Child's Name

Nickname ☐ Boy ☐ Girl

Address

Phone Number   Child's Primary Language

Mother's Name

Father's Name

Coordinator's Name

School

Teacher/Class

	YEAR	MONTH	DAY
Screening Date			
Birth Date			
Chronological Age			

SCORE SUMMARY

	Scaled Score Totals	Decision*				
		Other	Potential Problem	OK	Potential Advanced	
Motor						
Concepts						
Language						
DIAL-R Total						

* Use cutoffs found in Appendix E in the manual.
Cutoffs chosen:
☐ ±1.0 standard deviation
☐ ±1.5 standard deviation
☐ ±2.0 standard deviation
☐ other
Norm sample chosen:
☐ Census
☐ Caucasian
☐ Minority

OVERALL SCREENING DECISION

Potential Problem	OK	Potential Advanced

Decision based on:
☐ DIAL-R Total score   ☐ 1 area score
☐ 2 out of 3 area scores ☐ other
☐ all 3 area scores

RESULTS FROM OTHER SCREENINGS

	+	–	
Hearing			Does the child need to be referred for follow-up vision or hearing assessment? ☐ No ☐ Yes
Vision			If yes, check which: ☐ Hearing ☐ Vision

BEHAVIORAL OBSERVATION DECISION

Sum of observations checked for all three areas:

Does the child need to be referred for further social/affective assessment? ☐ No ☐ Yes
(See Appendix E in the manual for cutoffs.)

Additional comments on the child's behavior:

Order administered: _____

Motor Operator's Name _____

MOTOR	SCALED SCORE					Item Scaled Scores
	0 under 2 yrs.	**1** 2-3 yrs.	**2** 3-4 yrs.	**3** 4-5 yrs.	**4** 5-6 yrs.	
1. Catching	0	–	1	2	3	
2. Jumping, Hopping, and Skipping jumps: 0 1 hops: (right) 0 1 2 3 4 5 6 (left) 0 1 2 3 4 5 6 skips: 0-other 1-slide 2-step/hop or gallop 3-skip	0	1-2	3-8	9-12	13-16	
3. Building	0	1	2	3	4	
4. Touching Fingers	0	1	2	3	4	
5. Cutting	0-1	2	3	4	–	
6. Matching	0	1-7	8-9	10-11	12	
7. Copying	0	1-7	8-11	12-18	19-24	
8. Writing Name	0	–	–	1	2	
				Scaled Score Total (max. = 31)		

3. Building

6. Matching

I   O   +   □   △   ◊

E   N   D   S   ⅄   ⱦ

7. Copying

I	0 1 2	E	0 1 2
O	0 1 2	N	0 1 2
+	0 1 2	D	0 1 2
□	0 1 2	S	0 1 2
△	0 1 2	⅄	0 1 2
◊	0 1 2	ⱦ	0 1 2

BEHAVIORAL OBSERVATIONS
(Check all that apply.)

_____ unable to separate from adult

_____ cries/whines

_____ unwilling to answer questions

_____ perseverative; repeats what she or he says or does

_____ distractible; does not pay attention

_____ hyperactive; restless; fidgety; 'antsy'

_____ resistive; unwilling to try tasks

_____ disruptive; interrupts testing procedures

☐ Sum of Motor observations checked

FIGURE 8–5 *Continued*

Order administered: _____

Concepts Operator's Name _____

CONCEPTS	SCALED SCORE					Item Scaled Scores
	0 under 2 yrs.	**1** 2-3 yrs.	**2** 3-4 yrs.	**3** 4-5 yrs.	**4** 5-6 yrs.	
1. Identifying Body Parts	0	1-9	10-12	13-15	16-18	
nose neck chin ankle hair stomach shoulder hip ear knee chest waist teeth thumb heel tongue elbow wrist						
2. Naming Colors	0	1-7	8-15	16-18	—	
R O W G BL Y B BR P						
3. Counting (Rote)	0-2	3-4	5-8	9-10	11	
4. Counting (Meaningful)	0	1	3	5-7	9	
1 3 5 7 9						
5. Positioning	0	1-2	3	4	5	
on under corner between middle						
6. Identifying Concepts	0	1-14	15-20	21-26	27-28	
biggest big hot empty night longest long most more fastest fast littlest little cold full day shortest short least less slowest slow						
7. Naming Letters	0	—	—	1-10	11-16	
O B P E R W Y G						
8. Sorting Chips	0	—	—	1-4	5-8	
By color: R B Y						
By size: big little						
By shape: ○ □ △						

Scaled Score Total
(max. = 31)

BEHAVIORAL OBSERVATIONS
(Check all that apply.)

____ unable to separate from adult

____ cries/whines

____ unwilling to answer questions

____ perseverative; repeats what she or he says or does

____ distractible; does not pay attention

____ hyperactive; restless; fidgety; 'antsy'

____ resistive; unwilling to try tasks

____ disruptive; interrupts testing procedures

☐ Sum of Concepts observations checked

Order administered: _____

Language Operator's Name _____

LANGUAGE

	SCALED SCORE					Item Scaled Scores
	0 under 2 yrs.	**1** 2-3 yrs.	**2** 3-4 yrs.	**3** 4-5 yrs.	**4** 5-6 yrs.	
1. Articulating pin　　rabbit　　truck bed　　chair　　dress cup　　knife　　sandwich towel　　leg　　thumb hand　　fish　　mouth/teeth	0	1-14	15-26	27-29	—	
2. Giving Personal Data first name　sex　phone number last name　street age　city/state	0	1-3	4	5	6-7	
3. Remembering clapping:　A　B　C numbers:　A　B　C sentences:　A　B　C	0	1-3	4-5	6-7	8-9	
4. Naming Nouns cat　phone　comb plane　TV　pencil car　clock　ambulance	0	1-15	16	17	18	
5. Naming Verbs sleep　call　comb fly　watch　write drive　time　go to hospital	0	1-9	10-14	15-16	17-18	
6. Classifying Foods Tally: _____	0	1-2	3-4	5-6	7-8	
7. Problem Solving hungry:　0　1　2 dark room:　0　1　2 rain:　0　1　2 broken:　0　1　2	0	1	2-3	4-5	6-8	
8. Sentence Length	0	1-2	3	4	5-8	
			Scaled Score Total (max. = 31)			

BEHAVIORAL OBSERVATIONS
(Check all that apply.)

____ unable to separate from adult

____ cries/whines

____ unwilling to answer questions

____ perseverative; repeats what she or he says or does

____ distractible; does not pay attention

____ hyperactive; restless; fidgety; 'antsy'

____ resistive; unwilling to try tasks

____ disruptive; interrupts testing procedures

☐ Sum of Language observations checked

HOW I EVALUATE WITH PORTFOLIOS

I have used student portfolios to evaluate my kindergarten students for ten years. However, many changes have occurred in the portfolios over time as I have redefined their purpose and identified the criteria for effective portfolios. The purpose of student portfolios is to provide a record of each student's *process of learning* during the time he or she is in my classroom. Portfolio entries are made based on the following criteria:

■ They reflect the student's cognitive, social, emotional, and physical development.

■ They provide a visual record of the student's process of learning over time.

■ They encourage input from the student, teacher, and parent.

My student portfolios consist of a parent questionnaire, parent responses to conferences, individual assessment profiles, anecdotal records, and samples of student work (child selected as well as teacher selected). Because of the volume of materials that can accumulate in a portfolio, I have found a table of contents in the format of a checklist stapled inside the folder to be practical and efficient. As entries are made, I check the table of contents and can determine at a glance what has been included in the portfolio and what needs to be added.

The success of student portfolios as an evaluation tool depends on the appropriate assessment of the student, accurate documentation, and proper use of the information. Because of their importance, each of these is addressed separately.

Appropriate Assessment

Appropriate assessment is the process of observing, recording, and documenting children's work and how they do it. In my classroom, assessments are ongoing and occur as children go through the daily routines of signing in and participating in group time, share time, center time, and recess. I note which activities the children choose, how long they work on specific activities, and their process for completing activities. I observe students' learning styles, interest levels, skill levels, coping techniques, strategies for decision making and problem solving, and interactions with other children. My assessment tools are the materials and activities the children use as part of the regular classroom activities.

Accurate Documentation

Observations have little value unless they are accurately documented. To manage documentation more efficiently, I have developed or adapted a variety of forms to record *systematic assessments*. Throughout the year, I

Contributed by Linda Sholar, Sangre Ridge Elementary School, Stillwater, Oklahoma.

Decisions that have a major impact on children, such as enrollment, retention, or placement, are not made on the basis of a single developmental assessment or screening device, but must take into account other relevant information, particularly observations by teacher and parents.

Developmental assessment of children's progress and achievements is used to adapt curriculum to match developmental needs, to communicate with the child's family, and to evaluate the program's effectiveness.

Developmental assessments and observations are used to identify children who have special needs and/or who are at risk and to plan appropriate curriculum for them.

systematically assess individual children in each area of development and record this information on individual assessment profiles. I use a numbers and symbols system to describe the occurrence of behaviors or mastery of skills. Emphasis is on what each child can do, and each child's progress is compared with his or her prior work.

Number System	Symbol System
1 = Most of the time	* = Has full command
2 = Some of the time	+ = In control
3 = Not noticed	• = Needs time

I use a system to document skill proficiency when appropriate. The date of assessment and recordings (made with color-coordinated pencils) provide me with specific dated information about each child and allows me quickly to detect areas of growth. I have also developed several class evaluation forms that allow me flexibility in recording observations quickly yet accurately. These forms are especially useful in planning group and/or individual instruction.

I make *anecdotal records* (on Post-It notes) of unanticipated events or behaviors, a child's social interactions, and problem-solving strategies. I transfer these Post-Its to a class grid so I can determine at a glance which children I have observed. The anecdo-

tal records, along with the individual assessment profiles, become a part of each student's portfolio to be used for instructional planning and communicating with parents.

Throughout the year *samples of the student's work* are dated and included in the portfolio. Quarterly work samples that I select include cutting activities, writing numbers (each child decides how far he or she can write), and writing ABCs and any words the child can write independently (invented or conventional spelling). The children select samples of artwork and creative writing (e.g., journal entries, letters or drawing for parents).

Use of Information

I use assessment information to plan classroom instruction for individuals and groups, to identify children who may need special help, and to confer with parents and colleagues. During conferences, I share with parents the student's assessment profile for the different areas of development, and together we examine samples of the child's work that supports the assessment. Even though the progress is visually obvious, I can also point out less obvious progress as we view the samples. I give parents conference response forms and ask for comments or suggestions for additional portfolio entries. Using the portfolio, I am satisfied that I have gleaned an accurate assessment of and appreciation for each child's total

Developmental expectations based on standardized measurements and norms should compare any child or group of children only to normative information that is not only age-matched, but also gender-, culture-, and socioeconomically appropriate.

In public schools, there should be a developmentally appropriate placement for every child of legal entry age.[10]

Portfolios

Today many teachers use portfolios, a compilation of children's work samples, products, and teacher observations collected *over time* as a basis for assessment. Deci-

Assessment is no longer only paper-and-pencil tests measuring students' achievement. Children's work samples and products as part of a portfolio are used to evaluate and assess progress and achievement. Parents are now involved in discussions of goals for their children and in evaluations of progress toward these goals.

sions about what to include in portfolios vary, but examples include written work, artwork, audiotapes, pictures, models, and other materials that attest to what children are able to do. Some teachers let children put their best work in their portfolios; others decide with the children what will be included; others select themselves what to include. An important point to remember, and one often overlooked, is that portfolios are only one part of children's assessment. For example, at South Pointe Elementary (see page P of the color insert), teachers use computers to write written evaluations on each child each day.

LITERACY AND THE NATION'S CHILDREN

Literacy is an "in" word; we hear it in virtually all educational circles, and almost every early childhood educator is talking about how to promote it. It has replaced reading readiness as the primary objective of many kindergarten and primary programs. *Literacy* means the ability to read, write, speak, and listen, with emphasis on reading and writing well. To be literate also means reading, writing, speaking, and listening within the context of one's cultural and social setting.

Literacy is a hot topic in educational circles for a number of reasons. First, it is estimated that over 50 million Americans are functionally illiterate—at or below a fifth grade reading level. Furthermore, when we compare the U.S. literacy rate to that of other countries, we do not fare too well—many industrialized countries have higher literacy rates than the United States. Consequently, educators and social policy planners are always concerned about the inability of the schools to teach all children to read at more than a functional level.

Second, as discussed in chapter 1, businesses and industry are concerned about how unprepared the nation's work force is to meet the demands of the workplace. Critics of the educational establishment maintain that many high school graduates do not have the basic literacy skills required for many of today's high-tech jobs. Therefore, schools, especially at the early grades, are feeling the pressure to adopt measures that will give future citizens the skills they will need for productive work and meaningful living.

A third reason for the interest in children's literacy relates to a theme that recurs often in this book: the pendulum of change. Every fifteen or twenty years or so, a wave of reform swept the public schools. Usually reform movements contain elements of previous movements, as is the case with literacy. Many of the practices advocated in the name of making the nation literate are those used in the open education movement of several decades ago.

Literacy development is a major goal of the kindergarten curriculum. What is included in literacy development? What can kindergarten teachers do to promote children's literacy development?

Cultural and Social Processes

Literacy is viewed as a process that involves *both* cognitive and social activities. Presently, many reading and writing practices focus primarily on the cognitive—they are designed to give children mental skills such as word recognition or sound-word relationships. Teachers teach children to read using methods such as whole-word and phonetic analysis; these methods constitute the major portion of the reading program. Reading and writing are frequently taught as isolated, separate subjects and skills. Furthermore, reading and writing are often taught in ways that give them little meaning to children. Treating reading and writing as processes and skills that are separate from children's daily and immediate lives can lead to failure and retention. Fortunately, this approach to literacy is changing.

Emergent Literacy

Today, early childhood professionals use the term *emergent literacy* when talking about reading, writing, speaking, and listening. Professionals view literacy as a process that begins at birth, perhaps before, and continues to develop across the life span. Thus, with the first cry, children are considered to be beginning the process of language development. (See chap. 6 for a discussion of linguistic development.) This viewpoint takes literacy as a never-ending process, a continuum across the school years and into adulthood.

Emergent literacy themes emphasize using environmental and social contexts to support and extend children's reading and writing. Children want to make sense of what they read and write. The meaningful part of reading and writing occurs when children talk to each other, write letters, and read good literature or have it read to them. All of this occurs within a print-rich environment, one in which children see others read, make lists, and use language and the written word to achieve goals. Proponents of whole language maintain that this environment is highly preferable to previous approaches to literacy development.

The process of becoming literate is also viewed as a *natural* process; reading and writing are processes that children participate in naturally, long before they come to school. No doubt you have participated with or know of toddlers and preschoolers who are literate in many ways. They "read" all kinds of signs (McDonald's) and labels (Campbell's soup) and scribble with and on anything and everything.

The concept of emergent literacy, then, is based on the following beliefs about literacy and about how children learn:

- Reading and writing involve cognitive and social abilities that children employ in the processes of becoming literate and gaining meaning from reading, writing, speaking, and listening.

- Most children begin processes involved in reading and writing long before they come to school; they do not wait until someone teaches them. They should not have to wait to be taught. (Remember what Montessori said about early literacy.)

- Literacy is a social process that develops within a context in which children have the opportunity to interact with and respond to printed language and to other children and adults who are using printed language. In this context, children bring meaning to and derive meaning from reading and writing. Teachers and classrooms should encourage discussing and sharing knowledge and ideas through reading and writing.

- The cultural group in which children develop literacy influences how literacy develops and the form it takes. Children should also have opportunities to read the literature of many cultural groups in addition to their own.

Whole Language

Literacy is certainly a worthy national and educational goal. But how do educators go about accomplishing this agenda? The practice of choice in many school districts is the use of whole-language approaches to literacy development. *Whole language* is the use of all aspects of language—reading, writing, listening, and speaking—in the process of becoming literate. Children learn about reading and writing by speaking and listening; they learn to read by writing, and they learn to write by reading.

The following are common practices in implementing the whole-language approach:

- The use of *assisted reading*, in which the teacher first reads a story to the children then pauses on the second and following readings to allow the children to predict words and phrases. This process is repeated until the children are reading the story themselves.

- Making literacy *child centered,* so that reading and writing are purposeful and meaningful to the children

- *Accepting children's errors* as indicators of their developing literacy rather than their failure to read and write. As they write, for example, teachers encourage children to spell words as they think they should be spelled. "Invented spelling" is part of the language learning process, based on the theory that it is acceptable for a child to misread a word orally as long as comprehension and meaning is maintained.

- The use of *"quality" literature* that is interesting and exciting as both a motivation for reading and as a model for children's own writing

- The use of *predictable reading material*. For example, in the book *Goodnight Moon*, the phrase "goodnight moon" appears repeatedly throughout the text, so that when teachers and parents read this book to children, they can pause to let the children finish the pattern: "Goodnight chair, . . . " after which the child should—and usually does—respond, "Goodnight moon."

- The *integration of language with all subject areas*, so that children read and write across the curriculum—in science, social studies, math, and other areas—not just during reading class

- *Writing* is used as a way to help children communicate, with emphasis on helping children make sense of what they write rather than on the mechanics of writing
- The use of a *thematic approach*, such as "Who Am I," to provide a context for language learning and a means of integrating all the content areas. (In this particular theme, use science to explain children's circulatory systems and math to determine their average heart rates.)

Whole-language learning is supported by classroom procedures such as these:

- Providing quality literature: books, poems, and other types of language arts activities
- Pointing out uses of print materials, such as lists, books, greeting cards, magazines, menus, and phone books
- Journal writing
- Labeling classroom objects
- Having children dictate stories that are written down and reread to them
- Encouraging children to write, draw, and label their work
- Establishing an environment that encourages talking, listening, and interpreting written and oral language

Implications of Whole Language

Whole language has a number of implications for children and early childhood professionals. First, whole language represents a move away from subject-centered basic skills approaches to reading, writing, and learning. This approach leads to a second implication: Whole language is child centered, not subject centered. Third, "good" literature is used to help children learn to read and write. Fourth, there is a de-emphasis on phonics instruction as a primary focus of reading and a shift to using phonics as it evolves naturally and when necessary. Fifth, professionals use integrated/thematic approaches to provide a context and vehicle for promoting, nourishing, and developing children's literacy.

KINDERGARTEN CHILDREN AND TRANSITIONS

A *transition* is a passage from one learning setting, grade, program, or experience to another. Young children face many such transitions in their lives. They are left with baby-sitters and enter child care programs, preschools, kindergarten, and first grade. Depending on how adults help children make these transitions, they can be either unsettling and traumatic or happy and rewarding experiences.

For growing numbers of children, literacy development includes bilingual programs. As more children enter school with a home language other than English, professionals must include activities that help children maintain their home language as well as help them learn English.

The transition from home to preschool to kindergarten influences positively or negatively children's attitudes toward school. Under no circumstances should the transition from preschool to kindergarten or from kindergarten to first grade be viewed as the beginning of "real learning." Leaving kindergarten to enter first grade is a major transition. The transition may not be too difficult for children whose kindergarten classroom is housed in the same building as the primary grades. For others whose kindergarten is separate from the primary program or who have not attended kindergarten, the experience can be unsettling. Children with special needs who are making a transition from a special program to a mainstreamed classroom need extra attention and support, as we will discuss in chapter 11.

Parents and kindergarten professionals can help children make transitions easily and confidently in several ways:

- Educate and prepare children ahead of time for any new situation. For example, children and teachers can visit the kindergarten or first grade program the children will attend. Also, toward the end of the preschool or kindergarten year or as time to enter the kindergarten or first grade approaches, children can practice certain routines as they will do them when they enter their new school or grade.

- Alert parents to new and different standards, dress, behavior, and parent-teacher interactions. Preschool professionals, in cooperation with kindergarten teachers, should share curriculum materials with parents so they can be familiar with what their children will learn. Kindergarten professionals can do the same with first grade teachers.

- Let parents know ahead of time what their children will need in the new program (e.g., lunch box, change of clothing, etc.).

- Provide parents of special needs children and bilingual parents with additional help and support during the transition process.

- Offer parents and children an opportunity to visit programs. Children will better understand the physical, curricular, and affective climates of the new programs if they visit in advance. Professionals can then incorporate methods into their own program that will help children adjust to new settings.

- Cooperate with the staff of any program the children will attend, to work out a "transitional plan." Continuity between programs is important for social, emotional, and educational reasons. Children should see their new setting as an exciting place where they will be happy and successful.

The nature, extent, creativity, and effectiveness of transitional experiences for children, parents, and staff will be limited only by the commitment of all involved. If we are interested in providing good preschools, kindergartens, and primary schools, then we will include transitional experiences in the curricula of all the programs.

ISSUES IN THE KINDERGARTEN

In addition to the issues previously discussed—readiness, retention, transition programs—a number of other issues face professionals in regard to the kindergarten experience.

The Pushed-Down Curriculum

Perhaps you have visited a kindergarten program and left thinking, "Wow, a lot of what they're doing in kindergarten I did in first grade!" Many early childhood professionals would agree. The "pushed-down curriculum" is what happens when professionals teach kindergarten children as first graders and expect them to act like first graders and when the kindergarten curriculum resembles that of first grade. The kindergarten curriculum should challenge all children to do their best and provide them with social and cognitive skills they need for success, but it should also be appropriate for them.

A number of reasons account for the pushed-down (or "escalated") curriculum. First, beginning in 1957 there has been a decided emphasis on "academics" in U.S. education, particularly early childhood education (see chap. 2). Second, some parents believe an academic approach to learning is the best way to succeed in school and the work world. They may also see academics as one of the ways to compensate for the lack of experiences and opportunities prior to their child's school entry. The challenge for early childhood professionals in this regard is to educate parents about what is and is not appropriate for young children's learning.

What Happens When We Retain a Child?

More than likely some children in your own elementary classes were repeating the same grade. You probably remember them because they were bigger than you, or they were behavior problems, or they were in the "low" reading group. You took the presence of these children for granted and assumed children who had been retained were a natural part of the typical classroom. You concluded then, as you perhaps do now, that nonpromotion or retention is a good pedagogical device because it exposes children once again to the same material they have previously failed to learn. The fact that you can remember children who were repeating a grade is evidence that retaining children at least once, and perhaps two or three times in a school career, has a long, strong tradition in U.S. public and parochial education that continues today.

Along with the benefits of early education and universal kindergarten come disturbing and potentially disastrous side effects for children. Retained children, instead of participating in kindergarten graduation ceremonies with their classmates, are destined to spend another year in kindergarten. Many of these children are retained or failed because teachers judge them to be immature, or they fail to measure up to the district's or teachers' standards for promotion to first grade. Children are usually retained in the elementary years because of low academic achievement or low IQ. (In comparison, reasons for retention are different at the junior high level, at which students are generally retained because of behavior problems or excessive absences.)

When well-meaning professionals fail children, they do so in the belief that they are doing them and their families a favor. Professionals feel that children who have an opportunity to spend an extra year in the same grade will do better the second time around. Teachers' hopes, and consequently parents' hopes, are that these failed children will go on to do as well as (many teachers hold out the promise that they will do even better than) their nonretained classmates. But is this true? Do children do better the second time around?

Despite our intuitive feelings that children who are retained will do better, the research evidence is unequivocally to the contrary: children do not do better the second time around. In addition, parents report that retained children have a more pessimistic attitude toward school, with a consequently negative impact on their social-emotional development.[11]

The ultimate issue of retention is how to prevent failure and promote success. To achieve those goals, professionals will have to change their views about what practices are best for children and how to prevent the risk factors that create a climate for unsuccessful school experiences. As alternatives to retaining children in a grade, many school districts are implementing two kinds of programs. One is the developmental kindergarten, which, in essence, gives children two years to complete one year of kindergarten work. The second is transitional classes between kindergarten and first grade. However, these programs are controversial, as we discussed earlier.

Some school districts, including that in Dade County, Florida, have banned retention in kindergarten and first grade. Retention is possible, however, only in certain circumstances and with approval of the district superintendent.

High-Stakes Testing

Some kindergarten children still face *high-stakes testing*—a test that determines whether they will be promoted to first grade. Such tests, also known as *bench-mark* tests, are an effort to reduce *social promotion,* in which children are promoted so they can keep up with their age mates, their social peers. There are a number of reasons for movement away from high-stakes testing. First, such tests do not fit well with the newer curriculum approaches such as whole language and assessment processes such as portfolios. Second, high-stakes tests do not necessarily test what children really know. Third, these tests may be inappropriate for children of particular cultures. Fourth, many early childhood professionals believe it is not fair to children or their families to make a decision for or against promotion on the basis of one test.

The Graying of Kindergarten

There is a growing tendency for upwardly mobile parents to hold their children (especially sons) out of kindergarten for a year, for several reasons. First, when boys, who tend to be less mature than girls, have a birthday that makes them one of the youngest children in the class, they may not do as well as their parents expect. These parents want their children to be the oldest members of the kindergarten class, not the youngest. They reason that the older children will be the class leaders, will get more attention from the teacher, and have another year of school under their belt and therefore will be able to better handle the pushed-down curriculum. In other words, these children will be at the top of their class in all respects.

Second, parents who keep their children out of kindergarten for a year can afford to do this. Less well-to-do parents, on the other hand, want their children in school because they cannot afford day care or babysitters.

Until society and the schools really implement goal 1 of Goals 2000 ("Every child will enter school ready to learn") and until schools commit themselves to providing every child with the opportunity to learn to his or her fullest potential, the graying of kindergarten will likely continue.

Should Attendance Be Mandatory?

Although most children attend kindergarten, attendance is not mandatory for the majority of children, as we have seen. When kindergarten is not mandatory, this means that some children are left out, most likely those who would benefit most. On the other hand, as kindergarten becomes mandatory for more children, it will have tremendous implications for both the kindergarten and first grade curricula. In other words, as kindergarten becomes more institutionalized, it is likely that the curriculum will too.

QUALITIES OF A GOOD KINDERGARTEN TEACHER

1. Loves children (acceptance of various backgrounds and ability levels), respects children and parents
2. Patient, kind, caring, and understanding
3. Is a good listener
4. Promotes active learning, includes children's interests in the curriculum
5. Keeps up with current/new trends in education
6. Attends workshops and seminars regarding early childhood
7. Has a love for teaching kindergarten
8. Plans for learning, has a daily schedule, and is a short- and long-range planner
9. Is well organized
10. Has good classroom management
11. Has a good rapport with colleagues, parents, and children
12. Uses learning centers and has a child-centered classroom
13. Is innovative/creative
14. Can provide for all levels of students from enrichment to remedial
15. Instills a love of learning in students
16. Willing to give many extra hours
17. Has a desire and motivation to do a good job
18. Has a goal of wanting to ensure that each child is successful

Contributed by the kindergarten teachers at Croissant Park Elementary School, Broward County, Florida.

What Should the Kindergarten Curriculum Be Like?

Many different ideas prevail about what kindergarten and its curriculum should be like. While we will never have (and indeed it is not desirable that we should) a common kindergarten curriculum, the profession is far from agreement on what kindergarten should be like. Certainly professionals have to refocus their efforts toward developing a unified view of kindergarten and its proper role and place in the U.S. educational system.

WHAT LIES AHEAD? KINDERGARTEN'S FUTURE

From our discussions in this chapter, you may have several ideas about how kindergarten programs will evolve as we move into the twenty-first century. Add your ideas to the ones cited here:

- The trend in kindergarten education is toward full-day, cognitive-based programs. Kindergartens give public schools an opportunity to provide children with the help they need for later success in school and life. Children come to kindergarten programs knowing more than their counterparts of twenty years ago. Children with different abilities and a society with different needs require that kindergarten programs change accordingly.

Program in Practice

TEACHING IN THE KINDERGARTEN

"Mrs. Sholar, look. I lost my tooth. . . ."

"Teacher, you'll never guess what I have in here [as a ten-inch grass snake appears from a plastic butter tub], and it's not even slimy!"

"Who's the leader today?"

So begins a typical morning kindergarten class at Sangre Ridge Elementary School in Stillwater, Oklahoma.

Teaching involves establishing a classroom environment that promotes optimal learning and growth. For this to be done effectively, it is essential to identify basic beliefs about children and how they learn. These beliefs are reflected in the physical environment, academic agenda, and social climate of the classroom.

My challenge as a teacher is to create an environment in which the children feel safe and welcome so they are free to be risk takers in learning. Class rules established by the children, clearly displayed on the walls and referred to as needed, promote a feeling of physical safety and fairness among the children. Children's drawings on the classroom walls reflect current units of study and imply this room belongs to children whose work and ideas are valued. Scissors, glue, staplers, tape, and crayons are accessible to the children so they can exercise independence in helping themselves and assume responsibility for caring for themselves. Low tables are arranged to encourage easy movement from one learning activity to the next and to allow for individual and small group participation.

As the kindergarten children begin to feel comfortable in their classroom, I get to better know and understand them. They come from diverse backgrounds and enter the classroom at different stages of development and with unique learning styles. Regardless of how

each child learns, I want the children to see themselves as successful readers, writers, artists, mathematicians, and scientists. Children need an introduction and organized exposure to new information followed by opportunities to manipulate and interact with the new information. They learn best when they are actively involved in the learning process and when they are encouraged to wonder, for example, what will happen to the pumpkin seed if it is planted; to then experience planting and nurturing it; and to finally discover the network of roots just before the sprout pokes through the soil.

In kindergarten, I want the children to share experiences and develop as a community of learners in which teachers and children learn from each other in a noncompetitive environment. The process a child goes through to complete a task or learn a new concept is important. Answers are not automatically given, do not always come from the teacher, and often lead to more questions. As I question a child about how he made the green color on his picture when he had only red, yellow, and blue paint, he is encouraged to think about the process, experiment, and reach a conclusion. Other children learn from his explanation or may have their own explanation.

I want the children to experience learning as whole and natural and meaningful. Thematic units, carefully developed to integrate curriculum and skill areas, are adapted to class needs and interests. Concepts are presented in context, and it is often difficult to determine whether we are learning math or science or reading or writing. Learning is not preparation for the next grade in school; it is not even preparation for life. Rather, learning is life, and the classroom consists of real-life

Contributed by Linda Sholar, Sangre Ridge Elementary School, Stillwater, Oklahoma.

situations in which problem solving and learning occur because of real and obvious needs. When a child tells me she has made pictures for all her friends, I ask her to count them to see whether she has enough for everyone. When someone discovers the soap dispenser is out of soap, I suggest that child write a note for the custodian to remind him of the need. When the class disagrees about which book to read, we vote and experience democracy in action.

I want the children to be involved in making decisions about their own learning. Time is scheduled each day for children to select learning activities of their choice. All activities promote quality experiences and are supportive of current concepts and skills, so any choice is appropriate. As a child chooses, he decides what he is going to do first and how long he will work in the area. He may need a second plan of action if his first choice is already taken. He may decide to practice in the same area several days or to try a new activity each day or several activities in one day. His best work is a natural outcome since he is controlling what he does, when he does it, and how long he spends on the activity.

I want the children to see their parents as an integral part of their learning experience with teachers and parents working as a team. Parents need and often want to be involved in their child's school experience. Parent meetings and conferences, *K News* (our class newsletter), informal notes, and a parent bulletin board are useful tools of parental involvement in my classroom. An active "Helping Hands" program also encourages regular parent participation. In the classroom, parents interact with the children during center activities, read to individual children, or assist with special class events. A slide show set to music during our kindergarten class open house provides parents, who otherwise could not get into the classroom during the school day, the opportunity to see their children in action.

As we in education are bombarded with "new" ideas, commercial programs, and "easy" solutions or "cure-alls" for educating our youth, it is critical that we be authorities in our fields. We must be creative in the classroom, read professionally, attend workshops, discuss and share with colleagues, and most importantly continue to learn. We must learn from the very ones we teach and selectively make changes that are consistent with sound educational principles, personal philosophy, and results from classroom research. We must recognize our influence in the lives of children and be responsible to them.

As a teacher, I am continually challenged and rewarded. I am challenged to assess and plan for thirty-five unique individuals every day, helping them experience community without losing individuality. I am rewarded when I observe my five- and six-year-old children working together, offering another help or celebrating another's success. I am challenged to channel the energies and emotions of thirty-five sometimes fragile and sometimes not so fragile young spirits, knowing when to step in and guide and when to wait and watch. I am rewarded when I see these children developing self-control and working out conflicts in mutually acceptable ways. I am challenged to be genuine and "real" to my students. I am rewarded when middle school and junior high students return to my classroom to let their kindergarten teacher know what is happening in their lives because they know I care. As a teacher and the decisive factor in the classroom, I am challenged to be the best that I can be. I am rewarded daily when I observe my five- and six-year-old eager and trusting learners becoming the best that they can be.

Program in Practice

LONGFELLOW ELEMENTARY SCHOOL FOR THE VISUAL AND PERFORMING ARTS

An excellent example of restructuring at work in the early childhood arena is Longfellow Elementary School in Kansas City, Missouri, a magnet school for the visual and performing arts. Yvonne Clay's twenty-two kindergartners engage in an all-day program of basic skill instruction and drama, dance, music, and movement. Visual arts include painting, sketching, modeling with clay, and creative writing; the performing arts entail music, theater, and dance.

Drama plays a significant role in the curriculum and life of the kindergarten classroom. As Yvonne explains, "Drama and the other performing arts give children exposure to and experience with topics and people they would not otherwise have. Drama is in many ways a mirror of real-life events. I use drama to help children learn many important skills, concepts, and values. Drama is also a natural way of helping children learn through their bodies."

Yvonne gives these examples of drama activities in her kindergarten: "One of my groups reads in their basal reader a story of the rabbit and the hare. After the reading, the children acted out the story, and we empha-

sized expression and how the human voice—their voices—sounds in certain situations. Also, during Black History Month in February, the children did a 'Readers Theater' of the Rosa Parks Story. One group read the story and another group acted out the events. The children had a lot of fun getting ready. They made bus stop signs, made costumes out of clothing from the Salvation Army, and made a bus out of cardboard boxes with chairs for seats. I revised an existing script for the children and worked with the parents of the children who had reading parts. It was a great learning activity!"

Yvonne teaches readiness skills, reading (many of the children are reading at a first grade level or above by the end of the school year), math, social studies, science, writing, and creative movement—all integrated with drama. Support teachers provide instruction in art, music, physical education, computers, and Suzuki violin.

"I integrate academics into everything I do," explains Yvonne. "The visual and performing arts give children experiences to build their academics on. The arts also give children a chance to appreciate their self-worth at

- Kindergarten curricula will include more writing and reading. This literacy emphasis is appropriate and flows naturally out of whole-language programs. The challenge for all professionals is to keep literacy development from becoming a rigid, basic skills approach.

- Technology (see chap. 15) will be included more in both preschool and kindergarten programs. This technology inclusion is in keeping with the current growth of technology in all grade levels. However, as with many things, we think that earlier is better, so introducing technology early is seen as one way of making children in the United States computer literate. The feature on pages J

many levels and in different ways. Take, for example, a child like Alex, who struggles in reading. He really excels in dance. The experiences of being good in this area are a great benefit to him."

A number of important activities support the curriculum and make the kindergarten program unique.

Artist-in-Residence Program

The school district has an artist-in-residence program through which artists come into the school and classrooms to perform and teach. For example, a local, well-known puppeteer gave a performance, then taught the children about puppets. He worked with the children in making puppets and helped them give a performance with their puppets. In this way, a specific art activity is integrated into the curriculum and daily classroom activities.

Field Trips

The kindergarten children go every other month to various performing arts functions. These include trips to the ballet, symphony orchestra, plays, and other performances throughout the Kansas City area. Following the field trips, children's experiences are integrated into the curriculum. For example, after a trip to the zoo, some children may create an art product and others may choose to write about the experience.

Concluding Remarks

Community support for the Longfellow Magnet School is strong. According to Dee Davis, coordinator, early childhood, for the Kansas City Public Schools, "Families are enthusiastic about schools of choice for their children. They want and like to make choices on behalf of their children. Parents feel children do better in school when they study what interests them most."

The curriculum of the kindergarten program, with its focus on song and dance, is in many ways reminiscent of that supported by Froebel and other great educators. It is also significant that a school named for one of the nation's most celebrated poets—Henry Wadsworth Longfellow—should be involved in promoting learning through the arts.

and K of the color insert illustrates and emphasizes the following points: (1) technology, *as an instructional model* exists in growing numbers of early childhood programs, (2) technology is no longer something that can be feared or ignored by early childhood professionals, and (3) children are and can be very comfortable with and adept at technological applications to their lives and learning.

- Kindergarten will be viewed less as a place in which children get ready for school—and fail if they are not ready—and more as a place in which children learn and develop as part of the pre-K–12 schooling process.

READINGS FOR FURTHER ENRICHMENT

Boyer, Ernest L. *Ready to Learn: A Mandate for the Nation* (Princeton, NJ: Carnegie Foundation for the Advancement of Teaching, 1991)

> Boyer and the foundation lay out their seven steps for achieving goal 1—that every child in the United States will enter school ready to learn. This book should be read by all early childhood professionals.

Fisher, Bobbi. *Joyful Learning: A Whole Language Kindergarten* (Portsmouth, NH: Heinemann, 1991).

> A practical guide, full of ideas for how to implement a whole-language classroom throughout the school year. Links theory and practice so that kindergarten teachers can make learning joyful.

Fromberg, Doris P. *The Full-Day Kindergarten* (New York: Teachers College Press, 1987)

> Views young children as active, responsible, inquiring learners whose flexible thinking processes and social-emotional life must be encouraged and enhanced. Guidelines for creating unique kindergarten experiences combining academic instruction with nurturance to promote all areas of development.

Goffin, Stacy G., and D. A. Steglin, eds. *Changing Kindergartens: Four Success Stories* (Washington, D.C.: National Association for the Education of Young Children, 1992)

> An excellent book for parents, teachers, and principals who want to make kindergartens developmentally appropriate.

Graue, M. Elizabeth. *Ready for What? Constructing Meanings of Readiness for Kindergarten* (Albany: State University of New York Press, 1993)

> This book looks at readiness as an idea that is constructed by parents, teachers, and children as they interact in their neighborhoods and communities.

Walmsley, Bonnie Brown, Anne Marie Camp, and Sean A. Walmsley. *Teaching Kindergarten: A Developmentally Appropriate Approach* (Portsmouth, NH: Heinemann, 1993)

> Not a book, but rather a package of activities for the kindergarten teacher who wants to implement a developmentally appropriate program but does not know where to begin. Children's literature and theme based.

ACTIVITIES FOR FURTHER ENRICHMENT

1. Interview parents to determine what they think children should learn in kindergarten. How do their ideas compare to the ideas in this chapter and to your ideas?

2. Do you think as a teacher you are oriented toward cognitive skills or social-emotional play? Explain your reasons, and compare your response to those of your classmates.

3. As a teacher, would you support an earlier or later entrance age to kindergarten? If your local legislator wanted specific reasons, what would you tell him or her? Ask other teachers, and compare their viewpoints.

4. How might culture, socioeconomic background, and home life affect what should be taught to children in kindergarten?

5. Give examples from your observations of kindergarten programs to support one of these opinions: Society is pushing kindergarten children, or many kindergartens are not teaching children enough.

6. List special services school districts should provide to kindergarten children.

7. Compare the curriculum of a for-profit kindergarten, a parochial school kindergarten, and a public school kindergarten. What are the similarities and differences? Which would you send your child to? Why?

8. Do you think kindergarten should be mandatory for all five-year-old children? At what age should it be mandatory?

9. Should the results of a readiness test be the final word on whether a child is admitted to kindergarten? Explain your answer.

10. What are reasons for the current interest in helping children make transitions from one setting or agency to another? What are other transitions that early childhood educators should help children make, besides those mentioned in this chapter?

11. You have been asked to speak to a parent group about the pros and cons of contemporary approaches to literacy development in kindergarten. What major topics would you include?

12. Develop a list of suggestions for how parents can promote literacy in the home.

NOTES

1. From *All I Really Needed to Know I Learned in Kindergarten* by Robert L. Fulghum (New York: Villard Books, 1988), p. 6. Copyright © 1986, 1988 by Robert L. Fulghum. Reprinted by permission of Villard Books, a division of Random House, Inc.

2. Alec M. Gallup, "The 18th Annual Gallup Poll of the Public's Attitudes toward Public Schools," *Phi Delta Kappan* 68(1), pp. 55–56.

3. National Association for the Education of Young Children, "NAEYC Position Statement on School Readiness," *Young Children,* November 1990, p. 21.

4. Arnold Gesell and Catherine Amatruda, *Developmental Diagnosis: Normal and Abnormal Child Development* (New York: Harper & Row, 1941).

5. Caroline Pratt and Lucile C. Deming, "The Play School" in *Experimental Schools Revisited,* ed. Charlotte Winsor (New York: Agathon Press, 1973), p. 23.

6. Ernest L. Boyer, *Ready to Learn: A Mandate for the Nation* (Princeton, NJ: Carnegie Foundation for the Advancement of Teaching, 1992), pp. 136–143. Used by permission.

7. Jeffrey Burkart, "Developmental Kindergarten—In the Child's Best Interest?" *National Association of Early Childhood Teacher Educators* 10 (1989), pp. 9–10.

8. Friedrich Froebel, *Mother's Songs, Games and Stories* (New York: Arno, 1976), p. 136.

9. Cami Jones, *TEA Update: New Directions in Early Childhood Education* (Austin, TX: TEA Division of Curriculum Development, Prekindergarten and Kindergarten Education, 1991), pp. 9-11. Used by permission.

10. Sue Bredekamp, ed., *Developmentally Appropriate Practice in Early Childhood Programs Serving Children from Birth through Age 8,* expanded ed. (Washington, D.C.: National Association for the Education of Young Children, 1987), p. 13. © 1987 by NAEYC. Used by permission.

11. Lorrie A. Shepard and Mary Lee Smith, "Effects of Kindergarten Retention at the End of First Grade," *Psychology in the Schools* 24 (1987), pp. 346–357.

9

The Primary Years
The Process of Schooling

After you have read and studied this chapter, you will be able to:

☐ Assess the importance of the primary years for children, families, and the profession

☐ Describe the similarities and differences among preschool, kindergarten, and primary grade children

☐ Explain the physical, cognitive, language, psychosocial, and moral developmental characteristics of primary children

☐ Evaluate instruction and learning processes currently used in the primary grades and explain their implications for teaching and learning

☐ Analyze and discuss skills taught in the primary grades and processes of assessment and evaluation

☐ Implement processes and activities for teaching children how to "think"

☐ Identify issues involved in and assess the future of primary education

☐ Evaluate reasons for and ways in which education in the primary years is changing

RECLAIMING THE PRIMARY YEARS

In contrast to the renewed interest in infants, one might almost say that the years from six to eight are the forgotten years of early childhood and that primary children are frequently overlooked in terms of early childhood education. Although the profession defines early childhood as the period from birth to age eight, children from birth through kindergarten receive most of the attention; primary grade children are more often thought of as belonging to the elementary years. Indeed, the years from six to twelve are often referred to as the *middle years* or *middle childhood*, the years between early childhood and adolescence.

Seemingly, one of the major challenges facing the early childhood profession is to reclaim the years from age six through eight. If we are serious about the field of early childhood encompassing the years from birth to age eight, then we cannot focus research and training almost exclusively on the years up to age five, as we presently do. We act as though what comes before the primary years is much more important than what happens during the primary years. Lives are shaped in not only the early years but the primary years as well.

The primary years are an important time in life. The years from six to eight provide many opportunities for children to think, do, and become competent and self-assured persons. Early childhood professionals can and should play a major role in children's lives during these formative years as they do in earlier years.

WHAT ARE PRIMARY CHILDREN LIKE?

Physical Development

Two words describe the physical growth of primary age children: *slow* and *steady*. Children at this age do not make the rapid and obvious height and weight gains of the infant, toddler, and preschooler. Instead, they experience continual growth, develop increasing control over their bodies, and explore the things they are able to do.

From age five to seven, children's average weight and height approximate each other. For example, at six years, boys weigh forty-six pounds and are forty-six inches tall, while girls weigh forty-three pounds and are forty-five inches tall. At age seven, boys weigh fifty pounds and are forty-eight inches tall and girls, forty-eight pounds and forty-eight inches. The weight of boys and girls tends to be the same until about age nine, when girls pull ahead of boys in both height and weight. Wide variations appear not only in individual rates of growth and development, however, but also among the sizes of children in each classroom. The wide differences in physical appearances result from genetic and cultural factors, nutritional intake and habits, health care, and experiential background.

Motor Development

Primary children are adept at many motor skills. The six-year-old is in the *initiative* stage of psychosocial development; seven- and eight-year-old children are in the *industry* stage. Not only are children intuitively driven to initiate activities, they are also learning to be competent and productive individuals. The primary years are thus a time to use and test developing motor skills. Children at this age should be actively involved in activities that enable them to use their bodies to learn and develop feelings of purpose and competence. Their growing confidence and physical skills are reflected in games of running, chasing, and kicking. A nearly universal characteristic of children in this period is their almost constant physical involvement.

Differences between boys' and girls' motor skills during the primary years are minimal—their abilities are about equal. One implication for teachers is that they should not try to limit either boys' or girls' involvement in activities based on gender. We see evidence of the continuing refinement of fine-motor skills in the primary years in children's abilities to do many of the tasks they were previously unable to do or could do only with difficulty. They are now able to dress themselves relatively easily and attend to most of their personal needs, such as using utensils, combing their hair, and brushing their teeth. They are also more proficient at school tasks that require fine-motor skills, such as writing, artwork, and use of computers.

Cognitive Development

Children's cognitive development during the primary school years enables them to do things as first, second, and third graders that they could not do as preschoolers. A major difference between these two age groups is that the older child's thinking has become less egocentric and more logical (see chap. 4). The cognitive milestone that enables children between seven and eleven to think and act as they do is *concrete operational thought*; their reasoning, however, is still tied to the concrete. Logical operations are possible with concrete objects and referents in the here and now. Abstract reasoning comes later, in the *formal operation stage* during adolescence.

Moral Development

Jean Piaget and Lawrence Kohlberg are the leading proponents of a developmental concept of children's moral growth. Piaget identified the two stages of moral thinking typical of children in the elementary grades as the stage of *heteronomy*—being governed by others regarding right and wrong—and the stage of *autonomy*—being governed by oneself regarding right and wrong. As Piaget points out:

> Society is the sum of social relations, and among these relations we can distinguish two extreme types: relations of constraint, whose characteristic is to impose upon the individual from outside a system of rules with obligatory content, and relations of cooperation, whose characteristic is to create within people's minds the consciousness of ideal norms at the back of all rules. Arising from the ties of authority and unilateral respect, the relations of constraint therefore characterize most of the features of society as it exists, and in particular the relations of the child to its adult surrounding. Defined by equality and mutual respect, the relations of cooperation, on the contrary, constitute an equiliberal [sic] limit rather than a static system.[1]

The stage of heteronomy is characterized by *relations of constraint*. In this stage, children's concept of good and bad and right and wrong is determined by the judgments pronounced by adults. An act is "wrong" because a parent or teacher says it is wrong. Children's understanding of morality is based on the authority of adults and those values that "constrain" them.

Gradually, as children mature and have opportunities for experiences with peers and adults, moral thinking may change to *relations of cooperation*. This stage of personal morality is characterized by exchange of viewpoints between children and between children and adults as to what is right, wrong, good, or bad. This level of moral development is not achieved by authority but rather by social experiences within which children may try out different ideas and discuss moral situations. Autonomous behavior does not mean that children agree with other children or adults but that autonomous people exchange opinions and try to negotiate solutions.

Recall that in chapter 2 we discussed Lev Vygotsky's theory of the *zone of proximal development* and the importance of having children collaborate with more competent peers and adults for cognitive and social development. We can also see here, in Kohlberg's theory, the importance of social interactions and collaboration of adults and peers in children's moral development. According to Vygotsky, social interactions provide children opportunities for "scaffolding" to higher levels of thinking and behavior. Furthermore, Vygotsky said that part of the professional's pedagogical role was to challenge and help children move to higher levels of thinking and, in this case, moral development.

The stage of relations of constraint is characteristic of children up through first and second grades, while the stage of relations of cooperation is characteristic for children in the middle and upper elementary grades. The real criterion for determining which developmental stage a child is operating in, however, is how that child is thinking, not how old he or she is.

Kohlberg, a follower of Piaget, also believed children's moral thinking occurs in developmental levels. The levels and substages of moral growth as conceptualized by Kohlberg are preconventional, conventional, and postconventional.[2]

I: Preconventional Level (Ages Four to Ten)

Morality is basically a matter of good or bad, based on a system of punishments and rewards as administered by adults in authority positions. In stage 1, the *punishment-and-obedience orientation,* children operate within and respond to physical consequences of behavior. Good and bad are based on the rewards they bring, and children base judgments on whether an action will bring pleasure.

In stage 2, the *instrumental-relativist orientation,* children's actions are motivated by satisfaction of needs. Consequently, interpersonal relations have their basis in arrangements of mutual convenience based on need satisfaction. ("You scratch my back; I'll scratch yours.")

II: Conventional Level (Ages Ten to Thirteen)

During this level, morality is doing what is socially accepted, desired, and approved. Children conform to, support, and justify the order of society. Stage 3 is the *interpersonal concordance* or *"good boy/nice girl"* orientation. Emphasis is on what a "good boy" or "nice girl" would do. The child conforms to images of what good behavior is.

In stage 4, the *law-and-order* orientation, emphasis is on respect for authority and doing one's duty under the law.

III: Postconventional Level (Age Thirteen and Older)

Morality consists of principles beyond a particular group or authority structure. The individual develops a moral system that reflects universal considerations and rights.

Stage 5 is the *social-contract legalistic* orientation. Right action consists of the individual rights agreed on by all society. In addition to democratic and constitutional considerations, what is right is relative to personal values.

At stage 6, the *universal-ethical-principle* orientation, what is right is determined by universal principles of justice, reciprocity, and equality. The actions of the individual are based on a combination of conscience and these ethical principles.

Just as Piaget's cognitive stages are fixed and invariant for all children, so too are Kohlberg's moral levels. All individuals move through the process of moral development beginning at Level I and progress through each level. No level can be skipped, nor does an individual necessarily achieve every level. Just as intellectual development may become "fixed" at a particular level of development, so may an individual become fixed at any one of the moral levels.

Implications for Classrooms

The theories of Piaget, Kohlberg, and programs for promoting affective education have these implications for primary grade classroom practice:

- All professionals must like and respect children.
- The classroom climate must support individual values. Respect for children means respect for and acceptance of the value systems children bring to school.
- Professionals and schools must be willing to deal with issues, morals, and value systems other than those they promote for convenience, such as obedience and docility.
- A sense of justice must prevail in the schools, instead of the injustice that arises from imposing arbitrary institutional values.
- Children must have opportunities to interact with peers, children of different age groups and cultures, and adults to enable them to move to the higher levels of moral functioning.
- Students must have opportunities to make decisions and discuss the results of decision making. Children do not develop a value system through being told what to do or through infrequent opportunities for making choices and decisions.

SIGNIFICANCE OF THE PRIMARY YEARS

The primary years of early childhood education are significant because children are further inducted into the process of formal schooling. The preschool experience is often viewed as preparation for school, whereas with kindergarten (and increasingly with first grade) the process of schooling begins. How this induction goes will, to a large extent, determine how well children learn and whether they like the process of schooling.

Children's attitudes toward themselves and their lives are determined at this time. The degree of success now sets limits on life-long success as well as school success. Preparation for dealing with, engaging in, and successfully completing school tasks begins long before the primary grades, but it is during the primary grades that children encounter failure, grade retention, and negative attitudes. Negative experiences during this period have a profound effect on their efforts to develop positive self-image. Primary children are in Erik Erikson's *industry versus inferiority* stage. They want and need to be competent, and they should be given the opportunities to be so.

RESTRUCTURING THE PRIMARY SCHOOL

In chapter 1 we discuss the *restructuring* of early childhood programs in the United States today. Nowhere is this restructuring more evident than in the primary grades. Grassroots efforts, led by parents, teachers, and building- or program-level administrators are aimed at changing how schools are operated and organized, how teachers teach, how children are taught and evaluated, and how schools involve and relate to parents and the community. Accountability and collaboration are in; schooling as usual is out.

One such effort to help schools restructure is the nationally acclaimed "Comer Process," developed by James P. Comer of the Yale Child Study Center. This approach is detailed in this section's Program in Practice on page 350.

THE CONTEMPORARY PRIMARY SCHOOL

A lot of change has occurred in the primary grades over the past decade, with more on the way. Single-subject teaching and learning are out; integration of subject areas through such practices as whole language, thematic approaches, and literature-based programs are in. Students sitting in single seats, in straight rows, solitarily doing their own work are out; cooperative learning is in. Textbooks are out; projects and hands-on, active learning are in. Paper-and-pencil tests are out; student work samples and collaborative discussion of achievements are in. The teacher as director of all and "the sage on center stage" is out; facilitation, collaboration, cooperative discipline, and coaching are in. Letter grades and report cards are out; narrative reports, in which professionals describe and report on student achievement, checklists, which describe the competencies students have demonstrated, parent conferences, and other ways of reporting achievement are in.

In chapter 3, we discuss the death and rebirth of open education. South Pointe (see page P of the color insert) illustrates the rebirth in the 1990s of open education concepts and the child-centered movement. For those who thought the open education movement was dead, South Pointe is testimony to the fact it is alive and doing very well. In many respects, Dewey's progressive education ideas are finding fertile ground once again in the hearts and minds of early childhood professionals and parents who desire more personalized and developmental programs for young children.

South Pointe also illustrates another important educational movement: the operation of public education by private-sector companies. The operation of South Pointe by Educational Alternatives Inc. is not an aberration on the educational landscape. Rather, it represents the fulfillment of many trends already in place. For example, we have read about the creative and exemplary accomplishments of business and industry operating child care and preschool programs. Why can't they accomplish the same things for public education? Why not, indeed! This is but one of the many questions you should ask as you read the insert. In your questions lie the answers to the future directions of many early childhood programs.

THE SCHOOL DEVELOPMENT PROGRAM: THE COMER PROCESS

The School Development Program (SDP) model was established in 1968 in two elementary schools as a collaborative effort between the Yale Child Study Center and the New Haven Public Schools. The two schools involved were the lowest achieving in the city, with poor attendance and serious relationship problems among students, staff, and parents. Staff morale was low. Parents were angry and distrustful of the school. Hopelessness and despair were pervasive.

Because of preschool experiences in families under stress, a disproportionate number of low-income children presented themselves to the schools in ways that were understood as "bad," undermotivated, or appropriate on the playground, at home, or other places outside the school but inappropriate in school.

The school staffs lacked training in child development and behavior and understood school achievement solely as a function of genetically determined intellectual ability and individual motivation. Because of this, the schools were ill prepared to modify behavior or close the developmental gaps of their students. The staffs usually responded with low expectations.

To understand how such misalignments occur and how to overcome them in order to promote educational development, we began with the fact that a child develops a strong emotional bond to competent caretakers—usually parents—that enables them to help that child develop. Adequate development in social, psychological, emotional, moral, linguistic, and cognitive areas are critical for future academic learning. The attitudes, values, and behavior of the family and its social network strongly affect such development. A child whose development meshes with the mainstream values encountered at school will be prepared to achieve at the level of his or her ability. In addition, the meshing of home and school fosters further development. When a child's social skill are considered appropriate by the teacher, they elicit positive reactions. A bond develops between the child and the teacher, who can now join in supporting the overall development of the child.

By contrast, a child from a poor, marginal family is likely to enter school without adequate preparation. The child may arrive without ever having learned such social skills as negotiation and compromise. A child who is expected to read at school may come from a home in which no one reads, in which no parent ever read a bedtime story. It is because such circumstances differ from mainstream expectations that these children are often considered aggressive or "bad" and judged to have low academic potential.

Parents, for their part, take such problems as a personal failure or evidence of animosity from the mainstream. They lose hope and become less supportive of the school. Some parents, ashamed of their speech, dress, or failure to hold jobs, may become defensive and hostile, avoiding contact with the school staff. The result is a high degree of distrust between home and school. This degree of alienation between home and school makes it difficult to nurture a bond between child and teacher that can support development and learning.

We found that even when there was a desire to work differently, no mechanism was in place at the *building level* to allow parents, teachers, and administrators first to understand the needs, then to collaborate with and

Contributed by James P. Comer, M.D., director, School Development Program, Yale Child Study Center.

help each other address them in an integrated, coordinated way.

The model took shape in response to the conditions we found. Working collaboratively with parents and staff, we gradually developed our present nine-component model:

- Three mechanisms
- Three operations
- Three guiding principles

The three mechanisms consist of

- governance and management team, which consists of representatives of the parents, teachers, administrators, and support staff;
- a mental health or support staff team; and
- a parents' program.

The three operations are carried out by the governance and management team. These operations are

- the development of a comprehensive school plan with specific goals on the social climate and academic areas,
- staff development activities based on building-level goals in these areas (social and academic), and
- periodic assessment, which allows the staff to modify the program to meet identified needs and opportunities.

The three guiding principles and agreements are as follows:

- Participants of the governance and management team cannot paralyze the leader. On the other hand, the leader cannot use the group as a rubber stamp.

- Decisions are made by consensus to avoid "winner-loser" feelings and behavior.
- A *no-fault problem-solving* approach is used by all the working groups within the school, and eventually these attitudes permeate the thinking of most individuals.

As the governance and management team systematically addresses the problems and opportunities in the school, students, staff, and parents all begin to function more effectively. The staff development program helps the teachers gain the skills necessary to promote personal, social, and academic growth among students. As the hope and energy levels of the staff go up, so do the opportunities and motivation to devote time to planning, which leads to improved curriculum development and instruction.

Eventually the curriculum and the entire school experience begin to promote overall development among students. Significant academic and social behavior gains often follow.

Participation in both the day-to-day program in the classroom as well as school governance builds parents' confidence and competence as contributors to, and decision makers in, the community. Such enhancement of parents' social and academic skills has motivated many to return to school and complete their own high school and in some cases college education, which improves their employment opportunities.

The School Development Program is not a "quick fix," nor is it an "add-on." It is a different way of conceptualizing and working in schools and completely replaces traditional organization and management.

REASONS FOR CHANGES IN PRIMARY EDUCATION

Education in the primary grades is changing. Schooling in the elementary years has become a serious enterprise, for political, social, and economic reasons. First, educators, parents, and politicians are realizing that solutions to illiteracy, a poorly prepared work force, and many social problems begin in the first years of school, and even before. Second, the public is not happy about continuing declines in educational achievement. It wants the schools to do a better job teaching children the skills business and industry will need in the twenty-first century. Third, parents and the public in general want the schools to help solve many of society's problems (substance abuse, crime, violence, etc.) and turn around what many see as an abandonment of traditional American and family values.

THE NEW CURRICULUM FOR THE PRIMARY GRADES

In chapters 1, 7, and 8, we identify practices and programs that are child centered. The child-centered movement is alive and well in the primary grades also. We now discuss some of these practices.

The Self-Esteem Movement

In chapter 6, we examined Maslow's hierarchy of needs. One of these needs is for self-esteem, which is a positive feeling of self-worth and self-image. The self-esteem movement began in the 1980s as a way of improving children's achievement. The argument is that children do not or cannot achieve because of their poor self-worth. Proponents of self-esteem maintain that programs and practices to enhance self-esteem are particularly important for certain groups of children—minorities, females, and those at risk. Further, they maintain that the self-esteem of children is lessened by uncaring teachers and an indifferent school system.

Efforts to enhance students' self-esteem result in a number of practices:

- The use of praise as a means of recognizing and rewarding achievement. The use of praise is used also to make children feel special and comfortable with learning and to try to get children to do their best. Advocates of praising as a means of promoting self-esteem say it places less importance on the product and more on children's efforts. Unfortunately, in some cases, teachers have used praise too much, too often, and without a basis in solid achievement.

- The establishment of schools specifically designed to promote self-esteem and increase achievement through identity with one's culture

- Mentoring, role modeling and "shadowing" programs in which students are given opportunities to interact with successful people of their culture and socioeconomic backgrounds

However, not everyone agrees that the self-esteem movement is in children's best interests. Critics claim that teachers overpraise children, reward for little effort and achievement, and substitute praise and rewards for teaching. Further, they maintain that self-esteem results from achievement, not hollow praise.

Prosocial and Peace Education

There is a growing feeling among early childhood professionals that solutions to many societal problems, including war and violence, can be reduced and avoided. They believe efforts to achieve this goal should begin in the primary and preschool years. Consequently, emphasis is placed on *prosocial behaviors*—teaching children the fundamentals of peaceful living, kindness, helpfulness, and cooperation. Professionals can do several things to foster development of prosocial skills in the classroom:

- *Be a good role model for children.*   Teachers must demonstrate in their lives and relationships with children and other adults the behaviors of cooperation and kindness that they want to encourage in children.

- *Provide positive feedback and reinforcement when children perform prosocial behaviors.*   When children are rewarded for appropriate behavior, they tend to repeat that behavior. For example, you might say, "I like how you helped Tim get up when you accidentally ran into him. I bet that made him feel better."

- *Provide opportunities for children to help and show kindness to others.* Cooperative programs between primary children and nursing and retirement homes are excellent opportunities to practice helping and kind behaviors. (See the discussion on Stride Rite's Intergenerational Center in chap. 5.)

- *Conduct classroom routines and activities so they are as free as possible of conflict.*   At the same time, professionals can provide many opportunities for children to work together and practice skills for cooperative living. Learning centers and activities can be designed for children to share and work cooperatively.

- *When real conflicts occur, provide practice in conflict resolution skills.* These skills include taking turns, talking through problems, compromising, and apologizing. A word of caution regarding apologies: too often, an apology is a perfunctory response on the part of teachers and children. Rather than just saying the often empty words "I'm sorry," it is far more meaningful to help the child understand how the other child is feeling. Encouraging empathic behavior in children is a key to the development of prosocial behavior.

- *Conduct classroom activities based on multicultural principles and that are free from stereotyping and sexist behaviors* (see chap. 14).

- *Read stories to children, and provide literature for them to read that exemplify prosocial behaviors.*

- *Counsel and work with parents to encourage them to limit their children's television viewing, especially programs that are violent.*

- *Help children feel good about themselves, build strong self-images, and be competent individuals.*   Children who are happy, confident, and competent feel good about themselves and are more likely to behave positively toward others.

Program in Practice

"ROOTS AND WINGS"

Third grade is a year of great expectations and change. I am always curious to see how each child goes through his or her own individual metamorphosis. They walk into my classroom in August, timid and often immature. These little cocoons begin to mysteriously burst open after the Christmas break. Each child emerges in his or her own time and with his or her own identity. They are discovering who they are as well as what the world has to offer them. They flit around from place to place, friend to friend, and mood to mood, as would a butterfly in a garden. Spreading their wings, they take in all they can and then fly off for fourth grade in June.

"Third grade!" "Let's go!" "Third graders!" It is 8:10 *a.m.* in St. Mary's County, Maryland. At Lexington Park Elementary, with a student population of approximately 450, third graders are being called off their buses. Every school day at this time, third graders make their way through the school to mobile teaching units on the outside of the building. These units are home to sixty-eight third grade students. There are two third grade classrooms and a second-third grade combination classroom.

Let us take a look at a typical day in my third grade classroom. Welcome to Room 19. Students desks are arranged in groups of four to allow for cooperative learning teams. The standard listening, writing, and reading centers can be found at various locations around the room.

Students begin to arrive in the classroom at 8:15. At least one third of my twenty-six students eat breakfast in school. There is an ethnic mix of boys and girls in my classroom. The girls outnumber the boys by six. Cultural and economic backgrounds of the students differ as well. We are located near the Naval Air Warfare Center Aircraft Division at Patuxent River, Maryland. Therefore, many of our students' parents are either in some branch of the military or work for contractors affiliated with the base. Some parents commute the hour and a half to Washington, D.C. Single-parent families are here also.

Our day begins with a normal routine of checking in, sharpening pencils, ordering lunch, turning in homework, and the general welcoming of a new day. Today the morning work is to continue our language lesson on past-tense verbs and introduce the helping verbs *has, had,* and *have.* The math problem-solving entry in our math logbooks is to list coin combinations for $1.25. Today, an idea for the children's writing journal is to write about how it would feel to be a pine cone hanging on the top limb of a huge pine tree. Of course, students can self-select a journal topic.

After morning announcements, the plan of the day is discussed and morning work is reviewed. I am sure most teachers would agree that finding time in the day to teach everything can be difficult. Language and writing skills are one such aspect that must be practiced across the curriculum. Opportunities for writing are made available in all subject areas, including art.

Ohahyo is the Japanese good-day cheer heard echoing through our classroom this morning. (We have begun a unit on Japan.) Today we watch a video letter describing various Japanese trades and vocations. At the conclusion of the video, students vote to create handmade paper from cardboard egg cartons. The students work in their teams to formulate a materials list. During our wrap-up time, students update their Japan folders with required handouts and extra-credit assign-

Contributed by Barbara Lord, Lexington Park Elementary School, Lexington Park, Maryland.

ments. Japan is the third of four countries that will be studied this year. We began our study travel in our own country and focused on Washington, D.C. Ghana was the next country we visited. Upon completion of the Japan unit we will take our studies to India. The follow-up will be a field trip to Washington, D.C., where we will visit the embassies of the countries we have discussed, as well as the sites we read about when studying our nation's capital.

Third grade students benefit from the team teaching of science and social studies. My colleague teaches the concepts of science: simple machines, plant/animal life, the solar system, and weather. For four-week periods I teach social studies, and my colleague, Robin Harvey, teaches science. At the end of four weeks her students come to me for social studies and my students go to her for science. This approach reduces the strain of having to cover an extra subject. For teachers, every little bit of help in instruction is always welcome. Team teaching gives the students a chance to experience different teaching styles and methods.

Sharing the responsibility of educating our youth is an emphasis goal at Lexington Park Elementary School. We are fortunate to be involved in a community partnership with Naval Aviation Depot Operations Center (NADOC) at Patuxent River, Maryland. Personnel from NADOC volunteer time at our school as tutor buddies. Students identified under Chapter 1 are placed with tutors initially. However, any student showing need can receive support and assistance from a NADOC volunteer. As many as eight of my students benefit from this program. For example, tutors will reread stories with children, listen to stories children read, and review comprehension questions.

Partnerships, teams, and *sharing* are terms used frequently in my third grade classroom. St. Mary's County Public Schools and Johns Hopkins University were awarded a grant entitled Roots and Wings from the New American Schools Development Corporation. The goal of the New American School Development Corporation is to support restructuring efforts. Roots and Wings is one of eight grants funded nationally. Math Wings is a pilot component of the Roots and Wings program.

Piloting this math program provides for a unique teaching and learning experience. The units and lessons are sent from Johns Hopkins. The program involves cooperative learning teams. The daily plan includes class discussion, team investigation, partnered practice, and individual reinforcement with homework. The program allows students to invent their own methods to solve problems. Students have begun to accept ownership of Math Wings because their comments and concerns are welcomed and encouraged from Johns Hopkins. Students are free to provide constructive criticism about the lessons. Most students are supportive of the program. They are particularly fond of the use of manipulatives to reinforce skills that are taught.

Partnerships are also evident within our school in the special subjects classes. Music, media/computer lab, physical education, and art teachers are helpful in coordinating their lessons with our classroom curriculum. Because of limited classroom space, art and music classes are held in our classroom. The teacher carry supplies for instruction on carts. Students receive two sessions a week of physical education and music; media/computer lab and art are taught once a week.

After returning from an hour-long lunch and recess break, students are given the opportunity to participate in a class meeting. Everyday we take ten to fifteen minutes to celebrate achievement, discuss issues of concern, plan upcoming events, and learn ways in which we can make learning more successful.

In the afternoon, our theme of partnership extends from individual classrooms to every third, fourth, and fifth grade classroom. All three grade levels work together to teach Cooperative Integrated Reading and Composition (CIRC), yet another component of the Roots and Wings program. This program, involving the use of cooperative learning teams, allows third, fourth, and fifth grade students to be placed in a group at their individual reading level. My third graders enjoy working with students at different age and grade levels. Once students are grouped, their focus is to work together to achieve a common goal. The hour and a half CIRC block involves whole-class discussion, cooperative groupings, partnering activities, as well as individual assignments. This component of Roots and Wings has been in place for two years. Teaching and reading and writing through the CIRC process has proven to be effective in increasing student self-esteem as well as student achievement.

Our day has just about come to a close. Students return to their homeroom classrooms and prepare for dismissal. In the last few minutes of the school day, students unwind with a book, debrief with a friend, or jot down events of the day in their journals. Unless a child is picked up by a parent, all students ride a bus home from school. As the last bus is called, a few students are left behind who are involved in after-school programs. In still another component of Roots and Wings, students are able to enroll in computer club, homework center, tutoring, and even drama club. These activities are made available four days a week.

And so ends another day at Lexington Park Elementary. As I make my way through the maze of chairs and desks, I see several field trip forms left behind. Someone will be needing the language book that is lying on the floor in order to complete their homework tonight. Bits of paper and fragments of crayons—these are all part of the magical time and place we call third grade.

Teaching Thinking

The back-to-basics movement has been a dominant theme in U.S. education and will likely continue as a curriculum force. When we think of the basic skills, we generally think of reading, writing, and arithmetic, and many elementary schools allot these subjects the lion's share of time and teacher emphasis. Yet some critics of education and advocates of basic education do not consider the three Rs the ultimate "basic" of sound education. Rather, the real basic of education is *thinking*. The rationale is that if students can think, they can meaningfully engage in subject-matter curriculum and the rigors and demands of the workplace and life. As a result, teachers are including the teaching of thinking in their daily lesson plans.

In classrooms that emphasize thinking, students are encouraged to use their power of analysis, and teachers ask higher-level questions. Teachers are being encouraged to challenge their children to think about classroom information and learning material rather than merely memorize acceptable responses. So, instead of asking children to recall information, teachers are asking them to think critically about information, solve problems, and reflect. The following list describes some of the commonly taught thinking skills:

Commonly Taught Thinking Skills[3]

- *Analyzing*—examining something methodically; identifying the parts of something and the relationships between those parts
- *Inferring*—drawing a reasonable conclusion from known information
- *Comparing and contrasting*—noting similarities and differences between two things or events
- *Predicting*—forecasting what will happen next in a given situation, based on the circumstances
- *Hypothesizing*—developing a reasonable explanation for events, based on an analysis of evidence
- *Critical thinking*—examining evidence and arguments carefully, without bias, and reaching sound conclusions
- *Deductive reasoning*—applying general principles to specific cases
- *Inductive reasoning*—deriving general principles from an analysis of individual cases
- *Organizing*—imposing logical order on something
- *Classifying*—putting things into groups based on shared characteristics
- *Decision making*—examining alternatives and choosing one, for sound reasons
- *Problem solving*—analyzing a difficult situation and thinking creatively about how to resolve it

Implications for Professionals

Professionals who want to promote critical and creative thinking in children need to be aware of several things. First, children need the freedom *and* security to be creative thinkers. Many teachers and school programs focus on helping children learn the *right* answers to problems, so children soon learn from the process of schooling that there is only one right answer. Children may be so "right answer" oriented that they are uncomfortable with searching for other answers or consider it a waste of time.

Second, the environment must support children's creative efforts. Teachers must create classroom settings in which children have the time, opportunity, and materials with which to be creative. Letting children think creatively only when all their subjects are completed, or scheduling creative thinking for certain times, does not properly encourage it.

Third, creative *and* critical thinking must be *integrated* into the total curriculum, so that children learn to think across the curriculum, the entire school day, and throughout their lives.

Cooperative Learning

You can probably remember how, when you were primary school age, you competed with the other kids. You probably tried to see whether you could be the first to raise your hand. You leaned out over the front of your seat, frantically waving for your teacher's attention. In many of today's primary classrooms, however, the emphasis is on cooperation, not competition. Cooperative learning is seen as a way to boost student achievement and enhance self-esteem.

Cooperative learning is an instructional and learning strategy that focuses on instructional methods in which students are encouraged or required to work together on academic tasks. Students work in small, mixed-ability learning groups of usually four students who are themselves responsible for learning and helping their group members learn. In one form of cooperative learning, called "Student Teams—Achievement Division," four students—usually one high achiever, two average students, and one low achiever—participate in a regular cycle of activities, such as the following:

- The teacher presents the lesson to the group.
- Students work to master the material using worksheets or other learning materials. Students are encouraged not only to complete their work but also to explain their work and ideas to group members.
- Students take brief quizzes.[4]

Children in a cooperative learning group are assigned certain responsibilities; for example, there is a group *leader*, who announces the problems or task; a *praiser*, who praises group members for their answers and work; and a *checker*. Responsibilities rotate as the group engages in different tasks. Children are also encouraged to develop and use interpersonal skills, such as addressing classmates by their first names, saying "Thank you," and explaining to their group mates why they are proposing an answer. On the classroom level, five basic elements must be incorporated into the instructional process for cooperative learning to be successful:

1. *Positive independence.*   The students have to believe they are in the learning process together and that they care about one another's learning.
2. *Verbal, face-to-face interaction.*   Students must explain, argue, elaborate, and tie what they are learning now to what they have previously learned.
3. *Individual accountability.*   Every member of the group must realize that it is his or her own responsibility to learn.

In many of today's primary classrooms, the emphasis is on cooperation, not competition. Cooperative learning is seen as a way to boost student achievement and enhance self-esteem. Why is cooperative learning popular with teachers and students?

4. *Social.*   Students must learn appropriate leadership, communication, trust-building, and conflict resolution skills.

5. *Group processing.*   The group has to assess how well its members are working together and how they can do better.[5]

Proponents and practitioners of cooperative learning are enthusiastic about its benefits:

- It motivates students to do their best.
- It motivates students to help one another.
- It significantly increases student achievement.[6]

Supporters of cooperative learning maintain that it enables children to learn how to cooperate and that children learn from each other. And because schools are usually such competitive places, it gives children an opportunity to learn cooperative skills.

Not all teachers agree that cooperative learning is a good idea, however. They maintain that it is too time-consuming, because a group may take longer than an individual to solve a problem. Other critics charge that time spent on cooperative learning takes away time from learning the basic skills of reading, writing, and arithmetic.

Program in Practice

TEACHING THINKING WITH TEAM

Teaching Enrichment Activities to Minority Students, or TEAM, is a program designed to teach thinking skills, vocabulary development, and various enrichment activities in all subject areas to high-achieving minority students. Students are selected for the program according to teacher recommendation; test scores have nothing to do with the selection process. The purpose of the TEAM program is to compensate for environmental factors that might have hindered the child's ability and performance. The program is also designed to improve these students' thinking skills to enhance their prospects for access to academic excellence and/or gifted programs. The success rate of TEAM students entering a gifted program is 40 to 70 percent. The TEAM program has been successfully implemented since 1989 at Charles R. Hadley Elementary in Miami, Florida, with second and third grade students.

In a TEAM classroom, students' skills are improved by using a structured cognitive stimulation program, with highly sequential activities designed to stimulate thinking at the analytical level. Students also develop verbal reasoning skills, ability to make judgments, and strategies for questioning.

There is never a right or wrong answer in the TEAM classroom. If the student can justify an answer and sufficiently back it up, it is considered correct. Students are, however, consistently challenged to go beyond simple "yes" and "no" answers.

Implementing TEAM

A primary vehicle for TEAM program implementation in our classroom is provision of a comfortable environment. We have pillows where the children can go to read while lying down. We let them know they can accomplish whatever they put their minds to. We let the children know they will not be ridiculed, no matter what answer they give. They know that every question and answer is valued. We always emphasize the positive in our classroom. We feel that reinforcing the negative makes a child feel bad about him- or herself and, without positive self-regard, less likely to try to succeed. Most of our children come from an environment filled with negative feelings. Instead of adding to the negative feelings the child already has, we try to change those feelings into positive ones.

TEAM Strategies

We set high standards and expectations for our students—it seems that minimal expectations have been the norm in many of these children's previous classroom experiences. We could not help but wonder why. We have found that by raising our expectations for our students, we see a high level of accomplishment. We believe that teachers have the power to control student achievement by setting high expectations. If we want the best from our students, we should expect nothing but the best.

Our students are consistently involved in situations that require creative and imaginative responses. For Columbus Day, for example, we did a writing activity in which the students had to imagine that they were on one of the three ships. We first gave them facts about the voyage and the discovery, then they had to picture themselves as part of the crew.

Contributed by Sara P. Grillo, teacher, and Maria de la Torre, supervising teacher, Charles R. Hadley Elementary School, Miami, Florida.

What were the weather conditions? How did they eat? What kind of foods did they have? Was it a hard or easy voyage? Why? These types of activities get the children thinking, creating, and imagining. In this way, social studies and language arts are also incorporated into the curriculum. Subject areas in primary curricula tend to be isolated, so we strive to integrate all areas whenever possible.

We also incorporate the use of journals. Every morning, the children complete a journal entry using five or more sentences; for example, "My family is. . . ." The children express whatever feelings they wish. At the end of the week, we collect the journals, read them, and write back to the children. The children look forward to reading what we have written.

Another technique we use is brainstorming. This is an excellent way for students to share answers and express themselves. Students who have difficulty reading and writing can express themselves in this way—orally. Brainstorming is used in every subject. The students know their contributions will always be valued. Through this collaboration of thoughts and ideas, students are motivated for the lesson.

Cooperative learning is another facet of the TEAM program. Students are asked to work in pairs and groups to come up with solutions to problems. Structure in classrooms has generally been strict with regard to discipline and isolates children so that they work individually. Is this the way our society works? In our opinion, it is not. On the contrary, a well-functioning society is composed of members who share and work together toward a common goal. What better place to begin to learn the concept of cooperation than in the classroom? This is why we feel cooperative learning is crucial to a child's success in the outside world. Our students work in groups, share their ideas and thoughts, and evaluate each other. In our classroom, which is composed of a writing center, pillows, a computer, a listening station, magazines, books, newspapers, math manipulatives, and a hands-on science center, children circulate freely from center to center. Of course, there is an overall structure to classroom organization and scheduling, but the children are free to go to the center of their choice.

A TEAM for All

Any teacher, in any classroom, can teach children to think. As teachers, we need to be flexible and change with the times. Teachers cannot expect to do the same thing year after year, with different students who have different needs. A good teacher who sets high standards can accomplish anything.

Motivation is the key to all learning. If the teacher motivates the students, and the students are truly excited about learning, the process can begin. A teacher needs to build self-confidence and self-esteem in students. Teachers need to challenge students, let them take risks, provide for a comfortable environment, and expect the best from them. After all, the teacher is the *key* to any program, whether it succeeds or fails.

Given the new approaches in primary education, it makes sense that professionals would want to use a child-centered approach that increases student achievement. Furthermore, school critics say that classrooms are frequently too competitive and that students who are neither competitive nor high achievers are left behind. Cooperative learning would seem to be one of the better ways to reduce classroom competitiveness and foster "helping" attitudes.

CHARACTER EDUCATION

Character education is back in many elementary classrooms (and middle and senior high schools as well) across the United States, for several reasons. Society is alarmed by what it sees as a decline in moral values and abandonment of ethical values. The character education movement is also a reaction to the "anything goes" 1980s characterized by the savings and loan scandals and the "me first" and "I want everything—now" attitudes. Of course, society is also alarmed by substance abuse, teenage pregnancies, violence, and juvenile delinquency. Character education is seen as a way of reducing, and possibly, preventing these societal problems.

Character education programs seek to teach a set of traditional core values that will result in civic virtue and moral character. Some of these core values are honesty, kindness, respect, responsibility, tolerance for diversity, racial harmony, and good citizenship.

Efforts to promote character qualities and core values are evident in statewide efforts. For example, the state of Georgia has identified the following core values it wants all children to exhibit:[7]

Citizenship

Democracy: government of, by and for the people, exercised through the voting process

- Respect for and acceptance of authority: the need for and primacy of authority, including the law, in given circumstances
- Equality: the right and opportunity to develop one's potential as a human being
- Freedom of conscience and expression: the right to hold beliefs, whether religious, ethical or political, and to express one's views
- Justice: equal and impartial treatment under the law
- Liberty: freedom from oppression, tyranny or the domination of government
- Tolerance: recognition of the diversity of others, their opinions, practices and culture

Patriotism: support of and love for the United States of America with zealous guarding of its welfare

- Courage: willingness to face obstacles and danger with determination
- Loyalty: steadfastness or faithfulness to a person, institution, custom or idea to which one is tied by duty, pledge or a promise

Respect for the Natural Environment: care for and conservation of land, trees, clean air and pure water and of all living inhabitants of the earth

Many professionals view good literature as a good way to infuse character education in the curriculum. By reading literature that focuses on exemplary character traits and values, teachers can engage students in discussions and thinking about the importance of such traits in their own lives.

- Conservation: avoiding waste and pollution of natural resources

Respect for Others

Altruism: concern for and motivation to act for the welfare of others

- Civility: courtesy and politeness in action or speech
- Compassion: concern for suffering or distress of others and response to their feelings and needs
- Courtesy: recognition of mutual interdependence with others resulting in polite treatment and respect from them

Integrity: confirmed virtue and uprightness of character; freedom from hypocrisy

- Honesty: truthfulness and sincerity
- Truth: freedom from deceit or falseness; based on fact or reality
- Trustworthiness: worthy of confidence

Respect for Self

Accountability: responsibility for one's actions and their consequences

- Commitment: being emotionally, physically or intellectually bound to something
- Perseverance: adherence to action, belief or purpose without giving way
- Self Control: exercising authority over one's emotions and actions
- Frugality: effective use of resources; thrift

Self-Esteem: pride and belief in oneself and in achievement of one's potential

- Knowledge: learning, understanding, awareness

- Moderation: avoidance of extreme views or measures
- Respect for physical, mental and fiscal health: awareness of the importance of and conscious activity toward maintaining fitness in these areas

Work Ethic: belief that work is good and that everyone who can, should work

- Accomplishment: appreciation for completing a task
- Cooperation: working with others for mutual benefit
- Dependability: reliability, trustworthiness
- Diligence: attentiveness, persistence; perseverance
- Pride: dignity; self-respect; doing one's best
- Productivity: supporting one's self; contributing to society
- Creativity: exhibiting an entrepreneurial spirit; inventiveness; originality; not bound by the norm

WHOLE LANGUAGE

Whole language provides us an opportunity to return to our early childhood historic and philosophical roots (see chap. 2). Yetta Goodman, in her analysis of the whole-language movement, cites these historic influences:

- Comenius's concern for learner-centered pedagogy (see chap. 2),
- Piaget's support for active learning (see chap. 4),
- Vygotsky's belief in the relationship between the learning of the child and influences of the social setting (see chap. 4), and
- Dewey's advocacy of learner-centered education and integration of language arts into the curriculum (see chap. 2).[8]

The term *whole language* is used to convey the concept that language development, reading, writing, speaking, and listening are integrated and related processes. The following assumptions underlie the whole-language approach:

- Language and language learning are social activities; they occur best in a situation that encourages discussion and a sharing of knowledge and ideas.
- Language learning necessarily involves the risk of trying new strategies; error is inherent in the process.
- Reading and writing are context specific; what is learned about reading and writing is a reflection of the particular situation in which the learning is occurring.
- Reading and writing are content specific; what is learned about reading and writing reflects the particular situation in which the learning is occurring.
- Choice is an essential element for learning; there must be opportunities for students to select what they want to read and write about.
- Whole-language activities are those that support students in their use of all aspects of language. Students learn about reading and writing while listening; they learn about writing from reading and gain insights about reading from writing.

- Our role as teachers is best seen as "leading from behind" by supporting the language-learning capabilities of students indirectly through the activities we offer them.[9]

The Naturalness of Literacy Development

Educators today also stress the "naturalness" of children's literacy development. The case is made that many children learn to write and read in natural ways, many times on their own and without formal instruction. The example *par excellence* of this naturalness at work in literacy development is the many kindergarten and first grade children who come to school with rather well-developed writing and reading skills. Of course, Maria Montessori discussed this process as part of her program (see chap. 3).

The naturalness with which many children develop an interest in reading and writing *and* engage in the reading and writing processes at home and in preschool settings is frequently sharply contrasted with what many critics maintain is a less natural approach to teaching language arts. These "less than natural" approaches include what is frequently referred to as "sit down instruction" in which teachers teach children how to read and write. Other practices that critics label unnatural include the use of dittos and worksheets and mindless, repetitive exercises. For example, story starters, a technique by which teachers give children sentences to begin stories, can sometimes discourage writing and creativity. If every day a child is given a story starter that begins, "Today is Tuesday [or any other day of the school week], and it is cold outside . . . ," should it come as a surprise that the student soon loses interest in learning to write?

Efforts to promote a "natural" approach to reading and writing are seen in programs to involve parents in reading to their children at home, encouraging children and their families to use public libraries, and the growth of children's book clubs. The process of "being read to" in home and school is gaining in attention and popularity. Children who have been read to

- have developed crucial insights about written language being essential for learning to read and write;
- realize that written language, while related to it, is not the same as spoken language;
- have discovered that both spoken and written language can serve the same function; and
- have learned to follow plot and character development.[10]

Reading, Writing, and Literature

Learning to write and improving students' writing through reading is also receiving renewed emphasis today, which is why so many students are encouraged to read *good literature* as part of their reading/writing programs. This concept is affecting not only how children are taught (e.g., through literature); it is also influencing publishing companies. They are including more literature in their reading books.

The inclusion of literature in the reading/language arts curriculum is characterized by several important features:

- The inclusion of literature by well-known authors (e.g., Cynthia Rylant, A. A. Milne, Langston Hughes)
- The inclusion of the *unabridged* works of famous authors. Critics of the status of children's literacy have complained that rather than reading the "real thing," students have been subjected to the watered-down versions of famous authors. They cite this as one more example of the "dumbing-down" of textbooks and the curriculum.
- The use of literature as the context within which to teach reading and language arts skills

The Whole-Language Curriculum

A whole-language literacy program has a number of important components:

- It uses and incorporates *functional language;* that is, children are offered involvement with written language in and from the environment. Examples of the involvement of children in functional language include making signs and posters, writing letters, and making lists.
- It uses *predictable materials* such as signs, nursery rhymes, poems, as well as classical and contemporary children's stories. Predictable books are especially important because of their repetitive language, match between text and illustration, and familiar content.
- It incorporates *language experience* stories that evolve from the children's interests and activities.
- It uses *shared reading.* This is essentially a process in which teachers read favorite stories to children. This emphasis on shared reading has lead to the development of "big books." These oversized books enable teachers to involve children in a shared reading experience so they can see, participate, and feel that they are part of the process.
- It involves *story reading* in which children are read to one-on-one by older children, then the younger child reads to the older child. This process can also incorporate adults reading to children and vice versa.
- It uses *sustained silent reading,* which is a process in which a brief period of time is set aside daily so that everyone—children, teacher, principal, and in some schools custodians and cafeteria workers—read by themselves.
- It encourages children to *control their own learning* by initiating reading and writing activities. For example, they determine what books to read and when to read them.[11]

Child Centered and Humanistic

In terms of psychological and philosophical underpinnings, the whole-language approach to reading and writing is decidedly child centered and humanistic in both process and approach. In addition to its emphasis on incorporating children's interests in the reading/writing processes, whole language is decidedly Deweyan.

Besides the characteristics of whole-language instruction already mentioned, others help illustrate this approach's philosophical and pedagogical affiliation with the child-centered/progressive education movements. These characteristics are as follows:

1. A totally integrated approach to language instruction.
2. A focus on students' experiences and interests. Students self-select materials that have special meaning.
3. Students engage in writing regularly; they write about topics that are meaningful and interesting to them. Students' compositions become an integral part of the language arts program.
4. Students engage in oral language activities more frequently than they do in traditional classrooms.
5. Teachers are language models who participate in classroom language activities and read to children regularly.
6. The teacher as a researcher who observes students' learning as a basis for developing generalizations about how children learn the language arts.[12]

The Integrated Curriculum

The integrated curriculum is a natural progression from whole language, or whole language may be the result of attempts to integrate the curriculum. The integrated curriculum is an attempt to break down barriers between subject-matter areas and help children make connections between all content areas. In integrated learning, for example, children write in their journals about life in the United States and construct bar graphs about the height and weight of their classmates.

Authentic Writing

As a result of whole language, writing is becoming more *authentic;* that is, it is more concerned with the real world. Children are writing about real-life topics and issues—the environment, violence, how to help the homeless, and so forth. In today's contemporary classrooms, contrived writing is out the window and the real world is open for discussion and writing.

CHARACTERISTICS OF A PRIMARY PROFESSIONAL

When all is said and done, it is the professional who sets the tone and direction for classroom instruction and learning. Without quality professionals, a quality program is impossible. Quality primary professionals must possess all the personal qualities of humane, loving, caring people. In addition, they must be capable of interacting with very energetic young children. Unlike upper elementary children, who are more goal and self-directed, primary children need help in developing the skills and personal habits that will enable them to be independent learners. To help them develop

Program in Practice

USING COMPUTERS IN A FIRST GRADE CLASSROOM

Several years ago I introduced my first grade students to computers by dragging my own Atari computer to and from my classroom each day and using the television in my room as a monitor. A few years later, I was given an Apple IIE to use with my students. Then I upgraded to an Apple IIGS with a printer. Now, I have "graduated" to three networked IBM computers and a printer in my classroom. My class also goes to a Mac lab once a week. Most of my understanding of how young children work with computers has come from trial and error and observing my students as they work at the computer.

Often the first experiences that young children have with computers is through arcade-type games. They have played Nintendo, GameBoy, or some other form of video games extensively. When the children come into school and see computers, they automatically assume that we have provided them with a classroom arcade. One of the first questions that is asked is "Can I play the computer?" At that moment I teach the children to use the words *use* or *work at* instead of *play*. My next job is to help the children realize that the computers in my classroom will be used for something even more valuable than playing arcade games—learning!

Teaching Techniques

It is necessary to teach the children how to use the computers, just as you teach them about books, games, and other materials in the room. You can discuss general rules with the whole class, but specific hands-on training must be done in small groups. Often I can train a few children before or after school to use a new program. After they have had time to work through the program, they can help train their classmates during class time. Another training option is to use former students. This year some of my first graders are returning to their kindergarten teacher's room to help her introduce the computer to her children.

The trainers must understand that their job is to guide another child through the program. We have established a "hands off" rule. This means that the trainer may tell or point but cannot touch the keys. Usually I will have the trainer sit behind the child who is being introduced to a new program so that the keyboard is out of reach.

Once the program has been introduced, I allow each child to have adequate computer time. In our school, we have computer assisted instruction (CAI) programs in reading and math that our children should use daily. I have a file card for each child that contains the child's name and information necessary to get the program going. These cards are color coded into four groups that correspond with the colors that are used when the class is working in centers. The children flow from the independent center to the computer. I can place several cards by the keyboard. After the child has finished the lesson, he or she places his or her card in a plastic bag that is taped on the side of the computer, looks at the next card, and quietly taps that person on the shoulder to tell them that it is their turn. Of course, we have done some role playing with this procedure, as the first impulse of the children is to stand next to the computer and shout, "Jean, it's my turn at the computer!"

To eliminate confusion about which computer the child should use, I have placed stuffed animals on the top of each monitor. I

Contributed by Sarah Du Bosq, South Pointe Elementary School, Miami Beach, Florida.

sewed two or three strips of Velcro on the bottom of each animal and applied sticky-backed Velcro on the top of each monitor. The children know whether to go to the monkey, bunny, or puppy computer. I must admit that each year after the animals have been introduced, I usually find one or more of them hiding among the books or blocks. After the initial excitement of seeing the animals, the children realize their purpose and usually leave them alone.

I try to start the children flowing to the computers as early as I can each day. We try to maintain a continuous rotation. I feel that the time that is spent at the computer can be very valuable for each student. I view it more as one-to-one tutoring time rather than time away from direct teacher instruction.

Evaluation

It is important for the children to realize that the computer is a powerful learning tool if it is used properly. After the class has used the computer several times, I will begin to monitor their progress. In our CAI programs I can find out detailed information about an individual child's progress. Often I need to have mini-conferences with some of my students to help them learn to make the most of each session at the computer.

Shortly after we started working on the CAI math program, I realized that one child had gone to the computer thirteen times, while many others had only had three turns. I realized that Chris was staying at the computer after the first session was over. I also discovered that he had been spending most of his time clicking on the different "help" icons. In one ten-minute session, he had clicked on help fourteen times, attempted four problems, and done one correctly. I printed out Chris's

report, asked him to join me in a quiet corner of the classroom, and shared my revelations with him. After our discussion, Chris's attitude toward the computer changed drastically. He began to do only one session and enjoyed reporting his score to me each time.

Selecting Software

Searching for software can present many challenges. You must know the amount of memory your computer has and the type of software it can run. Sometimes you will find a program that is just what you have been searching for, but it will not work on your computer.

You should ask yourself several questions when looking for software: Will it meet students' instructional needs? Does it have teacher options so it can be individualized? Will it keep records of student progress? Is it easy for children to use? Is it "childproof"? Is it challenging enough to be used over a long period of time? [See chap. 15 for additional information on evaluating software.]

If you can preview the product, you need to try to use it the way a child would. In some programs it is very easy to exit the program by accident. I have watched a child moving icons around on the screen, not realizing that he has exited the program. I have also seen joy turn to frustration when a child has inadvertently clicked on something and the computer is no longer doing what the child has anticipated.

Some programs are wonderful but have a relatively short classroom life. After the children have mastered the concepts, they are ready to move on to other programs. If these programs are purchased by the school and kept in the media center, they may be cycled through several classrooms during the year. Teachers may also want to pool their resources by sharing different programs that they have purchased.

Several options may help you in your quest for great programs for your classroom. You can talk to other teachers about programs they have liked. Many conferences have material displays where you may find educational software. Sometimes a company will send you a program to preview. A variety of products can also be found at local retail stores, although these programs are designed primarily for home use and do not have the teacher options that you may want to use. Of course, you can look through catalogs, but often the description does not tell you enough about the product or has inaccurate grade recommendations.

Last year several teachers at my school searched for a good word processing program that would be appropriate for kinder-garten and first grade. We read about one interesting program in a catalog, but it indicated that it was appropriate for grades two through seven. We assumed that it would be too difficult for our children. After one of our teachers watched her six-year-old grandson using that program, she knew that it would be perfect for our needs. Now our children have a word processing program that they can use with ease.

Concluding Remarks

Reflecting on my attempt to bring computer technology into the classroom, I remember some of the frustration I felt as well as the joy of my students as we began to conquer this new machine together. I realize now that the rewards of this effort definitely outweigh any obstacles I had to overcome.

these skills and habits should be primary professionals' foremost goal. These guidelines will help implement that goal:

- *Plan for instruction.*   Planning is the basis for the vision of what professionals want for themselves and for the children. Professionals who try to operate without a plan are like builders without a blueprint. Although planning takes time, it saves time in the long run, and it provides direction for instruction.

- *Be the classroom leader.*   A quality professional *leads* the classroom. Some professionals forget this, and although children at all ages are capable of performing leadership responsibilities, it is the professional who sets the guidelines within which effective instruction occurs. Without strong leadership—not overbearing or dictatorial leadership—classrooms do not operate well. Planning for instruction helps a professional lead.

- *Involve children in meaningful learning tasks.*   To learn, children need to be *active and involved.* To learn to read they must read; to learn to write, they must write. Although these guidelines may seem self-evident, they are not always implemented. To learn, children need to spend time on learning tasks.

- *Provide individualized instruction.*   In a classroom of twenty-five or more children, a wide range of abilities and interests is apparent. The professional must provide for these differences if children are going to learn to their fullest. There is a difference between *individual* and *individualized* instruction; it is impossible to provide individual attention to all children all the time, but providing for children at their individual levels is possible and necessary. Educators are often accused of teaching to the average, boring the more able, and leaving the less able behind. This criticism can be addressed with individualized instruction. (See chap. 16 for more information about professionalism and becoming a professional.)

ASSESSMENT

Much of the primary school child's life is influenced by assessment of achievement. What children study, how they study it, and the length of time they study it are all evaluated in some way. Decisions about promotion are also made from assessment results. With so much emphasis on tests, it is understandable that the issue raises many concerns. Critics maintain that the testing movement reduces teaching and learning to the lowest common denominator—teaching children what they need to know to get the right answers. Many early childhood professionals believe that standardized tests do not measure children's thinking, problem-solving ability, or responsibility for their own learning. Furthermore, these critics of testing believe that the group-administered, objectively scored, skills-focused tests that dominate much of U.S. education do not support (indeed, they may undermine) many of the curricular reforms taking place today.

In response to such criticisms, testing and evaluation have undergone much change. Some of these changes are discussed next.

No matter what the content or purpose of a program, the key to successful teaching and learning is a well-prepared and child-centered teacher. What qualities of the primary professional would you add to the ones discussed in this chapter?

Authentic Assessment

Also referred to as *performance-based assessment,* authentic assessment is carried out through activities that require children to demonstrate what they know and are able to do. Meaningless facts and isolated information are considered un-authentic. Authentic assessment has the following traits:

- *Assesses children on the basis of their actual work.*   Work samples—often in a portfolio—exhibitions, performances, learning logs, journals, projects, presentations, experiments, and teacher observations are essential processes in authentic assessment.

- *Provides for ongoing assessment, over time, over the entire school year.*   Thus, a child's performance and achievement are continuously assessed, not just at the end of a grading period or at the end of the year through a standardized achievement test.

- *Is curriculum embedded.* Children are assessed on what they are actually doing in and through the curriculum.

- *Is a cooperative and collaborative process involving children, teachers, and in many cases parents.*   This is an attempt to move away from teacher-focused assessment and make assessment more child centered.

- *Is intended to help professionals and parents learn more about children.*   All areas—social-emotional, language, cognitive, and physical—are assessed. The whole child is evaluated rather than a narrow set of skills. In this sense, it is child centered and humane.

- *Assesses what* individual *children are able to do.* Authentic assessment evaluates what they as individuals are learning as opposed to measuring or comparing one child to another or children to children, as is so often the case.

- *Makes assessment part of the learning process.*   For example, third grader Haydee Bolado, as part of a project on the community, visited the recycling center. She made a presentation to the class and used the overhead projector to illustrate her major points, a poster board with pictures she had taken of the center, and several graphs to show which products are recycled most. In this way, she was able to demonstrate a broader range of what she had learned.

While early childhood professionals are enthusiastic about authentic assessment, some professionals are quick to point out the drawbacks inherent to it:

- It takes a lot more of the teacher's time to plan for and participate in a process of authentic assessment.

- Professionals need training to help them understand and apply authentic assessment.

- Some parents see the schools shift away from the traditional—traditional grading practices, traditional grades, and traditional testing—as a another sign of the fadism that schooling periodically undergoes. They want to stay with the traditional ways of doing things. (See the Guidelines for Appropriate Assessment on page 374.)

PROMOTION

Not surprisingly, with the new directions in primary education there is also a new look at grade failure and retention practices. Retention as a cure for poor or nonachievement is popular, especially with many professionals and the public. Despite the use of retention as a panacea for poor achievement, "the evidence to date suggests that achievement-based promotion does not deal effectively with the problem of low achievement."[13] Better and more helpful approaches to student achievement include strategies such as these:

- Using promotion combined with individualized instruction

- Promoting to a transition class in which students receive help to master skills not previously achieved

- Using after-school and summer programs to help students master skills

- Providing children specific and individualized help in mastery of skills

- Working with parents to teach them how to help their children work on mastery skills

Practices such as multi-age grouping, nongraded classrooms, and sustained instruction—in which one teacher stays with the same group of children for two to three years—are growing in popularity in the primary grades. One purpose is to help prevent failure and grade retention. What other advantages do you think these practices have?

GUIDELINES FOR APPROPRIATE ASSESSMENT

From a Position Statement of the National Association for the Education of Young Children and the National Association for Early Childhood Specialists in State Departments of Education

1. Curriculum and assessment are integrated throughout the program; assessment is congruent with and relevant to the goals, objectives and content of the program.

2. Assessment results in benefits to the child, such as needed adjustments in the curriculum or more individualized instruction and improvements in the program.

3. Children's development and learning in all domains—physical, social, emotional, and cognitive—and their dispositions and feelings are informally and routinely assessed by teachers' observing children's activities and interactions, listening to them as they talk, and using their constructive errors to understand their learning.

4. Assessment provides teachers with useful information to successfully fulfill their responsibilities: to support children's learning and development, to plan for individuals and groups, and to communicate with parents.

5. Assessment involves regular and periodic observation of the child in a wide variety of circumstances that are representative of the child's behavior in the program over time.

6. Assessment relies primarily on procedures that reflect the ongoing life of the classroom and typical activities of the children. Assessment avoids approaches that place children in artificial situations, impede the usual learning and developmental experiences in the classroom, or divert children from their natural learning processes.

7. Assessment relies on demonstrated performance during real, not contrived, activities, for example, real reading and writing activities rather than only skills testing.

8. Assessment utilizes an array of tools and a variety of processes, including, but not limited to, collections of representative work by children (artwork, stories they write, tape recordings of their reading), records of systematic observations by teachers, records of conversations ad interviews with children, and teachers' summaries of children's progress as individuals and as groups.

9. Assessment recognizes individual diversity of learning and allows for differences in styles and rates of learning. Assessment

From "Guidelines for Appropriate Curriculum Content and Assessment in Programs Serving Children Ages 3 through 8" in Sue Bredekamp and Teresa Rosegrant, eds., *Reaching Potentials: Appropriate Curriculum and Assessment for Young Children,* vol. 1, pp. 22–24 (Washington, D.C.: National Association for the Education of Young Children, 1992). Copyright © 1992 by NAEYC. Reprinted by permission.

• Identifying children who may need help before they enter first grade so that developmental services are provided early

• Using multiage grouping as a means of providing for a broader range of children's abilities and to provide children the benefits that come from multiage grouping

• Having a professional teach or stay with the same group of children over a period of several years as a means of getting to know children and their families takes into consideration children's ability in English, their stage of language acquisition, and whether they have been given the time and opportunity to develop proficiency in their native language as well as English.

10. Assessment supports children's development and learning; it does *not* threaten children's psychological safety of feelings of self-esteem.

11. Assessment supports parents' relationships with their children and does not undermine parents' confidence in their children's or their own ability, nor does it devalue the language and culture of the family.

12. Assessment demonstrates children's overall strengths and progress, what children *can* do, not just their wrong answers and what they cannot do or do not know.

13. Assessment is an essential component of the teacher's role. Since teachers can make maximal use of assessment results, the teacher is the *primary* assessor.

14. Assessment is a collaborative process involving children and teachers, teachers and parents, school and community. Information from parents about each child's experiences at home is used in planning instruction and evaluating children's learn-

ing. Information obtained from assessment is shared with parents in language they can understand.

15. Assessment encourages children to participate in self-evaluation.

16. Assessment addresses what children can do independently and what they can demonstrate with assistance since the latter shows the direction of their growth.

17. Information about each child's growth, development, and learning is systematically collected and recorded at regular intervals. Information such as samples of children's work, descriptions of their performance, and anecdotal records is used for planning instruction and communicating with parents.

18. A regular process exists for periodic information sharing between teachers and parents about children's growth and development and performance. The method of reporting to parents does not rely on letter or numerical grades but rather provides more meaningful, descriptive information in narrative form.

better and, as a result, provide better for children's educational and developmental needs. This approach is also called *sustained instruction*.

- Using a nongraded classroom. The nongraded classroom and *nongraded institution* go hand in hand. In the nongraded classroom, individual differences are recognized and accounted for. The state of Kentucky mandates nongradedness in grades 1 through 3. Advocates of nongradedness offer the following advantages:

Program in Practice

THE TWENTY-FIRST CENTURY PROGRAM IN INDEPENDENCE, MISSOURI

The Twenty-First Century Schools Program is a comprehensive child care program designed by Edward Zigler of Yale University's Bush Center for Child Development and Social Policy. It has served children from birth to twelve years of age and their families through a variety of services in the Independence, Missouri, school district since 1988.

The six components of the Twenty-First Century program are before- and after-school care for elementary school children, including half-day (flip-flop) care for kindergartners, child care for three- to five-year-olds, Parents as Teachers for parents with children birth to three years old, neighborhood day care providers network, information and referral, and medical screenings and referrals (Medicaid). Through these six components the Independence School District strives to provide for the social, emotional, physical, and intellectual growth of each child.

The Twenty-First Century program offers safe, high-quality child care that is accessible and affordable for families of children from two to twelve years of age. Parents pay a maximum of $26 per week for school-age child care and $63 per week for day care for preschoolers.

The program operates from 6:30 A.M. to 6:00 P.M. Before- and after-school care is provided in all thirteen Independence School District elementary buildings and one former elementary school building. The school-age child care program strives to build self-esteem and enhance the personal development of each child through crafts, physical activities, fine arts, music, field trips, computer work, and special events. Each child chooses from a variety of daily curriculum choices. An older child might spend thirty minutes in supervised homework, then decide to work on the computer. Physical activities for a younger child might be group exercises one day or outside team sports another. The curriculum is child centered, which enables each child to engage in activities that are of benefit physically, socially, and emotionally. The child's choice is the key.

Seven elementary school sites and one former elementary school building offer child care for children three to five. The Cognitively Oriented Curriculum/Project Construct approach is used in these day care programs. This approach focuses on the development of self-help skills, social skills, problem solving, and language. Children make choices from activity centers located around each room. Breakfast, lunch, and snack are included in the cost of the program.

More information on the Twenty-First Century Schools Program may be obtained by writing or calling school district superintendent Robert Watkins or school board president Phillip Parrino, Independence School District, 1231 S. Windsor, Independence, Missouri 64055; (816) 833-3433.

a. Opportunities for individualized instruction

b. An enhanced social atmosphere because older children help younger children and there are more opportunities for role modeling

c. Reduced or few, if any, retentions

d. Students do not have to progress through a grade-level curriculum in a lock-step approach with their age peers

Any effort to improve student achievement must emphasize helping children rather than using practices that threaten to detract from their self-image and make them solely responsible for their failure.

THE FUTURE OF PRIMARY EDUCATION

Although the educational system in general is slow to meet the demands and dictates of society, it is likely the dramatic changes seen in primary education will continue in the next decade. The direction will be determined by continual reassessment of the purpose of education and attempts to match the needs of society to the goals of the schools. Drug use, child abuse, the breakup of the family, and illiteracy are some of the societal problems the schools are being asked to address in significant ways.

Increasingly schools are asked to prepare children for their places in the world of tomorrow. All early childhood programs must help children and youth develop the skills necessary for life success. Even with the trend toward having children spend more time in school, we know that learning does not end with school and that children do not learn all they will need to know in an academic setting. It makes sense, therefore, to empower students with skills they can use throughout life in all kinds of interpersonal and organizational settings. Such skills include

- the ability to communicate with others, orally and in writing;
- the ability to work well with people of all races, cultures, and personalities;
- the ability to be responsible for directing one's behavior;
- the desire and ability for success in life—not as measured by earning a lot of money but by becoming a productive member of society; and
- the desire and ability to continue learning throughout life.

READINGS FOR FURTHER ENRICHMENT

Crompton, Rob. *Computers and the Primary Curriculum 3–13* (London: Falmer, 1989)

Comprehensive, up-to-date, and practical guide to the use of computers across a wide age range. Extensive use of color and samples of children's work to demonstrate the versatility of computers in schools.

Kamii, Constance. *Young Children Continue to Reinvent Arithmetic, 2nd Grade: Implications of Piaget's Theory* (New York: Teachers College Press, 1989)

Based on Piaget's theory and four years of research in public school. Traditional arithmetic teaching has been based on the assumption that arithmetic consists of rules that children must internalize. Kamii extends the theory from her earlier volume and provides new activities for second grade.

Paul, Richard, A. J. A. Brinker, and Marla Charbonneau. *Critical Thinking Handbook: K–3* (Rohnert Park, CA: Center for Critical Thinking and Moral Critique, 1987)

Designed to help teachers understand the process of critical thinking and how it can be taught. Provides general strategies for teaching thinking and shows how to adapt existing lesson plans to incorporate critical thinking activities.

ACTIVITIES FOR FURTHER ENRICHMENT

1. Interview parents and teachers to determine their views pro and con of nonpromotion in the primary grades. Summarize your findings. What are your opinions on retention?

2. Are you computer literate? Could you implement a program of computer literacy in a first grade? Why?

3. Survey children in first, second, and third grade to determine how many have computers in the home. Find out what software is most popular, whether the children like working on computers, and what suggestions they would make for using computers in the school. List five implications of your findings for you as an early childhood teacher.

4. List at least six reasons that early childhood professionals should know about child growth and development.

5. List five things primary teachers can do to promote positive assessment in the primary years.

6. In addition to the characteristics of primary teachers listed in this chapter, what others do you think are desirable? Recall your own primary teachers. What characteristics did they have that had the greatest influence on you?

7. You have been asked to submit ten recommendations for changing and improving primary education. Provide a rationale for each of your recommendations.

8. What other issues of primary education would you add to those mentioned in this chapter? How would you suggest dealing with them?

9. Do you think the primary grades are the neglected years of early childhood education? Why?

10. Identify five contemporary issues or concerns facing society, and tell how teachers and primary schools could address each of them.

11. Survey the homework practices and policies of school districts and teachers in your area. What specific things are professionals doing to promote more positive homework practices? What conclusions can you draw? What recommendations would you make?

12. Explain how first grade children's cognitive and physical differences make a difference in how they are taught. Give specific examples.

13. Of the three primary grades, decide which you would most like to teach, and explain your reasons.

14. What do you think are the most important subjects of the primary grades? Why? What would you say to a parent who thought any subjects besides reading, writing, and arithmetic were a waste of time?

NOTES

1. Jean Piaget, *The Moral Judgment of the Child,* trans. Marjorie Gabin (New York: Free Press, 1965), p. 395.

2. Lawrence Kohlberg, "The Claim to Moral Adequacy of a Highest Stage of Moral Judgment," *Journal of Philosophy* 70(18) (Oct. 25, 1973), pp. 630–646.

3. Scott Willis, "You CAN Teach Thinking Skills," *Instructor* 102(6) (Feb. 1993), pp. 44–45. Copyright © 1993 by Scholastic, Inc. Reprinted by permission.

4. R. E. Slavin, "Cooperative Learning and the Cooperative School," *Educational Leadership* 45 (1987), pp. 7–13.

5. R. Brandt, "On Cooperation in Schools: A Conversation with David and Roger Johnson," *Educational Leadership* 45 (1987), pp. 14–19.

6. Slavin, "Cooperative Learning," pp. 8–9.

7. Georgia Board of Education, Office of Instructional Services, Division of Student Support, *List of Core Values* (Atlanta: Author, 1992). Used by permission.

8. Yetta Goodman, "Roots of the Whole-Language Movement," *Elementary School Journal* 90 (1989), pp. 113–117.

9.   Judith M. Newman, "Introduction," in Judith
M. Newman, ed., *Whole Language: Theory
in Use* (Portsmouth, NH: Heinemann Educational Books, 1985), p. 5.

10.   Judith M. Newman, "Using Children's Books
to Teach Reading," in Judith M. Newman,
ed., *Whole Language: Theory in Use*
(Portsmouth, NH: Heinemann Educational
Books, 1985), p. 61.

11.   Ibid., pp. 62–63.

12.   Selected Characteristics from *Teaching Language Arts* by Barbara D. Stoodt. Copyright
© 1988 by Harper & Row Publishers, Inc.
Reprinted by permission of HarperCollins
Publishers, Inc.

13.   Monica Overman, "Practical Applications of
Research: Student Promotion and Retention," *Phi Delta Kappan* 67 (April 1986),
p. 612.

10

The Federal Government, Children, and Families
Building for the Future

After you have read and studied this chapter, you will be able to:

☐ Analyze the objectives of Head Start and other federal programs

☐ Explain the main features of the Head Start components

☐ Describe and explain the full range of services Head Start provides to children and their families

☐ Explain how and why Head Start has changed since its founding

☐ Analyze and evaluate Head Start's impact on children and families

☐ Clarify your personal values regarding the involvement of the federal government in educational programs

☐ Describe various ways the federal government supports early childhood programs

☐ Assess current attitudes toward federal support for early childhood programs

The federal government plays a major role in the lives of children, families, and early childhood professionals as a result of the programs it funds and supports. Federal initiatives have changed the nature, function, and scope of early childhood programs, and they will continue to function as a catalyst of change for early childhood programs. Much of what happens in early childhood programming is based in part on federal models and programs. Without the federal presence—laws, policies, and funding—the field of early childhood would not be as advanced as it is, nor would as many children receive the services they do.

Almost everyone is critical of the federal government, for what it does and does not do. Many complain that the government is not doing enough for the disadvantaged, needy, at-risk children and families as well as all families. However, the fact remains that the federal presence in early childhood programs is wide-ranging and influential. In this chapter we will examine some of these federal programs, functions, purposes, and effects.

FAMILIES AND POVERTY

Evidence from many sources indicates that when families' incomes are inadequate to meet their social and educational needs, parents and children are impaired in their ability to become contributing members of society. One of the most damaging consequences of poverty, however, is the effect it has on children's futures. Unfortunately, poverty tends to be generational. That is, when a family lives in poverty, the likelihood rises that their children—the next generation—will also be poor. What is more alarming, as we have seen in chapter 1, is that more families and their children are falling below the poverty line each year.

More than 50 million children are estimated to live in poverty, which means that their families' incomes are below the poverty guidelines set by the U.S. government. The effects of poverty are debilitating for both children and families. Being poor means more than being eligible for a free school lunch. It means poverty's children as a group are less healthy, live in inadequate housing, and do not have the opportunities for activities and experiences their wealthier counterparts have. Moreover, the increasing divorce rate, a phenomenon of the last several decades, brings economic consequences as well as social ones. A child in a household headed by a single female has a greater chance of being poor; the majority of low-income families are headed by females. Poverty, in this sense, has become feminized.

By federal definition, being poor means that you and your family do not have an income that allows you to purchase adequate health care, housing, food, clothing, and educational services. As of 1994, the federal government used the income levels in Table 10–1 (adjusted to family size and farm or nonfarm residence) to define the poverty level. (These figures change annually because of changing rates of inflation and the cost of living.)

The federal government plays a major role in the lives of children and families at home, at school, and in specific programs such as Head Start. Many federal programs help children learn new skills and behaviors and make a seamless transition to public schooling and other programs.

HEAD START: A TWO-GENERATION PROGRAM

History and Operating Principles

To help overcome the negative effects of poverty on the lives of adults and children, the federal government, in 1964, passed the Economic Opportunity Act. One of the main purposes of this act was to break intergenerational cycles of poverty by providing educational and social opportunities for children from low-income families. The act created the Office of Economic Opportunity, and from this office Project Head Start was developed and administered. Head Start was implemented during the summer of 1965, and approximately 550,000 children in 2,500 child development centers were enrolled in the program. The first programs were designed for children entering first grade who had not attended kindergarten. The portion of this childhood component of Head Start was literally to give children a head start on their first grade experience and, hopefully, on life itself.

Today, the National Head Start program has a budget of $3,326,285 and serves 713,903 children, or about 40 percent of those eligible. (Until the recent expansion of Head Start, which began in 1993, only about 25 percent of eligible children were served). There are 1,395 Head Start programs with a total of 37,221 classrooms. The average cost per child of the Head Start program is $3,758 annually. Head Start has a paid staff of 129,800 and 1,157,000 volunteers. A total of 13,854,000 children have been served by Head Start since it began.[1] Table 10–2 shows the racial and ethnic composition of Head Start programs, and Table 10–3 cites the ages of children served.

TABLE 10–1 Federal Family
Income Guidelines

Size of Family Unit	Income
1	$ 7,360
2	$ 9,840
3	$12,320
4	$14,800
5	$17,280
6	$19,760
7	$22,240
8	$24,720

Note: Guidelines are for all states except Alaska and Hawaii, the District of Columbia, and Puerto Rico.
Source: U.S. Department of Health and Human Services, Administration on Children, Youth and Families, Administration for Children and Families, Head Start Bureau, *Income Guidelines, 1994* (Washington, D.C.: Author, 1994).

TABLE 10–2 Racial and
Ethnic Composition of Head Start

Racial/Ethnic Group	Percentage of Enrollment
American Indian	4
Hispanic	24
Black	36
White	33
Asian	3

Source: Administration on Children, Youth, and Families, *Project Head Start Statistical Fact Sheet* (Washington, D.C.: January 1994), p. 2.

TABLE 10–3 Ages of Children
Served by Head Start

Age	Percentage of Enrollment
5 years and older	6
4 years	64
3 years	27
Under 3 years	3

Source: Administration on Children, Youth and Families, *Project Head Start Statistical Fact Sheet* (Washington, D.C.: January 1994), p. 2.

Head Start was established and operates according to the following premises:

1. Children who come from low-income families often have not received the cognitive, social, and physical experiences normally associated with success in first grade.

2. Many problems created by poverty can be alleviated or compensated for if children receive these experiences before they start school.

3. Intergenerational poverty cycles can be broken by providing educational and social opportunities for children early in their lives.

In our discussion of Head Start children, we often lose sight of the families from which they come. These are typical characteristics of Head Start families:

*   Fifty-five percent are headed by a single parent.
*   Fifty-two percent have one or two children.
*   Fifty-one percent have an annual income below $6,000.
*   Sixty-two percent have a primary caretaker between the age of twenty and twenty-nine.
*   Fifty-five percent have a primary caretaker with a GED or less education.
*   Sixty-seven percent belong to a minority group.
*   Seventy-four percent are receiving some type of welfare.
*   Forty-seven percent have heads of households who are unemployed.[2]

The Economic Opportunity Act required communities to create Community Action Agencies to coordinate programs and money for Project Head Start. The act further specified that any nonprofit organization could apply for operational money, develop a program, and operate a Head Start center; thus, organizations such as churches, parent groups, and public schools could design a Head Start program and apply to the Community Action Agency for funds. Later it was also possible for an agency to apply directly to the federal offices of Project Head Start for financing rather than to the Community Action Agency. Many organizations currently receive their money this way and are known as *single-purpose agencies*. While many Head Start programs were initially established by public school systems, most operated for only six to eight weeks during the summer. Presently, at the federal level, funding for Head Start comes through the Administration on Children, Youth, and Families (ACYF). Figure 10–1 shows the organizational structure that governs the operation of Head Start programs.

Head Start is intended to provide a comprehensive developmental program for preschool children from low-income families. The project is also committed to helping children achieve a positive outlook on life through success in school and daily life activities. The overall goal is to promote social competence by providing children with opportunities to achieve their potential in cognitive, language, socioemotional, and physical development.

FIGURE 10–1   Organizational Structure of Head Start

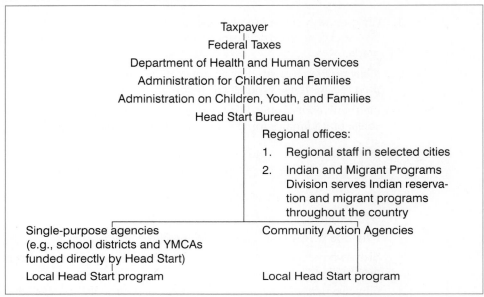

Agencies are permitted and encouraged to consider several program models and select the option best suited to children's needs and staff's capabilities and resources. Available program options are the center-based program option, the home-based program option, or approved locally designed variations.

The overall goal of Head Start is to bring about a greater degree of social competence in disadvantaged children. By social competence is meant the child's everyday effectiveness in dealing with his environment and later responsibilities in school and life. Social competence takes into account the interrelatedness of cognitive and intellectual development, physical and mental health, nutritional needs, and other factors that enable a child to function optimally. Head Start is a comprehensive developmental approach to helping achieve social competence. To this end, Head Start goals provide for:

A. The improvement of the child's health and physical abilities.

B. The encouragement of self-confidence, spontaneity, curiosity, and self-discipline which will assist in the development of the child's social and emotional health.

C. The enhancement of the child's mental processes and skills with particular attention to conceptual and verbal skills.

D. The establishment of patterns and expectations of success for the child, which will create a climate of confidence for his present and future learning efforts and overall development.

E. An increase in the ability of the child and his family to relate to each other and to others in a loving and supporting manner.

F. The enhancement of the sense of dignity and self-worth within the child and his family.

Head Start's approach is based on the philosophy that: (1) a child can benefit most from a comprehensive, interdisciplinary program to foster his development and remedy his problems, and (2) the child's entire family, as well as the community, must be involved.[3]

Implementation of these objectives occurs through Head Start child development centers, which provide a wide range of social, economic, educational, and physical services for children and their families.

Head Start Components

Head Start has the following program components: education, parent involvement, health services (including psychological services, nutrition, and mental health), social services, staff development, and administration.

Education

Objectives.   The educational program of Head Start is guided by the following objectives:

1. Provide children with a learning environment and the varied experiences which will help them develop socially, intellectually, physically, and emotionally in a manner appropriate to their age and state of development toward the overall goal of social competence.
2. Integrate the educational aspects of the various Head Start components in the daily program of activities.
3. Involve parents in educational activities of the program to enhance their role as the principal influence on the child's education and development.
4. Assist parents to increase their knowledge, understanding, skills, and experience in child growth and development.
5. Identify and reinforce experiences which occur in the home that parents can utilize as educational activities for their children.[4]

These educational objectives guide local programs in developing their own programs that are unique and responsive to the children, families, and communities they serve. Thus, there is really no national Head Start curriculum, although some people mistakenly believe there is. Many Head Start centers stress activities generally typical of nursery school/kindergarten programs, and ones associated with success in school such as taking and following directions, listening, and becoming accustomed to the routines and materials of learning.

Programmatic Direction.   One problem some Head Start centers have with the educational component of their programs is translating the national goals into meaningful local goals. This in turn results in uncertainty about the center's program, which makes it difficult for teachers to conduct appropriate activities. Head Start's educational objectives are sufficiently comprehensive to permit a grantee to conduct just about any kind of educational program it considers appropriate; here, however, lies the problem. When Head Start staff have appropriate preparation and are able to conceptualize what a good program should include, then working within the guidelines of the Head Start educational objectives is a strength. When personnel lack appropriate preparation, however, the program may not achieve intended goals. The good news is that 82 percent of Head Start teachers have degrees in early childhood education or the child development associate (CDA) credential.

The ACYF defines a part-day Head Start Program as one in which children attend less than six hours a day; full-day programs are those in which children attend six or more hours a day. Keep in mind that local grantees are free to develop their own programs within Head Start guidelines.

An example of a locally designed option is the use of family day care homes to provide full-day sessions for children. Metropolitan Dade County (Florida) uses this option to serve some of the three-year-old children the year before they enter a center-based four-year-old program. Grantees must demonstrate that these models address the needs of the local community.

This is a schedule for a full-day program at the Audubon Head Start program in Owensboro, Kentucky:[5]

8:00	Welcome children, health check, morning activities
8:15	Attendance, wash hands, helpers set table
8:30	Breakfast
9:00	Cleanup/Restroom
9:10	Large groups: circle time—music and movement
9:25	Explain Learning Centers
9:30	Learning Center time, brush teeth, individual objectives, small groups
10:50	Cleanup
11:00	Small group: mental health—Know Me/Know You; language—PEEK Kit
11:20	Prepare for lunch: wash hands, set table, food groupies, Chef Combo
11:30	Lunch
12:00	Cleanup/Restroom
12:10	Large group: story time
12:20	Outdoor play or indoor play (gross-motor)
1:20	Prepare to go home, recall day's activities
1:30	Departure

Performance Standards.   Since 1973, Head Start programs have had performance standards or requirements that must be met to continue receiving federal funds. These standards cover the component areas of education, health, nutrition, social services, and parent involvement. For example, according to the standards, educational objectives must be written to incorporate activities and services for meeting the needs of all children in the Head Start program. Each objective in all the component areas has a corresponding performance standard. Linking objectives to minimum standards of performance represents an admirable attempt by Head Start to strengthen its services.

Coordination with Public Schools.   Coordination of efforts, activities, and programs between Head Start and the public schools has not always been as functional and organized as it should be. Head Start is now pursuing a more collaborative, cooperative program of helping children and their families make the transition between Head Start programs and the public schools. To enhance these transition efforts, the ACYF, through the Head Start Coordination Project, awarded twelve states coordinating grants in 1991. These states are encouraged to develop collaborative projects with both public- and private-sector partners. In addition to promoting coordination and linkage between Head Start and other programs, the projects are expected to address state welfare reform, state-funded preschool programs, transition to public school, and mainstreaming children with disabilities.[6]

The Kentucky Department of Education has entered into an agreement with Head Start that aims to ensure that all eligible preschool children are enrolled and educated by either the public schools or Head Start and that the programs are of equal quality. This is a further example of the close working relationship Head Start hopes to forge with all public and private school systems.

Parent Involvement

From the outset, Head Start has been committed to the philosophy that if children's lives are to improve, corresponding changes must be made in their parents' lives. Part of the Head Start thrust is directed toward that end. Objectives for this program are as follows:

1. Provide a planned program of experiences and activities which support and enhance the parental role as the principal influence in their child's education and development.
2. Provide a program that recognizes the parents as:
    A. Responsible guardians of their children's well-being.
    B. Prime educators of their children.
    C. Contributors to the Head Start Program and to their communities.
3. Provide the following kinds of opportunities for parent participation:
    A. Direct involvement in decision making in program planning and operations.
    B. Participation in classroom and other program activities as paid employees, volunteers or observers.
    C. Activities for parents which they have helped to develop.
    D. Working with their own children in cooperation with Head Start staff.[7]

Employment.   It is required that parents and community members be given first chance at all entry-level positions. Therefore, it is not uncommon to find parents employed as aides and teachers in Head Start. The belief is that by helping parents learn, you also help their children learn. For example, parents who learn in the Head Start center that meal time is a time for conversation are more likely to model this behavior by talking to their children at home. In this respect, a great deal of emphasis is placed on Head Start teachers modeling appropriate behavior for parents so parents can model for their children.

Increasing Parent Income, Responsibility, and Pride.   Employing parents in Head Start centers is also a way to increase family incomes. Many parent volunteers have later been hired as bus drivers, cooks, aides, teachers, and directors (see this section's Program in Practice by Sarah Greene). As a result of seminars and training programs, some parents have gained the skills necessary to assume positions of increased responsibility, such as assistant teacher, teacher, and program director.

To make this process a reality, each Head Start center must create and implement a career development ladder with which employees and volunteers, through training and involvement, can move from one position to another with increased responsibility and pay. Jobs in Head Start are not viewed as dead-end positions. Of course, pay and responsibility are not the only benefits; self-image, an important factor in personal life, is also enhanced. Figure 10–2 shows a Head Start career ladder.

Policy Council.   Every Head Start program operates under policies established by a council that includes parents. If an agency receives money to operate three Head Start centers, each local center has a *parent committee,* and representatives from the parent committees serve on the policy council for the three programs. Half the policy council members are selected from among parents with children in the program, and half from interested community agencies (day care, family services) and parents who have previously had children in Head Start. Policies established by the council include determining the attendance area for the center and the basis on which children should be recruited, helping develop and oversee the program budget, and acting as a personnel and grievance committee.

The philosophy inherent in involving parents in a policy council is twofold. First, in many instances the people for whom programs are developed are the last to be consulted about them. The policy council system ensures that parents will have a voice in decisions. Second, parents have an opportunity to develop skills for operating programs and meetings. A basic concept of Head Start is to place people who lack certain skills in positions in which they can develop these skills, which they can then transfer to other settings with greater self-confidence. Those who question parents' abilities to make Head Start decisions must remember two points: (1) lack of formal education does not mean one cannot make good decisions, and (2) the policy council does not operate in a vacuum—it has the advice and guidance of the center director as well as educational consultants and the center teachers. Fifty-one percent of the policy council is made up of parents, and the other 49 percent of members represents agencies in the larger community.

Often, Head Start staff attend policy advisory committee meetings and offer comments and recommendations, but do not vote. Not all Head Start policy comes

FIGURE 10–2   Head Start
Career Ladder

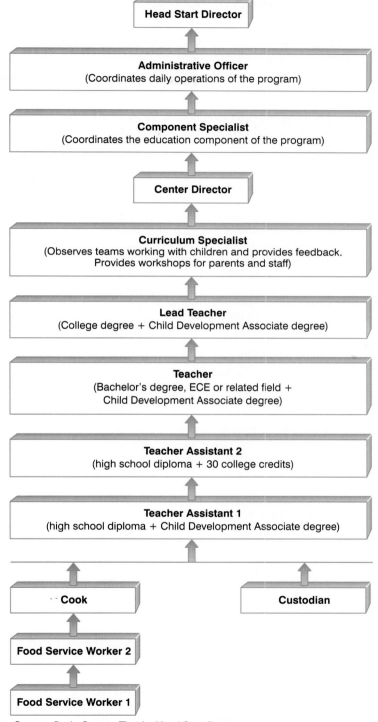

Source: Dade County, Florida, Head Start Program.

Program in Practice

HEAD START: A QUALITY COST-EFFECTIVE PROGRAM THAT WORKS

May 18, 1992, marked twenty-nine years of operation for Project Head Start. As the only national early intervention program, Head Start continues to provide enriched, comprehensive, early childhood education for low-income children. Head Start also offers a wide range of other services including health, nutrition, and social services, and emphasizes parent and community involvement in the development and operation of the program.

Countless reports and much research prove that for every dollar spent on the program, six dollars are saved, and that the Head Start graduate completes high school and beyond and makes better grades.

The list of positive outcomes goes on and on. However, having been involved with the program for twenty-six years in various capacities, I see so many successful aspects of the program that appear immeasurable. The most important, however, is the parent involvement component.

Head Start programs have a unique and special relationship with parents that does not yet exist in most organizations. Parents are truly treated as equal partners in the design of the local program and in the total involvement in their child's education. The relationship begins when local programs plan recruitment drives that include going into parents' neighborhoods, their churches, laundromats, and so forth. We demonstrate to the parents at the lowest edge of poverty that we want them and have no hesitation about being a part of their world. In fact, many of our staff live in the same neighborhood.

We continue to reach out to parents by holding our registration of the children during hours convenient for the working poor: early mornings and evenings, as well as Saturdays. Volunteers or staff care for their children during the registration period. Head Start staffers assist parents with the many federal forms that must be completed and they ask additional questions to get a very complete history of the child and family.

Patience, understanding, and respect underline the approach of the dedicated Head Start staff as they work with parents. Often, parents point to the warm environment that exists at Head Start centers as something that initially makes them feel welcome.

Once the child is enrolled, parents are oriented about the program. A parent from each classroom is selected to serve on the center committee, which has the responsibility of making decisions and recommendations about all activities at the center. For the first time in the lives of most parents, their opinion counts. Thus, a sense of pride and ownership develops about the Head Start center their child attends. Interested parents at the Manatee Head Start program in Bradenton, Florida, for instance, raised funds and purchased gifts

Contributed by Sarah M. Greene, chief executive officer, National Head Start Association.

directly from the policy council. The ACYF requires grantees to observe its performance standards and guidelines. In this sense, the policy council works within a framework designed by child development and human service experts. While staff make certain recommendations to the council about policy and procedures, the ultimate decisions as to how the program will operate, within the framework of the performance standards, are the responsibility of the policy council. Consequently, the

for each of their six centers including a VCR, an air conditioner, classroom supplies, popcorn poppers, and a microwave. They also sponsored a picnic at the park for the children.

From the center committee, parents are elected to serve on the Head Start policy council, which must be comprised of at least 50 percent parents. There, parents are trained to make all major policy decisions about the program, including the budget and grant application. At the policy council level, parents who at first are often too shy to speak out on an issue are making motions and raising questions by the close of the year. There are programs like Parents in Community Action, Inc., in Minneapolis, Minnesota, and Concerned Parents in Action, Inc., in Paterson, New Jersey, in which parents formed a corporation and are the administrators (grantees) for their programs.

Parents, recognized as the primary educators of their children, are encouraged to volunteer in all aspects of the program and participate in training programs that increase their knowledge, as well as attend workshops, seminars, and conferences.

I have met so many parents who relate that their Head Start experience inspired them to continue their education. Ophelia Brown, former Head Start parent and now director of one of the largest and most outstanding programs in the country in Miami, Florida, states, "I would never have thought about going back to school to get my high school diploma, not to mention getting my AA, then a BA and a MA if Head Start staff had not made me feel that I had the ability to achieve."

The success of Head Start's parent involvement program is crucial to helping the Head Start child continue successfully through school. Parents learn through Head Start that they must be active in the school system and community affairs. They must demonstrate to their children that they care and that their actions can positively impact their lives forever or their nonaction could leave them only to follow the vicious cycle of poverty.

Recently in Alexandria, Virginia, a group of minority parents (including two Head Start parents) filed a lawsuit against the local school board declaring discrimination against the selection process of kindergarten children. The suit was won!

Head Start has found the key to one day eradicating poverty. We touch parents in a way that makes them feel accepted and equal. We entrust them with responsibility, demonstrate genuine concern, and provide an opportunity for growth and self-achievement.

council does not necessarily do anything it wishes; rather, a group of people learn responsible action through making decisions about things that affect them.

Promoting Parent Activities.   Head Start parents often have different backgrounds, experiences, and life challenges than those of their more affluent counterparts. In addition, they have faced challenges that others have not. They have to

Head Start provides a comprehensive developmental health services program which includes a broad range of medical, dental, mental health, and nutrition services to preschool children. These programs are designed to promote children's physical, emotional, cognitive, and social development toward the overall goal of social competence. How do health services help achieve this goal?

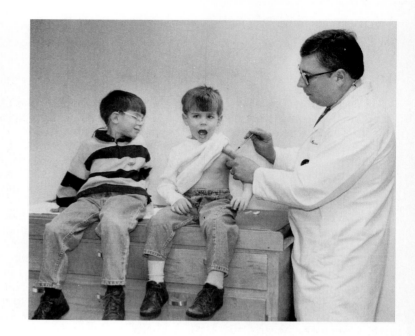

deal with the stress and uncertainty that result from unemployment, living on low incomes in poor housing, and dealing with personal problems without the support systems others take for granted. Head Start is committed to helping parents build on their strengths by offering them support and resources. Parents are invited to design activities and experiences that will provide for their and their families' growth and development. These activities are of three kinds: (1) education that adds to parents' knowledge and skills, (2) training activities to increase parents' understanding of their roles and functions within Head Start, and (3) activities that will enable parents to pursue their interests.

Funding for these parent development activities comes from regular Head Start funds, with the parents managing and administering the fund according to Head Start guidelines. Through such involvements, parents who have previously had a poor concept of education come to appreciate the power and value of education in their and their children's lives. Empowerment of parents is definitely a goal of Head Start.

Health Services

Head Start's health component delivers a comprehensive developmental program of medical, dental, mental health, and nutrition services to the child. Objectives for the medical and dental components are as follows:

1. Provide a comprehensive developmental health services program which includes a broad range of medical, dental, mental health, and nutrition services to preschool children, including handicapped children, to assist the child in his physical, emo-

tional, cognitive, and social development toward the overall goal of social competence.

2. Promote preventive health services and early intervention.

3. Provide the child's family with the necessary skills and insight and otherwise attempt to link the family to an ongoing health care system to ensure that the child continues to receive comprehensive developmental health care even after he leaves the Head Start program.[8]

Direct Service.   Child health services in public school settings usually consist of examinations and reports to the parent; corrective and remedial care are often left to the discretion of the parent. Head Start, however, assumes a much more active role. The child's current health status is monitored and reported to the parent, and, in cooperation with the parent, corrective and preventive procedures are undertaken. For example, if the child needs glasses, corrective orthopedic surgery, or dental care, services may be provided through the Head Start budget, although the pro-

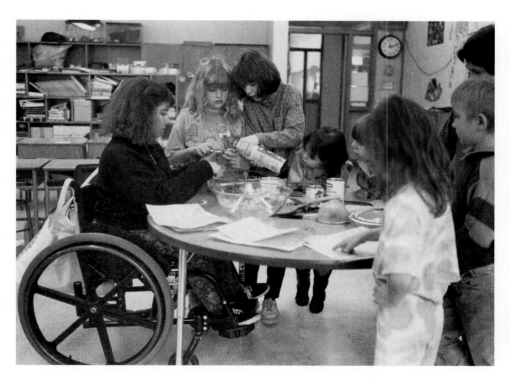

Nutrition plays an important role in children's and families' lives. For this reason, Head Start provides children with nutritious meals and snacks and opportunities to participate in activities that teach nutritional skills and information. What can early childhood professionals do to promote and support good nutrition in the lives of children and families?

gram usually works with social service agencies to provide services or money for health needs.

Regardless of the procedure, the parents' role in providing health care for the child is never bypassed. Although Head Start employees may take the child to the doctor or dentist, every effort is made to see that the parent receives support and assistance for securing appropriate services. For example, the community worker for the Head Start program might provide transportation for the parent, or if the parent has difficulty arranging an appointment with a specialist, the community worker might make arrangements. The philosophy inherent in this process supports the right of the parent as the primary teacher. An associated rationale is that through involvement in providing health services, parents learn how to provide for future needs.

Daily Health Education.   In addition to arranging medical examinations and care, each Head Start program teaches children how to care for their health, including the importance of eating proper foods and caring for their teeth.

TABLE 10–4   Head Start Menu Cycle

Monday	Tuesday	Wednesday	Thursday	Friday
Orange juice	Banana	Grape juice	Apple juice	Fruit cocktail
	Sausage patty			
Special-K	Grits	Cheerios	Cream of Wheat	Raisin Bran
Milk	Milk	Milk	Milk	Milk
Fish triangles	Spaghetti with meat sauce	Roast pork	Arroz con pollo (baked chicken)	Beef franks on bun
Peas	Lettuce & tomato salad	Collard greens	Chopped broccoli	Coleslaw
				Baked beans
Peaches	Apricots	Fruit cocktail	Pineapple tid-bits	Applesauce
Dinner roll	Garlic bread	White rice	Dinner roll	Hot dog bun
Tater tots	Salad	Fried plantains	Yellow rice (¼ cup)	Mustard/ketchup
Tartar sauce	Dressing			
Milk	Milk	Milk	Milk	Milk
Vanilla wafers (5)	Bread pudding (18 gm)	Graham crackers (2)	Cuban crackers (18 gm)	Saltines (4)
				Cheese cubes (½ oz.)
Pineapple juice	Milk	Milk	Orange juice	Milk

Source: Dade County, Florida, Head Start Program.

Nutrition. Head Start provides nutritious meals as well as nutrition education for children and their families. Objectives for the nutrition component are as follows:

1. Help provide food which will help meet the child's daily nutritional needs in the child's home or in another clean and pleasant environment recognizing individual differences and cultural patterns and thereby promote sound physical, social, and emotional growth and development.

2. Provide an environment for nutritional services which will support and promote the use of the feeding situation as an opportunity for learning.

3. Help staff, child, and family to understand the relationship of nutrition to health, factors which influence food practices, and a variety of ways to provide for nutritional needs and to apply this knowledge in the development of sound food habits even after leaving the Head Start program.

4. Demonstrate the interrelationships of nutrition to other activities of the Head Start program and its contribution to the overall child development goals.

5. Involve all staff, parents, and other community agencies as appropriate in meeting the child's nutritional needs so that nutritional care provided by Head Start complements and supplements that of the home and community.[9]

A basic premise of Head Start is that children must be properly fed to have the strength and energy to learn. This philosophy calls for teaching children good nutrition habits that will carry over for the rest of their lives and be passed on to their children. In addition, parents are given basic nutrition education so they, in turn, can promote good nutrition in their families. Such programs include seminars on buying food and reading and comparing grocery advertisements. One Head Start program in consumer education for parents and staff emphasized can sizes, number of servings per can, comparison of prices, nutritional value, and specific foods that can maximize dollar value.

Nutrition programs consist of a breakfast, snack, and lunch at the center. The menus are not traditional school cafeteria fare but rather food children like as well as that indigenous to their ethnic background (see Table 10–4). Generally, Head Start centers serve food family style—the food is served in bowls, and children help themselves whenever possible. Whatever a center's particular style, a meal is a vehicle for teaching skills and knowledge.

Mental Health Objectives. The mental health portion of the Head Start health services component has these objectives:

1. Assist all children participating in the program in emotional, cognitive, and social development toward the overall goal of social competence in coordination with the education program and other related component activities.

2. Provide handicapped children and children with special needs with the necessary mental health services which will ensure that the child and his family achieve the full benefits of participation in the program.

3. Provide staff and parents with an understanding of child growth and development, and appreciation of individual differences, and the need for a supportive environment.

4.   Provide for prevention, early identification, and early intervention in problems that interfere with a child's development.

5.   Develop a positive attitude toward mental health services and a recognition of the contribution of psychology, medicine, social services, education, and others to the mental health program.

6.   Mobilize community resources to serve children with problems that prevent them from coping with their environment.[10]

The Head Start concept of mental health focuses on early detection and prevention. Since spotting problems depends on the abilities of Head Start staff, training programs are initiated for that purpose. A Head Start program might hire a psychologist to help design and implement a diagnostic program through observation. The staff and parents would be trained to detect children's problems, and the psychologist would help the staff develop a set of prescriptions for dealing with particular behaviors. Thus, for example, a program to modify the behavior of an overly aggressive child would be developed and implemented under expert guidance. In addition, follow-up activities for use with the child in the center and home would also be devised.

Head Start also seeks to direct children and parents to existing mental health delivery systems such as community health centers. It does not intend to duplicate existing services but to help its clientele become aware of and utilize available services.

The mental health component of Head Start has undergone a policy shift over the years. In the beginning, programs emphasized direct services such as evaluating and treating children and their family. Now, the mental health services stress preventative activities designed to help staff, children, and families learn and practice skills for healthy living. Goals of this preventative program include improving self-concept; building positive relationships among children, peers, and staff; developing problem-solving skills; and learning how to manage stress.

Social Services

The social services component of Head Start assists families in their efforts to improve the conditions and quality of their family life. Social services are conducted *with* families, not for families. Families as a unit and individual family members are encouraged to use their strength to resolve issues and solve problems.

The social services worker (or family services coordinator) works with families to help them analyze and solve problems. Solutions often come as a result of liaison with existing agencies such as welfare departments, health agencies, and school systems. For example, if a family is not receiving its full welfare benefits or if it could benefit from family counseling, the social services worker would handle these problems through linkage with an appropriate public agency. Objectives for the social services component are these:

1.   Establish and maintain an outreach and recruitment process which systematically insures enrollment of eligible children.

2. Provide enrollment of eligible children regardless of race, sex, creed, color, national origin, or handicapping condition.
3. Achieve parent participation in the center and home program and related activities.
4. Assist the family in its own efforts to improve the condition and quality of family life.
5. Make parents aware of community services and resources and facilitate their use.[11]

Eligibility.   The social services component is responsible for enrolling those who are eligible for Head Start. After eligibility has been determined, the children must be enrolled. The basic criterion for admission to Head Start is family income level. Ninety percent of the children enrolled in a Head Start program must come from families that meet poverty guidelines; 10 percent may come from families above poverty levels.

Staff Development

Staff development is one of the major program goals of Head Start. Much of the parent training in child development and educational practices occurs through staff development programs. Training is usually conducted by professionals hired at the local level or representatives of the Head Start regional offices whose duties include assistance in designing training programs. Head Start programs also provide CDA training for their staffs (see chap. 5).

Administration

The Head Start administration component is designed to help local programs strengthen their administrative and management capabilities to bring about effective delivery of services. This component covers five major areas: program planning and management, personnel management, financial management, procurement and property management, and eligibility and enrollment.

Johnson & Johnson has given Head Start $1.2 million to provide administrative training for directors. The Head Start–Johnson & Johnson Management Fellows Program is designed to help directors develop the programs and management skills they need to implement their vision in addressing the challenges of Head Start expansion.

Improvements and Innovations

Traditionally, Head Start services have been delivered in five half- or whole-day programs, but there is a trend toward local options in service delivery. Under this approach, local Head Start programs are encouraged to plan, develop, and implement alternative ways to deliver services to children and parents.

Full-Day Programs

Many Head Start programs are planning to provide full-day services to children. Head Start personnel recognize more and more that half-day programs do not meet the full needs of parents or children.

Home-Based Option

All Head Start programs are encouraged to explore ways to deliver services directly to children in their home. This approach is based on the premise that the parent is the most important person in the child's life and the home the optimum place for growth and development. In brief, the local option encourages Head Start staff to plan programs that fit their needs and the needs of children and parents, while also taking into consideration the characteristics of the community they serve.

Local agencies may choose home-based programs as a means of delivering Head Start services, and today 578 Head Start programs operate a home-based program. Skilled home visitors assist parents in providing support services and developmental activities that children would normally receive in a center-based program. Presently, 4,396 home visitors serve more than 44,630 children and their families.

The primary difference between a center-based and a home-based option is that the home-based option focuses on parents in the home setting and is designed to help them participate in activities with their children. The home-based option is augmented by group socialization activities conducted at the center, in one of the family's homes, or somewhere else, such as a community center. The home-based option has these strengths:

1. Parent involvement is the very keystone of the program.
2. Geographically isolated families have an invaluable opportunity to be part of a comprehensive child and family program.
3. The individualized family plan is based on both a child and family assessment.

All Head Start programs enroll children with disabilities. They do this for several reasons. First, to provide services to and give a head start to as wide a range of children as possible; second, to provide services to the families of children with disabilities; third, to be a model of inclusion; and fourth, to integrate services with other community agencies. What other reasons can you think of?

4. The family plan is facilitated by a home visitor who is an adult educator with knowl-edge and training related to all Head Start components.

5. The program includes the entire family.[12]

According to Glenna Markey of the Bear River Head Start in Logan, Utah, there are several keys to making a home-based option work:

*   The home visitor must work with the parent, *not* the child. When *parents* work with their children, the intended results of the home-based option are achieved.

*   The home visitor must help the parent become a "child development special-ist," which ultimately benefits the parents' children and grandchildren.

*   The home visitor must try to do such a good job that the parent can do without him or her. In this sense, the home visitors put themselves out of a job!

*   The home visitor must assist the parent in identifying resources in the home environment that can be adapted for use in for helping children learn. When the home visitor supplies toys or materials and when these materials are no longer available, parents may think learning has to stop. Therefore, parents must be encouraged not to rely on commercial and store-bought materials. For exam-ple, brown grocery bags can be a coloring book, puzzles can be made out of cereal boxes, and tin cans can become musical instruments.[13]

Services to Children with Disabilities

At least 10 percent of Head Start enrollment must consist of children with disabili-ties. Nationally, 13.4 percent of all children enrolled in Head Start have a disability—mental retardation, autism, traumatic brain injury, health impairments, visual impair-ments (including blindness), hearing impairments (including deafness), emotional-behavioral disorders, speech or language impairments, orthopedic impairments, and learning disabilities.

To provide adequately for these children, staff and parents receive training in procedures related to the particular disabilities. Head Start also trains staff in identi-fication, treatment, and prevention of child abuse and neglect. (See chap. 11 for more information on educating children with disabilities.)

New Initiatives, Future Directions

Head Start has always been and remains in the vanguard of agencies involved in new and innovative programs. The following sections discuss some of Head Start's current ventures.

Comprehensive Child Development Program (CCDP)

The CCDP program is Head Start's involvement in infant-toddler programming. The purpose of this effort is to encourage intensive and comprehensive services to enhance the physical, social, emotional, and intellectual development of low-income children from birth to compulsory school age, including the provision of necessary support to their parents and other family members.

Services to infants and young children under this program include

- health services (including screening and referral),
- child care that meets state licensing requirements,
- early intervention services, and
- nutritional services.

Services for parents and other family members are intended to contribute to their children's healthy development. These include

- prenatal care;
- education in infant and child development;
- health, nutrition, and parenting services; and
- assistance in securing adequate income support, health care, nutrition assistance, and housing.

The Toddlers, Infants, Preschoolers and Parents (TIPP) project in Dade County, Florida, provides these services in a combined home/center model through four components: the Children's Center, which provides child development and child care; the Family Enrichment Center, which provides parenting skills, education, and training and employment; the Health Station, which furnishes health and nutrition services; and the Family Partners program, which engages in family advocacy.

Family Literacy

Head Start historically has been concerned about issues of family literacy, striving to increase family self-sufficiency and enable children to better benefit from educational and developmental opportunities. Head Start has set the following objectives:

- Exploration of the literacy needs of Head Start families: determining the families' levels of economic self-sufficiency and previous experience with literacy/adult education programs
- Dissemination of information on existing literacy programs to include a comprehensive listing of state and regional literacy volunteer programs, as well as descriptions of collaboration between Head Start programs and family literacy projects
- Improvement of all Head Start programs' capacity to promote family literacy—Head Start must build new resources and strategies and evaluate its contributions to family literacy development. The Head Start Bureau will support training and technical assistance, demonstration, and research/evaluation activities in support of this initiative.[14]

Family literacy programs vary in scope and strategy, but all recognize the impact literacy projects deliver when family needs are addressed.

There is a growing recognition of the roles fathers play in the growth, development, and education of children. As a result, Head Start is making a special effort to reach out and involve fathers. Here, a Head Start teacher explains to a father his child's program, activities, and achievement.

The Jackson County, Mississippi, Head Start has developed an innovative computer curriculum and computer lab that benefits 315 Head Start children and their parents as well as other adults. Three times a week three- and four-year-old Head Start children spend thirty minutes in the lab. When the children are not utilizing the lab, adults take courses. Instructors from the local Gulf Coast Community College use the Head Start Learning Center Lab to teach Head Start parents and employees of the county and local paper company.

The preschool program teaches children computer literacy, enhances the educational curriculum, and includes processes to improve children's speech. The adult program offers literacy training plus instruction for general equivalency diploma (GED) subjects in all curriculum areas.

Four Volunteer in Service to America (VISTA) volunteers work with parents to encourage their participation. They also accompany Head Start teachers and social workers on home visits to recruit other volunteers to support the program.

Father Involvement in Head Start

In 1991, the Region IV (Southeast) Administration for Children and Families (ACF) office held a family planning program. The focus of this meeting was a male involvement project. Several grants were awarded to initiate programs that would involve fathers or father figures in the Head Start program and to help them improve their lifestyle and community involvement.

Pinellas/Hillsborough (Florida) Head Start programs received a grant for a project: "Accepting the Leadership Challenge—A Special Head Start Project for Men." Fathers or father figures were recruited for this project through distribution of flyers and announcements at parent meetings. Participants attended a retreat that addressed goal setting, cultural sensitivity, and bonding. Projected outcomes for participants in the project are as follows:

- Higher self-esteem and belief in one's self
- Realistic goal setting, interrupting the failure traps of poor planning
- Improved interviewing techniques and employment readiness
- How to be a better parent and be aware of the child development process
- Life skills for personal health and mental well-being[15]

Head Start Transition Project

In our discussion of readiness in previous chapters, we have stressed Goal 1 of Goals 2000, which states that all children shall enter school ready to learn. Ready to learn, however, means more than "learning readiness." The new concept of readiness also includes schools' readiness to meet the needs of individual children at whatever level they may be. It also includes families' abilities to support the growth and development of children. All children are ready to learn provided they are in good health and come from a stable, nurturing, encouraging home. Early childhood programs including Head Start must provide a wide range of learning opportunities to meet the differences in children's functional levels, deliver services to families that help them provide a nurturing environment that enhances children's development, and enable parents to participate as full partners in the education of their children. Such a goal requires a comprehensive, interactive process that extends through the early childhood years.

Head Start has funded thirty-two sites in a transition project to determine the effects of the continuation of comprehensive services to Head Start graduates in the public schools. The purposes of this transition project are

1. to develop successful strategies where Head Start programs, parents, local education agencies, and other community agencies join together in a collaborative effort to plan and implement a coordinated and continuous program of comprehensive services to low-income children and their families beginning in Head Start and continuing through kindergarten and the first grades of public school;

2. to test the hypothesis that the provision of these continuous comprehensive services will maintain and enhance the early benefits attained by Head Start children and their families;

3. to determine the impact on children and families when comprehensive Head Start–like services are delivered over a period of time after the child has entered elementary school.[16]

The Santa Clara Office of Education (the Head Start grantee) and the Franklin-McKinley School District are collaborating on one of the thirty-two transition demonstration projects funded nationally. Santa Clara County, known across the country as "Silicon Valley," is a generally affluent county that nonetheless has areas of significant poverty. The Franklin-McKinley School District, located almost squarely in the middle of San Jose, is one such area where poverty, overcrowded housing, crime, and a myriad of other social problems are prevalent. Additional risk factors in the district include high rates of illiteracy among parents, a large number of limited-English-speaking students, high dropout rates, and little sense of community. There are virtually no middle- or upper-income families in the target school.

Key aspects of the transition project include these:

- Curriculum continuity throughout the early childhood years through implementation of the High/Scope approach in Head Start, kindergarten, and the primary grades (training, support, and equipment are provided for teachers)

- A series of transition activities (including parent meetings, visits to Head Start by the kindergarten teachers, and kindergarten trips by Head Start children and parents, with parallel activities for kindergarten to first grade and subsequent transitions) to help children and parents move confidently from Head Start to kindergarten and the early primary grades

- Facilitation of information transfers between Head Start and public schools, with special attention to the areas of special needs and health concerns

- Family case management and support, particularly in the areas of education, health, and social services, provided by bilingual Family Advocates (the project has Spanish-, Vietnamese-, and Cambodian-speaking staff)

- The establishment of a "Parent Place" at the schools for workshops and parent education activities (English as a Second Language, literacy, family math, employability, gang awareness and prevention, etc.), parent support groups, and drop-in

- Parent empowerment and involvement in the schools through classroom participation, parent workshops, linkage of transition project parents with existing school parent councils, opportunities for school and project decision making, and project governance through participation on the governing board

- Facilitation of parent-school communication through Family Advocate assistance with parent-teacher conferences, teacher outreach, and parent concerns

- Collaboration with existing community services, including Adult and Child Guidance Center (a local mental health agency), Gardner Health Clinic, Public Health Nursing, and Santee Neighborhood Action Center

The project has many unique features reflecting new directions for the education of at-risk children. The Franklin-McKinley School District is on a predominantly year-round school calendar and is committed to "one-stop shopping" through the provision of comprehensive services for children and families. For example, the district office houses a medical clinic that provides "free" services to all students; free van service is available to transport children and families to the clinic. A number of other community agencies and services are housed in the district office, including *Sí Se Puede* (It Can Be Done), a holistic, community-based program that addresses the needs of at-risk children through school and family programs; a gang awareness curriculum through the San Jose Police Department; and Project Crackdown, a neighborhood-based drug abatement and community-building program. Because of the cultural and linguistic diversity of the families in the district (97 percent of the transition project families are either Latino, Vietnamese, or Cambodian), Franklin-McKinley, Head Start, and the transition project place a high priority on programs that are culturally appropriate and relevant, as well as accessible to families with limited English skills.

Substance Abuse Prevention Curriculum

The Head Start Bureau has issued a new publication, *Head Start Substance Abuse Guide,* a resource book for Head Start grantees and other collaborating community programs. The guide helps grantees plan and carry out effective substance abuse strategies that will assist them in meeting the needs of their staff, families, and children. Head Start staff increasingly recognizes substance abuse as a problem affecting children and families in their communities.

Specific substance abuse strategies should accomplish the following goals:

- Strengthen staff capacity to respond to families who are involved with abuse of alcohol or drugs or who are vulnerable to involvement.
- Identify families vulnerable to or involved with substances.
- Help families receive sufficient and effective services from their communities.
- Assist families in supporting and nurturing their children.
- Make families aware of the health consequences associated with the abuse of substances.
- Provide extra support for children whose lives are affected by a family member's involvement with alcohol or drugs.[17]

Head Start programs play a major role in substance abuse prevention by

- offering prevention activities for families and staff;
- providing substance abuse information and education for family members and staff;
- developing formal ties with relevant agencies in the community so that substance abuse resources and referrals will be available for families who need them;
- providing a warm and supportive environment in which staff, adult family members, and children feel comfortable acknowledging and addressing a problem with substance abuse;
- adapting classroom curricula and resources to meet the special needs of children who demonstrate the harmful effects of exposure to alcohol or drugs, whether prenatally or from current family situations; and
- working with other community-based programs to reduce the violence and family stress associated with drugs.[18]

Head Start and the Homeless

Homelessness among families and children is on the rise (see chaps. 1 and 11), and Head Start agencies are responding. Over 541 grantees are serving homeless children in some capacity. Head Start programs relate that homeless children have one or more of the following characteristics: developmental delays; poor self-esteem; anxieties around food and possessions; overly compliant behavior with any adult person, which thus makes the child vulnerable to abuse; overly aware of parental responsibilities and problems; depression; and abnormal reactions to change. Also, homeless children are more likely to be in ill health and underimmunized.

In an effort to adapt to the needs of homeless families, the Head Start Bureau addresses the following areas:

- *Strong support for the staff.*   Promote achievable goals, providing each child and parent with positive experiences and training and support for staff.

- *Strong mental health component.*   Have available the services of a mental health professional who can address the needs of staff, parents, and children to help lessen staff burnout and better serve children and families.

- *A safe, reassuring environment through a structured daily environment.* Reduce levels of stimulation; maintain a simple schedule so each child knows what to expect; limit choices (not quantities) of toys and activities; plan for smaller class sizes; use more volunteers sensitive to the needs of homeless children.

- *Flexibility.*   Help staff deal with children leaving unexpectedly. The Berkely, Massachusetts, Head Start program has developed a special good-bye routine that includes a song, book, and discussion to help the children understand the process. Also, operate some classrooms in which all children are homeless; the days and hours of operation should be tailored to meet their specific needs. A Washington, D.C., Head Start program found that having early morning programs did not work for homeless families. Because of the active night life of the motel where they were housed, the morning hours were typically the time the children slept.

- *Transportation.*   Help ensure access to the program, particularly if the family is moved around in search of permanent housing.

- *Collaboration with the community.*   Cooperate with other community and state agencies; Head Start cannot address all the problems of the homeless.

- *Parental responsibilities/involvement.*   Focus and build on the family's strengths, and enable parents to build their capacity to cope with their life stresses; emphasize to parents the importance of their participation, which will enable them to better nurture and protect their children in areas such as health, nutrition, and education.

- *Make health screening a priority for homeless families.*   Refer the family as soon as they are enrolled to a local provider for medical appointments, and provide transportation.

Program in Practice

DAISY GIRL SCOUTS: A HEAD START ON LITERACY

Daisy Girl Scouts: A Head Start on Literacy— Playing in the World of Words is a demonstration project designed for girls to become Daisy Girl Scouts after their Head Start experience and thus continue to enhance the development of their potential and social competence. Like all other girls in the scouting program, Head Start graduates are encouraged to be in Girl Scouts throughout their school years and enjoy the life-long benefits from participation in a supportive environment like Head Start.

By initiating this coordinated effort with Head Start, Girl Scouts are acting on a national commitment to increase pluralism, reaching out with opportunities to girls from underserved, low-income populations. In this project, female Head Start graduates begin exploring the overall Girl Scout program. With an additional emphasis on getting a head start on literacy, age-appropriate activities encourage preliteracy skill development. Through the fun of "playing in the world of words"—active listening, storytelling, singing, dramatic play, dancing, drawing, and making things like their own Daisy Girl Scout scrapbooks—girls are learning to express themselves and understand others. Activities like these help them look forward to learning to read and succeed in school.

Head Start and Girl Scouts of America have joined forces to further the program goals of both agencies. Their cooperation is an excellent example of interagency involvement which benefits all children and their families.

- *Plan a mixed classroom.*   Have both homeless and nonhomeless children in the classroom to provide some stability to the program and contribute to everyone's opportunity to learn.

Family Service Centers

Head Start has awarded grants to forty-one programs in order to demonstrate ways its programs can work with other community agencies and organizations to deal effectively with the problems of substance abuse, illiteracy, and unemployment among Head Start families. The demonstration projects encourage families to participate in activities designed to

- reduce and prevent the incidence of substance abuse in Head Start families,
- improve the literacy of parents and other adults in Head Start families, and
- increase the employability of Head Start parents.[19]

Head Start II

With the expansion in 1993 of Head Start, federal officials are anxious to make significant improvements in the quality of the program. They are adopting new strategies to monitor and help assure the expansion will provide quality and integrity. Some of these include improved record keeping, staff training, and program monitoring. As Head Start moves toward what officials call a Head Start II model, increased funding will likely be allocated for adding more children, expansion to full-day and full-year programs, better facilities, staff training, and improved salaries.

Head Start in the 1990s

The National Head Start Association (201 N. Union Street, Suite 320, Alexandria, VA 22314) envisions the following goals for Head Start in the 1990s:

1. Establish full funding for all Head Start–eligible children.
2. Increase Head Start income eligibility guidelines to 133 percent of the poverty line. [This means in effect that families could earn about a third more income than specified by the poverty guidelines and still be eligible for Head Start participation. See Table 10–1 of this chapter.]
3. Ensure that Head Start can adapt to meet families' needs.
   a. Offer full-day, full-year Head Start.
   b. Make Head Start available during the summer months.
   c. Help families with infants and toddlers.
4. Identify areas of need relevant to Native American and migrant programs.
5. Continue the quality set-aside in the appropriation process to ensure Head Start quality issues are addressed. (About 25 percent of increases in the Head Start allocations are set aside to promote quality, as discussed earlier.)
   a. Support the quality of Head Start.[20]

Is Head Start Effective?

No question in early childhood education has been debated, discussed, considered, and examined more than whether Head Start makes a difference in children's lives. To the question "What do we know so far about Head Start?" Schweinhart and Weikart respond:

1. Short-, mid-, and long-term positive effects are available.
2. Adequately funded Head Start programs run by well-trained, competent staff can achieve the level of quality operation that will lead to positive effects.
3. Equal educational opportunity for all people is a fundamental goal of the great American experiment and good Head Start programs can make a sound contribution to the achievement of the goal.[21]

Additionally, in a study of children attending Head Start with other children, researchers concluded:

As a result of these analyses, we may conclude that participation in Head Start appeared to provide significant one-year gains on some measures of ability for low-income children. These gains, which could reasonably be attributed to children's participation in the Head Start program, were considerably more likely to accrue to Black children than to White children. Moreover, among Black children cognitive gains attributable to Head Start participation were more likely to occur in children with lower initial cognitive ability. It is important that the significant "Head Start advantage" was found in analytical designs that either controlled for test-specific ability or for general ability assessed at program entry, contrasting Head Start children with children of statistically comparable backgrounds who either had no preschool experience or who attended a non–Head Start preschool. Although the advantage of Head Start participation was clearer compared with no preschool experience, we conclude that there is evidence to support the superiority of Head Start over other preschool experience as well.[22]

One of the criticisms of Head Start is that the gains children make soon "fade out," generally by third grade. Barnett analyzed studies of Head Start's effectiveness and came to this conclusion: "In sum, there is considerable evidence that preschool programs of many types—including Head Start—have persistent effects on academic ability and success. There is no convincing evidence that these effects decline over time."[23]

What would seem to be important as Head Start expands its programs over the next decade is that it strives to offer quality programs for children and families. As such, it should focus on strengthening its educational component, continuing to involve parents in all the components, assuring staff are well prepared and trained, and providing a full range of comprehensive services for children and families.

What we must acknowledge is that the ability of Head Start to influence early childhood practice and make a difference in the lives of children and families is well established. Head Start is one of the most influential educational programs this country has had. This influence will likely continue and, in the process, empower families, communities, and professionals for the challenges of providing quality programs in the twenty-first century.

FOLLOW THROUGH

Operated through the public schools, Follow Through is a program designed to help children build on gains achieved in Head Start and other preschool programs. Existing programs are completing their projects, and federal officials are assessing whether additional projects are needed. Current funding for Follow Through is about $8.5 million. Unfortunately, Follow Through never became a national program and is conducted only in about forty schools throughout the country.

MIGRANT EDUCATION

In 1965, Congress authorized Title I of the Elementary and Secondary Education Act (ESEA) to provide public school programs for disadvantaged children. These funds, however, did not provide adequate services for the children of migrant workers; consequently, in 1966, ESEA Title I was amended by Public Law 89-750 to provide money specifically for the education of migrant children.

> Currently "migratory child" means a child (a) whose parent or guardian is a migratory agricultural worker or migratory fisherman; and (b) who has within the past twelve months moved from one school district into another (or, in a state comprising a single school district has moved from one school administrative area into another) in order to enable the child, the child's guardian, or a member of the child's immediate family to obtain temporary or seasonal employment in an agricultural or fishing activity.[24]

The Hawkins-Stafford Elementary and Secondary Improvement Act of 1988, PL 100-297, amended the migrant legislation, changing the ages of children served from five to seventeen years to three to twenty-one years. This amendment also required more parent involvement and planning of the migrant program. Currently, over 682,000 children are eligible for services, but only two-thirds of these receive them.[25]

Historically, migrant children have suffered educationally because their families seldom live in one place for any length of time. As a result, public schools have not always been willing to give migrant children the special attention they need. In addition, migrant children have had to work to supplement their families' incomes, which means that many do not attend school as often as they should, and others not at all. Without an education, migrant children are caught in the trap of illiteracy and inadequate job skills that prevents their escaping the cycle of poverty.

CHAPTER 1

Chapter 1 of the Hawkins-Stafford Act of 1988 serves about 5,327,000 children in about 75 percent of the nation's elementary schools. Of the children enrolled in Chapter 1, 7 percent are kindergarten children and 41 percent are children in grades K through 3. Funding for the 1991–92 program year was $6.2 billion.

The purpose of this program is to improve the educational opportunities of educationally deprived children by helping them succeed in the regular program of the local educational agency, attain grade-level proficiency, and improve achievement in basic and more advanced skills. These purposes are accomplished through such means as supplemental education programs, schoolwide programs, smaller class size, and increased involvement of parents in their children's education.

EVEN START

The federally funded Even Start Family Literacy Program combines adult literacy and parenting training with early childhood education in order to break cycles of illiteracy that are often passed on from one generation to another. Even Start is authorized by Part B of Chapter 1 of Title 1 of the Elementary and Secondary Education Act Reauthorization of 1988, as amended by the National Literacy Act of 1991. Even Start, operated through the public school system, provides family-centered education projects to help parents become full partners in the education of their children, assist children in reaching their full potential, and provide literacy training for their parents. Even Start projects are aimed at building on existing community resources to create a new range of services, integrating early childhood education and adult education for parents.

Even Start helps states address two of the Goals 2000 (see chap. 1). Goal 1 calls for all children in the United States to start school ready to learn. An important objective of this goal is for every parent to be their child's first teacher by devoting time each day to help him or her learn. Even Start also addresses Goal 5: that every adult American will be literate, possess the knowledge and skills necessary to compete in a global economy, and exercise the rights and responsibilities of citizenship. Current Even Start funding is about $110 million.

Eligible participants for Even Start are

- a parent of a child age birth through age seven if the parent is eligible for participation in an adult education program under the Adult Education Act, and

- a child from birth through age seven who is the child of an eligible parent and who resides in an elementary school attendance area designated for participation in programs under Chapter 1.

Children participating must take part in early childhood activities, and participating parents must take part in adult literacy activities, including activities in which the parents and children are involved together.[26]

Even Start funding is comprised of federal funds and a required local share as follows:

1. In the first year of the project's funding at least 10 percent of the total cost of the project

2. In the second year at least 20 percent of the cost of the project

3. In the third year at least 30 percent of the total cost of the project

4. In the fourth year at least 40 percent of the total cost of the project

The School District of Leon County, Florida, is collaborating with Florida First Start (a health program for children and families), Head Start, and many community-based organizations to establish five Family Resource Centers. Four of these centers are located in trailers at public school sites; one is at a housing complex. Twice a month parents and children ride the bus to the resource site. During the morning parents work with their children on early childhood activities, children return to their class for lunch, and parents attend their adult education classes and receive support services.

The support services for families include home visits focusing on parent-child activities, family activity nights, field trips, and special programs. The Parent Resource Center has books, toys, games, and materials for loan to families enrolled in the program.

The community offers a myriad of resources for the program. Child Care of South Florida helps with identification and recruitment of families as well as providing extended day activities for children. The Lee County Library, Lee County Literacy Council, and literacy volunteers of Lee County train volunteers and tutors. The Lee County School District's Vocational Adult and Community Education Program provides teachers for parents, adult learning materials, and training for parents, teachers, and volunteers. Technical assistance and program evaluation is provided by the University of South Florida.

FEDERAL SUPPORT FOR EARLY CHILDHOOD PROGRAMS

In addition to Head Start, Migrant Education, Chapter 1, and Even Start, the federal government plays a major role in funding other programs that involve and affect young children and their families.

Child Care

The federal government is one of the largest supporters of child care, in five ways. One way is through state agencies. Title XX of the Social Security Act provides monies to states in the form of "block grants." These monies are used to provide certain groups and classes of parents and children with child care. Some eligibility criteria under Title XX are that the parent receives Aid to Families with Dependent Children (AFDC), the parent receives a social security payment supplement, the gross income of the parent is below an eligibility level established by the state, or the parent belongs to a particular group (such as migrant farm workers) that is automatically eligible for child care services. Monies for child care under Title XX programs amount to over $700 million.

A second source of federal support for child care is the U.S. Department of Agriculture (USDA) Child Care Food Program. The USDA gives monies and commodities to child care centers and homes to support their nutrition programs. Children twelve years old and younger are eligible. The USDA provided over $700 million for the food program in fiscal 1992.

A third source of federal support is child care tax credits. Since 1975, parents can itemize the cost of child care as a deduction against their federal income taxes. Currently, the amount that can be deducted is based on a sliding scale. (See chap. 5 for an application of the scale.)

A fourth source of federal support to child care is employer support or employer sponsorship. The federal tax code allows employers certain tax breaks or benefits for providing child care for employees.

Last, a source of federal support comes through the government's role as an employer. Many federal agencies, including the CIA and the Internal Revenue Service, provide child care services for employees. Remember also the federal government's role in supporting military child care (see chap. 5).

The federal government will continue to play an influential role in all of education, ranging from services to pregnant women to higher education. While some people criticize the federal presence, which they see as control, others believe that without even greater federal support, issues of equality and quality cannot be adequately addressed. Regardless, the federal government will continue to play a dominant role in deciding who gets what kind of services. The challenge for early childhood professionals is to serve as advocates on behalf of children and their families and to influence federal policy so that programs, services, and monies are put to their best use.

READINGS FOR FURTHER ENRICHMENT

Beaty, Janice J. *Skills for Preschool Teachers*, 4th ed. (New York: Merrill/Macmillan, 1994)

Designed specifically for the Head Start, day care, and kindergarten worker, this book parallels the Child Development Associate Competencies; helpful for anyone contemplating this training program.

Zigler, Edward, and Susan Muenchow. *Head Start: The Inside Story of America's Most Successful Educational Experiment* (New York: Basic Books, 1992)

An interesting, behind-the-scenes account of the beginning and survival of Head Start. The authors draw on the lessons of Head Start to address some of today's most crucial and controversial lessons in education. They advocate that two of Head Start's most successful components, parent involvement and comprehensive services, be included in all early childhood programs.

Zigler, Edward, and Sally J. Styfco, eds. *Head Start and Beyond: A National Plan for Extended Childhood Intervention* (New Haven, CT: Yale University Press, 1993)

Zigler, one of the architects of Head Start, calls for combining that program with two other government-funded early childhood programs, Chapter 1 and Follow Through, which he says would result in more coordinated and cost-effective services for preschool and early elementary grade students.

ACTIVITIES FOR FURTHER ENRICHMENT

1. Accompany a Head Start home visitor on a home visit. Describe how home environments influence children's learning abilities.

2. Explain why you think Head Start and other programs are emphasizing a two-generation approach to the delivery of services. What are the pros and cons of such a delivery system?

3. Interview parents of Head Start children to find out what they feel has been the impact of Head Start on their family.

4. Visit a local school district and gather information about its federally supported programs. What kind of federal education programs does the district have? How is the money spent? Do you approve or disapprove of what you saw?

5. Visit several Head Start programs and compare and contrast what you see. How are they similar and different? How do you account for this?

6. Compare the schedule of a Head Start center in this chapter with a Head Start center in your community. Also compare the Head Start schedules to those of a preschool. What would you change? Be specific, and include your reasons.

7. Develop a list of pros and cons for involving parents in early childhood programs. What implications does this list have for teachers of young children? For Head Start programs? How do you feel about parent involvement in early childhood programs?

8. Develop a questionnaire you could give to parents to find out their needs and ideas about home-based and center-based early childhood programs. Which do they prefer?

9. Develop a set of criteria for deciding which families would be eligible for a home-based education program.

10. Conduct a poll of parents to find out how they think early childhood programs and schools can help them in educating their children, how they think they can be involved in early childhood programs, what specific help they feel they need in child rearing and educating, and what activities they would like in a home visitation program.

11. Contact the migrant education office in your area. What are the occupations of migrant parents? What are the major problems faced by these families? What services are being provided for them? Do you think the services to migrants are as effective and comprehensive as they should be?

12. Articulate the pros and cons of why you would or would not want to teach in a Head Start, Even Start, or other federally funded program.

NOTES

1. Administration on Children, Youth, and Families, *Project Head Start Statistical Fact Sheet* (Washington, D.C.: Author, January 1994), pp. 1–3.

2. Esther Kresh, *National Head Start Bulletin* 28 (May 1989), p. 9.

3. U.S. Department of Health and Human Services, *Head Start Program Performance Standards* (45 CFR §1304) (Washington, D.C.: U.S. Government Printing Office, November 1984), p. 4. Used by permission.

4. Ibid., pp. 8–9.

5. Schedule from Audubon Head Start, Owensboro, Kentucky.

6. Linda Likins, *National Head Start Bulletin* 40, p. 9.

7. *Head Start Program Performance Standards,* p. 58.

8. Ibid., p. 16.

9. Ibid., p. 38.

10. Ibid., pp. 30–31.

11. Ibid., p. 53.

12. E. Dollie Wolverton, "The Home-Based Option: Reinforcing Parents," *Head Start Bulletin* 12 (October/November 1986), p. 1.

13. Phone interview with author.

14. Clennie H. Murphy, Jr., "A Commitment to Family Literacy," *Head Start Bulletin* 30 (September 1989), p. 1.

15. *Accepting the Leadership Challenge: A Special Head Start Project for Men,* report from Pinellas and Hillsborough Programs, March 1992.

16. *Federal Register* 56(133), July 11, 1991, p. 318.

17. Raymond C. Collins and Penny R. Anderson, *Head Start Substance Abuse Guide: A*

Resource Handbook for Head Start Grantees and Other Collaborating Community Programs (Washington, D.C.: U.S. Department of Health and Human Services, Administration for Children and Families, Administration on Children, Youth, and Families, Head Start Bureau, January 1991), p. 4.

18. Ibid., p. 5.

19. U.S. Department of Health and Human Services, Administration on Children, Youth, and Families, Head Start Bureau, *Head Start: A Child Development Program* (Washington, D.C.: Author, n.d.).

20. National Head Start Association, *Legislative Notebook* (Alexandria, VA: Author, 1993).

21. Lawrence J. Schweinhart and David P. Weikart, "What Do We Know So Far? A Review of the Head Start Synthesis Project," *Young Children* 41(2) (January 1986), p. 50.

22. Valerie E. Lee, J. Brooks-Gunn, and Elizabeth Schnur, "Does Head Start Work? A 1-Year Follow-Up Comparison of Disadvantaged Children Attending Head Start, No Preschool, and Other Preschool Programs," *Developmental Psychology* 24(2), pp. 210–222. © 1988 American Psychological Corporation.

23. Steve Barnett, "Does Head Start Fade Out?" *Education Week,* May 19, 1993, p. 40.

24. *Federal Register* 42(134), July 13, 1977, p. 36080.

25. Interstate Migrant Education Council, *Migrant Education Policy Brief: Special Education* (N.p.: Author, September 1992), p. 2.

26. *Federal Register* 57(119), June 19, 1992, p. 2756230.

11

Teaching Children with Special Needs
Developing Awareness

After you have read and studied this chapter, you will be able to:

- ☐ Identify and use the terminology and legal definitions of children with special needs
- ☐ Assess the legal, political, moral, and social basis for mainstreaming and full inclusion of children in early childhood programs
- ☐ Write and defend a personal philosophy about teaching children with special needs
- ☐ Cite reasons for contemporary interest in special needs children
- ☐ Summarize the major provisions of and identify the implications of PL 94-142, PL 99-457, and PL 101-336 (ADA)
- ☐ Identify and evaluate issues relating to mainstreaming, full inclusion, and teaching children with disabilities
- ☐ Articulate reasons for and the basic components of an individual education program and individual family service plans
- ☐ Identify and explain the basis of programs for the gifted
- ☐ Develop methods for involving parents of special needs children in educational programs
- ☐ Examine definitions of child abuse and neglect
- ☐ Know and understand the role of the early childhood professional in identifying and reporting child abuse
- ☐ Understand the causes of stress in children's lives and what professionals can do to help children and families cope with stress

GLOSSARY OF TERMS

The following glossary of terms will help you have a clearer understanding of terms and concepts used throughout this chapter.

Adaptive education: An educational approach aimed at providing learning experiences that help each student achieve desired educational goals. The term *adaptive* refers to the modification of school learning environments to respond effectively to student differences and to enhance the individual's ability to succeed in learning such environments.[1]

Children with disabilities: Replaces former terms such as *handicapped*. Avoid the reversal of these words (i.e., *disabled children*).

Coteaching: The process by which a regular classroom professional and a special educator, or a person trained in exceptional student education, team-teach in the same classroom a group of regular and mainstreamed children.

Disability: A physical or mental impairment that substantially limits one or more major life activities.

Early education and care settings: Promotes the idea that all children learn and that child care and other programs *should* be educating children birth to age eight.

Exceptional student education: Replaces the term *special education;* refers to the education of children with special needs.

Full inclusion: The mainstreaming or inclusion of *all* children with disabilities into natural environments such as playground, family day care centers, child care centers, preschool, kindergarten, and primary grades.

Integration: A generic term that refers to educating children with disabilities along with typically developing children. This education can occur in mainstreamed, reverse mainstream, and full-inclusion programs.

Limited-English-proficient (LEP):   Describes people who have limited English skills.

Mainstreaming: The social and educational integration of children with special needs into the general instructional process, usually a regular classroom program.

Merged classroom: A classroom that includes—merges—children with special needs and children without special needs and teaches them together in one classroom. (See the Program in Practice describing the merged classroom.)

Natural environment: Any environment in which it would be natural for any child to be, such as home, child care center, preschool, kindergarten, primary grades, playground, and so forth.

Normalized setting: A place that is "normal" or best for the child.

Reverse mainstreaming: The process by which typically developing children are placed in programs for children with disabilities. In reverse mainstreaming, children with disabilities are the majority of the children.

Typically developing children: Children who are developing according to and within the boundaries of normal growth and development.

CHILDREN WITH SPECIAL NEEDS

Early childhood professionals and the public are very much involved in providing all children with an education appropriate to their physical, mental, social, and emotional abilities. In particular, the profession and society place a great deal of emphasis on educating children who have needs that other children do not. These children have disabilities, are gifted, or come from multicultural backgrounds; they often are discriminated against because of their disabilities, backgrounds, language, race, and gender. These conditions necessitate teaching strategies, programs, curricula, and new attitudes designed to meet all children's individual special needs.

Children with Disabilities

To understand programs for children with disabilities, it is important to know the federal government's definition. Public Law 101-476 defines children with disabilities this way:

> The term "children with disabilities" means children—
>
> A.   With mental retardation, hearing impairments including deafness, speech or language impairments, visual impairments, including blindness, serious emotional disturbance, orthopedic impairments, autism, traumatic brain injury, other health impairments, or specific learning disabilities; and
>
> B.   who, by reason thereof, need special education and related services.[2]

Public Law 101-336, the Americans with Disabilities Act (ADA) of 1990, defines disability this way: "The term 'disability' means, with respect to an individual, a physical or mental impairment that substantially limits one or more of the major life activities of such individual." A limitation of one or more major life activities would include a limitation on walking, hearing, vision, working, education, and so forth.

Several facets of the government's definition differ from the public's conception of children with disabilities. First, the federal definition is more comprehensive. Second, the public generally thinks of children with disabilities as those who have physical disabilities and not so much those who are emotionally or orthopedically impaired. Figure 11–1 shows the number of children with disabilities in the various categories; about 10 to 12 percent of the nation's children have disabilities.

Gifted and Talented Children

The Jacob K. Javits Gifted and Talented Students Education Act of 1988 defines gifted and talented children as those who "give evidence of high performance capability in areas such as intellectual, creative, artistic, or leadership capacity, or in specific academic fields, and who require services or activities not ordinarily provided by the school in order to fully develop such capabilities." The definition distinguishes between *giftedness*, characterized by above-average intellectual ability, and *talented*, referring to individuals who excel in such areas as drama, art, music, athletics, and leadership. Students can have these abilities separately or in combination. A talented five-year-old may be learning disabled, and an orthopedically disabled student may be gifted.

FIGURE 11–1   Number of Children with Disabilities in Various Categories

Disability	Numbers Served, 1991 (in thousands)
Specific learning disabilities	2,130
Speech or language impairments	987
Mental retardation	536
Serious emotional disturbance	391
Hearing impairments	58
Orthopedic impairments	49
Other health impairments	55
Visual impairments	23
Multiple disabilities	96
Deafness-Blindness	1
Preschool children with disabilities	445
Total for the year	4,771

Source: National Center for Education Statistics, *Digest of Education Statistics—1992* (ED 1.326:992), p. 64.

TEACHING IN THE MAINSTREAM

Today, many children with disabilities are taught in the *mainstream* when they enter preschool and primary grades. *Mainstreaming* is the process of serving young children with disabilities in natural environments. Natural environments are those environments in which children would normally be if they did not have a disability (child care centers, Head Start programs, preschool, kindergarten, primary grades, etc.). Specifically, mainstreaming refers to the process of taking a child from outside the mainstream, such as a special education center, and placing him or her in the mainstream, the natural environment. *Full inclusion* is the process of providing for children with disabilities in natural environments.

Mainstreaming and full inclusion (which also means serving a young child with a disability in a natural environment) differ from each other in that in full inclusion the child with a disability is assumed to be in the natural environment from the beginning. It is important to know this difference when planning full-inclusion programs because full-inclusion programs never have to have separate special education programs. The services provided in separate special education programs are now provided in full-inclusion programs in the natural environment by special professionals and other special services.

Mainstreaming can be interpreted to mean that children with special needs will be a part of the education system that traditionally has meant typically developing children and regular classrooms. In another sense, mainstreaming means that

Mainstreaming integrates children with disabilities into the least restrictive environment, often the regular classroom. Early childhood professionals must be able to work with children with disabilities and their families. What particular skills do you think are needed for working in a mainstreamed classroom? The description of the merged classroom in the Program in Practice feature will help you answer this question.

schools and other programs are returning special needs children to the system from which they have been excluded for over three-quarters of a century. A little over a decade ago, it was acceptable and thought to be educationally sound, legal, and humane to provide separate (but not always equal) education for special needs children outside the regular classroom. Even rarer was the mainstreamed preschool program, with little thought given to putting the very young children with disabilities in a regular program. It is no longer justifiable to do so when children can benefit from an educational program in the regular classroom. In mainstreaming, emphasis is on the concept of *normalcy*. This means that children are treated normally and educated as normally as possible.

All early childhood professionals should follow these guidelines for teaching in the mainstream:

- *Have a well-thought-out philosophy of education.* This approach is important no matter what kind of children you teach; however, it is absolutely necessary to think through your attitudes toward all children with special needs. *Everyone* who works with young children must have a positive attitude about providing the best for *all* children, period.

- *Know the nature of the children with special needs you will teach.*   Just as it is important to know about normal childhood growth and development, it is essential for you to know about different disabilities and how to provide appropriate programs for children with disabilities in the teaching-learning process.

- *Recognize that the profession is changing.*   More and more early childhood professionals are working closely with other professionals, especially special professionals, social workers and health professionals such as pediatricians and physical, speech/language, and occupational therapists. Early childhood professionals are expected to work cooperatively and collaboratively as team members in order to provide for children's needs and their family's needs. The concept and practice of one person providing for children's needs by her- or himself is an antiquated role for the contemporary early childhood professional.

FULL INCLUSION

Full inclusion is a growing trend designed to provide all special needs students in the regular classroom. Full inclusion is the mainstreaming or inclusion of *all* children with disabilities into natural environments such as playgrounds, family day care centers, child care centers, preschool, kindergarten, and primary grades. Public Law 94-142 requires *individualized* education for children with disabilities.

Today the philosophy of early childhood and other professionals is to mainstream all children regardless of their disabilities, with full inclusion the result. In the past, mainstreaming was used to place some children with disabilities in natural environments. Now full inclusion is becoming the accepted process for involving all children in natural environments.

Popularity of Full Inclusion

Full inclusion is currently popular and receiving attention for a number of reasons. First, court decisions and state and federal laws mandate, support, and encourage it. Many of these laws and court cases relate to extending to children and parents basic civil rights. For example, in the 1992 case of *Oberti v. Board of Education of the Borough of Clementon School District,* the judge ruled that Rafael, an eight-year-old with Down syndrome, should not have to earn his way into an integrated classroom.

Second, some parents of children with disabilities are dissatisfied with their children attending separate programs. They view these programs as a form of segregation. For example, in many cases, students with severe and moderate disabilities were taught in separate settings or in special education resource rooms.

Third, educators, parents, and children have had beneficial and rewarding experiences with full-inclusion programs. (See, for example, the Program in Practice features describing full inclusion on pages 426–429 and 438–439.)

However, full inclusion is not supported by everyone and is controversial for several reasons. First, not all parents want their children with disabilities taken from a

THE DIVISION FOR EARLY CHILDHOOD'S POSITION STATEMENT ON INCLUSION

Inclusion, as a value, supports the right of all children, regardless of their diverse abilities, to participate actively in natural settings within their communities. A natural setting is one in which the child would spend time had he or she not had a disability. Such settings include but are not limited to home and family, play groups, child care, nursery schools, Head Start programs, kindergartens, and neighborhood school classrooms.

DEC believes in and supports full and successful access to health, social service, education, and other supports and services for young children and their families that promote full participation in community life. DEC values the diversity of families and supports a family guided process for determining services that are based on the needs and preferences of individual families and children.

To implement inclusive practices DEC supports:

a. the continued development, evaluation, and dissemination of full inclusion supports, services and systems *so that options for inclusion are of high quality;*

b. the development of preservice and inservice training programs to prepare families, administrators, and service providers to develop and work within inclusive settings;

c. collaboration among all key stakeholders to implement flexible fiscal and administrative procedures in support of inclusion;

d. research that contributes to our knowledge of state of the art services; and

e. the restructuring and unification of social, education, health, and intervention supports and services to make them more responsive to the needs of all children and families.

Source: Division for Early Childhood of the Council for Exceptional Children, adopted April 1993, revised December 1993. Used by permission.

separate special education facility and placed in a full-inclusion program. Some parents believe that their children are not best served in either mainstream or full-inclusion programs but rather in separate special education settings.

In addition, many early childhood professionals feel that they do not have the training to provide for the disabilities of children who will be placed in their classrooms as a result of full inclusion. They also believe that they will not be able to provide for children with disabilities even with the assistance of aides and special support services. This perception implies that a great deal needs to be done to change the attitudes of early childhood professionals and provide them with the training that they need to work as successful professionals in full-inclusion settings.

Some people believe that the cost of full inclusion outweighs the benefits. On the other hand, some professionals think that the cost involved in separate special education facilities and programs can be used in full inclusion. Others believe that the cost can be no more and perhaps less than that of separate special education programs and facilities.

Finally, some believe that children with disabilities and their families are being provided with too many rights too soon and that this makes it difficult to keep up with changes and programs.

Program in Practice

THE MERGED CLASSROOM

What Is It?

The merged classroom is an innovative approach that allows all students to meet their full potential without pull-out programs or segregation. This environment merges general education students and students with special needs together in one classroom, with the general education teacher and the special education teacher serving as a team to coteach all the students.

Cooperative teaching, or coteaching, is when general and special educators work in a coactive, coordinated fashion to jointly teach academically and behaviorally heterogeneous groups of students in an educationally integrated setting. Both teachers are simultaneously present in the classroom and maintain joint responsibility for classroom instruction.

Merging classrooms with special education and general education students is the best way to meet individual needs. The focus is on the students' strengths, not their disabilities. The overall effectiveness of the merged program is based not only on the acquisition of academic skills but also on the quality interactions and friendships fostered among the children throughout the year.

The difference between mainstreaming or fully including isolated students in the general classroom environment and this merged program is that all students work at their ability level within the core curriculum to acquire academic skills; at the same time they are truly part of the class.

Why It Came About

Before developing this program, one of us taught first grade and the other a self-contained special education class. We established a friendship and discussed our frustra-

tions with the current system. "As the general educator, it seemed as though mainstreamed students were visitors in my classroom," remarks Kari. It was difficult to meet their needs, and I felt they missed connections due to their limited involvement in the classroom." Julie states, "As the special educator, I had always felt uncomfortable simply mainstreaming individual students into general education classrooms for a limited time each day. The students found it quite difficult to feel like true members of their mainstream classroom, and it was difficult for the general education teacher to assume ownership for their education."

We attempted merging our classrooms on a limited basis each day. Initially, this was just for opening exercises and physical education, although we planned thematic units together. After experiencing some success with the limited integration of our classes, we planned some cooperative group activities related to our theme of study and grouped our students heterogeneously for those activities.

Our success led to a pilot program fully merging a general education class of kindergarten and first grade students with a special education class of students with nonsevere disabilities in grades kindergarten, first, and second for summer school. The special education students in the class possessed a wide array of disabilities, including Down syndrome, cerebral palsy, childhood schizophrenia, learning disabilities, and Apert's syndrome.

We received positive feedback from administrators, parents, and children throughout the summer. Fueled by this experience, we were ready to try our hands with a full

Contributed by Kari Hull and Julie Morse, Lemon Avenue Elementary School, La Mesa, California.

school year. We are now in our second year of coteaching in a merged classroom.

How It Operates

Throughout the day, the children in our merged classroom are grouped in a variety of ways for instruction including large groups, split groups, cooperative groups, enrichment and remediation groups, and skill groups. Most of these groups are heterogeneous, with both general education and special education students. As the year progresses, we do find it necessary to have some homogeneous instructional groupings to teach specific skills.

At the beginning of the year, each child was individually assessed to determine his or her developmental skill levels in reading, math, and writing. Flexible instructional groups were formed based on the data taken from these assessments. Ongoing assessment and teacher observations are used to change student groupings as the needs arise. Our program is based on the whole-language model, which enables us to meet the wide range of developmental levels in our classroom.

We jointly plan the week's activities, and each of us assumes responsibility for our own heterogeneous reading and math groups. This approach is effective as it allows us to focus on the specific learning needs of each child rather than the entire classroom.

The weekly planning sessions are imperative to the success of the program as we make adaptations, discuss the progress of the children, and attend to the many details necessary to make each day run smoothly.

Another necessary ingredient of the merged program is a well-articulated behavior management program. We teach the students appropriate social skills and behavior and make them accountable through the use of a "star card" system that monitors behavior on a half-hourly basis.

What Is Life Like for the Children?

Other than the fact that there are two teachers and a full-time instructional aide, a larger class size, and two full-size classrooms, our class resembles any other class on our campus. However, in the merged classroom, diversity is seen as a strength, not a weakness or a problem. If you are a student in our classroom, the child sitting beside you may have autism, Down syndrome, cerebral palsy, a brain injury, or no disabilities at all. Laura Carpenter, a student in our class, exclaims, "This is a very fun class. It makes me happy!"

Jim and Anne-Marie Roach, parents of a general education student in our program, put it this way: "We really feel that it is important for children to develop an awareness of people with different backgrounds, be it ethnic, physical, religious, etc. Your classroom setting has helped Danny toward this awareness. It is rewarding to see children integrated in such a stimulating learning environment."

Pros

■ Cooperative teaching partners provide each other with a great professional support network to celebrate successes and to provide backup for less than positive circumstances that may arise.

■ The potential for burnout of the special education teacher is all but eliminated in the merged classroom.

■ The synergy, or collective energy, created in a coteaching environment ignites ideas and provides endless possibilities for teachers and students. Cooperative teaching allows for an effective use of each teacher's unique talents and abilities. As Nancy Kitson, a parent of a student in our program, puts it, "Dedication, enthusiasm, and consistency are the attributes that make these teachers a powerful team."

- Coteaching is a natural peer coaching situation as we practice new teaching strategies.

- The general education students in a merged classroom benefit from smaller instructional group sizes geared toward meeting their individual needs. This approach allows them to gain a keen understanding of the unique qualities and differences in others. They learn to value others for what they can do, not for what they cannot do.

- The merged classroom allows us to serve at-risk students who do not qualify for designated programs.

- The students with exceptional needs benefit from being part of a school community, forming relationships with regular education peers that transcend the walls of the classroom. The merged classroom provides these students with appropriate role models for behavior, social, and language skills.

- The merged classroom allows the teachers to move forward with the curriculum while each student is supported at their level within that curriculum.

Cons

- The amount of time necessary for joint planning and program development is immense.

- Differences in opinion can arise between the coteachers. Both teachers need to be willing to change the way they have done things in the past.

- There is an increased work load to maintain a quality program.

- Some people raise the objection that students with exceptional needs should be merged with students who are at the grade-appropriate level only. We feel that each student needs to be looked at as an individual and that for some, merging at an age-appropriate level creates frustration both academically and socially. Many students find their greatest success when they are working with general education students who are one to two years younger. We think the ideal situation would be a multiage setting for both general and special education students.

- Not all children with special needs can find success in a merged classroom. Last year, we had two boys, one with Down syndrome and severe behavioral problems and one who was severely emotionally disturbed. We found it difficult to meet their needs in a large classroom setting. As a result, they disrupted our class regularly, upsetting both teachers and students.

Overall, we have found the merged classroom to be a successful alternative to mainstreaming and integration of individual students with exceptional needs into general education classes. Coteaching in such a program is a viable method of instruction designed to meet the needs of diverse groups of children.

Julie describes next her experience with one student—a case exemplifying the potential successes contained within a merged classroom.

Matthew: A Case Study

I first met Matthew, a young boy with Down syndrome, when he was five and he joined my self-contained special education class. He presented himself as a very enthusiastic child with some preschool-level skills. His speech was unintelligible, but he still tried to converse with peers and adults. He did manifest some behavior problems when activities involved physical activity.

Matthew functioned very well in the self-contained setting, but I saw the need for involvement with general education peers. In January, he was mainstreamed into a kindergarten class for forty-five minutes per day. He experienced some success, but if activities were unstructured, he tended to become too rough with other children and the materials.

Before the next school year began, I searched for a kindergarten teacher who would integrate Matthew full-time for an entire year. I was fortunate to find someone willing to take on such a responsibility even though she had over thirty kindergartners in her class. Throughout this next year, I provided behavioral support for Matthew and left his kindergarten teacher to be in charge of his academic skills because he was ready and able to handle a kindergarten curriculum.

The year brought many successes. Matthew was accepted as a peer by the other children in the room. He was able to function within the academic setting with few behavior problems. However, the behavior problems continued to occur on the playground during physical activities.

Unfortunately, Matthew soon became treated as a mascot. The girls all tended to mother him, and the boys tended to cater toward him. This was something I had feared from the start. Matthew's teacher tried not to foster these behaviors, but the kids adored Matthew and saw him as needing their help. As a result, Matthew became very lazy. He continually looked to others for help, even when he did not need it, and the quality of his work diminished greatly. While the year was seen as an overall success, I felt very frustrated with the status thrust on Matthew, and I knew I had some bad habits to break.

The following year, Matthew became a part of our merged classroom. It was the perfect placement for him after being integrated in kindergarten. Matthew thrived in this environment. We set our expectations high from the start in order to break the bad habits he had developed the past year.

Matthew had not made the academic progress I felt he was capable of in kindergarten, so we set out to start him moving down the academic trail. Through the year, he learned to read emergent-level books with confidence, and he is doing his best at written language even though he still struggles greatly with oral language skills.

He has continued to be a part of our class this year and is a model student. He is now an independent worker and is treated by his peers as just another friend in class, not a mascot or someone who needs their help and guidance. He still experiences some behavior problems on the playground, but not everyone can be perfect.

Matthew is truly a merged classroom success story.

The merged classroom, with coteaching, is one approach to fully including children with disabilities with typically developing children. What are the advantages of the merged classroom? Of coteaching?

INTEREST IN SPECIAL NEEDS CHILDREN

The present interest in the education of special needs children prevails for several reasons. First, court cases and legal decisions have extended to special needs children the rights and privileges enjoyed by everyone. To ensure that these rights and privileges are accorded to children, parent involvement is a necessity. In some instances, court decisions have encouraged or ordered this involvement. In the absence of the special needs child's ability to be his or her own advocate, the courts, agencies, and parents assume that function.

Legislation enacted at the state and federal levels has specified that children with disabilities must receive a free and appropriate education. In essence, this legislation promotes and encourages development of programs for education of children with disabilities. This legislation also provides for parent involvement. Thus, professionals are involving parents of children with disabilities because they must.

Second, federal money is available to create programs for special needs children and greater social consciousness toward children with special needs. People recognize that those with disabilities have often been treated as second-class citizens and have been victims of oppression and degradation, so there is an effort to make reparations for past behavior and attitudes.

Third, many young people see teaching special needs children as a rewarding profession, with unlimited opportunities to contribute. These educators feel they can best serve society, children, and themselves by teaching, and devote their lives to helping these children.

Legislation enacted at the state and federal levels has specified that children with disabilities must receive a free and appropriate education. In essence, this legislation promotes and encourages development of programs for education of children with disabilities. The emphasis in early childhood programs is to mainstream children into a least restrictive environment.

Fourth, U.S. education emphasizes meeting the needs of individual children, and special needs children require special attention and accommodation.

Public Law 94-142

The landmark legislation providing for the needs of children with disabilities is PL 94-142. Section 3 of this law states:

> It is the purpose of this Act to assure that all handicapped children have available to them, within the time periods specified in section 612(2)(B), a free appropriate public education which emphasizes special education and related services designed to meet their unique needs, to assure that the rights of handicapped children and their parents or guardians are protected, to assist States and localities to provide for the education of all handicapped children, and to assess and assure the effectiveness of efforts to educate handicapped children.[3]

Public Law 94-142 provides for a free and appropriate education (FAPE) for all persons between the ages of three and twenty-one. The operative word is *appropriate;* the child must receive an education suited to his or her age, maturity, condition of disability, past achievements, and parental expectations. The common practice was to diagnose children with a disability and then put them in an existing program, whether or not that program was specifically appropriate. Now the educational program has to be appropriate to the child, which means that a plan must be developed for each child.

The child's education must occur within the least restrictive educational environment. *Least restrictive* means that environment in which the child will be able to receive a program that meets his or her specific needs—the regular classroom, if that is the environment in which the child can learn best. The least restrictive educational environment is not always the regular classroom; however, this law provides more opportunity to be with regular children.

The law requires *individualization of instruction* and *diagnosis*. Not only must the child's education be appropriate; it must also be individualized, taking into consideration the child's specific needs, disability, and preferences, as well as those of the parents. The key to the individualization process is another feature of the law that requires development of an individualized educational plan (IEP) for each child. This program must specify what will be done for the child, and how and when it will be done. The program must be in writing. In developing the IEP, a person trained in diagnosing disabling conditions, such as a school psychologist, must be involved, as well as a classroom professional, the parent, and, when appropriate, the child.

Several implications are associated with the IEP. One is that for the first time, on a formal basis, parents and children are involved in the educational determination of what will happen to the child. Second, the child must have a plan tailor-made or individualized for him or her. This approach assures accurate diagnosis and realistic goal setting, as well as responsible implementation of the program, which personalizes the process and increases the possibility of a more humane teaching-learning process.

The legislation specifies that parents and child will have a role in diagnosis, placement, and development of the IEP. Parents can state their desires for the child, and information parents have about the child's learning style, interests, and abilities can be considered in developing the educational plan. This process was not always possible or even considered necessary before passage of PL 94-142.

The law also provides for parents to initiate a hearing if they do not agree with the diagnosis, placement, or IEP. This provision gives the parents clout in encouraging public school personnel to provide a free and appropriate education for their child.

Function of the IEP

Using an individualized educational plan with all children, not just those with disabilities, is gaining acceptance with all early childhood professionals. Individualizing objectives, methodology, and teaching helps ensure that the teaching process will become more accurate and accountable.

The IEP has several purposes. First, it protects children and parents by assuring that planning will occur. Second, the IEP guarantees that children will have plans tailored to their individual strengths, weaknesses, and learning styles. Third, the IEP helps professionals and other instructional and administrative personnel focus their teaching and resources on children's specific needs, and it promotes the best use of everyone's time, efforts, and talents.

Fourth, the IEP helps assure that children with disabilities will receive a broad range of services from other agencies. The plan must not only include an educational component but also specify how the child's total needs will be met. If children can benefit from special services such as physical therapy, for example, it must be written into the IEP. This provision is beneficial not only for children but classroom professionals as well, because it broadens their perspective of the educational function.

Fifth, the IEP helps clarify and refine decisions as to what is best for children—where they should be placed, how they should be taught and helped. It also assures that children will not be categorized or labeled without discussion of their unique needs.

Finally, review of the IEP at least annually encourages professionals to consider how and what children have learned, whether what was prescribed is effective, and to prescribe new or modified learning strategies.

Implications for Parents

While the implications of PL 94-142 are far-reaching for children and adults with disabilities, its implications for involving parents in the educational process are especially important. To receive money under the provisions of the law or to continue receiving federal money for other programs, school districts must involve parents in the development of an educational program for their children. Involvement becomes the right of all parents of children with disabilities.

The second implication of this act is that parents' knowledge of their children must be included in the development of the educational plan. Also, parents are assured of continued involvement in their children's education in a number of ways. For example, the plans have to be reviewed and revised at least annually.

Furthermore, the law has due process features, which stipulate that if parents are not satisfied with their children's placement or the IEP, they have the right to appeal to higher authorities in the schools and, ultimately, to the courts. Child advocate agencies, organizations for citizens with disabilities, and civil rights groups advise parents of their rights and responsibilities under the provisions of this act.

Parents' Rights

Under the provision of PL 94-142, parents have these rights regarding their children's education:

1. Parents must give consent for evaluation of their children.
2. Parents have the right to "examine all relevant records with respect to the identification, evaluation, and educational placement of the child."
3. Parents must be given prior written notice whenever a change in "the identification, evaluation or educational placement of the child" occurs.

4. This written notice must be in the parent's native tongue.

5. Parents have an "opportunity to present complaints with respect to any matter relating to the identification, evaluation, or educational placement of the child."

6. Parents have the right to a due process hearing in relation to any complaint.

7. Parents have the right to participate in development of the IEP for their child.

8. Meetings to develop the IEP must be conducted in the parent's native tongue.

9. Meetings to develop the IEP must be held at a time and place agreeable to parents.

PL 94-142's most obvious benefit is to give children with disabilities access to the regular classroom. As mainstreaming continues and full inclusion becomes accepted and implemented, there will be more peer interaction among children with disabilities and typically developing children. The concept of *least restrictive environment* offers a great deal of opportunity for children with disabilities, which assures that all children will be educated and cared for.

Child Find

Public Law 94-142 provides for *Child Find* agencies to facilitate identification of children with disabilities. Child Find programs are operated by state and local agencies, including school districts. The major purposes of Child Find are to

*   locate and identify children and youth with disabilities,

*   conduct screening and assessment tests,

*   recommend educational and therapeutic services, and

*   refer parents to appropriate social service agencies.

Public Law 99-457

In 1986 Congress passed PL 99-457, the Education of the Handicapped Act Amendments—landmark legislation relating to infants, toddlers, and preschoolers with disabilities. Public Law 99-457 amends PL 91-230, the Education of the Handicapped Act (EHA), which was passed in 1970. Public Law 99-457 authorizes two new programs: Title I, Program for Infants and Toddlers with disabilities (birth through age two years), and Title II, Preschool Grants Program (ages three through five years). The Preschool Grants Program extends to children with disabilities between the ages of three and five the rights extended to the disabled under PL 94-142. This age group was included in PL 94-142 but often did not receive public school services because states had discretion as to whether to provide services to this age group.

The legislation recognizes that families play a large role in delivering services to preschool children with disabilities. Consequently, PL 99-457 provides that, whenever appropriate and to the extent desired by parents, preschoolers' IEPs will include instruction for parents. The legislation also recognizes the desirability of variations in program options to provide services to preschoolers with disabilities. Variations may be part-day home based and part- or full-day center based.

The Program for Infants and Toddlers authorized by PL 99-457 establishes a state grant program for infants and toddlers with disabilities, from birth to two years, who (1) are experiencing developmental delays in one or more of the following areas: cognitive, physical, language and speech, psychosocial, or self-help skills; (2) have a physical or mental condition that has a high probability of resulting in delay (e.g., Down syndrome, cerebral palsy); or (3) are at risk medically or environmentally for substantial developmental delays if early intervention is not provided. This program provides for early intervention for all eligible children. Early intervention services provided under 99-457 include these:

- A multidisciplinary assessment and a written individualized family service plan (IFSP) developed by a multidisciplinary team and the parents. Services must meet developmental needs and can include special education, speech and language pathology and audiology, occupational therapy, physical therapy, psychological services, parent and family training and counseling services, transition services, medical diagnostic services, and health services.

- An IFSP, which must contain a statement of the child's present levels of development; a statement of the family's strengths and needs in regard to enhancing the child's development; a statement of major expected outcomes for the child and family; the criteria, procedures, and timeliness for determining progress; the specific early intervention services necessary to meet the unique needs of the child and family; the projected dates for initiation of services; the name of the case manager; and transition procedures from the early intervention program into a preschool program.

Since PL 99-457 requires an IFSP, professionals need to know what these plans consist of and procedures for completing them. Although developing a program for individual children and/or their families is not the same as individualized instruction, it is important to know the differences between the two and how to conduct both processes.

Figure 11–2 shows one page from an IFSP developed by Child Development Resources in Lightfoot, Virginia, for a child. Note that the IFSP is for the beginning implementation stage, which accounts for why the section "Parents' Report of Progress Toward Outcome" is not yet filled in. As the plan is put into practice, this section will be completed. The entire IFSP is presented in Appendix C. An important document that merits close examination and study, this IFSP is a prototype and reflects the latest thinking in professionals' efforts to provide for special needs children and their families.

The following points should be kept in mind when striving for effective individual and family service plans:

- Methods and techniques of diagnostic and prescriptive teaching are essential as a basis for writing and implementing the IEP and the IFSP.

FIGURE 11–2 A Partial IFSP

Other Outcomes Desired by the Family

Outcome	Course of Action	Review/Modify (date)	Parents' Report of Progress Toward Outcome (date)
1. Kevin will have a smooth transition from CDR to the public schools (Fall 1995).	1a. Kevin's family and Lara will visit the Play Center to observe classrooms, therapies, and to meet the staff.	Feb. 1995	
	1b. Kevin will be referred to the Play Center by Lara with parent's permission.	Mar. 1995	
	1c. Kevin's parents and Lara will attend eligibility and IEP meetings as needed.	May/June 1995	
	1d. Kevin will attend Developmental Play Group more frequently in the spring to help him prepare for transition, if his parents desire.	Ongoing (starting late Spring 1995)	

Source: Child Development Resources, P.O. Box 299, Lightfoot, Virginia 23090. Used by permission.

- Working with parents is an absolute must for every classroom professional. You should learn all you can about parent conferences and communication, parent involvement, and parents as volunteers and aides (see chap. 13). In a sense, PL 94-142 and PL 99-457 mainstream parents as well as children.

- Working with all levels of professionals offers a unique opportunity for the classroom professional to individualize instruction. Since it is obvious that all professionals need help in individualizing instruction, it makes sense to involve all professionals in this process.

- As individual education becomes a reality for *all* children and families, professionals will need skills in assessing student behavior and family background and settings.

- Professionals must know how to identify sources of, and how to order and use, a broad range of instructional materials, including media. One cannot hope to individualize without a full range of materials and media. Professionals must regularly be concerned with students' visual, auditory, and tactile/kinesthetic learning styles. Some children in a classroom may learn best through one mode, other children through another. The classroom professional can utilize media, in particular, to help make teaching styles congruent with children's learning modalities (see chap. 14).

Completing the individualized family service plan and the individual educational plan is an important process, requiring the involvement of parents, children, and professionals.

TEACHING CHILDREN WITH DISABILITIES

As an early childhood educator, you will have children with special needs in your classroom (refer to Figure 11–1). These are some of the general types of special needs you will encounter in your classroom:

- *Visual impairment*—loss of visual functions sufficient to restrict the learning process

- *Hearing impairment*—slightly to severely defective hearing

- *Physical disability*—a condition that impedes normal development of gross- or fine-motor abilities

- *Speech impairment or communication disorder*—disorders of expressive or receptive language; stuttering, chronic voice disorders, or serious articulation problems affecting social, emotional, and educational achievement

- *Health impairment*—illnesses of a chronic and prolonged nature such as epilepsy, hemophilia, asthma, cardiac conditions, severe allergies, blood disorders, diabetes, and neurological disorders

- *Serious emotional disturbances*—outbursts of dangerous aggressiveness, self-destructiveness, severe withdrawal and uncommunicativeness, hyperactivity to the extent that it affects adaptive behavior, severe anxiety, depression, psychotic behavior, or autism

- *Specific learning disabilities*—disorders in one or more of the basic psychological processes involved in understanding or using language, spoken or written,

Program in Practice

THE OPEN DOOR PRESCHOOL, AUSTIN, TEXAS

The Open Door Preschool is a child care center that has successfully offered mainstreamed care since 1975. Addressing the problems created by the educational segregation of the preschooler with disabilities was the school's founding principle. The opportunity to play and learn with typically developing children helps prepare the child with disabilities for life in the mainstream. A mainstreamed preschool experience provides the opportunity to develop social skills as well as a strong self-concept; both of these help the child with disabilities participate successfully with typically developing peers.

Twenty-five to 30 percent of the enrollment of the Open Door are children with disabilities or those needing special care. A broad definition for "special needs" results in a great variety of skill levels. Children's skill level as well as their chronological age are considered when creating the composition of each class. Further, the nature of each special need is considered so that each class is man-

ageable in terms of supervision and routine care. These considerations result in classes that are defined more by developmental level than by age.

Jeffrey first came to the Open Door when he was twenty-three months old. His parents described him as a normal, active toddler, but they did report some problems at his previous preschool. Jeffrey's professional, however, immediately saw reason for concern about Jeffrey's abilities. When his family finally agreed to obtain some evaluations, we determined that Jeffrey was functioning at a fifteen- to eighteen-month-old level. A year later, Jeffrey is still in the Bluebird room, our youngest classroom. He is receiving speech and occupational therapy twice each week. His vocabulary has increased to over twenty words; he participates in many group activities; he loves music (the louder the better); and he enjoys drawing, painting, and water play. Jeffrey is well liked and accepted by his classmates, all of whom are a year younger than he is. He is very at

Contributed by Elizabeth Sears, training/technical assistance associate, Southwest Educational Development Laboratory, Austin, Texas.

that may manifest itself in imperfect ability to listen, think, speak, read, write, spell, or perform mathematical calculations

Resource Room

The resource room is one method of providing for children with disabilities in a mainstreamed setting. As the name implies, this classroom is an instructional setting that provides resources for students with disabilities and their professionals. A student who participates in the resource program is enrolled in the regular educational program and goes to the resource room regularly for special support, usually of an academic nature. Regular classroom professionals of the special needs students receive support through materials and ideas shared by resource professionals. In this way, professionals discover different approaches or alternative methods for

home with his two-year-old classmates, and he seems to function close to their level.

Emma came to the Open Door when she was four and a half. Her early childhood professionals and therapists placed her on an eighteen-month-old level. Because of her size, she was placed in our Sunshine room, which is primarily three-year-olds. Emma spent a year and a half in the Sunshine room. When she arrived each afternoon, she played quietly with toys. As the other children awoke from their naps, she greeted them with exuberant hugs and a twinkly-eyed smile. By the time Emma graduated to the Rainbow room with her classmates, she was a year and a half older than the others in the class. Despite her vocabulary of only four words, Emma's size required that she be with the oldest children in our school. The other children in the class knew Emma very well. She had been with most of them for at least a year. Her difficulties with speech, fine-motor tasks, and coordination did not prevent Emma from being included in many classroom activities. She enjoys being with her classmates. She scribbles as they draw, she struggles up the climber as they race up and down it, and she is right in the middle of any water play. Emma's loving hugs to all visitors are the finest greetings we can possibly give. Emma has helped many of the others at the Open Door learn to see how much everyone has to offer regardless of seemingly insurmountable hurdles.

Success stories at the Open Door are many. In our fifteen years of operation, we have turned away only one child, whose violent outbursts were uncontrollable. That was an incredibly painful experience for the staff. It is not only possible to mainstream children on the preschool level but also beneficial to all involved. The children with disabilities learn to interact with other children with whatever abilities they have; the typically developing children learn to see the abilities people have rather than focus on the abilities that are lacking or lagging behind.

meeting children's unique needs. The *resource professional* has training in special education and experience in teaching students with disabilities. The resource professional shares ideas with the other faculty members as well to promote positive attitudes toward all children.

The Transdisciplinary Team

The *transdisciplinary team approach* to children with special needs consists of *interdisciplinary* involvement across and among various health and social services disciplines. Members of the team can include any of these professionals: early childhood educator, physical therapist, occupational therapist, speech communication therapist, psychologist, social worker, and pediatrician. The rationale for the transdisciplinary approach is that a unified and holistic approach is the most effective way to provide resources and deliver services to children and their families.

Program in Practice

PRESCHOOL TREATMENT SERVICES: A COMMUNITY TEAM APPROACH TO THERAPY NEEDS FOR INFANTS AND CHILDREN IN COMMUNITY-BASED PROGRAMS

Alberta Children's Hospital in Calgary, Alberta, Canada, operates a unique outreach program to provide therapeutic intervention through mobile therapy teams to children with special needs in mainstreamed community settings.

Three community teams, each staffed by a speech/language pathologist, a physiotherapist, and an occupational therapist, travel daily throughout the city from their hospital base. Although some direct treatment is provided, the main focus is toward a collaborative approach in which goal setting and program implementation is a joint venture involving primary caregivers: parent, teachers, and aides. This is evidenced through the individual service plans (ISPs) formulated for each child. A psychologist and family support worker are available to provide support, education, and consultation to the team members, families, and community day care centers.

The program caseload consists of 150 infants and children having a broad range of disabilities and functioning levels. Intervention takes place in homes, family day homes, child day care centers, nursery schools, and preschool and school programs.

A significant feature of the program is the collaborative network established with twenty-five high-quality, community-based day care centers. A solid four-way partnership exists among the hospital teams, families, day care centers, and government funding agencies involved with special services for children with disabilities.

Philosophy

Central to the program philosophy is the belief that minimal separation from family and community life affords the best opportunity for children with disabilities to reach their maximum potential. The merging of knowledge and skills offered by therapists and primary caregivers facilitates the transfer of responsibility to family and community for the integration of therapy techniques into the child's daily activities.

The preschool treatment services program believes in

■   the principles of family-centered care,

■   the values and benefits of early intervention,

■   the value and benefits of inclusion of the child with special needs into family and community life, and

■   the strengthening of our working relationship with the community to achieve the child's optimal functioning abilities.

Objectives

Objectives of the outreach program are to

■   provide therapeutic intervention by direct treatment, demonstration teaching, and consultation;

Contributed by Ruth Cripps, former director, Community Outreach Services; Shirley Crozier, former coordinator of the community team; and M. Shirley Wormsbecker, program manager, Preschool Treatment Services, Alberta Children's Hospital.

- share knowledge and skills with primary caregivers and facilitate transfer of responsibility for therapy carry-over to family and community;

- help primary caregivers integrate treatment into daily routines;

- provide in-services, one-to-one consultation, and dialogue leading to increased knowledge and skills for parents, professionals, and related community staff;

- support, educate, and encourage parents to become informed advocates for their children; and

- provide educational presentations directed at increasing public awareness, knowledge, and involvement.

Program Model

The purpose, quantity, and type of assessment and intervention vary according to the needs of each child. It is essential, therefore, that the program and model of service delivery remain flexible. The program provides coordinated, continuous services for children from infancy to six years of age. A case manager oversees a child's intervention needs. The broad range of intervention can include therapy, education/coaching, family support, and community education and support.

A collaborative model is consistently followed, and everyone involved with the child is an integral member of the team. The team approach varies between interdisciplinary and transdisciplinary, according to the circumstances of each child, family, and community placement. To achieve maximum integration of the child's program into daily routine, the community team emphasizes teaching the necessary skills to parents and community caregivers. Over the past eighteen years, the program has assisted in the development of a strong cadre of community day care and preschool program staff whose enthusiasm and dedication to excellence are outstanding.

The mutual teaching-learning component of the model encompasses an exchange of skills and information within the team disciplines and between the teams and primary caregivers, as well as between the staff of community agencies and recreational programs. Sharing knowledge takes the form of demonstration teaching, writing skill-specific programs, and providing disability-specific materials. At times, the use of videos encourages mutual evaluation of skill acquisition. Sharing practical alternatives and creative responses to programming problems are the essence of frequent, short, and specific teaching sessions.

The community team pioneered the concept of integrating children with special needs into regular nonspecialized community settings. Although the model was initially developed for an urban setting, it has been adapted to the needs of several smaller regional cities and rural areas.

THE MATCH-UP MATRIX

Supports to Include All Children

The federal laws as well as state licensing and other regulatory agencies are no longer satisfied with the concept of "integrated" or "main-streamed" classroom environments. Previously, programs that chose to do so would bring a child with special needs into a "typical" classroom or "regular" program in which most or all of the other children had no identified special need. An increasing trend has been to design programs to serve children with and without identified disabling conditions in an "integrated" setting. Either of these arrangements would enable a child with special needs to be served in the least restrictive environment with their peers while receiving appropriate services to meet their needs.

In the past years, the idea of "inclusion" has emerged to describe the relationship between children with special needs and "regular" or typical classrooms. This concept provides that all students, with reasonable program and support accommodations and regardless of special needs or disabling condition, should be served in the same classroom as their peers. This policy has been mandated by law or by regulation in many states.

How is a preschool program or classroom teacher to decide what is "reasonable program and support accommodations"? How are parents to be a part of the process of supporting their child's inclusion in school activities? How will specialists know what services are required? How will early childhood staff identify their own training needs?

A match-up matrix is a way of thinking about such questions using a team approach. It asks all involved to discuss the issues based on information rather than emotion, prejudice, assump-tions, and/or false expectations. The setting resources are listed as they relate to an individual child's needs. The team that is attempting to make a placement decision examines each need as compared with the setting resources to deter-mine whether there is a match in each category. Actions to meet any unmet needs are identified and assigned a priority. With this strategy, a deci-sion can be made with concrete information regarding the program's abilities to meet the child's needs.

An Example

Two-and-a-half-year-old Adam has been diag-nosed with diplegic cerebral palsy (involvement of the lower extremities), with an accompanying seizure disorder resulting from a head injury he received in a car accident at eighteen months of age. Shortly after the accident, Adam received physical therapy through the hospital's out-patient services. On the recommendation of his therapist, Adam's parents are seeking to enroll him in a preschool.

Adam uses a walker to move around in his environment. Though he is able to do many things easily, he often asks for help. His lan-guage and cognitive skills have been assessed at or above age level; however, self-help skills have been affected by his gross-motor delays. Though seizures occurred frequently after the accident, with daily medication there has been no recurrence except with a high fever. Adam relates well to adults, though he sometimes appears unnecessarily dependent on them. He has limited opportunities to interact with children his own age. He has a teenage brother who seems to cater to him, both parents work, and a housekeeper/baby-sitter who watches him in his home. Both parents are concerned about Adam's care and want him to be happy.

In the match-up matrix of Adam's needs and the preschool's resources, we see a match in

Contributed by Mary Ann Wilson, director and associate professor of early childhood programs, Sullivan County Community College, Loch Sheldrake, New York; and Barry Pehrsson, chief executive officer, Southwinds, Inc., Middletown, New York.

many areas, including supports that exist and barriers that need to be overcome. A few actions are necessary (see Figure A) before the team can recommend that Adam enroll in the Sunshine Preschool. The greatest area of concern involves motor skills, with self-help activities a close second. The use of a walker in a busy classroom is possible, but the staff must organize the space differently for the ease of traffic patterns.

Adam's seating must be situated for easy use of the walker, and planning is needed to make sure that Adam will be able to maneuver easily around the classroom, especially in small spaces such as the bathroom. The physical therapist has offered to come to the preschool to share suggestions for Adam's independence. As with many young children who have not attended school, Adam will need help learning independent play and social skills with his peers. Though his parents have been assured that the seizure disorder is under control, the staff have requested specific information from the physician and neurologist to know what to expect and what to do if such an episode should occur.

As a result of the match-up matrix, the team has decided to take actions identified in the order of priority. Once completed, the team agrees to recommend that Adam be enrolled in the Sunshine Preschool. A team conference is planned to review progress at the end of two months of enrollment in school.

His parents decide to enroll Adam in the Sunshine Preschool. When they visit the program for the follow-up meeting, they are amazed by how much Adam can do for himself. They decide to send their teenage son to visit on his next school holiday, and they are beginning to understand the need to demand more independence in daily routines at home. Adam's physical therapist reports increase in his progress in their weekly sessions, particularly in Adam's motivation, compliance, and pride in his achievements.

Suggestions

The match-up matrix may show many areas in which a match does not easily occur between a program's resources and the child's needs. Supports may not be sufficient, or barriers might not be overcome with reasonable accommodations. In this case, the team may not recommend enrollment for a child. The match-up matrix can actually help the team identify programs or services that would be appropriate since the child's needs have already been outlined, and the match-up matrix defines what setting resources are needed to make the most appropriate placement decision. Thus, if an individual child or program do not "match" at a particular time, it is possible to define under what conditions the placement might be considered. If the child or the program is not "ready," the team can look forward to the time when the child or the program is indeed ready.

Programs no longer have the option to enroll children with special needs. It is a defined right of all children and families to be included in the same services and programs as their neighbors and peers, as much as reasonably possible. This policy of inclusion can only be a positive step toward mutual understanding and appreciation of skills, talents, and needs among adults as well as children.

FIGURE A A Match-Up Matrix for Adam at Sunshine Preschool

Resources	Staff Training and Information	Additional Expertise or Specialists
Child Needs		
Motor	S = Fine-motor and sensory activities available and age-appropriate. B = No experience with children using a walker	S = Licensed physical therapist can come to center twice weekly; classroom does gross-motor activities regularly. B = Parent will not be as actively involved; frequency reduced from three times weekly.
Language	S = Children's books, dramatic play and whole-language experiences available daily. B = None	None
Cognitive	S = Theme-based curriculum and pre-academic activities for problem solving and concept development. B = None	None
Social	S = Sufficient materials, ample space, trained supervision; child seldom shares materials and interacts primarily with adults, but staff has experience with these behaviors.	S = Parent willing to visit to help explain use of walker and cerebral palsy to children. B = No books, photos, dolls, or other items inclusive of children with special needs.
Self-Help	S = Child frequently asks for help in all self-help tasks. B = Though child is capable of participating in dressing, feeding, washing and toileting, currently leaves all to adult.	S = Therapist reports child is capable of nearly independent toileting and dressing with proper support. B = Needs adult help for all self-help and care activities.
Behavior	S = Affectionate, responsive and energetic child. B = Cries or tantrums at home as a refusal.	None
Medical	S = All staff certified in first aid and CPR. B = Lack information and experience in managing seizures, limited knowledge of cerebral palsy, staff concerned about restrictions for child.	S = Family doctor and neurologist will both write letters to center indicating no restrictions; complete medical history requested prior to admission for all children. B = No school nurse on premises.
Home	S = Preschool is close to home; parents can transport by taking turns; teenage brother at home willing to participate. B = Parents concerned child will be hurt physically through unsafe activities or emotionally by other children.	S = Program has open visitation for all family members and for friends. B = Need to design plan for children, staff, parents, and physical environment to assure smooth enrollment.

Key: S = Support; B = Barrier.

Note: Action priorities are determined in a team meeting of parents, teachers, specialists, and all other individuals concerned with the decision to enroll the child. Once the action items are completed, the child can be enrolled.

Equipment and Materials Needed	Peers Available	To Do
S = Classroom on first floor; a walker from home can remain at school; building is accessible by ramps. B = Monthly field trip sites need to be barrier-free; need extra person for trips.	S = Age-mates attend programs. B = Child has limited experience with age-mates—relies on adults for help to move.	1
None	S = Variety of children reflecting multicultural diversity. B = None	None
None	S = Children of various ages and development will provide opportunities to exchange experiences. B = None	None
B = No resource books or workshops attended by staff on "inclusion."	S = Other children enrolled with same and better developed social skills. B = Other children lack information or experience with handicapping conditions.	4
S = Budget has provision for adaptations. B = Bathroom needs bar for transfer to toilet; towel dispensers need to be lowered; art easel needs modification.	S = Other children also learning self-help skills. B = Parents must request participation at home to increase independence.	3
S = Positive guidance techniques used in classroom; videotapes available for parents to borrow.	S = Older children in class provide positive role models. B = Younger children in class display similar behaviors.	6
S = Parents can provide all seizure medications at home. B = Classroom must provide input on any behavior changes if and when medication is changed or should be changed.	S = Support group available for families through public health office. B = No other child with seizure disorder in program.	5
None	S = Parents given names of other parents to contact who have children in the program. B = No other parent of child with social need in program.	2

When mainstreaming children with disabilities into regular classrooms, professionals must make adjustments in human and educational resources. The match-up matrix can assist in making adjustments and decisions.

Members of the transdisciplinary team diagnose, prescribe, share information, and work cooperatively to meet children's needs. One of the members, usually the early childhood educator, heads the team, and other members act as consultants. The team leader carries out the instructions of other team members. A variation of this model is to have members of the team, such as the physical therapist, work directly with the child at specified times (e.g., twice a week) and provide activities and suggestions for the early childhood educator to implement at other times.

Children with Disabilities in Head Start Programs

Head Start services to children with disabilities consists of the following:

- *Outreach and recruitment.*   This effort is directed toward locating, identifying, and recruiting children with disabilities into Head Start. The most common sources for outreach are parents, public health departments, school systems, and newspaper articles.

- *Diagnosis and assessment of children with disabilities.*   Head Start staff members work with private diagnostic consultants to achieve this service.

- *Mainstreaming and special services.*   Special services include individualized instruction, parent counseling, and psychological and physical therapy.

- *Teaching and technical assistance.*   This service includes working with staff and parents to provide training for working with children with disabilities.

- *Coordination with other agencies.*   Head Start staff work closely with other agencies to identify, recruit, and offer services to children with disabilities and their families.

- *Summer Head Start.*   Many Head Start children who would otherwise probably not receive services before entering public school are served in summer programs.

Guidelines for Teaching Children with Disabilities

Professionals of children with disabilities can improve their teaching by emphasizing what children can do rather than what they cannot do. Children with disabilities have many talents and abilities, and professionals can help them fulfill their potentials as they would any other child. Teaching methods that are effective with typically developing children can be equally effective with children with disabilities. Conversely, many instructional activities that special professionals use with children with disabilities work just as well with typically developing children.

Professionals first need to diagnose what children are able to do, through observation, examination of work samples, professionally made tests, discussions with parents, examination of cumulative records, and discussions with other professionals.

Use of concrete examples and materials and multisensory approaches to learning are also important in teaching. Furthermore, all children need to be involved in learning activities. The professional must also model what children are to do rather than just tell them what to do. A good procedure is to tell children what they are to do, model a behavior or have a child who has already mastered a skill model it for others, have children perform the skill or task under supervision and give them corrective feedback, let children practice or perform the behavior, and involve the children in evaluating their performance.

Professionals should make learning interesting and the learning environment a pleasant, rewarding place to be. Also, a dependable classroom schedule is easier for children with disabilities because it gives them a sense of security and consistency.

Parent involvement, at both home and school, is one of the most effective ways to increase achievement for all children. In addition, every early childhood program should strive to have children become independent of others, especially professionals and parents.

REVERSE MAINSTREAMING

Reverse mainstreaming is receiving more attention in early childhood education today. In this model, typically developing children are placed in programs for children with disabilities. The children with disabilities are the majority. Usually, a group of two-thirds children with disabilities and one-third typically developing students functions well, but the optimum ratio for any program varies.

A number of assumptions are implicit in any model of reverse mainstreaming: (1) the instructional program and activities will be appropriate for both children with disabilities and typically developing students; (2) integration will have a positive rather than negative effect on both groups; (3) the program is pedagogically and administratively manageable.

Issues to consider in a program of reverse mainstreaming are as follows:

- Recruitment, identification, and selection of children to participate in the program

- Working with all parents, especially parents of the typically developing, to assure them that their children are receiving a good—even an above-average—educational experience

- Identification of services, equipment, materials, and necessary special professional training to assume an optimal program for all

The principal advantages of integrating a classroom that was previously only for children with disabilities are that typically developing students provide role models for behavior and skill development and the professional is able to maintain a perspective on normal growth and development.

MAKING TRANSITIONS

Transitional experiences from one setting to another are a must for all special needs children, especially those who have attended preschool in a special setting or a separate public school facility from the elementary school. To help the special needs child make a transition from one setting to another, the staffs of the sending and receiving agencies must cooperate in arrangements, activities, and plans. Consider these suggestions:

- Try to approximate certain features of the receiving environment. If the new classroom has a larger child-adult ratio, gradually get children used to working and functioning in larger groups.

- Help children become accustomed to social skills appropriate to the new environment. If children have been using a restroom inside the classroom but will have to go outside the classroom in the new school, help them practice this new routine.

- Use materials and activities as children will encounter them in the new setting. For example, get a set of textbooks a child will use and familiarize her with the format and activities.

- Approximate the kind and length of instructional activities children will be expected to participate in and complete.

- Visit the new school with children and their parents.

- Communicate with the receiving professional to share information about the child.

- Structure a social setting in the receiving classroom. Arrange a "buddy system" with the child in the new classroom.

- After the child has made the transition, visit the classroom to demonstrate a supportive, caring attitude to the receiving professional, parents, and child.

- The receiving professional has reciprocal responsibilities to make the transition as stress-free and rewarding as possible. Successful transitions involve all concerned: children, parents, professionals, administrators, and support personnel. (Other suggestions for transitional experiences are described in chap. 8.)

GIFTED CHILDREN

Practitioners Ann and Elizabeth Lupkowski believe young gifted children may display the following behaviors:

- *Long attention span.*   The attention span of gifted children is often longer than that of their peers. . . . Some young gifted children are able to work on projects for blocks of time as long as 45 minutes to 2 1/2 hours.
- *Creativity and imagination.*   Gifted children may have unique and innovative ideas for the use of common materials or unique names for possessions. . . . These children may also design unusual dramatic play situations, such as astronauts landing on the moon, and they often have imaginary friends or companions.
- *Social relationships.*   All children have varied social skills, and gifted children are no exception. They may be leaders of other children, with advanced social skills for their age, or they may prefer to be alone to work on their own interests. . . . Some gifted children may find innovative ways to settle disputes. Also, young gifted children may prefer to interact with older children and adults rather than with their same-age peers.
- *Number concepts.*   Some gifted children seem to be fascinated with numbers before they begin formal schooling.
- *Verbal skills.*   Gifted preschoolers may recognize letters early and show an early interest in printed matter. They may be interested in foreign languages and also exhibit correct pronunciation and sentence structure in their native language. Young gifted children may show an advanced vocabulary and may begin reading before they start school, although the significance of early reading as an indicator of giftedness has not been established.
- *Memory.*   Gifted children may show exceptional memories.
- *Specific interests.*   The young gifted child may show an in-depth interest in one or more areas and spend a great deal of time developing a collection of a class of objects, such as rocks or plastic animals.
- *Attention to detail.*   Gifted children often notice "insignificant" details in pictures and situations. They also enjoy making things more complex—elaborating on rules for games, for example.
- *High energy level.*   Some gifted children have been called hyperactive because of the high level of energy they show. These children also seem to need little sleep.
- *Reasoning ability.*   The ability to form analogies at a young age and to justify those responses may be another indicator of giftedness. . . . Perhaps the ability to successfully complete and justify this type of task is an indicator of advanced cognitive development.

- *Insight ability.*   Exceptional insight ability has been postulated as another characteristic of the intellectually gifted. They may be superior in insight ability because of the ability to sift out relevant information, blend those pieces of information, and add new information to appropriate information acquired in the past. These children have the ability to find solutions to complex problems.[4]

Pediatrician Michael Lewis has found four signs that most, but not all, gifted young children display during the first year of life:

1. *Sleep problems.*   These children either don't go to sleep easily, they wake up early, or they don't sleep long amounts of time. Any or all of these patterns may be present. While these kids give the impression that they are having some problems with sleeping, we don't think this is actually the case. Evidently, these children are exhibiting individual differences in sleep patterns: the only *problem* is that the parents don't get enough sleep.

2. *Alertness and attentiveness.*   One of the outstanding signs that parents report is that these children always look interested in what is going on around them. They are usually alert—their eyes are open, scanning the field, and they listen attentively. Indeed, they give you the feeling there is an inquisitive mind at work, even though it is the mind of a five-year-old.

3. *Early stranger fear or recognition.*   Normally, by eight months of age, children are smart enough to remember who they know and who they don't know. When they see a stranger they can compare the image of that person against the images of people they know. When it doesn't match anyone familiar, they become inhibited. Some of these children (about 70 percent) go on to become frightened and upset, a reaction we call stranger anxiety. This pattern normally shows itself in babies at about eight or nine months. In a large proportion of gifted children, we are seeing stranger anxiety showing itself in the third to fourth month of life. Not all gifted children we have seen show fearfulness; some just show interest. But, one way or another, all show early *recognition* that they see a stranger.

4. *Early language usage.*   Many children speak what seem to be intelligent sounds—"mama," "dada" and other words such as these—somewhere in the last quarter of the first year. However, we don't really consider them true words or true noun usage. It is the most complicated words, such as "boat" or "tree" or "dog," that we consider true noun usage. We have noticed that many gifted children start to produce these terms in the last quarter of the first year, when most children are still saying "mama," "dada," "cup," or other simple words.[5]

Gifted children may not display all these signs, but the presence of several of them can alert parents and early childhood professionals to make appropriate instructional, environmental, and social adjustments.

Mainstreaming the Gifted

Professionals tend to suggest special programs and sometimes schools for the gifted and talented, which would seem to be a move away from providing for these children in regular classrooms. Regular classroom professionals can provide for the gifted in their classrooms through enrichment and acceleration. *Enrichment* provides an opportunity for children to pursue topics in greater depth and in different ways than they normally might. *Acceleration* permits children to progress academically at their own pace.

In regular classrooms, professionals can encourage gifted children to pursue special interests as a means of extending and enriching classroom learning. They can use parents and resource people to tutor and work in special ways with these children and provide opportunities for the children to assume leadership responsibilities themselves. For example, they may be interested in tutoring other students who need extra practice or help. Tutoring can cut across grade and age levels. Students can also help explain directions and procedures to the class. Professionals can also encourage them to use their talents and abilities outside the classroom by becoming involved with other people and agencies and foster creativity through classroom activities that require divergent thinking (e.g., "Let's think of all the different uses for a paper clip"). Professionals must challenge children to think through the use of higher-order questions that encourage them to explain, apply, analyze, rearrange, and judge.

Many schools have resource rooms for the gifted and talented, in which children can spend a half-day or more every week working with a professional who is interested and trained in working with the gifted. There are seven ways to provide for the needs of gifted and talented children:

- *Enrichment classroom.*   The classroom professional conducts a differentiated program of study without the help of outside personnel.
- *Consultant professional.*   A program of differentiated instruction is conducted in the regular classroom with the assistance of a specially trained consultant.
- *Resource room–pullout.*   Gifted students leave the classroom for a short period of time to receive instruction from a specially trained professional.
- *Community mentor.*   Gifted students interact with an adult from the community who has special knowledge in the area of interest.
- *Independent study.*   Students select projects and work on them under the supervision of a qualified professional.
- *Special class.*   Gifted students are grouped together during most of the class time and are instructed by a specially trained professional.
- *Special schools.*   Gifted students receive differentiated instruction at a special school with a specially trained staff.[6]

Of the seven methods, resource room–pullout is the most popular.

INVOLVING SPECIAL NEEDS FAMILIES

Many of the procedures for involving parents can also be used with parents of children with special needs; however, professionals must consider the entire context of family life. The family's total needs must be met and educational, social, and medical problems addressed. It is important to work cooperatively with community agencies that can assist in delivering these services. Parents of children with special

Program in Practice

A GIFTED PRESCHOOL PROGRAM

The New Mexico State University Preschool for the Gifted is for gifted minority and majority children ages three to five who meet program eligibility criteria. The program's philosophy is that gifted leaders are critically needed in all fields. Failure to identify and foster giftedness at an early age, however, has resulted in a continuous waste to this precious human resource. It is a myth that gifted children succeed on their own. Without special help, many grossly underachieve. Thus, the program was established and is maintained on the assumption that services for the gifted should help such children maximize their potential to the benefit of themselves, as individuals, and society. Additional assumptions undergirding the program are that research on gifted children and their education has long-range benefits for all people, parents play a major role in the lives of their gifted children and should participate in their education, and services to economically disadvantaged gifted children constitute an investment for the future.

Goals and Objectives

Major goals of the program are to provide an ongoing (1) center for innovative, systematic research on gifted children, (2) model program for gifted minority and majority children, ages three to five, and (3) training site for pre-service and in-service professionals. Specific objectives for children include the following:

■ To develop a positive attitude toward themselves and learning

■ To encourage positive social values and interaction skills

■ To develop competency in basic skills

■ To broaden interests

■ To pursue talents and special interests

■ To advance breadth and depth of knowledge in academic and artistic disciplines

■ To develop and use convergent and divergent thinking skills

■ To appreciate and accept different cultures

How the Program Achieves Goals: Curriculum/Daily Schedule

The NMSU Preschool for the Gifted achieves its goals by organizing its program around three components as originally conceived by Dr. Margie Kitano, who served as the program's founder and original director. These components are (1) basic skill development, (2) thematic units, and (3) multicultural education (Kitano and Kirby, 1988). Individualized education programs (IEPs) are established at the beginning of each year in order to accomplish basic skills in important domains such as social-emotional and cognitive. If parents request, academic and preacademic goals are also established. Parent conferences are held during and at the end of the year to evaluate progress on IEP goals and other aspects of the program formatively and summatively.

With social studies as a template, thematic units such as energy are established and carried out over four- to six-week intervals. Field trips and guests often complement thematic units. During an energy unit, for example, students took a "walking trip" to the English Department's computer lab to experience electrical energy. Local language and cultural influences are also recognized. For instance, routine activities such as calendar time are carried out in both Spanish and Eng-

Contributed by S. W. Stile, professor, New Mexico State University, College of Education, Special Education/Communication Disorders, Las Cruces.

lish. Sign language is incorporated during activities as appropriate.

The following is the daily schedule for the program:

8:30–9:20   Self-select computer games, reading, science activities, board/card games, art, pretend (with adult interaction)

9:30–10:00   Circle time: whole-group stories, songs, calendar, sharing, unit study

10:00–10:20   Outdoor play: riding, sliding, sharing, digging, taking turns

10:20–10:35   Snack: table skills, sharing, language, nutrition

10:35–10:50   Story time/music

10:50–11:15   Individual and small-group work (basic skills on IEP/unit study/show and tell)

11:15   Dismissal

Criteria for Giftedness and Admission to the Program

An advisory committee made up of a parent of a preschool gifted child, a special educator, a school psychologist, a diagnostician, and a gifted education facilitator from the local public schools select children based on the following criteria:

■ Potential for benefiting from the program

■ Consistency of abilities with program goals

■ Evaluation of need, determined by the range and pattern of assessment scores

Screening/Diagnosis

A community screening effort is conducted each spring for sixty families who have responded to local newspaper and other media announcements. Screenings are held in NMSU's College of Education preschool classrooms on two consecutive Saturdays. Tests are administered by special education students and diagnostician interns under supervision of licensed diagnosticians. The following four instruments are used:

■ Raven Coloured Progressive Matrices

■ Stanford-Binet (4th ed.)

■ Thinking Creatively in Action and Movement (TCAM)

■ Woodcock-Johnson Tests of Achievement-R

Children who score in the superior range on either the Ravens, TCAM, or Woodcock-Johnson are invited back to participate in administration of the Stanford-Binet. Children are eligible for placement if they score in the superior range on *two* of the four instruments.

The assessment battery is under constant scrutiny. For example, the Kaufman Survey of Early Academic and Language Skills (K-SEALS) is being field-tested with children invited back for the intelligence testing. In addition, a parent nomination form is being validated with assistance from the NMSU Experimental Statistics Department. If the parent nomination data so indicate, this form will become part of the assessment battery.

Assessment results are entered into matrices and reviewed by the advisory committee. Students selected for the program are placed in slots vacated by students graduating to public or private kindergarten programs. Other eligible children are placed on a waiting list.

Summary

The NMSU Preschool for the Gifted was established to identify and foster giftedness at an early age. The program is hosted by the university and, in return, serves as a practicum and research site for students and interns in special education and related fields. A unit approach is employed to develop the preschool's curriculum using social studies as a base. IEPs are developed to address basic skills for each child. Eligibility and placement decisions are made by the program's advisory board in relation to results of testing in critical thinking, creativity, achievement, and intelligence. A typical day for a student includes self-selected or other activities, stories, outdoor play, snack with practice in table skills and conversation, music, and small-group and individual work on basic language and mathematics skills.

Reference

Kitano, M. K., and D. F. Kirby. *Gifted Education: A Comprehensive View* (Boston: Little, Brown, 1986).

needs frequently lack the support systems necessary for dealing with their and their children's needs. It is up to professionals to be supportive, help create support systems, and offer linkage to support systems.

Parents Need Help

Parents of special needs children need help, not sympathy, and help is often best when it is *self-help*. One barrier to self-help is the feeling of parents of the child with disabilities toward their child, themselves, and society. Hopelessness and helplessness may prevail. Parents may feel guilty, fearing they did something to cause the disability, and need support to escape from and deal realistically with their emotions.

Sometimes parents feel ashamed of their child and themselves and react by withdrawing from society, consciously or unconsciously attempting to protect themselves and the child from attention. Parents need help to see that there is nothing "wrong" with their children and that they are unique and interesting.

Mainstreaming has helped not only children with disabilities and their parents but all children and all parents. By extending certain basic rights and processes to the children with disabilities, all special needs children will be assured of these rights. It will not be long before all children will have IEPs written for them.

HISTORIC TIME LINE: SPECIAL NEEDS PROGRAMS

1963   PL 88-156 Maternal and Child Health Program is expanded.

1965   PL 89-313 Payments are made to states for children with disabilities, birth through age twenty, in state-operated programs.

1965   PL 89-97 Medicaid Program is established.

1967   PL 90-248 Early and Periodic Screening, Diagnosis, and Treatment Program (EPSDT) is added to Medicaid program.

1968   PL 90-538 Handicapped Children's Early Education Assistance Act creates Handicapped Children's Early Education Program (HCEEP); provides for model demonstration programs to acquaint public with problems and potentials of children with special needs.

1970   PL 91-230 Education of the Handicapped Act (EHA) is created; HCEEP is folded into part C of EHA.

1972   Head Start regulations require that 10 percent of enrollment opportunities be made available to children with disabilities.

1974   PL 93-644 Head Start program is amended to require that 10 percent of enrollment opportunities be made available to children with disabilities.

1975   PL 94-142 The Education for All Handicapped Children Act guarantees a free and appropriate education to children with disabilities ages five through twenty-one.

1983   PL 98-199 EHA is amended to allow use of funds for services to children with disabilities from birth.

1986   PL 99-457 authorized the Federal Preschool Program, which extended rights under PL 99-142 to children age three through five, and the Early Intervention Program, which established a state grant program for children from birth to two years old.

1990   Americans with Disabilities Act (ADA) requires access to public accommodations for all individuals regardless of disability. These public accommodations include child care centers and family child care homes.

1990   PL 101-476 Individuals with Disabilities Education Act (IDEA) provides services to children with disabilities from birth through age five.

1991   PL 102-119 Part H of IDEA is reauthorized and amended.

CHILD ABUSE AND NEGLECT

Many of our views of childhood are highly romanticized. We tend to believe that parents always love their children and enjoy caring for them. We also envision family settings are full of joy, happiness, and parent-child harmony. Unfortunately for children, their parents, and society, these assumptions are not always true.

The extent of child abuse is far greater than we might imagine. In 1992, an estimated 2,936,000 were reported to Child Protective Services (CPS) agencies as alleged victims of child maltreatment (e.g., physical abuse, neglect, sexual abuse, emotional maltreatment). This means that forty-five children per one thousand are reported each year; this number represents a 6 percent increase *per year* over the last decade.[7]

FIGURE 11–3   Guidelines for Detecting Abuse and Neglect

Kind of Abuse	Child's Appearance	Child's Behavior	Parent or Caregiver's Behavior
Physical	Unusual bruises, welts, burns, or fractures Bite marks Frequent injuries, explained as "accidental"	Reports injury by parents Unpleasant, hard to get along with, demanding, often disobeys, frequently causes trouble or interferes with others; breaks or damages things; or is shy, avoids others, is too anxious to please, too ready to let other people say and do things to him or her without protest Frequently late or absent, or comes to school too early or hangs around after school Avoids physical contact with adults Wears long sleeves or other concealing clothing Version of how a physical injury occurred is not believable (does not fit type or seriousness of the injury) Seems frightened of parents Shows little or no distress at separation from parents May seek affection from any adult	History of abuse as a child Uses unnecessarily harsh discipline Offers explanation of child's injury that does not make sense, does not fit injury, or offers no explanation Seems unconcerned about child Sees child as bad, evil, a monster, etc. Misuses alcohol or other drugs Attempts to conceal child's injury or protect identity of responsible party
Emotional	Less obvious signs than other types of mistreatment; behavior is best indication	Unpleasant, hard to get along with, demanding; frequently causes trouble, will not leave others alone Unusually shy, avoids others, too anxious to please, too submissive, puts up with	Blames or belittles child Cold and rejecting Withholds love Treats children unequally Seems not to care about child's problems

Source: U.S. Department of Health, Education, and Welfare, Office of Human Development Services, Administration for Children, Youth, and Families, Head Start Bureau, Indian and Migrant Programs Division, *New Light on an Old Problem*, DHEW Publication No. (OHDS) 78-31108 (Washington, D.C.: Author, 1978), pp. 8–11.

FIGURE 11–3   *continued*

Kind of Abuse	Child's Appearance	Child's Behavior	Parent or Caregiver's Behavior
Emotional (cont.)		unpleasantness from others without protest	
		Either unusually adult or overly young for age (e.g., sucks thumb, rocks constantly)	
		Behind for age physically, emotionally, or intellectually	
Neglect	Often dirty, tired, no energy	Frequently absent	Misuses alcohol or other drugs
	Comes to school without breakfast, often does not have lunch or lunch money	Begs or steals food	Disorganized, upset home life
		Causes trouble in school	Seems not to care what happens
		Often hasn't done homework	Isolated from friends, relatives, neighbors
	Clothes dirty or inappropriate for weather	Uses alcohol or drugs	Does not know how to get along with others
	Alone often, for long periods	Engages in vandalism, sexual misconduct	Long-term chronic illnesses
	Needs glasses, dental care, or other medical attention	Withdrawn or engages in fantasy or babyish behavior	History of neglect as a child
Sexual	Torn, stained, or bloody underclothing	Poor relationships with other children	Protective or jealous of child
	Pain or itching in genital area	Unwilling to participate in physical activities	Encourages child to engage in prostitution or sexual acts in presence of caregiver
	Has venereal disease	Engages in delinquent acts or runs away	Misuses alcohol or other drugs
		Says has been sexually assaulted by parent/caregiver	Frequently absent from home

Child abuse is not new, although it receives greater attention and publicity now than previously. Abuse, in the form of abandonment, infanticide, and neglect, has been documented throughout history. The attitude that children are property partly accounts for the history of abuse. Parents believed, and some still do, that they own their children and can do with them as they please.

The extent to which children are abused is difficult to ascertain but is probably much greater than most people realize. Valid statistics are difficult to come by because the interest in reporting child abuse is relatively new, and the definitions of child abuse and neglect differ from state to state and reports are categorized differently. Probably as many as one million incidents of abuse occur a year, but it is estimated that only one in four cases is reported.

Because of the increasing concern over child abuse, social agencies, hospitals, child care centers, and schools are becoming more involved in identification, treatment, and prevention of this national social problem. To do something about child abuse, those who are involved with children and parents have to know what abuse is. Public Law 93-247, the Child Abuse Prevention and Treatment Act, defines child abuse and neglect as:

> [t]he physical or mental injury, sexual abuse, negligent treatment or maltreatment of a child under the age of eighteen by a person who is responsible for the child's welfare under circumstances which indicate that the child's health or welfare is harmed or threatened thereby as determined in accordance with regulations prescribed by the Secretary.[8]

In addition, all states have some kind of legal or statutory definition for child abuse and treatment. Many states are defining penalties for child abuse.

Just as debilitating as physical abuse and neglect is *emotional abuse,* which occurs when parents, teachers, and others strip children of their self-esteem and self-image. Adults take away children's self-esteem through continually criticizing, belittling, screaming and nagging, creating fear, and intentionally and severely limiting opportunities. Emotional abuse is difficult to define legally and, most certainly, difficult to document. The unfortunate consequence for emotionally abused children is that they are often left in a debilitating environment. Both abuse and neglect adversely affect children's growth and development.

The guidelines in Figure 11–3 may help you identify abuse and neglect; however, one characteristic does not necessarily indicate abuse. You should observe the child's behavior and appearance over a period of time. Teachers should also be willing to give parents the benefit of the doubt about a child's condition.

These are other ways to deal with suspected abuse:

- You should be aware of the official policy and specific reporting procedures of your school system, and should know your legal obligations and the protections from civil and criminal liability specified in your state's reporting law. (All states provide immunity for mandated, good-faith reports.)

- Although you should be familiar with your state's legal definition of abuse and neglect, you are not required to make legal distinctions in order to report. Definitions should serve as guides. If you suspect that a child is abused or neglected, you should report. The teacher's value lies in noticing conditions that indicate that a child's welfare may be in jeopardy.

- Be concerned about the rights of the child—the rights to life, food, shelter, clothing, and security. But also be aware of the parents' rights—particularly their rights to be treated with respect and to be given needed help and support.

- Bear in mind that reporting does not stigmatize a parent as "evil." The report is the start of a rehabilitative process that seeks to protect the child and help the family as a whole.

- A report signifies only the *suspicion* of abuse or neglect. Teachers' reports are seldom unfounded. At the very least, they tend to indicate a need for help and support to the family.

- If you report a borderline case in good faith, do not feel guilty or upset if it is dismissed as unfounded upon investigation. Some marginal cases are found to be valid.

- Don't put off making a report until the end of the school year. Teachers sometimes live with their suspicions until they suddenly fear for the child's safety during the summer months. A delayed report may mean a delay in needed help for the child and the family. Moreover, by reporting late in the school year, you remove yourself as a continued support to both the child protective agency and the reported family.

- If you remove yourself from a case of suspected abuse or neglect by passing it on to superiors, you deprive child protective services of one of their most competent sources of information. For example, a teacher who tells a [children's protective services] worker that the child is especially upset on Mondays directs the worker to investigate conditions in the home on weekends. Few persons other than teachers are able to provide this kind of information. Your guideline should be to resolve any question in favor of the child. When in doubt, report. Even if you, as a teacher, have no immunity from liability and prosecution under state law, the fact that your report is made in good faith will free you from liability and prosecution.

- In the absence of guidance from the protective agency, the teacher can rely on several general rules for dealing with the abused or neglected child:

    Try to give the child additional attention whenever possible.

    Create a more individualized program for the child. Lower your academic expectations and make fewer demands on the child's performance—he or she probably has enough pressures and crises to deal with presently at home.

    Be warm and loving. If possible, let the child perceive you as a special friend to whom he or she can talk. By abusing or neglecting the child, someone has said in a physical way, "I don't love you." You can reassure the child that someone cares.

    Most important, remember that in identifying and reporting child maltreatment, you are not putting yourself in the position of autocrat over a family. The one purpose of your actions is to get help for a troubled child and family; the one goal is to reverse a situation that jeopardizes a child's healthy growth and development.[9]

Causes of Abuse

Why do parents and guardians abuse children? Those who have been responsible for a group of young children will better understand the reasons for child abuse than those who do not know young children. Child rearing is hard work; it requires patience, self-control, understanding, and restraint. It is entirely likely that most parents, at one time or another, have come close to behavior that could be judged abusive.

Stress is one of the most frequent causes of child abuse. Stressful situations arise from employment, divorce or separation, income, quality of family life, moving, death of a family member, violations of law, sickness or injury, and other sources. We are learning more about stress and its effect on health and the general quality of life. Parenting and teaching are stressful occupations, and parents and teachers often need support from professionals to manage stress.

Lack of parenting information is another reason parents abuse or neglect their children. Some parents do not know what to do or how to do it; these cases more frequently result in acts of omission or neglect than in physical violence. Frequently, the child does not receive proper emotional care and support because the parent is ignorant of this need. Lack of parenting information is attributable to several factors. First, in this mobile population, young parents often live apart from their own parents so grandparents have little opportunity to share child-rearing information. Second, the greater number of teenage parents means that many parents are neither emotionally nor cognitively ready to have children; they are really children themselves. We need a national effort to put parenting information into the curricula of every elementary and high school. Fortunately, a trend is beginning in this area.

A third reason for child abuse is the parent's cognitive and emotional state. How people are reared and parenting attitudes that are modeled for them have a tremendous influence on how they will rear their children. Methods of child rearing are handed down from generation to generation, and people who were abused as children are often abusive parents.

A fourth cause of abuse relates to unwanted and unloved children. We like to assume that every child is wanted and loved, but this is not the case. Some parents take out their frustration on their children, whom they view as barriers to their dreams and self-fulfillment. Or a parent may dislike a child because the child is a constant reminder of an absent spouse.

Some people believe a fifth reason for child abuse is the amount of violence in our society. Opponents of violence on television cite it as an example of people's callousness toward each other and poor role modeling for children.

A sixth cause of abuse can be attributed to parental substance abuse. Substance abuse creates a chaotic environment in which children cannot tell what to expect from their parents. Children of alcohol- or drug-using parents are often neglected because the parent is emotionally or physically absent when drunk or high. Substance-abusing parents are the kind of parents who forget to go to the store to buy food for a week. Because children of drug-using parents may not be physically abused, the signs of abuse may be subtle. A teacher might pick up clues that something is wrong at home if the child is not bringing lunch, is wearing the same clothes over and over again or clothes that do not fit, or has worn-out shoes because the parents have not noticed that new ones are needed. In general, drug use renders parents dysfunctional and unable to care for their children adequately.

To fully understand the causes and symptoms of abuse of children, we must consider the entire context of the family setting. Most abused children live in families that are *dysfunctional*. Dysfunctional families are characterized by parental mental instability, confused roles (a parent may function in the role of a child, which thus necessitates that the child function at an adult level), and a chaotic, unpredictable family structure

Program in Practice

THE TONE SCHOOL, TACOMA, WASHINGTON

The Tone School was established in 1988 to offer homeless students an education program that minimizes the disruption in their lives and facilitates their transition back into a permanent school setting.

Program goals include these:

■ Provide a safe nurturing educational environment for children in area shelters, in cars, under bridges, in abandoned buildings, and in other homeless settings.

■ Offer an instructional delivery system focused on individual diagnosis and prescriptive teaching.

■ Supply a full complement of support services needed to assist with the social and emotional impact of homelessness.

■ Assist in the eventual placement and follow-up of children in permanent school settings.

From the first day of enrollment, children start school immediately. Bus transportation is provided from all shelters and temporary housing sites. Within two days each student is clothed as needed from the school clothing bank. Each student is interviewed to assess educational and emotional needs and is given an orientation to the program. Additional counseling is provided for children in the classroom; parent counseling is offered when needed.

Parents are visited in the shelter to assess student and family needs and orient parents to the resources available to them. All health needs of the family are assessed, and health resources are made available to families by the school nurse.

The curriculum includes math, reading, social studies, health, science, art, music, physical education, plus swimming and computer literacy. The average length of stay for a student is about nineteen days. When students leave, the staff helps assure a good transition. Information is provided to the receiving school and teacher, including educational achievements, social-emotional development, and learning style. During the 1992 school year, Tone School served 278 students between the ages of five and fifteen.

and environment. The families are not functioning at a healthy level and are generally unable to care for and nurture a child's growth and development adequately.

Seeking Help

What can be done about child abuse? There must be a conscious effort to educate, treat, and help abusers or potential abusers. The school is a good place to begin. Another source of help is the federal government's National Center on Child Abuse and Neglect, which helps coordinate and develop programs and policies concerning child abuse and neglect. For information, write to the National Center on Child Abuse and Neglect, Children's Bureau, Office of Child Development, Office of Human Development, Department of Health and Human Services, P.O. Box 1182, Washington, D.C. 20012.

Child Help USA handles crisis calls and provides information and referrals to every county in the United States. Their hot line is 1-800-422-4453. The National

Committee to Prevent Child Abuse (NCPCA) is a volunteer organization of concerned citizens that works with community, state, and national groups to expand and disseminate knowledge about child abuse prevention. The NCPCA has chapters in all states; the address for its national office is National Committee to Prevent Child Abuse, 332 S. Michigan Avenue, Suite 1600, Chicago, Illinois 60604; 312-663-3520.

Child Abuse Prevention Curricula

Many curricula have been developed to help teachers, caregivers, and parents work with children to prevent abuse. The primary purposes of these programs are to educate children about abuse and teach them strategies to avoid it. Before using an abuse prevention curriculum with children, staff and parents should help select the curriculum and learn how to use it. Parent involvement is essential. As with anything early childhood professionals undertake, parents' understanding, approval, and support of a program make its goals easier to achieve.

Parents and caregivers should not assume, however, that merely teaching children with an abuse prevention curriculum ends their responsibilities. A parent's responsibility for a child's care and protection never ends. Likewise, professionals have the same responsibility for the children entrusted to them.

HOMELESS CHILDREN

Walking down a city street, you may have encountered homeless men and women, but have you seen a homeless child? Homeless children are the neglected, forgotten, often abandoned segment of the growing homeless population in the United States. The National Coalition for the Homeless estimates there are between 500,000 and 750,000 homeless youth, living in homeless families or on their own.

Homelessness has significant mental, physical, and educational consequences for children. Homelessness results in developmental delays and can produce high levels of distress. Homeless children observed in day care centers exhibited such problem behaviors as short attention spans, weak impulse control, withdrawal, aggression, speech delays, and regressive behaviors. Homeless children are at greater risk for health problems. It is estimated that over 40 percent of homeless children do not attend school, and, if they do enter school, they face many problems relating to their previous school problems (grade failure) and attendance (long trips to attend school). Fortunately, more agencies are responding to the unique needs of homeless children and their families.

Public Law 100-77, the Stewart B. McKinney Homeless Assistance Act of 1987, provides that "each State educational agency shall assure that each child of a homeless individual and each homeless youth have access to a free, appropriate public education which would be provided to the children of a resident of a State."[10]

CHILDHOOD STRESS

The scene of children being left at a child care center or preschool for the first time is familiar to anyone who has worked with young children. Some children quickly become happily involved with new friends in a new setting; some are tense, clinging fearfully to their parents. For many children, separation from the ones they are attached to is a stressful experience. Crying, fear, and tension are the *stress responses,* the symptoms or outward manifestations of children's stress.

Young children are subjected to an increasing number of situations and events that cause them fear and stress (see Figure 11–4). Some of the *stressors* include their parents' divorce, being left at home alone before and after school, parents who constantly argue, the death of a parent or friend, being hospitalized, living in a dangerous neighborhood, fears of nuclear war, poverty, riots, and child abuse. Children are also subjected to stress by parents who hurry them to grow up, act like adults, get into school, and succeed. Other causes of stress are the rush to early schooling, the emphasis on competency testing, and basic skills learning.

Parents and early childhood professionals are becoming aware of the effects stress can have on children: sickness, withdrawal, shyness, loss of appetite, poor sleep patterns, urinary and bowel disorders, and general behavior and discipline problems.

Many early childhood educators believe that one way to alleviate stress is through play. They feel children should be encouraged to play as a therapeutic antidote to the effects of stress. A second way to relieve stress in children is to stop hurrying and pressuring them. Many think children should be free from parental and societal demands so they can enjoy their childhood. Unfortunately, society is as it is; we cannot and should not want to return to the "old days." The tempo of twentieth-century America will continue to be hectic, and demands for individual achievement are increasing. As a result, the emphasis must be on helping children manage stress in their lives.

From preschool on, children should be taught stress reduction techniques, including relaxation and breathing exercises, yoga, physical exercises, meditation, and regular physical activity. Since we cannot slow the pace of society, we need to teach children coping skills. The amount and kinds of stress on children and its effect are causing more early childhood professionals to become involved in programs and agencies that work for solutions to societal issues that cause stress. In fact, reducing stress is one of the premier issues in early childhood education.

FIGURE 11–4   Common Childhood Fears and When to Expect Them

Infants	Toddlers	Preschool	School-Age
Strangers	Separation	Monsters	School
Separation	Toilets	Animals	Injury
Noises	Noises	Bedtime	Bullies
Falling	Bedtime	Day care	Teachers
	Day care	Death	Tests
			Getting lost

Source: Mark Rubinstein, "What Children Fear the Most," *Child* 4 (July/Aug. 1989), p. 42. Used by permission.

READINGS FOR FURTHER ENRICHMENT

Bailey, Donald B., Jr., and Mark Wolery. *Teaching Infants and Preschoolers with Disabilities* (New York: Merrill/Macmillan, 1992)

An informative and comprehensive book with a family-centered focus. Special emphasis is given to infants with disabilities and updates on the latest legislation.

Banks, James A., and Cherry A. McGee Banks, eds. *Multicultural Education: Issues and Perspectives* (Needham Heights, MA: Allyn & Bacon, 1993)

Provides professionals and caregivers with knowledge, insight, and understanding for working effectively with boys and girls; exceptional students; and students from various social class, religious, ethnic, and cultural groups. This book is based on the assumption that schools need reform to effectively provide for diverse groups.

Cook, Ruth E., Annette Tessier, and Virginia B. Armbruster. *Adapting Early Childhood Curricula for Children with Special Needs*, 3d ed. (New York: Merrill/Macmillan, 1992)

Useful helpful insights into early childhood curriculum and special needs children. Early childhood professionals can benefit greatly by learning how to adapt curriculum to the special needs of all children.

Haring, Norris G., Linda McCormick, and Thomas G. Haring, eds. *Exceptional Children and Youth: An Introduction to Special Education*, 6th ed. (New York: Merrill/Macmillan, 1994)

Focuses on the diversity of topics and issues facing professionals and all who work with exceptional children. Explores such areas as full integration of children with disabilities, prevention through early intervention, peer tutoring and social interaction, self-monitoring, and academic learning time.

Lewis, Rena B., and Donald H. Doorlag. *Teaching Special Students in the Mainstream*, 4th ed. (New York: Merrill/Macmillan, 1995)

Presents practical strategies for adapting standard instruction to meet the learning needs of all children in a mainstreamed classroom. Clear and informative account of providing for children with special needs; tips and practical advice.

Mercer, Cecil D., and Ann R. Mercer. *Teaching Students with Learning Problems*, 4th ed. (New York: Merrill/Macmillan, 1993)

Prepares regular classroom professionals, resource room professionals, remedial education professionals, and others for the challenges of individualized programming for students with behavior problems. Contains an in-depth discussion of peer tutoring, motivational techniques, professional coaching, and computer-assisted instruction.

Safford, Philip L. *Integrated Teaching in Early Childhood: Starting in the Mainstream* (White Plains, NY: Longman, 1989)

Demonstrates a teaching philosophy that enables all professionals in public schools and preschools to respond effectively and creatively to the special needs of all children. The practices advocated are all developmentally appropriate and designed to meet individual needs.

Thurman, S. Kenneth, and Anne H. Widerstrom. *Infants and Young Children with Special Needs: A Developmental and Ecological Approach* (Baltimore: Brookes, 1990)

Helps students examine theories of child development and their role in the education of children with special needs. It examines typical and atypical development in all areas, from birth to six. Good resource book.

Wang, Margaret C. *Adaptive Education Strategies: Building on Diversity* (Baltimore: Brookes, 1992)

Suggests innovative plans for the effective education of all students regardless of their background or level of ability. A practical step-by-step guide for developing, implementing, and evaluating adaptive education programs.

ACTIVITIES FOR FURTHER ENRICHMENT

1. Visit several public schools to see how they are providing individualized and appropriate programs for children with disabilities. What efforts are being made to involve parents?

2. Interview parents of children with disabilities. What do they feel are parents' greatest problems? What do they consider the greatest needs for their children? List specific ways they have been involved in educational agencies. How have educational agencies avoided or resisted providing for their or their children's needs?

3. Spend some time in a mainstreamed classroom. What specific skills would you need to become a good professional in such a setting?

4. What structural accommodations are being made in public buildings and schools to provide for people with special needs?

5. Visit a resource room. How is this setting different from a regular classroom? Would you want to be a teacher of children with disabilities in a setting other than a regular classroom? Why?

6. Visit agencies and programs that provide services for people with disabilities. Before you visit, list specific features, services, and facilities you will look for.

7. Compare and contrast a gifted program to a regular classroom setting.

8. What programs does the federal government support for children with special needs in your area? Give specific information.

9. Discuss with people of another culture their culture's attitudes toward people with disabilities. How are they similar or different from your attitudes?

10. John was convinced his two-year-old son was gifted. His wife, Yvonne, disagreed; she said their son was not independent enough. John insisted that the boy's advanced language development was the mark of a bright child. What suggestions would you make to help these parents settle their disagreement? Why might some parents think their children are gifted while other parents might not?

11. Use Mary Ann Wilson and Barry Pehrsson's match-up matrix with a child with disabilities and the primary classroom he or she will attend. Report your findings to your classmates.

12. Volunteer to teach a gifted child for six weeks. What special experiences did you provide? What did you learn? Would you want to teach the gifted? Why?

NOTES

1. Margaret C. Wang, *Adaptive Education Strategies: Building on Diversity* (Baltimore: Brookes, 1992), pp. 3–4.

2. Public Law 101-476, October 30, 1990, Stat. 1103.

3. *United States Statutes at Large,* vol. 89 (Washington, D.C.: U.S. Government Printing Office, n.d.).

4. Ann E. Lupkowski and Elizabeth A. Lupkowski, "Meeting the Needs of Gifted Preschoolers," *Children Today* (March/Apr. 1985), pp. 10–14.

5. Michael Lewis with Leslie Kane, "Early Signals of Gifted," *Mothers Today* (Jan./Feb. 1985), p. 14.

6. J. Gallagher, P. Weiss, K. Oglesby, and T. Thomas, *The Status of Gifted/Talented Education: United States Survey Needs, Practices, and Policies* (Los Angeles: National/State Leadership Training Institute on the Gifted and Talented, 1983).

7. National Center on Child Abuse Prevention Research, *Current Trends in Child Abuse Reporting and Fatalities: The Results of the 1992 Annual Fifty State Survey* (Chicago: National Committee to Prevent Child Abuse, 1993), pp. 2, 4.

8. *United States Statutes at Large,* vol. 88, pt. 1 (Washington, D.C.: U.S. Government Printing Office, 1976), p. 5.

9. U.S. Department of Health, Education, and Welfare, Office of Human Development, Office of Child Development, Children's Bureau National Center on Child Abuse and Neglect, *Child Abuse and Neglect: The Problem and Management: Vol. 2. The Roles and Responsibilities of Professionals,* DHEW Publication No. (OHD) 75-30074, pp. 70–72.

10. Public Law 100-77, the Stewart B. McKinney Homeless Assistance Act, Title VII-B, Subtitle B—Education for Homeless Youth, July 1987.

Guiding Children
Developing Prosocial Behavior

After you have read and studied this chapter, you will be able to:

☐ Distinguish among guidance, discipline, and punishment

☐ Explain the importance of helping children develop an internal locus of control

☐ Discuss a rationale for guiding children's behavior and helping them become responsible

☐ Evaluate the effectiveness of positive reinforcement in developing appropriate behaviors in children

☐ Interpret different reinforcement systems for managing behavior

☐ Develop a philosophy of guiding children's behavior

☐ Compare and contrast different theories of guiding children's behavior

☐ Identify the essential characteristics of effective behavior guidance

☐ Become conversant about issues related to discipline and young children

☐ Identify and implement appropriate child guidance practices

☐ Describe the peace education movement

Some Juvenile Crimes Down, but Trends Point Up

They are responsible for 14 percent of the nation's murders, 26 percent of all robberies and 44 percent of car thefts. They commit one-third of all burglaries and 16 percent of the rapes. They are America's children, and increasingly they are armed and dangerous.[1]

This lead-in material paints a pretty grim picture of the nation's youth. The local media and U.S. newspapers underscore public and professional interest in children's behaviors at home, on the streets, and in early childhood programs. The public sees children, at ever younger ages, being mean and nasty to their peers and adults. They also see young children as victims of violence and crime by ever-younger children.

Who is to blame? Certainly parents receive their share. But the public also blames the educational system for allowing and even promoting uncivilized behavior. Parents interpret children's misbehavior as one indicator that educators have gone "soft" on discipline. Educators are accused of not teaching children to act civilly and for not having the manners, morals, and behavior necessary for living in civilized society.

Contemporary society also receives its share of blame for the way children act. There is national concern about the breakup of the family, the breakdown of moral standards, violence on television, widespread substance use, rampant crime, and general disrespect for authority. These trends are seen as evidence of parental and societal erosion of authority and discipline beginning in the earliest years. Again, many believe that current social ills are caused by parents' and educators' failures to discipline children.

The present and future behavior and misbehavior of children is the subject of much debate. Parents and the public look to early childhood professionals for assistance in helping children learn how to live in a democratic society.

DISCIPLINE DEFINED

So if America sees its children as undisciplined, the flip side is that they need discipline. But what does the term *discipline* mean? *Discipline* comes from the Latin word *disciplin,* which means to instruct or teach. And this is what all who have any responsibility for children should do—discipline or *teach* them how to guide and direct their own behavior and get along with others. The emphasis is on *teaching* children how to become responsible for guiding and directing their own behavior.

Viewed as teaching, discipline is a process of helping children build positive behaviors. From this perspective, discipline (teaching) involves *behavior guidance*, a process by which *all* children learn to control and direct their own behavior and become independent and self-reliant. In this view, behavior guidance is a process of helping children develop skills useful to them over a lifetime. Professionals' and parents' roles are to (a) guide children toward developing self-control, (b) encourage children to be independent, (c) meet their intellectual and emotional needs, (d) establish expectations for children, (e) organize appropriate behaviors and arrange environments so self-discipline can occur, and (f) change their own behavior when necessary.

The goal of most parents and professionals is to have children behave in socially acceptable and appropriate ways that contribute to and promote living in a democratic society. (It will be helpful here to review the core values outlined in chap. 9 on pp. 362–364.) Since this goal is never really fully achieved, we should view guidance of children's behavior as a process of learning by doing. Children cannot learn to develop appropriate behaviors and learn to be responsible by themselves. Just as no one learns to ride a bicycle by reading a book on the subject, children do not learn to guide themselves by being told what to do all the time. Maria Montessori often remarked that "discipline is not telling." Children must be shown and taught through precept and example. Children need opportunities to develop, practice, and perfect their abilities to control and guide their own behavior. They need the guidance, help, support, and encouragement of parents and early childhood professionals.

Thus, effective guidance of children's behavior at home and in early childhood programs consists of these essential elements:

- Knowing yourself
- Knowing child development
- Meeting children's needs in individually and culturally appropriate ways
- Helping children build new behaviors and skills of independence and responsibility
- Establishing appropriate expectations
- Arranging and modifying the environment so that appropriate, expected behavior and self-control are possible
- Modeling appropriate behavior
- Avoiding creating or encouraging behavior problems
- Involving parents and families
- Promoting empathy and prosocial behavior

Let us take a closer look at each of these essential elements.

Knowing Yourself

The first rule in guiding children's behavior is to *know yourself*. Unless you know your attitudes toward discipline and behavior, it will be hard to practice a rational and consistent program of guidance and discipline. So, develop a philosophy of discipline. What do you believe about child rearing, discipline, and children?

Knowing yourself and what you believe also makes it easier for you to share with and counsel parents about discipline. Today, many parents find the challenges of child rearing overwhelming. They do not know what to do and consequently look to professionals for help. Knowing what you believe, based on sound principles of how children grow, develop, and learn, enables you to work with parents confidently.

Knowing Child Development

It may be overstating the obvious, but the foundation for guiding the behavior of all the children we teach and care for is to know what they are like. Unfortunately, not all professionals are as knowledgeable about children as they should be. This means that they expect behaviors of some children that are more appropriate for younger or older children, and here lies the problem. Children do not behave well when professionals expect too much or too little of them based on their development or when they expect them to behave in ways that inappropriate for them as individuals. So, a key for guiding children's behavior is to know—really know—what they are like. This is one reason child development information is presented in this book (see, for example, the Program in Practice features discussing infants and toddlers in chap. 6).

Self-Regulation

Self-regulation is the ability to comply with a request; initiate and cease activities according to situational demands; modulate the intensity, frequency, and duration of verbal and motor acts in social and educational settings; postpone acting on a desired object or goal; and generate socially approved behavior in the absence of external monitors. Self-regulation is a lifelong goal, not necessarily something that children achieve in the early years. We are always in the process of refining our ability to self-regulate our behavior.

Having knowledge about when and how young children are able to regulate their own behavior makes it easier to guide their behavior. The stages of development of self-regulation in the early years are outlined in Figure 12–1. The figure also illustrates the behavioral features of each stage as well as parent and professional behaviors that promote self-regulation.

The child development information provided you in chapters 6 through 9 will help you match your expectations to children's abilities.

Meeting Children's Needs

Part of knowing child development and knowing children is knowing and meeting their needs. Abraham Maslow felt that human growth and development was oriented toward *self-actualization,* the striving to realize one's potential. He felt that humans are internally motivated by five basic needs that constitute a hierarchy of motivating behaviors, progressing from physical needs to self-fulfillment. Maslow's hierarchy (see Figure 6–6 for the graphic representation of the hierarchy) moves through physical needs, safety and security needs, belonging and affection needs, and self-esteem needs culminating in self-actualization. Let us look at an example of each of these stages and behaviors to see how we can apply them to guiding children's behavior.

- *Physical needs.*   Children's abilities to guide their behavior depends in part on how well their physical needs are met. Children do their best in school, for example, when they are well nourished. Thus parents should provide for their

FIGURE 12–1   The Development of Self-Regulation

Phases in the Development of Self-Regulation	Age	Features	Caregiver Roles
Neurophysiological modulation	Birth to 2 or 3 months	Development of clearly defined periods of wakefulness; development of schemes to self-soothe, e.g., nonnutritive sucking.	Provide interactions and opportunities for stimulation; provide routines of eating and sleeping.
Sensorimotor modulation	3 months to 1 year	Ability to engage in sensorimotor acts and change an act in response to events. Modulations help infants become aware of their own actions in holding, reaching, and playing. When infants differentiate their own actions from those of others, the potential for self-regulation emerges.	Provide caregiver–infant interactions; provide activities for the infant.
Control	1 year to 18 months	Shows awareness of social and task demands defined by caregiver. Can initiate, maintain, modulate, or cease physical acts, communication, and emotional signals.	Provide patterns of communication and interaction. Provide opportunities for toddlers to notice the effects of their actions. Call attention to expectations. Channel the toddler into desired activities.
Self-control	2 years or older	Compliance and emergent abilities to delay an act or request and to behave according to caregiver and social expectations in the absence of external monitors.	Continue to provide and call attention to expectations. Avoid "controlling" toddlers' behaviors. Avoid being critical of behaviors.
Self-regulation	3 years or older	Growing ability to adapt and regulate behavior to set behavioral demands.	Continue to provide and call attention to expectations. Encourage independence, provide verbal interaction, and give reasons for behavior.

Source: Adapted from Claire B. Kopp, "Antecedents of Self-Regulation: A Developmental Perspective," *Developmental Psychology* 18 (March 1982), p. 200. Copyright 1982 by the American Psychological Association. Adapted by permission.

children's nutritional needs by giving them breakfast. Professionals should also stress the nutritional and health benefits of eating breakfast. The quality of the environment is also important. If classrooms are dark and noisy and smell of stale air, children cannot be expected to "behave." Children also need adequate rest to do and be their best. The amount of rest is an individual matter, but many young children need eight to ten hours of sleep. A tired child cannot meet many of the expectations of schooling.

- *Safety and security.*   Children should not have to fear parents or professionals and should feel comfortable and secure at home and school. Asking or forcing children to do school tasks for which they do not have the skills makes them feel insecure, and when children are afraid and insecure, they are under a great deal of tension. Consider also the dangers many urban children face, such as crime, drugs, and homelessness, or the insecurity of children who live in an atmosphere of domestic violence. So, in addition, part of guiding children's behavior includes providing safe and secure communities/neighborhoods. (See chap. 13 for a discussion of developing social capital.)

- *Belonging and affection.*   Children need love and affection and the sense of belonging that comes from being given jobs to do, being given responsibilities, and helping make classroom and home decisions. Love and affection needs are also satisfied when parents hold, hug, and kiss their children and tell them "I love you." Professionals meet children's affectional needs when they smile, speak pleasantly, are kind and gentle, treat children with courtesy and respect, and genuinely value each child for who she or he is. An excellent way to show respect for children and demonstrate to them belonging and affection is to greet them personally when they come into the classroom, center, or home. A personal greeting helps children feel wanted and secure and promotes feelings of self-worth. In fact, all early childhood programs should begin with this daily validation of each child.

- *Self-esteem.*   When children view themselves as worthy, responsible, and competent, they act that way. Children's views of themselves come primarily from parents and professionals. Experiencing success gives them feelings of high self-esteem, and it is up to parents and professionals to give all children opportunities for success. The foundation for self-esteem is success and achievement.

- *Self-actualization.*   Children want to use their talents and abilities to do things for themselves and be independent. Professionals and parents can help children become independent by helping them learn to dress themselves, go to the restroom by themselves, and take care of their environments. They can also help children set achievement and behavior goals ("Tell me what you are going to build with your blocks") and encourage them to evaluate their behavior ("Let's talk about how you cleaned up your room").

These points highlight the need for professionals and parents to consider children's basic needs in the process of helping them guide and develop responsibility for their behavior.

Children have a basic need for love and affection and are more capable of responsible behavior when this need is met. Meeting the full range of children's needs as outlined by Maslow's hierarchy is an excellent way to help children guide their own behavior.

Helping Children Build New Behaviors

Locus of Control

Helping children build new behaviors means that we help them learn that they are primarily responsible for their own behavior, that the pleasures and rewards for appropriate behavior are internal, from within them as opposed to always coming from outside (i.e., from the approval and praise of others). This concept we refer to as *locus of control*—the source or place of control. The preferred and recommended locus of control for young and old alike is internal. We want children to control their own behavior. When the locus of control is external, children are controlled by others; they are always told what to do and how to behave. We must try to avoid developing an external locus of control in children.

It would be naive, however, to think that a child is born with this desired inner-directed locus of control. Instead, the process of helping children develop an internal locus of control begins at birth and continues through the early childhood years. In fact, developing an inner locus of control is a never-ending process that goes on throughout life.

One of the criticisms of programs and practices in which children's behaviors are constantly reinforced through praise and rewards is that this approach promotes an external locus of control (i.e., the person providing the reinforcement and the reinforcement itself). The argument goes that children behave only because someone else is telling them to and rewarding them for the behavior. Rewards, such as genuine praise and other means of reinforcement, are entirely proper when used wisely and appropriately. Everyone likes praise, and there should be praise for honest efforts. We will discuss this point further shortly.

Empowering Children

Helping children build new behaviors creates a sense of responsibility and self-confidence. As children are given responsibility, they develop greater self-discipline, so that professionals and parents have to provide less guidance and children are less of a "discipline problem." Ironically, many professionals and parents hesitate to let children assume responsibilities, and without responsibilities, children are bored and frustrated and become discipline problems—the very opposite of what is intended. Guidance is not a matter of professionals getting children to please them by making remarks such as "Show me how perfect you can be," "Don't embarrass me by your behavior in front of others," "I want to see nice groups," or "I'm waiting for quiet." Rather, it is important to instill in children a sense of independence and responsibility for their own behavior. For example, you might say, "You have really worked a long time cutting out the flower you drew. I like how you kept working on it until you were finished. Would you like some tape to hang it up with?"

Helping children and warmly supporting their efforts is one of the most effective and humane forms of guidance. In addition, supporting children's efforts enables them to become independent of adults and do things for themselves. Identify some ways professionals can support children in their efforts to do things for themselves.

Parents and professionals can do a number of things to help children develop new behaviors:

- *Give children responsibilities.*   All children, from an early age, should have responsibilities, that is, tasks that are their job to do and for which they are responsible. Being responsible for completing tasks and doing such things as putting toys and learning materials away promotes a positive sense of self-worth and conveys to children that in a community people have responsibilities for making the community work well.

- *Give children choices.*   Life is full of choices—some require thought and decisions; others do not. But every time you make a decision, you are being responsible and exercising your right to decide. Children like to have choices, and choices help them become independent, confident, and self-disciplined. Learning to make choices early in life lays the foundation for decision making later. These are some guidelines for giving children choices:

    Give children choices when there are valid choices to make. When it comes time to clean up the classroom, do not let children choose

Very young children can begin to learn responsibility by picking up and putting away their toys, but parents and professionals must arrange the environment to promote that kind of responsibility. Although this child may be putting toys in the basket as a kind of game, caregivers and parents can reinforce this type of behavior through positive responses.

whether they want to participate, but let them pick between collecting the scissors or the crayons.

Help children make choices. Rather than say "What would you like to do today?" say "Sarah, you have a choice between working in the wood-working center or the computer center. Which would you like to do?"

When professionals do not want children to make a decision, they should not offer them a choice.

In the High/Scope curriculum (chap. 4), children select what activities they will participate in and then are accountable for their choices. Making choices is key to developing in children responsible behavior that internalizes the locus of control.

- *Support children.*   Early childhood professionals must support children in their efforts to be successful. They can arrange the environment and make opportunities available for children to be able to do things. Successful accomplishments are a major ingredient of positive behavior.

Establishing Appropriate Expectations

Expectations relate to and set the boundaries for desired behavior. Expectations are the guideposts children use in learning to direct their own behavior. Like everyone, children need guideposts along life's way.

Professionals and parents need to set appropriate expectations for children, which means they must decide what behaviors they expect of children. When children know what parent and professionals expect, they can better achieve those expectations. Up to a point, the more we expect of children, the more and better they achieve. Generally, professionals and parents expect too little of most children.

However, having expectations for children is not enough. Professionals have to help children know and understand what the expectations are *and* help them meet these expectations. Some children will need little help in meeting expectations; others will need demonstration, explanation, encouragement, and support as they learn to meet expectations.

Setting Limits

Setting limits is closely associated with establishing expectations and relates to what is unacceptable behavior. For example, knocking over a block tower built by someone else and running in the classroom are generally considered unacceptable behaviors. Setting clear limits is important for three reasons:

1. It helps professionals clarify in their own minds what they believe is unacceptable *based on their knowledge of child development, children, their families and their culture.* When professionals do not set limits, inconsistency can occur.
2. Setting limits helps children act with confidence because they know which behaviors are acceptable.
3. Limits provide children with security. Children want and need limits.

In a High/Scope classroom (see chap. 4), children are encouraged to make choices about what activities they will engage in and how they will accomplish the activity. Giving children choices is an excellent way to help them develop independence and responsibility.

As children grow and mature, the limits change and are adjusted to developmental levels, programmatic considerations, and life situations.

Classroom Rules

Although I like to talk about and think in terms of expectations and limits, most early childhood professionals think and talk about rules. This is fine, but here are some additional guidelines.

Plan classroom rules from the first day of class. As the year goes on, you can involve children in establishing classroom rules, but in the beginning, children want and need to know what they can and cannot do. For example, rules might relate to changing groups and bathroom routines. Whatever rules you establish, they should be fair, reasonable, and appropriate to the children's age and maturity. Keep rules to a minimum; the fewer the better. For example, in Cindy Gajdos's classroom of four-year-olds at the Texas Women's University Nursery School, the rules are simple, few, and consistently enforced:

1. Be gentle with your friends.
2. We are all friends at nursery school.
3. Use an inside voice.
4. Keep your feet on the floor.
5. Use your words when you have a problem.

The children are reminded of these rules and are encouraged to conform to them. Four-year-olds can realistically be expected to follow these guidelines, so there is less chance for misbehavior. Children are able to become responsible for their own behavior in a positive, accepting atmosphere within which they know what the expectations are for them. Review the rules, and have children evaluate their behavior against the rules. You can have expectations without having rules. If you have activities ready for children when they enter the classroom, you establish the expectation that upon entering the classroom, they should be busy.

Arranging and Modifying the Environment

Environment plays a key role in children's ability to guide their behavior. For example, if parents want a child to be responsible for taking care of his room, they should arrange the environment so he can do so, by providing shelves, hangers, and drawers at child height. Similarly, a professional should arrange the classroom so children can get and return their own papers and materials, use learning centers, and have time to work on individual projects.

In child care centers, early childhood classrooms, and family day care homes, professionals arrange the environment so that it supports the purposes of the program and makes appropriate behavior possible. Sandra Crosser provides the following suggestions for organizing the early childhood classroom:

1. Is there an open area large enough for the entire group to meet together?
2. Does the physical arrangement of work centers allow for quiet areas to be located away form noisier activities?
3. Are centers arranged within the classroom so that they are defined by low boundaries, such as room dividers, shelves, tables, floor mats, or tape? Can the teacher see over and around equipment so that all children are visible at all times?
4. Are most materials located where children can reach them without asking the teacher for help?
5. Is there a place for everything?
6. The busier and more involved the children are, the less likely they are to exhibit behavior problems.
7. Are routines set?[2]

The Classroom as Reinforcer

Behavior modification strategies can also be applied to the physical setting of the classroom. The classroom should be arranged so that it is conducive to the behaviors the professional wants to reinforce. If a professional wants to encourage independent work, there must be places and time for children to work alone. Disruptive behavior is often encouraged by classroom arrangements that force children to walk over other children to get to equipment and materials. A professional may find that the classroom actually contributes to misbehaviors. The atmosphere of the classroom or the learning environment must be such that new behaviors are possible.

Although professionals want to encourage independence, they often make the children ask for materials, which the professional must then locate. This practice discourages independence.

The same situation applies in the home. If a parent wants a child to keep her room neat and clean, it must be possible for the child to do so. The child should also be shown how to take care of her room. The parent may have to lower shelves or install clothes hooks. When the physical arrangement is to the child's size, the child can be taught how to use a clothes hanger and where to hang certain clothes. A child's room should have a place for everything; these places should be accessible and easy to use.

A Rewarding Environment

The classroom should be a place where children can do their best work and be on their best behavior. It should be a rewarding place to be. Components of an environmentally rewarding classroom are

- opportunities for children to display their work,
- opportunities for freedom of movement (within guidelines),
- opportunities for independent work, and
- a variety of work stations and materials based on children's interests.

Time and Transitions

Generally more important to adults than children, time plays a major role in every program. Some guidelines in relation to time and its use are these:

1. Do not waste children's time. They should be involved in interesting, meaningful activities from the moment they enter the center, classroom, or family day care home.
2. Do not make children wait. When children have to wait for materials, their turn, and so forth, provide them with something else to do, such as listening to a story or playing in the block center. When children have to wait, problems can occur, because children like to be busy and involved.

Transitions are times when children move from one activity to another. They should be made as smoothly as possible. In one program, teachers sing "It's Cleanup Time" as a transition from one activity to cleanup and then to another activity.

Routines

Establish classroom routines from the beginning. Children need the confidence and security of a routine that will help them do their best. A routine also helps prevent discipline problems, because children know what to do and can learn to do it without a lot of disturbance. Parents need to establish routines in the home; if the child knows the family always eats at 5:30 P.M., he can be expected to be there. A professional must also be consistent. Consistency plays an important role in managing behavior in both the home and classroom. If children know what to expect in terms of routine and behavior, they will behave better.

Modeling Appropriate Behavior

We have all heard the maxim "Telling is not teaching." Nevertheless, we tend to teach by giving instructions. Professionals soon realize, however, that actions speak louder than words. We encourage children to be impolite when we are impolite to them. How will students learn what it means to be courteous if they are not shown courtesy?

Children see and remember how other people act. The child then tries the act, and if this new action brings a reward of some kind, the child repeats it. The leading proponent of the modeling approach to learning is Albert Bandura, who believes that most behavior people exhibit is learned from the behavior of a model or models. He thinks children tend to model behavior that brings rewards from parents and professionals.

A model may be someone whom we respect or find interesting and whom we believe is being rewarded for the behavior he or she exhibits. Groups may also serve as models. For example, it is common to hear a professional in an early childhood classroom comment, "I like how Cristina and Carlos are sitting quietly and listening to the story." Immediately following such a remark, you can see the group of children settle down to listen quietly to the story. Models children emulate do not necessarily have to be from real life; they can come from television and books. In addition, the modeled behavior does not have to be socially acceptable to be reinforcing.

The early childhood professional should use the following techniques to help children learn through modeling:

- *Showing.*   The professional shows children where the block corner is and how and where the blocks are stored.

- *Demonstration.*   The professional performs a task while students watch. For example, the professional demonstrates the proper way to put the blocks away and how to store them. Extensions of the demonstration method are to have the children practice the demonstration while the professional supervises and to ask a child to demonstrate to other children.

- *Modeling.*   Modeling occurs when the professional practices the behavior expected of the children. Also, the professional can call children's attention to the desired behavior when another child models it.

- *Supervision.*   Supervision is a process of reviewing, insisting, maintaining standards, and following up. If children are not performing the desired behavior, you will need to *review* the behavior. You must be consistent in your expectations of desired behavior. Children will soon learn they do not have to put away their blocks if you allow them not to do it even once. Remember, you are responsible for setting up the environment to enable the children's learning to take place.

Professionals need to model and demonstrate social and group-living behaviors as well, including using simple courtesies (saying "Please," "Thank you," "You're welcome," etc.) and practicing cooperation, sharing, and respect for others.

Avoiding Problems

Parents and professionals actually encourage a great deal of children's misbehavior. Professionals see too much and ignore too little. Parents expect perfection and adult behavior. If parents and professionals focus on building responsible behavior, there will be less need to solve behavior problems.

Ignoring inappropriate behavior is probably one of the most overlooked strategies for managing an effective learning setting and guiding children's behavior. Ironically, many professionals feel guilty when they use this strategy. They believe that ignoring undesirable behaviors is not good teaching. While ignoring some inappropriate behavior is an effective strategy, ignoring behavior must be combined with positive reinforcement of desirable behavior. Thus, one ignores inappropriate behavior and at the same time reinforces appropriate behavior. A combination of positive reinforcement and ignoring can lead to desired behavior.

When a child does something good or is on-task, reward him or her. Use verbal and nonverbal reinforcement and privileges to help assure that the appropriate behavior will continue. Catch children being good; that is, look for good behavior. This helps improve not only individual behavior but group behavior as well.

Writing contracts for certain work experiences is a great way to involve the child in planning his or her own work and behavior. Rules to follow in contracting are to keep contracts short and uncomplicated, make an offer the child cannot refuse,

Modeling appropriate behavior and demonstrating for children how to act and do things are two of the most important and easily accomplished means of helping children learn to guide their behavior.

make sure the child is able to do what you contract for, and pay off when the contract is completed.

Involving Parents and Families

Involving parents and families is a wonderful way to gain invaluable insights about children. Furthermore, parents and professionals must be partners and work cooperatively in effectively guiding children's behaviors.

Another important rule in guiding behavior is to *know your children.* A good way to learn about the children you teach is through home visits. If you do not have an opportunity to visit the home, a parent conference is also valuable. Either way, some of the information you should gather is the child's health history and interests; the child's attitude toward schooling; the parents' educational expectations for the child; what school support is available in the home (e.g., books, places to study); home conditions that would support or hinder school achievement (such as where the child sleeps); parents' attitudes toward schooling and discipline; parents' support of the child (e.g., encouragement to do well); parents' interests and abilities; and parents' desire to become involved in the school.

The visit or conference offers an opportunity for the professional to share some ideas with the parents. You should, for example, express your desire for the child to do well in school; encourage the parents to take part in school and classroom programs; suggest (if asked) ways to help the child learn; describe some of the school programs; give information about school events, projects, and meetings; and explain your beliefs about discipline.

Working with and involving parents also provides professionals opportunities to help parents with parenting skills and child-related problems. The foundation for children's behavior is built in the home, and some parents unwittingly encourage and promote children's misbehavior and antisocial behavior. In many ways, parents promote antisocial behavior in their children by using punitive, negative, and overly restrictive punishment. In particular, when children are enrolled in child care programs at an early age, professionals have an ideal opportunity to help parents learn about and use positive discipline approaches to child rearing. (Chap. 13 is devoted entirely to parent, family, and community involvement.)

Promoting Empathy and Prosocial Behavior

In considering life in the 1990s, there is a trend toward reflecting back on the 1980s as a decade of greed and selfishness—the me generation. With this in mind, professionals are now focusing on helping children learn how to share, care for, and assist others. We call these and similar behaviors *prosocial behaviors.*

Parents and professionals want to encourage *altruistic behavior* in children, that is, intentional behaviors that benefit others. Part of altruistic behavior involves *empathy,* the ability to vicariously feel another person's emotions and feelings. As mentioned in chapter 4, Piaget believed that young children are egocentric, which prevents them from having empathy for others. This is another area in which

Piaget's theory is being modified and updated based on continuing research. We now know that children as young as two and three years of age are quite capable of being empathetic.

Parents and professionals can do a number of things to promote prosocial behaviors that will enable children to show concern for others; help others through acts of kindness and sharing; and respond to the conditions of others through affection, comfort, sympathy, joy, and love:

1. *Model behaviors that are caring, loving, and helping.*   When young children see adults helping others, sharing with others, and comforting others in distress, then they too learn that such behaviors are important and worthwhile. Parents and professionals should also provide children opportunities to see other children and adults modeling prosocial behaviors. Organizations such as Junior Girl Scouts, Brownies, Cub Scouts, and others that traditionally engage in helping activities offer a social context for children to see people helping others and for them to do the same.

2. *Provide opportunities to engage children in helping and service to others.*   For example, beginning in the toddler years, children can visit with the elderly, bringing them treats and artwork. What is important is for professionals to offer children the chance to engage in helping others in meaningful ways.

3. *Parents and professionals can help children "put themselves in someone else's place" by asking them how they think about a particular situation or event.*   For example, a caregiver might ask,"How do you think Laura feels because you won't share your toys with her?"

Parents and professionals want to promote the intrinsic development of empathy, that is, a desire to engage in sympathetic behaviors because it is the right and good thing to do. They should avoid rewarding children for these behaviors. When rewards are the consequences of empathy and helping, then children learn that acts of helping or kindness are based on these external rewards. Certainly children can and should be complimented for doing good things, and they should be encouraged to assist others. However, they should not learn that the reward is the reason for helping others. Helping and kindness are the rewards themselves.

COOPERATIVE DISCIPLINE

Cooperative discipline is the name of a classroom management program published by American Guidance Service (Circle Pines, MN 55014). It encourages teachers, parents, administrators, and parents to work as a team in helping students choose appropriate behaviors.[3]

Cooperative Living and Learning

Apart from implementing a commercial program, early childhood professionals can do a lot to promote cooperative living in which children help each other direct their behavior. Recall from chapter 2 our discussion of Vygotsky's theory of social relations. Children are born seeking social interactions, and social relations are necessary for children's learning and development. Peers help each other learn.

Children's natural social groups and play groups are ideal and natural settings in which to help children assist each other in learning new behaviors and being responsible for their own behavior. The classroom as a whole is an important social group. Classroom meetings in which professionals and children talk can serve many useful functions. They can talk about expected behaviors from day to day ("When we are done playing with toys, what do we do with them?"), review with children what they did in a particular center or situation, and help them anticipate what they will do in future situations ("Tomorrow morning when we visit the Senior Citizen Center . . ."). In all these situations, children are cooperatively engaged in thinking about, talking about, and cooperatively learning how to engage in appropriate behavior. Furthermore, children can help identify a particular problem or misbehavior and discuss appropriate behavior.

The teacher and child also form an important social group that influences behavior. The teacher can model a particular behavior, engage a child in a discussion of behavior, and compliment the child on behavior.

Professionals must initiate, support, and foster a cooperative, collaborative learning community in the classroom in which children are involved in developing and setting guidelines and devising classroom and, by extension, individual norms of behavior. Professionals "assist" children but do not do things for them, and they ask questions that make children think about their behavior—how it influences the class, themselves, and others. This process of cooperative living occurs daily. Discussions grow out of existing problems, and guidance is provided on needs of children and the classroom.

The account of the Stride Rite Intergenerational Day Care Center in the color insert illustrates the importance and benefits of social interactions across age ranges. Children helping the elderly and the elderly helping children have many social, cognitive, and behavioral benefits.

Teaching Conflict Management and Resolution[4]

Quite often, conflicts result from children's interactions with others. Increasingly, early childhood professionals are advocating teaching children ways to manage and resolve their own conflicts.

Teaching conflict resolution strategies is important for several reasons. First, it makes sense to give children the skills they need to handle and resolve their own conflicts. Second, teaching conflict resolution skills to children enables them to use these same skills as adults. Third, the peaceful resolution of interpersonal conflicts contributes, in the long run, to world peace. In this sense, peace curricula and attempts to teach children behaviors associated with peacemaking begin with harmony in the child care and preschool classroom families. When professionals involve children in efforts to resolve interpersonal behavior problems peacefully, they intuitively learn that peace begins with them.

Strategies used to teach and model conflict resolution include these:

- *Talk it over.*   Children can learn that talking about a problem often leads to a resolution and reveals that there are always two sides to an argument. Talking also helps children think about other ways to solve problems. Children can and should be involved in the solution of their interpersonal problems *and* classroom and activity problems.

- *Model resolutions.*   Caregivers can model resolutions for children: "Erica, please don't knock over Shantrell's building because she worked hard to build it"; "Barry, what is another way (instead of hitting) you can tell Pam that she is sitting in your chair?"

- *Teach children to say "I'm sorry."*   Saying "I'm sorry" is one way to heal and resolve conflicts. It can be a step toward good behavior. Piaget maintained that prior to the stage of concrete operations (before the age of seven), young children do not have the cognitive maturity to take another's point of view. Since they cannot "decenter," it is difficult for them to know how others feel and therefore to be sorry for something. Thus, the very young are not cognitively able to learn to say "I'm sorry" and have real conviction that they indeed are sorry. Nevertheless, children need to be reared in an environment in which they see and experience others being sorry for their inappropriate actions toward others.

- *Do something else.*   Teach children to get involved in another activity. Children can learn that they do not always have to play with a toy someone else is playing with. They can get involved in another activity with a different toy. They can do something else now and play with the toy later. Chances are, however, that by getting involved in another activity they will forget about the toy they were ready to fight for.

- *Take turns.*   Taking turns is a good way for children to learn that they cannot always be first, have their own way, or do the prized activity. Taking turns brings equality and fairness to interpersonal relations.

- *Share.*   Sharing is a good behavior to promote in any setting. Children have to be taught how to share and how to behave when others do not share. Children can be helped to select another toy rather than hitting or grabbing. Again, keep in mind that during the early years children are egocentric, and acts of sharing are likely to be motivated by expectations of a reward or approval such as being thought of as a "good" boy or girl.

BEHAVIOR MODIFICATION

A popular approach to guidance based on behavior rather than on feelings is *behavior modification.* An important concept of behavior modification is that all behavior is caused. Everyone acts the way they do for reasons, although the reasons may not always be apparent; in fact, children do not always know why they behave a certain way. How often have you heard the expressions "He didn't know what he was doing," "I don't know why she acts like she does," "I can't understand why I did that," and "I didn't know what I was doing"?

A second basic concept is that behavior results from reinforcement received from the environment. American psychologist Edward L. Thorndike (1874–1949) observed that the consequences of one's behavior influence future behavior. He formalized this observation in his learning principle, the *law of effect*. If a satisfying condition follows a behavior, the child tends to repeat that behavior, and the strength of the stimulus-response connection increases. If an unsatisfying condition follows a behavior, the individual tends not to repeat that behavior, and the stimulus-response connection weakens or disappears. The law of effect points out how important the quality of feedback is for behavior.

This law has gradually come to be known as the *imperial law of effect,* which says that the consequences of particular responses determine whether the response will be continued and therefore learned. In other words, what happens to an individual after acting in a particular way determines whether he or she continues to act that way. If a child cries and is immediately given a cookie, and this happens several times, that youngster will probably learn that crying is a good way to get cookies. And the cycle continues: receiving cookies reinforces crying behavior. We should understand that this behavior is not always planned; a child does not necessarily think, "I'm going to cry because I know Mom will give me a cookie." The child may have cried; the mother, to stop the crying, gave a cookie to the child, who then associated the two events.

B. F. Skinner (1904–1990) is given credit for many of the technological and pedagogical applications of behavior modification, including programmed instruction. Skinner also emphasized the role of the environment in providing people with clues that reinforce their behavior.

In behavior management, we are concerned with behavior modification, or changing behavior. As used in our discussion, *behavior modification* means the *conscious* application of the methods of behavioral science, with the intent of changing children's behavior. Professionals and parents have always been concerned with changing children's behavior, but it is implicit in the term *behavior modification* that we mean the conscious use of techniques to change behavior.

Behaviorists maintain that all behavior is learned and, in this sense, all behavior is caused by reinforcers from which individuals gain pleasure of some kind. The problem, however, is that professionals and parents have usually changed children's behavior without realizing it. Professionals and parents should be more aware of the effect they have on children's behavior. To use power ignorantly and unconsciously to achieve ends that are basically dehumanizing to children is not good teaching practice. For example, when a child first comes to school, she may not understand that sitting quietly is a desirable behavior that many schools and professionals have established as a goal. The professional may scold the child until she not only sits quietly but sits quietly and bites her nails. The professional did not intentionally set out to reinforce nail biting, but this is the child's terminal behavior, and the professional is unaware of how it happened.

Reinforced Misbehavior

We must recognize that professional and parent behavior, attitude, predisposition, and inclination can cause a great deal of child misbehavior. Many children misbehave because their misbehavior is reinforced. For example, children enjoy receiving attention; therefore, when a child receives any kind of attention, it reinforces the behavior the child exhibited to get that attention. A child who is noisy receives attention by being scolded. The chances of his exhibiting the same behavior (talking to the child beside him) to elicit attention from the professional is greatly increased as a result of the reinforcement.

We sometimes encourage children to do sloppy work or hurry through an activity when we emphasize finishing it. We may give children a paper with six squares on it to color and cut out and say, "After you color all the squares, I will give you a pair of scissors so you can cut the squares out." The child may hurry through the coloring to get to the cutting. We would do better to concentrate on coloring first, then cutting.

Positive Reinforcement

When we talk about positive reinforcement, we are talking about providing *rewards* or *reinforcers* that promote behaviors professionals and parents decide are desirable. *Positive reinforcement* is maintaining or increasing the frequency of a behavior following a particular stimulus. What the child receives, whether candy, money, or a hug, is the *reinforcer*, the *reinforcement*, or the *reward*. Generally, a positive reinforcer is any stimulus that maintains or increases a particular behavior.

These are verbal reinforcers: "Good," "Right," "Correct," "Wonderful," "Very good," "I like that," "Good boy/girl," "That's great!" and "I knew you could do it." Professionals can also use nonverbal behavior to reinforce children's behavior and learning; for example, a nod, smile, hug, pat on the head or shoulder, standing close to someone, eye contact, paying attention, or even a wink show children that you approve of their behavior or are proud of what they are doing.

The classroom can be set up to provide a positively reinforcing environment. If it is organized to help make desired behaviors possible, provides opportunities for novelty and children's control over their environment, and reflects children's desires, interests, and ideas, children will tend to try to live up to the expectations the setting suggests.

Understanding Behavior

Another extremely important concept of behavior modification focuses on external behavior rather than the causes of behavior; that is, professionals and parents should generally not be concerned with *why* a child acts as he or she does. This idea usually takes some getting used to, because it is almost the opposite of what we have been taught. Professionals particularly feel it is beneficial to know why a child acts the way he or she does, and they spend a great deal of time and effort trying to determine motivations. If Gloria is fidgety and inclined to daydream, for example, the professional may spend six weeks investigating the causes. He learns that Gloria's mother has been divorced three times and ignores her at home. On the basis of this information, he concludes that Gloria needs help but is no closer to solving her problem than he was six weeks previously. A professional's time and energy should be spent developing strategies to help children with their behavior. Sometimes underlying causes help us deal with the behavior we wish to modify, but we need to recognize that the behavior a child exhibits is the problem, and it is behavior that we need to attend to.

Providing Guidance

Children are generally unable to act or think their way out of undesirable behavior. Parents and professionals may say, "You know how to act," when indeed the child does not know. Professionals also often say, "He could do better if he wanted to." The problem, however, is that the child may not know what he wants to do or may not know what is appropriate. In other words, he needs an organized procedure for how to act. Building new behavior, then, is a process of getting children to act in new ways.

A common approach to behavior management is "talking to" and reasoning. As children often do not understand abstract reasoning, it does not generally have the desired effect. The child is likely to behave the same way, or worse. This often leads to a punishment trap, in which the professional or parent resorts to yelling to get the desired results. The behavior we want children to demonstrate must be within their ability. For instance, children cannot pay attention to and be interested in a story that is based on concepts that are too advanced for their comprehension or that is read in a monotonic, unenthusiastic voice. Although *Charlotte's Web* is a children's classic, we cannot expect a group of three-year-olds to sit still and listen attentively as it is read aloud.

REINFORCING BEHAVIOR
Appropriate Reinforcers

A reinforcer is only as effective as the child's desire for it. In other words, if the reinforcer has the power to reinforce the behavior that precedes it, then it will work. A method used to determine the nature of a reinforcer is the *Premack principle*. David Premack determined that behaviors with a high probability of occurrence can be used to reinforce behaviors with a low probability of occurrence. For example, activities children participate in when they have free time are often what they like to do best. Professionals can use these activities to reinforce desired behaviors.

Using the chalkboard or art easels is a highly desirable activity in many early childhood classrooms. Therefore, professionals can provide extra time to use them to reinforce desired behavior. Rewards that children help select are most likely to have a desired effect on behavior. Privileges children often choose are watering the plants, feeding classroom pets, washing chalkboards, running errands, going outside, playing games with friends, leading games, enjoying extra recess, passing out papers and supplies, using audiovisual equipment, doing flash cards, and cutting and pasting. Figure 12–2 shows typical reinforcers in an early childhood setting.

FIGURE 12–2   Reinforcers Used in Early Childhood Settings

Primary Reinforcers		**Conditioned Reinforcers**		
Reinforce behavior without the respondent's having much previous experience with the item		Reinforce as a result of experiences the respondent has had with the reinforcer		
Food		**Verbal—praise**		
Juice	Raisins	"I like the way you . . ."		
Celery	Cheese	"Great"	"Fine"	"A-okay" "Tremendous"
Carrots	Fruit	"Right on"	"Wow"	"Excellent"
		"Beautiful"	"Way to go"	"Fantastic"
		"Terrific"	"Super"	"Fine job"
		Nonverbal		
		Facial	*Gestures*	*Proximity*
		Smile	Clapping of hands	Standing near someone
		Wink	Waving	
		Raised eyebrow	Forming an okay sign (thumb + index finger)	Shaking hands
		Eye contact		Getting down on child's level
			Victory sign	Hugging, touching
			Nodding head	Holding child's arm up
			Shrugging shoulders	
		Social (occur in or as a result of social consequences)		
		Parties		
		Group approval		
		Class privileges		

Praise as a Reinforcer

Praise is probably the most frequent method of rewarding or reinforcing children's behavior. Praise is either general or specific. Specific praise is more effective because it describes the behavior we want to build. The child has no doubt that she is being praised and what she is being praised for. For example, if a child picks up her blocks and you say, "Good, Laura," she may or may not know what you are referring to, but if you say "Laura, you did a nice job of putting your blocks away," Laura knows exactly what you are talking about.

Parents and professionals should approach children positively. A positive approach builds self-esteem. We help build positive self-images and expectations for good behavior by complimenting children and praising them for the things they do well. Every child has praiseworthy qualities.

Contingency Management

Professionals frequently find it helpful to engage in *contingency contracting* or *contingency management* to reinforce behavior. With this strategy, the child might be told, "If you put the materials away when you're done with them, you can use the chalkboard for five minutes." Sometimes contingency management is accompanied by a written contract between the professional and student, depending, of course, on the child's age and maturity.

When parents or professionals manage a contingency, they must be sure they have thought through its consequences. For example, if a parent says, "If you don't clean up your room, you have to stay there until you do," the child may choose not to clean up his room but to stay there and play with his toys. In this case, he does not have to do as he was told and is rewarded for not doing it.

Token System

Reinforcement works best when it occurs at the time of the behavior we want to reinforce. Also, the sooner reinforcement follows the desired behavior, the better it works. Particularly when building new skills or shaping new behaviors, it is important to reinforce the child immediately. To provide immediate reinforcement, some professionals use tokens, such as plastic disks, buttons, trading stamps, or beans, which the child later trades for an activity. If the children like to use the art easel, the professional might allow a child to exchange ten tokens for time at the easel. When a child performs appropriate tasks and exhibits professional-specified behavior, he or she receives a token.

Time-Out

Time-out is another practice professionals and parents often use. In fact, it is the most favored form of discipline used by parents (see Figure 12–3). Time-out is the removal of a child from an activity because he or she has done something wrong.

FIGURE 12–3   Methods of
Discipline Favored by Parents

Type of Discipline	Percentage of Parents
Using time-out	38
Lecturing (in a nice way)	24
Spanking	19
Taking away television privileges	15
Scolding (not in a nice way)	15
"Grounding" them	14
Taking away allowance	2

Source: "Parental Discipline," *Education Week,* May 19, 1993, p. 3. Reprinted with permission from *Education Week.*
Note: Percentages do not add up to one hundred because parents use more than one method.

Presumably, the time-out gives the child an opportunity to think about the misbehavior. After a set amount of time or when the child says he or she can behave (which, of course, *all* children say), the child is allowed to return to the activity.

Professionals should use time-out only when it is appropriate to children's developmental levels. This strategy is inappropriate for infants' and toddlers' developmental levels, but infrequent use is sometimes effective with preschoolers. Time-out is generally not effective as a guidance technique, because it is debatable whether young children will "think" about what they did wrong. Additionally, time-out is usually irrelevant to the inappropriate behavior, so children do not make a connection between the poor behavior and the punishment.

Children are energetic and impulsive, so it is effective to use *preventive guidance* techniques that catch problems before they happen, or "prevent" them. Examples of preventive guidance are appealing room arrangement, effective scheduling, minimal waiting time, and an interesting, active curriculum. These approaches are far more effective than using "band-aid" strategies to guidance such as time-out.

Development of Autonomous Behavior

Implicit in guiding children's behavior is the assumption that they can be, should be, and will be responsible for their own behavior. The ultimate goal of all education, according to Constance Kamii, a noted Piaget expert, is to develop *autonomy* in children, which means "being governed by oneself."

Early childhood educators need to conduct programs that promote development of autonomy. One aspect of facilitating autonomy is exchanging points of view with children.

When a child tells a lie, for example, the adult can deprive him of dessert or make him write 50 times "I will not lie." The adult can also refrain from punishing the child and, instead, look him straight in the eye with great skepticism and affection and say, "I really can't believe what you are saying because. . . ." This is an example of an exchange of

A CULTURAL BASIS FOR CLASSROOM MANAGEMENT

It is easy for professionals to believe that behavior and discipline are separate aspects of classroom management. This feeling goes along with the notion that children are children and through their energetic, active involvement in their environment and their lack of experience and maturity, misbehavior inevitably occurs. We must recognize, however, that it is almost impossible to separate children and how they behave from the cultural environments in which they are reared. Environment determines to a great extent the kind of behavior management children expect and will respond to. Unless professionals or caregivers are aware of these cultural conditions, they may not discipline children appropriately, and children will respond negatively to the discipline.

Some examples will help us understand this cultural reality. In a second grade classroom, Ms. González, a new teacher, has difficulty controlling the class. The class as a whole does not listen to her, although she uses many of the techniques taught in her college classes. She believes her colleagues are firmer with their students than she feels she should be. Finally, in frustration, she asks the teacher in the next classroom, "What am I going to do?" Her friend tells her that one reason for her difficulty is that the children come from families in which a "heavy hand" is the natural way of punishment, and the children are accustomed to feeling that an adult is not serious unless some form of physical punishment accompanies a command. The friend goes on to explain to Ms. González that, while it is not necessary for her to punish the children, it will be necessary, at least in the beginning, for her to be firmer in following up her directions. She cannot ask that something be done and expect it to be done until she is able to build a basis for this kind of behavior.

In a child care classroom, Ms. Chan is concerned about the three-year-old children's lack of independence. Many are still on bottles and cannot dress themselves, and some cannot use eating utensils. During a conference with the director, Ms. Chan learns that it is customary in the culture of the children's homes for parents to overprotect and extend the period of dependency. A mother is viewed as a good parent when she does many of the things for her child that other cultures expect the child to do for him- or herself at three or four years of age. These parents value extended dependency.

In conferences with parents and staff, Ms. Chan will have to decide which areas are most important for the children's successful functioning in the center and teach those skills and behaviors. Although it is important that she understand the parents' attitudes, she must explain the necessity of certain independent behaviors in the center. She should also solicit the parents' help. She will concentrate her efforts in the beginning on helping the children dress themselves and learn how to feed themselves.

points of view that contributes to the development of autonomy in children. The child who can see that the adult cannot believe him can be motivated to think about what he must do to be believed. The child who is raised with many similar opportunities can, over time, construct for himself the conviction that it is best eventually for people to deal honestly with each other.[5]

The ultimate goal of developing autonomy in children is to have them regulate their own behavior and make decisions about good and bad, right and wrong (when they are mature enough to understand these concepts), and how they will behave in relation to themselves and others. Autonomous behavior can be achieved only when

Parents and professionals should encourage children, at an early age, to do things for themselves so they may become self-directive and autonomous. This includes allowing children to practice and develop self-help skills such as drinking from a cup.

a child considers other people's points of view, which can occur only if they are presented with viewpoints that differ from their own and are encouraged to consider them in deciding how they will behave. The ability to take another person's point of view is largely developmental. It is not until around age eight, when children become less egocentric, that they are able to decenter and see things from other people's points of view. Autonomy is reinforced when professionals and parents allow sufficient time and opportunities for children to practice and perform tasks for themselves. Independence is also nurtured when children are allowed to use problem-solving techniques and learn from their mistakes.

Rewards and punishment tend to encourage children to obey others without helping them understand how their behavior was appropriate or inappropriate. Even more importantly, they have not had an opportunity to develop rules of conduct to govern their behavior. Children can be encouraged to regulate and be responsible for their own behavior through what Piaget referred to as "sanctions by reciprocity." These sanctions "are directly related to the act we want to sanction and to the adult's point of view, and have the effect of motivating the child to construct rules of conduct for himself, through the coordination of viewpoints."[6]

Examples of sanctions by reciprocity include exclusion from the group, when children have a choice of staying and behaving or leaving; taking away from children the materials or privileges they have abused, such as not allowing them to use certain materials while leaving open the opportunity to use them again if they express a desire to use them appropriately; and helping children fix things they have broken and clean up after themselves. A fine line separates sanctions by reciprocity and punishment. The critical ingredient that balances the scales on the side of reciprocity is professionals' respect for children and their desire to help them develop autonomy rather than blind obedience.

Physical Punishment

Is it possible to guide children's behavior without punishment? More and more, professionals agree that it is. Whether parents and professionals should spank or paddle as a means of guiding behavior is an age-old controversy. Some parents spank their children, following a "No!" with a slap on the hand or a spank on the bottom. This form of punishment can be an effective means of controlling a child's behavior when used in moderation immediately following the misbehavior. Some parents and religious groups base their use of physical punishment on their religious beliefs. Yet, what some parents do with their child in the home is not acceptable for others to do outside the home, where spanking is considered an inappropriate form of guidance. In fact, in some places, such as Florida, physical punishment in child care programs is legislatively prohibited.

Several problems with spanking and other forms of physical punishment persist. First, physical punishment is generally ineffective in building behavior in children. Physical punishment does not show children what to do or provide them with alternative ways of behaving. Second, adults who use physical punishment are modeling physical aggression. They are, in effect, saying that it is permissible to use aggression in interpersonal relationships. Children who are spanked thus are more likely to use aggression with their peers. Third, spanking and physical punishment increase the risk of physical injury to the child. Spanking can be an emotionally charged situation, and the spanker can become too aggressive, overdo the punishment, and hit the child in vulnerable places. Fourth, parents, caregivers, and teachers are children's sources of security. Physical punishment takes away from and erodes the sense of security that children must have in order to function confidently in their daily lives. In short, the best advice regarding physical punishment is to avoid it; use nonviolent means for guiding children's behavior.

In the long run, parents and early childhood professionals determine children's behavior. In guiding the behavior of children entrusted to their care, professionals and others must select procedures that are appropriate to their own philosophies and children's particular needs. Guiding children to help them develop their own internal system of behavior control benefits them more than a system that relies on external control and authoritarianism. Developing self-discipline in children should be a primary goal of all professionals.

READINGS FOR FURTHER ENRICHMENT

Canter, Lee, and Marlene Canter. *Assertive Discipline: A Take-Charge Approach for Today's Educator* (Santa Monica, CA: Canter, 1986)

> Lee Canter is the leading proponent of "assertive discipline"; based on principles of assertiveness training, this approach encourages professionals and parents to take charge of the discipline process; it derives its popularity from the self-help movement of the 1970s and 1980s.

Greenberg, Polly. *Character Development: Encouraging Self-Esteem and Self-Discipline in Infants, Toddlers and Two-Year-Olds* (Washington, D.C.: National Association for the Education of Young Children, 1991)

> Twelve thoughtful essays, with practical, problem-solving points of view for professionals who care about developing good people while working with young children.

Kostelnik, Marjorie J., Laura C. Stein, Alice Phipps Whiren, and Anne K. Soderman. *Guiding Children's Social Development* (Cincinnati, OH: South-Western, 1988)

> Helps professionals relate to children in ways that will help them maximize their potential. Describes generic principles and skills adaptable to any early childhood setting.

Marion, Marian. *Guidance of Young Children, 3d ed.* (New York: Merrill/Macmillan, 1991)

> A practical guide for helping early childhood educators and others guide young children. Examines the three critical factors in guidance: children, adults who work with children, and the environment.

Putnam, Joyce, and J. Bruce Burke. *Organizing and Managing Classroom Learning Communities* (New York: McGraw-Hill, 1992)

> A general overview to classroom management using a learning community view of the classroom. The authors treat classroom management as a function of educational goals and view teaching as the creation of positive learning cultures.

ACTIVITIES FOR FURTHER ENRICHMENT

1. List five pros and cons of the advantages and disadvantages of using rewards to stimulate and reinforce desired behaviors.

2. What is the difference between normal behavior and acceptable behavior? Give an example of a case when normal behavior may not be acceptable and another when acceptable behavior may not be normal.

3. Observe an early childhood classroom. What reinforcement system (implicit or explicit) does the professional use to operate the classroom? Do you think the professional is aware of the systems of reinforcement in use?

4. Behavior modification is practiced by parents and professionals without their being aware of what they are doing or the processes they are using. Observe a mother-child relationship for examples of parental behavioral management. What rewards does she offer? What was the child's resultant behavior? After further observation, answer these questions for the professional-child relationship. In both situations, what are some ethical implications of the adult's actions?

5. Observe an early childhood classroom to see which behaviors earn the professional's attention. Does the professional pay more attention to positive or negative behavior? Why do you think the professional acts the way he does?

6. A mother says her four-year-old daughter will not keep her room neat; it is always a mess, and she cannot get the child to put anything away. Develop specific strategies you could give this parent to use in helping her keep the child's room in order. Design a floor plan and show furnishings that would help a child keep her room neat.

7. While observing in a primary classroom, identify and examine aspects of the physical

setting and atmosphere that could influence classroom behavior. Can you suggest improvements?

8. List ten behaviors you think are desirable in toddlers, ten for preschoolers, and ten for kindergartners. For each behavior, give two examples of how you would encourage and promote development of that behavior.

9. Interview five parents of young children to determine what they mean when they use the word *discipline*. What implications might these definitions have for you if you were their children's professional?

10. List five methods for guiding children's behavior. Tell why you think each is effective, and give examples.

11. Do you believe in the adage "Spare the rod and spoil the child"? Where does this saying come from? What does it mean? Do you think the implications of this saying are appropriate for today's children?

12. Explain, with examples, why it is important for professionals and parents to agree on a philosophy of behavioral guidance.

NOTES

1.   Warren Richey, "Some Juvenile Crimes Down, but Trends Point Up," *Sun-Sentinel*, Oct. 18, 1993, p. 1.

2.   Sandra Crosser, "Managing the Early Childhood Classroom," *Young Children* (Washington, D.C.: National Association for the Education of Young Children, 1992), pp. 22–25.

3.   Linda Albert, *Cooperative Discipline: Classroom Management That Promotes Self-Esteem—Leader's Guide* (Circle Pines, MN: American Guidance Service, 1990), p. 5.

4.   George S. Morrison, *Education and Development of Infants, Toddlers, and Preschoolers* (Glenview, IL: Scott, Foresman, 1988), pp. 254–255.

5.   Constance Kamii, *Number in Preschool and Kindergarten* (Washington, D.C.: National Association for the Education of Young Children, 1982), p. 23.

6.   Ibid., p. 77.

13

Parent, Family, and Community Involvement
Keys to Successful Programs

After you have read and studied this chapter, you will be able to:

☐ Identify changes in contemporary society and families and the influences these changes have on children, families, and early childhood programs

☐ Cite reasons for the importance of parent, family, and community involvement programs

☐ Explain the importance of involving all parents and families represented in early childhood programs

☐ Expand your understanding of family involvement, and develop a personal philosophy regarding its purposes and benefits

☐ Identify ways early childhood professionals and others can encourage and support programs for involving families and communities

☐ Plan a program for assessing parent/family needs and involving parents and families in early childhood programs

INTEREST IN PARENT, FAMILY, AND COMMUNITY INVOLVEMENT

Changes in Schooling

Schooling used to consist mostly of teaching children social and basic academic skills. But as society has changed, so has the content of schooling. Early childhood programs have assumed many of the functions and responsibilities of parents. Part of the broadening of the role and function of early education and schooling includes helping parents and families meet their problems *and* involving them in decisions regarding the ways programs function.

Readiness Goal

As a result of Goal 1—the readiness goal—of Goals 2000 (formerly America 2000; see chap. 1), professionals are now trying to help children come to school ready to learn. Such efforts also focuses attention on parents as the first teachers of their children. One of the first such programs is Parents as Teachers (PAT), a home-school partnership designed to give children a good start in life by maximizing children's overall development during the first three years of life. Authorized by Missouri's Early Childhood Development Act in 1984, PAT is a model for other programs throughout the country. It provides *all* parents with information about children's development and activities that promote language, intellectual, and social development.

Political and Social Forces

The rediscovery of the need to strengthen the relationship between families and schools is partly the result of political and social forces. The consumer movement of the last several decades convinced families that they should no longer be kept out of their children's schools. Families believe that if they have a right to demand greater accountability from industries and government agencies, they can also demand effective instruction and care from schools and child care centers. Families have become more militant in their demand for quality education, and schools and other agencies have responded by seeking ways to involve families in the quest for quality. Professionals and families realize that mutual cooperation is in everyone's best interest.

In response to the changing landscape of contemporary society, early childhood professionals are working with parents in developing programs for helping them and their children develop to their fullest and lead productive lives. Early childhood professionals are very supportive of such efforts, as shown in Tables 13–1 and 13–2. Also, U.S. teachers believe that *the* highest priority of public education is to strengthen parents' roles in their children's education (see Table 13–3). For their part, 56 percent of the public believes that a lack of parental involvement with children's education is a serious problem in education today; 26 percent believe it is a somewhat serious problem.[1]

TABLE 13-1   Support for Early Childhood Education and Parental Involvement

Question: *One approach to more successful public education is to help students begin their formal schooling well prepared to learn. Should the federal government make the following one of its highest priorities in education, a lower priority to pursue if funds can be made available, or should no additional resources be spent on it?*

	Highest Priority (%)	Lower Priority (%)	No New Resources (%)	Not Sure (%)
Base: 1,000				
Programs helping disadvantaged parents work with their children to encourage learning	69	27	4	*
Fully funding Head Start	61	29	8	1

Source: L. Harris and Associates, The Metropolitan Life Survey of the American Teacher (New York: Metropolitan Life Insurance, 1993), p. 18. Used by permission.

TABLE 13-2   Support for Programs to Help Increase Parental Involvement

Question: *One approach to more successful public education is to help students begin their formal schooling well prepared to learn. Should the federal government make programs helping disadvantaged parents work with their children to encourage learning one of its highest priorities in educaiton, a lower priority to pursue if funds can be made available, or should no additional resources be spent on it?*

		School Level	School Location	Teacher Ethnicity		
Base	**Total 1,000**	**Elementary 438**	**Inner City 123**	**White 914**	**Black 58**	**Hispanic 29**
Higheset priority (%)	69	75	82	67	88	72
Lower priority (%)	27	22	14	29	7	25
No new resources (%)	4	3	4	4	5	3
Not sure (%)	*	*	1	1	—	—

Source: L. Harris and Associates, *The Metropolitan Life Survey of the American Teacher* (New York: Metropolitan Life Insurance, 1993), p. 18. Used by permission.

TABLE 13–3   Priorities for Public Education

Question: *If you had to pick one of the following as the area that should be given the highest priority or second highest priority in public education policy in the next few years, which would it be?*

	Highest Priority (%)	2nd Highest Priority (%)	Net 1st & 2nd Highest Priority (%)
Base: 1,000			
Strengthening parents' roles in their children's education (%)	54	26	80
Improving and expanding early childhood education programs including Head Start for preschool children (%)	26	35	61
Establishing tough standards (%)	12	22	34
Improving safety in and near schools (%)	8	16	24
Not sure (%)	1	1	

Source: L. Harris and Associates, *The Metropolitan Life Survey of the American Teacher* (New York: Metropolitan Life Insurance, 1993), p. 23. Used by permission.

Indeed, parents and the public at large view parent involvement as an important factor in children's success in school. Ninety-five percent of parents with children in school and 97 percent of people with no children in school think it is important to encourage parents to take a more active part in educating their children.[2]

Family Involvement: A New Paradigm

In response to changing families, children, and society, programs are shifting away from parent involvement to family involvement. This represents a major paradigm shift in early childhood education. We examined reasons for this shift in chapter 1. Essentially, professionals have recognized that children live in families and that it makes sense to work with all the people who live in a family in efforts to help children *and* the family members.

For example, in a family in which one or more family members are illiterate, it makes a great deal of sense to develop their literacy while developing the child's literacy. In one family literacy program operated with Chapter 1 funding (see chap. 10) in the Dade County (Florida) school system, computers and literacy software are loaned to parents for thirty-day periods for use in the home. Chapter 1 personnel provide assistance for using the hardware and software.

Many families today are under great stress from poverty, single parenting, mobility, unemployment, and underemployment. Families often lack closeness and the income to get necessary support services. More early childhood and other professionals are acknowledging the need to make such programs available to parents and families.

   Ellen Galinsky of the Families and Work Institute (see chap. 16) identifies the following as ways in which family involvement is different from parent involvement:[3]

- The parent-child relationship is strengthened.
- The family is the client.
- Adult needs are met.
- Parents' strengths are recognized and built on.

John Dewey (see chap. 2) believed the school should act as a bridge between home and society (community). This is what is happening today. More partnerships are being formed and professionals are building bridges that result in family-centered education. This process is depicted in Figure 13–1.

   The *family-centered model* employed by early childhood programs today recognizes that family problems are interrelated and affect all members of the family. A child may come to school with underdeveloped language skills because language development is viewed as the school's job. Children of drug-addicted parents are at risk for poor achievement and dropping out. Family-centered programs seek to address these and other risks in the home and community.

   As recently as a decade or so ago, there was much talk about family involvement, but not much of it was going on. Times have changed. Now early childhood professionals not only talk about the importance and benefits of family involvement; they also seek and implement significant ways to involve families. Family involvement has come into its own in early childhood education.

FIGURE 13–1   Building Bridges Between the School, Home, and Community

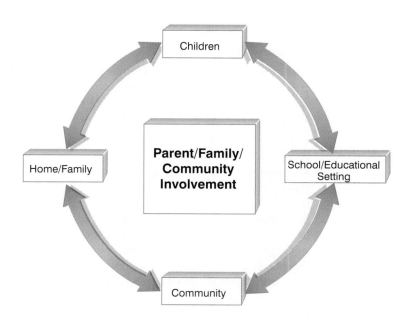

WHO IS A PARENT?

A parent is anyone who provides children with basic care, direction, support, protection, and guidance. Accordingly, a parent can be single, married, heterosexual, gay, lesbian, a cousin, aunt, uncle, grandparent, a court-appointed guardian, a brother, a sister, an institution employee, a surrogate, a foster parent, or a group such as a commune. These changing patterns of who parents are have important implications for early childhood professionals, because these are individuals whom they seek to involve.

WHAT IS A FAMILY?

Just as we have changed our thinking about parents, so too must we change our thinking about families. Families have undergone radical changes during the 1980s and 1990s. Children are born into many different kinds of families, and families create for children a wide variety of living arrangements (see Figure 13–2). These family structures affect, in obvious and subtle ways, children's development and how early professionals relate to them.

For statistical and reporting purposes, the U.S. Census Bureau classifies family households into three types: married couple families, families with male householders (no wife present), and families with female householders (no husband present). A *household* is defined as the person or persons who comprise a family unit. A *family* is defined as two or more persons living together who are related by birth, marriage, or adoption. The term *householder* has replaced "head of family." Table 13–4 illustrates how families have changed over the years.

Types of Families

Nuclear Family

Our concept of the family is undergoing radical redefinition. The *nuclear family*, consisting of two parents and one or more children, is no longer the unit in which many children live. We must recognize that as society changes, so do families (see chap. 1 for statistics.)

Extended Families

An *extended family* consists of families, grandparents, aunts, uncles, brothers, sisters, and sometimes cousins, living together as a unit or sharing feelings of kinship through close geographic proximity and shared concern and responsibility for family matters. In an extended family, children may be reared by other family members, particularly grandparents. Grandparents acting as parents is a growing phenomenon in the United States. When grandparents act as parents and in an extended family situation, it is not uncommon for a grandparent to respond to a note from a professional for a conference about a child's school progress. Sometimes an unperceptive professional interprets this as a sign that families do not care, when it is actually a normal state of affairs in a family in which everyone

FIGURE 13–2   Kinds of Families

- *Nuclear family*—married couple and child(ren)
- *Single-parent family*—headed by a mother or father
- *Stepfamily*—a family in which the children belong to one spouse or the other
- *Blended family*—a family that consists of his and her and their children
- *Foster family*—people who provide care and protection for children in their homes
- *Extended family*—a family that includes relatives
- *Gay-lesbian family with child(ren)*
- *Dual-wage-earning family*
- *Single-wage-earning family*
- *Second time around family*—having one or more children, natural or adopted, after the first children are grown
- *Grandparent family*—grandparents raising children
- *Couples without children*
- *Biological family*—a family in which all children are biological children of both parents
- *Adoptive family*—a family in which all children are adoptive children of both parents
- *Biological mother-stepfather family*—a family in which all children are biological children of the mother and stepchildren of the father
- *Biological father-stepmother family*—a family in which all children are biological children of the father and stepchildren of the mother
- *Joint biological-step parents*—a family in which at least one child is a biological child of both parents and another child is a step child of one or both parents
- *Joint biological-adoptive family*—a family in which at least one child is a biological child of both parents and at least one child is an adoptive child of both parents
- *Joint biological step–adoptive family*—a family in which at least one child is a biological child of one parent and a stepchild of the other parent and at least one child is an adopted child of both parents

accepts responsibility for children's growth and development. The extended family may well be the type to which more and more families turn as a means of support and assistance in child rearing.

Single-Parent Families

With the increase in the divorce rate and new attitudes toward child rearing, single-parent families are increasing, and single fathers rearing dependent children is commonplace, not a rarity. Also, some people choose to be single families through

TABLE 13–4   Eight Ways Families Have Changed

	1970	1980	1990	1992	% Change		
					70–80	80–90	90–92
1. Married couples	44,755,000	49,112,000	52,317,000	52,457,000	10	7	0.26
2. Married couples with children	25,532,000	24,961,000	24,537,000	24,420,000	–2	–1.7	–0.5
3. Male householder (no spouse) with children	341,000	616,000	1,153,000	1,283,000	81	87	11
4. Female house- holder (no spouse) with children	2,858,000	5,445,000	6,599,000	7,043,000	91	21	7
5. Marriages	2,159,000	2,390,000	2,448,000	2,362,000	11	3	–3.5
6. Divorces	708,000	1,189,000	1,175,000	1,215,000	68	–1	3.4
7. Avg. size per household	3.14	2.76	2.63	2.62	–12	–5	–0.4
8. Avg. size per family	3.58	3.29	3.17	3.17	–8	–4	*

Source: Compiled with data from the U.S. Bureau of the Census.

adoption, artificial insemination, or one of the other procedures that are possible through the latest reproductive technologies (again, see chap. 1).

Stepfamilies and Blended Families

A *stepfamily* is one parent with children of his or her own and a spouse. When two people, each with children of their own, marry, they form a *blended, merged,* or *reconstituted family*. These families have "his" children and "her" children; if they have children together, a third level of sibling relationships is added with "their" children.

Foster Parent Families

A *foster family* is one that cares for, in a family setting, children who are not its own. Foster families are usually screened by the agencies that place children with them, and sometimes the children are relatives. Foster families occasionally adopt the children they care for, but even if not, the children sometimes remain in the foster home for extended periods.

A major crisis facing many social service agencies today is a lack of qualified foster care families that has resulted in part from the reluctance of some to be foster

GRANDMOTHER PARENT

Albertha Reese, sixty-two, watches her two granddaughters ride their bikes on the sidewalk in front of their housing project. Albertha raised ten children of her own and did not plan on raising another family. But, as she explains, "my daughter is addicted to crack. She don't think much about being a mother. She's not around much, so it's up to me. I'm all the girls got." The girls, Dominique, six, and Sholanda, eight, are good students at PS 204 two blocks away. "I really keep after them to do well in school," says Albertha. "But it's hard, with the peer pressure and all. I'd like the girls to go to college, but I don't know where the money will come from. It's hard making ends meet as it is. All I get is public assistance and food stamps. We'll manage, though. I tell them, 'Your grandmother loves you. We'll find a way.'"

parents. Many agencies are vigorously attempting to recruit, identify, and train foster families, especially from minority groups.

Gay and Lesbian Families

While many people do not want to talk about or recognize the growing number of gay and lesbian families, the fact is that the number is increasing. Estimates of the number of children living with gay and lesbian parents is about 7 million. Gay and lesbian parents have the same ability to parent as do heterosexual parents. The unique problems that generally arise in their parenting are coping with prejudice and helping their children understand how their family is similar to and different from others. Furthermore, children who are reared by gay and lesbian parents are no more likely to grow up to be gay and lesbian than are children from heterosexual families.

Research has this to say about the children of gay and lesbian parents: "There is no evidence to suggest that psychological development among children of gay men or lesbians is compromised [endangered] in any respect relative to that among offspring of heterosexual parents."[4]

IMPLICATIONS OF FAMILY PATTERNS FOR EARLY CHILDHOOD PROFESSIONALS

Support Services

There are many ways for professionals to help children and families in these days of changing family patterns. They may, for example, help develop support services for families and parents. Support can extend from being a "listening ear" to organizing support groups and seminars on single parenting. Professionals can help families link up with other agencies and groups, such as Big Brothers and Big Sisters and

Families continue to change and, as they do, early childhood professionals must adapt and adopt new ways of involving them and providing for their needs. Growing numbers of fathers have sole responsibility for rearing their children. What can professionals do to assure the involvement of single fathers in their programs?

Families without Partners. Through newsletters and fliers, professionals can offer families specific advice on how to help children become independent and how to meet the demands of single parenting, stepfamilies, and other family configurations.

Child Care

Another way professionals can help is to make arrangements for child care services. More families need child care, and early childhood personnel are logical advocates for establishing child care where none exists, extending existing services, and helping to arrange cooperative baby-sitting services.

Avoiding Criticism

Professionals should be careful not to criticize families for the jobs they are doing. They may not have extra time to spend with their children or know how to discipline them. Regardless of their circumstances, families need help, not criticism.

Similarly, professionals should not be judgmental; they should examine and clarify their attitudes and values toward family patterns and remember that there is no "right" family pattern from which all children should come.

Professionals also need to address the issue of changing family patterns in the educational experiences they arrange. They must offer experiences children might not otherwise have because of their family organization. For example, outdoor activities such as fishing trips and sports events can be interesting and enriching learning experiences for children who may not have such opportunities.

Program Adjustments

Professionals need to adjust classroom or center activities to account for how particular children cope with their home situations. Children's needs for different kinds of activities depend on their experiences at home. Opportunities abound for role-playing situations, and such activities help bring into the open situations that children need to talk about. Use program opportunities to discuss families and the roles they play. Make it a point in the classroom to model, encourage, and teach effective interpersonal skills.

Sensitivity

There are also specific ways to approach today's changing family patterns. For example, avoid having children make presents for both parents when it is inappropriate to do so and awarding prizes for bringing both parents to meetings. Replace terms like *broken home* with *single-parent family*. Be sensitive to the demands of school in relation to children's home lives. For instance, when a professional sent a field-trip permission form home with the children and told them to have their mothers or fathers sign it, one child said, "I don't have a father. If my mother can't sign it, can the man who sleeps with her sign it?" Seek guidance and clarification from families about how they would like specific situations handled; for example, ask whether they want you to send notices of school events to both parents.

Seeking Training

Request in-service training to help you work with families. In-service programs can provide information about referral agencies, guidance techniques, ways to help families deal with their problems, and child abuse identification and prevention. Professionals need to be alert to the signs of all kinds of child abuse, including sexual.

Increasing Parent Contacts

Finally, professionals should encourage greater and different kinds of parent involvement through visiting homes; talking to families about children's needs; providing information and opportunities to parents, grandparents, and other family members; gathering information from families (such as interest inventories); and keeping in touch with parents. Make parent contacts positive.

Why Is Parent and Family Involvement Important?

By now you may have asked yourself, "Why should I be bothered with parent and family involvement?" The most compelling reason for involving families is the effect it has on improving children's achievement. Research shows that family involvement in almost any form improves student achievement, regardless of the family's cultural or socioeconomic background. When children have a quality school program and supportive and involved families, they do better on academic and social skills. Children see family involvement as a sign that their families value education. When their

Home visits are becoming more a part of efforts to provide a full range of services to children and families. Home visits offer an excellent way to gather information about families, to share information with them, and to let them know they are respected partners in the process of education.

families are involved in their program, they recognize that their families are not just "leaving them off" and forgetting them.

Many professionals realize that they are more likely to achieve their program goals effectively when they encourage family involvement. In turn, families are more inclined to join the effort to improve the teaching-learning process. Every parent has a duty to be involved in some way in his or her children's education or any program that provides a major service to them and their children. In fact, specific legislation, especially as it relates to programs that receive federal and state funds, such as Head Start, mandates family involvement, particularly for families with special needs children (see chaps. 10 and 11).

Evidence shows that families are more supportive of programs with which they have direct and meaningful involvement. If early childhood professionals want support for quality programs, family involvement is a certain way to achieve it.

WHAT IS PARENT/FAMILY INVOLVEMENT?

Swick sees family involvement as a threefold process: (1) a partnership between families and professionals and their helpers in the community; (2) a developmental process that is built over a period of time through intentional planning and effort of every team member; and (3) a process by which families and professionals work, learn, and participate in decision-making experiences in a shared manner.[5]

Based on these three essentials—a partnership, a developmental process, and shared decision-making—parent/family involvement is defined as *a process of helping families use their abilities to benefit themselves, their children, and the early childhood program*. Families, children, and the program are all part of the process; consequently, all three parties should benefit from a well-planned program of family involvement. Nonetheless, the focus in parent/child/family interactions is the family, and early childhood professionals must work with and through families if they want to be successful.

Four Approaches to Parent and Family Involvement

In looking at and designing programs of parent and family involvement, early childhood professionals may proceed in several different ways.

Task Approach

The most common and traditional way to approach parent and family involvement is through a task orientation. This method seeks to involve parents in order to get assistance completing specific tasks that support the school or classroom program. In this orientation, faculty, staff, and administration work to involve parents and other family members as tutors, aides, attendance monitors, fundraisers, field trip monitors, and clerical helpers. This is the type of parent and family involvement many professionals are comfortable with and the sort that usually comes to mind when planning for some kind of parent or family involvement. However, although this type of parent involvement has many benefits, by itself it does not represent a sufficient program of family involvement.

Process Approach

In a process orientation, families are encouraged to participate in certain activities that are important to the educational process, such as curriculum planning, textbook review and selection, membership on task forces and committees, professional review and selection, and helping to set behavior standards. This approach is becoming popular, because professionals realize the importance of sharing these processes and decisions with parents, family members, and members of the community. Parents and others need preparation and support for this kind of involvement. Some professionals may think parents lack the necessary skills to help in certain areas, but with some assistance and an opportunity to participate, many family members are extremely effective.

Developmental Approach

A developmental orientation seeks to help parents and families develop skills that benefit themselves, children, schools, professionals, and families and, at the same time, enhance the process of family growth and development. This humanistic orientation is exemplified in such programs as cooperative preschools, community schools, and Head Start.

Comprehensive Approach

A comprehensive approach to parent and family involvement includes elements of all the preceding approaches, especially the developmental approach (see Figure 13–3). It goes beyond all of the other three approaches, however, in that it makes the family the *center* or *focus* of activities. This method does not seek involvement from parent or family members for the sake of involvement or the benefit of a particular agency. Rather, it works with, in, and through the family system to empower, assist, and strengthen the family. As a result, all family members are helped, including children.

The comprehensive approach seeks to involve parents, families, and community persons in school processes and activities, including decisions about the school. It also provides parents choices about which school or program their children will attend. Over the past decade, *choice,* the process of permitting parents to select the school their children will attend, has gained popularity. Some states and many school districts allow parents to enroll their children in the schools of their choice. While most parents of preschool children have had this choice based on the fact that they pay for their children's education, many public school parents have not. Now many do, which has helped change the public's attitude toward them.

A comprehensive program also provides involvement through family development and support programs. Many programs are not only encouraging involvement in family-centered programs; they are providing them. These family support programs include parenting programs, home visitations, substance abuse education

FIGURE 13–3   Comprehensive Approach to
Parent/Family Involvement

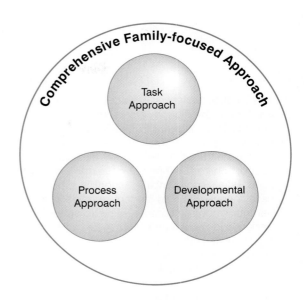

and treatment programs, discussion and support groups, job training and referral programs, basic skills training programs, and linking parents to existing community resource programs.

Methods for Involving Parents and Families

As early childhood professionals develop programs of parent and family involvement, the following tips can prove helpful.

Develop a Positive Attitude

The first and primary prerequisite for effective involvement is the right attitude. Professionals have to *want* parent and family involvement in early childhood programs; otherwise, the process will not be as effective as it should be. A professional must not feel threatened by parents and families and must sincerely believe that family involvement will increase opportunities for all.

Get to Know Parents and Families

Professionals in all programs must get to know their parents and families—their needs, strengths, and conditions. One good way to do so is through *home visits.* Home visits are now used more and more as a means for

- demonstrating to parents and families that professionals and programs are sincere in their efforts to provide education and support and that professionals are approachable persons and programs are approachable places;

Program in Practice

MOBILIZING PROVIDERS, PARENTS, AND CHILDREN: THE HEALTH LEARNERS PROJECT

The Healthy Learners Project is a collaborative formed by Florida International University and the Dade County Public Schools. It is a family empowerment initiative designed to build parental and institutional capacities to support children's healthy development and successful performance in school. The project uses a consortium of leaders, providers, and parents working together with the school to design and reconfigure the delivery of a variety of services in a culturally responsive, consumer-guided, cohesive manner.

Building on the African belief that it takes a "village to educate and raise a child," Fienberg/Fisher Elementary School serves as the hub of the family support village. The school, with an enrollment of a thousand and 92% of its student body receiving free school lunch, is located in south Miami Beach. This is a multicultural, multigenerational community that has rapidly become a mecca for actors, models, and tourists.

Forty parents, known as Rainmakers, have been trained in outreach skills, communication, referrals, and interviewing techniques focusing on family strengths. Having identified such barriers as lack of information in the community, inability to help their children complete homework, increased absen-

teeism, and safety concerns, to name a few, these parent aides together with the school and service providers offer their expertise in reducing these barriers.

Rainmakers have developed and implemented a number of initiatives that have become institutionalized at Fienberg/Fisher as well as other schools locally and nationally. The following discussion will give a broad overview of some of the initiatives currently underway at Fienberg/Fisher Elementary School.

RAIN (Referral and Information Network)

Using a consumer-guided, consumer-run approach, a parent-to-parent information center known as RAIN was opened in September 1991. This center, housed on the school campus, has served over four hundred families from Fienberg/Fisher as well as other members of the community. Families wishing to receive assistance with their rent and utilities; looking for a new apartment; needing help filling out applications for public assistance; and needing food and medical vouchers, clothing, and furniture are referred by the teachers, school counselors, or other service providers to the Rainmakers.

Contributed by Tonia Alameda, Fienberg/Fisher Elementary School.

- providing opportunities for professionals to get to know parents and families "on their turf," without territorial barriers, which sets a positive atmosphere for continuing involvement;

- opening up lines of communication between parents, families, and early childhood programs and developing a sense of partnership;

- enhancing relationships between families and early childhood programs;

The Homework Club

Realizing that families lived in crowded studio apartments and that appropriate space to do homework was unavailable, the Rainmakers requested space in the school for students to complete their homework before going home. Students from kindergarten to sixth grade attend a one-hour homework club after school four days a week. Responding to the increasing need to serve more students, the Boys and Girls Club provides funding for four teachers to assist the Rainmakers. Approximately two hundred children are currently enrolled in the Homework Club.

Home Intervention Teams

Created to increase the attendance in the school, these teams are mobilized by the Rainmakers according to the specific crisis. For example, when a lice crisis threatened to close down the school, the Rainmakers created the "Lice Busters" campaign in which a team of Rainmakers visited the homes of children with excessive absenteeism to provide the necessary treatment. In other cases, Rainmakers have provided families with the necessary services in order to expedite the child's prompt return to the classroom.

Funds from the Danforth Foundation support a full-time social worker who serves as the family advocate and ten parent aides (Rainmakers) as well as in-kind services from professors from the Department of Social Work at Florida International University and Miami University in Oxford, Ohio. A service integration grant from the Department of Health and Human Services as well as the Danforth funds have helped to leverage such resources as the four after-school teachers for the Homework Club from the Boys and Girls Club, a counselor from Jewish Family Services, a job developer from the Department of Labor, two attorneys and a paralegal from Legal Services of Greater Miami, a domestic violence counselor from the Department of Justice Assistance, a full-time therapist from the Children's Psychiatric Center, and social work students from Florida International University. Through Public Education Capital Outlay (PECO) funds, the Dade County Public School system has recently awarded Fienberg/Fisher Elementary School $750,000 for the acquisition of a facility to house the previously mentioned agencies that comprise the full-service school initiative. In addition to these agencies, this facility will house Bright Horizon—a parent resource center, RAIN, and a day care operated by the Rainmakers.

Parts of this project are being replicated in eleven schools in South Florida, three in California, five in Colorado, and twelve in Ohio.

- delivering to parents and families services that support them as parents and first teachers of their children and that enhance their skills as parents and family members;
- assessing the home environment as a means for continuing involvement, help, and support;
- helping children feel "special" and good about themselves as a result of their seeing and knowing that their teacher or caregiver cares; and
- offering opportunities to identify parent and family strengths and weaknesses.

FIGURE 13–4 Four Types of Parents

+ Supportive of child (for example, often encourages) + Active participant (for example, helps child with homework)	– Not supportive of child (for example, ignores child) + Active participant (for example, comes if food is provided)
+ Supportive of child (for example, cares for well-being) – Inactive participant (for example, rarely comes to school activities)	– Not supportive of child (for example, is abusive) – Inactive participant (for example, no communication with school)

Source: Judith A. Vandergrift and Andrea L. Greene, "Rethinking Parent Involvement," *Educational Leadership* (Sept. 1992), p. 59. Reprinted with permission of the Association for Supervision and Curriculum Development. Copyright 1992 by ASCD. All rights reserved.

Meet Parents at Their Level

It is important to demonstrate a willingness to provide opportunities for involvement and engagement at families' levels. For example, Vandergrift and Greene identify four types of parents (see Figure 13–4).

While there are other ways of viewing parents, viewing them in the context of Figure 13–4 provides a framework for meeting their needs and providing for involvement. What is important is that families have meaningful involvement, not the kind they feel is wasting their time and talents and that delivers services of little value.

Meet Parents' Needs

In addition to meeting parents on their levels, professionals must also meet parents' needs in authentic ways. One way to do this is to use Maslow's hierarchy of needs (see chap. 6) to identify needs and then develop appropriate strategies to address them. Figure 13–5 illustrates how to use Maslow's hierarchy in a process of parent involvement.

Plan

Planning is a critical factor for a successful program of parent and family involvement. Determine what families will do before they become involved, but be willing to change plans after determining parent strengths, weaknesses, and needs. Seek creative ways to involve *all* families. Some families, regardless of their level of education, are threatened by school and school-like settings. Help them overcome these fears. Provide for all levels of abilities, desires, and needs. Do not expect the same participation from every parent or family to want to do the same thing or to have the same needs. Regardless of how much or little parents can or want to be involved, give them the opportunity to participate.

FIGURE 13–5   Parents' Needs and Ways to Meet Them

Parents' Needs	How Head Start Helps	Community Resources

Physiological:
   Food
   Clothing
   Shelter
   Health
	Identifies resources for parents; makes referrals and follow-up	Public assistance, Aid to Dependent Children; public housing, food programs, health clinics, alcohol and drug abuse programs, weight control programs, Planned Parenthood

Safety:
   Job security
   Environmental safety
   Civil rights
	Identifies resources; makes referrals; educates parents about rights and satisfaction of grievances	Civil laws, including antidiscrimination, housing, consumer, and health legislation; legal aid; employment training; social security benefits; union and job contracts

Social:
   Affection
   Friendship
   Family ties
   Group membership
	Provides opportunities for socializing and recreation, developing parenting skills, planning and participating in center activities	Churches; neighborhood community organizations; mental health programs, including individual, family, and group counseling; Parents without Partners; senior citizens centers

Esteem:
   Self-confidence
   Independence
   Competency
   Knowledge
   Recognition
   Appreciation
   Respect
	Provides opportunities for participating in policy groups and training for decision making and participation in civic activities; recognizes contributions, skills, and services of parents; refers to community resources for skills and career development, adult education	Adult education programs, church and community organizations, political and civic groups, volunteer services

Self-fulfillment:
   Development of
   personal abilities,
   skills, creativity
	In addition to those cited already, provides opportunity for unique individual parent contributions; refers to community resources for individual development	In addition to those cited already, Art and cultural activities; groups promoting human growth and potential

Source: U.S. Department of Health and Human Services, Administration for Children and Families, Administration for Children, Youth, and Families, Head Start Bureau, *A Handbook for Involving Parents in Head Start,* prepared by Associate Control, Research, and Analysis, Inc., DHHS Publication No. (ACF) 91-31187 (Washington, D.C., U.S. Government Printing Office, 1991), p. 36.

Work with and Through Families

Let parents, families, and community members help organize and operate the program of family involvement. In such an approach, the professional's functions will be as follows:

- Develop a program rationale and structure, including philosophy and goals. Determine what you want to do and what families want and need.
- Train families for effective involvement. For example, in the RAIN program described earlier, parents and community members receive forty hours of training—twenty hours learning how to work with parents, families, and agencies and twenty hours visiting homes and learning about community concerns.
- Supervise the program, including planning with the parents, seeking additional community support, and making sure efforts are achieving their intended purposes.
- Evaluate the overall effectiveness of the program, including each parent's performance.

Activities for Involving Families

Unlimited possibilities exist for family involvement, but a coordinated effort is required to build an effective, meaningful program that can bring about a change in education and benefit all concerned: families, children, professionals, and community. Families can make a significant difference in their children's education, and with the professional's assistance, they will be able to join professionals and schools in a productive partnership. The following are examples of activities that allow for significant family involvement.

An important part of parent/ family involvement is linking families with community services. Why is there an increased emphasis on linking families with services? What kinds of services would families be most likely to need?

Schoolwide Activities

*   *Workshops*—to introduce families to the school's policies, procedures, and programs. Most families want to know what is going on in the school and would do a better job of parenting and educating if they knew how.
*   *Family nights, cultural dinners, carnivals, and potluck dinners*—to bring families and the community to the school in nonthreatening, social ways.
*   *Adult education classes*—to provide the community with opportunities to learn about a wide range of subjects.
*   *Training programs*—to give parents, family members, and others skills as classroom aides, club and activity sponsors, curriculum planners and policy decision makers. *When parents, family members, and community persons are viewed as experts, then empowerment results.*
*   *Support services such as car pools and baby-sitting*—to make attendance and involvement possible.
*   *Fairs and bazaars*—to involve families in fund-raising.
*   *Performances and plays*—especially ones in which children have a part tend to bring families to school; however, the purpose of children's performances should not be to get families involved.

Communication Activities

*   *Telephone hot lines.*   Hot lines staffed by families can help allay fears and provide information relating to child abuse, communicable diseases, and special events. Telephone networks are also used to help children and parents with homework and monitor latchkey children (see chap. 5).
*   *Newsletters.*   Newsletters planned with parents' help are an excellent way to keep families informed about program events. Newsletters can also include curriculum information and activities. Newsletters in parents' native languages help keep minority-language families informed.
*   *Home learning materials and activities.*   A monthly calendar of activities is one good way to keep families involved in their children's learning.

Educational Activities

*   *Participation in classroom and center activities.*   While not all families can be directly involved in classroom activities, those who can should be encouraged. Those who are involved must have guidance, direction, and training for these involvements. Involving parents and others as paid aides is an excellent way also to provide employment and training. Many programs, such as Head Start, actively support such a policy.
*   *Involvement of families in writing individualized education programs (IEPs)* for special needs children. Involvement in writing an IEP is not only a legal requirement but also an excellent learning experience (see chap. 11).

Service Activities

- *Resource libraries and materials centers.*   Families benefit from books and other articles relating to parenting. Some programs furnish resource areas with comfortable chairs to encourage families to use these materials.

- *Child care.* Families may not be able to attend programs and become involved if they do not have child care for their children. Child care makes their participation possible and more enjoyable.

- *Respite care.*   Some early childhood programs provide respite care for parents and other family members, which enables them to have periodic relief from the responsibilities of parenting a chronically ill child or a child with disabilities.

- *Service exchanges.*   Service exchanges operated by early childhood programs and other agencies help families in their needs for services. For example, one parent provided child care in her home in exchange for having her washing machine repaired. The possibilities for such exchanges are endless.

- *Parent support groups.*   Parents need support in their roles. Support groups can provide parenting information, community agency information, and speakers.

- *Welcoming committee.*   A good way to involve families in any program is to have other families contact them when their children first join a program.

Decision Activities

- *Hiring and policy making.*   Parents and community members can and should serve on committees that set policy and hire staff.

- *Curriculum development and review.*   Parents' involvement in curriculum planning helps them learn about and understand what constitutes a quality program and what is involved in a developmentally appropriate curriculum. When families know about the curriculum, they are more supportive of it.

Parent-Professional Conferences

Significant parent involvement can occur through well-planned and -conducted parent-professional conferences. Such conferences are often the first contact many families have with school. Conferences are critical from a public relations point of view and as a vehicle for helping families and professionals accomplish their goals. These guidelines will help professionals prepare for and conduct successful conferences:

- *Plan ahead.*   Be sure of the reason for the conference. What are your objectives? What do you want to accomplish? List the points you want to cover and think about what you are going to say.

- *Get to know the parents.*   This is not wasted time; the more effectively you establish rapport with a parent, the more you will accomplish in the long run.

- *Avoid an authoritative atmosphere.*   Do not sit behind your desk while the parent sits in a child's chair. Treat parents and others like the adults they are.

- *Communicate at the parent's level.*   Do not condescend or patronize. Instead, use words, phrases, and explanations the parent understands and is familiar with. Do not use jargon or complicated explanations, and speak in your natural style.

- *Accentuate the positive.*   Make every effort to show and tell the parent what the child is doing well. When you deal with problems, put them in the proper perspective: what the child is able to do, what the goals and purposes of the learning program are, what specific skill or concept you are trying to get the child to learn, and what problems the child is having in achieving. Most important, explain what you plan to do to help the child achieve and what specific role the parent can have in meeting the achievement goals.

- *Give families a chance to talk.*   You will not learn much about them if you do all the talking, nor are you likely to achieve your goals. Professionals are often accustomed to dominating a conversation, and many parents will not be as verbal as you, so you will have to encourage families to talk.

- *Learn to listen.*   An *active* listener holds eye contact, uses body language such as head nodding and hand gestures, does not interrupt, avoids arguing, paraphrases as a way of clarifying ideas, and keeps the conversation on track.

- *Follow up.*   Ask the parent for a definite time for the next conference as you are concluding the current one. Another conference is the best method of solidifying gains and extending support, but other acceptable means of follow-up are telephone calls, written reports, notes sent with children, or brief visits to the home. While these types of contacts may appear casual, they should be planned for and conducted as seriously as any regular parent-professional conference. No matter which approach you choose, advantages of a parent-professional conference follow-up are these:

    Families see that you genuinely care about their children.

    Everyone can clarify problems, issues, advice, and directions.

    Parents, family members, and children are encouraged to continue to do their best.

    It offers further opportunities to extend classroom learning to the home.

    You can extend programs initiated for helping families and formulate new plans.

- *Develop an action plan.*   Never leave the parent with a sense of frustration, not knowing what you are doing or what they are to do. Every communication with families should end on a positive note, so that everyone knows what can be done and how to do it.

Children and Conferences

A question frequently asked is "Should children be present at parent-teacher conferences?" The answer is "Yes, of course." The only caveat to the yes response is "If it is appropriate for them to be present," and in most instances it is appropriate.

There are a number of benefits for the child's and other family members' being present:

- Children have much to contribute. They can talk about their progress and behavior, offer suggestions for improvement and enrichment, and discuss their interests.
- The *locus of control* is centered in the child. Children learn they have a voice and opinions and others think this is important and are listening.
- Children's self-esteem is enhanced because they are viewed as an important part of the conference and because a major purpose of the conference is to help them and their families.
- Children learn that education is a cooperative process between home and school.

Telephone Contacts

When it is impossible to arrange a face-to-face conference as a follow-up, a telephone call is an efficient way to contact families. (Some families, however, do not have a telephone.) The same guidelines apply as to face-to-face conferences; in addition, remember these tips:

- Since you cannot see someone on a telephone, it takes a little longer to build rapport and trust. The time you spend overcoming families' initial fears and apprehensions will pay dividends later.
- Constantly clarify what you are talking about and what you and the families have agreed to do, using such phrases as "What I heard you say then . . ." or "So far, we have agreed that. . . ."
- Do not act hurried. There is a limit to the amount of time you can spend on the phone, but you may be one of the few people who cares about the parent and the child. Your telephone contact may be the major part of the families' support system.

Involving Single-Parent Families

Sometimes, family involvement activities are conducted without much regard for single-parent families. Professionals sometimes think of single-parent families as problems to deal with rather than people to work with. Involving single-parent families need not present a problem if professionals remember some basic points.

First, many adults in one-parent families are employed during school hours and may not be available for conferences or other activities during that time. Professionals must be willing to accommodate families' schedules by arranging conferences at other times, perhaps early morning (breakfast), midmorning, noon (lunch), early

Parents can be involved and informed through telephone conferences. For many of today's busy parents, the telephone is an ideal means of communication between the home and the early childhood program. Increasing numbers of professionals now have telephones in their classrooms for easier communication.

afternoon, late afternoon, or early evening. Some employers, sensitive to families' needs, give released time to participate in school functions, but others do not. Professionals and principals need to think seriously about going to families rather than having families always come to them. Some schools have set up parent conferences to accommodate families' work schedules, while some professionals find that home visits work best.

Second, professionals need to remember that such families have a limited amount of time to spend on involvement with their children's school and their children at home. When professionals confer with single-parent families, they should make sure (1) the meeting starts on time, (2) they have a list of items (skills, behaviors, achievements) to discuss, (3) they have sample materials available to illustrate all points, (4) they make specific suggestions relative to one-parent environments, and (5) the meeting ends on time. One-parent families are more likely to need child care assistance to attend meetings, so child care should be planned for every parent meeting or activity.

Third, illustrate for single-parent families how they can make their time with their children more meaningful. If a child has trouble following directions, show families how to use home situations to help in this area. Children can learn to follow directions while helping families run errands, get a meal, or help with housework.

Fourth, get to know families' lifestyles and living conditions. A professional can easily say that every child should have a quiet place to study, but this may be an impossible demand for some households. Professionals need to visit some of the homes in their community before they set meeting times or decide what family involvement activities to implement or what they will ask of families during the year. All professionals, particularly early childhood professionals, need to keep in mind the condition of the home environment when they request that children bring certain items to school or carry out certain tasks at home. When asking for a parent's help, the professional needs to be sensitive to the parent's talents and time constraints.

Fifth, help develop support groups for one-parent families within the school, such as discussion groups and classes on parenting for singles. Professionals must include the needs and abilities of one-parent families in their family involvement activities and programs. After all, single-parent families may be the majority of families represented in the program.

Language-Minority Parents and Families

The developmental concept of family involvement is particularly important when working with language-minority families. Language-minority parents are individuals

Building positive relationships with single parents and other family members is an important part of the education process. Time spent talking with parents about how you and the program can help their chidren learn is time well spent. Furthermore, such interaction provides opportunities for the involvement to be culturally sensitive.

whose English language proficiency is minimal and who lack a comprehensive knowledge of the norms and social system, including basic school philosophy, practice, and structure. Language-minority families often face language and cultural barriers that greatly hamper their ability to become actively involved, although many have a great desire and willingness to participate in their children's education.

Because the culture of language-minority families often differs from the majority in a community, those who seek a truly collaborative community, home, and school involvement must take into account the cultural features that can inhibit collaboration. Traditional styles of child rearing, family organization, attitudes toward schooling, organizations around which families center their lives, life goals and values, political influences, and methods of communication within the cultural group all have implications for parent participation.

Language-minority families often lack information about the U.S. educational system, which can result in misconceptions, fear, and a general reluctance to respond to invitations for involvement. Furthermore, the U.S. educational system may be quite different from what language-minority families are used to in a former school system. They may have been taught to avoid active involvement in the educational process, with the result that they prefer to leave all decisions concerning their children's education to professionals and administrators.

The U.S. ideal of a community-controlled and -supported educational system must be explained to families from cultures in which this concept is not as highly valued. Traditional roles of children, professionals, and administrators also have to be explained. Many families, and especially language-minority families, are quite willing to relinquish to professionals any rights and responsibilities they have for their children's education, and they need to be taught to assume their roles and obligations toward schooling.

Culturally Sensitive Family Involvement

The following are some suggestions provided by Janet González-Mena for working with families:

- Know what each parent in your program wants for his or her child. Find out families' goals. What are their caregiving practices? What concerns do they have about their child? Encourage them to talk about all of this. Encourage them to ask questions. Encourage the conflicts to surface—to come out in the open.

- Become clear about your own values and goals. Know what you believe in. Have a bottom line, but leave space above it to be flexible. When you are clear, you are less likely to present a defensive stance in the face of conflict. When we are ambiguous, we come on the strongest.

- Become sensitive to your own discomfort. Tune in on those times when something bothers you instead of just ignoring it and hoping it will go away. Work to identify what specific behaviors of others make you uncomfortable. Try to discover exactly what in yourself creates this discomfort. A conflict may be brewing.

- Build relationships. When you do this, you enhance your chances for conflict management or resolution. Be patient. Building relationships takes time, but it enhances communications and understandings. You'll communicate better if you have a relationship, and you'll have a relationship if you learn to communicate.

- Become effective cross-cultural communicators. It is possible to learn these communication skills. Learn about communication styles that are different from your own. Teach your own communication styles. What you think a person means may not be what he or she *really* means. Do not make assumptions. Listen carefully. Ask for clarification. Find ways to test for understanding.

- Learn how to create dialogues—how to open communication instead of shutting it down. Often, if you accept and acknowledge the other person's feelings, you encourage him or her to open up. Learn ways to let other know that you are aware of and sensitive to their feelings.

- Use a *problem-solving* rather than a *power* approach to conflicts. Be flexible—negotiate when possible. Look at your willingness to share power. Is it a control issue you are dealing with?

- Commit yourself to education—both your own and that of the families. Sometimes lack of information or understanding of each other's perspective is what keeps the conflict going.[6]

Teenage Parents

As we learned in chapter 1, teenage parenting is on the rise. At one time, most teenage parents were married, but today the majority are not. Also, most teenage families elect to keep their children rather than put them up for adoption and are rearing them within single-parent families. Teenage families frequently live in extended families, and the child's grandmother often serves as the primary caregiver. Regardless of their living arrangements, teenage families have the following needs:

- *Support in their role as families.*   Support can include information about child-rearing practices and child development. Regardless of the nature and quality of the information given to teenage families, they frequently need help in implementing the information in their interactions with their children.

- *Support in their continuing development as adolescents and young adults.*   Remember that younger teenage parents are really children themselves. They need assistance in meeting their own developmental needs as well as those of their children.

- *Help with completing their own education.*   Some early childhood programs provide parenting courses as well as classes designed to help teenage-parent dropouts complete requirements for a high school diploma. Remember that a critical influence on children's development is the mother's education level.

As early childhood programs enroll more children of teenage families, they must be attentive to creatively and sensitively involving these families as a means of supporting the development of families and children.

Involving Fathers

More fathers are involved in parenting responsibilities than ever before. Over one-fifth of preschool children are cared for by their fathers while their mothers work outside the home.[7] The implication is clear: early childhood professionals must make special efforts to involve all fathers in their programs.

More professionals recognize that fathering and mothering are complementary processes. Definitions of nurturing are changing to include the legitimate and positive involvement of fathers in children's lives. Many fathers are competent caregivers, directly supervising children, helping set the tone for family life, providing stability to a relationship, supporting the mother in her parenting role and career goals, and personifying a masculine role model for the children. More fathers, as they discover or rediscover these parenting roles, turn to professionals for support and advice.

There are many styles of fathering. Some fathers are at home while their wives work; some have custody of their children; some are single; some dominate home life and control everything; some are passive and exert little influence in the home; some are frequently absent because their work requires travel; some take little interest in their homes and families; some are surrogates. Regardless of the roles fathers play in their children's lives, early childhood professionals must make special efforts to involve them.

Involving Other Caregivers

Often children of two-career families and single families are cared for by nannies, au pairs, baby-sitters, and housekeepers. Whatever their titles, these adults usually play significant roles in children's lives. Many early childhood programs and schools are reaching out to involve them in activities such as professional conferences, help with field trips, and supervision of homework. The involvement should occur with families' blessing and approval for a cooperative working relationship.

COMMUNITY INVOLVEMENT

A comprehensive program of family involvement has, in addition to families, professionals, and schools, a fourth important component: the community. More childhood professionals realize that neither they alone nor the limited resources of their programs are sufficient to meet the needs of many children and families. Consequently, early education professionals are seeking ways to link families to community services and resources. For example, if a child needs clothing, a professional who is aware of community resources might contact the local Salvation Army for assistance.

Professionals can do these things to increase their effectiveness in parent-community involvement:

- Become familiar with the community and community agencies by walking around the neighborhood to locate resource agencies and meet the people who staff them and by using the telephone book to contact community agencies.
- Compile a list of community agencies and contact persons for immediate referral and use.

Only by helping families meet their needs and those of their families and children will there be opportunities for children to reach their full potential. For this reason alone, regardless of all the other benefits, family involvement programs and activities must be an essential part of every early childhood program. Families should expect nothing less from the profession, and we, in turn, must do our very best for them.

DEVELOPING SOCIAL CAPITAL

We are all familiar with the idea of capital as wealth. But there is another kind of capital, *social capital,* that consists of the social relations that exist in the family or community.[8] Family social capital consists of such things as the attention, nurturance, support, and help family members can provide children in their learning and development. When family members provide these things to children, then the social capital is high. When they do not, then the social capital is low.

For example, merely having adults in the home does not mean there is a wealth of social capital. If parents are consumed by their own problems, backgrounds, and socioeconomic status (e.g., substance abuse, unemployment, spouse abuse, divorce, employment stress, lack of education, etc.), then the social capital is low. Professionals may not realize this. If they expect parents to help children with their homework, for example, they may hold such expectations without an understanding of or little regard for the social capital that exists in the home for accomplishing this task. Another example: a family with well-educated family members and a high socioeconomic status may have the potential for high social capital. Their attention, however, may be focused outside of the home, or perhaps they, too, are consumed with problems of single parenting, divorce, and so on. Thus, they offer little support, help, and encouragement to the children. In this case, low social capital also prevails.

Much the same applies to the community. A community that has a system in place that provides for children and families (e.g., makes available parks, playgrounds, senior citizen centers/community centers, violence- and drug-free environments, a caring attitude) is high on social capital and supports children and families.

Schools and professionals must work with families and communities to help develop social capital and the means to use it in the education and development of children and families.

> When families and communities are weak, the school lacks a resource that is central to its effectiveness in educating children. Lessons learned from a past in which social capital was abundant can obscure a central fact: *The effectiveness of schools in settings*

The social capital of a neighborhood and community supports the ability of early childhood programs to provide quality services and of families to educate and rear their children well. For these reasons, early childhood professionals have a responsibility to help communities develop social capital. What social capital of your community supports the education of young children? What social capital is needed to support the process?

where the social capital of family and community is weak depends upon the rebuilding of that social capital. This can be a task for agencies other than the school, but it is a task which is in the interest of no party more than that of the school. In such a setting, a school must in its own interests take on new activities to accomplish its task of educating children. If the school is to accomplish this task of (that is, if children are to learn, and not merely be taught), then it must help rebuild the family and community social capital that facilitates learning.[9]

Family-centered programs that acknowledge parents as the first teachers of their children; help them develop skills, knowledge, and abilities; and link them to community agencies are serious about developing and utilizing the social capital of family members. The social capital of the school's neighborhood, in turn, can be enhanced via community-centered programs linking the early childhood program with community agencies (e.g., churches, businesses, social service agencies, community centers, governmental agencies).

Program-Business Involvement

One good way to build social capital in the community is through school-business involvement. More early childhood programs are developing this link as a means of strengthening their programs and helping children and families. For their part, businesses are anxious to develop the business-school connection in efforts to help schools better educate children. Basically, businesses' efforts at involvement consists of four types:[10]

- *Adopt-a-school.*   Existing in about 40 percent of the elementary schools, this is the most popular type of involvement. Businesses provide tangible goods and services to schools such as guest speakers, employee tutors, small grants, and products. For example, companies such as Burger King and McDonald's provide professionals with coupons for food items. They in turn use these as incentives for achievement, appropriate behavior, literacy involvement, and so forth.

- *Project driven.*   A business or businesses join with a school or program with the intent of bringing about change. The training of Head Start administrators (see chap. 10) illustrates this kind of involvement. Other examples are found in chapter 5.

- *Reform oriented.*   An individual company or a consortium gets involved to change a variety of practices throughout a district or agency.

- *Policy change.*   Business leaders and organizations help develop or influence legislation and public policy. For example, a group of businesses known as the Business Roundtable seeks to promote programs of school choice in thirty states.

The challenge to early childhood professionals is quite clear. Seeking ways to involve parents in school activities is no longer a sufficient program of parent involvement. Today, the challenge is to make families the focus of our involvement activities. Anything less will not help families and children access and benefit from the opportunities of the twenty-first century.

National Organizations

National programs dedicated to family involvement are a rich resource for information and support. Some of these are listed here:

- Center on Families, Communities, Schools and Children's Learning, 605 Commonwealth Avenue, Boston, Massachusetts 02215; 617-353-3309 (The center's address and phone number are the same as IRE's.)

- Families United for Better Schools, 31 Maple Wood Mall, Philadelphia, Pennsylvania 19144; 215-829-0442. This is an organization of families working to help other families work for better schools.

- Institute for Responsive Education (IRE), 605 Commonwealth Avenue, Boston, Massachusetts 02215; 617-353-3309

- National Committee for Citizens in Education (NCCE), 900 Second Street NE, Suite 8, Washington, D.C., 20002-3557; 800-638-9675. This organization seeks to inform families of their rights and to get them involved in the public schools.

- The Home and School Institute, 1201 16th Street NW, Washington, D.C. 20036; 202-466-3633

- National Congress of Parents and Teachers (The National PTA), 700 N. Rush Street, Chicago, Illinois 60611; 312-787-0977

READINGS FOR FURTHER ENRICHMENT

Brizius, Jack A., and Susan E. Foster. *Generation to Generation: Realizing the Promise of Family Literacy* (Ypsilanti, MI: High/Scope, 1993)

> Offers a practical, thorough discussion of literacy issues and how they impact the family unit. Includes guidance for setting up community programs.

Fruchter, Norm, Anne, Galletta, and J. Lynne White. *New Directions in Parent Involvement,* ERIC Document ED 360683 (Washington, D.C.: Academy for Educational Development, 1992)

> Describes eighteen parent involvement programs that have given parents greater roles and responsibilities in the education process.

National Task Force on School Readiness. *Caring Communities: Supporting Young Children and Families* (Washington, D.C.: National Association for the Education of Young Children, 1991)

> Suggests a blueprint for achieving the first national education goal: "Every child will enter school ready to learn." Stresses that efforts for helping children achieve this goal must be family and community centered.

Powell, D. R. *Families and Early Childhood Programs* (Washington, D.C.: National Association for the Education of Young Children, 1989)

> Offers an in-depth, critical review of the growing literature on rationales for working with parents, relations between families and early childhood programs, and promising strategies for addressing home-school relations.

Swap, Susan McAllister. *Developing Home-School Partnerships:From Concepts to Practice* (New York: Teachers College Press, 1993)

> Provides an overview of, and practical suggestions for, professionals who want to strengthen ties with parents.

ACTIVITIES FOR FURTHER ENRICHMENT

1. Arrange with a local school district to be present during a parent-teacher conference. Discuss with the teacher, prior to the visit, his or her objectives and procedures. After the conference, assess its success with the teacher.

2. List the various ways early childhood professionals communicate pupils' progress to families. What do you think are the most and least effective ways? What specific methods do you plan to use?

3. You are responsible for publicizing a parent meeting about how the school plans to involve families. Describe methods and techniques you would use to publicize the meeting.

4. List six reasons that early childhood professionals might resist involving families. For each of the reasons for resistance, give two strategies for overcoming these resistances.

5. You have just been appointed the program director for a family involvement program in first grade. Write objectives for the program. Develop specific activities for involving families and providing services to them.

6. Visit social services agencies in your area, and list the services they offer.

    a. Describe how professionals can work with these agencies to meet the needs of children and families.

    b. Invite directors of social services to meet with your class to discuss how they and early childhood professionals can work cooperatively to help families and children.

7. Ask five low socioeconomic and five middle-income families how they think early childhood programs and schools can help them in educating their children, how they think they can be involved in early childhood programs, what specific help they feel they need in child rearing/educating, and what activities they would like in a home visit program.

8. What functions do you feel the family should exercise but does not? What family functions could be better accomplished by other agencies? Do you think education about gender roles is better accomplished in the home or by an external educational agency? What functions do you feel the family you came from should have performed but did not? What functions did they perform that you do not agree with?

9. As families change, so, too, do the services they need. Interview families in as many settings as possible (e.g., urban, suburban, rural), from as many socioeconomic backgrounds as possible, and from as many kinds of families as possible. Determine what services they believe can help them most, then tell how you as a professional could help provide those services.

10. Develop a set of guidelines that a child care center could use to facilitate the involvement of fathers, language-minority families, and families of children with disabilities.

11. What are today's most serious parenting problems? How can early childhood professionals help families with these problems?

NOTES

1. "How Americans Grade Their School System," *Business Week*, Sept. 14, 1992, p. 85.

2. Stanley M. Elam, Lowell C. Rose, and Alec M. Gallup, "The 25th Annual Phi Delta Kappa/Gallup Poll," *Phi Delta Kappan* (Oct. 1993), p. 149.

3. Personal conversation with the author.

4. Charlotte J. Patterson, "Children of Lesbian and Gay Parents," *Child Development* 63(5) (Oct. 1992), p. 1036.

5. Kevin J. Swick, *Inviting Parents into the Young Child's World* (Champaign, IL: Stipes, 1984), p. 115.

6. Janet González-Mena, "Taking a Culturally Sensitive Approach in Infant-Toddler Programs," *Young Children* (Jan. 1992), pp. 8–9. Used by permission.

7. Deborah L. Cohen, "More Fathers Take On Role of Child Care, Study Finds," *Education Week*, Sept. 29, 1993, p. 12.

8. James S. Coleman, *Parental Involvement in Education*, ED 1.2:P75/6 (Washington, D.C.: U.S. Government Printing Office, 1991), p. 7.

9. Ibid., pp. 13–14.

10. "Saving Our Schools," *Business Week*, Sept. 14, 1992, p. 71.

Multiculturalism
Education for Living in a Diverse Society

After you have read and studied this chapter, you will be able to:

- ☐ Use and apply the language and terminology associated with multicultural education
- ☐ Explain and discuss the implications of multicultural contemporary society for schooling
- ☐ Choose and apply ways for infusing multicultural content in curriculum, programs, and activities
- ☐ Develop and defend a philosophy of teaching for multicultural awareness and understanding
- ☐ Implement multicultural programs and practices in centers and classrooms
- ☐ Identify and discuss issues relating to multiculturalism
- ☐ Educate yourself and young children for living in a diverse society

GLOSSARY OF TERMS

The following terms will assist you as you study this chapter.

Antibias: An active/activist approach to challenging prejudice, stereotyping, bias, and the "isms"[1]

Bias-free: Programs, activities, materials and behaviors that are free from biased perceptions, language, attitudes, and actions

Bilingual education: "The use of two languages for the purposes of academic instruction with an organized curriculum that includes, at a minimum, (1) continued primary language (language 1) development, (2) English (language 2) acquisition, and (3) subject matter instruction through (language 1) and (language 2). Bilingual education programs assist limited-English-proficient (LEP) students in developing literacy both in English and the primary language to a level at which they can succeed in an English-only classroom. Programs may also include native speakers of English [these are children whose primary language is English and are learning a second language]."[2]

Diversity: Describes various cultures, ethnic groups, socioeconomic groups, languages, and gender identities that exist in society at large and early childhood programs in particular. Diversity is seen as a positive rather than negative state. Consequently, diversity is celebrated, studied, and respected. Additionally, early childhood professionals try to ensure that cultural diversity exists in curriculum, teaching, caregiving practices, and activities.

Infusion: A process of integrating multicultural perspectives into the curriculum, as well as promoting content awareness, sensitivity, knowledge, and behaviors. Infusion is used as a means of transforming existing or new curricula so that they are truly multicultural.

Language maintenance: "The preservation of a native language when a second language is learned as opposed to displacement of the native language by the second language"[3]

Limited-English-proficient (LEP) parents: "Parents whose children have been identified as limited-English-proficient and/or who are also limited in their proficiency in English"[4]

Limited-English-proficient (LEP) student: "A student whose primary language is other than English and who does not comprehend, speak, read, or write at a level necessary to receive instruction only in English with native English-speaking peers"[5]

Mainstream: "In the field of bilingual education, this term refers to the monolingual English curriculum or classroom."[6] (See chap. 11 for a full discussion of mainstream and mainstreaming.)

Multicultural education: Multicultural education is education that prepares students to live, learn, communicate, and work to achieve common goals in a culturally diverse world by fostering understanding, appreciation, and respect for people of other ethnic, gender, socioeconomic, language, and cultural backgrounds.

Nonsexist: Attitudes and behaviors that convey that the sexes are equal.

MULTICULTURAL CHILDREN

Multiculturalism in today's society is expressed in many ways. Children come from cultures different from that of the majority population. These children are members of minority cultures such as Asian American, Native American, African American, and Hispanic. Many cities and school districts have populations that express great diversity. For example, the Dade County, Florida, school district has children from 122 countries of the world, each with their own culture. Figure 14–1 shows how minority culture groups have contributed to the 12.5 million ethnic population increase in major metropolitan areas.

Multicultural children may have special learning needs and quite often special language needs. Children may need help because of differences in behavior based on cultural customs and values. Children also come from many socioeconomic backgrounds; as indicated in Figure 1–10, many families and their children live in poverty. According to the U.S. Bureau of the Census (1991, unpublished data), 3.7 million, or one out of four, children under age six live in poverty. These children are also part of the multicultural composition of society.

As an early childhood educator, you will want to promote multicultural aware-ness in your classroom. In its simplest form, *multicultural awareness* is the appreci-ation for and understanding of peoples' cultures, socioeconomic status, and gender. It also includes understanding one's own culture. The terms and concepts for describing multicultural awareness are not as important as the methods, proce-

FIGURE 14–1   Contributions to the Ethnic Population Increase in the Fifty Largest U.S. Metropolitan Areas during the 1980s

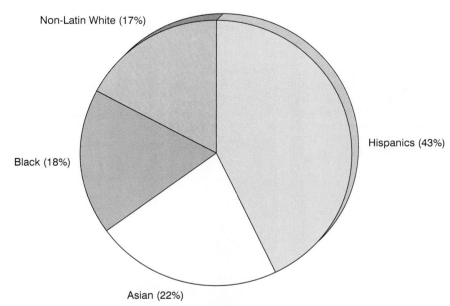

Source: "Ethnic Growth," *Miami Herald*, Apr. 30, 1991, p. 1.

dures, and activities for developing meaningful early childhood programs. Some early childhood professionals assume they are promoting multicultural awareness when they are actually presenting only a fragment of the concept. Multicultural awareness in the classroom is not the presentation of other cultures to the exclusion of the cultures represented by children in the class. Rather, multicultural awareness programs and activities focus on other cultures while at the same time making children aware of the content, nature, and richness of their own. Learning about other cultures concurrently with their own culture enables children to integrate commonalities and appreciate differences without inferring inferiority or superiority of one or the other.

In chapter 1 we stressed the diverse nature of U.S. society. We emphasize it again here. The reality today is that the United States is a multicultural country, as conveyed in Figure 14–2. Early childhood professionals must prepare themselves and their children to live happily and productively in this society.

MULTICULTURAL EDUCATION

James Banks, noted author and multicultural educator, states that multicultural education consists of three things: an idea or concept, an educational reform movement, and a process. Banks identifies each of these three in the following ways:

1. Multicultural education incorporates the idea that all students—regardless of their gender and social class and their ethnic, racial, or cultural characteristics—should have an equal opportunity to learn in school.

2. Multicultural education is also a reform movement that is trying to change the schools and other educational institutions so that students from all social-class, gender, racial, and cultural groups will have equal opportunity to learn.

Today's society is multicultural and diverse. Early childhood professionals must consider gender and multicultural and socioeconomic factors when planning the environment, programs, and activities.

FIGURE 14–2   U.S. Population by Race/Ethnic Groups

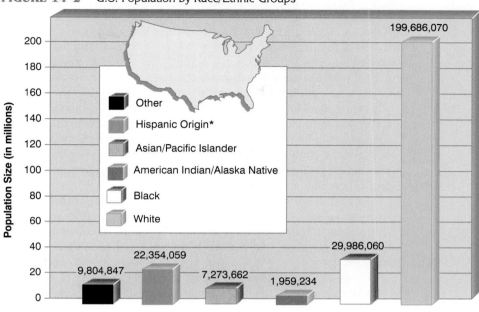

*Persons of Hispanic origin may be of any race.
Source: "What Is U.S. Population Distribution by Race/Ethnic Groups?" *NCBE Forum,* newsletter of the National Clearinghouse for Bilingual Education, 16(3), March 1993, p. 4. Used by permission.

3. Multicultural education is also a process whose goals will never be fully realized. Educational equality, like liberty and justice, are ideals toward which human beings work but never fully attain. Racism, sexism, and discrimination against people with disabilities will exist to some extent no matter how hard we work to eliminate these problems. When prejudice and discrimination are reduced toward one group, they are usually directed toward another group or they take new forms. Because the goals of multicultural education can never be fully attained, we should work continually to increase educational equality for all students.[7]

Generally, definitions of multicultural education used to guide daily program and classroom practice incorporate Banks's first definition. For example, the state of Florida defines multicultural education as

education that prepares students to live, learn, communicate and work to achieve common goals in a culturally-diverse world by fostering understanding, appreciation and respect for people of other ethnic, gender, socioeconomic, language and cultural backgrounds.[8]

A number of things are worth noting in both Banks's and the Florida definition of multicultural education. First, both call early childhood professionals—indeed, everyone—to develop an awareness of the diverse nature of contemporary society. Children in the United States are multicultural children. In many early childhood programs, Anglos are the minority population. Furthermore, 32 million people—14 percent of the population—speak a language other than English in the home, which is an increase of 8.9 million (38 percent) since 1980.[9] Because more children are multicultural, the early childhood curriculum must accommodate to meet their particular individual and cultural needs.

The multicultural nature of today's students has important implications beyond early childhood programs and extends to their life outside the program as well. Multiculturalism influences and affects work habits, interpersonal relations, and a person's general outlook on life. Early childhood professionals must also take these multicultural influences into consideration when designing curriculum and instructional processes.

Second, both definitions of multicultural education call our attention to the *inclusive* nature of multicultural education. Notice that in addition to ethnicity and culture, multicultural education also entails gender, socioeconomic status, and language. In this sense, the nature of multicultural education has been significantly expanded compared to how it was viewed a decade or so ago. Frequently, individuals with disabilities are also included in efforts to promote multicultural education and understanding. This approach is evident in Banks's definition of multicultural education as a process.

VistaKids programs address some basic fundamental challenges of educating the United States' increasingly diverse population (see pages L and M of the color insert). For instance, how can early childhood professionals use technology to help millions of immigrant children become literate in their native language and English? How can professionals help assure that multicultural children will not become technological illiterates? The answers to these questions are not easy to give or implement.

VistaKids programs also represent another reality: the willingness of the private sector and special interest groups to fund and support programs for young children. In fact, this trend is one of the great changes in early childhood education over the last decade and will continue.

MULTICULTURAL INFUSION

Today, early childhood professionals emphasize *infusing* multiculturalism into their curriculum, programs, and practices. *Infusion* means that multiculturalism is a part of children's and families' daily lives. Efforts at promoting multiculturalism in an early childhood program have implications far beyond the program itself. A primary goal of multicultural education is to change the lives of children and their families.

In a larger perspective, infusion strategies are used to assure that multiculturalism becomes a part of the entire center, school, and home. For example, some infusion processes used by early childhood programs are (1) teaching to children's learning styles, (2) promoting and using conflict resolution strategies (see chap. 12), (3) encouraging cooperative learning, (4) fostering cultural awareness, and (5) welcoming parent and community involvement for all families. Listed here are some strategies to help make instructional programs sensitive and responsive to diversity:

- *Contributions.*   Professionals should add to classroom activities, as appropriate, the accomplishments of women, individuals with disabilities, and people from different cultural groups.
- *Themes.*   Early childhood professionals may select themes that help strengthen children's understanding of self, their culture, and the cultures of others. Literature choices from a variety of cultures can help children identify cultural similarities and encourage understanding and tolerance.
- *Issues.*   Topics such as prejudice, stereotyping, discrimination, and segregation can and should be discussed in early childhood classrooms.
- *Selection of instructional materials.*   When picking materials for use in their programs, early childhood professionals can use the following criteria:

  Make sure people of color and many cultural groups are represented.

  Make sure the materials do not include stereotypical roles and language.

  Make sure there is gender equity—that is, that boys and girls are represented equally and in nonstereotypical roles.

  Make sure that historic information is accurate and nondiscriminatory.

  Make sure people of all cultures are represented fairly and accurately.

THE MULTICULTURAL EARLY CHILDHOOD PROFESSIONAL

How can the early childhood professional respond to the challenge of infusing and including multiculturalism in the early childhood curriculum? The following sections offer some suggestions.

Use Currently Popular Child-Centered Approaches

Many of the things early childhood professionals and children do in programs and classrooms can be used to infuse multiculturalism into the curriculum. For example, in cooperative learning, the teacher can form groups to address issues of communication and equity (see chap. 9 for more information about cooperative learning). Whole language offers many opportunities to use multicultural literature (see later discussion). The point is that the professional who truly desires a multicultural setting, curriculum, and program will seek to do this within the everyday life of the classroom and through instructional practices.

Use Good Literature

Many early childhood educators use literature to infuse multiculturalism into their programs. Literature is selected that emphasizes peoples' habits, customs, and general living and working behaviors. Through this approach, professionals stress the

Program in Practice

IMPLICATIONS OF LATINO CHILD DEVELOPMENT FOR EARLY CHILDHOOD PROFESSIONALS

In order to provide appropriate programs and services to Latino populations (i.e., people whose origins are Mexican, Puerto Rican, Cuban, Central or South American, or some other Spanish origin) residing in the United States, early childhood professionals must begin to understand what aspects of the developmental process are "culturally specific" and what aspects are universal or common to all humans regardless of cultural background. This differentiation is not easily made. One of the primary reasons for our lack of understanding is the absence of systematic research targeting minority children in general. Much of what we know is often based on data that implicitly or explicitly compares low-income minority children against middle-class Anglo populations. The problem with this approach is that minority children's development tends to be viewed as less optimal when compared to their middle-class counterparts. Early childhood professionals must base their understanding of minority children's development within their own particular cultural context.

Given this guideline, what do we know about the Latino child's growth and development that is "culturally specific" and that has implications for how programs and services should be structured? First, we know that cultural background and socioeconomic background are highly interrelated so that what we think may be "culturally specific" may be more a function of the group's adaptation to their socioeconomic conditions. When social class is similar, differences between middle-income Anglos and middle-income Latinos may decrease. For example, research shows that maternal teaching strategies are different when comparing low-income Latinos and middle-income Anglos. However, differences substantially decrease when comparisons are made between middle-income Latinos and middle-income Anglos.

Social class standing is an important indicator of available resources such as the quality of housing, employment opportunities, medical services, and, most importantly, the quality of educational programs. For Latinos residing in the United States, their level of acculturation also plays an important role. *Acculturation* refers to the degree to which an individual is able to function effectively in the dominant culture. This quality includes the ability to speak the language, knowledge of the dominant group's values, and cultural expressions (e.g., foods, art). These factors play a major role in determining an individual's ability to adapt to the wider society. Therefore, the early childhood professional must begin to appreciate the relationship between social class standing and acculturation and those behaviors that stem from living in different socioeconomic situations.

Second, in understanding Latino child development, it is important to cultivate an awareness of Latino parents' orientation to children and examine how this affects the goals of child rearing. Previous research on parental beliefs suggest that cultural background is an important determinant of parental ideas. The type of competence parents expect of young children may vary from culture to culture. For low-income immigrant Latino parents, expectation for their children's skill development may differ from Latinos born in the United States. That is, foreign-born Latinos perceive the behavioral capabilities of young children as developing later than do U.S.-born Latinos. It may be that low-income

Contributed by Marlene Zepeda, California State University, Los Angeles.

immigrant Latinos have a more maturational orientation to children's development so that the early emphasis on cognitive stimulation promoted in the United States is somewhat inconsistent with their expectations.

A maturational approach to child rearing may stem from the social and historic backgrounds of Latino groups living in the United States. In cultures in which children are expected to take part in the cultural activities of adults, such as sibling caretaking and economic maintenance of the family, certain parent-child interaction patterns will emerge. Thus, in more rural, traditional culture, parents may socialize their children by stressing observation and immediate assistance in task development rather than explicit instruction, which tends to be valued by middle-class U.S. parents. On the other hand, in U.S. culture children are segregated into age-graded classrooms in which information is given in bits and pieces over an extended period.

Early childhood professionals need to consider how parental orientation may differ from the specific goals and objectives of a particular intervention program. When working with immigrant families it is sometimes appropriate to indicate how the expectations of the school explicitly differ from the group's orientation. For many immigrant families, adaptation and innovation are a way of life, and accepting different ways of doing things is part and parcel of the immigrant experience. However, for second-generation or more acculturated groups reared in the United States, such explicit contrast may not suffice. In these instances, the practitioner must become familiar with the degree of acculturation that characterizes the group and adjust their services accordingly.

Third, Latinos hold certain values and beliefs that are important for childhood socialization. The following sections discuss an overview of important core values and beliefs that will vary in individual families depending on their acculturation level, socioeconomic standing, and ethnic loyalty. It is very important to see these core values as broad generalizations subject to adaptations to local conditions.

Familialism

This value is viewed as one of the most important culture-specific values of Latinos. *Familialism* refers to strong identification and connections to the immediate and extended family. Behaviors associated with familialism include strong feelings of loyalty, reciprocity, and solidarity. Familialism is manifested through the following: (1) feelings of obligation to provide both material and emotional support to the family, (2) dependence on relatives for help and support, and (3) reliance on relatives as behavioral and attitudinal referents.

Respeto

Associated with familialism is the cultural concept of *respeto,* which is an extremely important underlying tenet of interpersonal interaction. Basically, *respeto* refers to the deference ascribed to various members of the family or society because of their position. Generally speaking, respect is accorded to the position and not necessarily the person. Thus, respect is expected toward elders, parents, older siblings within the family, and teachers, clergy, nurses, and doctors outside the family. With respect comes deference; that is, the person will not question the individual in the authority position, will exhibit very courteous behavior in front of them, and will appear to agree with information presented to them by the authority figure.

Bien Educado

If a person exhibits the characteristics associated with *respeto,* then they are said to be *bien educado.* What is important here is that the term *education* is not formal education but the acquisition of the appropriate social skills and graces within the Latino cultural context. For traditional Latinos, someone could have honors from Harvard University, but if he or she did not conform to this system, the person would be considered badly educated.

Conclusion

Incorporation of important cultural values and beliefs into the professional's interpersonal conduct provides families with a semblance of cultural continuity and maintains feelings of self-respect. The professional can accomplish this by demonstrating high degrees of courtesy, understanding that indirect communication on the part of the child and parent is a reflection of *respeto* to teachers as authority figures, and viewing the broader family configuration as an important resource for understanding Latino family dynamics. Within this general framework, the professional must accommodate individual differences and local community conditions.

similarities and differences regarding how children and families live their *whole* lives. This approach removes multiculturalism from merely stressing differences or only teaching about habits and customs.

Multicultural literature is fast becoming a well-established part of early childhood education. Previously, much of early childhood multicultural literature focused on African Americans and the customs of children in other countries. Today, multicultural literature is more representative of cultural groups living in the United States. Books are also more *authentic.* This means they are written by authors from a particular culture, they present true-to-life accounts both past and present, and they are well illustrated. The following books are representative of the rich selections now available:

The Last Princess by Fay Stanley (New York: Four Winds Press, 1991). This is a biography of nineteenth-century Hawaiian Princess Ka'iulani and her efforts to keep business interests from taking over Hawaii.

Nine-In One Grr! Grr! by Blia Xiong (San Francisco: Children's Book Press, 1989). A story of the Hmong tribe. When the great god Shao promises Tiger nine cubs each year, Bird comes up with a clever trick to prevent the land from being overrun by tigers.

Family Pictures by Carmen Lomas Garza (San Francisco: Children's Book Press, 1990). The author describes, in bilingual text and illustrations, her experiences growing up in a Hispanic community in Texas.

Many contemporary instructional practices such as cooperative learning are excellent ways to promote collaboration, cooperation, and positive interpersonal relations. What other practices would you use to help all children get along with and work well with others?

The Invisible Hunters by Harriet Rohmer (San Francisco: Children's Book Press, 1987). Set in seventeenth-century Nicaragua, this Miskito Indian legend illustrates the impact of the first European trader on traditional life.

Tar Beach by Faith Ringgold (New York: Crown, 1991). A young girl dreams of flying above her Harlem home, claiming all she sees for herself and her family. Based on the author's quilt painting of the same name.

Bigmama's by Donald Crews (New York: Greenwillow Books, 1991). Visiting Bigmama's house in the country, young Donald Crews finds his relatives full of news and the old place and its surroundings, just the same as the year before.

Assess Your Attitudes Toward Children

The following are questions early childhood professionals can ask to help assess their attitudes toward young children and their families to help assure that they are multiculturally sensitive:

- Do you have different expectations of children from different neighborhoods? For example, do you expect a higher level of work from students who live in affluent neighborhoods than from those who live in trailer parks?

- With which children do you feel most comfortable? Are you influenced by what children wear? The positions their parents hold? The color of their skin? Some people believe men have higher levels of intelligence than women and that those with lighter skin colors are smarter than those who are dark-skinned. Some people perceive those with an affluent, white-collar lifestyle as being "smarter, better, and more civilized" than those from working-class communities.

- What do you know about the children's communities? In order to provide schooling relevant to the lives of students, teachers need a sense of the child's world view. What is it like living in the community? What roles and relationships are most important? Do you understand the nuances of student nonverbal and verbal communication?

- What connections do you feel to the children's community? Society has changed drastically in the past twenty years. Few children attend neighborhood schools in large urban districts; instead, many students of all colors have become accustomed to long bus rides. In addition, few teachers teach in their neighborhood; instead, they may drive ten miles [or more] to another community.

- Do you expect your children to learn your ways of teaching, or do you find out in which modes of instruction children learn best? When teaching in a multicultural manner, do not try to mold the child to fit your manner of teaching. Instead learn about the child and your teaching changes to affirm the child. One effective strategy is to use culturally familiar examples when discussing new concepts. For example, a teacher was giving a lesson in how people can provide themselves with complete proteins every day without eating meat. The teacher asked her predominantly Mexican-American class what they ate for dinner. Some of the kids said "pizza." Other students said "spaghetti," while others yelled out "tortillas and beans." The teacher then explained that if they ate tortillas, which are made from grains, with their beans, they were getting a complete protein. The example helped to make connections between an abstract scientific concept and students' personal lives.[10]

Use These Processes

Gloria Boutte and Christine McCormick[11] suggest six processes that will help teachers assure they conduct authentic multicultural programs and activities:

1. *Building multicultural programs.*   This means that teachers will seek to develop and conduct programs that are multicultural. Teachers and caregivers must truly want to have a classroom, center, and program that is multicultural in materials, programs, and attitudes. Such programs should include the similarities and differences in peoples and culture.

2. *Showing appreciation of differences in others.*   To achieve this goal, early childhood educators must model the behavior they want in their children and colleagues. For example, professionals should respond positively to children's language, avoid correcting, and show appreciation and encouragement. In authentic classrooms— as opposed to unaware one—professionals demonstrate appreciation of other cultures and viewpoints.

3. *Avoiding stereotypes.*   The culturally aware professional realizes that "Hispanic" is not one culture but that it includes children from many countries and cultures. The culturally sensitive professional does not predict failure for certain cultural groups but has high hopes, aspirations, and expectations for all children and believes all children are capable of learning.

4. *Acknowledging differences.*   Professionals must believe children are different, acknowledge children are different, and plan curriculum and programs that reflect and authentically demonstrate that children are different. Children's cultures and family backgrounds are viewed as assets, not deficits.

5. *Discovering diversity within the classroom.*   Professionals really get to know children and their families by visiting in their homes, by talking to them, by exploring the communities in which they live, and by involving parents, family members, and the community in the program.

6. *Avoiding pseudo multiculturalism.*   Authentic professionals address the needs of all children and are sensitive to all cultures of all children. Sometimes people mistakenly think they are promoting multiculturalism by focusing exclusively on teaching about and infusing one culture into the curriculum and program.

Follow These Guidelines

Early childhood professionals must keep in mind that they are the key to a multicultural classroom. These guidelines can help you in teaching multiculturalism:

-   Recognize that all children are unique. They all have special talents, abilities, and styles of learning and relating to others. Provide opportunities for children to be different and use their abilities.

-   Promote uniqueness and diversity as positive.

-   Get to know, appreciate, and respect the cultural backgrounds of your children. Visit families and community neighborhoods to learn more about cultures and religions and the ways of life they engender.

-   Infuse children's culture (and other cultures as well) in your teaching.

-   Use *authentic* situations to provide for cultural learning and understanding. For example, a field trip to an open-air market (e.g., Little Haiti, a neighborhood in Miami) provides an opportunity for understanding firsthand many of the details about how people conduct their daily lives. Such an experience provides wonderful opportunities for writing, cooking, reading, and endless possibilities for the dramatic play area. What about setting up a market in the classroom?

-   Use authentic assessment activities to assess fully children's learning and growth. A portfolio (see chaps. 8 and 9) provides an ideal way to assess children in nonbiased and culturally sensitive ways. The point is that early childhood professionals should use varied ways of assessing children.

-   Infuse culture into your lesson planning, teaching, and caregiving. Use all subject areas—math, science, language arts, literacy, music, art, and social studies—to relate culture to all the children and all you do.

-   Use children's interests and experiences to form a basis for planning lessons and developing activities. This approach makes students feel good about their backgrounds, cultures, families, and experiences. Also, when children can relate what they are doing in the classroom to their out-of-school experiences, their learning is more meaningful to them because it is connected to their daily lives.

-   Be proud of and secure in your culture. Children will ask about you, so you should share with them your background.

HEAD START AND MULTICULTURAL PROGRAMMING

Head Start has identified the following principles as a framework for multicultural programming:[12]

- Every individual is rooted in culture.
- The cultural groups represented in the communities and families of each Head Start program are the primary sources for culturally relevant programming.
- Culturally relevant and diverse programming requires learning accurate information about the culture of different groups and discarding stereotypes.
- Addressing cultural relevance in making curriculum choices is a necessary, developmentally appropriate practice.
- Every individual has the right to maintain his or her own identity while acquiring the skills required to function in our diverse society.
- Effective programs for children with limited English-speaking ability require continued development of the primary language while the acquisition of English is facilitated.
- Culturally relevant programming requires staff who reflect the community and families served.
- Multicultural programming for children enables children to develop an awareness of, respect for, and appreciation of individual cultural differences. It is beneficial to all children.
- Culturally relevant and diverse programming examines and challenges institutional and personal biases.
- Culturally relevant and diverse programming and practices are incorporated in all components and services.

DIFFERENT CHILDREN, DIFFERENT LEARNING STYLES

Every person has a unique learning style. Although every person's learning style is different, we can cluster learning styles for instructional purposes. It makes sense to consider these various styles and account for them in early childhood programs when organizing the environment and developing activities.

What do we mean, exactly, by learning styles?

Learning style is the way that students of every age are affected by their (a) *immediate environment,* (b) *own emotionality,* (c) *sociological needs,* (d) *physical characteristics,* and (e) *psychological inclinations* when concentrating and trying to master and remember new or difficult information or skills. Children learn best *only* when they use their learning style characteristics advantageously; otherwise they study, but often forget what they tried to learn.[13]

Learning styles consist of the following elements:

- *Environmental*—sound, light, temperature, and design

- *Emotional*—motivation, persistence, responsibility, and the need for either structure or choice
- *Sociological*—learning alone, with others, or in a variety of ways (perhaps including media)
- *Physical*—perceptual strengths, intake, time of day or night energy levels, and mobility
- *Psychological*—global/analytic, hemispheric preference, and impulsive/reflective

The elements of individual learning styles are depicted in Figure 14–3.

Providing for children's learning styles helps professionals respond appropriately to diversity in their programs. One of the most effective ways to begin is by diagnosing each individual student's learning style. A useful device for doing this is the *Learning Style Inventory,* developed by Rita Dunn, Kenneth Dunn, and Gary Price. A second thing that professionals can do is provide for children's individual learning styles through classroom practices and adaptations. For example, Dunn, Dunn, and Price suggest the following ways to adapt the learning environment to children's individual learning styles.[14]

Noise Level

Provide music on earphones or earplugs (to avoid distractions for those who need quiet); create conversation areas or an activity-oriented learning environment separately from children who need quiet. *Or* establish silent areas: provide individual dens or alcoves with carpeted sections; suggest earphones or earplugs without sound to insulate against activity and noise.

Light

Place children near windows or under adequate illumination; add table or desk lamps. *Or* create learning spaces under indirect or subdued light away from windows; use dividers or plants to block or diffuse illumination.

Authority Figures Present

Place children near appropriate professionals and schedule periodic meetings with them; supervise and check assignments often. *Or* identify the child's sociological characteristics, and permit isolated study if self-oriented and peer groupings if peer oriented, or multiple options if learning in several ways is indicated; interact with collaborative professional.

Visual Preferences

Use pictures, filmstrips, films, graphs, single-concept loops, transparencies, computer monitors, diagrams, drawings, books, and magazines; supply resources that require reading and seeing; use programmed learning (if student

FIGURE 14–3 Diagnosing Learning Styles

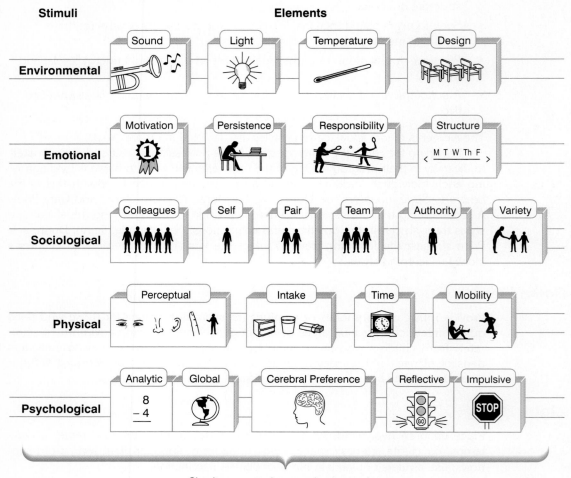

Simultaneous and successive processing

Source: From M. C. Carbo, R. Dunn, and K. Dunn, *Teaching Students to Read through Their Individual Learning Styles* (Boston: Allyn & Bacon, 1986), p. 3. Copyright © 1986 by Allyn & Bacon. Reprinted by permission.

needs structure) and written assignments and evaluations. Reinforce knowledge through tactile, kinesthetic, and then auditory resources. *Or* use resources prescribed under the perceptual preferences that are strong. Use several multisensory resources such as videotapes, sound-filmstrips, television, and tactile/kinesthetic material. Introduce information through child's strongest perceptual preference.

Tactile Preferences

Use manipulative and three-dimensional materials; resources should be touchable and movable as well as readable; allow such children to plan, demonstrate, report, and evaluate with models and other real objects; encourage them to keep written or graphic records. Reinforce through kinesthetic, visual, and then auditory resources. *Or* use resources prescribed under the perceptual preferences that are strong. Use several multisensory resources such as videotapes, sound-filmstrips, television, and real-life experiences such as visits, interviewing, building, designing, and so on. Introduce information through activities such as baking, building, sewing, visiting, or acting; reinforce through visual, auditory, and kinesthetic methods. Introduce information through child's strongest perceptual preference.

Kinesthetic Preferences

Provide opportunities for real and active experiences in planning and carrying out objectives; visits, projects, acting, and floor games are appropriate activities for such individuals. Reinforce through tactile, visual, and then auditory resources. *Or* use resources prescribed under the preferences that are strong. Use several multisensory resources such as videotapes, sound-filmstrips, television, and tactile/manipulative materials. Introduce information through "real-life" activities (e.g., planning a part in a play or a trip); reinforce through tactile resources such as electroboards, task cards, learning circles, and so forth; then reinforce further visual and auditory resources.

Mobility

Provide frequent breaks, assignments that require movement to different locations, and schedules that permit mobility in the learning environment; require results, not immobility. *Or* provide a stationary desk or learning station where most of the child's responsibilities can be completed without requiring excessive movement.

DIFFERENT CHILDREN, DIFFERENT INTELLIGENCES

Piaget's theory of intelligence (see chap. 4) is based primarily on one intelligence, logical-mathematical. In his book *Frames of Mind*,[15] Howard Gardner hypothesizes that rather than one overall intelligence, there are at least seven distinct intelligences (see chap. 2):

- Linguistic
- Logical-mathematical
- Spatial
- Musical
- Bodily kinesthetic
- Interpersonal
- Intrapersonal

Further, Gardner maintains that all children possess all seven of these intelligences, although some intelligences may be stronger than others. This accounts for why children have a preferred learning style, different interests, likes and dislikes, habits, preferred lifestyles, and career choices.

These seven intelligences imply that students have unique learning styles appropriate to the particular intelligences. Consequently, early childhood professionals should consider children's learning styles and make efforts to accommodate their teaching styles, activities, and materials to them. Figure 14–4 will help you make the connection using Gardner's theory.

SEXISM AND SEX-ROLE STEREOTYPING

Reasons for the concern about sexism and sex-role stereotyping are the same as those that have promoted interest in multiculturalism in general and nondiscrimination in particular.

The Civil Rights movement and its emphasis on equality provides an impetus for seeking more equal treatment for women as well as minority groups. Encouraged by the Civil Rights Act of 1964, which prohibits discrimination on the basis of race or national origin, civil rights and women's groups successfully sought legislation to prohibit discrimination on the basis of sex. Title IX of the Education Amendments Acts of 1972, as amended by Public Law 93-568, prohibits such discrimination in the schools:

> No person in the United States shall, on the basis of sex, be excluded from participation in, be denied the benefits of, or be subjected to discrimination under any education program or activity receiving Federal financial assistance.[16]

Since Title IX prohibits sex discrimination in any educational program that receives federal money, early childhood programs as well as elementary schools, high schools, and universities cannot discriminate against males or females in enrollment policies, curriculum offerings, or activities.

The women's movement (see chap. 1) has encouraged the nation, educational institutions, and families to examine how they educate, treat, and rear children in relationship to sex roles.

There is yet another reason for the nation's interest in sexism. A recent survey conducted by the American Association of University Women (AAUW) reveals that four out of five students in grades 8 to 11 are sexually harassed in school. Sexual harassment was defined as "unwanted and unwelcome sexual behavior which interferes with your life."[17] The AAUW research further revealed that

- girls receive significantly less attention from classroom teachers than do boys;
- African American girls have fewer interactions with teachers than do white girls, despite evidence that they attempt to initiate interactions more frequently;
- sexual harassment of girls by boys—from innuendo to actual assault—in our nation's schools is increasing.[18]

FIGURE 14–4   Seven Styles of Learning

Type	Likes To	Is Good At	Learns Best By
Linguistic Learner *"The Word Player"*	read write tell stories	memorizing names, places, dates and trivia	saying, hearing and seeing words
Logical/Mathematical Learner *"The Questioner"*	do experiments figure things out work with numbers ask questions explore patterns and relationships	math reasoning logic problem solving	categorizing classifying working with abstract patterns/relationships
Spatial Learner *"The Visualizer"*	draw, build, design and create things daydream look at pictures/slides watch movies play with machines	imagining things sensing changes mazes/puzzles reading maps, charts	visualizing dreaming using the mind's eye working with colors/pictures
Musical Learner *"The Music Lover"*	sing, hum tunes listen to music play an instrument respond to music	picking up sounds remembering melodies noticing pitches/ rhythms keeping time	rhythm melody music
Bodily/Kinesthetic Learner *"The Mover"*	move around touch and talk use body language	physical activities (sports/dance/acting) crafts	touching moving interacting with space processing knowledge through bodily sensations
Interpersonal Learner *"The Socializer"*	have lots of friends talk to people join groups	understanding people leading others organizing communicating manipulating mediating conflicts	sharing comparing relating cooperating interviewing
Intrapersonal Learner *"The Individual"*	work alone pursue own interests	understanding self focusing inward on feelings/dreams following instincts pursuing interests/ goals being original	working alone individualized projects self-paced instruction having own space

Source: Chart from "Different Child, Different Style" by Kathy Faggella and Janet Horowitz in *Instructor,* September 1990, p. 52. Copyright © 1990 by Scholastic Inc. Reprinted by permission.

The AAUW results are revealing in several ways, and they have many implications for early childhood professionals. First, the findings reveal the extent of sexual harassment. Second, the data show that 85 percent of the girls surveyed and 76 percent of the boys say they have been sexually harassed. Some may have thought or think that sexual harassment is something only girls experience, but this data indicate the extent to which boys are also harassed. Third, the data from the survey reveal that the psychological effects of sexual harassment are more profound for girls than boys. Seventy percent of the girls and 24 percent of the boys reported that the experience made them very or somewhat upset.

These data should cause early childhood professionals to be concerned about the roots of sexism and sexual harassment and to realize that these practices have their beginnings in the early years in practices found in homes, centers, and preschools. Early childhood professionals must continue to examine personal and programmatic practices, evaluate materials, and work with parents for the purpose of eliminating sexism and to assure that girls—indeed, all children—will not be short-changed in any way.

The *Federal Register* defines *sexism* this way:

> The collection of attitudes, beliefs, and behaviors which result from the assumption that one sex is superior. *In the context of schools*, the term refers to the collection of structures, policies, practices and activities that overtly or covertly prescribe the development of girls and boys and prepare them for traditional sex roles.[19]

Research consistently demonstrates that boys receive more attention in classrooms than do girls. This is but one example of the unequal treatment of girls. Early childhood professionals must examine their personal and programmatic practices, evaluate materials, and work with parents for the purpose of eliminating sexism and to assure that girls—indeed, all children—will not be short-changed in any way.

On the basis of sex, parents and society begin at a child's birth to teach a particular sex role. Probably no other factor plays such a determining role in life as does identification with a sex role. It was once thought that certain characteristics of maleness or femaleness were innate; but it is now generally recognized that sex role is a product of socialization, role modeling, and conscious and unconscious behavior modification. Culturally, certain role models are considered appropriate for males and certain ones suitable for females. Traditional male roles center around masculinity, traditional female roles around femininity.

Society imposes and enforces certain sex roles. Schools, as agents of socialization, encourage certain behaviors for boys and different ones for girls. Parents, by the way they dress their children, the toys they give them, and what they let them do, encourage certain sex-role behaviors. Parents also model behaviors for their children and tell them to act "like your mother" or act "like your father." Parents and teachers also modify, shape, and reinforce sex-role behavior. "Don't act like a girl," or "Play with this—this is for boys," or "Don't play with that—only girls do that," and "Boys don't cry" are a few of the ways they modify behavior toward one sex role or the other.

Educators disagree as to whether children can or should be reared in an non-stereotyped environment. Some say children have a right to determine their own sex roles and should therefore be reared in an environment that does not impose arbitrary sex roles. Rather, the environment should be free from sex-role stereotyping to encourage the child to develop his or her own sex role. Other educators say it is impossible not to assign sex roles. In addition, they argue that development of a sex role is a difficult task of childhood and that children need help in this process.

It is too simplistic to say one will not assign or teach a particular sex role. As society is now constituted, differentiated sex roles are still very much in evidence and likely to remain so. Parents and teachers should provide children with less restrictive options and promote a more open framework in which sex roles can develop. These are some ways to provide a non-sex-stereotyped environment:

- *Provide opportunities for all children to experience the activities, materials, toys, and emotions traditionally associated with both sexes.*   Give boys as well as girls opportunities to experience tenderness, affection, and the warmth of close parent-child and teacher-pupil relationships. Conversely, girls as well as boys should be able to behave aggressively, get dirty, and participate in what are typically considered male activities, such as woodworking and block building.

- *Examine the classroom materials you are using and determine whether they contain obvious instances of sex-role stereotyping.*   When you find examples, modify the materials or do not use them. Let publishers know your feelings, and tell other faculty members about them.

- *Examine your behavior to see whether you are encouraging sex stereotypes.*   Do you tell girls they cannot empty wastebaskets, but they can water the plants? Do you tell girls they cannot lift certain things in the classroom because they are too heavy for them? Do you tell boys they should not play with dolls and "boys aren't supposed to cry"? Do you reward only females who are always passive, well behaved, and well mannered?

- *Have a colleague or parent observe you in your classroom to determine what sex-role behaviors you are encouraging.*   We are often unaware of our behaviors, and self-correction begins only after the behaviors are pointed out to us. Obviously, unless you begin with yourself, eliminating sex-role stereotyping practices will be next to impossible.

- *Determine what physical arrangements in the classroom promote or encourage sex-role stereotyping.*   Are boys encouraged to use the block area more than girls? Are girls encouraged to use the quiet areas more than boys? Do children hang their wraps separately—a place for the boys and a place for the girls? All children should have equal access to all learning areas of the classroom; no area should be reserved exclusively for one sex. In addition, examine any activity and practice that promotes segregation of children by sex or culture. Cooperative learning activities and group work offer ways to assure that children of both sexes work together.

- *Counsel with parents to show them ways to promote nonsexist child rearing.*   If society is to achieve a truly nonsexist environment, parents will be the key factor, for it is in the home that many sex-stereotyping behaviors are initiated and practiced.

- *Become conscious of words that promote sexism.*   For example, in a topic on community helpers, taught in most preschool and kindergarten programs at one time or another, many words carry a sexist connotation. *Fireman, policeman*, and *mailman* are all masculine terms; nonsexist terms are *firefighter, police officer*, and *mail carrier.* You should examine all your curricular materials and teaching practices to determine how you can make them free from sexism.

- *Examine your teaching and behavior to be sure you are not limiting certain roles to either sex.*   Females should not be encouraged to pursue only roles that are subservient, submissive, lacking in intellectual demands, or low paying. Some specific things you can do in your teaching are these:

  Give all children a chance to respond to questions. Research consistently shows that teachers do not wait long enough after they ask a question for most children, especially girls, to respond. Therefore, quick responders—usually boys—answer all the questions. By waiting longer you will be able to respond to girls' answers.

  Be an active professional. Just as we want children to engage in active learning, so too professionals should engage in active involvement in the classroom. This helps assure that you will get to interact with and give attention to all children, not just a few.

  Help all children become independent and do things for themselves. Discourage behaviors and attitudes that promote helplessness and dependency. Discourage remarks such as "I can't because I'm not good at. . . ."

Examine your classroom management and behavioral guidance techniques (see chap. 12). Are you treating both sexes and all cultures fairly and in individual and culturally appropriate ways?

Use portfolios, teacher observations, and other authentic means of assessing children's progress (see chap. 9) in order to provide bias-free assessment. Involving children in the evaluation of their own efforts is also a good way of promoting positive images of themselves.

- *Do not encourage children to dress in ways that lead to sex stereotyping.*   Females should not be encouraged to wear frilly dresses, then forbidden to participate in an activity because they might get dirty or spoil their clothes. Children should be encouraged to dress so they will be able to participate in a wide range of activities both indoors and outdoors. This is an area in which you may be able to help parents if they seek your advice. Or, you may want to discuss how dressing their child differently can contribute to more effective participation.

BILINGUAL EDUCATION

For most people, *bilingual education* means that children (or adults, or both) will be taught a second language. Some people interpret this to mean that the child's native language (often referred to as the *home language*)—whether English, Spanish, French, Italian, Chinese, Tagalog, or any of the other 125 languages in which bilingual programs are conducted—will tend to be suppressed. For other people, bilingual education means the child will become proficient in a second language. The Bilingual Education Act, Title VII of the Elementary Secondary Education Act (ESEA), sets forth the federal government's policy toward bilingual education:

> The Congress declares it to be the policy of the United States, in order to establish equal educational opportunity for all children and to promote educational excellence (A) to encourage the establishment and operation, where appropriate, of educational programs using bilingual educational practices, techniques, and methods, (B) to encourage the establishment of special alternative instructional programs for students of limited English proficiency in school districts where the establishment of bilingual education programs is not practicable or for other appropriate reasons, and (C) for those purposes, to provide financial assistance to local educational agencies.[20]

Reasons for Interest in Bilingual Education

Diversity is a positive aspect of U.S. society. Ethnic pride and identity have caused renewed interest in languages and a more conscious effort to preserve children's native languages. Sixty years ago, foreign-born individuals and their children wanted to camouflage their ethnicity and unlearn their language because it seemed unpatriotic or un-American; today, however, we hold the opposite viewpoint.

A second reason for interest in bilingual education is an emphasis on civil rights. Indeed, much of the concept of providing children with an opportunity to know, value, and use their heritage and language stems from people's recognition that they have a right to them. Just as extending to children with disabilities is very much evident today, so is doing the same to children and their languages. This extending of rights to children—in this case, a right to preserve their native language and learn English—is part of the view of children as people with rights (see chap. 1).

Yet another reason for bilingual interest is the number of people who speak a language other than English. According to the Census Bureau, 31.8 million, or one in seven, residents of the United States speak a language other than English, with Spanish now the second most common language other than English. Figure 14–5 shows the twenty-five most common languages (other than English) spoken in the home. Pay particular note to the fastest-growing languages, such as Mon-Khmer, spoken by Cambodians. Taken as a group, the Asian school-age population is expected to double by 2020.

These data show that the chances you will work with parents, children, and families in a language other than English is increasing. They also give you some idea what languages parents and children you work with will speak. Moreover, these increases will necessitate a need to develop culturally appropriate material and activities. As individual professionals and as a body of professionals, we cannot ignore the need for appropriate curriculum materials for children of all cultures. To do so runs the risk of adding to the risk of language-minority children being cut off from mainstream life and the American dream. Finally, there is a need to develop training programs for early childhood professionals that will enable them to work in culturally sensitive ways with parents, families, and children.

Types of Bilingual Programs

Early childhood programs and schools can make several responses to children's language learning. First, they can use an *immersion* program, in which children typically are placed in a program in which English is the exclusive language and all instruction is conducted in English. A teacher may or may not know the child's native language. The goal of an immersion program is to have children learn English as quickly and fluently as possible. Little if any effort is made to maintain or improve the child's native language ability.

A second response is to provide a *transitional* bilingual program, in which children study in their native language until they become proficient in the second language, usually English. In transitional programs, children are generally taught mostly in their native language for four or five years. About sixty to ninety minutes a day is devoted to English instruction. The goals of transitional bilingual education are twofold: (1) to help children acquire concepts and skills through their native language while becoming proficient in English and (2) to preserve, maintain, and enhance the child's native language and culture.

FIGURE 14–5   The Twenty-Five Languages Most Commonly Spoken at Home

Language	Total Speakers over 5 Years Old	Percentage Change from 1980
Spanish	17,339,172	50.1
French	1,702,176	8.3
German	1,547,049	–3.7
Italian	1,308,648	–19.9
Chinese	1,249,213	97.7
Tagalog	843,251	86.6
Polish	723,483	–12.4
Korean	626,478	127.2
Vietnamese	507,069	149.5
Portuguese	429,860	19.0
Japanese	427,657	25.0
Greek	388,260	–5.4
Arabic	355,150	57.4
Hindi, Urdu, and related	331,484	155.1
Russian	241,798	38.5
Yiddish	213,064	–33.5
Thai	206,266	131.6
Persian	201,865	84.7
French Creole	187,658	654.1
Armenian	149,694	46.3
Navajo	148,530	20.6
Hungarian	147,902	–17.9
Hebrew	144,292	45.5
Dutch	142,684	–2.6
Mon-Khmer	127,441	676.3

Source: "The Top 25 Languages," *New York Times,* Apr. 28, 1993, p. A10, from U.S. Census Bureau data. Copyright © 1993 by the New York Times Company. Reprinted by permission.

Texas Essential Elements for Bilingual Education

The following are the Texas Early Childhood Essential Elements for bilingual prekindergarten and kindergarten education:

Prekindergarten Bilingual

1. *Communicative development.*   The student shall be provided opportunities to:
   A. receive instruction of basic concepts of the school environment in the primary language
   B. learn to expand oral language spoken on topics relevant and meaningful for young learners

      i.   respond to storytelling or spoken discourse in verbal and/or non-verbal ways

      ii.   listen to literary selections daily for personal enjoyment and language acquisition, appreciate the sound devices of rhyme and rhythm, and comprehend meaning of written texts presented orally

      iii. recognize simple variation in language depending on social contexts

      iv. understand the meaning of words in spoken discourse

      v.   understand the meaning of Spanish sentence structures (e.g., statements, questions, commands) in spoken discourse, and

      vi. acquire Spanish sounds and intonation patterns by listening to spoken discourse

  C. learn to speak in social and school settings

      i.   participate in nonverbal communication through gesture, pantomime, and facial expression

      ii.   engage in a conversation by sharing ideas and opinions with others

      iii. talk about what is observed through the five senses

      iv. relate events from personal experiences

      v.   engage in creative drama activities

      vi. use speech for a variety of functions (e.g., greetings, apologies, requests, information giving, seeking); and

      vii. develop awareness of word order in spoken interactions.

2. *Literacy.* The student shall be provided opportunities to:

  A. experience a print-rich environment in the classroom

  B. participate in dictated stories and reading, group charts, labelling, personal dictation; and

  C. participate in independent writing (e.g., using marks, scribbles, invented spellings).

3. *Culture.* The student shall be provided opportunities to:

  A. learn the behaviors of the school culture

  B. respect differences in behavior and expressions of others

  C. value one's own family language and traditions; and

  D. discuss what families do together.

Kindergarten Bilingual

4. *Communicative development.* The student shall be provided opportunities to:

  A. respond to storytelling or spoken discourse in verbal and/or non-verbal ways

  B. listen to literary selections daily for personal enjoyment and language acquisition

      i.   appreciate the sound devices of rhyme and rhythm

      ii.   comprehend the meaning of written texts presented orally; and

      iii. predict probable outcome.

  C. respond to various language functions (e.g., greetings, following directions, requests, giving information, seeking information)

      D.   recognize simple variation in language depending on social contexts including formal and informal pronouns

      E.   understand the meaning of words in spoken discourse

      F.   understand the meaning of Spanish sentence structures (e.g., statements, questions, commands) in spoken discourse

      G.   acquire Spanish sounds and intonation patterns by listening to spoken discourse

      H.   participate in nonverbal communication through gesture, pantomime, and facial expression

      I.   communicate meaningfully in one-to-one and small group situations

      J.   engage in creative drama activities; and

      K.   narrate events from personal experience.

5.   *Literacy.*   The student shall be provided opportunities to:

      A.   experience a print-rich environment in the classroom

      B.   participate in dictated stories and reading, group charts, labeling, personal dictation

      C.   participate in independent writing (e.g., using marks, scribble, invented spellings)

      D.   discriminate sound for each letter of the alphabet

      E.   discriminate visual shapes and forms of letters

      F.   understand the direction of conventional print

      G.   respond to storytelling by:

         i.   telling what the story is about

         ii.   recalling important facts and details

         iii.   arranging events in sequential order; and

         iv.   distinguishing between real and make-believe

      H.   make choices of children's literature for individual viewing; and

      I.   keep a notebook of daily drawings, scribbles, pictures, or emerging writing to represent experiences.

6.   *Culture.*   The student shall be provided opportunities to:

      A.   learn the behaviors of the school culture

      B.   respect differences in behavior and expressions of others

      C.   value one's own family language and traditions; and

      D.   discuss what families do together.[21]

Issues in Bilingual Education

As you might expect, programs for helping children learn English are controversial. Critics of immersion programs assert that when the focus is only on teaching English, children are at risk for losing the ability to speak and use their native language. On the other hand, proponents of immersion programs maintain that English is the language of schooling and U.S. society, and it is in children's best interests to learn

English as quickly and fluently as possible. Further, they maintain that it is the parents' responsibility to help maintain native language and culture. For their part, parents want their children to be successful in school and society. Some regret that their children have not maintained their native language because of the role it plays in culture and religion.

Critics of transitional bilingual programs maintain that it takes children too long to learn English and that it is too costly to try and maintain a child's native language. On the other hand, proponents of transitional programs say it makes sense to help children learn English while preserving native language and culture.

AMERICAN INDIAN AND ALASKA NATIVE EDUCATION

A resurgence has surfaced in the preservation and teaching of native languages by many American Indian groups, partly because of a revived interest in Native American issues and concerns, a national report, and the passage of several federal laws. The national report of the Indians Nations at Risk Task Force says that if Native American children are to succeed, then barriers such as "the loss of native-language ability and the wisdom of the older generations" must be overcome. The report also encourages that native languages be used in the home and reinforced in the schools. In addition, the Native American Languages Act of 1990 urges "all educational institutions serving Indians to include native-language instruction in their curricula."

ANTIBIAS CURRICULUM

The goal of an *antibias* curriculum is to help children learn to be accepting of others regardless of gender, race, ethnicity, socioeconomic status, or disability. Children participating in an antibias curriculum are comfortable with diversity and learn to stand up for themselves and others in the face of injustice. Additionally, in this supportive, open-minded environment, children learn to construct a knowledgeable, confident self-identity.

Young children are constantly learning about differences and need a sensitive teacher to help them form positive, unbiased perceptions about variations among people. As children color pictures of themselves, for example, you may hear a comment such as "Your skin is white and my skin is brown." Many teachers are tempted, in the name of equality, to respond, "It doesn't matter what color we are—we are all people." While this remark does not sound harmful, it fails to help children develop positive feelings about *themselves*. A more appropriate response might be "Tabitha, your skin is a beautiful brown, which is just right for you; Christina, your skin is a beautiful white, which is just right for you." A comment such as this positively acknowledges each child's different skin color, which is an important step for developing a positive self-concept.

Through the sensitive guidance of caring teachers, children learn to speak up for themselves and others. By living and learning in an accepting environment, children find that they have the ability to change intolerable situations and can have a positive impact on the future. This is part of what empowerment is all about, and it begins in the home and early childhood programs. It is important, then, that the antibias curriculum starts in early childhood and continue throughout the school years.

CHILDREN OF POVERTY

Although everyone imagines the United States as a land of opportunity, a large number of the nation's children may not realize the dream of becoming all that they can be. More and more children are subject to the disadvantages and long-term destructive consequences poverty engenders. To be poor means getting a poor start in life. In the United States, 21.9 percent of all children under eighteen live in poverty (see chap. 10 for the poverty income guidelines).[22] This rate is more than double that of other major industrialized nations (see Figure 14–6).

FIGURE 14–6   Percentage of Children Living in Poverty in Industrialized Nations

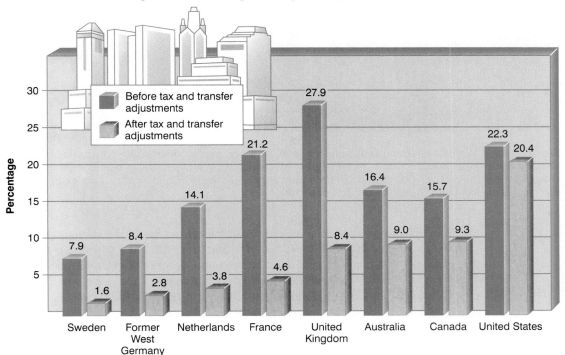

Source: "Children in Poverty," *Education Week,* Sept. 29, 1993, p. 3, from United Nations Children's Fund data. Reprinted with permission from *Education Week.*

Homelessness is not something that only happens in other communities or on television. Homeless children and their families are a growing part of society. Early childhood professionals must find ways to meet the needs of homeless children and to provide them with education and other services which will enable them to reach their full potential.

Early childhood professionals are seeking ways to provide educational and preventive social services to poor children and their families to enable them to develop their potential so as to lead healthy and successful lives. Certainly, agencies such as Head Start have done many good things for the poor and disadvantaged, but it is not enough. Only about 25 percent of the children who need Head Start services receive them, and Head Start does not start soon enough—many children actually need a head start on Head Start. However, as we discussed in chapter 10, Head Start has received increased funding, and the possibility exists for more funding.

The facts from all the data that we have indicate that we are not doing the best we can for our children. We must be strong advocates for and on behalf of poor children and their families if we are to have any hope of helping assure that more children will not slide below the poverty line. We must—for the sake of our children, for all our sakes—provide for our children as though they truly are our greatest wealth. We cannot and should not settle for anything less.

READINGS FOR FURTHER ENRICHMENT

Banks, James A. *Teaching Strategies for Ethnic Studies* (Boston: Allyn & Bacon, 1991)

Deals with specific teaching strategies, goals, current trends, and a rationale for ethnic content in the curriculum.

Banks, James A., and Cherry McGee Banks. *Multicultural Education: Issues and Perspectives*, 2d ed. (Boston: Allyn & Bacon, 1993)

Two of the country's leading authorities in multicultural issues and programming provide a comprehensive and informative discussion of many issues involved in multicultural education today.

Baruth, Leroy. *Multicultural Education of Children and Adolescents* (New York: Addison-Wesley, 1992)

Addresses the need of multicultural education for children today. Various cultures are highlighted, and their impact on society is noted to illustrate how multiculturalism can be taught to children in the school as well as in the home.

Booth, Tony, Will Swann, Mary Masterson, and Patricia Potts. *Curricula for Diversity in Education* (New York: Routledge, 1992)

Provides many interesting, informative ideas for integrating multicultural activities and promoting appreciation of and respect for diversity in early childhood programs.

Comer, James P., and Alvin Poussaint. *Raising Black Children* (New York: Plenum, 1990)

A highly readable and comprehensive guide that focuses on the special concerns of black parents. Offers advice on over a thousand child-rearing questions. Includes topics such as self-esteem, positive discipline, racism, and getting along with others.

Cushner, Kenneth, Averil McClelland, and Philip Stafford. *Human Diversity in Education: An Integrative Approach* (New York: McGraw-Hill, 1992)

Provides an integrated discussion of the various forms of human diversity in schools. Stresses how individuals can become functioning group members in classrooms and other settings.

Darder, Antonia. *Culture and Power in the Classroom* (New York: Bergin & Garvey, 1991)

The author analyzes multicultural education as it appears in the United States today and addresses issues that confront teachers in classrooms in which most of the students are from different cultures. Darder gives tools teachers can use to practice multicultural education and also a guide to help them evaluate their own perspectives of multiculturalism.

Diaz, Carlos, ed. *Multicultural Education for the 21st Century* (Washington, D.C.: National Education Association, 1992)

A selection of readings relating to aspects of multicultural imperatives for education, effective teaching practices, role of gender and achievement in schooling, evaluation of the multicultural classroom, and teacher education programs.

Gollnick, Donna M., and Philip C. Chinn. *Multicultural Education in a Pluralistic Society*, 3d ed. (New York: Merrill/Macmillan, 1990)

Provides an overview of the microcultures to which children belong and gives specific ideas for how professionals can use pluralism to implement multicultural education.

Jensen, Mary, and Zelda Chevalier. *Issues and Advocacy in Early Education* (Boston: Allyn & Bacon, 1990)

> Discusses many important issues relating to early childhood education. A chapter on multicultural education challenges some misconceptions about multicultural education and the role of the teacher.

Lynch, James. *Education for Citizenship in a Multicultural Society* (New York: Cassell Villiers House, 1991)

> The book deals with local, national, and international information to teach citizenship and education in a multicultural world.

Sleeter, Christine E. *Empowerment through Multicultural Education* (Albany: State University of New York Press, 1991)

> A good reference for ideas and information on how multiculturalism empowers all children, including those living in low-income housing and speaking minority languages.

Sparks, Louise Derman, and the ABC Task Force. *Anti-Bias Curriculum: Tools for Empowering Young Children* (Washington, D.C.: National Association for the Education of Young Children, 1989)

> Helps early childhood professionals assist children in learning to think critically, solving problems, and discussing difficult issues of justice so as to develop healthy self-images. Also helps professionals examine their own biases.

Tiedt, Pamela L., and Iris M. Tiedt. *Multicultural Teaching*. 3d ed. (Boston: Allyn & Bacon, 1990)

> Assumes that multicultural understandings are essential for the education of all children and that all education is multicultural. Helps teachers learn how to encourage children to think about multiculturalism in the world around them.

ACTIVITIES FOR FURTHER ENRICHMENT

1. Choose ten children's books and evaluate them for multicultural content. Decide how you would use these materials to promote awareness and acceptance of diversity.

2. Interview field experience students regarding their ethnic origins and positive classroom experiences relating to culture. Explain how these comments would influence the curriculum you would teach and how you would present it.

3. Interview people in your community to determine typical attitudes toward and means of punishment of children in different cultures. Be specific, so you can be aware of similarities and differences. What implications do these have for the teacher's role in reporting child abuse?

4. Examine children's readers and supplemental materials to determine instances of sexism. What recommendations would you make to change such practices?

5. Observe children in both school and non-school settings for examples of how dress reflects sex stereotyping and how parents' behaviors promote sex stereotyping.

6. The environment and certain materials may promote sexism, and they do play a powerful role. Examine the environment of classrooms and homes to determine the extent of sexist practices. Make recommendations based on your findings.

7. Stories and literature play an important role in transmitting to children information about themselves and what to expect.

    a. What books and literature played an important role in your growing up?

    b. Identify five children's books and give reasons why you think they would be good books to use with children.

8. Survey ten teachers and your classmates, asking them what the term *multicultural* means. What are the similarities and differences? What recommendations would you make based on these definitions?

9. Interview principals to discover how they are dealing with issues of multiculturalism in their schools. What are they doing to actively promote a truly multicultural setting?

10. Cite at least five ways in which culture determines different child-rearing patterns. Identify five implications these different approaches have for early childhood professionals.

NOTES

1. Louise Derman-Sparks and the ABC Task Force, *Anti-Bias Curriculum: Tools for Empowering Young Children* (Washington, D.C.: National Association for the Education of Young Children, 1989), p. 3.

2. Division of Human Resource Development, Florida Atlantic University Multifunctional Resource Center, *Empowering ESOL Teachers: An Overview. Vol. II* (Tallahassee: Florida Department of Education, 1993), App. A., Glossary, Sections, VII–X, pp. i–vi.

3. Ibid., p. v.

4. Ibid.

5. Ibid.

6. Ibid., p. vi.

7. James A. Banks, "Multicultural Education: Characteristics and Goals," in James A. Banks and Cherry McGee Banks, eds., *Multicultural Education: Issues and Perspectives,* 2d ed. (Boston: Allyn & Bacon, 1993), pp. 3–4. Used by permission.

8. Florida Department of Education, *Multicultural Education in Florida, Multicultural Education Review Task Force Report* (Tallahassee: Florida Department of Education, 1991), p. ix.

9. *NCBE Forum,* newsletter of the National Clearinghouse for Bilingual Education, 16(3) (March 1993), p. 4.

10. Valerie Ooka Pang and Jesús Nieto, "Multicultural Teaching," *Kappa Delta Pi Record* 29(1) (Fall 1992), pp. 25–27.

11. Gloria S. Boutte and Christine B. McCormick, "Authentic Multicultural Activities: Avoiding Pseudomulticulturalism," *Childhood Education* (Spring 1992), pp. 140–144. Reprinted by permission of the Association for Childhood Education International, 11501 Georgia Ave., Suite 315, Wheaton, MD. Copyright © 1992 by the Association.

12. U.S. Department of Health and Human Services, Administration for Children, Youth, and Families, *Multicultural Principles for Head Start Programs,* CYF-IM-91-03 (Washington, D.C.: U.S. Government Printing Office, March 1991), pp. 5–6.

13. Marie Cabo, Rita Dunn, and Kenneth Dunn, *Teaching Students to Read through Their Individual Learning Styles* (Boston: Allyn & Bacon, 1991), p. 2. Copyright © 1991 by Allyn & Bacon. Adapted by permission.

14. Rita Dunn, Kenneth Dunn, and Gary Price, *Learning Style Inventory* (LSI) (Lawrence, KS: Price Systems, 1987), pp. 14–19. Material adapted by permission.

15. Howard Gardner, *Frames of Mind* (New York: Basic Books, 1983).

16. *Federal Register,* June 4, 1975, p. 24128.

17. Millicent Lawton, "Four of Five Students in Grades 8 to 11 Sexually Harassed at School, Poll Finds," *Education Week,* June 9, 1993, p. 5.

18. American Association of University Women, "What the Research Reveals," *The AAUW Report: How Schools Shortchange Girls: Executive Summary* (Washington, D.C.: Author, 1992), p. 2. Copyright © 1992, the American Association of University Women Educational Foundation.

19. *Federal Register,* Aug. 11, 1975, p. 33803.

20. Statute 2372, Section 703.

21. Cami Jones, *TEA Update: New Directions in Early Childhood Education* (Austin: TEA/Division of Curriculum/Prekindergarten/Kindergarten, 1991), pp. 12-13.

22. Robert Pear, "Poverty in U.S. Grew Faster Than Population Last Year," *New York Times,* Oct. 5, 1993, p. A10.

15

Technology and Early Childhood
Education for the Twenty-First Century

After you have read and studied this chapter, you will be able to:

☐ Assess the importance and extent of technology use in contemporary society

☐ Determine the role, place, and scope of technology in early childhood programs

☐ Evaluate the meaning of technological literacy and its implications for young children and early childhood professionals

☐ Appraise the nature of multicultural technology and how it applies to the changing nature of the U.S. population

☐ Assess how technology supports and facilitates children's learning and thinking

☐ Examine the role of assistive technology in helping children with disabilities be fully included in centers and classrooms

☐ Evaluate the extent to which technology influences how early childhood professionals teach and how children learn

GLOSSARY OF TERMS

The following terms will help you be more familiar with and conversant about technology and technological processes.

Binary number system: A system using only two digits, 0 and 1, to represent all numbers. This system is used in computers because an electrical circuit has two states: off and on.

Bit: The smallest unit of information in a computer. It is an abbreviation for *binary digit*.

Byte: A string of eight bits. A byte represents a number or character. *K* is used to stand for 1,024 bytes. (*K* means 1,000.) *Megabyte* equals 1,000 K. (*Mega* means a million.) This designation is important because it is how the power of computers is determined. (See also *RAM*.)

CD-ROM (compact disk–read only memory):   A disk that looks like an audio CD. Includes color graphics, text, and full-motion video.

Digital: Computers perform their operations with quantities represented by electronic digits (0s and 1s representing on and off), in the RAM memory.

Electronic bulletin board: Electronic networks in which people can leave messages for anyone accessing that network. Literally public bulletin boards that are electronic.

E-mail: An electronic computer network that enables professionals and children to exchange information and create electronic ties with others. For example, my E-mail address is MORRI-SON@SERVAX.FIU.EDU. Any person linked to Internet (see definition on page 571) can communicate with me electronically through E-mail. E-mail and electronic bulletin boards are often linked together. As a result, persons can "post" notices on electronic bulletin boards and read the responses through their E-mail.

Hard disk: A sealed disk used to store data. It stores more information and runs (works) faster than a floppy disk. Hard disks come in many sizes, from 80 to 500 megabytes. The bigger the better, because much of today's software takes large amounts of disk space.

Hardware: The equipment of technology. Hardware includes computers, monitors, keyboards, VCR players, disk drives, mice, and printers.

Hypermedia: Software that enables the user to access or link to other media such as graphics, audio, video, animations, and so forth, through a process known as *branching*. For example, you could read a small biography on Mozart, click a button to hear a symphony, and click another button to read about the influence of his music on the film industry.

Interactive: When a person is communicating one-on-one with the computer. The person operating the computer gives the computer a command, the computer reacts, another command is given, and so forth. An example of a noninteractive process is when the computer operator gives

THE COMPUTER GENERATION

A recent front-page headline of the *New York Times* stated in an uncharacteristically unstaid way, "Computer Age Tots Trading Building Blocks for Software." The writer of the article asked, "Is a generation emerging that will be computer literate before it is literate?" He then answered his own question: "Many people seem to think so."[1]

Children today are technological persons. Their growth and development have consisted of large doses of television, videos, electronic games, and computers in the home and shopping center. Everyday newspapers, television, and other forms of

a command and the computer finishes the task, process, or program without further instructions from the operator. Typically, drill-type software for young children is considered noninteractive or passive. An open-ended product, such as a software drawing program, would be considered interactive.

Internet: An international computer network that links nodes (computer systems) at participating government agencies, educational institutions, and commercial entities. The Department of Defense started the network in 1969. Today, Internet consists of over 5,000 interconnected networks. Quite an electronic highway!

Megabyte: One million bytes

Modem: Hardware, either internal or external, that connects to a telephone line and converts computer language into one that can be sent over the telephone lines. The modem transforms the computer's digital signals (0s and 1s) to analog signals (sound).

Mouse: An attachment that enables users to manipulate the cursor by hand—by moving the mouse and clicking a switch—rather than by using keyboard commands. A *trackball* performs the same function but is connected to the keyboard.

Multimedia: The integration of still pictures, motion pictures, text, and sound with reading, writing, drawing, problem solving, searching, and creating. This definition is different from a common use of the word to mean the use of various media hardware such as television, computers, projectors, and so forth.

RAM: Stands for *random access memory*, to cite how much memory a computer has (e.g., 640 K of memory). RAM is important because software packages specify how many megabytes of RAM are required to run them.

Scanner: An input device that copies pictures and words into the computer by turning the visual representations (analog) into digital information that can be reproduced on the computer screen or printed.

Software: The programs, systems, data, games, and information that are stored on disks and tapes used in computers and other hardware.

Soundboard: Hardware that is built into the computer or an additional accessory used to digitize speech or music.

Telecommunications: The process of using telephone lines and a computer(s) to communicate with another computer. *Satellite dishes* play an important role in telecommunications and in *distance learning,* that is, the delivery of classes in which the teacher is not physically present. Telecommunications, such as E-mail, involves a computer, modem, telephone line, and telecommunications software.

Virtual reality: A computer-based simulated environment that users seem to enter and that seems real for the participant.

popular media chronicle the latest technological benefits to society. What once was exceptional is now commonplace. What were once thought of as miracles are now everyday products used in medical technology, education, the home, and office. Computers were once huge, power-hungry machines that filled rooms the size of small houses. Today, powerful computers are small enough to sit on students' desks, and more and more students have laptop computers they easily carry back and forth from home to school. Some computers are now designed even to fit in the palm of your hand!

During the past few years, home computing has grown in popularity. IBM, Apple, and other computer manufacturers have introduced computers targeted for the home market. Manufacturers design software to entertain and educate adults and children in a home setting. Publishers of educational software for school use now design many of their newest titles with families in mind as well.

John Dewey said that education is a process of living, not a process of preparing students for the future. Dewey's observation is as meaningful now as it was then. Early childhood professionals must incorporate computers and other technology into their programs and children's lives.

TECHNOLOGY: A DEFINITION

Technology is the application of scientific, material, and human resources to the solution of human needs. Technology is of immense benefit to all humankind. Using this definition, technology goes beyond computers and video games. Part of children's becoming technologically literate requires that they have experiences with the full range of available technological resources.

We find application of technology to early childhood programs through computers, computer programs, television, videodiscs, tape recorders, cassettes, and assistive technology. These forms of technology have many applications for teaching. Consequently, early childhood professionals must consider the full range of technology that is applicable to their classrooms, centers, and activities.

Technological Literacy

We cannot speak or think about technology as though it were apart from what goes on in the everyday world, and children are aware of this. Many children are very savvy about technology and its use. For example, elementary school children iden-

Computers are fast becoming a common part of the home environment. Many children come to school familiar with computers and other technology. Other children have had very limited exposure. Professionals have to accept the challenge of meeting all children's technological needs.

FIGURE 15–1 Children's Computer Use at School

Group	Pre-K–Kindergarten (%)	Grades 1–8 (%)
Male	13.9	52.9
Female	15.6	51.7
White	17	58.4
Black	7.4	35.7
Hispanic	10.1	40.2

Source: Compiled from data from U.S. Department of Commerce, Bureau of the Census, *Current Population Survey, 1991*.

tify computer users as persons who are "detectives, auto mechanics, insurance agents, police officers, newspaper reporters, astronauts, telephone operators, airline pilots, architects, computer programmers and travel agents."[2] (Read how a preschooler solved a teacher's computer problem in Susie Armstrong's vignette in chap. 3.)

Technological literacy, the ability to understand and apply technology to meet personal goals, is increasingly viewed as important as the traditional components of literacy—reading, writing, speaking, and listening. Advocates of technological literacy maintain that students need to be able to read and write on-line as well as with books and paper and pencil, that they need to speak on the phone and with voice mail and to participate in video-conferencing as well as in face-to-face conversations, and that they must develop skills in presenting their knowledge and products with multimedia. In fact, many educators fear that the United States may be creating a new class of illiterates—children who do not have access to computers and other technology and who do not know how to use and apply technology. Figure 15–1 indicates that many children still do not use computers in the public schools, with African-American children in particular using computers less than other children. It may be that students do not use computers because they do not have access to them and/or their teachers do not incorporate the use of computers in curricula and activities.

THE TECHNOLOGY OF TEACHING AND LEARNING

Much of the application of technology to curriculum and instruction, especially as it is applied to children with special needs, is attributable to B. F. Skinner. Skinner introduced to education and teaching the concept of *programmed learning*, in which what students are to learn is programmed or arranged in a progressive series of small steps from simple or basic to complex. Students are rewarded or reinforced with the right answer after each small step, a concept in keeping with Skinner's belief that knowing that one has answered a question correctly (in other words, *positive feedback*) is a powerful motivating force for children.

Several advantages of programmed learning are that learning is broken down into small, manageable units; students use the program themselves; and students progress at their own rate. Today, software programs designed to teach colors, numbers, and numerous other concepts use many of Skinner's ideas. For example, as students select a response, they are "rewarded" with the right answer, and, in many software programs, a voice responds saying, "Good job, [name of the child]." In other programs, a musical tone or other sound signals a right answer. The software is programmed so that a right answer advances the program to the next frame, story, or problem. If the student provides an incorrect response, the software is programmed to ask the same question again or provide a review scenario and ask another question. Well-written software provides for appropriate feedback, reinforcement of concepts, and review.

However, many early childhood professionals question whether Skinner's approach to learning is developmentally appropriate for young children, especially when applied to software programs as described here. They stress the need to avoid drill-type software and lessons, frequently referred to as "electronic ditto sheets." Rather, they advocate that children be involved in open-ended software that promotes discovery learning. Further, they stress that developmentally appropriate software enables children to be "in command" rather than being controlled by the software, as often happens in drill-type software. (See "The Computer-Enriched Kindergarten" feature later in this chapter.)

COMPUTERS IN EARLY CHILDHOOD PROGRAMS

Computer literacy is knowledge about, understanding of, and the ability to use computers. Computer literacy also includes an understanding of the social and educational implications of computers; that is, computers play an important part in daily living and computers can help us learn. Computers are used for many different things and in many different ways. Children can explore and understand the way computers are used and can learn that computers are built and programmed by people. Critical to computer literacy is a child's attitude toward computers and their applications. This feeling should be one of confidence and willingness to learn more about and become involved with computers and computer technology. Such an attitude comes naturally when children are involved in appropriate activities and software.

Three problems confront early childhood teachers in implementing an effective program of computer instruction: their personal acceptance of computers, decisions about how to use computers in early childhood programs and classrooms, and assuring themselves that computers do not have a negative influence on children. Teachers cannot afford to decide not to use computers and technology. When they do, they risk having technologically illiterate children; denying children access to skills, knowledge, and learning; and not promoting an attitude of acceptance of technology into their everyday lives. Rather, they must promote access to technology and develop creative ways to involve children.

Multicultural Technology

The United States is a changing society. By 2010, one third of all U.S. youth will live in California, Florida, Texas, and New York. In Texas and California, 57 percent of these youth will be nonwhite; in New York and Florida, 53 percent.[3] What is the implication of the growing multicultural nature of the United States? One is that the *appropriate* use of technology can help promote children's literacy development, especially the learning of English and their own native language. Technology has to do more than provide children skills they can use in shopping center arcades and on home video games. It has to help students learn the social, language, and cognitive skills they need for successful learning and living.

Second, school districts are searching for ways to teach basic skills to an increasingly diverse population of students. Increasingly, they look to technology for ways to achieve their goals of literacy learning for all children and their families. They are collaborating with computer companies to develop hardware and software to assist them in this task.

Bilingual Education Technology

The Florida Department of Education, the Dade County, Florida, Public Schools, and the Jostens Learning Corporation in San Diego, California, cooperatively developed "Technology-Assisted Language Learning for K–12 ESOL Students." The program was designed so it would also be appropriate for English for Speakers of Other Languages (ESOL) programs across the nation. Total development cost of this program exceeded $6 million.

One part of this program is designed to help Spanish-speaking students in kindergarten and primary grades become fluent in English. It introduces them to the sounds and rhythms of the English language through literature, rhymes, and songs. Eight thematic units include on- and off-line activities that work together to help nonindependent and beginning-level students acquire the basic vocabulary and concepts they need to succeed in the English-speaking classroom. These units use animation, full-color graphics, sound, role plays, games, small-group activities, and collaborative groups. Figure 15–2 depicts the contents of the K–3 component and shows the steps to English language development.

Such collaborative efforts between a software company and school districts are commonplace. Whereas the bilingual/multicultural software market was once somewhat ignored, businesses now realize there is growing need for programs and software to meet the needs of a diverse population.

Multicultural Infusion Through Technology

Technology is also used to infuse multiculturalism into the curriculum of early childhood classrooms. Videos provide an excellent way to do this. One such video is *Children's Songs around the World,* an interactive video that contains music of traditional songs from Mexico, China, Israel, Brazil, and other countries.

FIGURE 15–2 Steps to English Language Development

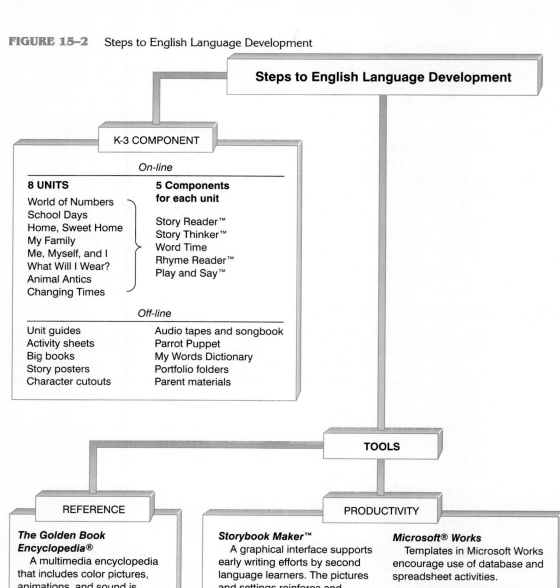

Steps to English Language Development

K-3 COMPONENT

On-line

8 UNITS

World of Numbers
School Days
Home, Sweet Home
My Family
Me, Myself, and I
What Will I Wear?
Animal Antics
Changing Times

**5 Components
for each unit**

Story Reader™
Story Thinker™
Word Time
Rhyme Reader™
Play and Say™

Off-line

Unit guides
Activity sheets
Big books
Story posters
Character cutouts

Audio tapes and songbook
Parrot Puppet
My Words Dictionary
Portfolio folders
Parent materials

TOOLS

REFERENCE

***The Golden Book
Encyclopedia®***
  A multimedia encyclopedia that includes color pictures, animations, and sound is available for student research. Text-to-speech technology supports second language learners.

English Express™
  The on-line picture dictionary has pictures grouped by themes and by alphabetical order.

PRODUCTIVITY

Storybook Maker™
  A graphical interface supports early writing efforts by second language learners. The pictures and settings reinforce and extend students' developing vocabularies.

Chart Maker
  This semantic mapping tool allows students to manipulate information and ideas and enables them to display relationships.

Microsoft® Works
  Templates in Microsoft Works encourage use of database and spreadsheet activities.

The Jostens Learning Writing Processor
  This easy to use writing tool includes a dictionary, a thesaurus, and a spell checker.

The Writing Center™
  Allows students to do their own desktop publishing.

Source: Jostens Learning, 9920 Pacific Heights Blvd., Suite 100, San Diego, California 92121-4330. Used by permission.

At Bank Street College, the Center for Children and Technology has researched what software designers need to consider in order to achieve a multicultural balance in their products. The center recommends including the following four elements to help assure multiculturally appropriate software: history, culture, language, and art.

Application of Technology to Early Childhood Programs

Three interesting processes are apparent in the growth of technological applications in early childhood programs. First, computer technology is being used in unique ways to help children learn. Second, more hardware and software is used to assist professionals to help children learn. Third, professionals are embracing technology as a way of helping them *manage* instruction, keep records, report to parents, and communicate with colleagues and other professionals. For example, teachers and the children at South Pointe Elementary (see chap. 9) keep a daily computer record of each child's activities, achievement, and progress. This is used as one basis for planning, assessment, and reporting to parents. Hardware and software packages such as Apple's Early Learning Solution help professionals build a portfolio of materials for each child.

A number of different approaches to and philosophies of facilitating and promoting children's learning through computers are possible. The vignettes on pages 578 to 586 will help you appreciate and understand two of these approaches. In the Writing to Read Program by IBM, children are involved in learning literacy through the use of a somewhat structured approach. The computer and software are seen as a central element of teachers teaching and children learning. On the other hand, in "The Computer-Enriched Kindergarten," computers are seen as a means of providing open-ended discovery learning, problem solving, and computer competence. As you read these two sections, list the ways they are similar and different and then write a paragraph explaining which approach you support.

TECHNOLOGY AND CHILDREN WITH SPECIAL NEEDS

Technology can help children with special needs learn and their teachers teach. Technology helps children with vision impairments see and children with physical disabilities read and write. Technology helps developmentally delayed children learn the skills they need to achieve at their appropriate levels and enables children with disabilities to substitute one ability for another and receive the special training they need. Technology permits children with special needs to enjoy, through the process of learning, knowledge, skills, and behaviors that might otherwise be inaccessible to them. Technology *empowers* children with special needs; that is, it enables them to exercise control over their lives and the conditions of their learning. It enables them to do things previously thought impossible.

In addition, technology changes people's attitudes about children with disabilities. For example, whereas children with disabilities may be viewed by some as not being able to participate fully in regular classrooms, they now recognize that instead

(Text continues on p. 586.)

Program in Practice

VOY A LEÉR ESCRIBIENDO: WRITING TO READ

Writing to Read is a computer-based reading and writing program for kindergarten and first grade students. It combines technology with educational techniques. Writing to Read is based on the assumption that children best learn to read by being taught how to write. With this program, young children learn to write what they can say and read stories they have written. The program builds on a child's natural language growth, which typically includes a 2,000- to 4,000-word vocabulary when entering kindergarten. In many traditional programs, the kindergartner is expected to learn to read only six to eight words, but in Writing to Read, the child is able to write any word in his or her vocabulary.

This instructional method builds writing and reading skills before a youngster has mastered all the complexities of spelling. A phonemic spelling system is used in which the sounds of spoken English are represented by a selected set of forty-two phonemes. To learn these phonemes, five learning stations are provided that address visual, auditory, and tactile modalities. Once children have learned these phonemes, they can write anything they can say, including such motivating words as *tyrannosaursus rex, boa constrictor,* and *skateboarding.* A distinction is made between invented and standard spelling, but while in the Writing to Read Center, children spell words the way they sound without worrying about correct spelling. Children make a natural transition to conventional spelling as they read standard spelling in textbooks and literature.

There are several expected outcomes for children involved in this program. First, children become fluent and productive writers. Students are expected to write words, sentences, or stories every day while in the cen-

ter. By the end of first grade, a number of children are writing multichapter books. Children become confident about their writing ability, and writing becomes a part of their basic repertoire of skills at a very young age.

Five learning stations work together to provide an active and motivating learning environment. The stations include Computer, Work Journal, Writing/Typing, Listening Library, and Make Words.

We will follow a typical kindergarten child during her daily hour in the Writing to Read Center in my classroom. Cecilia began the program in December after a two-week orientation. She is in a class of thirty-three kindergarten children in South Bay Union School District, located in California on the Mexican border. The district has a substantial percentage of low-income, single-parent families, as well as a high level of limited English-speaking students. (Students who are being taught in Spanish participate in the Spanish version of Writing to Read called *Voy a Leér Escribiendo,* or VALE.)

The Writing to Read Center is located in a separate room not far from the kindergarten. I had already passed out the small books called Work Journals to all the children in the classroom before they entered the center. The children have been assigned their first station while in the classroom, so they walk into Writing to Read and proceed directly to that station to begin work. Cecilia and her partner John have been assigned first to the Computer Station. Ms. Allas, the lab assistant, has already loaded the correct disk into the computer. At this station, Cecilia will work with her partner while responding to instructions given by the computer "voice." The computer will instruct the partners to say and type the

Contributed by Kathie W. Dobberteen, former kindergarten teacher, South Bay Union School District, Imperial Beach, California.

Amanda Torres and her teacher, Kathie Dobberteen, at the Writing to Read Center. Today's teachers emphasize writing as a means of promoting readiness and overall literacy development.

sounds of one of the thirty words included in the lesson. Cecilia works at this station for approximately fifteen minutes, which provides enough repetition to learn the sounds in a Cycle word such as *cat*.

After Cecilia and John have completed their work at the Computer Station, they proceed to the Work Journal Station. Here they listen to a taped lesson that reinforces the sounds they have just learned. They write sounds and words in their Work Journal. After the partners have completed the Work Journal Station, they are free to choose their next station. An important goal

of the Writing to Read program is to help children become responsible for their own learning.

Cecilia decides she would like to write something on the computer today, so she goes to the typing section of the Writing/Typing Station, which contains eight word processors. She finds her own story disk and loads it into the computer. She recently had a birthday and wants to write about the ring she received as a gift. Cecilia is a very independent kindergartner and writes her story without assistance. When she has finished, she prints her story on the printer, removes her disk, and puts it away.

The next stop is the Writing Table, where Cecilia proudly reads her story to me. Cecilia receives a lot of specific praise for her creation (see Figure A).

Cecilia has just enough time to go to the Make Words Station, where she can select manipulatives (hands-on learning materials) to form words. Today she chooses letter stamps and a stamp pad to write her mom a note. She stamps "I love you, Mom" and draws lots of hearts around the edge of the paper.

There are usually groans when I signal that it is time to clean up the center to go back to the classroom. Children, while actively learning, also have a great deal of fun.

FIGURE A   Cecilia's Story

cecilia june 9 a roobe is red and a
dimin is cler sum peple find dimins
in cavs and in tunls and mostle
dimins go with enetes I hav regs with
dimins and i dont wair them becus
thair icspensiv and tha fol vair ese
    the end

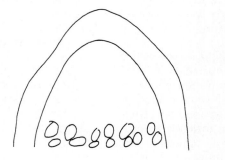

Tomorrow, when the class comes to Writing to Read, Cecilia will probably be assigned to the Listening Library Station because she did not have time to go to that station today. There she will listen to high-quality children's literature (literature written by famous authors) while tracking the story in the book. This process helps reinforce the sound-symbol relationship in context and teach standard spelling because children see correct spelling in the books. Cecilia will also have a chance to go to the Writing Table, which is part of the Writing/Typing Station. Here, she will work with pencil and paper while I encourage her writing.

I see many strengths in the Writing to Read program. First, it provides for all the readiness levels of the student in my kindergarten class by encouraging developmentally appropriate activities that can be adjusted to meet students' needs. Self-esteem is enhanced because children are not categorized into high, middle, and low groups, and they develop a "can-do" attitude. Children can progress and review at their own rate because the computer allows for individualized learning.

Children in Kathie Dobberteen's class using the Writing to Read Center. Dobberteen believes children need involvement in literacy development that will provide success and a basis for learning to read and write well.

Program in Practice

THE COMPUTER-ENRICHED KINDERGARTEN

One by one the class of kindergartners enters the recently silent room. Some burst in energetically; others are sleepily led by their parents. As part of their daily routine, the children spend a few minutes exploring the room, looking at the new activities that they will be able to choose later. The activities for this day are familiar ones for these children: painting on the easel, constructing hand puppets, decorating the dramatic play area, arranging pattern sticks, and using computers.

"I want the children to feel just as comfortable using computers as they do using blocks or crayons or pencils," says Nancy Edwards, master teacher of the University of Delaware Kindergarten. Computers have been part of this classroom for the past ten years, and with the growing availability of suitable software for young children, computers have become increasingly integrated in the developmentally appropriate education of young children.

It is time to begin the day, and twenty energetic five-year-olds sit cross-legged on the group-time rug. "Our calendar person today is Sharla!" Nancy announces, and a child bounces to the front board. With the teacher's guidance, Sharla announces the day and date and determines from the month's calendar pattern the color of today's square. "Pink, white, red, red, pink, white, red, red," Sharla points to the previous days. "Today has to be pink!" Sharla has followed the program of the calendar in the same way the computer follows a preset program.

After calendar time, Nancy draws the children's attention to the various activities available to them for the day, including several related to the week's theme of beavers, and dismisses them to the different areas of the

room. While Christine, Joshua, and Will enter the cardboard beaver lodge in dramatic play, Christopher and Orion set about constructing their City of Doom in the block area, Sharla and Catherine put on smocks before painting, and Ronnie heads for the Macintosh near the front of the room.

Ronnie holds the computer's mouse comfortably and navigates through Kid Desk (the file manager that organizes the programs that the students may access) and into Spelunx, his favorite program. As soon as Xavier hears the familiar drum rhythms that accompany the program, he rushes to fill the empty seat next to Ronnie. "I can get into every cave in this program. You want me to show you?" Xavier offers. "Do you know how to get to the room that shows Pluto and Saturn and the planets?" Ronnie asks. Xavier nods vigorously, "Yeah, you got to click on the left tunnel. No, this left tunnel," pointing to the screen as Ronnie controls the mouse.

Spelunx is one of the newest wave of software programs that combines state-of-the-art graphics and sound with an open-ended, exploration design, which allows children to exercise problem-solving abilities and communication skills while developing computer competence. Children refine these cognitive and social skills while using the computer, just as they can while engaged in more traditional activities. "I had heard all about using the computer to create 'microworlds' for the kids to explore, but it never really made sense to me until I saw this program," Nancy Edwards comments. "When the kids are moving through the various caves and tunnels in Spelunx, their language is no different from what I hear them use when they're in a dramatic play setting, like the beaver lodge. They

Contributed by Bernadette Caruso, University of Delaware Kindergarten.

are using the computer to play, I mean *really play*, in the way that lets them explore an entirely new environment."

At a nearby table, Amy is arranging colored Popsicle sticks to match the patterns suggested on the direction board. The student teacher designed this activity to foster small-motor coordination, but by simply propping up the direction board against an empty shoe box, the teacher has re-created the horizontal-vertical situation common to the computer keyboard-screen relationship. Mastering this activity will help Amy feel more comfortable using the computer, as well as increase her fine-motor dexterity.

Shawn has discovered the Macintosh in the rear of the room. Clicking on the picture of his teacher, he smiles as he hears Nancy's recorded voice welcome the kindergartners to the computer. "I'm the skateboard," Shawn whispers as he selects his icon from a class list in Kid Desk. "This is my desk," he declares proudly as a colorful dinosaur-decorated desktop is displayed. "Listen to this!" Shawn clicks on the representation of an answering machine, and Nancy's voice again is heard, "Hi, Shawn! Have fun on the computer today." Shawn laughs, "She's talking to me!"

A student teacher approaches the computer with Hannah in tow. "Shawn, Hannah would like to play the computer, too, and since there is still one chair empty here, there is room to share with her, OK?" Shawn scoots his chair slightly, and Hannah takes a seat. After watching silently for a few moments, Hannah requests that Shawn open up the jellybean game. "Which is that?" Shawn asks, and Hannah offers to show him. Taking the mouse, Hannah selects Millie's Math House and navigates to the appropriate game. "Here, see, you gotta put that many jellybeans

on the cookie," indicating the number on the screen.

After several correct responses, Hannah pushes the mouse to Shawn so he can try. "I don't want to put that many on. I don't like jellybeans." With Hannah's assistance, Shawn contentedly creates cookies that match his preferences rather than the computer's, and he continues with the game. Unlike drill-and-practice programs, a developmentally appropriate piece of software allows the children to experiment with various responses without being "punished" by a buzzing sound or negative reply. The children have the chance to ask, "What would happen if . . . ?" and then are able to test their hypotheses.

Computers are probably the most versatile material a kindergarten room can have. Nancy agrees. "A computer can provide activities that promote language development, or art, or math skills, or all of them at once," she says. In an appropriate program, while the children are playing the game, they are also engaged in problem solving and discussion with peers.

Several minutes later, Shawn decides to move to the block area. Hannah immediately exits the math game and navigates to her own desk icon on the Macintosh. Opening the program Storybook Weaver, she declares, "I have this one at home, so I'm really good at it. I like it 'cause I like to draw pictures, and I can't draw a Pegasus by myself, but with the computer, I can."

After a short snack break, the children assemble on the rug to share the objects they have brought from home. Today's designated object is a favorite book, so the group circle is filled with proud readers, holding well-loved copies of such classics as *Where the Wild Things Are* and *The Cat in the Hat*. Stephen waves his book happily. "Look, Nancy! My book is the same one we have on the computer!" And, indeed, the paperback copy of Mercer Mayer's *Just Grandma and Me* that Stephen holds is the same story that is told through an interactive CD-ROM program. Available in the classroom since the first day in September, this program allows the children to explore inside the animated illustrations while the computer reads the text aloud, in English, Spanish, or Japanese.

Programs like Just Grandma and Me and A Silly Noisy House (another CD-ROM program) provide a welcoming introduction to computers for young children, since they allow unlimited exploration with no predetermined right or wrong answers. The child can place the cursor on almost any object on the screen and get a positive response, in the form of character animation or music. "It gives the child a feeling of immediate success," Edwards says. "That's especially important for those children who may be hesitant to try something new. It gets them on the computer, and there is no chance to fail."

Dr. Daniel Shade, director of the Technology in Early Childhood Project, believes that good pieces of software, like A Silly Noisy House, do just that: put the child in control, allow exploration, and offer success. Mastering these pieces of software gives children a strong sense of power; now they can use a tool that grown-ups use in the real world—not a scaled-down version or a pretend computer, but a real, working piece of technology.

In this area of technology, the boundaries that have traditionally separated the child's world from the adult's are fading. For instance, Jill brought to share time a minibook she created: a single page of information on beavers she printed out from an on-line encyclopedia on her home computer. "More and

more of our share times include some kind of computer activity," Nancy notes. "It could be a picture or story the child creates on the computer, or an experience of using the parents' machines." Hannah illustrates this by sharing, along with her book, a bookmark she designed on her home version of Storybook Weaver.

Before dismissing the children to free-choice time, the teacher directs their attention to the Apple II computer near the door. "Boys and girls, some of you might have noticed today that we've put out a new piece of software. It's called Tracks, and I know that Josh tried it this morning. Josh, can you tell us what this program does?" Josh squirms under the class's attention and responds quietly, "I built a beaver lodge." "You did? Just like we're doing in the dramatic play area? That's great!" Nancy encourages. "Boys and girls, maybe some of you would like to look at the program and see how it can help you build a beaver lodge on the computer. Or, you can take apart the lodge that the computer built and see what's inside. Since Josh is the expert at Tracks, you can ask him for help if you need it." With the wide range of early childhood software available, almost every topic covered in the classroom can be supported on the computer—including beavers.

While several children move to examine the new program, others approach the art table to complete a beaver puppet. By "reading" the rebus cards provided, the young students are practicing early literacy skills, as well as developing their abilities to follow picture directions and process step-by-step instructions. The refinement of these skills, part of any developmentally appropriate early childhood classroom, is also necessary for successful computer use; with minimal adaptation, the beaver puppet construction becomes a way to foster computer accomplishment. "The *last* thing this activity is," the teacher remarks, "is an art project."

While Xavier and Catherine build their puppets, Maria and Tara are busily working on an Apple machine. At the request of a teacher, Maria is showing Tara how to make her own story with the Stone Soup program. "See, you click on the green box, then you pick up the guy you want, and you click him into the picture. OK, now you can type here on the keys. See, these are called keys. And your name comes up on the picture! OK, you ready to print? You click on the picture of the paper, and you tell the computer to print. Is the printer ready? OK, print!" The two girls rush to the side of the Imagewriter to watch their color printout emerge.

Maria is the class expert for Stone Soup. After reading the book to the class and having them act out the story, Nancy introduced the children to the software program of the same name. Maria decided she would create her own Stone Soup book, and has diligently devoted some time of every day for two weeks to her project. Each day, Maria independently loads the program, chooses a page of the animated story, rearranges, adds and removes objects, and types invented text to build her own story. When asked why she decided to use the computer for her project rather than crayons or paints, Maria replies, "The computer makes it an easier time. Crayons don't know what I want the picture to look like, and I can't make them look right. The computer knows how I want it to look, and then I can make it do what I want." Daniel Shade describes this as *scaffolding*; like Hannah with her Pegasus, Maria is using the computer as a tool to assist her in producing a picture that she can describe and understand but cannot yet create on her own. The computer extends the child's natural abilities and will support her until she develops the physical and cognitive skills necessary to master the task independently.

Although the computer is assisting the child, it does not *control* her. As our expert Maria explains, "The computer helps me start, but I tell it what to do, 'cause I use the command keys." The emphasis this classroom's teacher places on the computer as a tool, operated by the child and helpless without the child's direction, is evident in Maria's explanation; this child knows that *she* is in control of the *machine*, not the other way around.

Mary Minker, a teacher in the University of Delaware Preschool, has recently begun to use computers in her classroom of four-year-olds but can already see the impact of this sense of control. "After the children are exposed to some programs where they can feel successful, they are really confident in their status as computer users. In the beginning of the year, I made sure all my student teachers were thoroughly familiar with the programs so they could help the children. Well, now I have a brand new group of student teachers, and it's the children who are teaching them how the computers work! The children are very proud of what they can do on the machines."

These children should be proud of their accomplishments. Often, they master complex computer skills that adult users would find difficult. For example, Sharla ends her activity time on KidPix, a graphics program. Rather than being content with the simple painting and drawing options, Sharla chooses to take a predrawn graphic and alter it to her own specifications. Selecting the picture of a horse, Sharla uses the Stamp Editor function to enlarge the picture and change the color, one pixel at a time, to make the horse look more like one of her favorite toys. Instead of the standard brown horse, this young computer user now has a custom-made stamp of a pink horse with a purple mane and blue spots. "Now it's a picture of My Pretty Pony!" Sharla declares.

As the day's session comes to an end, the children proudly display the work they have completed. In this technology-enriched classroom, the students are fortunate enough to include computer printouts along with the traditional fingerpaintings and puppets. But more than just creating printouts, these children are developing the confidence and abilities of computer users, which allow them to say, "Look what I did! I did it all by myself with the computer!"

Software References

Explore-a-Classic: Stone Soup (William K. Bradford Publishing, 1989)

Explore-a-Science: Tracks (William K. Bradford Publishing, 1989)

Just Grandma and Me by Mercer Mayer (Broderbund Software, Inc., 1992)

Kid Desk (Edmark Software Corporation, 1992)

Kid Pix (Brøderbund Software, Inc., 1991)

Millie's Math House (Edmark Software Corporation, 1992)

Silly Noisy House by Peggy Weil (The Voyager Company, 1991)

Spelunx (Brøderbund Software, Inc., 1992)

Storybook Weaver (MECC, 1992)

of being segregated in separate programs, children can be fully included in regular classrooms with the assistance of technology.

Computer technology is a valuable tool to those who work with children with special needs. A child with cerebral palsy speaks his first words by choosing words on a communication speech board that is under his control. A speech synthesizer then pronounces the words. Deaf children learn to hear as speech vibrations are transformed into tactile patterns they can feel. An autistic child, assumed to be deaf and without speech, speaks her first words after manipulating the Logo turtle. (Logo is a programming language developed for children that enables them to produce screen graphics.)

The number of such applications grows daily. For example, the 1992 Lekotek *Software Resource Guide*[4] lists over three hundred software programs suited for children aged two through fourteen with mental, physical, behavioral, sensory, and learning disabilities.

Assistive Technology

Assistive technology covers a wide range of products and applications. "Assistive technology for children with disabilities ranges from such simple devices as adaptive spoons and switch-adapted, battery-operated toys to complex devices such as computerized environmental control systems."[5] Single switches, the most common, are used with software that scans the options available. All the child needs to do is hit the switch. There are all kinds of switches, such as pads, puff, and eyebrow (see Figure 15–4).

Figures 15–3, 15–4, and 15–5 illustrate some of the applications of assistive technology in early childhood settings. In Figure 15–4 we see how alternative keyboards can be used to emulate joystick and mouse inputs. The large keyboard in front of the girl is used to produce up, down, left, and right cursor movement and mouse button action. Figure 15–5 shows how professionals can create and use activity choice boards to help children learn how to make selections and take turns.

The field of early childhood education is undergoing dramatic changes through integration with the field of special education. As a result, early childhood professionals are adopting assistive technology to help children and their families. Opportunities for using many forms of technology are available to very young children, from birth to age three. Some of these include powered mobility, myoelectric prostheses, and communication devices. Infants as young as three months have interacted with computers, eighteen-month-old children have driven powered mobility devices and used myoelectric hands, and two-year-olds have talked via speech synthesizers. Children with severe physical disabilities learn how to use switches and scanning techniques.

Technology is particularly important for children with disabilities who depend on and need assistive technology to assist them to communicate, learn, and be mobile. The use of assistive technology to help children with disabilities received great impetus through PL 101-476, the Individuals with Disabilities Education Amendments of 1990. This law amended PL 99-457, the Education of the Handicapped Amendments of 1986. Specifically, PL 101-476 expanded the nature of services that can be provided to young children with disabilities. In particular, the law identifies assistive technology as a service that is to be provided to young children. Public Law 100-407, the Technology Related Assistance for Individuals with Disabilities Act of 1988, defines *assistive technology* as "any item, device or piece of equipment that is used to increase, maintain, or improve the functional abilities of persons with disabilities."

An extremely important issue in the use of assistive technology with young children is the appropriateness of such technology.

> Assistive technology is appropriate if it meets the following criteria:
>
> First, a technology should respond to (or anticipate) specific, clearly defined goals that result in enhanced skills for the child.
>
> Second, a technology should be compatible with practical constraints, such as available resources or the amount of training required to enable the child, his family, and the early childhood educator to use the technology.
>
> Third, a technology should result in desirable and sufficient outcomes. Some basic considerations for children with disabilities are related to (1) ease of training the child and his family to use and care for the technology; (2) reasonable maintenance and repair, with regard to time and expense; and (3) monitoring of the technology's effectiveness.[6]

FIGURE 15–3 Emulators for Joystick and Mice. (a) The joystick and mouse shown require a certain amount of manual dexterity. So, other devices such as the emulator boards shown in (b) and (c) enable a child to achieve the same purpose possible with a mouse or joystick.

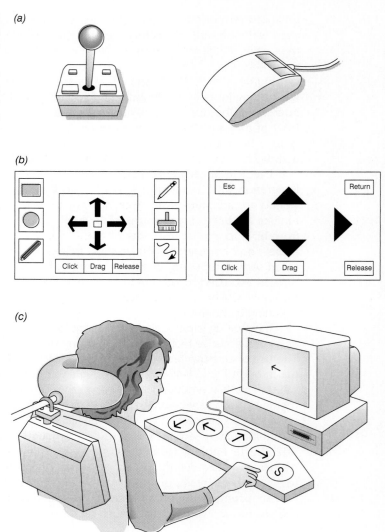

(a)

(b)

(c)

Source: Gregory Church and Sharon Glennen, *The Handbook of Assistive Technology* (San Diego: Singular Publisher Group, 1992), p. 150. Used by permission.

FIGURE 15–4 Switches for Children with Paralysis. Eye blinks activate the switch (a), a sip-and-puff switch (b), and a muscle tension switch (c).

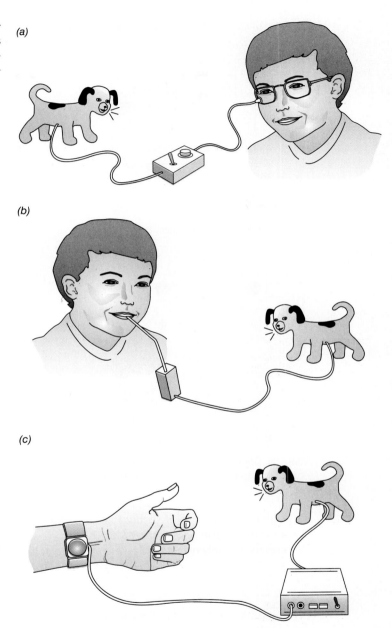

(a)

(b)

(c)

Source: Gregory Church and Sharon Glennen, *The Handbook of Assistive Technology* (San Diego: Singular Publisher Group, 1992), p. 181. Used by permission.

FIGURE 15–5 Play Activity Choice Boards

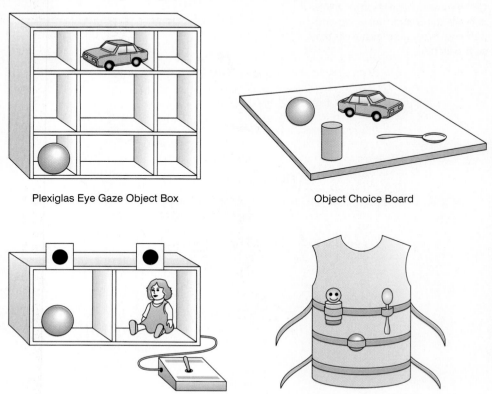

Plexiglas Eye Gaze Object Box

Object Choice Board

Scanning Choice Board with Switch

Play Vest with Objects

Source: Gregory Church and Sharon Glennen, *The Handbook of Assistive Technology* (San Diego: Singular Publishing Group, 1992), p. 186. Used by permission.

The mere application of technology therefore is not enough. Professionals have to be sensitive to the above criteria as they work with children, families, and other professionals in applying technology to learning settings and children's special needs.

SOFTWARE FOR YOUNG CHILDREN

The quantity and quality of software for children is growing. More children are coming "on-line" as part of their learning to read, write, and compute. For example, Figure 15–2 identifies some of the software designed to help children learn language.

Not all software is good software. Good teachers have always evaluated the materials they use with their children. Now they must also assess the software that children use. Figure 15–6 (see page 592) provides one set of evaluative criteria that teachers may use.

Assistive technology enables children with disabilities to participate in regular classrooms and to learn skills and behaviors not previously thought possible. Technology will play an even greater role in children's learning in the years to come.

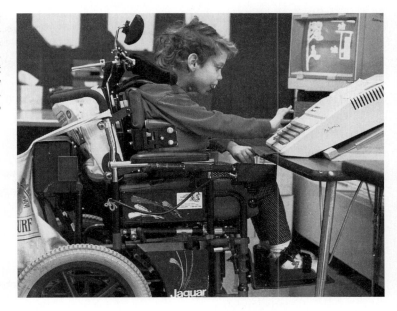

Figure 15–7 shows the outstanding software of 1992 and 1993 as evaluated by the criteria given in Figure 15–6. This software was announced at the 1992 and 1993 NAEYC Conferences.

INTEGRATED LEARNING SYSTEMS

Integrated learning systems (ILSs) are networked systems that present groups of children with lessons on their individual computers from programs of lessons and activities stored in a central computer. They are frequently criticized as electronic workbooks with an emphasis on rote learning. As Clements and his colleagues point out, "Evaluations of these systems show moderate effect on basic skill; however, one must question other aspects of ILSs, especially diminished teacher and learner control. In too many cases ILSs represent a triumph of bureaucratic efficiency over young children's development."[7]

Proponents, however, maintain that contemporary versions are more sophisticated, with graphics and lessons that pace each individual's learning. The popularity of ILSs seems to be growing. For example, in 1994, the Palm Beach County (Florida) school district spent $25 million to install 7,500 computer work stations in the district's seventy-five elementary schools. This project, in conjunction with Computer Curriculum Corporation, represents the largest installation of a computer-based learning system in the nation. The software of the program, SuccessMaker, includes full-motion video, animation, computer graphics, and digitized sound to provide an interactive learning environment in mathematics, reading, language arts, writing, science, and life skills.

FIGURE 15–6 Haugland/Shade Software Evaluation Form

Evaluated by: _____   Date: _____

Title:_____   Cost: _____

Publisher: _____

Concepts: _____

Description: _____

Comments: _____

Criteria	Rating	Characteristics
Age Appropriate	____	Realistic concepts; appropriate methods
Child Control	____	Actors not reactors; child sets pace; can escape
Clear Instructions	____	Verbal instructions; simple and precise directions; picture choices
Expanding Complexity	____	Low entry, high ceiling, learning sequence is clear; teaches powerful ideas
Independence	____	Adult supervision not needed after initial exposure
Process Orientation	____	Process engaged, product secondary; discovery learning, not skill drilling; intrinsic motivation
Real-World Model	____	Simple, reliable model; concrete representations; objects function
Technical Features	____	Colorful; uncluttered realistic graphics; animation loads and runs quickly; realistic corresponding sound effects or music; sturdy disks
Transformations	____	Objects and situations change; process highlighter
Trial and Error	____	Children test alternative responses
Sub Total		
Anti-Bias Deduction	____	Multiple languages; universal focus; mixed gender and role equity; people of color; differing ability or age; diverse family styles

Ratings:
 1— Software reflects all the characteristics within a criteria.
 .5— Software reflects at least half the characteristics within a criteria.
 0— Software reflects less than half the characteristics within a criteria.
Software receiving a total score of 7.0 or above is considered developmentally appropriate.

Source: Susan W. Haugland, director, Kids Interacting with Developmental Software, Department of Environmental Sciences, Southeast Missouri State University, Cape Girardeau, Missouri; and Daniel D. Shade, director, Technology in Early Childhood Habitats, Department of Individual and Family Studies, University of Delaware, Newark.

FIGURE 15–7   Haugland and Shade's 1992 and 1993 Developmentally Appropriate Software Awards

Category	Program(s)	Publisher
Creativity and the arts	• Kid Pix	Broderbund Software
	• Kid Works 2	Davidson & Associates
Creative problem solving	• Facemaker, Golden Edition	Queue, Inc.
Language arts	• My Words	Hartley Courseware, Inc.
	• Paint with Words	MECC
	• Storybook Theatre	Wings for Learning
	• Storybook Weaver	MECC
Math and science	• EZ Logo: Revised Edition	MECC
	• Learn about Plants	Sunburst
	• Millie's Math House	Edmark
Multicultural	• The Legend of Raven	W. K. Bradford
Problem solving	• Thinkin' Things	Edmark
Thematic focus	• The Farm	Kidware II
	• Zoo Keeper	Davidson & Associates
User accessibility	• Kid Desk	Edmark

OTHER TECHNOLOGICAL APPLICATIONS

Synthesizers

During the 1990s, technology has had an expanding impact on music education. New technologies, such as the synthesizer, help children learn music better. Synthesizers are capable of producing sounds from 120 different instruments and contain many songs that are built into the system. A synthesizer makes it possible to easily teach many skills, such as instrument recognition, and gives children the ability to play simple melodies.

CD-ROM

A CD-ROM disk is exactly like an audio compact disk; it is made of aluminum with an acrylic cover. Data are recorded as tiny pits in tracks in the aluminum layer and are read by a laser beam reflecting off those pits. About 660 megabytes fit on one disk, which corresponds to more than 250,000 typed pages!

The potential of the CD-ROM in the schools is practically unlimited in terms of function and content. Some excellent CD-ROM programs are available for classroom use, such as The Golden Book Encyclopedia and The San Diego Zoo Pre-

Program in Practice

AN INTERACTIVE LEARNING SYSTEM IN PROGRESS: GALAXY CLASSROOM

GALAXY Classroom is the nation's only inter-active satellite education network exclusively designed for elementary students. The $24 million GALAXY Classroom network broad-casts uniquely designed, noncommercial video programs as part of its language arts and science curricula. Through the use of fax machines, students can communicate with their peers in other GALAXY Classrooms in twenty-one states, the District of Columbia, and Mexico. GALAXY Classroom is an educa-tional initiative of Hughes Aircraft operated by the Los Angeles–based GALAXY Institute for Education, a nonprofit organization. The insti-tute receives support from the National Sci-ence Foundation and other major founda-tions.

A Day in the Life of GALAXY Classroom

8:30 A.M. CST, Hammond, Indiana   Sec-ond graders at Lafayette Elementary School crowd excitedly around the fax machine as letters come in from their new GALAXY friends in the Bronx, New York.

9:55 A.M. PST, Los Angeles, Califor-nia   An engineer monitors the DirectTV satellite as the GALAXY Classroom network prepares to broadcast SNOOPS, a third to fifth grade science program, to schools across the United States and Mexico.

12:50 P.M. EST, Washington, D.C.   Third grade teacher Christine Kane glances at the clock on the wall of John Eaton Elementary. In two minutes GALAXY will broadcast the sec-ond part of the SNOOPS series "The Case of the Full Moon Bandits." Christine opens the GALAXY equipment cabinet. When she clicks on the twenty-six-inch color television set, her students become quiet in anticipation.

10:00 A.M. PST, Norwalk, California   Third grade teacher Bob Rayburn looks at his wristwatch and then at the VCR to make sure the red record button is lit. He will record the

Contributed by Stephanie Brea, the GALAXY Institute for Education.

---

sents the Animals. Both these make use of pictures, sound, and animation in addi-tion to text and are also very easy to use.

Videodiscs

Videodiscs are similar to musical compact disks. They are larger, about twelve inches, and store pictures, charts, and other information as well as words and music. The videodisc is inserted into a disc player, and students watch the program on the classroom television. When the videodisc is attached to a computer, the pro-gram becomes "interactive"; that is, students can search for specific information, replay, and pinpoint specific information they need according to their individual questions and learning needs.

Spanish version of the program and play it for the class later. Because of the large number of Hispanic children in his class, Bob likes to trade off showing the GALAXY video drama in English and Spanish. Bob further strengthens his students' skills in both languages by using GALAXY's specially designed materials and newsletters in Spanish and English.

1:15 P.M. EST, Hickman, Kentucky Principal Linda Littlejohn thumbs through a GALAXY theme guide as she watches the GALAXY science curriculum program with some third grade students. Alice, a student, writes notes to use later to collect fingerprint data for Cornelius, a SNOOPS character. She will use the GALAXY computer E-mail to send the data to "Data Base" so that it might be used in the next broadcast.

2:00 P.M. CST, Austin, Texas A second grader sends a fax to his satellite friend Nadine at Mary Lin Elementary in Atlanta, Georgia, about the feathers and birds' nests he collected for his science project. He also proposes a new joint science project for their classes.

2:30 p.m. PST, Salem, Oregon Principal John Trujillo is watching a third grade classroom perform hands-on chromatography experiments based on "The Case of the Full Moon Bandits." Their results will help them solve the mystery of the program and learn about patterns and substances. They will fax their results to other GALAXY schools to compare results with their peers just like real scientists do. . . .

Another advantage of videodiscs is that the disc player can access two different soundtracks, a digital and an analog track. Each track in turn has a right and a left channel, just like your stereo system has a left and a right speaker. Videodisc manufacturers use this availability of multiple audio channels to add the soundtrack in other languages, music, or a combination of both.

Videodisc manufacturers are responding to the growing need for multilingual and multicultural software. The Optical Data Corporation of Warren, New Jersey, developed the first electronic textbook. Called Windows on Science, a science curriculum for grades K through 6, it has a separate Spanish soundtrack and is also available in an all-Spanish version. Texas adopted this electronic textbook, gaining the distinction of being the first state to use such material.

Audio

Audio support for computers provides many important instructional advantages. It helps students in reading skills development in a way that was previously possible only by means of the human voice. It supports understanding of vocabulary and on-screen text and can provide additional background or setting information. It is also essential for teaching phonetic features of language. Audio feedback gives students immediate information about their lesson responses. Not only are correct answers acknowledged, but the reasons why they are correct are often reinforced. In the event of an incorrect response, audio guidance often suggests approaches that may lead to a right answer.

Television

Joan Ganz Cooney, originator of *Sesame Street* and chair of the Executive Commit-tee of Children's Television Workshop, believes that the technology of television has three important strengths: it is accessible, it is cost-effective, and it works.[8] An example of the strengths of television applied to early childhood education is the Sesame Street Preschool Education Program Initiative (PEP). PEP is a national edu-cational program for preschool children in child care centers and family day care homes. Created around *Sesame Street* viewing, PEP uses storybook reading and related activities to promote and stimulate children's natural curiosity for learning. By 1996, it is estimated that 2.3 million children will participate.

RESEARCH AND TECHNOLOGY

Research provides us with much valuable information about the influence of tech-nology on children, their responses to technology, and how technology helps them

Technology includes more than computers. Listening stations such as this one are an exam-ple of technology applied to children's learning. When selecting materials for children to use at listening stations and other centers, professionals should choose those that are developmentally appropriate.

learn. In one study involving kindergarten and third grade children, researchers found that computers cultivated and sustained children's attention and concentration. Even while using television as a distractor during a twenty-seven-minute lesson, kindergarten children spent 69 percent and third graders 86 percent of their time attending to the computer. The researchers concluded:

> Computers can provide an intrinsically interesting learning environment for children that promotes attention, concentration to the task at hand, and reduced distractibility to competing environmental stimuli. Like television, computers appear to sustain attention by a rather effortless process. This effortless attentional process can be directed towards educational computer content that is worthy of children's sustained attention.[9]

Researchers have conducted many studies regarding the effects of technology on children's behavior, achievement, and literacy development. This research shows that technology and appropriate software, used in the right ways, promotes active learning, problem solving, literacy, and social-emotional development.[10] Furthermore, children exposed to developmental software—that is, software specifically identified as having the potential to support children's development—demonstrated gains in intelligence, nonverbal skills, structural knowledge, long-term memory, and complex memory. In addition, when developmental software is reinforced with supplemental activities, then children also show gains in verbal skills, problem solving, abstractions, and conceptual skills.[11]

Involving Parents Through Technology

In Los Angeles, there is a ninety-minute program in which principals, teachers, and parents explain to parents the changes that are occurring in the California classrooms as schools move to implement a new language arts curriculum. Parents can call a toll-free number to ask questions or clarify information. Although teleconferencing is no substitute for human interaction, it is a way in which parents can be aware of and involved in their child's school's issues.

EARLY CHILDHOOD PROFESSIONALS AND TECHNOLOGY

Early childhood professionals have to make decisions about their roles in and use of technology. Clements and his colleagues believe professionals have three choices:

> An important decision must be made among three paths that differ in the goals and types of computer applications. Those traveling the first path use simple computer games for "rewards" or occasionally use drill software but do not integrate it into their wider educational program. Those traveling on the second path integrate drill and other structured software activities into their programs. Those traveling on the third path use problem-solving software and tools such as word processors, Logo, and drawing programs to extend and enrich their children's education.

Research suggests that the first path leads nowhere: teachers might better invest efforts and resources elsewhere.

The second path is educationally plausible. Well-planned, integrated computer activities can increase achievement in cost-effective ways. . . .

The third path is more challenging—in time, in effort, in commitment, and in vision. This path alone, however, offers the potential for substantive educational innovation consonant with NAEYC guidelines and those of other professional organizations.[12]

ISSUES IN TECHNOLOGY

Early childhood professionals must consider a number of issues in their use and selection of technology and software.

Equity

All children must have equitable access to technology that is appropriate for them. While some may think that a worthy goal is to see that all children spend the same amount of time on the computer, all children may not need the same time. Some children may have to spend more time in order to achieve mastery of the objectives.

Equity consists of more than access and time. Equity also includes the idea that all children will learn how to use technology and appropriate software so that they are technologically literate. Having one group, socioeconomic class, or gender be more comfortable with, skillful with, and proficient in technology means that inequities and *technological illiteracy* result. We must avoid creating a generation of "have nots" of technology.

Equity also means that all children have opportunities to use good software. In particular, it means that children are not drilled to death with electronic worksheets as a means of attempting to raise their or their school's achievement test scores.

Antibias

As discussed in chapter 14 and elsewhere throughout this text, all professionals must take into consideration the diversity present in contemporary society. When professionals select materials, *including computer software, videos, films and other technologically based applications,* they must make sure these materials include depictions of children and adults of color, with differing abilities and ages, and that these materials are nonstereotypic of gender, culture, and socioeconomic class. The software industry has made progress in this regard but still has a long way to go in order to meet antibias criteria in their products. Professionals must evaluate all software they purchase and continually advocate for nonbiased software.

Sue Haugland offers these suggestions when evaluating software:

- Software should be available in multiple languages.
- Software should portray diverse environments and cultures as well as characteristics of all environments.

Equity is a critical issue in the use of technology. All children should have the opportunity to become technologically literate, regardless of their culture, gender, or socioeconomic status. How can professionals assure that equity exists in all programs?

- Software should maintain gender equity; that is, both sexes are represented and there should be equity in their roles.
- Software should have heterogeneous representation, African-Americans, Hispanics, Asians, etc.[13]

Integration

Technology should be integrated into the early childhood curriculum and learning environment as much as possible. Technology should be part of the classroom organization so its use can help promote cooperative learning and achieve learning outcomes for children. For example, a computer/technology center could be one of the centers found in early childhood classrooms that children have access to as they would any other center. In this way, the technology would be used as much as possible. And, just as important, such a center would have software that enables children to work independently, with little or minimal adult supervision.

Appropriate Use

Use of technology should not be something children get to do only when they have completed other tasks. Technology should not be used as a reward or as something children get to do only after they have done other activities, nor should it be a supplemental activity. Rather, it should be an integrated part of the early childhood program.

Drill versus Discovery

A major controversy among early childhood professionals involves the purpose of computers in the classroom. On the one hand, some say that drill-and-practice programs that emphasize helping children learn colors, numbers, vocabulary, and skills such as addition have no place in the early childhood program. They say that only software that encourages learning by discovery and exploration is appropriate. On the other hand, some professionals see drill-and-practice software as a valuable means for children to learn concepts and skills they so desperately need to succeed in school. The VistaKids program (see pages L and M of the color insert) is an example of using skill-based software to help children develop literacy and English language competency.

Of course, in this case, as with so many things, a middle ground offers an appropriate solution. Many children like drill-and-practice programs and the positive feedback that often comes with them. In fact, many children can and do spend long periods of time working on such programs.

One point is that this is not all these children should do or have the opportunity to do these programs. Second, not all children like or do well with skill-drill programs. A third point is that all children should have access to a wide variety of software and instructional and learning activities that are appropriate to them as individuals. This is what a developmentally appropriate curriculum is all about, and it applies to technology and software as well.

Higher-Order Learning

Technology can support and facilitate critical educational and cognitive processes such as cooperative learning, group and individual problem solving, critical thinking, reflective practices, analysis, inquiry, process writing, and public speaking. Also, technology can promote metacognition, that is, thinking about thinking.

Computer Literacy

Children and their teachers need to be computer literate, and this goal should direct the computer program of the primary grades. An effective program of computer literacy can be developed with the following guidelines:

1. Computer literacy must be defined comprehensively, including two general areas: learning *with* computers and learning *about* computers.

2. However, decisions concerning what children learn about computers should be made not by asking, "What can we teach kids about computers?" but rather by asking, "What understandings about computers, their impact on our world, and their uses are *developmentally appropriate* for, and *educationally relevant* to, young children?" This question implies that lectures on the history of computers or rote

memorization of computer components terminology should not be included in the curriculum. Only when meaningful concepts can be actively learned should they be considered for inclusion.

3.   For both general areas, educators should (a) decide first how and when to use computers to accomplish the goals of early education and (b) integrate these uses into the curriculum, while (c) remaining consistent with the beliefs, principles, and practices of the program.

These guidelines have several important ramifications. For example, they imply that the development of the "whole child" will be given first and primary consideration; there will not be a "computers" unit that is separate from work in social studies, science, language arts, and so on; and *individual children will have different needs, interests, and abilities and, therefore, will learn different things about computers and will use them in different ways*. This should be welcomed as well as accepted; no effort should be made to force all children to "master" all aspects of computer literacy. Instead of one definition of computer literacy for all, teachers should determine what computers can do to help a particular child reach a particular goal.[14]

THE FUTURE

Undoubtedly you have heard the saying "You haven't seen anything yet." This remark applies to technology and its application to all school settings from prekindergarten through grade 12. For example, Florida has launched an initiative called School Year 2000 in which technology will be used to improve instruction, management, and student services. The vision of School Year 2000 is that each student will acquire the foundational skills and competencies to succeed as an adult in the information age. Needless to say, such a vision begins in the early years.

What will have to happen in order to bring tomorrow to the classrooms today? First, early childhood professionals must decide themselves to use technology and gain the training necessary to be computer literate. Second, professionals must dedicate themselves to the developmentally appropriate use of technology and software. Third, professionals must recognize that technology and all its applications are not just add-ons to the curriculum or activities to do only when there is time or to reward children for good behavior or achievement. Technology and software are here to stay, and they can, like text-based materials, help children learn to their fullest potential.

ACTIVITIES FOR FURTHER ENRICHMENT

1.   Visit classrooms in your local school districts. What evidence of the integration of technology into the curriculum can you find? What conclusions can you draw from your data?

2.   Interview early childhood professionals in your school district. What barriers do they say they must contend with in their efforts to include technology in the curriculum? What implications do these barriers have for what early childhood professionals can accomplish?

3.   Why are some early childhood professionals slow to adopt computers and other technology in their classrooms? What suggestions would you give for how to facilitate this process?

4. Visit a computer (technological) magnet school in your area to determine how computers and other technologies are integrated in the curriculum. What technology was available that you did not think would be? What technology was not available that you thought should be?

5. Some teachers and parents think young children should not be introduced to computers. Interview five parents and teachers.

    a. List reasons why they might feel this way.

    b. Do you agree that young children should not be introduced to computers?

    c. How young is "too young"?

6. Visit a center or program that provides services to children with disabilities. Cite five ways in which technology is used to implement the curriculum, help teachers teach, and promote children's learning.

7. With the use of BASIC or any other computer language, develop a game for students in grades K through 3.

8. Choose a particular theme, and write a lesson plan to show how you would integrate technology into a kindergarten classroom.

9. Write a four-paragraph report in which you explain your views of the use of technology in early childhood programs. Present this to a center director, school principal, or similar person for feedback. Set up a conference for discussion and reaction.

READINGS FOR FURTHER ENRICHMENT

Beynon, John, and Hugie Mackay (Eds.). *Computers into Classrooms: More Questions Than Answers* (Bristol, PA: Falmer, 1993)

> Critically examines computers and their use in teaching and learning. Provides much interesting information and raises many issues that need to be addressed by teachers who wish to bring themselves and their children into the technological age.

Buckleitner, W. *High/Scope Buyer's Guide to Children's Software 1993* (Ypsilanti, MI: High/Scope, 1993)

> High/Scope's annual survey of programs for children aged three to seven. Over five hundred software programs reviewed. Includes descriptions, ratings, award-winning programs, a glossary, and a national directory of software producers.

Church, Gregory, and Sharon Glennen (Eds.). *The Handbook of Assistive Technology* (Baltimore, MD: Singular Publishing Group, 1992)

> Covers all key areas of assistive technology and offers information about establishing, maintaining, and expanding assistive technology services for young children and youth. Contents include such topics as "Adaptive Toys and Environmental Controls" and "Integrating Assistive Technology in the Classroom and Community."

Geiser, Paul G., and Mygna Futrell. *Teachers, Computers, and the Curriculum: Microcomputers in the Classroom* (Boston: Allyn & Bacon, 1990)

> Introduces teachers to computer terms and uses and suggests ways to integrate the technology into teaching activities.

Papert, Seymour. *The Children's Machine: Rethinking School in the Age of the Computer* (New York: Basic Books, 1993)

> Papert is the popularizer of Logo; in this book he envisions a future for education in which computers restore the wonder to learning.

Salpeter, Judy. *Kids and Computers: A Parent's Handbook* (Carmel, IN: SAMS, 1992)

> Helps parents bring computers into their home life, with detailed software reviews. Makes the computer experience a successful and pleasurable one for the entire family.

Sewell, David. *New Tools for New Minds: A Cognitive Perspective on the Use of Computers with Young Children* (New York: St. Martin's, 1990)

> Draws attention to the close relationships among educational software, classroom computer use, and cognitive development. The use

of computers is seen as promoting effective teaching and learning.

Warger, Cynthia (Ed.). *Technology in Today's Schools* (Alexandria, VA: Association for Supervision and Curriculum Development, 1990)

Describes successful approaches for using technology to improve curricula.

NOTES

1.   Joshua Mills, "Computer Age Tots Trading Building Blocks for Software, *New York Times* (Feb. 13, 1994), p. A1.

2.   Roberta H. Barba, "Assessing Children's Attitudes towards Computers: The Draw-a-Computer User Test," *Journal of Computing in Childhood Education*, 2(1) (1990), p. 13.

3.   U.S. Bureau of the Census, 1991.

4.   Pam *Ross,* ed., *Software Resource Guide* (Evanston, IL: National Lekotek Center, 2100 Ridge Ave., Evanston, IL 60201; (708) 328-0001).

5.   Loretta Holder-Brown and Howard P. Parette, Jr., "Children with Disabilities Who Use Assistive Technology: Ethical Considerations," *Young Children* (Sept. 1992), p. 74.

6.   Ibid., pp. 74–75.

7.   Douglas H. Clements, Bonnie K. Nastasi, and Sudha Swaminathan, "Young Children and Computers: Crossroads and Directions from Research," *Young Children* (Jan. 1993), p. 57.

8.   Joan Ganz Cooney, "Not a Moment to Waste," *Electronic Learning*, 12(6) (Mar. 1993), p. 54.

9.   Sandra L. Calvert, Caitlin Brune, Maria Eguia, and Jean Marcato, *"Attentional Inertia and Distractibility during Children's Educational Computer Interactions."* Poster session presented at the biennial meeting of the Society for Research in Child Development, Seattle, Washington, April 1991.

10.   Clements et al., pp. 56–64.

11.   Susan W. Haugland, "The Effects of Computer Software on Preschool Children's Developmental Gains," *Journal of Computing in Childhood Education,* 3 (1992), pp. 15–30.

12.   Clements et al., p. 63. Used by permission of the National Association for the Education of Young Children.

13.   Susan W. Haugland, "Maintaining an Anti-Bias Curriculum," *Day Care and Early Education* (Winter 1992), pp. 44–45.

14.   Douglas H. Clements, *Computers in Early and Primary Education.* (Needham Heights, MA: Allyn & Bacon, 1985), pp. 52-53. Copyright © 1985 by Allyn and Bacon. Reprinted by permission.

16

Early Childhood Professional Development

Becoming a Professional

After you have read and studied this chapter, you will be able to:

☐ Analyze the relationship among early childhood professionals' attitudes, character, and children's development

☐ Explain qualities of early childhood professionals that are worthy of emulation

☐ Value and identify with the philosophies of early childhood professionals and teachers of the year

☐ Identify important themes and concepts that contribute to becoming a good professional

☐ Plan for and begin to implement essential attitudes, skills, and behaviors that will enable you to have a joyful, productive, and professional career

☐ Write a personal and meaningful philosophy of early childhood education

☐ Devise a personal plan for becoming an early childhood professional

THE EARLY CHILDHOOD PROFESSIONAL

The term *professional* is used a lot. But how would you explain it to someone who asked you, "Who is an early childhood professional?" What does *professional* mean? *An early childhood professional is well paid and knowledgeable and demonstrates high-quality performance, which results in better outcomes for children.*[1] According to this definition, then, there are three essential elements of being an early childhood professional:

1. *Good pay.*   Demonstration of professional knowledge and behavior implies that individuals will be adequately compensated.
2. *Knowledge.*   This consists of what professionals need to know in order to be effective in any position they hold.
3. *Demonstration of quality through performance.*   Another way to put it is that the early childhood professional engages in competent and informed practice. As a contemporary saying goes, being able to talk the walk is not enough. You have to be able to walk the talk. The professional puts knowledge and skills into practice.

Table 16–1 outlines professional categories as identified by the National Association for the Education of Young Children. These categories reflect the latest thinking of the profession in its efforts continually to enhance professionalism in early childhood education.

Teaching is and should be a joyful experience for those who dedicate themselves to it. The profession demands and young children deserve the best from all who work with young children and their families.

TABLE 16–1   Definition of Early Childhood Professional Categories

This table is designed to reflect a continuum of professional development. The levels identify levels of preparation programs for which standards have been established nationally.

Early Childhood Professional Level VI

Successful completion of a Ph.D. or Ed.D. in a program conforming to NAEYC guidelines; OR

Successful demonstration of the knowledge, performance, and dispositions expected as outcomes of a doctoral degree program conforming to NAEYC guidelines.

Early Childhood Professional Level V

Successful completion of a master's degree in a program that conforms to NAEYC guidelines; OR

Successful demonstration of the knowledge, performance, and dispositions expected as outcomes of a master's degree program conforming to NAEYC guidelines.

Early Childhood Professional Level IV

Successful completion of a baccalaureate degree from a program conforming to NAEYC guidelines; OR

State certificate meeting NAEYC/ATE certification guidelines; OR

Successful completion of a baccalaureate degree in another field with more than 30 professional units in early childhood development/education including 300 hours of supervised teaching experience, including 150 hours each for two of the following three age groups: infants and toddlers, 3- to 5-year-olds, or the primary grades; OR

Successful demonstration of the knowledge, performance, and dispositions expected as outcomes of a baccalaureate degree program conforming to NAEYC guidelines.

Early Childhood Professional Level III

Successful completion of an associate degree from a program conforming to NAEYC guidelines; OR

Successful completion of an associate degree in a related field, plus 30 units of professional studies in early childhood development/education including 300 hours of supervised teaching experience in an early childhood program; OR

Successful demonstration of the knowledge, performance, and dispositions expected as outcomes of an associate degree program conforming to NAEYC guidelines.

Early Childhood Professional Level II

II.   B.   Successful completion of a one-year early childhood certificate program.

II.   A.   Successful completion of the CDA Professional Preparation Program OR completion of a systematic, comprehensive training program that prepares an individual to successfully acquire the CDA Credential through direct assessment.

Early Childhood Professional Level I

Individuals who are employed in an early childhood professional role working under supervision or with support (e.g., linkages with provider association or network or enrollment in supervised practicum) and participating in training designed to lead to the assessment of individual competencies or acquisition of a degree.

Source: "NAEYC Position Statement: A Conceptual Framework for Early Childhood Professional Development, 1994," *Young Children,* 49(3), p. 74. Copyright © 1994 by the National Association for the Education of Young Children. Reprinted by permission.

The Knowledge Base of the Profession

What is the knowledge that early childhood professionals need to possess? The following list describes what the early childhood profession identifies as the content of the profession. To work effectively with all young children—infants and toddlers, preschoolers, and primary school–age children (including those with special needs)—all early childhood professionals must

- demonstrate a basic understanding of the early childhood profession and make a commitment to professionalism;

- demonstrate a basic understanding of child development and apply this knowledge in practice;

- observe and assess children's behavior for use in planning and individualizing teaching practices and curriculum;

- establish and maintain an environment that ensures children's safety and their healthy development;

- plan and implement a developmentally appropriate program that advances all areas of children's learning and development, including social, emotional, intellectual, and physical competence;

- establish supportive relationships with children and implement developmentally appropriate techniques of guidance and group management;

- establish positive and productive relationships with families; and

- support the uniqueness of each child, recognizing that children are best understood in the context of family, culture, and society.[2]

These items represent the *core knowledge* of the profession. Figure 16–1 shows how the acquisition of this core knowledge integrates with the ongoing process of becoming a professional. In this sense, the professional, at the moment of entry into the field, *at whatever level,* undertakes the responsibility to engage in increasing levels of preparation and knowledge acquisition. The expanding cone of the knowledge one gains throughout the process of becoming a professional is shown in Figure 16–2.

The Process of Becoming a Professional

The acquisition of core knowledge throughout one's professional life has embedded in it the process of continuous professional development. When does a person step over the line from being a nonprofessional to being a professional? When, if ever, does a person become a "finished" professional, so that they do not have to do anything more about becoming a professional? These are not easy questions to answer. Rather than trying to answer them directly, it makes more sense to answer them this way: a person is always in the process of becoming a professional. The professional is never a "finished" product and is always studying, learning, changing, and *becoming* a professional. The teachers of the year that you read about in this chapter would not think of themselves as "completed" professionals. All would say that there is more they need to learn and more they can do. This process of continuous professional development is depicted in Figure 16–3.

FIGURE 16–1   Core Knowledge in the Early Childhood Profession

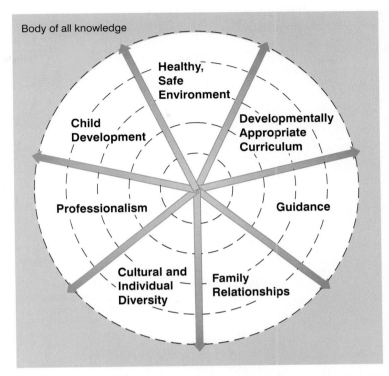

The dotted lines indicate stages of professional development achieved by the acquisition of recognized credentials that are based on professional standards of preparation. Moving from the innermost circle—the precredential level—individuals demonstrate knowledge required for the Child Development Associate (CDA) Credential and associate, baccalaureate, and advanced degrees. The arrows denote the continuum that extends from knowledge necessary for implementing effective practice to knowledge necessary for the generation and translation of knowledge; core knowledge is embedded within the larger body of all knowledge.

Source: From "Of Ladders and Lattices, Cores and Cones: Conceptualizing an Early Childhood Professional System," by Sue Bredekamp and Barbara Willer, 1992, *Young Children,* 47(3), p. 49. Copyright © 1992 by the National Association for the Education of Young Children. Reprinted by permission.

Becoming a professional means you will participate in training and education beyond the minimum needed for your present position. You will also want to consider your career objectives and the qualifications you might need for positions of increasing responsibility. The National Academy of Early Childhood Programs specifies staff qualifications and training appropriate for positions in early childhood programs that you should review to determine how they apply to your career and life goals (see Figure 16–4 on p. 612).

FIGURE 16–2   The Expanding
Knowledge Base

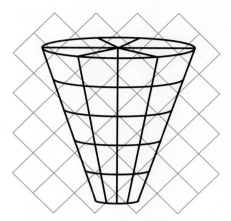

The cone reflects the expanding knowledge base obtained
by participating in a comprehensive, articulated system of
professional development.

Source: From "Of Ladders and Lattices, Cores and Cones:
Conceptualizing an Early Childhood Professional System," by
Sue Bredekamp and Barbara Willer, 1992, *Young Children,*
47(3), p. 50. Copyright © 1992 by the National Association for
the Education of Young Children. Reprinted by permission.

In 1991, the National Association for the Education of Young Children, with a
grant from the Carnegie Corporation of New York, established the National Institute
for Early Childhood Professional Development. The Institute will conduct efforts to
achieve an articulated, coordinated professional development system.

Qualities of Early Childhood Professionals

Currently, there is a great deal of discussion about quality in early childhood programs, which is directly related to the quality of the professionals in these programs.
And, as you discovered throughout this book, merely discussing quality is not sufficient—professionals must involve themselves in activities that will promote quality in
their lives and the lives of the children they teach and care for.

Anyone who has contemplated teaching has probably asked, "Am I the kind of
person suited for a career in early childhood education?" This is a difficult question
to answer honestly. However, the following are qualities early childhood professionals should demonstrate: love and respect for children, knowledge of children and
their families, caring, compassion, courtesy, dedication, empathy, enthusiasm,
friendliness, helpfulness, honesty, intelligence, kindness, motivation, patience, sensitivity, trust, understanding, and warmth. Home and early school experiences are critical for developing these qualities. So if we want these qualities in our future professionals, we need to promote them *now,* in our teaching of young children. Toward

FIGURE 16–3   A Continuum of Becoming a Professional

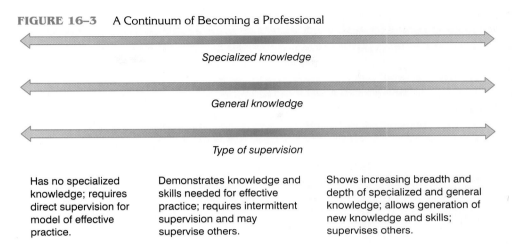

Specialized knowledge

General knowledge

Type of supervision

| Has no specialized knowledge; requires direct supervision for model of effective practice. | Demonstrates knowledge and skills needed for effective practice; requires intermittent supervision and may supervise others. | Shows increasing breadth and depth of specialized and general knowledge; allows generation of new knowledge and skills; supervises others. |

Source: From "A 'New' Paradigm of Early Childhood Professional Development," by Barbara Willer and Sue Bredekamp, *Young Children,* 48(4), p. 65. Copyright © 1993 by the National Association for the Education of Young Children. Reprinted by permission.

that end, professionals might well concentrate on nurturing in themselves what is probably the most important of these characteristics: caring.

As a professional, you will live and work in classrooms, programs, and other settings in which things do not always go smoothly, in which children do not always learn ably and well, in which children are not always clean and free from illness and hunger, in which children's and parents' backgrounds and ways of life are different from yours. If you truly care, being an early childhood professional is not easy. Caring means you will lose sleep trying to find a way to help a child learn to read, that you will spend your own money to buy supplies, that you will spend long hours planning and gathering materials. Caring also means you will not leave your intelligence, enthusiasm, or talents outside the classroom but will bring them into the center, classroom, administration offices, and board of directors meetings or wherever you can make a difference in the lives of children and their families.

PREPARING FOR A CAREER IN EARLY CHILDHOOD EDUCATION

A career as an early childhood professional can be greatly rewarding for those who want it to be. Discussed next are some things you can do to make your career happy and productive for you, children, and families.

Go where the opportunities are. Sometimes people lock themselves into a particular geographic area or age range of children. Some locations may have an oversupply of professionals, while other areas, especially urban, have a chronic shortage of professionals. Cities usually offer challenging and rewarding opportunities. There will always be a job for one who is willing to go where the jobs are.

FIGURE 16–4   Staff Qualifications and Development

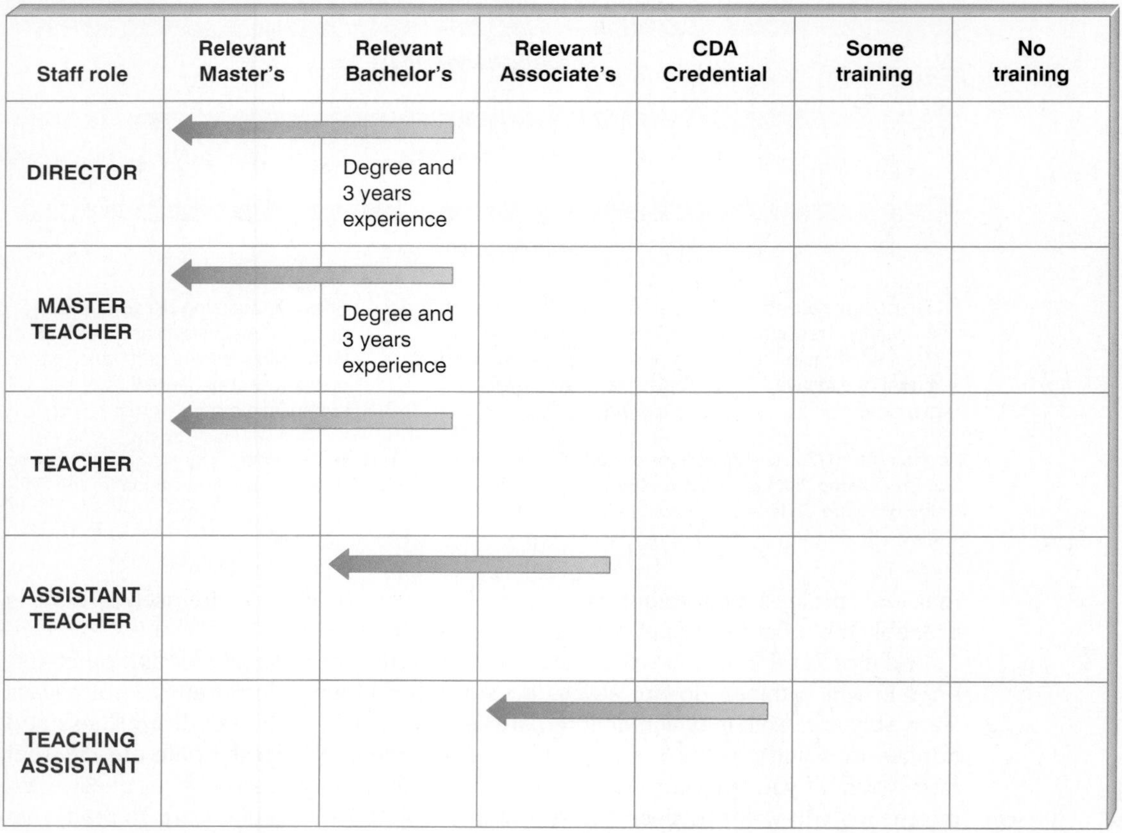

Staff role	Relevant Master's	Relevant Bachelor's	Relevant Associate's	CDA Credential	Some training	No training
DIRECTOR		Degree and 3 years experience				
MASTER TEACHER		Degree and 3 years experience				
TEACHER						
ASSISTANT TEACHER						
TEACHING ASSISTANT						

This figure does not include specialty roles such as educational coordinator, social services director, or other providers of special services. Individuals fulfilling these roles should possess the knowledge and qualifications required to fulfill their responsibilities effectively.

Source: National Academy of Early Childhood Programs, *Accreditation Criteria and Procedures of the National Academy of Early Childhood Programs,* rev. ed. (Washington, D.C.: National Association for the Education of Young Children, 1991), p. 31.

Seek every opportunity for experiences with all kinds of children in all kinds of settings. Individuals often limit themselves to experiences in one setting (e.g., the public schools) and ignore church schools, child care programs, private and non-profit agencies (e.g., March of Dimes, Easter Seal Society, etc.), baby-sitting, and children's clothing stores as venues to broaden and expand their knowledge of children. These experiences can often be work related and doubly rewarding. Though these positions may pay little or nothing, be willing to volunteer your services, because volunteer positions have a way of leading to paid positions. Many career possibilities and opportunities can become available this way.

Before committing yourself to training for one teaching specialty, volunteer in at least three different areas of education to find out exactly what age and field of education you are most interested in. Do other volunteer work with children in activities such as recreation, social events, or scouting.

Honestly analyze your attitudes and feelings toward children. Do you really want to work with young children, or would you be happier in another field? During your experiences with children, you should constantly test your attitudes toward them and their families. If you decide that working with children is not for you because of how you feel about them, then by all means do not teach.

Honestly believe that all children are capable of learning. Some parents lament that those who work with young children act as though their children cannot learn because of their culture or socioeconomic background. All children have the right to be taught by a professional who believes they are capable of learning to the fullest capacity.

Explore the possibilities for educational service in fields other than the public school. Do not limit your career choices and alternatives because of your limited conception of the teacher's role. Students often think teacher education prepares an individual only to teach. Other opportunities for service are available in religious organizations; federal, state, and local agencies; private educational enterprises; hospitals; libraries; and social work. Do not feel pressured to choose a major during your first year or two in college. Take a variety of electives that will help you in career choices, and talk to vocational counselors. Do not make up your mind too quickly about teaching a certain grade level or age range. Many teachers find out, much to their surprise, that the grade level they *thought* was best for them was not. Remain flexible about a grade or subject to teach.

Seize every educational opportunity to enhance your training program and career. Through wise course selection, weaknesses can be strengthened and new alternatives explored. For example, if your program of studies requires a certain number of social science credits, use them to explore areas such as sociology and anthropology, which have fascinating relationships to education. Electives that practicing teachers sometimes wish they had taken in college are typing, first aid, audiovisual aids and media, behavior modification/management, special education, creative writing, and arts and crafts. Of course, a teacher can never have too strong a background in child development.

Start now to develop a philosophy of education and teaching. Your philosophy should be based on what you believe about children and the learning process, how you think children should be taught, and your present values. A philosophy of teaching serves as a guide for classroom practice. Many teachers fill the school day and children's lives with unrelated activities, without considering whether they match their objectives. So much of teaching is based on no philosophy at all. In fact, your philosophy may be the only guide to help you teach, for as surprising as it may seem, many schools operate without a written philosophy.

GROWING FROM A STUDENT TO A PROFESSIONAL

My first encounter with professionalism occurred as an undergraduate student at Stephen F. Austin State University in Nacogdoches, Texas. I majored in child development and family living because I enjoyed working with young children and wanted to understand their growth and development. A professor recommended that it was a good professional move to join the National Association for the Education of Young Children. She added that a resumé indicating professional involvement is often useful in interviewing. I joined but never attended any meetings or functions.

After graduation, I moved to Denton, Texas, to attend graduate school at Texas Woman's University, again majoring in child development. While attending graduate school, I taught three- and four-year-old children at the Texas Woman's University Nursery School. The director of the nursery school, Mrs. Barbara Jackson—my supervisor, mentor, and friend—encouraged me to rejoin NAEYC. I joined but again did not attend any functions the first year. The local affiliate, Denton AEYC, asked Mrs. Jackson to present her wonderful "Science for Preschool Children" session at the spring workshop. Mrs. Jackson asked me if I would help her. This was the beginning of my professional involvement! Little did I know what a beginning it was.

Aside from serving as support at the workshop (Mrs. Jackson really *did* everything), I also made the signs to label our activities. For the next workshop, Dr. Velma Schmidt and Dr. Arminta Jacobson asked me to make signs because they liked the ones I had previously made. Who would have thought sign making would be my ticket to professionalism? After becoming involved at this minimal level, I was asked to serve as a member of the Workshop Planning committee. I played a low-key role, primarily following the lead of others. The next year I was asked to serve as chairperson of the Week of the Young Child (WOYC) committee. The Week of the Young Child is designed to bring attention to the needs of young children.

Immediately after receiving my doctoral degree in child development, I moved to Austin, Texas, while my husband attended law school. In Austin, I taught at the Open Door, a mainstreaming preschool near the University of Texas. Almost immediately after I began teaching in the four-year-old class, the director, Jill Gronquist, encouraged me to join the Austin Association for the Education of Young Children (AAEYC) as cochair of the Public Education and Speakers Bureau committee. The next year, Jill resigned her office as vice president for community relations and asked that I fill her position. Intimidated by the responsibility, I nonetheless attended a summer board meeting. The board was a delightful group of preschool and child care pro-

Contributed by Cindy Haralson, child development specialist, Dade County Public Schools.

Basing your teaching on a philosophy will make the difference between filling children's school days with unrelated activities and filling them with activities directed toward helping them learn and develop to their fullest potential. As you develop your philosophy during preservice training, discuss it with friends, professors, and in-service teachers, and be willing to revise it as you gain new knowl-

fessionals, and I slowly began to feel comfortable in the position. As fate would have it, a primary responsibility of the community relations vice presidency is to plan and implement the Week of the Young Child. Fortunately, Bibi Somyak, who teaches four-year-olds at First English Lutheran Child Development Center, beautifully orchestrated the first WOYC of my term. Writing WOYC information for inclusion in the AAEYC newsletter was essentially the extent of my involvement.

As the second Week of the Young Child during my vice presidency rolled around, the responsibility was mine. I was busy in a new position with the Internal Revenue Service. The IRS Austin Service Center and Compliance Center had been designated by the federal government to implement a model on-site child care center for the employees of the IRS, Department of Veterans Affairs, and the Department of the Treasury. With the assistance of many qualified professionals, I planned and implemented a program to serve a hundred children between the ages of six weeks and six years. With the help of my friend Joanne Polasek, I planned and held a successful mall fair during the WOYC for Austin children and their families. We also held our annual Parade to the Capitol, in which youngsters and their parents and teachers march to the capitol and are entertained by children's musicians. At the Capitol, a proclamation is read declaring the day as Texas Children's Day during the Week of the Young Child. The events are intended to emphasize to the community the needs of young children and receive local media coverage.

At the IRS, while simultaneously teaching child development at Austin Community College, I feel I accomplished significant professional growth. Through association with professionals such as Elizabeth Sears, director of the Open Door; Sandra Hamilton, department chairperson of child development at Austin Community College; and Gale Spear, a Bank Street College of Education graduate who is director of the Austin Community College Child Care Center as well as a college instructor at ACC, I learned about child advocacy and the importance of vocalizing concerns about quality child care. Through these associations, I have grown in my commitment to young children and to my profession. Such issues now influence my life greatly—whom I vote for, what type of program with which I am willing to be associated, keeping up with legislation that affects children and their families, and keeping up-to-date in our field's professional literature.

The road was long as I evolved into a committed professional, but I feel it was worth the wait. Of course, all previous developments in my career affect my present functioning. I have learned a lot as I become increasingly involved in my field and look forward to learning and growing more in the years to come.

edge and insights. Developing a philosophy will not automatically make you a good teacher, but it will provide a foundation on which to build a good teaching career. (An added benefit of developing a philosophy is that it will help you respond professionally during job interviews.)

Volunteer activities provide an excellent opportunity to expand your vision of working with young children and to learn new skills. You should not hesitate to seek out appropriate volunteer activities as a way to enhance your personal and professional growth.

Examine your willingness to dedicate yourself to teaching. Acquaint yourself thoroughly with what teaching involves. Visit many different kinds of schools. Is the school atmosphere one in which you want to spend the rest of your life? Talk with several teachers to learn what is involved in teaching. Ask yourself, "Am I willing to work hard? Am I willing to give more time to teaching than a teaching contract may specify? Are teachers the kind of people with whom I want to work? Do I have the physical energy for teaching? Do I have the enthusiasm necessary for good teaching?"

Honestly analyze your feelings and attitudes toward working with young children. Not everyone has the skills or temperament required for effective teaching of young children. Matching your abilities to the children you can work with best is an important part of becoming a professional.

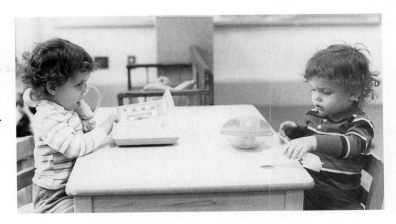

As you enter the teaching profession, several other suggestions will help you find your career more productive and rewarding. Let us consider some of them next.

Adjust to the ever-emerging new careers of teaching and society. All careers are molded by the needs of society and the resources available. Many teachers and schools waste potential and miss opportunities because of their unwillingness to adjust to changing circumstances and conditions.

Be willing to improve your skills and increase your knowledge. Many professionals choose to do this by returning to school, which is usually encouraged by state certification requirements for permanent or continuing certification. Many teachers fulfill the requirements through a master's degree. A trend in teacher certification is to allow accumulation of a specified number of "points," gained through college credits, in-service programs, attendance at professional meetings and conferences, and other professional involvements. These points then count toward certification and take the place of college courses.

Reading is one method of self-improvement; a less obvious method is to force change by periodically teaching at different grade levels. By changing grade levels, teachers gain new insights into and perspectives on children and teaching. Whatever method you choose for self-improvement, you should recognize the need for constant retraining. While some school districts do provide opportunities for retraining, most of the responsibility will be yours.

Be willing to try new things. Some new teachers get in a rut immediately upon entering the profession. They feel their college education has provided them with the one right way to teach children. This attitude results in a preconceived, fixed notion of what teaching is. These teachers become so preoccupied with fulfilling this image of good teaching that they seldom relax enough to try new ideas. Despite the number of new ideas and methods available, it is surprising how few the average teacher tries. Even though sometimes trying something new may arouse opposition from your colleagues, do not let that possibility deter you.

Be enthusiastic for teaching and in your teaching. Time and again the one attribute that seems to separate the good teacher from the mediocre is enthusiasm.

Even if you were not born with enthusiasm, *trying* to be enthusiastic will help a great deal.

Maintain an open-door policy in teaching. Welcome into your classroom parents, colleagues, college students, and all who want to know what schools and centers are doing. Teaching need not be a lonely profession.

DEVELOPING A PHILOSOPHY OF EDUCATION

A philosophy of education is a set of beliefs about how children develop and learn and what and how they should be taught. Your philosophy of education will be quite personal. There may be similarities between your philosophy and that of another teacher, but what you believe is unique with you. You should not try to mold your philosophy to match another's; your philosophy should reflect *your* beliefs.

As we discussed earlier, your philosophy will guide and direct your daily teaching. Your beliefs about how children learn best will determine whether you individualize instruction or try to teach the same thing to everyone in the same way. Your philosophy will determine whether you help children do things for themselves or whether you do things for them. The following paragraphs describe some ways to go about developing your philosophy.

Read widely in textbooks, journals, and other professional literature to get ideas and points of view. A word of caution: When people refer to philosophies of education, they often think only of historic influences. This is only part of the information available for writing a philosophy. Make sure you explore contemporary ideas as well, for these will also have a strong influence on you as a professional.

If you have not written your philosophy, these headings will help you get started:

- I believe the purposes of education are . . .
- I believe that children learn best when they are taught under certain conditions and in certain ways. Some of these are . . .
- The curriculum of any classroom should include certain "basics" that contribute to children's social, emotional, intellectual, and physical development. These basics are . . .
- Children learn best in an environment that promotes learning.
- Some of the features of a good learning environment are . . .
- All children have certain needs that must be met if they are to grow and learn at their best. Some of these basic needs are . . .
- I would meet these needs by . . .
- A teacher should have certain qualities and behave in certain ways. Qualities I think important for teaching are . . .

Have other people read your philosophy. This helps you clarify your ideas and redefine your thoughts, because your philosophy should be understandable to others. (They do not necessarily have to agree with you.)

Talk with successful teachers and other educators. (The following accounts of the Teachers of the Year are evidence that a philosophy can help a person become an above-average teacher.) Talking with others exposes you to others' points of view and stimulates thinking.

Evaluate your philosophy against this checklist:

___ Does it accurately relate my beliefs about teaching? Have I been honest with myself?

___ Is it understandable to me and others?

___ Does it provide practical guidance for teaching?

___ Are my ideas consistent with each other?

___ Does what I believe make good sense?

___ Have I been comprehensive, stating my beliefs about (1) how children learn, (2) what children should be taught, (3) how children should be taught, (4) the conditions under which children learn best, and (5) the qualities of a good teacher?

A GOOD TEACHER: A LESSON FROM HISTORY

It is worthwhile looking at the history of early childhood education for ideas about good teachers. In fact, we need look no further than Froebel, father of the kindergarten:

> I understand it thus. She [the mother] says, "I bring my child—take care of it, as *I* would do"; or "Do with my child what is right to do"; or "Do it better than I am able to do it." A silent agreement is made between the parents and you, the teacher; the child is passed from hand to hand, from heart to heart. What else *can* you do but be a mother to the little one, for the hour, morning or day when you have the sacred charge of a young soul? In hope and trust the child is brought to you, and you have to show yourself worthy of the confidence which is placed in your skill, your experience and your knowledge.[3]

ETHICAL STANDARDS FOR THE PROFESSION

A professional is an ethical person. The profession of early childhood education has a set of ethical standards to guide our thinking and behavior. As an early childhood educator, you will want to be a good teacher as judged by the profession. The National Association for the Education of Young Children has developed both a Statement of Commitment and a Code of Ethical Conduct (Appendix D). This is the Statement of Commitment:

> As an individual who works with young children, I commit myself to furthering the values of early childhood education as they are reflected in the NAEYC Code of Ethical Conduct.

(Text continues on page 625.)

TEACHERS OF THE YEAR

Dodie Magill, Kindergarten Teacher, 1993 South Carolina Teacher of the Year, Pelham Road Elementary School, Greenville, South Carolina

Teaching is more than imparting facts and knowledge to students. Teaching is helping to instill in children a love for learning that will inspire them to continue the education process throughout their lives. I believe that outstanding teachers accomplish this in a variety of ways.

They begin by working to build a positive self-concept in each child. A student should feel successful and special in his or her own way. Understanding that each child has a unique "time clock" for growth and development, teachers must respect the uniqueness of each child. In my classroom, each child is a very important person. Weekly a VIP is chosen who takes home a small bulletin board and returns proudly the next day to share photographs of him- or herself and family members with the class.

In addition to teaching children to believe in themselves, we must expect the best from each child. Through encouragement and support, we can guide children through challenges and help them meet their full potential. By encouraging children with hugs, smiles, and pats on the back, teachers can inspire their students to attempt new challenges. By building on their strengths and emphasizing their success, children learn that risks are worthwhile. In my classroom, children earn "Pelham Road Community Cash" for extra math work that they may spend in our Math Store.

Teachers must make learning relevant for their students and do this by providing hands-on experiences. Young children are not abstract thinkers. They need to have their learning rooted in concrete experiences. What child will forget how peanut butter is made when they have uprooted the peanut plant, roasted the peanuts, shelled and ground them, and then spread the mixture on crackers to eat?

I try to make learning "come alive" for my students. Dressing up as "Betty Balanced Meals" during a study of food groups or as "Mr. Taste Bud" while we study our five senses, I capture their attention. Through these performances I also demonstrate that imagination and creativity are valuable qualities.

Technology must play an integral part of an effective teacher's classroom. By encouraging children to use computers as a basic tool for learning, we are helping prepare them for the real world, which is dependent on technology.

Because young children do not differentiate knowledge by subjects, they learn best if their learning is integrated. Using a unit approach, I weave together each content area to relate to our theme. Weekly, I shop for the groceries needed for our snack center. The nutritious foods we eat daily extend math, science, language, and social studies concepts. The sound "p" is made memorable when children make their own personal pepperoni pizzas, and the concept of "half" becomes real when children cut their own sandwiches into two equal parts.

As teachers we must provide experiences for our students to become independent thinkers who are responsible for their own behavior and capable of making good decisions for themselves. By setting appropriate limits for children and enforcing rules consistently, I can set their boundaries. By modeling behavior that shows caring and concern for others, I teach them how to respond to their peers. By allowing children to choose learning centers that interest them and yet require that certain tasks be done within that time frame, I am helping them learn to use their time wisely and responsibly.

Actively involving parents is another important job for teachers. I encourage parents to participate in my classroom in such ways as recording stories and letters the children dictate to them. They accompany us on field trips, make play dough, or share their favorite storybooks with the class. I frequently telephone parents, send notes home, and make home visits to keep them informed of their child's progress. I keep them up-to-date of our class activities through weekly newsletters that often contain ideas for activities they can do at home.

Helping children feel a part of their school and community is another role of teachers. At the beginning of the school year, I help my students feel comfortable in their new school surroundings by using "The Gingerbread Man" story. After returning to the cafeteria oven to get the gingerbread men we have baked, we discover that they have all escaped! By following clues left by the little men, we meet workers in our school who assist us in finding the cookies.

Feeling a part of the "real-world" community is equally important. By taking field trips related to our units of study, inviting guests into our classroom to share their experiences, and finding ways we can serve others in the community, we are learning to be responsible members of society. From riding on a real horse to discovering how an automated teller machine gives money out of the bank, children experience community life firsthand.

Whenever I am introduced as a "kindergarten teacher," I usually receive the response of a prolonged "Ohhhh." Although I am never sure if the "Ohhhh" is intended in sympathy, condescension, or amazement, I am always tempted to explain like this:

"Yes, I teach kindergarten.

"Where else can learning be as much fun as play because their learning occurs through play?

"Where else can I get fifty hugs a day and not have to ask for them?

"Where else can former kindergartners stop by in the mornings to get their own hugs on their way to first, second, or even fifth grade?

"Where else can I receive a crayoned portrait of myself with the words inscribed 'I love you'?

"Where else can I forget my own problems because my students need me to help solve theirs?

"Where else can I laugh, dance the 'Hoky-Pokey,' crow like a rooster, or oink like a pig, and not be thought foolish?

"Yes, I teach kindergarten, and I'm proud to be the first partner with parents as children embark on lifelong learning."

Violet Geib, First Grade Teacher, 1993 Pennsylvania Teacher of the Year, Stiegel Elementary School, Manheim, Pennsylvania

My philosophy is a result of my own nontraditional educational journey and the outstanding teachers I have met along the way. The feelings I bring to teaching are an expression of this philosophy.

Compassion—Remember how heavy the school door is for a first grader, how it feels if everyone laughs, how a happy note rises to the top of your backpack, how special a hug makes you feel, what adventures wait inside the covers of a book.

Creativity—Develop a theme that crosses curriculum using language arts, math, social studies, and science. Respond to situations as they occur, and recognize the potential inherent in each experience. A "happy circle" discussion, a picture, a current event, a shared book have each been the genesis for a theme. Create a happy, aesthetically pleasing environment from "at home" materials, children's creations, and books. Collect and save these creations and books to present as authentic assessment to families to validate positive progress along the way.

Commitment—To children and my job. Valuing what I do allows me to work long hours after the school day. I can always answer the question "What were you doing at school so late tonight?"

"I couldn't wait for the morning to get started on tomorrow!"

Enthusiasm—I am fortunate to have a profession that pays me to do what I enjoy most, allows me to learn, and allows me the autonomy to develop an ever-changing learning environment. As a child I loved every day of school (in spite of a mile walk each way), I loved to read (even though I personally owned only two books), I loved a stimulating discussion (even if I lost the argument), and I loved discovering and experimenting with new ideas (even if the arena was only a one-room school). Teaching, for me, is the sharing of this love.

My beliefs spill into my classroom by incorporating these qualities daily. The rewards are unlimited: A hug from John as he goes out the door with these words, "You're the best teacher I ever had." (Remember, he only had one other teacher before me!) Ken jumping up from the reading table shouting, "I can read! I can read!" when the sound of a vowel supplied the missing clue he needed. Dereck, of whom a neighbor said, "All that boy does is run wild," choosing to write story after story in the classroom. Allowing Bingo, our stuffed dog, to go home with "Katie" to soften the hurts of an abusive mother. Filling the empty valentine bag for "Larry" so he could hand them out the next day to his friends. Preparing an exciting room for all those who need beauty and motivation to offset the drabness and apathy of their home environment. Having so many mothers involved in my room who want to help that I can no longer afford to buy each of them a gift at the end of the year. Hearing the positive comments of those same parents at our summer picnic in my backyard. But, the best reward is seeing the children succeed!

My style reflects my belief that compassion, creativity, commitment, and enthusiasm are all essential to teaching. My room reflects my strong feelings about the importance of literature; an integrated curriculum; choice for interest and cooperative learning; freedom to explore, discover, experiment; and opportunities to write. Woven throughout you will find that reading is the thread that ties it all together.

Diane Cutshall, Second Grade Teacher, 1993 Indiana Teacher of the Year, Indian Meadows Elementary School, Fort Wayne, Indiana

I became a teacher to be a part of children's academic, social, and emotional growth. I believe I make a positive difference in the lives of my students by inviting success. I establish a trusting relationship with them by building a sense of family beginning the first day of school. I want my students to feel accepted and supported, so I provide a variety of activities that help us get to know one another well. Each day we begin with "What's Happening." Children sharing their experiences with one another enables them to work well together in the classroom. Once a week I have lunch with a group of five students. This is not a reward but an opportunity for me to know them in a different setting.

I reach out to students who need something beyond the school day. I invite them to spend time with my family on the weekends and during the summer. This year one of my students spent a Saturday afternoon having lunch at my home, then going to a movie with my family. Students have joined my family on other outings such as spending afternoons at the pool, taking bike rides, attending festivals, and even gathering vegetables from my garden! I regularly attend my students' ball games or recitals. This helps me build rapport and reinforces my commitment to them as valuable individuals.

Each day I provide my students with meaningful activities designed to help them become self-motivated and confident learners. It is my goal that each of them continue to achieve long after they leave my classroom. By creating an environment conducive to taking risks, my students feel safe enough to experiment and question. They are actively involved in their learning so it is meaningful for them.

As a whole-language teacher, I plan themes that integrate the curriculum. In addition to the social studies and science topics, my students help choose the other themes we study. Last year they chose to learn more about space, ecology, sports, families, fairy tales, animals, and nature. Although the children chose the topics and made decisions about what projects they wanted to share with the class, my expectations for their learning were developmentally appropriate and intellectually challenging.

My students read, write, and discuss daily to improve reading and writing skills. They solve real-world problems and use a wide variety of manipulatives to understand concepts.

My students learn they are capable of making predictions and testing theories, not just repeating information. I facilitate this journey by motivating, communicating, and nurturing. It is my job to provide the tools and background knowledge to foster growth.

Developing a partnership with parents ensures greater success with children. I value the knowledge parents have about their children, so I ask them to write a letter describing the learning qualities they see in their second graders. This letter may include any information that would help me know my students better. Weekly newsletters are sent home describing math concepts taught, problem-solving lessons, reading and writing workshop activities, and other pertinent information. Also, parent volunteers are utilized weekly to help facilitate learning in my classroom.

I work with my students to develop responsibility and independence. I am a good listener and, above all, an advocate for *all* children. The most rewarding aspect of teaching is the mutual affection my students and I share. No other job can offer the satisfaction I feel when a student meets with success.

Nancy B. Royal, Kindergarten Teacher, 1993 Georgia Teacher of the Year, Elm Street Elementary School, Newman, Georgia

To teach is to have a direct influence on the lives of those you instruct. As a teacher of young children, I believe in the development of the total child. It is my responsibility to provide readiness experiences that will help each child strive for his or her full potential in all areas of growth and development—physical, social, emotional, and intellectual. I endorse a hands-on approach to learning in which children experience firsthand the concepts to be explored. Believing that a child learns by doing, I feel that it is important for me to provide as many language-rich, success-oriented experiences as possible to expand the child's knowledge of the world.

In my opinion, an outstanding teacher centers his or her philosophy around a positive approach to instruction. Children need to develop a positive self-concept as they experience success in the classroom, and the teacher has the responsibility for providing activities that will promote a feeling of personal worth for students. In the classroom of such a teacher, children know that they are loved and experience warmth, trust, acceptance, and understanding. Mistakes are accepted and discussed. A positive, enthusiastic atmosphere motivates and encourages students to try new activities and reach new goals.

I understand also that an outstanding teacher is one who can successfully bridge the gap between home and school. He or she accomplishes this task by communicating frequently and openly with parents. The teacher realizes that parents should be given the opportunity to share in their children's accomplishments and takes time to inform them when there is a need for help, support, or reinforcement. The outstanding teacher seeks innovative ways to blend what is going on in the classroom with the children's everyday experiences at home.

The outstanding teacher works also to bridge the gap between cultures. He or she strives to understand the cultural background of the students and create an atmosphere in the classroom in which differences are accepted. Meeting the diverse needs of these individuals with varying backgrounds and abilities becomes a vital mission for the teacher. He or she must be willing to patiently reteach and reinforce for the low achiever, while constantly challenging those who are developmentally ready for more difficult skills. An outstanding teacher must always focus on the individual—that person's background, strengths, needs, personality, and feelings—to remain effective in the classroom.

As a teacher of young children, my most rewarding moments are those in which the children themselves feel the greatest sense of pride and accomplishment. Whether it is the first time a child comes into the room without tears after leaving Mom, or writes his name for the first time, or types her first story in the computer lab, my rewards come often in the kindergarten classroom. Whether it is a unit on "Rabbits" or "Rockets," I still get very excited when I have planned, gathered materials, and implemented a new whole-language unit for the first time. When I see the children excited about learning, I am rewarded. When I see parents interested, excited, and involved in my classroom activities, I am again fulfilled as we become partners in the children's education. I love teaching, and I find daily rewards in the classroom that keep me motivated and excited year after year.

I try to demonstrate my love for preschoolers by the experiences I provide in my classroom. Through the use of thematic units centered around quality literature, my boys and girls experience many varied hands-on activities that integrate skills throughout our curriculum. In a unit as the one on "Hats," skills from language, math, science, writing, art, and social studies are all integrated and taught throughout the day. To foster language development, I try to provide a language-rich environment in which students are totally immersed in the language.

I seek new ways to blend the work of my students at both home and school. I strive to involve parents by sending home weekly newsletters to inform them of our activities. In an effort to send a little bit of school home, I have developed video packets of learning materials that go with each of my units. The children can take home these packets for parents to use as they work with their children. The packets have books, games, and activities, as well as videos of my reading the books and offering ideas and suggestions to parents of ways to use the games and materials. Positive parental responses to the use of these video packages indicate that parents welcome the opportunity to share some of our class experiences at home. By completing the activities at home with their children, parents seem to gain confidence in working with their children, and they appear to be better able to recognize other teaching opportunities at home.

The outstanding teacher must realize the need to form partnerships among schools, parents, businesses, and communities. Schools can no longer be effective if viewed in isolation. Rather, they must join with the entire community in assuming responsibility for educating today's children. Educators must be willing to reach beyond the walls of the classroom to promote collaborative efforts aimed at reaching families and students. It is critical that we provide fresh, creative, and conducive parent education programs and that we employ innovative and effective early intervention strategies. We, as educators, must work to foster acceptance of diversity, whether it be in developing understanding of different cultures, family structures, or economic backgrounds. It is our responsibility to equip students with life-long learning by teaching skills and concepts that will enable children to function productively in the future.

To the best of my ability I will:

Ensure that programs for young children are based on current knowledge of child development and early childhood education.

Respect and support families in their task of nurturing children.

Respect colleagues in early childhood education and support them in maintaining the NAEYC Code of Ethical Conduct.

Serve as an advocate for children, their families and their teachers in community and society.

Maintain high standards of professional conduct.

Recognize how personal values, opinions, and biases can affect professional judgment.

Be open to new ideas and be willing to learn from the suggestions of others.

Continue to learn, grow, and contribute as a professional.

Honor the ideals and principles of the NAEYC Code of Ethical Conduct.[4]

THE EARLY CHILDHOOD PROFESSIONAL AND THE WORLD OF TOMORROW

In preparing to undertake the professional challenges of the next century, many people try to forecast what life will be like. As a result of this forecasting, essential features of the future are evident that will help influence and determine the nature of the professional's necessary core knowledge, skills, and behaviors:

- Learning will be considered a lifelong process. All early childhood professionals will be expected to engage in a process of continuous learning, growth, and development across their life span.

- More services to children will be delivered in and through the family system. This means that early childhood professionals will need to know adult growth and development and how to meet adult needs.

- The United States will become an even more diverse country. Diversity training must be an essential part of the training of early childhood professionals, enabling them to work with children, parents, and families from all cultural and socioeconomic backgrounds.

- Even more money will be spent on educating young children and their families. Early childhood education will continue to be a source of great interest and the focus of the public's attention. This means that early childhood professionals will have to assume their rightful role in helping allocate resources and assure that they are wisely used.

- Technology will play an even greater role in learning *at all levels*. As indicated in chapter 15, part of professional development involves developing technological literacy in oneself and a willingness to foster technological literacy in children.

As an early childhood educator, you must be prepared to take your place in a world in which learning is valued and respected. You should also be prepared to

A PROFESSIONAL AT WORK

I have always used my work to address pressing societal questions faced in my own life or that I see in the lives of those around me. So, it is not surprising that I turned to the study of work and family life in the early 1980s. I had just completed a study of parental growth and development that resulted in the book *The Six Stages of Parenthood* and a study of exemplary child care in the United States that led to the book *The New Extended Family: Day Care That Works.*

Both of those research projects involved extensive interviewing of parents. In both, parents seemed to be telling a similar story. They were struggling to manage everything they had to do, trying to do their best at work and at home, feeling unsure of how they were supposed to feel or act because they had so few role models. When times were rough—such as "rush hour" in the morning, getting everyone ready to leave, or "arsenic hour" in the evening, trying to spend time with the children and get dinner on the table when energy was at its lowest ebb— parents blamed themselves. They had the feeling that other people were managing, were enjoying quality time with their children, were having meaningful discussions at the dinner table rather than refereeing family fights. In blaming themselves, I felt that parents did not realize that families had changed faster than the institutions of society, such as the workplace and the school, and that the problems were both inevitable and prevalent.

From these observations of parents, my first study on work and family life was shaped. The purpose of this study was to ascertain those aspects of work and family life that were associated with more conflict or more success in balancing job and family responsibilities. We found that it was more than the proverbial lack of time that caused problems. Of particular importance were demanding jobs and nonsupportive supervisors.

We went on to identify the aspects of supervisors' behavior that made the biggest difference. Of note was a study we did in a series of small factories that included interviews with children and the workers' husbands and wives. In our interviews with children, we asked them what their parents' union could do that would improve the quality of their family life. First, however, we had asked their parents to guess what their children might say. The parents, by and large, thought that their children would seek more time with their parents. According to the children, "more time would be nice," but far more important was their parents' coming home "less wired." When we asked the children what made their parents wired, they knew. They spoke to us about a boss who was asking a mother to do too much work, a new coworker that a father was supposed to train but the coworker did not speak English, or fights and tension on the assembly line. The children also had techniques for handling their parents when they came home wired, from jumping in the bathtub to escape conflict to picking a fight "because there is going to be a fight eventually and I might as well get it over with."

When the parents heard these messages from their children, they determined to take action. Through our research project, the workers bargained for the right to bring work-family problems to management several times a year. At the next such meeting, agreement was reached to bring in someone to teach conflict resolution skills on the assembly line.

Contributed by Ellen Galinsky, copresident, Families and Work Institute, 330 Seventh Ave., New York, New York.

In 1988, Dana Friedman and I decided that the time was right for an organization devoted to work and family. After a year's work, the Families and Work Institute (thus named because families come first) opened its doors in July 1989. The purpose of the institute is to serve as a center for policy research and a national clearinghouse for information on issues related to the changing work force and the changing family. We have a so-called litmus test for determining which projects we take on. We look for issues that are beginning to crest, around which there is a growing debate but little information. Instead, the debate is being fueled by assumption and opinion. We then design nonpartisan studies to inform the debate.

An example of this approach was our study of parental leave. Completed in May 1991, just as federal legislation was heading toward passage in the Senate, the study showed that 91 percent of businesses, small and large, had no problems in complying with their state mandates. This study informed the federal debate as well as that in numerous state legislatures, and it was mentioned frequently when the Family and Medical Leave Act was passed in 1993 and signed into law by President Clinton.

Other studies have been designed to inform federal policy making. For example, we are conducting several studies that examine the impact of improvements in state child care regulations on parents, the child care marketplace, and quality itself. In Florida, new regulations require improved ratios, increased hours of training, and a child development associate degree or its equivalent for every twenty children in a center. We are studying the impact of these regulatory changes.

Not all our studies are designed to inform public policy; some have the express intent of affecting practice. For example, the Florida study should be able to help us understand how various ways of reaching a child development associate degree affect the provisions of child care quality. Does an apprentice system matter, for instance? Are some methods of professional preparation better than others? Likewise, our *Study of Children in Family Child Care and Relative Care* has a second component in which we investigate how different family child care training programs affect the provision of quality care. Again, we should be able to examine the elements of training to see which are most effective.

Another study we conducted on parent-teacher relationships has also been useful in thinking about teacher preparation. We found that the teachers' attitudes were significantly predictive of better or worse relationships with parents. For example, teachers who thought that mothers should not work reported less supportive relationships. The mothers must have sensed something too because when teachers disapproved of their working, they also reported less supportive relationships. Most important from this study was the finding that ethnic and social class differences between teachers and parents were predictive of worse relationships. This observation leads to a call for teachers to have diversity training just as employees in corporations are doing.

Our studies are also aimed at affecting business practice. Our recently released *National Study of the Changing Work Force,* sponsored by thirteen corporations and two foundations, found that workers today were more likely to be committed and loyal to their employers and more willing to go the extra mile to help companies succeed when their environment was positive. This and other findings from the study are being used by companies for long-range strategic planning.

An important aspect of the work of the Families and Work Institute is disseminating information. We receive and respond to more than a thousand callers a month requesting information. We hold conferences for the business community and the early childhood field. We have published nine books and have several more in the final stages of completion. Finally, members of

our staff are frequent presenters at conferences throughout the United States and abroad.

It has been an exciting time since the founding of the Families and Work Institute. Creating something new is never easy, but the pressure to do the highest-quality work within the uncertainties of obtaining funding is well worth the challenge. The joy is in the constant opportunity to frame important questions, design new ways of answering them, learn from our findings, and share those learnings with others. The joy is in doing work that matters.

devote your career to continually learning new skills and gaining new knowledge.

- Business and industry will play an even larger role in the education and support of services, including education for children and families. Early childhood professionals must be prepared to work cooperatively and collaboratively as professionals with this sector of society. Indeed, these linkages provide a challenging opportunity to expand and enrich early childhood programs.

- The time we are living in is much different than what society was like a decade ago. As a result, the role of the early childhood professional will continue to change and evolve. You have read in many places throughout this book how and the extent to which these changes are taking place. Not only must professionals reconceptualize their own roles, they must also rethink what is best for children and their families.

  This reconceptualization of roles and responsibilities is critical for the professional in the twenty-first century. For example, early childhood professionals seldom think of themselves as part of one of the most effective crime prevention programs there is, but it is so. For example, the High/Scope Perry Preschool Study found that children born in poverty who participated in a high-quality, active-learning preschool program at ages three and four have fewer criminal arrests than adults who received no preschool program as children.[5]

- We will see a stronger movement toward professionalizing teaching, which is already evident from our previous discussion of professionalism. The professionalization of teaching is part of the national effort to improve education. The public recognizes, albeit belatedly, that real and lasting changes in education will occur when teachers are trained as professionals and treated as professionals. The emphasis on professionalism will require teachers to assume more responsibility for their own behavior and their professional development.

- We will see an intensification of training as professionalism demands higher levels of competence. A bachelor's degree may become a five-year program. Early childhood teachers and child care workers will probably have to take additional training through the CDA, in-service training, or college-related courses. Early childhood professionals will be challenged and often required to demonstrate professionalism through courses, workshops, and certificate programs.

- Changes in professional education will take place. There is growing pressure from state departments of education, professional groups, and public policy makers to require education colleges to eliminate or greatly reduce the number of education courses at the undergraduate level. In fact, legislation in Texas limits to fifteen the number of credit hours an education major can take at the undergraduate level. These kinds of regulations and restrictions are usually made by people who see little value in education courses; they assume that if you know your content area, you can teach it. How much calculus a first grade teacher needs to know, for instance, is not usually addressed. Nonetheless, efforts to limit education courses will likely continue.

- Early childhood programs will begin to serve different types of children in different ways. This is particularly true as a continuing impact of PL 94-142 and PL 99-457. There are more young children with disabilities, birth to age five, in programs designed to meet their and their families' needs. This situation means new programs will be developed, and teachers will be trained or retrained to provide appropriate services.

    The fields of early childhood education and early childhood special education are fast becoming one. As full inclusion reaches more programs, professionals have to be trained in both areas to appropriately meet the needs of all children and their families.

- Professional roles will expand. A higher degree of professionalism will bring greater responsibility and decision making. The role of early childhood professionals will continue to be reconceptualized. Teachers will be trained to work

Early childhood professionals have an obligation to help children learn correct behaviors and how to guide their actions. Hoping someone else or some other agency will do it is not satisfactory. Not only must professionals reconceptualize their own roles, they must also rethink what is best for children and their families.

with parents, design curriculum materials, plan programs for paraprofessionals, and work cooperatively with community agencies, including business and industry.

Many schools currently operate a system of differentiated staffing and employ teachers and aides with differing role functions, levels of responsibility, training, and salary. Also, as the currently popular school-based management movement grows, more teachers will be involved in decisions about how schools operate and how and what children will learn.

Differentiated staffing will be accompanied by differentiated teaching. There will be closer attention to different learning styles. Greater attention to learning styles will also involve greater use of concrete learning materials, self-selected activities, and students as tutors.

- Professionals and community agencies will develop more collaborative, cooperative relationships. Teaching is an integral part of the broader range of human services and helping professions. The sharp lines that have traditionally separated social work, the health professions, and education are gradually blurring. Unfortunately, members of these professions are often reluctant to admit that other professionals can provide meaningful services that complement their own. There is also a trend toward resolving social problems through interdisciplinary programs, to which each profession contributes its particular expertise (see chap. 11).

Involvement in the early childhood profession can be a joyful experience for those who dedicate themselves to it. The profession demands, and young children deserve, the best of teachers and caregivers. Becoming a good professional requires a lot of hard work and dedication. All who call themselves "professional" must accept the challenges and responsibilities that are part of the title.

READINGS FOR FURTHER ENRICHMENT

Goffin, S. G., and J. Lombardi. *Speaking Out: Early Childhood Advocacy* (Washington, D.C.: National Association for the Education of Young Children, 1988)

A practical guidebook about how public policy is made and what you can do to influence decisions in favor of children's best interests.

Hatkoff, Amy, and Karen Kelly Klopp. *How to Save the Children* (New York: Simon & Schuster, 1992)

Hatkoff was director of volunteerism at the Prince George Hotel in New York City. The

Prince George was the largest welfare hotel in the world, housing more than two thousand children. Out of her experiences came the two hundred specific suggestions in the book on things people can do to help children. This is an excellent clearinghouse of ideas, addresses, and phone numbers for individuals who want to get involved.

Kidder, Tracy. *Among Schoolchildren* (Boston: Houghton Mifflin, 1989)

This best-selling and highly acclaimed book traces a year in the life of Chris Zajac, an elementary teacher in Holyoke, Massachusetts. The reader shares Zajac's successes and failures as she teaches her ethnically mixed fifth grade class.

Morgan, G., S. Azer, J. Costley, A. Genser, I. Goodman, J. Lombardi, and B. McGinsey. *Making a Career of It: The State of the States Report on Career Development in Early Care and Education* (Washington, D.C.: National Association for the Education of Young Children, 1993)

Contains key findings, promising practices, and policy recommendations for planning and improving regulation, delivery, and financing of early childhood training.

ACTIVITIES FOR FURTHER ENRICHMENT

1. Recall the teachers who taught you. List which characteristics you would imitate and which you would try to avoid as a teacher.

2. You are in charge of the professional development of a child care center for the coming year. Identify ten topics for in-service training that you think would be appropriate for all professionals in the center.

3. Some people think that caring for and teaching young children requires little or no professional training. Write a two-page report refuting this belief.

4. Reflecting on your years in the primary grades, what experiences do you consider most meaningful? Why? Would these experiences be valid learning experiences for children today? How and why?

5. With two or three of your classmates, brainstorm and compile a list of competencies for early childhood teachers that are (a) generic, that is, applicable to all teaching, and (b) specific for early childhood education. Have professors of education and in-service teachers respond to your list.

6. Talk with other professionals about careers that relate to children and parents. How did they come to their jobs? Is there evidence that they planned for these careers? Do you think you would enjoy an alternative career in education? Why?

7. Write and share your philosophy of education with your classmates. Have them critique it for comprehensiveness, clarity, and meaning. How do you feel about the changes they suggested?

8. List the reasons you have decided to become an early childhood professional. Share and compare the list with your classmates. What conclusions can you draw from the lists?

9. Read the accounts of Teachers of the Year. Write a report about what impressed you most about their accounts, what outstanding qualities these teachers demonstrate, and why they were able to become Teachers of the Year.

10. List ten characteristics and qualities you think are essential for an early childhood professional. Compare your list with one of your classmates. How are they similar and different?

NOTES

1. Barbara Willer and Sue Bredekamp, "A 'New' Paradigm of Early Childhood Professional Development," *Young Children,* 47(3) 1993, p. 63.

2. Ibid., p. 64. Copyright © 1993 by the National Association for the Education of Young Children. Reprinted by permission.

3. Friedrich Froebel, *Mother's Songs, Games, and Stories* (New York: Arno, 1976), p. xxxiii.

4. Stephanie Feeney and Kenneth Kipnis, "A New Code of Ethics for Early Childhood Educators!" *Young Children,* 45 (1989), p. 29.

5. Lawrence J. Schweinhart, H. V. Barnes, and David P. Weikart, *Significant Benefits: The High/Scope Perry Preschool Study through Age 27* (Ypsilanti, MI: High/Scope, 1993), p. xv.

CDA Competency Goals and Functional Areas

COMPETENCY GOALS	FUNCTIONAL AREAS
I. To establish and maintain a safe, healthy learning environment	1. Safe: Candidate provides a safe environment to prevent and reduce injuries.
	2. Healthy: Candidate promotes good health and nutrition and provides an environment that contributes to the prevention of illness.
	3. Learning Environment: Candidate uses space, relationships, materials, and routines as resources for constructing an interesting, secure, and enjoyable environment that encourages play, exploration and learning.
II. To advance physical and intellectual competence	4. Physical: Candidate provides a variety of equipment, activities, and opportunities to promote the physical development of children.
	5. Cognitive: Candidate provides activities and opportunities that encourage curiosity, exploration, and problem solving appropriate to the developmental levels and learning styles of children.

Source: The Council for Early Childhood Professional Recognition, *Essentials for Child Development Associates Working with Young Children* (Washington, D.C.: Author, 1991), pp. 103–463 ff. Used by permission.

COMPETENCY GOALS	FUNCTIONAL AREAS

	6. Communication: Candidate actively communicates with children and provides opportunities for support for children to acquire, and use, verbal and nonverbal means of communicating thoughts and feelings.
	7. Creative: Candidate provides opportunities that stimulate children to play with sound, rhythm, language, materials, space, and ideas in individual ways and to express their creative abilities.
III. To support social and emotional development and provide positive guidance.	8. Self: Candidate provides physical and emotional development and emotional security for each child and helps each child to know, accept, and take pride in himself or herself and to develop a sense of independence.
	9. Social: Candidate helps each child feel accepted in the group, helps children learn to communicate and get along with others, and encourages feelings of empathy and mutual respect among children and adults.
	10. Guidance: Candidate provides a supportive environment in which children can begin to learn and practice appropriate and acceptable behaviors as individuals and as a group.
IV. To establish positive and productive relationships with families	11. Families: Candidate maintains an open, friendly, and cooperative relationship with each child's family, encourages their involvement in the program, and supports the child's relationship with his or her family.
V. To ensure a well-run, purposeful program responsive to participant needs	12. Program Management: Candidate is a manager who uses all available resources to ensure an effective operation. The Candidate is a competent organizer, planner, record keeper, communicator, and a cooperative co-worker.
VI. To maintain a commitment to professionalism	13. Professionalism: Candidate makes decisions based on knowledge of early childhood theories and practices, promotes quality in child care services, and takes advantage of opportunities to improve competence, both for personal and professional growth and for the benefit of children and families.

B

Highlights of the United Nations Convention on the Rights of the Child

■ Every child has the inherent right to life, and States shall ensure, to the maximum, child survival and development.

■ Every child has the right to a name and nationality from birth.

■ When courts, welfare institutions or administrative authorities deal with children, the child's best interests shall be a primary consideration. The child's opinions shall be given careful consideration.

■ States shall ensure that each child enjoys full rights without discrimination or distinctions of any kind.

■ Children should not be separated from their parents, unless by competent authorities for their well-being.

■ States should facilitate reunification of families by permitting travel into, or out of, their territories.

■ Parents have the primary responsibility for a child's upbringing, but States shall provide them with appropriate assistance and develop child-care institutions.

■ States shall protect children from physical or mental harm and neglect, including sexual abuse or exploitation.

■ States shall provide parentless children with suitable alternative care. The adoption process shall be carefully regulated and international agreements should be sought to provide safeguards and assure legal validity if and when adoptive parents intend to move the child from his or her country of birth.

■ Disabled children shall have the right to special treatment, education and care.

■ The child is entitled to the highest attainable standard of health. States shall ensure that health care is provided to all children, placing emphasis on preventive measures, health education and reduction of infant mortality.

■ Primary education shall be free and compulsory; discipline in schools should respect the child's dignity. Education

Source: United Nations, *Convention on the Rights of the Child* (New York: United Nations Department of Public Information, 1993), pp. 4–8. Reprint 24717—May 1993—20M; Publication Source DPI/1101, United Nations. Used by permission.

should prepare the child for life in a spirit of understanding, peace and tolerance.

- Children shall have time to rest and play and equal opportunities for cultural and artistic activities.

- States shall protect the child from economic exploitation and work that may interfere with education or be harmful to health and well-being.

- States shall protect children from the illegal use of drugs and involvement in drug production or trafficking.

- All efforts shall be made to eliminate the abduction and trafficking of children.

- Capital punishment or life imprisonment shall not be imposed for crimes committed before the age of 18.

- Children in detention should be separated from adults; they must not be tortured or suffer cruel and degrading treatment.

- No child under 15 should take any part in hostilities; children exposed to armed conflict shall receive special protection.

- Children of minority and indigenous populations shall freely enjoy their own culture, religion and language.

- Children who have suffered maltreatment, neglect or detention should receive appropriate treatment or training for recovery and rehabilitation.

- Children involved in infringements of the penal law shall be treated in a way that promotes their sense of dignity and worth and that aims at reintegrating them into society.

- States should make the rights in the Convention widely known to both adults and children.

Individualized Family Service Plan

NAME: Kevin Taylor
DATE OF BIRTH: 5/24/93
AGE: 19 mos., 19 days
DATE OF ASSESSMENT &
   IFSP MEETING: 1/13/95
DATE OF REPORT: 1/25/95
SERVICE COORDINATOR: Lara Clark

LEGAL GUARDIAN: Bob & Tammy Taylor
ADDRESS: 242 American Drive
   Williamsburg, VA 23188
PHONE: 555-0303

PERTINENT HISTORY

This is Kevin's third assessment at Child Development Resources (CDR). He has been in the Infant-Parent Program since November 1992 because of his diagnosis of Down syndrome, developmental delays, and medical complications. Since his last assessment, Kevin has received weekly home visits from Lara Clark and several motor consultations from a physical therapist. Kevin has not been able to attend Developmental Play Group owing to his ongoing illnesses.

    Kevin continues to have upper-respiratory infections and ear infections. He has been receiving his medical care at Williamsburg Community Hospital. Kevin is scheduled to have an ear, nose, and throat (ENT) consultation at the Children's Hospital of the King's Daughters in February. Since Kevin's surgery in June 1994, his health has greatly improved. He was weaned off oxygen in September and is no longer required to use the apnea monitor (which checks a child's breathing—it sounds an alarm if the child stops breathing). Kevin continues to get breathing treatments as needed for congestion. He has not been hospitalized since his surgery in June.

Source: Child Development Resources, Lightfoot, Virginia. Used by permission. The author would like to thank CDR for graciously contributing this material.

Kevin's hearing and vision have not been formally tested since his stay in the neonatal infant care unit (NICU) after his birth. His parents will continue to monitor his condition, but at this time there are no concerns. His hearing may be evaluated when he goes for the ENT in February.

CHILD ASSESSMENT

ASSESSMENT TEAM MEMBERS

Tammy Taylor	Parent
Lynda Olive	Speech pathologist
Lisa Davis	Occupational therapist
Lara Clark	Infant development specialist

ASSESSMENT INSTRUMENTS USED

Early Learning Accomplishment Profile (E-LAP)—selected sections

Receptive-Expressive Emergent Language Scale (REEL)

The Infant Scale of Communicative Intent

Uzgiris-Hunt Scales of Infant Development (Dunst)—selected sections

Fewell Play Assessment Scale

Social-Emotional Developmental Profile (SEED)

Hawaii Early Learning Profile (HELP)—selected sections

Peabody Developmental Motor Scales

Family observations and report

Clinical observations

STRENGTHS, CONCERNS, AND DEVELOPMENTAL LEVELS

Kevin played for about an hour during the assessment with a variety of toys and people. Along with his mother, Kevin showed the team many of the social games he enjoys playing. He likes to play a game in which his mother counts, "1-2-3," and then he vocalizes a prolonged "Aah." Kevin raises both hands in the air when his mother asks, "How big is Kevin?" After he raises his hands, she says, "So big." He likes to make raspberries and prolonged "s" and "f" sounds. He also babbles (repeats consonant-vowel combinations), most frequently with the "d" sound. He also frequently uses single consonant-vowel combinations such as "da." He was observed to use the "n," "m," and "t" sounds as well in such combinations. Signs for some major concept words have been introduced to Kevin, but he is not yet copying them.

Kevin very quickly and consistently found the source of many sounds occurring in the assessment room. He shows, by turning to look or getting excited, that he knows the names of his family members. When his name is called, he stops what he is doing and turns to look at the person speaking. He shows by his actions that he knows what "ball" and "music" mean, which are favorite things. He tries to put his arms up in response to someone saying, "Do you want up?" He sometimes tries to move one of his arms in response to "bye-bye." He also seems to know what "down" means. He understands simple requests such as "clap-clap" or "dance." He understands what

"Come here" means when a hand gesture accompanies it. When he is holding something and an adult requests, "Give it to me" with an accompanying hand gesture, he will hold out the object to them but not yet release it. Kevin likes to look at books and will do so for several minutes. He does not yet point to the pictures when they are named.

Kevin has learned to sit by himself for a few minutes. When a toy falls behind him, he has difficulty reaching around to pick it up and topples over backward. When he wants to get down from a sitting position, Kevin is able to twist at his waist and lower himself down with his hands, although his movements are fast, and sometimes he bumps his head on toys or objects that get in his way. He has not yet learned to get into a sitting position from lying on his back or stomach by himself. When on his stomach on the floor, Kevin pushes up on his hands with his arms straightened. He is able to reach for toys in front of him while holding himself up in this position with his other arm. Frequently he pushes himself up onto his hands and knees and rocks back and forth. He has recently learned to move himself forward on the floor by lunging forward on his stomach in an inchworm type of a crawl. When held in a standing position with support at his hips and chest, Kevin takes most of his weight on his feet. Occasionally, he will stand while leaning his upper body on furniture and with support given to his hips. His mother reports that he enjoys kneeling on the sofa and rocking himself at home. Standing and kneeling activities are good to help Kevin strengthen the muscles of his hips and legs.

Kevin uses his hands and eyes together to play with toys in a variety of ways. He has learned to bring his hands together in front of him to bang toys together he is holding or to clap his hands. When given a plastic stick, he used it to bang on a drum purposefully. Kevin took blocks out of a container. He banged the blocks together when his mother told him to "clap clap" the blocks, then he flung a block. He frequently threw other toys he was holding as well. This is a typical stage children go through, and it shows us that Kevin is learning to let go of toys when he wants to. At home, Kevin is just beginning to learn to put things back into containers. His mother has Kevin put his toys into a very large basket. Kevin occasionally points his index finger as he is playing to point in the air or sometimes to poke into the hole of a toy. He uses his index finger and thumb together to work some toys, like the lever of a pop-up box. Often, if he does not get the toy to work with his finger, he will use his whole hand to bang the toy.

Kevin is showing signs that he is ready to give up his bottle, but he will not yet take much fluid from a cup. He usually will hold his mouth open and let the liquid run out or spit it out, especially if it is milk. His mother has tried thickening the liquids without much success. Kevin will eat pureed table foods or baby foods. He will also take semisolids of a thick, even texture. He rejects many foods having an uneven texture to them. Observation of Kevin eating indicated that his gag reflex is elicited very far forward on his tongue. Kevin is also beginning to use the thumb side of his hand to pick up tiny objects like Cheerios from his tray, but he has not yet figured out how to put them in his mouth to eat them.

Kevin shows skills at the seven- to eight-month level in the areas of gross-motor and receptive-language development. His expressive-language skills are scattered from six to eight months. He shows skills at the nine- to eleven-month level in the area of fine-motor development. Kevin's cognitive skills range from eleven to fifteen months and his social skills from twelve to fifteen months. In the area of self-help development, Kevin is demonstrating skills at the nine-month level. He is eligible for CDR's Infant-Parent Program and Part H services of

IDEA (Individuals with Disabilities Education Act) because of his diagnosis of Down syndrome and developmental delays. (Part H of IDEA applies to infants and toddlers and requires an IFSP.)

FAMILY CONCERNS, RESOURCES, AND PRIORITIES

Kevin's parents are most concerned about his developmental progress. They would like to see Kevin be able to sit more steadily, kneel at furniture to play, drink more from a cup, and play with a variety of toys. They are anxious to see the ENT with hopes of decreasing Kevin's ear infections.

Since Kevin will turn two this spring, he will be old enough to attend the public school program in the fall. Kevin's family has looked at other available community programs and decided to start the eligibility process this spring for the Hometown public school program. Lara Clark and other CDR staff will assist Kevin's family through the transition process as requested by the Taylors.

OUTCOMES RELATED TO CHILD DEVELOPMENT

OUTCOME: Kevin will begin to feed himself.

OBJECTIVES/CRITERIA	STRATEGIES	PERSONS RESPONSIBLE	REVIEW/ MODIFY (DATE)	STATUS REPORTED BY (DATE)
1. Kevin will take take more liquids from a cup and less from the bottle.	1a. Activities from *Pre-Feeding Skills*: pp. 240–242, 301–302; 1b. *HELP* curriculum: pp. 472, 473, 481, 490.	Family Members, Primary Service Provider, Develop. Play Group Staff	5/95	
2. Kevin will eat foods with a variety of textures and with mixed textures.	2a. Activities from *Pre-Feeding Skills*: p. 231, Option 5, p. 232, Option 7, p. 225, Option 1, p. 226, Option 4. 2b. *HELP* curriculum: pp. 468, 470–471.	"	5/95	
3. Kevin will use his thumb and index finger together to pick up and feed finger foods to himself.	3a. *Learning Through Play* curriculum: pp. 158D, 179A; 3b. *HELP* curriculum: pp. 336; 343, 476.	"	7/95	

OUTCOMES RELATED TO CHILD DEVELOPMENT

OUTCOME: Kevin will use his eyes and hands together to play with a variety of toys in new ways.

OBJECTIVES/CRITERIA	STRATEGIES	PERSONS RESPONSIBLE	REVIEW/ MODIFY (DATE)	STATUS REPORTED BY (DATE)
1. Kevin will make visible marks on paper with crayons.	1a. *HELP* curriculum: pp. 344, 328, 353;	Family Members, Primary Service Provider, Develop. Play Group Staff	5/95	
2. Kevin will put various toys, objects, and shapes into different-sized openings of containers.	2a. *HELP* curriculum: pp. 65, 346, 354; 2b. *Learning Through Play* curriculum: pp. 208–209,B.		6/95	
3. Kevin will use his index finger to point to pictures, push buttons of toys, and poke into holes of toys while he plays.	3a. *HELP* curriculum: pp. 342, 351, 89.	"	7/95	

OUTCOME: Kevin will strengthen the muscles of his arms, shoulders, legs, hips, stomach, and back in order to help him move in new ways and more independently.

OBJECTIVES/CRITERIA	STRATEGIES	PERSONS RESPONSIBLE	REVIEW/ MODIFY (DATE)	STATUS REPORTED BY (DATE)
1. Kevin will prevent himself from falling backwards and sideways while sitting by using his arms to catch himself.	1a. *HELP* curriculum: p. 250; 1b. Tilting games on a large ball or an adult's lap; 1c. *Positioning for Play: Home Activities for Parents* pp. 95, 99, 105, 107.	Family Members, Primary Service Provider, Develop. Play Group Staff	5/95	
2. Kevin will pivot or twist around in a circle while he is sitting to get toys placed out of reach.	2a. *HELP* curriculum: p. 256.	"	7/95	
3. Kevin will get into a sitting position from lying on hips, stomach, or back without help.	3a. *HELP* curriculum: p. 241.	"	6/95	
4. Kevin will play with his toys while maintaining a kneeling position at furniture.	4a. *Positioning for Play: Home Activities for Parents* pp. 125, 127, 129.	"	5/95	
5. Kevin will stand while holding onto a support.	5a. *HELP* curriculum: p. 242; 5b. *Positioning for Play: Home Activities for Parents* pp. 137, 139, 143–5.	"	7/95	

OUTCOMES RELATED TO CHILD DEVELOPMENT

OUTCOME: Kevin will use more sounds, signs, and words to communicate with others.

OBJECTIVES/CRITERIA	STRATEGIES	PERSONS RESPONSIBLE	REVIEW/ MODIFY (DATE)	STATUS REPORTED BY (DATE)
1. Kevin will use gestures to say "yes," "no," and "good-bye" and to play games.	1a. *HELP ... at Home* curriculum: pp. 46, 67, 151; 1b. *Learning Through Play* curriculum: pp. 170C, 193C.	Family Members, Primary Service Provider, Develop. Play Group Staff	5/95	
2. Kevin will begin to use words and/or signs to name, request, protest, say good-bye, greet, and refuse.	2a. *HELP ... at Home* curriculum: pp. 152, 164, 166, 167; 2b. *Learning Through Play* curriculum: p. 194D; 2c. *The Comprehensive Signed English Dictionary.*	" "	6/95	

OUTCOMES RELATED TO CHILD DEVELOPMENT

OUTCOME: Kevin will understand more of the words, signs, phrases, and sentences that others use to communicate with him.

OBJECTIVES/CRITERIA	STRATEGIES	PERSONS RESPONSIBLE	REVIEW/ MODIFY (DATE)	STATUS REPORTED BY (DATE)
1. Kevin will show by his actions that he knows the names of some common objects.	1a. *Help ... at Home* curriculum: pp. 48, 51; 1b. *Learning Through Play* curriculum: pp. 167C, 192B; 1c. *Comprehensive Signed English Dictionary.*	Family Members, Primary Service Provider, Develop. Play Group Staff	3/95	
2. Kevin will show by his actions that he understands simple questions and one-step requests.	2a. *HELP ... at Home* curriculum: pp. 47, 57, 58; 2b. *Learning Through Play* curriculum: p. 192A.	"	6/95	

OTHER OUTCOMES DESIRED BY THE FAMILY

OUTCOME	COURSE OF ACTION	REVIEW/ MODIFY (DATE)	PARENTS' REPORT OF PROGRESS TOWARD OUTCOME (DATE)
1. Kevin will have a smooth transition from CDR to the public schools (Fall 1995).	1a. Kevin's family and Lara will visit the Play Center to observe classrooms, therapies, and to meet the staff.	Feb. 1995	
	1b. Kevin will be referred to the Play Center by Lara with parent's permission.	Mar. 1995	
	1c. Kevin's parents and Lara will attend eligibility and IEP meetings as needed.	May/June 1995	
	1d. Kevin will attend Developmental Play Group more frequently in the spring to help him prepare for transition, if his parents desire.	Ongoing (starting late Spring 1995)	

EARLY INTERVENTION SERVICES

1. Weekly home visits with Lara Clark, primary service provider
2. Feeding consultation visits with Lynda Olive as needed
3. Weekly Developmental Play Group and Wednesday Parent Group from 9:30 to 11:30 A.M.
4. Transition Play Group on Fridays from 9:30 to 11:30 A.M.
5. Transportation to and from Developmental Play Group if needed
6. Reassessment in four to six months
7. Service coordination, including transition planning

PROJECTED DATES AND DURATION

The services listed here will begin immediately and continue for four to six months.

PAYMENT ARRANGEMENTS FOR SERVICES

Early intervention services will be provided by Child Development Resources with partial payment by the family's health insurance for any reimbursable services. The services will be provided at no cost to the family.

IFSP MEETING PARTICIPANTS

I had the opportunity to participate in the development of this plan. I understand the program plan and I give permission to the Infant-Parent Program to carry out the plan leading toward the agreed-on outcomes. I/We also agree to carry out the plan as it applies to my/our role in the provision of services.

_____

Parent/Legal Guardian Signature(s)

_____

Date

I had the opportunity to participate in the development of this program. I do not agree with this plan and I do not give my permission to the Infant-Parent Program to carry out the plan.

_____

Parent/Legal Guardian Signature(s)

_____

Date

The following individuals participated with the family in the development of the IFSP. Each individual understands and agrees to carry out the plan as it applies to his/her role in the provision of services.

_____

Lynda T. Olive   Lisa Davis
M.Ed., CCC-SLP/A   M.S., OTR/L

_____

Lara M. Clark
M.Ed.

Treatment plans will be followed as outlined in this IFSP.

_____

J. Mellon, M.D.

_____

Date

The National Association for the Education of Young Children Code of Ethical Conduct

PREAMBLE

NAEYC recognizes that many daily decisions required of those who work with young children are of a moral and ethical nature. The NAEYC Code of Ethical Conduct offers guidelines for responsible behavior and sets forth a common basis for resolving the principal ethical dilemmas encountered in early childhood education. The primary focus is on daily practice with children and their families in programs for children from birth to eight years of age: preschools, child care centers, family day care homes, kindergartens, and primary classrooms. Many of the provisions also apply to specialists who do not work directly with children, including program administrators, parent educators, college professors, and child care licensing specialists.

Standards of ethical behavior in early childhood education are based on commitment to core values that are deeply rooted in the history of our field. We have committed ourselves to:

Appreciating childhood as a unique and valuable stage of the human life cycle

Basing our work with children on knowledge of child development

Appreciating and supporting the close ties between the child and family

Recognizing that children are best understood in the context of family, culture, and society

Source: This Code of Ethical Conduct and Statement of Commitment was prepared under the auspices of the Ethics Commission of the National Association for the Education of Young Children. The commission members were Stephanie Feeney (chairperson), Bettye Caldwell, Sally Cartwright, Carrie Cheek, Josué Cruz, Jr., Anne G. Dorsey, Dorothy M. Hill, Lilian G. Katz, Pamm Mattick, Shirley A. Norris, and Sue Spayth Riley. Copyright © 1992 by the National Association for the Education of Young Children. Reprinted by permission.

Respecting the dignity, worth, and uniqueness of each individual (child, family member, and colleague)

Helping children and adults achieve their full potential in the context of relationships that are based on trust, respect, and positive regard

The Code sets forth a conception of our professional responsibilities in four sections, each addressing an arena of professional relationships: (1) children, (2) families, (3) colleagues, and (4) community and society. Each section includes an introduction to the primary responsibilities of the early childhood practitioner in that arena, a set of ideals pointing in the direction of exemplary professional practice, and a set of principles defining practices that are required, prohibited, and permitted.

The ideals reflect the aspirations of practitioners. The principles are intended to guide conduct and assist practitioners in resolving ethical dilemmas encountered in the field. There is not necessarily a corresponding principle for each ideal. Both ideals and principles are intended to direct practitioners to those questions which, when responsibly answered, will provide the basis for conscientious decision making. While the Code provides specific direction for addressing some ethical dilemmas, many others will require the practitioner to combine the guidance of the Code with sound professional judgment.

The ideals and principles in this Code present a shared conception of professional responsibility that affirms our commitment to the core values of our field. The Code publicly acknowledges the responsibilities that we in the field have assumed and in so doing supports ethical behavior in our work. Practitioners who face ethical dilemmas are urged to seek guidance in the applicable parts of this Code and in the spirit that informs the whole.

SECTION I: ETHICAL RESPONSIBILITIES TO CHILDREN

Childhood is a unique and valuable stage in the life cycle. Our paramount responsibility is to provide safe, healthy, nurturing, and responsive settings for children. We are committed to supporting children's development by cherishing individual differences, by helping them learn to live and work cooperatively, and by promoting their self-esteem.

IDEALS

I-1.1   To be familiar with the knowledge base of early childhood education and to keep current through continuing education and in-service training.

I-1.2   To base program practices upon current knowledge in the field of child development and related disciplines and upon particular knowledge of each child.

I-1.3   To recognize and respect the uniqueness and the potential of each child.

I-1.4   To appreciate the special vulnerability of children.

I-1.5   To create and maintain safe and healthy settings that foster children's social, emotional, intellectual, and physical development and that respect their dignity and their contributions.

I-1.6   To support the right of children with special needs to participate, consistent with their ability, in regular childhood programs.

PRINCIPLES

P-1.1   Above all, we shall not harm children. We shall not participate in practices that are disrespectful, degrading, dangerous, exploitative, intimidating, psychologically damaging, or physically harmful to children. *This principle has precedence over all others in this Code.*

P-1.2   We shall not participate in practices that discriminate against children by denying benefits, giving special advantages, or excluding them from programs or activities on the basis of their race, religion, sex, national origin, or the status, behavior, or beliefs of their parents. (This principle does not apply to programs that have a lawful mandate to provide services to a particular population of children.)

P-1.3   We shall involve all of those with relevant knowledge (including staff and parents) in decisions concerning a child.

P-1.4   When, after appropriate efforts have been made with a child and the family, the child still does not appear to be benefitting from a program, we shall communicate our concern to the family in a positive way and offer them assistance in finding a more suitable setting.

P-1.5   We shall be familiar with the symptoms of child abuse and neglect and know and follow community procedures and state laws that protect children against abuse and neglect.

P-1.6   When we have evidence of child abuse or neglect, we shall report the evidence to the appropriate community agency and follow up to ensure that appropriate action has been taken. When possible, parents will be informed that the referral has been made.

P-1.7   When another person tells us of their suspicion that a child is being abused or neglected but we lack evidence, we shall assist that person in taking appropriate action to protect the child.

P-1.8   When a child protective agency fails to provide adequate protection for abused or neglected children, we acknowledge a collective ethical responsibility to work toward improvement of these services.

P-1.9   When we become aware of a practice or situation that endangers the health or safety of children, but has not been previously known to do so, we have an ethical responsibility to inform those who can remedy the situation and who can keep other children from being similarly endangered.

SECTION II: ETHICAL RESPONSIBILITIES TO FAMILIES

Families are of primary importance in children's development. (The term *family* may include others, besides parents, who are responsibly involved with the child.) Because the family and the early childhood educator have a common interest in the child's welfare, we acknowledge a primary responsibility to bring about collaboration between the home and school in ways that enhance the child's development.

IDEALS

I-2.1   To develop relationships of mutual trust with the families we serve.

I-2.2   To acknowledge and build upon strengths and competencies as we support families in their task of nurturing children.

I-2.3   To respect the dignity of each family and its culture, customs, and beliefs.

I-2.4   To respect families' childrearing values and their right to make decisions for their children.

I-2.5   To interpret each child's progress to parents within the framework of a developmental perspective and to help families understand and appreciate the value of developmentally appropriate early childhood programs.

I-2.6   To help family members improve their understanding of their children and to enhance their skills as parents.

I-2.7   To participate in building support networks for families by providing them with opportunities to interact with program staff and families.

PRINCIPLES

P-2.1   We shall not deny family members access to their child's classroom or program setting.

P-2.2   We shall inform families of program philosophy, policies, and personnel qualifications, and explain why we teach as we do.

P-2.3   We shall inform families of and, when appropriate, involve them in policy decisions.

P-2.4   We shall inform families of and, when appropriate, involve them in significant decisions affecting their child.

P-2.5   We shall inform the family of accidents involving their child, of risks such as exposures to contagious disease that may result in infection, and of events that might result in psychological damage.

P-2.6   We shall not permit or participate in research that could in any way hinder the education or development of the children in our programs. Families shall be fully informed of any proposed research projects involving their children and shall have the opportunity to give or withhold consent.

P-2.7   We shall not engage in or support exploitation of families. We shall not use our relationship with a family for private advantage or personal gain, or enter into relationships with family members that might impair our effectiveness in working with children.

P-2.8   We shall develop written policies for the protection of confidentiality and the disclosure of children's records. The policy documents shall be made available to all program personnel and families. Disclosure of children's records beyond family members, program personnel, and consultants having an obligation of confidentiality shall require familial consent (except in cases of abuse or neglect).

P-2.9   We shall maintain confidentiality and shall respect the family's right to privacy, refraining from disclosure of confidential information and intrusion into family life. However, when we are concerned about a child's welfare, it is permissible to reveal confidential information to agencies and individuals who may be able to act in the child's interest.

P-2.10   In cases where family members are in conflict we shall work openly, sharing our observations of the child, to help all parties involved make informed decisions. We shall refrain from becoming an advocate for one party.

P-2.11   We shall be familiar with and appropriately use community resources and professional services that support families. After a referral has been made, we shall follow up to ensure that services have been adequately provided.

SECTION III: ETHICAL RESPONSIBILITIES TO COLLEAGUES

In a caring, cooperative work place human dignity is respected, professional satisfaction is promoted, and positive relationships are modeled. Our primary responsibility in this arena is to establish and maintain settings and relationships that support productive work and meet professional needs.

A—RESPONSIBILITIES TO CO-WORKERS: IDEALS

I-3A.1   To establish and maintain relationships of trust and cooperation with co-workers.

I-3A.2   To share resources and information with co-workers.

I-3A.3   To support co-workers in meeting their professional needs and in their professional development.

I-3A.4   To accord co-workers due recognition of professional achievement.

PRINCIPLES

P-3A.1   When we have concern about the professional behavior of a co-worker, we shall first let that person know of our concern and attempt to resolve the matter collegially.

P-3A.2   We shall exercise care in expressing views regarding the personal attributes or professional conduct of co-workers. Statements should be based on firsthand knowledge and relevant to the interests of children and programs.

B—RESPONSIBILITIES TO EMPLOYERS: IDEALS

I-3B.1   To assist the program in providing the highest quality of service.

I-3B.2   To maintain loyalty to the program and uphold its reputation.

PRINCIPLES

P-3B.1   When we do not agree with program policies, we shall first attempt to effect change through constructive action within the organization.

P-3B.2   We shall speak or act on behalf of an organization only when authorized. We shall take care to note when we are speaking for the organization and when we are expressing a personal judgment.

C—RESPONSIBILITIES TO EMPLOYEES: IDEALS

I-3C.1   To promote policies and working conditions that foster competence, well-being, and self-esteem in staff members.

I-3C.2   To create a climate of trust and candor that will enable staff to speak and act in the best interests of children, families, and the field of early childhood education.

I-3C.3   To strive to secure an adequate livelihood for those who work with or on behalf of young children.

PRINCIPLES

P-3C.1   In decisions concerning children and programs, we shall appropriately utilize the training, experience, and expertise of staff members.

P-3C.2   We shall provide staff members with working conditions that permit them to carry out their responsibilities, timely and nonthreatening evaluation procedures, written grievance procedures, constructive feedback, and opportunities for continuing professional development and advancement.

P-3C.3   We shall develop and maintain comprehensive written personnel policies that define program standards and, when applicable, that specify the extent to which employees are accountable for their conduct outside the work place. These policies shall be given to new staff members and shall be available for review by all staff members.

P-3C.4   Employees who do not meet program standards shall be informed of areas of concern and, when possible, assisted in improving their performance.

P-3C.5   Employees who are dismissed shall be informed of the reasons for the termination. When a dismissal is for cause, justification must be based on evidence of inadequate or inappropriate behavior that is accurately documented, current, and available for the employee to review.

P-3C.6   In making evaluations and recommendations, judgments shall be based on fact and relevant to the interests of children and programs.

P-3C.7   Hiring and promotion shall be based solely on a person's record of accomplishment and ability to carry out the responsibilities of the position.

P-3C.8   In hiring, promotion, and provision of training, we shall not participate in any form of discrimination based on race, religion, sex, national origin, handicap, age, or sexual preference. We shall be familiar with laws and regulations that pertain to employment discrimination.

SECTION IV: ETHICAL RESPONSIBILITIES TO COMMUNITY AND SOCIETY

Early childhood programs operate within a context of an immediate community made up of families and other institutions concerned with children's welfare. Our responsibilities to the community are to provide programs that meet its needs and to cooperate with agencies and professions that share responsibility for children. Because the larger society has a measure of responsibility for the welfare and protection of children, and because of our specialized expertise in child development, we acknowledge an obligation to serve as a voice for children everywhere.

IDEALS

I-4.1   To provide the community with high-quality, culturally sensitive programs and services.

I-4.2   To promote cooperation among agencies and professions concerned with the welfare of young children, their families, and their teachers.

I-4.3   To work, through education, research, and advocacy, toward an environmentally safe world in which all children are adequately fed, sheltered, and nurtured.

I-4.4   To work, through education, research, and advocacy, toward a society in which all young children have access to quality programs.

I-4.5   To promote knowledge and understanding of young children and their needs. To work toward greater social acknowledgement of children's rights and greater social acceptance of responsibility for their well-being.

I-4.6   To support policies and laws that promote the well-being of children and families. To oppose those that impair their well-being. To cooperate with other individuals and groups in these efforts.

I-4.7   To further the professional development of the field of early childhood education and to strengthen its commitment to realizing its core values as reflected in this Code.

PRINCIPLES

P-4.1   We shall communicate openly and truthfully about the nature and extent of services that we provide.

P-4.2   We shall not accept or continue to work in positions for which we are personally unsuited or professionally unqualified. We shall not offer services that we do not have the competence, qualifications, or resources to provide.

P-4.3   We shall be objective and accurate in reporting the knowledge upon which we base our program practices.

P-4.4   We shall cooperate with other professionals who work with children and their families.

P-4.5   We shall not hire or recommend for employment any person who is unsuited for a position with respect to competence, qualifications, or character.

P-4.6   We shall report the unethical or incompetent behavior of a colleague to a supervisor when informal resolution is not effective.

P-4.7   We shall be familiar with laws and regulations that serve to protect the children in our programs.

P-4.8   We shall not participate in practices which are in violation of laws and regulations that protect the children in our programs.

P-4.9   When we have evidence that an early childhood program is violating laws or regulations protecting children, we shall report it to persons responsible for the program. If compliance is not accomplished within a reasonable time, we will report the violation to appropriate authorities who can be expected to remedy the situation.

P-4.10   When we have evidence that an agency or a professional charged with providing services to children, families, or teachers is failing to meet its obligations, we acknowledge a collective ethical responsibility to report the problem to appropriate authorities or to the public.

P-4.11   When a program violates or requires its employees to violate this Code, it is permissible, after fair assessment of the evidence, to disclose the identity of that program.

Index

The Author

George S. Morrison, Ed.D., is professor of early childhood and elementary education at Florida International University, where he teaches courses in early childhood education, curriculum and instruction, and elementary education. Professor Morrison's accomplishments include a Distinguished Academic Service Award from the Pennsylvania Department of Education, an Outstanding Alumni Award from the University of Pittsburgh School of Education, and an Outstanding Service Award from Florida International University.

Dr. Morrison is the author of other books on early childhood education, child development, and curriculum. His professional affiliations include the National Association for the Education of Young Children (NAEYC), National Association of Early Childhood Teacher Education (NAECTE), the Society for Research in Child Development (SRCD), the World Organization for Early Childhood Education (OMEP), the Association for Supervision and Curriculum Development (ASCD), the American Educational Research Association (AERA), the Association of Teacher Educators (ATE), and Phi Delta Kappa. He is also the founder and sponsor of the Early Childhood Education Club at Florida International University.